MANAGING CULTURAL DIFFERENCES

In today's global business environment, it is vital that individuals and organizations have sophisticated global leadership skills. Communication and understanding of different cultures is paramount to business success.

This new edition of the bestselling textbook, *Managing Cultural Differences*, guides students and practitioners to an understanding of how to do business internationally, providing practical advice on how competitive advantage can be gained through effective cross-cultural management. Crises in the Middle East, the weakening of some emerging markets, and the value of diversity and inclusion are just a few examples of contemporary issues discussed in this text, which also introduces a completely new chapter on global business ethics.

With a wealth of new examples, case studies, and online materials, this textbook is required course reading for undergraduates, postgraduates, and MBA students alike, as well as being a vital tool for anybody selling, purchasing, traveling, or working internationally.

Neil Remington Abramson Having worked as a consultant and manager in the private sector for many years, Neil Abramson completed his MBA and PhD at the Richard Ivey School of Business, Western University. He is a professor of International Strategy (ret.) at Simon Fraser University. An East Asia specialist, Abramson researches the building of effective, harmonious, and ethical cross-national business relationships. He has published in the *Journal of International Business Studies*, *Management International Review*, *Journal of Business Ethics*, and *Organization Studies*. As president of the SFU Faculty Association, he led its successful unionization.

Robert T. Moran Bob Moran began his professional career in Japan as a Catholic priest whose responsibilities in Japan for five years included working as a playing coach for the best hockey team in Japan. It was during this experience that he learned that "culture counts" and living and working in a new and complex culture required new skills. He ended his professional career as a Professor Emeritus at Thunderbird School of Global Management, USA. At Thunderbird he was voted by students 16 times Outstanding Professor in International Studies. As a consultant and presenter in Executive Education Programs he has worked for Exxon Mobil, Novartis, Singapore Airlines, Toyota, JCB, Volvo, General Motors, and many other global organizations. Academic institutions he has worked with include Thunderbird, SMU, Stanford, Wharton, Babson and others. The book *Managing Cultural Differences* is an overview of what he has learned and taught about leadership in complex, changing global business environments.

Praise for the Tenth Edition:

"The new newest edition of *Managing Cultural Differences* is outstanding. It outlines important skill sets and excellent international background for today's global managers and leaders. I highly recommend it to CEOs and their management teams."

> – *Harry Owens Jr., MD MIM CPE, Private Consultant,*
> *International Health Programs/Projects, USA*

"With increasingly globalized markets, our workplaces today are much more diverse and complex. The tenth edition of *Managing Cultural Differences* is a must-read for people looking to become effective managers and deal makers, and to master the delicate aspects of international business."

> – *Lucy Li, National Director of Client Segment Strategy,*
> *Business Financial Services, Royal Bank of Canada*

"A timely new edition that is thought provoking and superbly easy to delve into. This is a fuss free read that skilfully marries key globalization, leadership and inter-cultural ideas and concepts with great illustrations from social and business practice. The addition of two new chapters on the topical themes of leadership in an increasingly challenging global world as well as global business ethics is to be welcomed and a richly informative addition from a reader's perspective, be they international business studies students or global leadership practitioners."

> – *Randhir Auluck, Associate Head of School, School of Marketing and Management,*
> *Coventry University, UK*

"In a world growing ever closer, the need for cultural translation to enable increased functionality is more important than ever. This book is a new tool for the business toolbox, which offers not just a path forward, but actionable examples that can be used today."

> – *Harold S. Back, President, Core Financial Corporation, USA*

"This new edition continues to generate enhanced understanding of cultural differences in a business context, and offers tools for managing effectively. I highly recommend it to students of International Business."

> – *Hemant Merchant, PhD, Professor of Global Business,*
> *University of South Florida St. Petersburg, USA*

Praise for the previous editions:

"[R]ich with new stories, examples and suggestions … contains required information for anyone interacting in a culture other than their own."
 – *Warren Wilhelm, DBA Harvard Business School, President, Global Business Alliance*

"[T]his book will continue to be my guide for working with European and global clients."
 – *Karen Green, Organizational Development Consultant, Karity HR Solutions, UK*

"[A] must read for managers and leaders working cross-culturally."
 – *Jeffrey Kolanchick, Leadership Development Advisor, Saudi Aramco, Saudi Arabia*

"[A] terrific springboard for understanding the complexities, challenges and rewarding of running global operations."
 – *J.T. Battenberg, III, Chairman of the Board/CEO Delphi Automotive Systems*

"[M]erits the classification as the Gold Standard of cross-cultural textbooks."
 – *Richard D. Mahoney, PhD, Thunderbird School of Global Management*

"[O]ne of the best organized books on the subject."
 – *The HRD Review*

"[A] rich, almost encyclopedic array of advice, case studies and examples … an excellent book."
 – *Academy of Management Review*

MANAGING CULTURAL DIFFERENCES

Global Leadership for the 21st Century

TENTH EDITION

Neil Remington Abramson and
Robert T. Moran

Routledge
Taylor & Francis Group

LONDON AND NEW YORK

Tenth edition published 2018
by Routledge
2 Park Square, Milton Park, Abingdon, Oxon, OX14 4RN

and by Routledge
711 Third Avenue, New York, NY 10017

Routledge is an imprint of the Taylor & Francis Group, an informa business

First edition published by Gulf Publishing Company, Houston, Texas 1979
Ninth edition published by Routledge 2014

British Library Cataloguing-in-Publication Data
A catalogue record for this book is available from the British Library

Library of Congress Cataloging-in-Publication Data
Names: Abramson, Neil R., 1953- author. | Moran, Robert T., 1938- author. |
Harris, Philip R. (Philip Robert), 1926– Managing cultural differences.
Title: Managing cultural differences / Neil R. Abramson and Robert T. Moran.
Description: Tenth Edition. | New York : Routledge, 2018. | Revised
edition of the authors' Managing cultural differences, 2014. | Includes
bibliographical references and index.
Identifiers: LCCN 2017007985| ISBN 9781138223455 (hardback) |
ISBN 9781138223684 (pbk.) | ISBN 9781315403984 (ebook)
Subjects: LCSH: International business enterprises–Management. |
Management–Cross-cultural studies. | Acculturation. | Cross-cultural studies.
Classification: LCC HD62.4 .H37 2014 | DDC 658.1/8–dc23
LC record available at https://lccn.loc.gov/2017007985

ISBN: 978-1-138-22345-5 (hbk)
ISBN: 978-1-138-22368-4 (pbk)
ISBN: 978-1-315-40398-4 (ebk)

Typeset in Berthold Akzidenz Grotesk
by RefineCatch Limited, Bungay, Suffolk

Visit the companion website: www.routledge.com/cw/moran

To my wife Haruyo and my all-grown-up family: Rutsu, Ikkei, Karen and Tomoka. Thanks for all the care and support you give me. To my teachers: Alan Haynes, Dick Henshel, Harry Lane, Trevor Fisher, and so many more. Thanks for helping me come to where I am. In faith, hope and love.

Neil Remington Abramson

To Elizabeth, Sarah, Molly, Rebecca, Benedict and of course Virgilia. You bring much joy into our home.

Robert T. Moran

CONTENTS

EXHIBITS

FOREWORD

Each day I drive down the road to my office, which connects New Delhi, the capital city of India, to the home of the Taj Mahal—Agra. From the humble bullock cart to the technological and engineering marvel—the latest limousine; from the farmer carrying his harvest to the market to the Ivy League-educated executive; from the cows, to the trucks and the crowded buses, everyone seemingly has equal right to space on the road. Yet in all of this chaos, each person seems to be headed somewhere with intent.

One often wonders what overseas visitors, especially businesspeople, would think of this on their first visit to India. Would the Westerners, who are perhaps "goal-focused," ponder how they will meet their objectives in this chaos? Would the Chinese, who are perhaps used to "order," contemplate on how they will meet their objectives? What is the Indian, who is used to "ambiguity," thinking? What if they are actually members of the same global company; perhaps part of the same team that has been tasked with executing a time-limited project?

Having worked with Japanese, Indian, American, and British MNCs, I am often reminded of my early days in one of the first Indo-Japanese joint ventures in India, almost three decades ago, when the Indian and the Japanese teams prepared two entirely different time plans for setting up the same project in India. One of the major points of contention, fairly simple as it may seem, was the time it would take to bring component parts from the South to the North of India, a journey of over 2,000 km. The Indian team gave ten days, and the Japanese five in their respective estimates. This variance applied to most other activities in the project plan as well, with the overall project estimate varying from 18 to 30 months depending on who one asked. The matter was resolved amicably at 26 months after both teams were asked to experience the 2,000 km journey by traveling together.

After this episode, which is described below in greater detail, all other issues of contention fell into place, as both teams made it a point to experience all areas of difference together and develop countermeasures for each activity. A joint team made the presentation to the Indo-Japanese Board. The joint venture went on to become a huge success. What brought this about was the underlying and unwritten understanding of one another's point of view, taken in the context of *culture*.

India is a land of 1.2 billion people, with 22 official languages, 1,596 dialects, and seven major religions; where chaos seems the only order; where the day after tomorrow could mean any day after two; where people are comfortable with making improvisations based on context on a continual basis to accommodate the constantly changing plans of others. And yet, there are world class companies, extremely successful, operating in India.

So, let's return to the 2,000 km journey from the South to the North. On the very first day we had to postpone our departure because of a "bandh" (a general strike) called by a Southern state to protest a river water-sharing dispute that went back over five decades. We set-off on the second day and had several interesting experiences together. Road signage in India is difficult to come by, so one often had to stop to ask local passersby for directions. The directions are "approximate"—turn right from the yellow house with the clothes line, left from the small biscuit shop, etc. Also, since we in India often speak only three languages each, and there is often no overlap among the 22 languages officially recognized, communication cannot be taken for granted.

We passed trucks with broken axles, not because their quality was substandard, but because overloading was the norm and not the exception. We were invited into homes for meals, though we were complete strangers—and of course we accepted some invitations. Food was often served on banana leaves or in "thaalis" (a round steel tray). The entire meal was served simultaneously, including the dessert. Our Japanese guests noticed that the food was mixed by the person eating it in the proportion that he or she liked it best. It was therefore "approximate." In contrast, in the West and even in Japan, precise quantities are served, and those by course.

Our Japanese colleagues, being used to "precision, tight tolerances, and just-in-time," began to understand that at least within the new joint venture and its supply chain, an enormous cultural change from "approximation" to "precision" would be required. It was this understanding that was the critical factor that laid the foundation for a successful joint venture. Needless to mention, our Japanese colleagues made extensive notes at every stage.

I first had the privilege of meeting Professor Moran in India and later in the UK during modules he was conducting for our future global leadership team based on the title of his book, *Managing Cultural Differences*. In a program comprising seven distinct modules covering finance, strategy, operation, etc., his module was rated as the very best—the most appropriate and relevant, and he personally as the most articulate professor—by the participants, our future leaders representing Brazil, China, India, the UK, and the USA. It enabled the participants to better understand one another, especially in a cultural context, and therefore arrive at synergistic decisions during these discussions. The unspoken "whys" of the opinions of one another were much better appreciated. Most participants recommended that this be the very first module in the future!

Most global managers, aspiring or otherwise, are challenged by a highly dynamic environment even in the land of their own birth, which only becomes more complex as they step onto the shores of others. It is how they are able to empower themselves to leverage the power of culture to maximize organizational performance in a cross-cultural environment that will determine their ultimate success. To my mind, it is not humanly possible or even necessary to be an expert in all cultures, but it is important for us to develop a local cultural sensitivity within an overall global context.

In its tenth edition, the authors maintain the theme that our global world is changing (witness the Brexit vote in the UK and the 2016 presidential win of Mr. Trump in the USA, among many other world changes). As a result, complex and sophisticated skills are increasingly necessary for today's global leaders, managers, and travelers.

There are two new chapters in the tenth edition. Chapter 7, "Lessons for global leaders," focuses *not* on theories of global leadership, but on some things we know about the *behaviors of skilled* global leaders. Chapter 9, "Global business ethics," suggests ways to build trust and relationships across cultures. Other chapters have been reorganized and there is much new material. New material and sections have been added in Chapters 11–18. Each chapter begins with a short list of learning objectives for the reader.

I would like to thank Professors Moran and Abramson for penning this edition, with special thanks to Professor Moran for asking me to write this Foreword to the tenth edition.

Managing Cultural Differences is a must-learn and must-read text for every business school; in fact, for every aspiring and practicing business leader. This edition improves an already classic business text and is perhaps the most comprehensive, easy to relate to, and therefore to understand, that I have had the pleasure of reading.

I am sure all readers will benefit immensely from it, as I have.

Vipin Sondhi
MD and CEO
JCB India Limited
March 14, 2017

PREFACE

Since the ninth edition of *Managing Cultural Differences* was published there have been many changes in our global world. Some of these changes are political, some are wars that continue to destroy and kill innocent people, and all have significant economic consequences that impact the quality of life of those most needing help.

Many copies of *Managing Cultural Differences* have been sold in the United Kingdom and the United States, where Brexit narrowly passed in 2016 and Donald Trump was elected president of the United States. In both cases the winners argued that economic nationalism would make Britain and the United States better off. We don't believe this will happen under Trump or May, but we believe trading between nations will continue and a wall will create many more problems than it was intended to solve.

We believe, more than ever, that anyone working in our diverse world needs more sophisticated and common-sense leadership skills. We need individuals who are curious, open, and who don't believe the world gets better when our side wins all the time. Racism, sexism, xenophobia, and other -isms haven't worked for any country in the past and they won't work now.

In the tenth edition of *Managing Cultural Differences* we have kept these three words but added a subtitle. The title is now *Managing Cultural Differences: Global Leadership for the 21st Century*. There are two new chapters, one on Global Ethics and another on Behaviors of Skillful Leaders. We have also kept a lot of the old "good stuff" and we continue to strive for a balance between theory and practice.

We especially strive to write so that readers will remember a few points from every chapter and use some of what they remember, and hope in so doing they will add value to their personal and professional lives.

Neil Abramson, *Vancouver, British Columbia, Canada*
Robert Moran, *Paradise Valley, Arizona, United States*

ACKNOWLEDGMENTS

This is the tenth edition of *Managing Cultural Differences*. Over the years many people have contributed in many ways to making this book what it is today. We thank you all.

Again we acknowledge Vipin Sondhi, the Managing Director and CEO of JCB India, for writing the Foreword. He is an executive of exceptional skill.

Natalie Tomlinson is wonderful to work with. As a small thanks to her we were able to recommend some special restaurants in Naples prior to her first visit. Although this is not part of our professional vocabulary usage, we both think you are "cool" Natalie.

Georgia Lessard is always easy to work with and *Managing Cultural Differences*, tenth edition, was no exception.

We acknowledge and thank Haruyo Abramson who solved complex formatting difficulties.

We also thank the many professors, reviewers, and readers of previous editions who gave us feedback and suggestions. We incorporated many in this edition.

1 GLOBAL LEADERSHIP, CULTURE, AND A CHANGING WORLD

We begin Chapter 1 and *Managing Cultural Differences*, tenth edition, with six actual situations involving managing cultural differences and global leadership skills.

After reading the first three chapters of the book, all should have a good understanding of the basis of the misunderstandings and be able to identify alternative responses that might have good results.

There is no perfect "road map" for success in a global world. There are, however, "global road mapping skills."

Situation 1

Question from a European to a Chinese HR director concerning attendance at a company-sponsored course:

> Do you think Mr. Zhao will be able to come to the course next week, as I would like to make hotel reservations for him and the hotel is quite full?

Answer:

> It is possible he may have to attend a meeting in Shanghai.

Follow-up question two days later, before the course begins, sent by email:

> I am following up our earlier conversation and am wondering if Mr. Zhao will be attending the course?

**L
E
A
R
N
I
N
G

O
B
J
E
C
T
I
V
E
S**

After reading and studying concepts/examples and illustrations in Chapter 1, readers should:

1   Reflect on any prejudices or biases they might hold about other peoples or cultures.
2   Be convinced that "culture counts" more than ever in today's global world.
3   Understand the importance of learning the national character and management philosophies of their global counterparts.
4   Be aware of some of their global skills.
5   Begin to see events and issues from their own and from the other's perspective.

Answer by email:

As I told you previously, he will NOT attend.

Result: A significant misunderstanding between the Chinese HR director and the Westerner. The HR director ignored the Westerner at work for several days.

Situation 2

A few days after Michael had arrived in Japan, he was reading and replying to emails received from his new Japanese colleagues. He was willing to support them as much as possible, and was keen to be accepted by the new organization as the new boss. He, therefore, carefully worded his email replies. He also tried to provide advice and guidance whenever he felt it could be useful for his Japanese colleagues.

One email he had received had important documents attached and had been widely distributed by his colleague. Unfortunately, a draft had not been shared with him prior to distribution. Both the mail text and the document had been prepared very carefully by his Japanese colleagues, and the content was almost perfect. Overall, Michael was very pleased.

However, Michael decided that he should provide some feedback to his Japanese colleagues. He wanted to ensure that in the future he would have the chance to review such important documents before they were sent out. So he added his reply:

The documentation you had put together and sent out was very well done. I thank you very much for your hard work and would kindly ask you to consider my thoughts when preparing these kinds of documents. Perhaps, in the future, you can share the draft version with me prior to sending it out.

Best regards, Michael

After his Japanese colleagues received his reply, they got together to discuss corrective actions as they felt very committed to meeting all the expectations of their new boss. Thinking he was very angry, they tried to find out what went wrong on their side, how to then reply to their boss, and how to establish a special review process. But even after longer discussions, they found no serious mistakes, and everybody was unsure about how to proceed.

Situation 3

Our legal person is very intelligent and an excellent negotiator. She was born in Germany but has spent many years in the US and Canada. One would think she was an American by the way she presents herself and by her accent. During negotiations, I have noticed that she speaks very quickly, with never-ending sentences. I can only imagine what the Chinese thought. I believe they were not following her and were getting a little frustrated. Also, the lawyer was not patient. She would not let them question or make any comments.

Situation 4

Guus Hiddink, the coach of the South Korean soccer team in the 2002 World Soccer Games held in South Korea and Japan, experienced the following:

He learned that the younger players on the team tended to pass to the more senior "strikers" in consistent patterns. Recognizing this as a "problem," he brought the team together, told them that for the honor of their country and in order to do well in the upcoming games, they had to pass to the person who seemed to be in the best position to score. The team agreed.

However, there was little change in the pattern of passing after his "pep talk."

Situation 5

As an American, my first Christmas party in Switzerland was an enlightening experience. I had only been in the country for about three months and was just getting to know a few of my co-workers. We were all sitting at the traditional long Swiss-style tables, and our table had about 20 people. This included our "big" boss, a few of his direct reporters, and my peers and me. After dinner and a few glasses of wine, the conversation started to get very "questionable." So I just sat back to see what was going to happen and how everyone else was going to take this.

The situation was that the American "big boss" and a few of his direct reporters (Spanish) began saying some things about a female (American) colleague's body directly to her. I said "Wow" to myself and watched the American woman become increasingly uncomfortable, but no one challenged any comments.

Situation 6

Barbara had a PhD in chemistry, as did her boss with whom she had a good working relationship. Barbara was frustrated because her boss had never given her any positive feedback on her work. The only time any feedback was offered was when Barbara made a mistake and, in this case, the feedback was negative and strong.

The world has changed, and so must people living in this changed global world. But not everything has changed.

The premise of this book is simple: just as no two individuals are exactly the same, neither are two nations of societies. However, the people in the same culture share certain things in common that are not necessarily shared by people of another culture. This is the reality.

Our goal is to help readers think or rethink many aspects related to the attitudes and skills we all need to survive and thrive in today's global environment. Or, to write it more simply: to learn to live and work with differences. Hence, the title of our book, *Managing Cultural Differences.*

In the early stages of socialization, the parents or caregivers of children from all cultures have a major influence on how their children behave and their values and attitudes. The parental influence example illustrates this point.[1]

AN EXAMPLE OF PARENTAL INFLUENCE

When I began delivering executive seminars for a particular large global company about eight years ago with a professional colleague, his presentations to executives were good but not great, according to the ratings of attendees. Feedback was that they were a little too academic in contrast with a different style that included "stories" to illustrate academic points. Over the years, he has included more and more stories to illustrate what he wants participants to remember and use.

I suspect some of his stories have fabricated elements, but he recently told the following, which illustrated to me the influence of parents on children:

> My wife is Republican and listens regularly at home and in the car to conservative talk shows. Often, our two boys are in the car with her. I am registered Independent but often vote for a Democrat, and I voted for Obama. My wife voted for McCain, the Republican candidate in 2008.

> On election day, the boys went to bed at the regular time, but I stayed up till it was clear Obama would win. I was thrilled. My wife was depressed.
>
> My younger son, who was nine years old at the time, got up first and asked me, "Dad, who won?" When I told him Obama won, he began to weep uncontrollably. I hugged him and told him it is going to be OK that Obama won, and don't worry.
>
> He then said, "But Obama will tax my allowance." When I told him that Obama was not going to tax his $2.00-a-week allowance, he stopped crying.
>
> Parents, indeed, influence their children.

As parents and caregivers gradually lose their ability to influence their children, teachers, religious leaders, and textbooks, as well as their children's friends and peers, become increasingly major influences in their lives. The following examples are from textbooks in several different countries, taken from an article in *The Economist*. They are illustrations of how governments and school districts in selected countries attempt to control ideology by the textbooks they allow and what is written in them. The examples cited are from the Georg Eckert Institute,[2] which studies textbooks from 160 countries, covering history and geography.

- In Saudi Arabian textbooks, "The Jews and Christians are enemies of the true believers" is written and probably results in intolerance toward Jews and Christians.
- In China, there was an attempt to introduce a curriculum of national education that omitted the events of the Cultural Revolution and Tiananmen Square.
- In Japan, textbooks whitewash and gloss over Japanese World War II war crimes.
- In the US, many textbooks play down slavery and the killing of many Native American tribes.
- In an Israeli textbook, Palestinians are depicted as refugees, farmers, and terrorists.
- In the US in 2012, about 25 percent of students in public schools are Hispanic, yet most of the main characters in children's texts read by Hispanics are white.

We believe that children are not born with prejudice, it is learned. Bias and the resulting xenophobia are present in most, if not all, cultures. In fact, we could say we live in xenophobic times—for proof, just pick up any newspaper and you can see prejudice toward people who are not quite like us, and minority groups, that is often accompanied by cruelty.

In Andrew Solomon's wonderful book *Far from the Tree*,[3] he writes that most children share some traits with their parents or caregivers. He calls these "vertical identities," which are passed down through strands of DNA and cultural/family traditions. Solomon cites skin color, language, religion, and nationality as examples.

There are also acquired traits, which he refers to as horizontal identities that are different from one's parents and are acquired from a peer group. Being gay is a horizontal identity as most gay kids are born of straight parents.

Some things have *not changed* or changed very little over the past few years: Russia is still the largest country in the world by size; Everest is the tallest mountain; the Nile is the longest river—179 miles longer than the Amazon; the Sahara is the largest desert by far; Greenland is the largest island; China has the most people; and Tokyo is the world's largest city by population: 38,000,000. But did you know the facts in the Did You Know box?

DID YOU KNOW?

- Twenty-five percent of the population in China with the highest IQs and 28 percent in India are greater than the total population of North America. This has implications for parents, teachers, and politicians—China and India have more honor kids than most, if not all, countries have kids in total.
- China will soon be the number-one English-speaking country in the world by population.
- Every six minutes, 60 babies are born in the US, 244 babies are born in China, and 351 babies are born in India.
- In the US, one out of two people are working for a company for whom they have worked less than five years.

Vérité en-deça des Pyrénées, erreur au delà. (There are truths on this side of the Pyrenees that are falsehoods on the other.)[4]

In 1492, Christopher Columbus set sail for India, going west … he called the people he met "Indians" and came home and reported to his king and queen, "The world is round." I set off for India 512 years later … I went east … I came home and reported only to my wife and only in a whisper, "The world is flat."[5]

The real voyage of discovery consists not in seeking new landscapes but in having new eyes.

Marcel Proust, French novelist, 1871–1922

The important thing is not to stop questioning. Curiosity has its own reason for existing.

Albert Einstein

Source: From *Did You Know?* by Karl Fisch and Scott McLeod. Adapted by Sony BMG. Full presentation can be viewed at www.youtube.com/watch?v=jpEnFwiqdx8.

ENCOURAGING CURIOSITY IN CHILDREN

Although I wouldn't encourage my two-year-old to stick his fingers down a spider hole in the African soil where he is being raised, I try to foster his sense of curiosity and his desire to learn. Can he climb and make it to the top of the water tank? Sure; I will be right behind him. What does that flame feel like? Let's find out; I'll guide his fingers close enough to it so he won't get burned.

Today, academics, psychologists, teachers, parents, and even business leaders are being encouraged to not only be curious themselves but to nurture curiosity in their employees. Curiosity is linked to innovation, exploration, drive, growth, and solving challenges … and to learning about other people and cultures.

Most people are comfortable with what they know and with ideas and people that are very much like themselves.

Curiosity leads to learning and to seeing with new eyes what is in our rich resource world.

Source: Rebecca Moran, pilot in Tanzania, 2004–2013.

In the twenty-first century, leaders in business, government, and the professions cope with the phenomenon of globalization. It prompts them to cross borders more frequently and to communicate with persons from other cultures, either in person or electronically. This chapter provides a rationale and an imperative for all individuals working "globally" to understand and respect their counterparts, and to develop the skills required to work effectively in today's complex world. Ways to analyze and understand other cultures are presented, along with how to use the suggested strategies. Seeing global issues through "multiple lenses" or "by hearing with new ears" is also important.

Why does the world appear flat to some, round to others, and what are the advantages or disadvantages of either? Thomas Friedman writes about his insights during an interview with Nandan Nilekani, CEO of Infosys Technologies Limited:

"Outsourcing is just one dimension of a much more fundamental thing happening today in the world," Nilekani explained. "What happened over the last (few) years is that there was a massive investment in technology, especially in the bubble era, when hundreds of millions of dollars were invested in putting broadband connectivity around the world, undersea cables, all those things." At the same time, he added, computers became cheaper and dispersed all over the world, and there was an explosion of software email, search engines like Google, and proprietary software that can chop up any piece of work and send one part to Boston, one

LEARNING OBJECTIVES

LEARNING OBJECTIVES

part to Bangalore, and one part to Beijing, making it easy for anyone to do remote development. When all of these things suddenly came together around 2000, added Nilekani, they created a platform where intellectual work, intellectual capital, could be delivered from anywhere. It could be disaggregated, delivered, distributed, produced, and put back together again—and this gave a whole new degree of freedom to the way we do work, especially work of an intellectual nature.... And what you are seeing in Bangalore today is really the culmination of all these things coming together.[6]

The point is, the playing field in the global marketplace is being leveled for some, and thus "flat." That is an advantage for many and a disadvantage for others. In either view, cultural competing is a requirement. Culture does count.

The coauthors of this book have worked for global organizations for many years. In the 1960s and early 1970s, we had to convince many business and government leaders that "culture counts." From the industrialized world, the perspective often voiced was: "We tell them what to do, and if they want to work with us, they do it." This is rarely or never the situation today.

We no longer have to convince anyone with any global experience that *culture counts*. And when organizations, nongovernmental organizations (NGOs), and political organizations ignore, dismiss, or minimize culture, the costs are often significant. This chapter will present proven frameworks, models, and paradigms relevant to working skillfully in today's global business and geopolitical world. We believe managing cultural differences skillfully for all individuals, organizations, NGOs, and governments from all countries is a human and business imperative. Understanding the environment is a fundamental requirement for maintaining a competitive advantage. To successfully adapt to changes in the environment is a requirement for survival. Culture impacts relationships and business operations. Schein states it profoundly:

> Consider any complex, potentially volatile issue—Arab relations, the problems between Serbs, Croats, and Bosnians, corporate decision-making, getting control of the U. S. deficit, or healthcare costs, labor/management relations, and so on. At the root of the issue, we are likely to find communication failures and cultural misunderstandings that prevent the parties from framing the problem in a common way, and thus make it impossible to deal with the problem constructively.[7]

Also supporting the notion that "culture" is important is Alan Greenspan, former chairman of the US Federal Reserve. Greenspan stated that he originally believed that capitalism was "human nature."[8]

After the collapse of the Soviet economy, however, he concluded that "it was not human nature at all, but culture." Culture is finding its place of significance in the experience of global individuals.

Cultures have always been distinct, mostly separate and independent. Over the past 100 years, and especially during the last 25, cultures and nations have remained unique, but have become increasingly more interconnected in complex and nonobvious ways. This book covers many topics, but the threads of culture, differences, and leadership run throughout.

> In the early 1990s, I happened to come across early 1960s economic data on Ghana and South Korea, and I was astonished to see how similar their economies were at that time. These two countries had roughly comparable levels of per capita gross national product (GNP); similar divisions of their economy among primary products, manufacturing, and services; and overwhelmingly primary product exports, with South Korea producing a few manufactured goods. They were also receiving comparable levels of economic aid. Thirty years later, South Korea had become an industrial giant with the fourteenth largest economy in the world. No such changes had occurred in Ghana, whose per capita GNP was now about one-fifteenth that of South Korea's. How could this extraordinary difference in development be explained? Undoubtedly, many factors played a role, but it seemed to me that culture had to be a large part of the explanation. South Koreans value thrift, investment, hard work, education, organization, and discipline. Ghanaians had different values.[9]

In short, culture counts.

Diamond's[10] statement that "We all know that history has proceeded very differently for peoples from different parts of the globe" is one we can all agree with. The specific data that humans all came from Africa are not disputed. Diamond asks why different people develop in different ways. His answer: "History followed different courses for different peoples because of differences in peoples' environments, not because of biological differences among peoples themselves."[11]

Change is also a part of our daily lives, and impacts all. If culture counts, managing cultural differences or skillfully leading in a global world becomes of paramount importance. Most of the following events took place after the year 2000 and share aspects of culture, differences, conflict, consequences, and leadership.

"An internationalist without being indifferent to members of one's tribe." Albert Einstein wrote these words in a letter to a friend in 1919. Einstein was a genius, but these words suggest he was also quite wise.

The following examples are relevant and from the experiences of Robert Moran.[12] He was born in Canada, where he lived for 25 years, then moved to Japan and later settled in the US. His stories, therefore, have a North American flavor.

Example 1: *A friendly encounter*

In our neighborhood, trash is picked up every Monday and Thursday. I was born and spent my early years in Canada, and everyone then called the trash "garbage." One of my early chores as a young boy was to take out the garbage.

I still take out the garbage, usually on a Sunday night for an early Monday morning pickup. One Sunday, as I left a full bucket on our street, I met a neighbor who was taking her dog for a walk. We exchanged friendly pleasantries, and she asked about our adult children. She was genuinely interested.

"Elizabeth is still living and working in France," I said, "and we are about to have a second American/French grandchild." I told her that Sarah was working in Taiwan, Molly was in San Francisco working for the Gap, Rebecca was a volunteer bush pilot in Tanzania, flying medical personnel to the Masaai, and Ben, our youngest, was in West Africa finishing his first year as a Peace Corps volunteer.

Our neighbor looked at me and, in a matter-of-fact way, responded: "Well, at least you have one 'normal' one."

We believe our five adult children are all "normal," at least most of the time. Working and living in San Francisco—and working in Taiwan—are equally "normal" in today's world.

Example 2: *You can't trust the French*

Many years before the above encounter, around the 1990s, I took a sabbatical from the Thunderbird School of Global Management, where I have been a faculty member since 1976. With two stuffed duffel bags each, my spouse and I left for France with our five young children. I was going to teach at a grande école—a French Ivy League university—in the suburbs of Paris. We wanted our children to learn another language and have a genuine experience of another culture.

For several weeks, we had not yet met any other foreigners as we tried to find an affordable used car, a house to rent, and schools for our children. We had only met French people who, without exception, helped us figure out how things worked in their sometimes-bureaucratic country.

Our youngest child, Ben, however, who was seven at the time, had met an American whose name was Jack, and he asked if Jack could come over and have dinner with us. We immediately agreed. As it was my turn to cook, with the help of my eldest daughter, we decided that fish—four trout from the local marché—would be the entree.

As Jack was our guest, I presented the fish on a platter to him first. As I did this, my daughter said, from across the table, "Be careful, everyone, there may be some small bones in the fish." Jack, also seven years old, looked at me and responded, "Okay … (sigh).… You know, you just can't trust the French."

Surprised at his comment, I asked him where he had first heard it. "My mother says that all the time," he responded.

Later that night, when I was dropping him off at his home, I met Jack's mother. She told me that she hated living in Europe and wanted to go home to the US. She was lonesome, missed her friends, and did not really like living in France.

Of course, there is nothing abnormal about being lonely and finding a new environment. But her feelings and attitudes clearly influenced Jack, who might not have responded as he did if his mother was happier in France.

Example 3: *The all-American girl*

Last spring, as my work at the university slowed down, my spouse and I were able to spend a little more time together, and we were ready for a new adventure. So we rented a small house in the French countryside, thinking that we would spend our time studying French, the first language of two of our grandchildren.

When my spouse told one of her friends that we were leaving for several weeks, her friend responded: "That's not for me—I'm an all-American girl!"

Remaining an "all-American" would be a safe bet, I suppose, if the world in which we live had not changed drastically since the 1990s due to huge forces of globalization. In fact, leading economists comfortably predict that in a generation the center of worldwide economic activity will shift out of the US and into Asia, where countries are already preparing to take over this role.

Our world has been most influenced by the victors of a war that concluded over half a century ago—namely, the US, Western Europe, and Russia—but rising economic powers such as India, Brazil, and China are increasingly asserting themselves in the international arena. The US will no longer be able to maintain its role as sole superpower.

But many people, including global businessfolk, to my great alarm, believe otherwise.

In order for all people to better prepare themselves for this tectonic shift, a new way of thinking is necessary. Those who learn new ways of living in a globalized world will have the tools necessary to step forward and participate, and even lead. Those who stick to being "all-American," however, will in all likelihood be left out of the process altogether.

Indeed, being a *global American* is, in many ways, just as important for all Americans as being a *global company* is for most, if not all, American organizations if they are to succeed in today's world. Companies that were late in adapting to the new global economy are struggling to catch up. The same must also be true for Germans, Japanese, Saudis, Indians, Nigerians, and people of all nations.

Such a shift in paradigm is not impossible. About 500 years ago, after the earth was discovered to rotate around the sun, humanity had to give up the then-held belief

L
E
A
R
N
I
N
G

O
B
J
E
C
T
I
V
E
S

that the earth was at the center of the universe. It simply wasn't. Giving up old ideas or ideas that don't work, or ideas that are inaccurate, is difficult.

New skills and attitudes are required for businesspeople, students, and all individuals to find our way in a new and rapidly changing world. Being at ease in other cultures, and having the global awareness and curiosity that is necessary to follow the rapid transformations taking place outside our borders—*and even inside of them*—are important ingredients in a global psyche.

Global people are already active in the fields of politics, business, academics, healthcare, and in other professions and walks of life. Indeed, millions—yes, millions—of individuals already live and work in countries other than their own. But today, it is increasingly important that every person develop a global attitude as well. We can no longer leave this to government or business leaders.

Importantly, the major issues that the world may be facing in this century—that is, tectonic shifts in the global economy, terrorism, global warming and increased pollution, mass migration, and the threat of global epidemics (just to name a few)—are not issues that any country, even if it wanted to, could deal with alone. An increased collaboration with other countries and organizations across a wide spectrum of cultures will be fundamental to overcoming these challenges.

Not only global Americans, but also global French, Saudi, Chinese, and others

One final incident demonstrates an important motivation that I have held since the 1990s.

During executive business seminars that I teach, I am often asked "Is it only Americans who have to be global? What about the rest of the world?" I usually respond by relating the following incident.

Many years ago, in New York, I was in the office of a senior vice president of a very large US-based company. A person who reported to the senior vice president, and who had just returned from Asia to conclude an important contract, was invited to meet me. During the meeting, he told me that the deal in Asia should be canceled as, he explained, "They don't understand us, or our business, and they are arrogant."

The senior vice president, in my presence, responded angrily: "If they are arrogant, don't understand us—or whatever—I expect you to be that much more skillful. If you tell me how bad anyone else is again, I'll fire you."

Talk about tension!

A global person

Warren Buffett, the CEO of Berkshire Hathaway and one of the world's most successful, influential, and wealthy individuals, is quoted as saying: "Only when the tides goes out do you find out who is not wearing a bathing suit."

Globalization is exposing most countries to more interactions and relationships with people and products from other countries, yet many people from different countries are not prepared to work, live, and prosper in a global and highly competitive new world.

In an Apple white paper,[13] the authors cited a 2002 National Geographic study as follows:

> Eighty-five percent of 18- to 24-year-old Americans were unable to locate Afghanistan and Iraq on a map, despite the fact that the United States was at war or publicly preparing for war in both countries. Sixty-nine percent were unable to locate Great Britain, and 29% were unable to find the Pacific Ocean.

In a more recent example, also from the US, Timothy Egan[14] asked, are we "smarter than an immigrant?" He wrote:

> Can you name all three branches of government or a single Supreme Court justice? He said that most Americans cannot, and 90% of new immigrants can.

He also wrote: "A recent survey of Donald Trump's supporters in Texas found that 40% believed that Acorn will steal the upcoming elections." But Acorn has been out of existence for six years.

A third-party candidate running for president in 2016 was asked during a TV interview his opinion in solving the problems in Aleppo. He responded, "What is Aleppo?" Two weeks later, he was asked to name a foreign leader of a country who he admired or respected. He couldn't name any government head, let alone one he admires.

But what is a global person? A global person does not believe that his/her nation is the best at everything and that everyone else wants to be just like him/her—rather, he/she is aware that other cultures of the world have lives and viewpoints different from his/her own. A global person may not speak more than one language or have lived in another country. He/she may not even own a passport. However, a global person is aware of and interested in the issues of people around the world. He/she is empathetic and sensitive, and has skills in interacting with people who may not look like, talk like, smell like, or act like him/her.

"Worldmindedness"—a global awareness of other cultures and people (in many ways, the opposite of hate and fear)—is a trait that can be taught, just like language.

The growing importance of other countries in the global arena should not be a threat, but an opportunity for cultural education, growth, and creativity.

In the *Sage Handbook of Intercultural Competence*,[15] many models and paradigms are identified to describe an interculturally competent individual. In most models, there are a knowledge component (knowledge of self, knowledge of other cultures, etc.), a skill component (showing respect, listening, accurately interpreting meanings, etc.), and an attitudinal component (globally minded, not believing one's way is the best or only way, etc.). All can be learned. Knowledge is easier to acquire than a skill to act on. Learning a skill is easier than transforming an ethnocentric attitude. We will start with culture and a short definition: "Culture is the way we do things here."

It is important to remember the following, however:

1   All people are to some extent like all other people—this is the universal aspect which all humans share. All people are to some extent unique—this is the individual aspect, and no two human beings are exactly the same. All people are to some extent like some other people—this is the cultural aspect which we share, in part, with people from our own tribe (as Einstein said).

2   Culture is learned. This learning is on the basis of the following statements:

An individual's early childhood experiences exert a lasting effect on his/her personality. Psychologists, sociologists, anthropologists, and others accept this. The issues being studied are the critical ages and the specific experiences. The early childhood experiences and parenting practices vary from culture to culture. As a result, if a child of a US white woman were to be adopted by a Chinese couple living in a village in China, that child would learn to speak, read, and write Chinese, and behave like most of the other children in the village, but look more like the US mother than any others in the village. He or she would behave like a Chinese boy or girl and learn Chinese values.

We begin with culture.

CULTURE

Culture is a distinctly human means of adapting to circumstances and transmitting this coping skill and knowledge to subsequent generations. Culture gives people a sense of who they are, of belonging, of how they should behave, and of what they should be doing. Culture impacts behavior, morale, and productivity at work, and includes values and patterns that influence company attitudes and actions. Culture is dynamic. Cultures change . . . but slowly. Culture is often considered the driving force behind human behavior everywhere. The concept has become the context to explain politics, economics, progress, and failures. In that regard, Huntington[16] has written:

It is my hypothesis that the fundamental source of human conflict in this new world will not be primarily ideological or primarily economic. The great divisions among humankind and the dominating source of conflict will be culture.

Culture and cultural identities are shaping the patterns of cohesion, disintegration, and conflict in the post-Cold War world. Global politics is being reconfigured along cultural lines—peoples and countries with similar cultures are coming together. Peoples and countries with different cultures are coming apart.

Prior to entering a new market, forming a partnership, or buying a company, organizations spend time and money on "due diligence." What is forgotten or minimized in both business and politics is "cultural due diligence." The following models or frameworks on cultural analysis might be important in any due diligence exercise that has a cultural component. Chomsky et al.,[17] for example, demonstrate the ability to master an incredible wealth of factual knowledge, and these skills exemplify political due diligence. Lewis[18] demonstrates the importance of cultural due diligence for business. Globally minded individuals do this routinely.

The following ten categories are a means for understanding either a macroculture or a microculture, and can be useful for studying any group of people, whether they live in the rural south of the US, India, the bustling city of Hong Kong, Bangalore, Arusha in Tanzania, or Baghdad in Iraq.

Sense of self and space. The comfort one has with self can be expressed differently by culture. Self-identity and appreciation can be manifested by humble bearing in one culture and by macho behavior in another. Americans have a sense of space that requires more distance between individuals than do Latins or Arabs.

Communication and language. The communication system, verbal and nonverbal, distinguishes one group from another. It is estimated that there are fewer than 7,000 human languages today.[19] Apart from the multitude of "foreign" languages, some nations have 15 or more major spoken languages (within one language group there are dialects, accents, slang, jargon, and other such variations). The meanings given to gestures, for example, often differ by culture (see examples in Chapter 2).

Dress and appearance. This includes the outward garments and adornments, as well as body decorations that tend to be culturally distinctive. We are aware of the Japanese kimono, the African headdress, the Englishman's umbrella, and the Polynesian sarong.

Food and feeding habits. The manner in which food is selected, prepared, presented, and eaten often differs by culture. One man's pet is another person's delicacy. Americans love beef, yet it is forbidden to Hindus, while the forbidden food in Muslim and Jewish culture is pork, eaten extensively by the Chinese and others. Using one's hands, chopsticks, or knives and forks to eat also varies by location.

Time and time consciousness. Sense of time differs by culture—some are exact and others are relative. Generally, Germans are precise about the clock, while many Latins are more casual. In some cultures, promptness is determined by age or status. Thus, in some countries subordinates are expected on time at staff meetings, but the boss is the last to arrive. Yet, there are people in some other cultures who do not bother with hours or minutes, but manage their days by sunrise and sunset.

A FRIENDLY SOLUTION

Guillaume is a fast-paced expatriate pilot originally from Paris. He drives quickly and walks with purpose. Naturally friendly, he chats with locals—when he has time. On his way to work, he is often late and rarely has time; he blames this on the local pace.

Rebecca, also an expatriate pilot, understands the local culture and works with it. Without rush and little effort, she moves mostly unhindered.

On her drive to work, she slows down to give an airport worker a ride. It is here that Guillaume goes zipping by.

A minute later, Guillaume comes to a skidding halt at the airport gate, where his morning's frustrations begin.

The guard is stirring his tea. He waits until the dust settles, then looks up to see an expatriate in a hurry. He puts down his mug and stretches his arms. He checks the weather, slides on his jacket, and strolls out to open the gate. The process takes no more than two minutes, but it drives the fast-paced pilot crazy every morning.

When the gate finally swings open, it is for Rebecca, who coasts through with a wave and friendly smile. The guard is still inspecting Guillaume's car.

Guillaume will check in at his plane four minutes late again. For him, working in this culture is frustrating and full of unnecessary delays.

The pace at which different cultures operate varies drastically across the globe. For most Westerners, time is money and life is rushed; but far from Wall Street, Swahili culture moves with the saying "Hurry, hurry, and you'll lose the blessings."

A hurried expatriate in Africa can expect to be slowed down.

Rebecca, who has lived all over the world, has found a solution that seems to work for her everywhere. Regardless of her rush, she takes time to greet people. As a result, when the guard at the gate sees her coming, he has the gate open before she arrives. By slowing down to be friendly, she is able to maintain her fast pace. Unlike Guillaume, she arrives at her plane smiling and on time.

When it comes to dealing with cultural differences, there is nothing more important than being friendly.

Source: Ezra Jay, pilot in Tanzania, 2013.

Relationships. Many cultures fix human and organizational relationships by age, gender, status, and degree of kindred, as well as by wealth, power, and wisdom. The family unit is the most common expression of this characteristic, and the arrangement may go from small to large—in a Hindu household, the joint family may include, under one roof, mother, father, children, parents, uncles, aunts, and cousins. In fact, one's physical location in such houses may also be determined, with men on one side of the house and women on the other.

Relationships between and among people vary by category—in some cultures, the elderly are honored, whereas in others they are ignored; in some cultures, women must wear veils and appear deferential, while in others the woman is considered the equal, if not the superior, of the man.

Values and norms. The values of a culture, or subculture, determine behavior. From the value system, a culture sets norms of behavior for that society. These acceptable standards for membership may range from work ethic or pleasure to absolute obedience or permissiveness for children, from rigid submission of the wife to her husband to a more equal relationship. The globalization process and telecommunications are leading to the development of some shared values that cross borders and express planetary concerns, such as protection of the environment.[20]

Beliefs and attitudes. Possibly the most difficult classification is ascertaining the major belief themes of a people, and how this and other factors influence their attitudes toward themselves, others, and what happens in their world. People in all cultures seem to have a concern for the supernatural that is evident in their religions and religious practices. Western culture seems to be largely influenced by the Judeo–Christian–Islamic traditions, while Eastern or Asian cultures have been dominated by Buddhism, Confucianism, Taoism, and Hinduism. Religion, to a degree, expresses the philosophy of a people about important facets of life and is influenced by culture, and vice versa.

Mental process and learning. Some cultures emphasize one aspect of brain development over another, so that one may observe striking differences in the way people think and learn. Anthropologist Edward Hall maintains that the mind is internalized culture, and the mental process involves how people organize and process information. Life in a particular locale defines the rewards and punishment for learning or not learning certain information or in a certain way, and this is confirmed and reinforced by the culture. For example, Germans stress logic, while logic for a Hopi Indian is on the basis of preserving the integrity of his/her social system and all the relationships connected with it.

Work habits and practices. Another dimension of a group's culture is its attitude toward work—the dominant types of work, the division of work, and the work habits or practices, such as promotions or incentives. Work has been defined as exertion or effort directed to produce or accomplish something. Some cultures espouse a work ethic in which all members are expected to engage in a desirable and worthwhile activity. In other societies, this is broadly defined to include cultural pursuits in music and the arts or sports. For some cultures, the worthiness of the activity is narrowly measured in terms of income produced, or the worth of the individual is assessed in terms of job status.

These ten general classifications are a basic model for assessing a particular culture. It does not include every aspect of culture, nor is it the only way to analyze culture. This approach enables one to examine a people systemically. The categories are a beginning means of cultural understanding as one travels and visits different cultures. Likewise, the model can be used to study the microcultures within a majority national culture. All aspects of culture are interrelated, and to change one part is to change the whole. There is a danger in trying to compartmentalize a complex concept like culture, while trying to retain a sense of its whole. Culture is a complex system of interrelated parts that must be understood holistically.

The speaker was an "expert" on doing business in the Middle East. During his presentation he repeated a variation of the "golden rule" that, to him, was fundamental for working in the oil-producing states in the Gulf: "He who has the gold makes the rules."

In cross-cultural conflict situations, are the rules and outcomes always determined by those who have the gold? Does the stronger always win? What happens, for example, when a German who has learned order hierarchy is assigned to manage a team of Italians who may be less orderly?

What happens when a Harvard-trained physician accepts a position in the Middle East as head of a department and, after asking his colleagues from a number of countries their future plans so that he can prepare a five-year projection of staffing needs, is told he has made an error and caused the morale in the department to decline?

What happens when an Australian company representative changes the dates of scheduled seminars because they interfered with his vacation?

Social scientists and others who have studied or experienced conflict have been well aware of its destructive element, which was observed in wars, strikes, family disruption and disharmony. But recently, the notion that conflict—managed well—could serve some useful purposes has become more prevalent.

But what is conflict? Simply stated, conflict begins when one perceives that the other has frustrated, or is about to frustrate, some right. This frustration may result from actions that range from intellectual disagreement to physical violence. Whatever the definition, the management of conflict is a major issue at the personal and organizational level of a company.

Many people are beginning to view conflict as a healthy, natural, and inevitable part of all relationships. This belief implies that problems can be addressed directly, and that people are motivated to search for solutions. Hence the importance, from the perspective of those who believe that conflict is healthy, of understanding the conflict process and the dynamics of conflict episodes.

If we add an international or intercultural perspective to conflict, however, there is added complexity. The frustration, which precipitated the conflict, may be based on a different cultural perception of the situation.

When participants in a conflict are from the same culture, they are more likely to perceive the situation in basically the same way and organize their perceptions in similar ways. The person involved in cross-cultural conflicts must be careful not to assume that the perception and values of the persons involved in the conflict are the same.

The methods used by a society for dealing with conflicts reflect the basic values and philosophy in that society. In the Arab world, *mediation* is critical in resolving disputes. Confrontation almost never works—especially if the rules are made by those who have the gold. Mediation allows for saving face and mutual understanding, and is rooted in a realism that all conflicts do not have neat solutions.

The Chinese, on the other hand, have learned to internalize conflict and seem to ignore it. Conflict is not healthy, desirable, or constructive.

If we begin by trying to understand the basic values and philosophy of those involved, we might then be able to develop acceptable means for solving some of the cross-cultural conflicts. Perhaps less obvious to those embroiled in conflicts, we also need to be respectful and maintain cordiality—even when we disagree.

Source: adapted by Robert Moran in 2016 from a speech he delivered in Europe.

SYSTEMS APPROACH TO CULTURE

There are many different anthropological approaches to cultural analysis, and many prefer to use a coordinated systems approach as an alternative to understanding other cultures. A system, in this sense, refers to an ordered assemblage or combination of correlated parts that form a unitary whole.[21]

Kinship system. The family relationships and the way a people reproduce, train, and socialize their children; the typical North American family is a nuclear and rather independent unit. In many countries, there may be an extended family that consists of several generations held together through the male line (patrilineal) or through the female line (matrilineal). Such families have a powerful influence on child rearing, and often on nation building.

Educational system. How young or new members of a society are provided with information, knowledge, skills, and values may be formal and informal within any culture. How people learn varies by culture.

Economic system. The manner in which the society produces and distributes its goods and services is in some ways an extension of the family; in Japan it is group-oriented. Until recently, the world was divided into capitalistic or socialistic economic blocs, and economies were labeled *First World* (advanced free enterprise systems); *Second World* (socialist or communistic societies based on centralized planning and control); and *Third World* (developing nations moving from the agricultural to industrial or postindustrial stages). These categories are now outdated. Today, economies are mixed—some supposed Third World economies have high-technology sectors, as in India and China; and Second World countries, formerly in the European Eastern Bloc, are now free-market economies. Another trend beyond national economies is toward regional economic cooperatives or associations that cut across national and ideological boundaries, such as is happening with the North American Free Trade Agreement (NAFTA) and the European Union. Macroeconomics is the study of such systems. Globalization critics say it benefits only the elite. In fact, "a less open world would hurt the poor most of all."[22]

Political system. The dominant means of governance for maintaining order and exercising power or authority. In some cultures it is tribal, where chiefs rule; others have a ruling royal family with an operating king, while some prefer democracy.

Religious system. The means for providing meaning and motivation beyond the material aspects of life; that is, the spiritual side of a culture or its approach to the supernatural may lift a people to great heights of accomplishment, as is witnessed in the pyramids of Egypt and the Renaissance of Europe. It is possible to project the history and future of India, for instance, in terms of the impact of its belief in reincarnation, which is enshrined in its major religion. Diverse national cultures can be somewhat unified under a shared religious belief in Islam or Christianity, for example. In some countries, Islam is becoming the basis for governance, legal, and political systems. In others, religion dominates legal and political systems, such as in Israel. Unfortunately, history demonstrates that in the name of religion, zealots and extremists may engage in culturally repressive behavior, such as religious persecution, ethnic cleansing, terrorism of nonbelievers, and even "holy" wars. Many religions also teach that their religious beliefs are the correct ones and other religious beliefs are wrong.

Association system. The network of social groupings that people form, whether in person or electronically, may range from fraternal and secret societies to professional/trade associations. Some cultures are very group-oriented and create formal and informal associations for every conceivable type of activity (e.g., the culture in the US). In some countries, families organize into clans, finding it difficult to work together for the common national good, as in Afghanistan and Iraq.

Health system. The concepts of health and wholeness, well-being, and medical problems differ by culture. Some countries have witch doctors, spiritual remedies, and herb medications. Others, like India, have fewer government-sponsored social services, while Britain has a system of socialized medicine. The US is in the midst of a major transition in its healthcare and delivery system, and there is increasing emphasis on universal coverage, prevention, and wellness health models. Medical practitioners can be culturally biased. For example, Western medicine tended to ignore folk medicine, especially in Asia and Africa.

Recreational system. What may be considered play in one culture may be viewed as work in another, and vice versa. In some cultures, "sport" has considerable political implications; in others, it is solely for enjoyment; while in still others, it is big business. Some cultures cherish the creative and performing arts, providing financial support for artists and musicians. Certain types of entertainment, such as a form of folk dancing, seem to cut across cultures.

KEY CULTURAL TERMINOLOGY

The specialists who make a formal study of culture use terms that may be helpful to those trying to comprehend the significance of this phenomenon in business or international life.

Tradition

This is a very important aspect of culture that may be expressed in unwritten customs, taboos, and sanctions. Tradition can program a people as to what are proper behaviors and procedures relative to food, dress, and certain types of people, and what to value, avoid, or de-emphasize. As the song on the subject of "tradition" from the musical *Fiddler on the Roof* extols:

> Because of our traditions, we keep our sanity. . . . Tradition tells us how to sleep, how to work, how to wear clothes. . . . How did it get started? I don't know—it's a tradition. . . . Because of our traditions, everyone knows who he is and what God expects of him![23]

Traditions provide a people with a "mindset" and have a powerful influence on their moral system for evaluating what is right or wrong, good or bad, and desirable or not. Traditions express a particular culture, giving its members a sense of belonging and uniqueness. But whether one is talking of a tribal or national culture, or of a military or religious subculture, traditions should be reexamined regularly for their relevance and validity. Mass global communications stimulate acquisition of new values and behavior patterns that may more rapidly undermine ancient, local, or religious traditions, especially among women and young people worldwide.

The following struck the authors' imagination when a manager for a high-tech company brought it to our attention; namely, tradition and superstition express themselves when numbering floors in a hotel. We added some observations of our own as well (see Exhibit 1.1).

EXHIBIT 1.1 COUNTING ELEVATOR FLOORS

It is quite normal in the US to see the thirteenth floor absent in the selection of floors on the elevator directory panel. This is due, of course, to our cultural bias regarding the number 13 as being "unlucky." By omitting it in the numbering sequence of the hotel floors, one avoids the anxiety of a superstitious customer. After entering the Hai-Li Hotel elevator in China and punching in my floor selection, I quickly noticed that not only was number 13 absent, but 14 was as well. As one rose to the higher floors in the hotel, one passed from floor number 12 to floor number 15. I mentioned this to my friends, and they assured me that the Chinese culture had an aversion to an unlucky number as well, only it was number 14. So our culturally astute hotel had decided to delete both numbers, thus showing their sensitivity (and respect) to both cultures, while showing favor to neither. Similarly, in some countries, the custom is to designate the entrance floor as the "ground" floor, while the next floor becomes labeled the "first" floor, as the numbering continues upward. This is confusing to foreigners from countries where the entrance area from the street is known as the "first floor"; the problem worsens when more floors are being built underground—when entering, the visitor may find him or herself on the second or even third floor. Even basements are being built downward in levels 1, 2, 3, etc., and may be given exotic names after fruit or flowers. All this shakes up the staid and makes the world more interesting.

E
X
H
I
B
I
T

1.1

Some of these cultural variables have been researched and a "cultural profile" developed by Schmitz[24] for many countries. There are ten concepts in the model:

1   *Environment*. Social environments can be categorized according to whether they view and relate to people, objects, and issues from the orientation of *control* (change environment), *harmony* (build balance), or *constraint* (external forces set parameters).

2   *Time*. A *past* orientation is indicated by placing a high value on pre-established processes and procedures. A *present* orientation is indicated by placing a focus on short-term and quick results. A *future* orientation is indicated by placing a focus on long-term results.

3   *Action*. Social environments can be distinguished by their approach to actions and interactions. An emphasis on relationships, reflection, and analysis indicates a *being* orientation. A focus on task and action indicates a *doing* orientation.

4   *Communication*. An emphasis on implicit communication and reliance on nonverbal cues indicates *high-context* orientation. A *low-context* orientation is indicated by a strong value placed on explicit communication.

5   *Space*. Cultures can be categorized according to the distinctions they make between *public* and *private* spaces.

6   *Power*. Social environments can be categorized by the way they structure power relationships. A *hierarchy* orientation is indicated by a high degree of acceptability of differential power relationships and social stratification. An *equality* orientation is indicated by little tolerance for differential power relationships and the minimizing of social stratification.

7   *Individualism*. An emphasis on independence and a focus on the individual indicate an *individualistic* orientation. An emphasis on affiliation and subordination of individual interest to that of a group, company, or organization indicates a *collectivistic* orientation.

8   *Competitiveness*. An emphasis on personal achievements, individual assertiveness, and success indicates a *competitive* orientation. Valuing quality of life, interdependence, and relationships indicates a *cooperative* orientation.

9   *Structure*. Environments that value adherence to rules, regulations, and procedures are considered *order*-oriented and prefer predictability and minimization of risk. Environments that value improvisation exhibit a *flexibility* orientation and tend to reward risk-taking, tolerate ambiguity, and value innovation.

10 *Thinking*. Cultures can expect, reinforce, and reward either a *deductive* approach (an emphasis on theory, principles, concepts, and abstract logic) or an *inductive* approach (emphasis on data, experience, and experimentation). They may also either emphasize a *linear* approach (analysis and segmentation of issues) or a *systemic* approach (synthesis, holism, and the "big picture").

Of course, it is important to keep in mind that these constructs are not rigid, and material diversity illustrates this. The concepts can be considered as along a continuum, where extremes are unlikely and placement is relative; it is this that leads us to Hofstede's research.

Can we profile people from other countries?

We can tell you in eight minutes if you have a global mindset . . . or something like that. That statement was listed on a promotional brochure of an educational institution to measure one's "global mindset" by completing a questionnaire in eight minutes. That is an extreme claim, and false.

It is an accurate statement to state that all we can see about our fellow humans is their behavior. We can't see "global mindset," for example. For that matter, we cannot see "culture" or "values" or "assumptions" or "prejudice"—but we can see the BEHAVIOR of individuals who are behaving or talking in a way demonstrating prejudice or bias or racism.

In asking the question "Why do individuals behave the way they behave?" we believe we have to consider three factors. The first is culture. People from the same culture are alike in some ways because they share many aspects of the same cultures previously discussed in this chapter. But they are also in many ways unique, so in understanding BEHAVIOR, we also have to consider PERSONALITY. That is each person's uniqueness. The 2017 population of China is over 1,300,000,000 (one billion, three hundred million), and no two Chinese are exactly the same but there are some aspects of being Chinese that all Chinese share. We must also consider CONTEXT, as we are to some extent influenced by where, when, who, the seriousness or trivialness of the issue, etc. Dr. Geert Hofstede was the first to systematically study aspects of national character that have business and global interaction implications, and we begin with him.

BUT REMEMBER, THESE TRAITS ARE JUST STARTING POINTS AS WE SEEK TO UNDERSTAND THE BEHAVIOR OF ANY GLOBAL RELATIONSHIP.

Hofstede's early research

To create opportunities for collaboration, global leaders must learn not only the customs, courtesies, and business protocols of their counterparts from other countries, but must also understand the national character, management philosophies, and mindsets of the people. Hofstede, a European research consultant, has helped identify important dimensions of national character. He firmly believes that "culture counts" and has identified four dimensions of national culture:

1   *Power distance*—indicates "the extent to which a society accepts that power in institutions and organizations is distributed unequally."

2   *Uncertainty avoidance*—indicates "the extent to which a society feels threatened by uncertain or ambiguous situations."

3   *Individualism*—refers to a "loosely knit social framework in a society in which people are supposed to take care of themselves and of their immediate families only." Collectivism, the opposite, occurs when there is a "tight social framework in which people distinguish between in-groups and out-groups; they expect their in-group (relatives, clan, organizations) to look after them, and in exchange for that owe absolute loyalty to it."

4   *Masculinity*—with its opposite pole, *femininity*, expresses "the extent to which the dominant values in society are assertiveness, money, and material things, not caring for others, quality of life, and people."[25]

A significant dimension related to leadership in Hofstede's original study of 40 countries is the power distance dimension. He assigned an index value to each country on the basis of mean ratings of employees on a number of key questions.[26]

Exhibit 1.2 shows the positions of the 40 countries on the power distance and uncertainty avoidance scales, and Exhibit 1.3 shows the countries' positions on the power distance and individualism scales.

The US ranked 15th on power distance, 9th on uncertainty avoidance (both of these are below the average), 40th on individualism (the most individualist country in the sample), and 28th on masculinity (above average).

In Hofstede's study, the US ranked 15th out of 40 on the power distance dimension. If this had been higher, then the theories of leadership taught in the US might have been expected to be more Machiavellian. We might also ask how US leaders are selected. Most are selected on the basis of competence, and it is the position of the person that provides his or her authority in the US, which is, theoretically at least, an egalitarian society. In France, which has a higher power distance index score, there is little concern with participative management but great concern with who has the power.

Even today, French industry and the managers who run it are a mixture of the old and the new. France is still, in some ways, a country of family empires with many paternalistic traditions. There is also a remnant of a feudalistic heritage that is deeply rooted within the French spirit, which could account for the very conservative and autocratic nature of their business methodology. Hofstede has shown that in countries with lower power distance scores than the US, such as Sweden and Germany, there is considerable acceptance of leadership styles and management models that are even more participative than those that presently exist. Industrial democracy and codetermination is a style that does not find much sympathy in the US.

Hofstede has demonstrated that in Germany there is high uncertainty avoidance and, therefore, industrial democracy is brought about first by legislation. In Sweden, where uncertainty avoidance is low, industrial democracy was started with local experiments. Hofstede[27] continues as follows:

EXHIBIT 1.2 POSITIONS OF 40 COUNTRIES ON THE POWER DISTANCE AND UNCERTAINTY AVOIDANCE SCALES

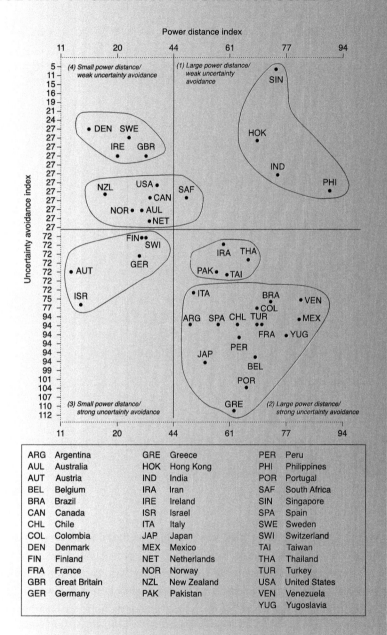

ARG	Argentina	GRE	Greece	PER	Peru
AUL	Australia	HOK	Hong Kong	PHI	Philippines
AUT	Austria	IND	India	POR	Portugal
BEL	Belgium	IRA	Iran	SAF	South Africa
BRA	Brazil	IRE	Ireland	SIN	Singapore
CAN	Canada	ISR	Israel	SPA	Spain
CHL	Chile	ITA	Italy	SWE	Sweden
COL	Colombia	JAP	Japan	SWI	Switzerland
DEN	Denmark	MEX	Mexico	TAI	Taiwan
FIN	Finland	NET	Netherlands	THA	Thailand
FRA	France	NOR	Norway	TUR	Turkey
GBR	Great Britain	NZL	New Zealand	USA	United States
GER	Germany	PAK	Pakistan	VEN	Venezuela
				YUG	Yugoslavia

Source: Hofstede, G. *Cultures Consequences: International Differences in Work-Related Values.* Beverly Hills, CA: Sage Publications, 1984.

EXHIBIT 1.3 POSITIONS OF 40 COUNTRIES ON THE POWER DISTANCE AND INDIVIDUALISM SCALES

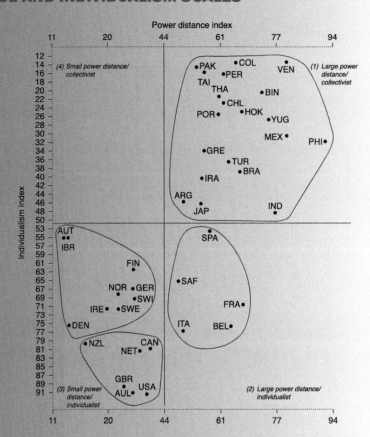

Source: Hofstede, G. *Cultures Consequences: International Differences in Work-Related Values.* Beverly Hills, CA: Sage Publications, 1984.

The crucial fact about leadership in any culture is that it is a complement to subordinateship. The Power Distance Index scores ... are in fact based on the values of people as *subordinates*, not on the values of superiors. Whatever a naive literature on leadership may try to make us believe, a leader cannot choose his style at will; what is feasible depends to a large extent on the cultural conditioning of his/her subordinates. I therefore show ... a description of the type of subordinateship that, other things being equal, a leader can expect to meet in societies at three different levels of Power Distance, and to which his/her leadership has to respond. The middle level represents what most likely is found in the US environment.

Where does this leave us as global managers? Perhaps we pick and choose, and adopt what is appropriate in the home culture. The matter is brought into focus as we examine a specific management system. The underlying assumptions regarding leadership in the US are clearly seen in the practice of management by objectives (MBO). This assumes that a subordinate is independent enough to negotiate meaningfully with a superior (not too high of a power distance), that both the superior and the subordinate are willing to take risks (a low uncertainty avoidance), and that performance is important to both (high masculinity).

Hofstede continues to demonstrate the importance of cross-cultural research as MBO is applied to Germany.

> Let us now take the case of Germany. This is also a below-average Power Distance country, so the dialogue element in MBO should present no problem. However, Germany scores considerably higher on Uncertainty Avoidance; consequently, the tendency towards accepting risk and ambiguity will not be present to the same extent. The idea of replacing the arbitrary authority of the boss by the impersonal authority of mutually agreed-upon objectives, however, fits the low Power Distance, high Uncertainty Avoidance cultural cluster very well. The objectives become the subordinates' "superego."[28]

The consequences of Hofstede's conclusions are significant. Leadership, decision-making, teamwork, organization, motivation, and in fact everything managers do are learned. Management functions are learned, and they are on the basis of assumptions about one's place in the world. Managers from other business systems are not "underdeveloped" American managers.

Professor House and the GLOBE Study[29]

Similar in some ways with Hofstede but adding new dimensions and concepts, Robert House led a research project that attempted to measure culture "in country, industry, and organization." House used data from over 17,000 middle managers from 951 organizations in the food processing, financial services, and telecommunications industries in 58 countries. He also identified the characteristics of outstanding leaders and "least desirable" traits. The results showed differences in cultures, with some aspects of leadership and some "charismatic and team-oriented" traits valued by all countries. But first a description of the nine dimensions that "capture the similarities and/or differences in norms, values, beliefs—and practice—among societies."

Exhibit 1.4 shows the nine dimensions used to differentiate between cultures.

EXHIBIT 1.4 NINE DIMENSIONS

Power distance	The extent to which people in a culture expect others to be treated equally.
Uncertainty avoidance	The extent to which risk is avoided.
Humane orientation	The degree a culture rewards altruistic behavior.
Collectivism I (institutional)	The degree to which institutions in a culture reward sharing resources.
Collectivism II (in-group)	The degree to which people in a culture express pride in their organizations.
Assertiveness	The degree to which individuals are aggressive in their relationships.
Gender egalitarianism	The degree to which men and women are equally valued.
Future orientation	The extent to which individuals exhibit future-oriented behaviors.
Performance orientation	The degree to which a culture rewards performance and excellence.

On the basis of his research using the above dimensions, House was able to place the 61 countries into culture clusters (for example, the Latin American culture contains the countries of Guatemala, El Salvador, Argentina, Venezuela, Costa Rica, Colombia, Ecuador, Mexico, Bolivia, Brazil; and the Nordic Europe cluster includes Denmark, Sweden, and Finland). Within the cluster there is significant similarity, but between clusters there are differences.

Of particular relevance to our book is the global list of traits exhibited by outstanding leaders, which they describe as "exceptionally skilled at motivating, influencing, or enabling you, others, or groups to contribute to the success of the organization or task."

Listed below in rank order are the most desirable traits and the least desirable traits:

Most Desirable
- Integrity
- Inspirational
- Visionary
- Performance-oriented
- Team integrator
- Decisive
- Administratively competent
- Diplomatic
- Collaborative team orientation
- Self-sacrificial
- Modesty

Least Desirable
- Humane
- Status-conscious
- Conflict-inducer
- Procedural
- Autonomous
- Face-saver
- Nonparticipative
- Autocratic
- Self-centered
- Malevolent

Although the traits were not described in any detail, the meaning of most is self-evident, and most people who are leaders in their business organization would probably agree with the two lists. It would be interesting to ask leaders from various countries how "exceptional leaders" in their countries demonstrate or behave in a way that shows "inspirational," "diplomatic," "self-sufficient," or "humane," "conflict-inducer," or "procedural," for example. We believe there would be significant and important cultural differences with the responses to this question.

Bond's Confucian cultural patterns

Another researcher, Michael H. Bond, believes that the taxonomies developed by Western scholars have a Western bias.[30] In his research, he found four dimensions of cultural patterns: integration, which refers in a broad sense to the continuum of social stability; human-heartedness, which refers to values of gentleness and compassion—people who score highly on this dimension value patience, courtesy, and kindness toward others; moral discipline refers to a sense of moderation in daily activities; and the Confucian work dynamic indicates an individual's orientation to life and work. According to Bond, the behaviors that are exhibited along this continuum are consistent with the teachings of Confucius.

Kong Fuzi, renamed Confucius by Jesuit missionaries, was a Chinese civil servant who lived during the Warring States Period about 2,500 years ago. He sought to determine ways in which Chinese society could move away from fighting among themselves so that through discipline, human relationships, ethics, politics, and business relationships they could be more harmonious. He was well known for his wisdom and wit, and was regularly surrounded by followers who recorded his teachings. Confucianism is a set of practical principles and ethical rules for daily life.

Confucius taught that people should be educated, skilled, hard-working, thrifty, modest, patient, and unrelenting in all things. Human nature is assumed to be inherently good, and it is the responsibility of the individual to train his or her character in these standards of behavior.

Exhibit 1.5 represents a clear and simple framework for understanding cultural differences along several dimensions and will be valuable for any person working in the global world.

Many other researchers, including Fons Trompenaars and Charles Hampden-Turner, have studied culture and written persuasively on culture's impact on global business in the twenty-first century.

EXHIBIT 1.5 CONTINUUM OF CULTURAL VARIABLES

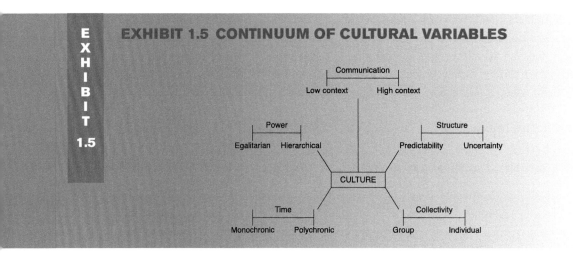

CULTURAL UNDERSTANDING AND SENSITIVITY

And does culture explain everything?

As one works and lives in other cultures, most come to realize there are no good cultures or bad cultures in every aspect. Most also come to believe there are no perfect cultures, including their own.

The recent book *Why Nations Fail*,[31] by Daron Acemoglu and James Robinson, asks the question "Why are there significant differences in the standard of living between rich countries and poor countries?"

The authors begin by describing theories and realities that do NOT answer the question adequately. The first inadequate answer, according to the authors, is the "geography hypothesis" which purports to explain the differences between rich and poor countries by differences in geography. "Many poor countries, such as those in Africa, Central America, and South Asia, are between the tropics of Cancer and Capricorn. Rich nations, in contrast, tend to be in temperate zones." Many social scientists and well-known authors use this as an explanation, arguing that people in warm or hot areas of the world tend to be lazy and don't work hard.

The other widely promoted theory to explain national differences in prosperity is the "cultural hypothesis." Acemoglu and Robinson write that culture explains, in part, world inequality.

> Yes, in the sense that social norms, which are related to culture, matter and can be hard to change, but mostly no, because those aspects of culture often emphasized—religion, national ethics, African or Latin American values—are just not important for understanding how we got here and why the inequities in the world persist.

The "ignorance theory" is also inadequate to explain differences. This theory asserts that inequality exists because no one knows how to help poor countries become more prosperous.

So what is the explanation? The authors demonstrate that nations fail because nations differ on the rules of how an economy works and the incentives that motivate their people. They cite the following to support their answer. Most people in North Korea are poor without entrepreneurial initiative or creativity, and much of their education is propaganda. After school, most enter the army for ten years. They cannot own property or own a business.

In South Korea, most receive a good education (in recent studies, their students at most levels in math and science are among the world's best); they can borrow money to start a business or build a home on property they own. The authors call economic institutions in South Korea "inclusive," as they allow the majority of people to make the best use of their talents and skills in their economic activities; this results in advances in technologies and innovation. North Korea's economic institutions are referred to as "extractive" because "such institutions are designed to extract income and wealth from one subset of society to benefit a different subset." They use many examples from different centuries in different geographical locations to explain *why nations fail*.

The global leader, sensitive to cultural differences, appreciates a peoples' distinctiveness and effectively communicates with individuals from different cultures. A global leader does not impose his/her own cultural attitudes and approaches. Thus, by respecting the cultural differences of others, we will not be labeled as "ethnocentric," defined in *The Random House Dictionary* as:

> Belief in the inherent superiority of one's own group and culture; it may be accompanied by a feeling of contempt for those considered as foreign; it views and measures alien cultures and groups in terms of one's own culture.

Through cross-cultural experiences, we become more broad-minded and tolerant of cultural "uniqueness." When this is coupled with some formal study of the concept of culture, we not only gain new insights for improving our human relations, but we become aware of the impact of our native culture. Cultural understanding may minimize the impact of culture shock and maximize intercultural experiences, as well as increase professional development and organizational effectiveness. Cultural sensitivity should teach us that culture and behavior are relative and that we should be more tentative, and less absolute, in human interaction.

The first step in managing cultural differences effectively is increasing one's general cultural awareness. We must understand the concept of culture and its characteristics before we can fully benefit from the study of cultural specifics and a foreign language.

Further, we should appreciate the impact of our specific cultural background on our own mindset and behavior, as well as those of colleagues and customers with whom we interact in the workplace.[32] This takes on special significance within a more diverse business environment, often the result of increasing migration from less developed to more developed economies.

In the March 20, 2009, *Herald Tribune* article by Nicholas D. Kristof, he wrote:

That's because there's pretty good evidence that we generally don't truly want good information—but rather information that confirms our prejudices. We may believe intellectually in the clash of opinions, but in practice we like to embed ourselves in the reassuring womb of an echo chamber.

He ended his article:

So perhaps the only way forward is for each of us to struggle on our own to work out intellectually with sparring partners whose views we deplore. Think of it as a daily mental workout analogous to a trip to the gym: if you don't work up a sweat, it doesn't count.

GLOBAL TRANSFORMATIONS

To stay globally competitive, more and more corporations are increasing their investments and activities in foreign countries. US engineers can work on a project during the day, and then send it electronically to Asia or elsewhere for additional work while they sleep. Such trends represent an enormous challenge for cross-cultural competence. C-Bay Systems in Annapolis, Maryland, for instance, transmits US physicians' dictations about patients to their subsidiary operations in India where they are transcribed into English, sent back to headquarters by computer, and then the completed version is sent on to the medical office from which the communication originated.

Another example of "going global" is seen in personalized service firms such as law and accounting. These professions are increasingly engaging in cross-border activities, hiring local practitioners who comprehend their own unique culture, language, and legal or accounting systems. The need for international expertise and capital is one reason for this trend. Companies of professionals are forming alliances with their foreign counterparts, such as the Alliance of European Lawyers. To be successful, the acquisition process then requires an integration of *national, organizational*, and *professional cultures*. Under these circumstances, culture becomes a critical factor ensuring business success, particularly with the twenty-first century trend toward economies of scale favoring large, multidisciplinary, and multinational professional service organizations.[33]

In only 10 percent of 191 nations are the people ethnically or racially homogeneous. Never before in history have so many inhabitants traveled beyond their homelands, either to travel or work abroad, or to flee as refugees. In host countries, the social fabric is being reconfigured and strained by massive waves of immigrants, whether legal or illegal.[34]

Many corporate and government leaders, business students, and citizens still operate with dated mindsets regarding the world, the people in various societies, the nature of work, the worker, and the management process itself.

Thus, today's leaders are challenged to create new models of management systems. For that to happen, managers and other professionals must become more innovative and recognize the contribution of each individual or unit to the effective workings of the whole.

As the late Peter Drucker consistently observed, the art and science of management is in its own revolution, and many of the assumptions on which management practice was based are now becoming obsolete.

Foreign competition and the need to trade more effectively overseas have forced most corporations to become more culturally sensitive and globally minded. Managing people from different cultures is receiving the attention of business students as well as those in education and human resource development. Global management is a component in most executive education training programs worldwide.

According to Rhinesmith:[35]

Global managers must reframe the boundaries of their world . . . of space, time, scope, structure, geography and function; of functional, professional, and technical skills from a past age; of thinking and classification relative to rational to intuitive, national versus foreign, we versus they; of cultural assumptions, values and beliefs about your relations with others, and your understanding of yourself.

How do companies foster and create effective global managers? What is a global manager? Companies with worldwide operations are pondering these questions, plus many others. They find that the human resource component of the answer is, at times, more limiting than the capital investment in globalization. Bartlett and Ghoshal[36] state:

Clearly, there is no single model for the global manager. Neither the old-line international specialist nor the more recent global generalist can cope with the complexities of cross-border strategies. Indeed, the dynamism of today's marketplace calls for managers with diverse skills. Responsibility for worldwide operations belongs to senior business, country, and functional executives who focus on the intense interchanges and subtle negotiations required. In contrast, those in middle management and front-line jobs need well-defined responsibilities, a clear understanding of their organization's transnational mission, and a sense of accountability.

Sheridan[37] found three clusters of leadership competencies and included intrapersonal competencies, interpersonal competencies, and social competencies. The following seven Cs apply not only to US leaders, but to global leaders also. Her summary is shown in Exhibit 1.6.

Self-perception and others' perception of you

Intentions are important but, like culture, perceptions count. And for the present and foreseeable future, what happens in our global world will be to a large extent influenced

EXHIBIT 1.6 INTERCULTURALLY COMPETENT LEADER

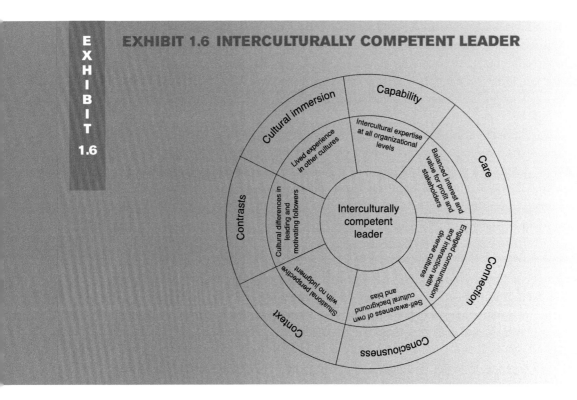

by the US. China is increasingly becoming a world power. The US is involved in many global economic, political, and religious disputes and conflicts. But in this complex, rapidly changing yet interconnected global world, the influence of even the most powerful is highly limited.

Now consider these comments, which provide a contrast.[38]

Americans, almost alone in the world, have a serious . . . even simplistic belief that their country is a force for enduring good. They acknowledge it does not always get it right, that at times its antics fall far short of its highest ideals, but all but the most hardened cynics really believe in America as a force for freedom and prosperity and in the universality of these goals. This belief is born of the country's history, religion, and culture.

. . . It is this self-faith as much as anything that defines and differentiates Americans from most of the rest of the world. There is not much doubt that outside the United States, American intentions, especially under the Bush administration, are regarded with a degree of suspicion and resentment . . . it is not hard to see why this self-belief evinces such cynicism around the world. The United States' record–supporting tyrants, even in places such as Iraq, where it eventually topples them–is hardly unblemished. At times, America's commitment to liberty has looked a little selective.

Denial

Most individuals, at some time in their lives, deny realities. In families, children deny that their parents are alcoholic, and women deny that their husbands are abusive. Similarly, in business organizations and academic institutions, "realities" are suppressed, "feelings" and emotional reactions are not considered, and intellectualization exercises force new realities into old paradigms.

The humorous parody in the American Way box illustrates the denial of a country's competitiveness problem and a misdiagnosis. This example is American, but it can easily apply to most countries.

THE AMERICAN WAY

The Americans and the Japanese decided to engage in a competitive boat race. Both teams practiced hard and long to reach their peak performance. On the big day, they both felt ready.

The Japanese won by a *mile*.

Afterward, the American team was discouraged by the loss. Morale sagged. Corporate management decided that the reason for the crushing defeat had to be found, so a consulting firm was hired to investigate the problem and recommend corrective action.

The consultant's findings: The Japanese team had eight people rowing and one person steering; the American team had one person rowing and eight people steering. After a year of study and millions spent analyzing the problem, the consulting firm concluded that too many people were steering and not enough were rowing on the American team.

So, as race day neared again the following year, the American team's management structure was completely reorganized. The new structure: four steering managers, three area steering managers, one staff steering manager, and a new performance review system for the person rowing the boat to provide work incentive.

That year the Japanese won by *two* miles.

Humiliated, the American corporation laid off the rower for poor performance and gave the managers a bonus for discovering the problem.

In this oversimplification, in the first race the Americans were overconfident and denied they had a competitiveness problem. In preparation for the second race, there was a serious misdiagnosis. Hamel states it well:

To fully understand our competitive advantage/disadvantage, we have to go deeper, and look at our "genetic coding"—that is, our beliefs, our managerial frames. It is these beliefs that restrict our perceptions of reality and degrees of freedom. To be successful, a company needs "genetic variety." Our challenge must be to get outside our restrictive managerial frames.

If you want to enlarge your managerial frames, you must be curious about how the *rest of the world thinks*—and you must *have humility*. The real competitive problem is not that our institutional environment is hopelessly unhelpful, but that our managerial frames are hopelessly *inappropriate to the next round of global competition.*[39]

CONCLUSIONS

Two additional skills are of fundamental importance today for global people. The first skill is *listening* to understand (see additional concepts in Chapter 2). Many global leaders, particularly of nation-states, do not seem to possess this skill to a high degree. Listening is a symbol of respecting the dignity of others.

The second is the skill of locating and using many very sophisticated *cultural interpreters*. It is impossible for any individual, given the complexity of culture, to have a free understanding of other systems. However, cultural interpreters, individuals from each culture, can teach leaders. Having listened and been a student with cultural interpreters as teachers, the global leader is equipped to face the many opportunities and challenges that will be continually presented.

Having a sense of culture and its related skills is a unique human attribute. Culture is fundamentally a group of problem-solving tools for coping in a particular environment. It enables people to create a distinctive world around themselves, to control their own destinies, and to grow. Sharing the legacy of diverse cultures advances our social, economic, technological, and human development. Culture can be analyzed in a macrocontext, such as in terms of national groups, or in a micro sense, such as within a system or organization. Increasingly, we examine culture in a global sense from the perspective of work, leadership, or markets.

Because management philosophies and practices are culturally conditioned, it stands to reason that there is much to be gained by including cultural studies in all management or professional development. This is particularly relevant during the global transformation under way. Culturally skilled leaders are essential for the effective management of emerging global corporations as well as for the furtherance of mutually beneficial world trade and exchange. In these undertakings, the promotion of cultural synergy by those who are truly global managers will help us to capitalize on the differences in people, while ensuring their collaborative action.

Learning to manage cultural differences is a means for all persons to become more global in their outlook and behavior, as well as more effective personally and professionally. When cultural differences are understood and utilized as a *resource*, then all benefit.[40] When they are not, the costs are significant. We end with a dilemma when a "boss" is good at many things but is not a good listener. This will also serve as a transition to the concepts in Chapter 2.

IS THE BOSS A GOOD LISTENER?

"If my boss and the president of our company would stay at home and do what they're best at doing, we'd have fewer problems in France." These words were uttered privately to me recently. The engineer who had this opinion had just returned to France with his French boss, the company managing director, from Asia. Both considered the trip not very successful. Why?

Listening skills

High-level executives make it to the top for many reasons. Among them is the ability to make quick decisions that more often than not have positive results. These same executives are often rather articulate in conceptualizing issues. As a result, the executive spends more time talking than listening. The skill of articulation carried to the extreme can become a liability because there is little or no listening.

Western education seems to emphasize articulation over the acquisition of listening skills, which are essential to international business. In the US, for example, Professor Lyman Steil of the University of Minnesota pioneered scientific research on listening, and discovered that it is the communication competency that is used most, but the one that is taught least.

We learn to listen and talk before we read and write. Should we have difficulties with reading, writing, and talking, we will receive special assistance while at school. Not so with listening. Listening is a complex activity. The average person speaks around 12,000 sentences every day. The average person can speak at about 150 words per minute, while the listener's brain can absorb around 400 words per minute. What do we do with this spare capacity? Unfortunately, many of us do nothing. We become bored. A good listener is seldom bored, and uses this extra capacity to listen to the entire message and to analyze more fully the meanings behind the words.

Many people are just "polite listeners" and are not listening—they are just waiting their turn to speak and are perhaps rehearsing their lines.

"*Active listening*," however, involves a listener with very definite responsibilities. In active listening, the listener strives for complete and accurate understanding, for empathy, and to actively assist in working out problems.

Listening fulfills a vital function. The listener provides feedback to the speaker concerning the latter's success in transmitting a message clearly. In doing this, the listener exerts some influence over future messages that might or might not be sent.

The ability to listen is especially important when persons from low-context cultures communicate with persons from high-context cultures.

If your boss isn't a good listener, perhaps he or she should stay home.

(This concept will be discussed in Chapter 2.)

MIND STRETCHING

1   How did your parents/caregivers influence you?

2   Can you have a global mindset and be a proud Canadian or French or…?

3   Do you believe the world is really "flat," and what does this mean?

4   How can you see events and issues through multiple lenses?

5   When confronted with cultural differences, why do we often dig in and believe our way is right rather than listen?

6   What is your opinion regarding the Prophet Mohammed cartoon controversy?

7   In five years, with your "futurist hat" on, how would you describe our "global world"?

NOTES

1   Moran, Robert T. Journal notes, 2013.

2   "It Ain't Necessarily So," *The Economist*, October 13, 2012.

3   Solomon, A. *Far from the Tree: Parents, Children and the Search for Identity*. New York: Scribner, 2012.

4   Pascal, B. *Pensées*, Vol. 60, 1670, p. 294.

5   Freidman, T. "It's a Flat World, After All," *New York Times Magazine*, April 3, 2005.

6   Freidman, T. *The World Is Flat: A Brief History of the Twenty-First Century*. New York: Farrar, Strauss and Giroux, 2005, pp. 6–7.

7   Schein, E. H. "On Dialogue, Culture and Organizational Learning," *Organizational Dynamics*, Vol. 22, No. 2, 1993, pp. 40–51.

8   Brooks, D. "It's Culture That Counts," *International Herald Tribune*, February 21, 2006.

9   Harrison, L. and Huntington, S. P. (eds.). *Culture Matters*. New York: Basic Books, 2000, p. 111.

10   Diamond, J. *Guns, Germs, and Steel*. New York: Norton and Company, 1999, p. 13.

11   Ibid., p. 25.

12   Moran, Robert T. Personal journal, 2010.

13   *Global Awareness and Education: American's Test for the 21st Century*. Apple Inc., February 2007.

14   Egan, T. "The Dumbed Down Democracy," *New York Times*, Opinion Page, August 26, 2016.

15   Deardorff, D. K. (ed.). *The Sage Handbook of Intercultural Competence*. Thousand Oaks, CA: Sage, 2009.

16   Huntington, S. *The Clash of Civilizations and the Remaking of World Order*. New York: Simon & Schuster, 1996.

17   Chomsky, N., Mitchell, P. R., and Schoeffel, J. (eds.). *Understanding Power*. New York: Vintage, 2002.

18   Lewis, R. D. *The Cultural Imperative*. Yarmouth, ME: Intercultural Press, 2003.

19   *Science & Culture*, January/February 2008.

20   Freidman, *The World Is Flat*.

21   Miller, J. G. *Living Systems*. Niwot, CO: University Press of Colorado, 1994. See also *Systems Research and Behavioral Science*, Wiley Interscience, online.

22   *The Economist*, October 1, 2016.

23   Stein, J. "Tradition," *Fiddler on the Roof*. Harnick, S., lyrics, Bock, J., music, 1964.

24   Schmitz, J. *Cultural Orientations Guide*. Princeton, NJ: Princeton Training Press, 2003, pp. 10–12.

25   *Science & Culture*, January/February 2008.

26   Ibid.

27 Hofstede, G. *Cultures Consequences: International Differences in Work-Related Values*. Beverly Hills, CA: Sage, 1984. See also Hofstede, G. *Cultures and Organizations: Software of the Mind*. London: McGraw-Hill, 1991.

28 Hofstede, *Cultures and Organizations: Software of the Mind*.

29 For our summary, we have chosen to use the article "Leader Effectiveness and Culture: The GLOBE Study," published by the Center for Creative Leadership in 2014.

30 Lustig, M. W. and Koester, J. *Intercultural Competence: Interpersonal Communication Across Cultures*, 5th edn. New York: Allyn and Bacon, 2005.

31 Acemoglu, D. and Robinson, J. *Why Nations Fail*. New York: Crown Business, 2012.

32 Thiederman, S. *Bridging Cultural Barriers to Success: How to Manage the Multicultural Workforce*. Lexington, MA: Lexington Books, 1990; Thiederman, S. *Profiting in America's Multicultural Workplace*. Lexington, MA: Lexington Books, 1991.

33 *The Economist*, August 29, 1998, p. 59.

34 Harris, P. R. In Simons, G., Abramms, B., Hopkins, A., and Johnson, D. (eds.), *The Cultural Diversity Handbook*. Princeton, NJ: Pacesetter Books, 1996.

35 Rhinesmith, S. H. *A Manager's Guide to Globalization*, 2nd edn. Chicago, IL: Irwin/ASTD, 1996, p. x.

36 Bartlett, C. A. and Ghoshal, S. "What is a Global Manager?" *Harvard Business Review*, September/October, 1992, p. 131.

37 Sheridan, E. *The Global Business Leadership*. Burlington, MA: Elsevier, 2009.

38 Baker, G. "The Land of the Free Enjoys the Thrill of Being a Force for Good," *Financial Times*, April 12–13, 2003.

39 Hamel, G. "Pushing the Envelope of Global Strategy and Competitiveness," a summary of remarks by Gary Hamel for the Executive Focus International 1993 Executive Forum, February 12, 1993.

40 Gesteland, R. R. *Cross-Cultural Business Behavior: Marketing, Negotiating, and Managing Across Cultures*. Copenhagen: Copenhagen Business School Press (Handelshojskolens Forlag), 1999.

2 GLOBAL LEADERS AND INTERCULTURAL COMMUNICATIONS

We can ignore race (skin color) on a political level but we can't ignore that ethnic differences exist on a social level—especially between different cultures. We have to value differences (as opposed to using them as reasons to discriminate)—essentially going beyond ignoring, recognizing or tolerating differences to actually appreciating them, to cast culture in the light of strengths instead of weaknesses. . . . Portraying differences as strengths is the first step in eliminating bias.

Brent Massey[1]

Wouldn't it be great to have x-ray vision into other people's personalities—to know what they are thinking, what they care deeply about, their likes and dislikes? If we did have x-ray vision, then we'd know how to best approach people, how to pique their interest in our ideas, resolve a conflict, strike a bargain, or simply help them feel more at ease relating to us. . . . How do you "read" the other person quickly to discover what strategy is best?

Paul D. Tieger and Barbara Barron-Tieger[2]

Cross-cultural communication looks at how people from differing cultural backgrounds communicate, in similar and different ways among themselves, and how they endeavor to communicate across cultures. Intercultural communication studies situations where people from different cultural backgrounds *interact*.

Wikipedia[3]

L
E
A
R
N
I
N
G

O
B
J
E
C
T
I
V
E
S

After reading and studying the concepts, examples, and illustrations in Chapter 2, readers should be able:

1   To learn and make allowance for cultural differences affecting intercultural communication. These include: low-context versus high-context cultures; fast versus slow messaging cultures; personal space preferences; monochronic versus polychronic time cultures; body language; and eye contact.
2   To identify four Jungian styles of communication characteristic in particular cultures based on national characters. Readers will understand how these styles affect communication, interaction, and relationship building. Readers will learn how each interaction style behaves negatively when under situational stress.
3   To identify in which national cultures each of the four communications styles are most likely to be found as the predominant communications preferences based on national character.

INTRODUCTION

Back in the last century, most people who worked in business spent between 70 and 90 percent of their time communicating, mainly verbally but also in writing, with superiors, co-workers, subordinates, clients or customers, friends or acquaintances, or media.[4] These days, with smartphones, tablets, email, texting, Facebook, Twitter, and interactive electronic media, much of our "alone" time is spent with, or in relation to, others as well. Much of what used to be verbal communication—talking and making presentations—has been replaced with electronic written communication. A recent study by Adobe found that white-collar workers in the US were spending an average of 4.1 hours of their working days checking their work email and responding.[5] This represented 20.5 hours per week or 1,000 hours in a year.

These days, people may attend meetings and conferences by Skyping on their laptops or even their smartphones rather than attending in person. People set-up personal and business networks using Facebook, Twitter, Line, Viber, and other similar apps that limit the recipients to a select few that may include members from any number of national cultures from around the world. Hence, it is much easier for us to engage in cross-cultural communications electronically than it was for businesspeople in past generations, and given workplace diversity, it is easy for us to do so without even being aware because we cannot see the person receiving our email or text messages.

Our electronic communication may be very conditioned by our own culture, even in ways of which we are not conscious, and may be received in ways we did not intend because of the different culture-based interpretations of the recipient. We must, therefore, try to communicate in ways that seem to be received appropriately—as we intended—and to avoid culturally inappropriate interactions. Sometimes it will only become apparent that we have communicated inappropriately for a particular receiver based on his/her response, and so we need to know how to repair unintended damage and get back on track.

The generally accepted definition of communication has been altered to some degree by the electronic internet age. In times past, its first definition was that there was a sender and a receiver. The sender conveyed ideas, feelings, and/or information to the receiver. Successful communication occurred if the receiver understood the message in the same sense that the sender intended. These days, this definition has been replaced by what used to be the third most important definition, based on frequency of usage. Now the simple transmission or conveyance of the message has become the first definition of communication in modern dictionaries, and the vehicle for transmission—letter, email, or text message—has become the second. Achieving mutual understanding may now be only the third most important definition. In other words, in common usage it may be sufficient in order for communication to occur to simply send a message, whether it is understood by the receiver or not. At the university, when a receiver claims that she/he did not receive a particular communication, the sender consults his/her mailbox of sent messages and says "Oh yes, I sent that message on such-and-such date," as if that is the end of the matter. The sender is not concerned whether the receiver had understood the intention of the message, or misgauged its importance among the dozens of emails and messages received daily. The sender did not, and does not, expect any confirmation from the receiver that his/her message has been received, and simply assumes it has been understood.

In business, however, the sender usually still has as his/her goal to influence the receiver in some way. A salesperson is trying to influence particular customers or clients to purchase specific products or services in specific amounts by a certain date. Marketers are trying to influence manufacturers to be more responsive to perceived customer needs, while manufacturers seek to reduce manufacturing costs by increasing acceptance of mass-produced products while reducing numbers of special orders. Managers seek to provide feedback to their subordinates—reinforcing positive behaviors and reducing negative behaviors. Senior managers are trying to ensure that those reporting to them understand the company's strategic plan, and are effectively organizing their assigned resources to achieve their assigned productivity goals. All of these kinds of goals require that the receiver not only understand what the sender is trying to communicate, but also, from the sender's point-of-view, that the receiver is moved to actions intended by the sender.

The sender's task is made considerably more complicated by the vagaries of intercultural communication. The sender may make culturally based assumptions about what constitutes appropriate communication that would be considered inappropriate assumptions in the receiver's culture. When the receiver makes the appropriate assumptions of his/her own culture, she/he may interpret the message in ways the sender did not intend, and likely could never have predicted based on his/her own cultural assumptions about appropriate communication.

A good example of this is email. There are cultures that favor "fast messaging" communication, and other cultures that favor "slow messaging" communication. In fast messaging cultures like the US, Canada, and so on, it is considered entirely appropriate to send relevant information and requests by email to strangers, hoping to expedite outcomes. In slow messaging cultures like China, Saudi Arabia, and so on, businesspeople want to build relationships prior to conducting business, and strangers are treated quite differently from friends. Outcomes may usually only be expedited between friends who trust each other's intentions, and usually, if it's a complicated request, friends telephone or visit each other rather than emailing. Email is perceived as only appropriate for handling simple issues like expeditiously providing relevant information.

Other issues that profoundly affect intercultural communication include high-context versus low-context cultures, timing preferences in terms of monochronic and polychronic cultures, body language and eye contact, and whether people have cultural preferences about how physically close they should be when interacting in person. Many of these considerations are discussed in this chapter.

In addition, recent empirical research has demonstrated that national cultures have "national characters" that differ in predictable ways from culture to culture.[6] Inkeles defines national character as follows:

> We propose that character should be taken literally to mean the dispositions built into the personalities of the individuals who make up a society, and that national character be the sum of such qualities across the individuals who make up a national population ... approached through a broad and wide-ranging conception of the human personality ... rest[ing] on measurement, on the systematic use of psychological tests and attitude and value surveys drawn from representative national samples.[7]

Research on national character was prominent during the middle of the twentieth century but fell out of favor later, when it was associated with justifying racial stereotypes based on assertions of genetically based differences unsupported by empirical evidence. It has now been rehabilitated with mounting empirical evidence that "populations having the same ethnic origin manifest quite different psychosocial character when located in different national settings," irrespective of race.[8] Individuals with very different ethnic origins have been shown to have the same national character when present together in the same national culture.

Cognitive and personality psychology theory and research has supported these observations. Personality research has established that humans-as-species share the same limited number of categories of cognitive preferences regardless of their cultural orientations.[9] These human personality dimensions exist as genetically based endogenous dispositions that vary in strength from individual to individual.[10] They also differ in the distribution of frequencies of specific personality dimensions from culture to culture. Costa and McCrae[11] argued that cross-national differences in cognitive preference seemed to result from frequency differences in national cultural gene pools. These differences in frequencies of cognitive preferences affect what may be considered communications norms from culture to culture. If known, communications senders could predict the probable information-processing preferences they might expect to encounter in specific cultures, and design their communications accordingly.

The Jungian personality model[12] represents an established basis for predicting national character. It is based on three bipolar sets of opposites, producing eight factors.[13] Four of these factors are related particularly to communications preferences.[14] Myers[15] created the more familiar Myers–Briggs Type Indicator (MBTI), perhaps the most popular personality assessment tool, by adding a fourth bipolar dimension to the Jungian model, resulting in 16 personality types. Massey[16] conducted a study of 104 national cultures using MBTI theory that may be used to establish the national characters for each culture based on the Jungian model.

In this chapter, and throughout *Managing Cultural Differences*, we have chosen to use the Jungian model with its eight factors for two important reasons. First, although the MBTI has been the most well-known application of Jungian personality theory throughout the late twentieth and early twenty-first centuries, the latest leading-edge "depth typology" theory development and research has concentrated on Jung's original personality model.[17] Second, modern depth typology has combined Jung's personality types with Myers' MBTI model and John Beebe's " 'eight function–attitude eight archetype' model" to initiate "a new generation of personality type models" with a remarkable ability to "illuminate interpersonal differences and common ground."[18] The model also predicts how each communication style becomes dysfunctional when individuals perceive themselves to be under high stress, and what you should do to repair the situation. In conjunction with Massey,[19] we are able to predict, in this chapter, the predominant communications problems that will be encountered between individuals representing different national characters. The Jungian model, and its impact on cross-cultural communication, will be explained later in this chapter.

A few words of caution about our approach are appropriate. When we argue with Massey that a nation has a predominant psychological national character that significantly impacts its style of communication, that does not mean that everyone from that national culture is like that. Stereotyping should be avoided. All four of the communication styles that we identify from the Jungian model exist in every country, but one of the four will be most evident. You have to learn through personal interaction how best to communicate individually with every foreign counterpart you encounter. Our goal is simply to help communication senders predict what kind of communications strategies will be most effective in various national cultures. These predominant national styles give you a place to begin your communication—the approach most likely to succeed on average.

INTERCULTURAL COMMUNICATION: INTRODUCTION

When we study international business, we might have a tendency to believe that the cultures in North America, Europe, and Japan are the most important to consider in terms of achieving effective communication. Many of the most successful multinational enterprises have originated from these areas. However, the odds are that you will have to communicate far beyond this circle of cultures over the course of your management career. Our world's population exceeds seven billion. If, however, the global population were only 1,000 people, it would have the following composition:[20]

- 52 North Americans (including 47 Americans and 5 Canadians);
- 150 Europeans (including Western, Eastern, and Russian);
- 6 Australians and New Zealanders;
- 584 Asians (including 200 Chinese and 167 Indians);
- 124 Africans;
- 84 Latins and South Americans.

In addition, when we hear that English is the international language of commerce, it is all too easy to forget how few speak it as their native language. If the global population again were only 1,000 people, about 50 percent of the people would speak the following as their first languages:

- 165 Mandarin;
- 86 English;
- 83 Hindi/Urdu;
- 64 Spanish;
- 58 Russian;
- 37 Arabic.

The other 50 percent speak Bengali, Portuguese, Indonesian, Japanese, German, French, and 200 other languages. Communication, indeed, can be challenging in this global village.

Effective communication across cultural and linguistic boundaries is difficult. It involves learning to use flexible approaches to listen, observe, and speak according to the specific situation at hand. Before a person is able to communicate effectively with people from different cultures, it is important to know about their culture, language, history, and where they live. The following is a list of questions that require a little more knowledge and sophistication. They are adapted from the booklet, "So You're Going Abroad: Are You Prepared?"[21] These are the kinds of questions you want to be able to answer as part of your preparations for an international assignment that could facilitate your communicating effectively with locals. Can you answer the questions for any country in which you have worked or done business in the past?

1   There are many contemporary and historical people of whom a country is proud. Can you name a politician, a musician, a writer, a religious leader, a sports figure?

2   Are you familiar with that country's basic history? Date of independence? Relationship to other countries?

3   What are some routine courtesies that people are expected to observe in that country?

4   How do they greet each other? Foreigners?

5   What do you know about their major religions?

6   Are there role differences between men and women?

7   What kinds of foods are traditional?

8   What kind of humor is appreciated?

9   What is the relationship between that country and your country?

Intercultural communication is a process whereby individuals from different cultural backgrounds attempt to share meanings. In the classical anthropological sense, culture refers to the range of human phenomena that cannot be attributed to genetic outcomes. Specifically, "culture" has two meanings.[22] First, it comprises the evolved human capacity to classify and represent experience symbolically, and to act with imagination and creativity. Second, it includes all the distinct ways in which people in different geographic locations classify and represent their experiences and act creatively. *Material* culture includes physical artifacts. *Intangible* culture includes language, customs, beliefs, values, mores, and so on, passed on from generation to generation. With communication, we are most concerned with the intangible. Lustig and Koester[23] provide definitions of communications. For example, intercultural communication is "the presence of at least two individuals who are culturally different from each other on such important attributes as their value orientations, preferred communication codes, role expectations, and perceived rules of social relationship."

Much of what constitutes intercultural communications is nonverbal, consisting of cultural conventions as to how communications should be organized and focused, and how individuals should place themselves in relation to each other when communicating. It has been estimated that as much as 80–90 percent of communication is nonverbal in that it involves no exchange of words.[24]

THE COMMUNICATION PROCESS

Effective communications is difficult enough even with your spouse and loved ones. For that reason, it makes sense for us to review the communication process in general before considering the added complications of effective intercultural communications.

Communication is a process of circular interaction involving a sender, receiver, and message. In the most basic terms, the sender sends a message to the receiver. When the receiver understands what the sender means, successful communication has occurred. In human interaction, the sender or receiver may be a person or a group of people. The message conveys meaning through the medium or symbol used to send it (the how), as well as in its content (the what). Essentially, people tend to selectively perceive information and judge its relevance and importance in the context of their own perceptual preferences. An individual's self-image, needs, values, expectations, goals, standards, cultural norms, and personality affect the way input is received and interpreted. Two people can thus receive the same message and understand it as having two entirely different meanings. They actually perceive the same object or information differently. Communication, then, is a complex process of linking up or sharing perceptual fields between sender and receiver. The effective communicator builds a bridge to the world of the receiver. When the sender is from one cultural group and the receiver from another (and in the communication process, this is reciprocal), the human interaction is intercultural communication.

Once the sender sends the message, the receiver analyzes the message in terms of his or her particular field of experience and pattern of ideas. He/she essentially decodes the message, interpreting it for meaning, and encoding and sending back a response. Thus, communication is a circular process of interaction.

The communicator, whether as an individual from a cultural group or as a member of an organization, exhibits or transmits many kinds of information. First, the intended message is communicated on verbal and nonverbal levels. We also communicate unintended, or unconscious, messages on verbal and nonverbal levels. The latter includes a whole "silent language" including voice tone, gestures, facial expressions, and body language. According to Hall,[25] 80–90 percent of the message you send, or interpret as the receiver, is based on this silent language. The person is both a medium of communication and a message. This silent language is particularly influenced by culture in ways people are often not aware.

Listening

Listening is at the heart of all successful communications. We listen to both the words and the nonverbal signaling. We learn to listen and talk before we read and write.

Listening is a complex activity. The average person speaks approximately 12,000 sentences every day at about 150 words per minute, while the listener's brain can absorb around 400 words per minute. This means the listener always has the capacity to understand. What do we do with this spare capacity? We become bored. We assume we know what is being said. We think about what we are going to say whenever he/she is finished speaking. We interrupt. A good listener understands that without good listening, there will be poor results. He/she uses this extra capacity to listen to the entire message and to more fully analyze the meanings behind the words.

Listening means different things to different people. It can mean different things to the same person in different situations. There are two types of positive listening behaviors:

1   *Information gathering* is a form of listening. Its purpose is the absorption of information, both stated and nonverbally signaled. Information gathering is not the same as

interpretation. As soon as we start interpreting what someone is saying, it is possible to lose track of anything else he/she is saying.

2   *Active listening*[26] requires that the listener demonstrate to the speaker that he/she really understands what is being said. We *paraphrase* the speaker by saying what we think he/she means. We *perception check* how we understand the speaker to be feeling about what he/she is saying. We *summarize* briefly before making our own response, so the speaker will understand we are discussing the points he/she has made. Active listening is what our normal listening mode should be, but we rarely do it fully because it is work, and because it feels artificial if we are not used to doing it.

There are also some negative forms of listening that are more likely to cause difficulties and result in poor outcomes. These include:

1   *Polite listening* is listening just enough to meet the minimum social requirements by being able to make a relevant response or changing to a relevant alternate topic. If we are thinking what to say next, then we are not really listening.

2   *Defensive listening* is based on finding points that can be disputed in order to maintain our own positions against whatever the speaker is saying.

3   *Offensive listening* looks for opportunities to trap or trip up an opponent with his/her own words. A lawyer, when questioning a witness, listens for contradictions, irrelevancies, and weakness.

The positive forms of listening, especially active listening, are above all a sharing of oneself with another. It is impossible for one to become an active listener without becoming involved with the speaker. Listening demonstrates a respect and concern that words alone cannot fully express. It has the unique power of diminishing the magnitude of potential communication problems. By speaking to someone who actively listens, a speaker has the sense of already accomplishing something. He/she knows that the message has been successfully transmitted. And the listener exerts some influence over the speaker when it is the listener's turn to speak. Both know that they are talking about the same topic and that the listener has understood the speaker's points. This makes the speaker more interested in what the response will be when it is his/her turn to listen.

MODELS OF INTERCULTURAL COMMUNICATION

Traditional Western models of communication are a reflection of Western cultural and philosophical thought. The early models depicted communication as a linear process, and were deemed process models including the source, message, channel, and receiver.[27] The sender was regarded as the one responsible for the success of the communication because he/she took responsibility for the contents of the message.[28]

Current models tend to be more sociological and to highlight the effect of culture. For example, one model includes the sender, message, channel, noise, receiver, feedback, and cultural context.[29] Noise is defined as the perceptions of, and the cultural backgrounds of, each communicator. Cultural filters are the noise for both the sender and receiver.[30] We agree, however, with recent research[31] asserting that the language and signaling used in communication are not separable from its cultural context. Therefore, culture should not be viewed as noise, but rather as a key ingredient within the practice of communication. Culture influences how language is formed, how the linguistic communication is understood, and impacts how the language is constructed.[32] Because we do not view culture as peripheral to communication, the values[33] that are espoused as part of one's culture become highly salient. One's values are the basis for judging whether actions are considered "right or wrong." So, failing to understand predominant values within a society and failing to concede that an individual person has a particular set of beliefs will both lead to poor communication.[34]

Our own view is that intercultural communication seeks to understand how people from different countries and cultures act, communicate, and perceive the world around them. On the one hand, it considers the effect of culture in determining how individuals encode messages, the mediums they choose to transmit messages, and the ways they interpret messages. On the other hand, it also studies situations in which people from different cultural backgrounds interact. While language is an important component, intercultural communication also focuses on social attributes, thought patterns, and cultural contents. The fields of anthropology, cultural studies, linguistics, psychology, and even philosophy all participate in identifying its key attributes.

There are many theories in all these disciplines that seek to explain how intercultural communications works and how to do it successfully. Our own approach recognizes that individuals engage in culturally moderated behaviors that may be consciously adopted as normative patterns of everyday life, or unconsciously adopted as habitual patterns of communicating within their own particular cultural group. Our approach also recognizes that, while in the past, the identification of cultural differences was the paramount concern, more recently the role of cultural similarities in simplifying communication challenges has become a more important consideration.

Variables in the communication process

Samovar and Porter[35] identified a number of variables in the communication process whose values were determined to some extent by culture. Each variable influences our perceptions, which in turn influence the meanings we attribute to behavior. In order to work effectively in a multicultural environment, one should recognize these and study the cultural specifics of the country or area to be visited.

Values are abstract and generalized principles defining appropriate and inappropriate behavior, believed to apply in all situations. Members of a cultural group feel a strong and emotionally toned commitment that becomes a standard for judging others' actions. Values provide the generalized standards of behavior that are expressed in more specific and concrete ways in social norms. For example, Western Christian and Middle-Eastern Islamic societies have a strong value commitment to the principle of charity offered to monetarily or socially disadvantaged individuals.

Social norms define rules or standards for evaluating what behavior is considered socially acceptable. Norms are guidelines as to the ranges of behavior considered appropriate and applicable in particular situations. In the example offered above, Western Christian and Middle-Eastern Islamic societies accept a generous range of what constitutes acceptable expressions of charity, including nonfinancial contributions.

Attitudes are emotionally toned psychological states that predispose us to behave in certain ways. Attitudes differ from values in being situational in their application while values are understood to apply in all cases.

Stereotypes are sets of attitudes that cause us to attribute qualities or characteristics to a person on the basis of the group to which that individual belongs. Stereotypes are outsiders' beliefs about groups. They constitute assumptions and/or generalizations, based on experience, that allow an educated guess about how someone or some group will behave that allow us to organize and understand our environment. Stereotypes aid us in predicting behavior and reduce our feelings of uncertainty. Stereotypes may be dangerous, however, when we apply them to any individual member from that group. This is especially a concern in cross-cultural communication. We can say that a stereotype is useful in suggesting how we should approach an unknown stranger, but as we learn about that person we should abandon general assumptions for specific individual knowledge. There is no guarantee that any individual from a specific culture will behave as members of that culture generally behave according to the stereotype.

The *social organization* of cultures is another variable that influences one's perceptions. Hofstede and Hofstede[36] developed a cultural dimensions theory based on five value dimensions and their impact on national cultural organizational culture (see Chapter 1 for Hofstede's earlier work). They argued that these five values dimensions strongly influenced social organization (and individual behavior) in predictable directions.

Roles in a society are expectations within a culture concerning behavior that may affect communication. Some roles have very prescriptive rules. Gender is an obvious example. In Western business, there is an expectation of gender equality that may not be found in various conservative cultures. Western companies typically send female expatriates to conservative societies, Saudi Arabia for example, where the rights of women are not as well established. These female expatriates are usually treated as foreigners rather than as women, assuming they are not members of the ethnic group to which they have been sent. Merchant[37] observed that the role of female expatriates may be affected by their gender; as much by their own stereotypical expectations about the culture they have been sent to, as by how they are actually treated.

Language skill in a host country is acknowledged as important. Many believe, however, that a competent interpreter can be helpful and, at times, necessary even if we speak the native language. A competent interpreter may help us understand the deliberations of those we negotiate with. An interpreter is also helpful to ensure that the opposite side's translator is providing an accurate translation of our own statements. An interpreter may, therefore, be useful even if you do speak the local language.

NONVERBAL COMMUNICATION

Earlier in this chapter, we noted that 80–90 percent of communication was nonverbal in that it involved no exchange of words.[38] Hall, an anthropologist generally acknowledged as the founder of the intercultural communications field,[39] observed that much of what anyone communicated was done unconsciously. There was an "out-of-awareness" level of communication[40] on the part of the "speaker" that was received at an out-of-awareness level by the receiver. Intercultural communications could be influenced profoundly and negatively without the conscious awareness of either side. Because neither side was aware of this level of communication, it represented an uncontrolled dimension of interpersonal communication operating at the level of the unconscious. The purpose of the following sections is to acquaint you with these unconscious media and their effects on intercultural communication.

Low- and high-context communication

Hall makes a vital distinction between high- and low-context cultures, and how this impacts communications. A *high-context culture* uses more vague forms (or high-context) communications. Information is either understood to be in the physical context or internalized in the person (they assumed to know the background) so that less has to be communicated in the explicit words or message. Japan, Saudi Arabia, and Spain are cultures characterized by high-context communications.

On the other hand, a *low-context culture* employs more direct (or low-context) forms of communications. It is assumed that receivers need the context around the communication and so most information is contained in explicit codes, such as words. Germany, and many northern European countries, are low-context cultures as are the US and Canada.

When individuals communicate, they attempt to find out how much the listener knows about whatever is being discussed. In a low-context communication, the listener is assumed to know very little and must be told practically everything. In high-context cultures, the listener is already "contexted" and therefore does not need to have much background information.

When communicating with individuals of our own culture, we can more readily assess the communication cues so that we know when our conversation, our ideas, and words are being understood and internalized. However, communication between high- and low-context people is often fraught with impatience and irritation on both sides. Low-context communicators may provide more information than high-context receivers feel necessary, and be regarded by the latter as repetitive and even disrespectful of others' time. High-context communicators may not provide enough information or background for low-context listeners, and be regarded as difficult to understand, or even as holding back. High-context communicators may feel that they are expected to be almost disrespectfully blunt just to get their messages across to low-context listeners.

When communicating across cultures, communication misunderstandings can occur, but they are usually not serious and can be rectified. Exhibit 2.1 is an excellent example of a low-context question responded to by a very high-context Middle-Eastern communicator.

E
X
H
I
B
I
T

2.1

EXHIBIT 2.1 MIDDLE EAST LOW-/HIGH-CONTEXT COMMUNICATION

"How many days did it take?" I asked.

"I will tell you. We watered at al Ghaba in the Amairi. There were four of us, myself, Salim, Janazil of the Awamir, and Alaiwi of the Afar; it was in the middle of summer. We had been to Ibri to settle the feud between the Rashid and the Mahamid started by the killing of Fahad's son."

Musallim interrupted, "That must have been before the Riqaishi was Governor of Ibri. I had been there myself the year before. Sahail was with me and we went there from…."

But al Auf went on, "I was riding the three-year-old I had bought from bin Duailan."

"The one the Manahil raided from the Yam?" Bin Kabina asked.

"Yes. I exchanged it later for the yellow six-year-old I got from bin Ham. Janazil rode a Batina camel. Do you remember her? She was the daughter of the famous gray which belonged to the Harahaish of the Wahiba."

Mabkhaut said, "Yes, I saw her last year when he was in Salala, a tall animal; she was old when I saw her, past her prime but even then a real beauty."

Al Auf went on, "We spent the night with Rai of the Afar."

Bin Kabina chimed in, "I met him last year when he came to Habarut; he carried a rifle, 'a father of 10 shots,' which he had taken from the Mahra he had killed in the Ghudun. Bin Mautlauq offered him the gray yearling, the daughter of Farha, and 50 riyals for this rifle, but he refused."

Al Auf continued, "Rai killed a goat for our dinner and told us…." But I interrupted: "Yes, but how many days did it take you to get to Bai?" He looked at me in surprise and said, "Am I not telling you?"

Source: Thesiger, W. *Arabian Sands*. London: Penguin Books, 1991.

When communicating across cultures, communication misunderstandings can occur, but they are usually not serious and can be rectified. Exhibit 2.2 illustrates a communication misunderstanding that had grave results. It is the transcript of the conversation between the captain, copilot, and controller on the Avianca flight that crashed on Long Island, New York, in 1991.

Slow versus fast messaging preferences

There has been a tremendous emphasis on fast messaging in European and North American cultures in last the few years. The days of "snail" mail, telephones with or without answering

EXHIBIT 2.2 AN EMERGENCY

Captain to Copilot: "Tell them we are in emergency."
Copilot to Controller: "We are running out of fuel."
Controller: "Climb and maintain 3,000."
Copilot to Controller: "Uh, we're running out of fuel."
Controller: "I'm going to bring you about 15 miles northeast and then turn you back.... Is that fine with you and your fuel?"
Copilot: "I guess so."
The jet ran out of fuel and crashed.

The communication misunderstanding involves the high- and low-context communication styles. It can be seen from this dialogue between the pilot, copilot, and controller that there was a critical misunderstanding between the copilot, who was Colombian (native language Spanish and high-context), and the American controller, who was a low-context communicator. "Emergency" is low-context. "We are running out of fuel" is more high-context (literally, all airplanes, once they take off, are running out of fuel). The controller's last question, "Is that fine with you and your fuel?" is more high-context. The controller could have asked, "Are you declaring a fuel emergency?" If the controller had asked this question, perhaps the copilot would have responded "yes" because he or she had just heard the pilot say "Tell them we are in emergency."

Unless global leaders are aware of the subtle differences, communication misunderstandings between low- and high-context communicators can result. Japanese communicate by not stating things directly, while Americans usually do just the opposite—often declaring "Spell it all out, please." The former looks for meaning and understanding in what is not said—in the nonverbal communication or body language, in the silences and pauses, in relationships and empathy. The latter is not as used to interpreting nonverbal communication and emphasizes sending and receiving accurate messages directly, by stating clearly what is meant.

machines, pagers, and even taking your time answering email, are receding quickly into the past. These days we carry smartphones and tablets and prefer to send text messages because email can be too slow. People who still don't have smartphones or tablets have become "dinosaurs" and may be left out because it's too hard to get an immediate answer. We prefer someone easier to access. One study showed that the predominant form of communication for people between ages 35 and 50 was email, but texting was preferred for people younger than 35. Even telephone conversations are becoming passé (except for Skype); reserved for telephone salespersons and older folks who haven't really discovered the twenty-first century. This creates a communication barrier between older and younger people.

Even slow-message-preferring cultures like China and Japan are getting into the act. In China, for example, text messaging is a way to get around the state censors that try to monitor and restrict freedom of speech, and do a pretty thorough job with the internet and email.

Hall and Hall observed, however, there were both fast and slow methods for sending messages, and that some cultures preferred slower while others preferred faster. Exhibit 2.3 indicates sources for fast and slow messaging. Note that the fast and slow equivalents are given side by side.

Hall and Hall[41] observed that part of the difference between the fast- and slow-message cultures was the quality of interpersonal relationships that cultures valued. In Japan, personal relationships tended to take a long time to develop and solidify, and were based on knowing a lot about, and having a lot in common with, another.

EXHIBIT 2.3 FAST AND SLOW MESSAGES

Fast messaging	Slow messaging
Prose	Poetry
Headlines; news summaries	Books
A communiqué	An ambassador
Propaganda	Art
Cartoons	Etchings
TV commercials	TV documentaries
Television, radio and internet	Print
Quick, easy, familiarity	Slow, deep relationships
Ideologies	Culture
Telephone (becoming slower)	Telephone answering machines
Email	Mail from the post office
Texting	Telephone

The same was true in China. Western businesspeople understand that to build valuable relationships in China, you have to spend the time to develop trust and personal feelings for each other through cooperation, finding shared interests and goals, handling disagreements constructively, and being reliable over a long period of time.

These considerations pose a red flag for twenty-first-century Euro-North American businesspeople. Fast messaging has become the norm in these cultures. It is, however, a very culture-laden practice. Even though business cultures in other cultures—China, or India, for example—have adopted it as well, it may not build effective relationships in slow messaging cultures. If, however, we receive emails and texts from our Asian associates, we should not be surprised. There are fast and slow messages in every culture.

Space preferences

Hall and Hall[42] consider perceptions of appropriate spatial boundaries in terms of territoriality and personal space. Different cultures also have different conceptions about what constitutes an appropriate amount of personal space. This is the "bubble" of space left between individuals communicating with each other. In northern Europe, these bubbles are quite large, but as you go south to France, Italy, Greece, and Spain, the expected size decreases. A space considered "intimate" in Northern Europe, or for Americans of Northern European ancestry—less than two feet separating—would be considered normal conversing distance between bodies in Southern Europe. In Japan and China, people accept levels of crowding in public spaces that would be considered unacceptable in Europe or North America. Violation of these norms—too close or too far apart—may produce a feeling of discomfort, whether you are conscious of it or not.

Time preferences

Hall and Hall[43] distinguish between monochronic and polychronic time. In monochronic cultures such as the US, Canada, Western Europe, and Japan, time is experienced as linear, like a road that goes from past to future. Time naturally divides into segments, and is efficiently scheduled. There is a strong emphasis on using time efficiently and saving it wherever possible. It's almost sinful to lose or waste time. People burdened with priorities learn at time management courses how to handle less important tasks in as little time as possible.

Latin America and Southern Europe are examples of polychronic cultures. They are in almost every way the antitheses of monochronic cultures. A much greater emphasis is placed on involvement with people, and one's schedule to complete individual interactions that take longer. Japan is an interesting combination because the culture is monochronic in the way schedules are kept with foreigners, and public transport runs exactly on time. However, interpersonal relationships are often conducted polychronically. Exhibit 2.4 highlights the major differences between the two.

EXHIBIT 2.4 MONOCHRONIC VERSUS POLYCHRONIC PEOPLE

E X H I B I T 2.4

Monochronic people	Polychronic people
Do one thing at a time	Do many things at once
Focus intently on their work	Easy to distract; constantly interrupted
Committed to the job	Committed to people and relationships
Deadlines and schedules rigidly kept	Schedules are objectives, to be kept if possible
Emphasize and expect promptness	Need for promptness depends on the relationship
Tend to be low-context and need lots of background information and context	Tend to be high-context and already know or think they know
Adhere to plans with determination	Plans may change easily
Used to short-term relationships	Build lifelong relationships

Source: Hall, E. T. and Hall, M. R. *Hidden Differences*. Garden City, NY: Anchor Doubleday, 1985, pp. 18–19.

Electronic communications media (texting, email, social media, websites, and so on) are far more popular in monochronic cultures because they save time. We should be aware, however, that individuals in polychronic cultures could feel uncomfortable with these technologies or see them as emanating from people that they do not, and will not, have significant relationships with. Therefore, they might not respond as efficiently as we hoped, or might not place as much value on relationships with us because we had not spent the time they preferred in face-to-face contact. Despite the historical tensions Chinese feel about Japan, Chinese businesspeople have reported that they preferred to do business with Japanese rather than Western sellers because the Japanese took the time to build personal relationships. If North American sellers sold the Chinese a product, that was the last you saw of them for years until they thought maybe you might need something else. The Chinese called this approach "disposable relationships."[44] It was also a difference between polychronic and monochronic relationships.

International body language

Do your actions really speak louder than your words? A study by Ting-Toomey[45] found that up to 65 percent of a message's meaning is sent through body language, or physical signaling. It contributes to at least three reasons for cross-cultural conflict. First, the same signal carries different meanings in different cultures. Second, many nonverbal signals are sent in each interaction, making interpretation ambiguous. Third, personality, gender, socioeconomic status, and the situation may all produce variants in bodily signaling, adding to confusion.[46] Exhibit 2.5 lists the many types of body language.

EXHIBIT 2.5 TYPES OF NONVERBAL COMMUNICATION

- Hand, arm, and head gestures;
- facial expressions;
- body posture and bearing;
- interpersonal distance (proxemics);
- degree of and nature of eye contact;
- degree of and nature of interpersonal touch;
- symbolic messages derived from specific colors;
- attitude and behavior toward time, and the use of time;
- attitude and behavior toward food, and the use of food;
- voice pitch, inflections, speed of verbal communications;
- use of silence.

Source: Ting-Toomey, S. *Communicating Across Cultures*. New York: Guilford Press, 1999.

Nonverbal signals or gestures are used in all cultures, and understanding the differences can help us become better cross-cultural communicators. Furnham[47] reported an example of similar body language cues having different cultural reactions. He said, "Research in the United States has shown that tips tend to be larger if the waiter touches the diner . . . and if the waiter gives a big and 'authentic' initial smile." However, in the UK that same body language exhibited by a waiter may result in no tip at all. Body language is frequently culturally distinct.

International body language can fall under three categories, the first two of which can create problems:

1   A gesture can mean something different to others than it does to you. For example, the A-OK gesture, as used in the US, means that things are fine, great, or that something has been understood perfectly. But Brazilians interpret it as an obscene gesture, and to the Japanese it means money.

2   A gesture can mean nothing to the person observing it. Scratching one's head or drawing in breath and saying "sah" are common Japanese responses to embarrassment. One can miss these cues as these gestures may have no particular meaning in one's native culture.

3   A gesture can mean basically the same in both cultures and the meaning is accurately communicated with few possible misunderstandings.

Hand and arm gestures

Most people use their hands when speaking, to punctuate the flow of conversation, refer to objects or persons, and mimic and illustrate words or ideas. Often, gestures are used in place of words. Generally, Japanese speakers use fewer words and fewer gestures than Canadian speakers. French, including French-Canadians, use more of both. Italians use much more.

In Canada, patting a small child on the head usually conveys affection. But in Malaysia and other Islamic countries, the head is considered the source of one's intellectual and spiritual powers. It is sacred and should not be touched. Australians signal "time to drink up" by folding three fingers of the hand against the palm, leaving the thumb and little finger sticking straight up and out. In China, the same gesture means "six."

To get someone's attention or to summon a waiter or waitress is often a problem. This task requires different gestures in different countries. For example, in restaurants in North American countries, one would call a waiter or waitress quietly, "sir," "miss," or "waiter," raise a finger to catch his or her attention, or tilt one's head to one side. Do not snap your fingers. In the Middle East, clapping one's hands is effective. In Japan, extend your arm slightly upward, palm down, and flutter your fingers. In Spain and Latin America, extend your hand, palm down, and rapidly open and close your fingers. In Brazil, make a "hissing" sound.

Eye contact

In many Western cultures, a person who does not maintain good eye contact is regarded as slightly suspect. Those who avoid eye contact are unconsciously considered unfriendly, insecure, untrustworthy, inattentive, and impersonal. By contrast, Japanese children are taught in school to direct their gaze at the region of their teacher's Adam's apple or tie knot. As adults, Japanese lower their eyes when speaking to a superior as a gesture of respect. In Canadian First Nations cultures, those who seek and maintain eye contact are the ones considered suspicious and questionable.

In Latin American cultures and some African cultures, such as Nigeria, prolonged eye contact from an individual of lower status is considered disrespectful. By contrast, the polite English person is taught to pay strict attention to a speaker, to listen carefully, and to blink his or her eyes to let the speaker know he or she has been understood as well as heard.

INTERCULTURAL COMMUNICATION GUIDELINES

Achieving successful intercultural communication can be a challenging—even daunting—task. Interculturally, you need to study the culture you will be working with, and to understand the key ways it is different from your own. When you are the speaker, you have to be sensitive to values, norms, and attitudinal differences so that you don't make your receiver uncomfortable. You need to be informed and watch to provide the right context (high or low), and the right messaging speed, without intruding on your receiver's personal space bubble. You need to be sensitive as to how he/she regards the time you are taking, making sure your gestures are appropriate, and whether you should make continuous, occasional, or no eye contact. There are skilled international personnel who can do all this and more as easily as we might ride a bicycle. They have been doing it a long time. It takes a long time to get good at intercultural communication. And it's difficult to prescribe what each individual reader needs to concentrate on because each one of us is different.

There are, however, some general guidelines that everyone should be aware of while building up sensitivity to all the potential pitfalls in intercultural communication. Exhibit 2.6 summarizes a number of behaviors research has identified as useful for intercultural effectiveness.

Guidelines for using English with non-English speakers

On average, most Europeans speak more than one language. For example, Switzerland, a relatively small country, has three official languages: French, German, and Italian. Canada has two official languages, English and French, and while not nearly all citizens are bilingual, it sure is helpful if an Anglo-Canadian can speak passible French in the province of Quebec, where only French is officially recognized. The typical Japanese studies English as well as other languages. English is becoming a second language in China and most Chinese students coming to study in North America are reasonably fluent or working hard to become so. This is not the case for most US citizens who, even when they study a foreign language, often lack fluency. Americans generally expect to conduct their business in English, either because their local contacts have learned English or through the use of interpreters.

The good news for these Americans and other native English-speaking people is that English has become a global language and is recognized in many places around the world as the language of commerce. Many international businesspeople have learned English as

EXHIBIT 2.6 RESEARCH-IDENTIFIED BEHAVIORS MOST IMPORTANT FOR INTERCULTURAL EFFECTIVENESS

- Demonstrate respect (verbally and nonverbally).
- Respond to people in a nonjudgmental, non-evaluative manner.
- Recognize that your exact knowledge, beliefs, and perceptions are unique and valid only for yourself.
- Demonstrate empathy.
- Listen carefully and try to show you've understood by saying what you think the speaker has said.
- Have tolerance for ambiguity.
- Turn off your behavioral auto-pilot and actively manage how you interact with others.
- Demonstrate a willingness to adopt different roles and adapt your behaviors.

E X H I B I T 2.6

a second language (ESL). The bad news is that even though ESL people are usually doing their best to function in English, they may not have as good a command of the language as you might hope. And the pronunciation accents of some ESL English speakers may require a lot of practice to understand.

You could rely on interpreters if one is available or affordable. Translation does, however, have downsides. It is slow, since what one says in English must be translated bit by bit, so less detail may be communicated. Translators often do not provide a full translation of what is being said. Sometimes translators lack the specialized vocabulary to accurately translate business concepts. There is also the problem of equivalence of concepts between languages. The same word may mean something quite different from language to language. For example, in English, "consensus" means that everyone agrees. In Japanese, it means that the other party is willing to agree but expects you to compromise on some other later point. Sounds like compromise, but if you didn't know, you could get in trouble later not realizing the other side believed you owed them one in return.

In any event, you will often find yourself doing intercultural communication with ESL people whose command of English may not be as good as a native English speaker. This can easily lead to misunderstandings. You may only discover these when the final contract is produced in both native languages, and you have the one in their language back-translated into English (a good practice). Riddle and Lanham[48] proposed some guidelines for handling these kinds of situations, and others are based on the authors' experience:

1   Use simple English. Practice using the most common 3,000 words in English; that is, those words typically learned in the first two years of language study. Avoid uncommon words—for example, use "witty" rather than "jocose," or "effective" rather than "efficacious."

2   In writing, use maximum punctuation—for example, use commas that help clarify the meaning, but that could technically be omitted.

3   Conform to basic grammar rules more strictly than is common in everyday conversation. Make sure that sentences express a complete thought, that pronouns and antecedents are used correctly, and that subordination is accurately expressed. A Japanese associate finds the lack of rigid English grammatical and pronunciation rules frustrating because both are clearly defined in Japanese.

4   Avoid the use of idiom and slang.

5   With international associates unfamiliar with your culture, you may be required to make lengthy explanations of an analogy you thought was self-evident that your counterparts found confusing or obscure.

6   When speaking or writing to someone you do not know well, use their last name and keep the tone formal while expressing personal interest or concern. In Germany, people are often uncomfortable with the American practice of using only first names.

7   Oral presentations should be made plainly, clearly, and slowly, using visual aids whenever possible.

8   Important face-to-face or telephoned international business communications should be confirmed by email, fax, or letter, preferably in both languages.

9   Written brochures, proposals, and reports should be translated into the native language of the receiver or client. However, you should send both the English material and its translation. In China, for example, carrying an English brochure is a status symbol that others may envy even if no one can read it. Too often, it is only the English brochure that is sent, communicating nothing but ignorance.

10   Communication by email, texting, or through websites has the disadvantage that you do not know the receiver's culture, values, norms, and so on. You don't see the nonverbal response. As fast messages from a monochronic culture, possibly high-context if little context is provided, with a strong expectation of a fast response, there are many possibilities for ineffective communications. If it is important, it is best to stick with email and provide considerably more context than would be normal within North American electronic communication.

Companies work hard not only to ensure accurate translations, but also to achieve fortuitous translations. Accurate and fortuitous translation is dependent upon knowledge of the intended group's culture and how their cultural values influence their perceptions. For example, Sang and Zhang[49] provide examples of English corporate names translated into Mandarin Chinese. The goal in each case was to achieve a sound similar to that of the English, while highlighting positive Chinese values to create a basis for corporate trust:

■   Ford = Fu Te, or Fortune and Uniqueness;
■   Nike = Nai Ke, or Endurance and Victory;
■   Desis (a pesticide company) = Di Sha Si, or Enemy, Kill, Dead.

When Exxon first entered Japan it chose "Enco" as its name. This turned out to mean "stalled car" in Japanese. Coca-Cola's first name in Asia employed Chinese characters that produced the right sounds but meant "Bite the wax tadpole."

PERSONALITY PSYCHOLOGY AND INTERCULTURAL COMMUNICATIONS

The Jungian model[50] of personality types is an information-processing model based on three bipolar scales. Initially, personality has two *attitudes*. In order to function as a sentient being, a person must be oriented outward to perceive and communicate with his/her external environment; this is called *extraversion*. At the same time, a person must also be oriented inward so as to be able to think about what is happening in the external environment and to problem-solve; this is called *introversion*. Individuals are either primarily extraverted or primarily introverted in their orientation, but in practice must be both. The attitude, extraverted or introverted, that an individual primarily prefers will be a part of his/her *dominant* personality type. The less favored, but still essential, attitude will be part of that individual's *auxiliary* personality type. Individuals primarily relate to their worlds through their dominant personality type, but are balanced in their functioning by their auxiliary personality type. Quenk observes that the auxiliary type functions with, on average, 87 percent of the conscious energy of the dominant, affecting individual consciousness to a somewhat lesser extent than the dominant.[51]

Those whose dominant attitude is extraverted are called extraverts. Extraverts are oriented primarily toward their "outer worlds," preferring interaction and communication with other people to thoughtful reflection.[52] Kummerow et al. observed that extraverts were more likely to initiate social interactions, enjoyed communicating with others, wanted to communicate in person through talking, and wanted to connect with others through conversation.[53] Thorne and Gough[54] found extraverts to be gregarious and talkative, with a strong interest in being with others. By contrast, introverts (dominant attitude is introverted) were primarily interested in their own thoughts and/or feelings and uninterested in communicating with others. They preferred personal reflection,[55] solving issues on their own, and focusing on tasks rather than other people.[56] Myers agreed,[57] observing that extraverts were primarily involved with an outer world of people and objects, while introverts were primarily concerned with an inner world of concepts and ideas.

We concluded from these discussions that a Jungian psychological profile would contain an extraverted preference, and an introverted preference. One would be "dominant" in the sense that an individual would be more likely to be oriented in its direction with its preferences. The second would be "auxiliary," and somewhat less strong, in the sense that it would balance the limitations of the dominant one. The auxiliary would always have the opposite attitude to the dominant so that an individual could relate to both outer communications with others, and private inner thinking and problem-solving.[58]

In addition to attitude, Jung observed that humans required two functions related to gathering and evaluating information in order to engage in action. Relevant information needed to be perceived, and then its value needed to be assessed before useful communication (extraverted) or problem-solving (introverted) could be initiated. Jung[59] called some people *perceivers* because they put a higher value on information collection. Others he called *judgers* because they put a higher value on judging the quality of the information once it was collected. Jung proposed two basic and opposite perceiving functions called *Sensing* and *iNtuiting*. He proposed two basic and opposite judging functions called *Thinking* and *Feeling*. The dominant personality type would be either *perceiving* (sensing or intuiting) or *judging* (thinking or feeling). The auxiliary type would be the opposite of the dominant, either perceiving or judging, because normally functioning humans require both abilities in order to make decisions and take actions. Myers[60] summarized as follows.

Good type development, therefore, demands two conditions: first, adequate but by no means equal development of a judging process and a perceptive process, one of which predominates, and, second, adequate but by no means equal facility in using both the extraverted and introverted attitudes, with one predominating. When both conditions are met, the person's type development is well balanced.

Eight personality types result from these three bipolar opposites, extraversion/introversion, sensing/intuiting, and thinking/feeling. Beebe[61] has offered three-word descriptions of each intended to capture the essence of each based on many years of in-depth typology psychiatric practice (see Exhibit 2.7).

A psychological profile, individual or as a national character, would include both an extraverted type related to communication and interaction with others, and an introverted type related to individual reflection and problem-solving. Regardless of which was dominant or auxiliary, the extraverted type would influence interpersonal communications, and the introverted one individual problem-solving. In this chapter we will only consider how the extraverted type styles impact communications. In Chapter 11 we will consider the introverted reflection and problem-solving types in terms of their effects on strategic thinking. In Chapters 12 (Middle East), 14 (East Asia), 15 (South and Southeast Asia, and Australia), and 18 (Canada and the US), we will compare full national character profiles (extraverted and introverted) to consider how differences affect cross-national interactions.

Jungian personality types and individual communications styles

An individual's communication style (Se, Ne, Te, or Fe) is based on whether sensing (Se), intuiting (Ne), thinking (Te), or feeling (Fe) is the individual's extraverted preference for interacting with others. Following Exhibit 2.7, we see that Fe is the most concerned with building

EXHIBIT 2.7 EIGHT JUNGIAN PERSONALITY TYPES

Personality type	As it appears to others	As it is intended	At its most developed
Extraverted Sensing (Se)	Engaging	Experiencing	Enjoying
Extraverted iNtuiting (Ne)	Entertaining	Envisioning	Enabling
Extraverted Thinking (Te)	Regulating	Planning	Enforcing
Extraverted Feeling (Fe)	Validating	Affirming	Relating
Introverted Sensing (Si)	Implementing	Verifying	Accounting
Introverted iNtuiting (Ni)	Imagining	Knowing	Divining
Introverted Thinking (Ti)	Naming	Defining	Understanding
Introverted Feeling (Fi)	Judging	Appraising	Establishing the Value

Source: Beebe, J. *Energies and Patterns in Psychological Type: The Reservoir of Consciousness.* London: Routledge, 2016.

EXHIBIT 2.7

positive interpersonal relationships. They are perceived to validate others' efforts, and intend to affirm and relate to others. By contrast, Te is primarily concerned with achieving objective results regardless of relationships. Te people are seen as intending to regulate task achievement efforts, and their intention is to both plan and enforce the achievement of those plans. Ne is primarily concerned with creativity and new ideas. Ne people entertain others with their interesting and creative ideas, but they believe they have envisioned better ways that will enable themselves and others to achieve better results. Following are more detailed descriptions.

Se and Ne are perceiving functions (see above). *Se* individuals emphasize information perceived from the five senses and often have a remarkable, and even photographic, memory for what something looked, sounded, felt, tasted, or smelled like. *Ne* individuals de-emphasize the importance of sensory information, regarding it as merely the appearance of a more basic reality or underlying truth. Intuiting people are understood to be effective in reading between the lines, imagining possibilities, and seeing connections between ideas, theories, events, and objects that may elude the more practical sensors.

Se individuals want to hear about the facts—what happened—and are more concerned with the practicality of getting things done. They trust their experience, approach problems in realistic and pragmatic ways, and prefer to approach problems using tried-and-true methods that have been shown to work. In contrast, Ne individuals tend to discount the importance of all these sensing preferences. They are more abstract, imaginative, intellectual, theoretical, and future-oriented. They eschew traditional methods, hoping to find new ways of doing things that might be more effective (getting the right things done) or efficient (getting things done right). It is estimated that in the American population, approximately 65 percent are Se, and 35 percent are Ne.[62]

Te and Fe are judging functions (see above). *Te* individuals employ a relatively impersonal and rational judging process. Thinkers intend to be fair, firm, critical, skeptical, and to apply principles, or what they consider fundamental truths. *Fe* individuals employ a relatively personal judging process that takes account of personal feelings and preferences—one's own and those of others. Feelers intend to be friendly, sympathetic, empathetic, and try to care for others' needs and concerns in their decision-making. They value warm, trusting and cooperation-based harmonious relationships, and are willing to sacrifice some effectiveness or efficiency to maintain positive relationships.

Te individuals appear more logical and analytical in their communications and value these qualities in others' communications to themselves. They may appear critical and brusque because they tend to be more self-interested and like to win their points. At the same time, thinkers intend to be fair and apply the same standards to everyone, including themselves, without bias, and regardless of existing relationships. By contrast, Fe individuals may appear more sensitive, and because they hope to please others, they are more likely than thinkers to express personal appreciation or compliment the work achievements of others, or to look for extenuating circumstances to give people another chance when things are not going well. It's important to note that thinkers do not appreciate the willingness of feelers to excuse performance deficits, while feelers do not like the perceived insensitivity and personal criticism of thinkers' communications. It is estimated that in the American population, 65 percent of males and 35 percent of females are thinkers, while 35 percent of males and 65 percent of females are feelers.[63]

In summary, we have four psychologically and genetically based[64] communications styles whose reliability and validity have been demonstrated many times.[65] Se and Ne individuals place a higher priority on collecting information than judging its importance. Te and Fe individuals place their priority on judging the value of information they have at their disposal. All four styles exist in all known cultures, but one will be found to be more characteristic of communications in each national culture.

Specifically, these extraverted attitude-functions are described as follows.[66]

- *Extraverted Feeling (Fe)*: Fe individuals are concerned to conform to established cultural patterns and societal norms of interaction and relationship. Their behavior is generally polite, considerate, and sensitive to the needs and expectations of those around them. Fe individuals understand situationally appropriate behavior, and build friendly relationships based on cooperation, shared interests, mutual benefits, and developing trust. They have a value commitment to altruism and will sacrifice their own interests for others. Fe individuals have a knack for maintaining harmony in relationships. They are skilled in establishing empathy and rapport, cooperating, saying the right thing at the right time, and serving others.

- *Extraverted Sensing (Se)*: Se individuals have an extremely accurate sense and memory of factual information about the external environment. They seek specifics and details related to their involvements and remember even the smallest elements. Therefore, they have a very accurate memory of what was previously communicated. Se individuals focus on the facts and have little interest in theory or precedents, and do not want to be limited by others' rules or expectations. They are never late for appointments. At the same time, Se individuals enjoy excitement and fun, are loveable, and make good company. They may be cultured in the sense of being connoisseurs of wine or art—anything where a fine, detailed knowledge is required.

- *Extraverted Thinking (Te)*: Te individuals understand the external environment to be governed by logical and structured processes of cause and effect. Their goal is to organize the external environment and its inhabitants. They tend to see things very dualistically, definitely in terms of "black and white" and "true and false," and have logical and impersonal reasons for their assertions and actions. Anyone and anything that agrees with their reasoning is "right." Anyone and anything disagreeing is "wrong." Te individuals are strong in planning, organizing, directing, and controlling capabilities, with a strong need for closure. They do not regard their feelings for others as important, and are not good at giving positive feedback.

- *Extraverted iNtuition (Ne)*: Ne individuals appear disorganized to others but may be immensely creative in their thinking. They are quickly able to understand and interpret complex situations, see connections between ideas or events that seem disparate to others, and are skillful in reading between the lines in interpersonal interaction to see the true motives and feelings of others. Ne individuals generate high levels of enthusiasm for new projects, constantly generating new ideas, processes and/or procedures for achieving outcomes. They make innovative entrepreneurs though they tend to become bored easily and move onto new projects without finishing old ones. They value minority rights and liberal social change.

It is easy to calculate your own Jungian attitude-functions using one of the free Jungian, MBTI, or Keirsey personality instruments on the internet.[67] Exhibit 2.8 gives the 16 four-letter MBTI or Keirsey personality types that these instruments would calculate as yours and their equivalent primary and auxiliary Jungian attitude-functions. The percentage of respondents scoring each personality type is derived from an international sample.[68] However, it should be remembered that type and attitude-function distributions vary by national culture and this is an overall international convenience sample of all those who have participated in this online consulting service.

EXHIBIT 2.8 DOMINANT AND AUXILIARY ATTITUDE-FUNCTION PREFERENCES BASED ON MBTI ASSESSMENT

MBTI personality type	Number scoring this type (%)	Dominant attitude-function	Auxiliary attitude-function
ISFJ	13.8	Si	Fe
ESFJ	12.3	Fe	Si
ISTJ	11.6	Si	Te
ISFP	8.8	Fi	Se
ESTJ	8.7	Te	Si
ESFP	8.5	Se	Fi
ENFP	8.1	Ne	Fi
ISTP	5.4	Ti	Se
INFP	4.4	Fi	Ne
ESTP	4.3	Se	Ti
INTP	3.3	Ti	Ne
ENTP	3.2	Ne	Ti
ENFJ	2.5	Fe	Ni
INTJ	2.1	Ni	Te
ENTJ	1.8	Te	Ni
INFJ	1.5	Ni	Fe

Source: Career Testing and Career Direction, "How Rare Is Your Personality Type?" www.careerplanner.com (retrieved September 16, 2016).

Jung's attitude-functions and communications styles

An interesting point is that it is always the extraverted attitude-function that you see when you interact with someone, regardless of whether that attitude-function is dominant or auxiliary. If a person's dominant attitude is extraverted, then she/he interacts with others from his/her dominant attitude-function, and what-you-see-is-what-you-get (WYSIWYG). WYSIWYG means that because you are observing the dominant attitude-function (because it is extraverted), you are directly communicating with the attitude-function that will make the person's final decision. Communications are easier and more likely to influence outcomes if you are in direct communications with the aspect of the person that will make the decision. If, however, a person's dominant attitude is introverted, then she/he interacts with others from his/her auxiliary extraverted attitude-function and his/her true thinking is less evident.

Using the data from Exhibit 2.8, the overall frequencies of these attitude-functions may be calculated to predict the relative likelihood that they will be encountered in one's communication activities. Exhibit 2.9 indicates the probability that a person you are communicating with will be exhibiting a dominant extraverted Fe, Se, Te, or Ne attitude-function.

Jung's attitude-functions and national character

There have been surprisingly few attempts to determine the attitude-functions characteristic of national cultures, or to ascertain national character on a global basis, even though this information could help international business personnel to prepare for the communications and interaction preferences of local counterparts in different countries. Such information

EXHIBIT 2.9 DISTRIBUTION OF EXTRAVERTED ATTITUDE-FUNCTIONS ENCOUNTERED IN INTERNATIONAL COMMUNICATIONS

Attitude-function	Dominant (%)	Auxiliary (%)	Total (%)	WYSIWYG (% of attitude-function dominant)
Extraverted Sensing (Se)	12.8	14.2	27.0	47.4
Extraverted Feeling (Fe)	14.8	15.3	30.1	49.2
Extraverted Thinking (Te)	10.5	13.7	24.2	43.4
Extraverted iNtuition (Ne)	11.3	7.7	19.0	59.5
Totals	49.4	50.9	100.3	49.9 (Average)

Source: Career Testing and Career Direction, "How Rare is Your Personality Type?" www.careerplanner.com (retrieved September 16, 2016).

could be as useful as, for example, Hofstede's[69] assessments of the average power distance, uncertainty avoidance, individualism, and masculinity work value scores discussed in Chapter 1, in providing a sense of how national cultures clustered together into like and unlike groups.

One interesting attempt to assign characteristic MBTI personality types, and Jungian attitude-functions to national cultures was that of Massey.[70] His study was qualitative in nature, relying on face-to-face interviews either with individuals, or focus groups of individuals from many national cultures, plus hundreds of email discussions about how individual respondents in these many countries conducted their lives and their business. Then, based on his training and experience, and the information collected, Massey classified each culture as to its psychological national character. His study fulfilled most of Inkeles' criteria for identifying predominant dispositions built into the personalities of the individuals that make up a national population based on measurement, psychological testing, and surveys of attitudes and values.[71] Massey argued that the value of his analysis was in helping "anyone doing international business"[72] understand in which countries they would feel most comfortable, and be most effective communicating and working with local counterparts.

Using Massey's study, it was possible to produce some interesting clusters of national cultures based on their Fe, Se, Te, and Ne communications preferences, as presented in Exhibit 2.10. Note that even though Massey's study included over 100 nations, we have mostly only considered the top 20 nations, which account for about 95 percent of international trade.

EXHIBIT 2.10 SE, FE, TE, NE DOMINANT OR AUXILIARY EXTRAVERTED ATTITUDE-FUNCTION NATIONAL COMMUNICATION STYLE CLUSTERS

Geographic area	Extraverted Sensing (Se)	Extraverted Feeling (Fe)	Extraverted Thinking (Te)	Extraverted iNtuiting (Ne)
North America	None	Canada	US	None
Latin America	Mexico, Argentina	None	None	Brazil
East Asia	China, Philippines, Indonesia	Japan, South Korea, Taiwan	None	None
South and Southeast Asia	Thailand	Singapore, Malaysia, Vietnam	Australia	India
Middle East	Turkey, Iraq, Israel	Iran	None	Saudi Arabia
Europe		None	Germany, France, United Kingdom	Italy, Spain, Russia
Africa	South Africa	Nigeria	None	None

Source: Massey, B. *Where in the World Do I Belong?* USA: Jetlag Press, 2006.

The *Se cluster* was the largest, with ten countries including China, the world's largest economy by purchasing power parity[73] (PPP) in 2016, and two strong emerging markets in Mexico and Turkey. The *Fe cluster* was second largest, with nine countries including Japan, the world's fourth largest economy (2016, PPP), and Canada, as well as the strong emerging markets of South Korea and Vietnam. The *Ne cluster* was tied for smallest with five countries including the strong emerging markets of Russia, Saudi Arabia, and India. India is the world's third largest economy (2016 PPP). The *Te cluster* was also tied for smallest with five countries, but these included the US, Germany, France, and the UK. The US is the world's second largest economy (2016, PPP). Germany is fifth largest, the UK sixth, and France seventh.

Given that Fe, Se, Te, and Ne each represent a different communication style with different goals and behaviors, many communications difficulties could be predicted for representatives of the world's major economies, especially dealing with each other. It is a fair assumption that businesspeople from national cultures within the same cluster would experience fewer communications dissonances and difficulties with business counterparts. It is also a fair assumption that more communications difficulties would occur when businesspeople interacted with counterparts not only from a different national cluster but also a different communication style than their own. For example, referring back to Exhibit 2.7, Se communicators, the largest group of countries, appear to others to "engage" an issue or situation, intending to "experience" it for themselves, and will ultimately "enjoy" it based on their process of involvement. Beebe[74] argued that engaging and experiencing meant having a hands-on encounter with an issue or situation—having to be involved in an embodied way so that it came to be sufficiently real for them to satisfactorily understand it. Se needs to understand the issue or situation intimately in all its detail by touching, and being touched by, it. So, Se is very detail-oriented, very focused on the objective situation. Fe communicators, the second largest group in Exhibit 2.10, are primarily oriented toward the interpersonal dynamics of the stakeholders related to the situation. They are not engaged in the objective details like Se. Ne communicators generally engage their imaginations to think of creative alternatives rather than focusing either on the details of the existing situation, or the interpersonal dynamics.

English-speaking (US, UK, Australia), and European Union (Germany, France, UK) representatives might face greater than average cross-national communications difficulties because their preference for Te-style communications is relatively uncommon among major trading nations, and their focus is quite different from Se, Fe, or Ne.

The best way to illustrate the potential difficulties of the Te communication preferences is by offering examples.

1   *Te* (US, UK, Germany, France, Australia) *communications with Se* (China):
    a.   Te communications are impersonal and analytical. They regard interpersonal feelings, positive or negative, as unimportant and do not express them easily. By contrast, Se communications put value on having fun and building positive interpersonal relationships.

b. Te communications are strongly focused on planning, organizing, directing, and controlling, and leading others and situations. Se individuals have little interest in being limited by others' rules or expectations.

c. Te communications apply dualistic "black and white" and "true and false" dichotomies as governing principles to themselves and others. They would argue counterparts are wrong where they disagree with what Te regards as "true" and evident. Se individuals focus mainly on the facts in the specific situation and are not interested in theories or precedents established in other situations. Chinese culture is not dualistic and tends to regard opposites as complementary.

d. In addition, Se individuals are extremely accurate in their memories about anything that was said, proposed, or intimated in both formal and informal interactions. They will remember and act on minutiae that Te counterparts may not recall.

2   *Te* (US, UK, Germany, France, Australia) *communications with Fe* (Japan, Canada, Iran):

a. Fe communications focus primarily on polite and considerate behavior that is sensitive to the needs of the business counterpart. Fe individuals are adept at following their cultural patterns of genteel interaction with the goal of building cooperation, jointly shared goals, mutual benefits, and eventual trust. The Te style of impersonal and analytical communications that discount interpersonal feelings is antithetical for Fe.

b. Fe communications seek harmonious relationships based on mutual cooperation and compromise. Te attempts to control the planning, organizing, directing, controlling, and leading of projects do not offer easy compromise.

c. Fe culture is relatively altruistic in the sense of value commitments intended to improve relationships and society at large. Te communications may be perceived as relatively self-interested insofar as it seeks to control events and situations.

3   *Te* (US, UK, Germany, France, Australia) *communications with Ne* (Russia, Saudi Arabia, Brazil):

a. Ne communications appear disorganized. Te will rapidly seek to re-organize mutual communications through their strong preferences and capabilities for planning, organizing, directing, and controlling.

b. Ne individuals are very creative in suggesting new and untried ideas based on unexpected connections that more conventional thinkers have not seen. Te tends to rely on more conventional ideas and established information and precedents.

c. Ne individuals begin new relationships and projects with enthusiasm but easily become bored and lose interest if dissatisfied with their counterparts or the rejection of their proposed innovations. Te insistence on "right versus wrong" ways of proceeding may produce this disinterest.

d. Ne individuals are extremely perceptive in reading between the lines to intuit the true motives of their communications counterparts. Te communication is relatively controlling and self-interested and this cannot be easily disguised from Ne.

The point of these illustrations is that most of what Te communicators regard as normal communications goals and practices may produce dissatisfaction, conflict, and reduced prospects for success for Se, Fe, or Ne counterparts. The same is true in reverse.

Se, Fe, and Ne communicators may encounter similar levels of stress dealing with each other. Some of these comparisons are made in Chapters 12, 14, and 15. You are also able to predict communications difficulties yourself, between Fe and Se for example, using the descriptions provided above.

Attitude-functions under stress

Under conditions of extreme stress, or sickness, extraverted function-attitudes may behave quite differently in terms of their communications processes (see Exhibit 2.11).[75]

The "inferior" attitude-function may be manifested. This inferior attitude-function is the opposite of an individual's dominant attitude-function[76] and is normally consciously denied, representing attitudes and behavioral preferences that an individual's dominant personality regards as repugnant, immoral, and even culturally inappropriate.[77]

Because the dominant personality denies its existence, the inferior remains autonomous from the individual's conscious intentionality and works behind the scenes, causing neurotic or compulsive behavior.[78] Because the inferior attitude-function is repressed early in life and never develops, it produces behavior that is childish, uncontrolled and primitive if and when it emerges from unconsciousness.

Under conditions of stress, fatigue, illness and/or drug abuse,[79] an individual's consciousness may be overshadowed by his/her inferior attitude-function[80] and his/her behavior will change in predictable directions depending upon the dominant attitude-function. Descriptions of the eight inferior attitude-functions are found in Exhibit 2.11. These descriptions are derived from Thompson,[81] Bayne,[82] Quenk,[83] Sharp,[84] von Franz,[85] and Jung.[86]

The point here is simple. If you observe your counterparts communicating in ways described in Exhibit 2.11, they are probably showing the effects of too-great stress. They will feel embarrassed when they regain control. You should not take offense. It would be best to take a break just to give them time to regain their self-control.

EXHIBIT 2.11 CHARACTERISTIC DOMINANT ATTITUDE-FUNCTION BEHAVIOR WHEN STRESSED

Unstressed dominant attitude-function	Relevant national cultures	Stressed shadow function behavior
Extraverted Sensing (Se): Shadow is primitive Ni	Argentina, Australia, Greece, Indonesia, Iraq, Israel, Mexico, Pakistan, Philippines, South Africa, Thailand, Turkey	Normal easy-going agreeableness disappears. Becomes withdrawn, pessimistic, and tired. Suspicious of counterpart motives. Feels persecuted. Worries she/he will become ill. Excessive appetite. Triggered by excessive structuring of activities; elimination of alternatives; excessive future focus.
Extraverted Feeling (Fe): Shadow is primitive Ti	Canada, Malaysia, Nigeria, South Korea, Taiwan	Normal optimism, enthusiasm, and interest in others disappears. Becomes depressed and withdrawn. Feels things are hopeless. Becomes cynical about prospects. Triggered by lack of counterpart trust; conflict; pressure to conform.
Extraverted Thinking (Te): Shadow is primitive Fi	France, Germany, UK, US	Feels strong invisible loyalty. Acts like a faithful friend. Absolute, childlike, and sentimental feelings for and about others. Becomes cranky and irritable. Escalates small irritations into major confrontations. Triggered by others violating Te values; others' emotional outbursts.
Extraverted iNtuiting (Ne): Shadow is primitive Si	Brazil, India, Italy, Russia, Spain, Saudi Arabia, Spain	Becomes withdrawn and depressed. Small issues make Ne obsessive, picky, and upset. Becomes cranky, irritable, and escalates small irritations into major confrontations. Triggered by physical exhaustion, and/or excessive focus on facts.

Source: Abramson, N. R. "Do the Chinese Seek Relationship? A Psychological Analysis of Chinese–American Business Negotiations Using the Jungian Typology." *Journal of Global Business*, Vol. 16, No. 31, 2005, pp. 7–22.

CONCLUSIONS

The most basic skill that global leaders must cultivate is learning how to effectively communicate and listen cross-culturally. To facilitate our interactions with persons who do not share our values, assumptions, or learned ways of behaving requires new competencies and sensitivities so that those very cultural differences become resources. The complexities of the communication process have been reviewed here from the perspectives of personality differences associated with national cultures, and nonverbal cross-cultural behaviors such as body language and gestures.

The personality-based communications differences likely represent genetic differences that exist to differing degrees in the gene pools of different national cultures. Others, like context, time orientation, messaging speed, personal space, and expectation of eye contact are more likely habitual expectations based on the norms of the culture you are most comfortable with. Having had all of these factors that negatively impact communication brought to your attention, it becomes your conscious choice whether to try to ameliorate their effects when others look uncomfortable. Even genetically based personality factors are not inevitable when you are apprised of them and intend to overcome their potentially negative effects. Learning to take account of all these factors can be mind stretching (see below), and it takes years to achieve proficiency.

Awareness of nonverbal communications is especially critical for successful intercultural communications. You may create a negative impression and even damage a relationship simply by behaving in what are considered normal ways within your own cultural background. Cultures concerned with maintaining harmony and "face" (respect) are especially sensitive to body language. In China, for example, even the appearance of unexpressed frustration or anger upon one's face is equivalent or worse than a fully expressed angry argument in North America. Some Chinese say that they will give Westerners "three strikes," or nonverbal mistakes, but then they will be "out" and excluded from further consideration. With some Chinese it takes only one "fly ball" to be out and so it is essential to behave appropriately, regardless of your inner feelings.

MIND STRETCHING

1 Canada is the largest trading partner of the US including both imports and exports. A typical American businessperson has a dominant extraverted Te attitude-function that dominates his/her communications style. A typical Anglo-Canadian businessperson has an dominant Fe extraverted attitude-function that similarly dominates his/her communications. What communications pitfalls would you expect them to experience when negotiating a business relationship? How will their discussions go if they experience too much stress? Which is likely to

experience the toughest stress the soonest? How may they best proceed to handle their difficulties?

2   The UK has voted to leave the European Union. Assuming the British negotiators are Te dominant, what difficulties would you anticipate in their communications with their French and German counterparts who are also Te communicators? Massey says the Belgians are Fe dominant, and senior EU executives are Belgian. What is likely to be their response to the negotiations?

3   Do you prefer fast or slow messaging? Does that preference affect the quality of relationships you are able to build with your friends, and with strangers you meet? Try discussing this in a group with age, sex, gender, and cultural differences between members.

4   In your personal life, do you have many friends who are different from you? How are they different? Are they different in personality, ethnicity, culture, or are most of your friends of your own cultural background? Why do you choose certain people to be your friends and not others, or is it your choice?

5   How much time do you spend understanding another person's perspective? Or do you prefer to try to persuade others to change and adopt your own perspective?

NOTES

1   Massey, B. *Where in the World Do I Belong?* USA: Jetlag Press, 2006.
2   Tieger, P. D. and Barron-Tieger, B. *The Art of Speed-Reading People*. Boston, MA: Little, Brown and Company, 1998.
3   https://en.wikipedia.org/wiki/Cross-cultural_communication (retrieved April 12, 2017).
4   Kotter, J. P. "What Effective General Managers Really Do," *Harvard Business Review*, Vol. 60, No. 6, 1982, pp. 156–167.
5   Dewey, C. "The Dirty Time-Suck That Is Email," *Vancouver Sun*, October 4, 2016, p. NP6.
6   Inkeles, A. *National Character: A Psycho-Social Perspective*. New Brunswick, NJ: Transaction Publishers, 2015.
7   Ibid., p. x.
8   Ibid., p. ix.
9   See McCrae, R. R. and Costa, P. T. Jr. *Personality in Adulthood: A Five-Factor Theory Perspective*, 2nd edition. New York: Guilford Press, 2003. Costa, P. T. Jr. and McCrae, R. R., *Revised* NEO *Personality Inventory (NEO-PL-R) and* NEO *Five Factor Inventory (NEO-FFI) Professional Manual*. Odessa, AZ: Psychological Assessment Resources, 1992. Seagal, S. and Horne, D. *Human Dynamics: A New Framework for Understanding People and Realizing the Potential of Our Organizations*. Waltham, CA: Pegasus, 1997.
10 McCrae, R. R., Costa, P. T. Jr., and Yik, M. S. M. "Universal Aspects of Chinese Personality," in M. H. Bond (ed.), *The Handbook of Chinese Psychology*. Hong Kong: Oxford University Press, 1996, pp. 189–207.
11 Costa and McCrae, *Revised NEO Personality Inventory*.
12 Jung, C. G. *Psychological Types*. Princeton, NJ: Princeton University Press, 1976.
13 For example, Thompson, H. L. *Jung's Function-Attitudes Explained*. Watkinsville, GA: Wormhole Publishing, 1996.

14 The other four Jungian personality factors are related to individual problem-solving and will be discussed in detail in Chapter 11. In Chapters 12, 14, 15, and 18, the eight factors are combined to produce national characters and discussed in terms of how the differences between national characters affect negotiations across cultures. These discussions comparing national characters emphasize the problems that English-speaking nationals (American, British, Canadian, and Australian) and EU nationals (German and French) would typically encounter negotiating in a number of national cultures in these regions.

15 Myers, I. B. *Gifts Differing: Understanding Personality Type*. Palo Alto, CA: Davies-Black, 1995.

16 Massey, *Where in the World Do I Belong?*

17 Hunziker, M. *Depth Typology: C. G. Jung, Isabel Myers, John Beebe and the Guide Map to Becoming Who We Are*. n.p.: Write Way Publishing Company, 2016.

18 Ibid., pp. 9–10 passim.

19 Massey, *Where in the World Do I Belong?*

20 Meadows, D. H. "If the World Were a Village of 1,000 People," in D. Aberley (ed.), *Futures by Design: The Practice of Ecological Planning*. Philadelphia, PA: New Society Publishers, 1994.

21 Moran, R. T. "So You're Going Abroad: Are You Prepared?" self-published, 10th printing, 2003.

22 Macionis, G. and John, L. *Sociology*, 7th Canadian edition. Toronto, ON: Pearson Canada, 2010, p. 53.

23 Lustig, M. W. and Koester, J. *Intercultural Competence*. New York: Addison-Wesley, 1998.

24 Hall, E. T. *The Silent Language*. Garden City, NY: Anchor/Doubleday, 1959.

25 Hall, *The Silent Language*.

26 Gordon, T. *Leader Effectiveness Training: L.E.T. (Revised)*. New York: Perigee Trade, 2002.

27 Clausen, L. "Corporate Communication Challenges: A 'Negotiated' Cultural Perspective," *International Journal of Cross-Cultural Management*, Vol. 7, No. 3, 2007, pp. 317–332.

28 Ibid.

29 Jandt, F. E. *Intercultural Communication: An Introduction*, 2nd edition. Thousand Oaks, CA: Sage, 1998.

30 Ibid.

31 Liddicoat, A. J. "Communication as Culturally Contexted Practice: A View from Intercultural Communication," *Australian Journal of Linguistics*, Vol. 29, No. 1, 2009, pp. 115–133.

32 Ibid.

33 Nordby, H. "Values, Cultural Identity and Communication: A Perspective from Philosophy of Language," *Journal of Intercultural Communication*, Vol. 17, No. 6, 2008, p. 1.

34 Ibid.

35 Samovar, L. A. and Porter, R. E. *Intercultural Communications: A Reader*. Belmont, CA: Wadsworth Publishing, 1988.

36 Hofstede, G. and Hofstede, G. J. *Cultures and Organizations: Software of the Mind*, 2nd edition. New York: McGraw-Hill, 2005.

37 Merchant, H. "Olly Racella in Bangkok," in H. Merchant (ed.), *Competing in Emerging Markets: Cases and Readings*. New York: Routledge, 2007, pp. 139–155.

38 Hall, *The Silent Language*.

39 Rogers et al., "Edward T. Hall."

40 Hall, *The Silent Language*, p. 62.

41 Ibid.

42 Hall, E. T. and Hall, M. R. *Hidden Differences*. Garden City, NY: Anchor Doubleday, 1985.

43 Ibid.

44 Abramson, N. R. and Ai, J. X. "Using Guanxi-Style Buyer–Seller Relationships in China: Reducing Uncertainty and Improving Performance Outcomes," *International Executive*, Vol. 39, No. 6, 1997, pp. 765–804.

45 Ting-Toomey, S. *Communicating Across Cultures*. New York: Guilford Press, 1999.

46 Ibid.

47 Furnham, A. "Actions Speak Louder than Words," *Financial Times*, April 4, 1999.

48 Riddle, D. L. and Lanham, Z. D. "Internationalizing Written Business English: 20 Propositions for Native English Speakers," *Journal of Language for International Business*, Vol. 1, 1985, pp. 1–11.

49 Sang, J. and Zhang, G. "Communication across Languages and Cultures: A Perspective of Brand Name Translation from English to Chinese," *Journal of Asian Pacific Communication*, Vol. 18, No. 2, 2008, pp. 225–246.

50 Jung, *Psychological Types*.

51 Quenk, N. L. *Was That Really Me? How Everyday Stress Brings Out Our Hidden Personality*. Palo Alto, CA: Davies-Black Publishing, 2002.

52 Bayne, R. "Psychological Type as a Model of Personality Development," *British Journal of Guidance and Counselling*, Vol. 16, No. 2, pp. 167–175.

53 Kummerow, J. M., Barger, N. J. and Kirby, L. K. *Work Types*. New York: Warner Books, 1997.

54 Thorne, A. and Gough, H. *Portraits of Type*. Palo Alto, CA: Consulting Psychologists Press, 1991.

55 Bayne, R. *The Myers–Briggs Type Indicator: A Critical Review and Practical Guide*. London: Chapman & Hall, 1995.

56 Kummerow et al., *Work Types*.

57 Myers, *Gifts Differing*.

58 For more on extraversion versus introversion, see Bayne, *The Myers–Briggs Type Indicator*. Also see Tieger and Barron-Tieger, *The Art of Speed-Reading People*.

59 Jung, *Psychological Types*.

60 Myers, *Gifts Differing*, cited in Quenk, *Was That Really Me?*, p. 22.

61 Beebe, J. *Energies and Patterns in Psychological Type: The Reservoir of Consciousness*. London: Routledge, 2016.

62 For more on Sensing versus iNtuiting, see Bayne, *The Myers–Briggs Type Indicator*. Also see Tieger and Barron-Tieger, *The Art of Speed-Reading People*.

63 Ibid.

64 See McCrae and Costa, *Personality in Adulthood*. See also Berger, J. M. *Personality*, 6th edition. Belmont, CA: Thompson Wadsworth, 2004.

65 Bayne, *The Myers–Briggs Type Indicator*.

66 See Abramson, N. R. "Do the Chinese Seek Relationship? A Psychological Analysis of Chinese–American Business Negotiations Using the Jungian Typology," *Journal of Global Business*, Vol. 16, No. 31, 2006, pp. 7–22. Also Thompson, *Jung's Function-Attitudes Explained*; and Sharp, D. *Personality Types: Jung's Model of Typology*. Toronto, ON: Inner City Books, 1987.

67 Google "free personality test." Hit the "16Personalities" one (https://16personalities.com). As a back-up, Google "keirsey temperament sorter." Hit "Personality Test–Keirsey.com" (www.keirsey.com/sorter). It's free as long as you do not buy all the reports.

68 Career Testing and Career Direction, "How Rare Is Your Personality Type?" www.careerplanner.com (retrieved September 16, 2016).

69 Hofstede, G. *Cultures Consequences: International Differences in Work-Related Values*. Beverley Hills, CA: Sage Publications, 1984.

70 Massey, *Where in the World Do I Belong?*

71 Inkeles, *National Character*

72 Ibid., back cover.

73 Purchasing power parity (PPP) tries to adjust nominal GDP for the actual cost of living in different countries based on the real exchange rates of currencies. The US economy is larger than that of China using nominal GDP. The rankings of world economies in 2016 are from Wikipedia, "List of Countries by GDP (PPP)," https://en.m.wikipedia.org/wiki/List_of_countries_by_GDP_(nominal) (retrieved September 27, 2016).

74 Beebe, *Energies and Patterns in Psychological Type*.

75 Quenk, *Was That Really Me?*.

76 Hopcke, R. H. *A Guided Tour of the Collected Works of C. G. Jung*. Boston, MA: Shambhala, 1999.

77 Johnson, R. A. *Owning Your Own Shadow: Understanding the Dark Side of the Psyche*. San Francisco, CA: Harper, 1991.

78 Hopcke, *A Guided Tour*.

79 Quenk, *Was That Really Me?*.

80 Thompson, L. *Personality Type: An Owner's Manual*. Boston, MA: Shambhala, 1998.

81 Ibid.

82 Bayne, *The Myers–Briggs Type Indicator*.

83 Quenk, N. L. *Beside Ourselves: Our Hidden Personality in Everyday Life*. Palo-Alto, CA: Davies-Black Publishing, 1993.

84 Sharp, *Personality Types*.

85 von Franz, M. L. "The Inferior Function," in M. L. von Franz and J. Hillman (eds.), *Lectures on Jung's Typology*. Woodstock, ON: Spring, 1986.

86 Jung, *Psychological Types*.

3 GLOBAL LEADERS LEARNING IN RESPONSE TO CHANGE

Those whose perspective is limited are likely to err in judgment, taking wrong turns, making bad judgments, and inflicting harm on others. For the sake of our mutual benefit and prosperity, therefore, we should strive to actively broaden our horizons, striving to constantly widen our vision. . . . Nothing is more dangerous than to go through life assuming that you understand everything. Rather, we should think we do not understand at all and let others teach us and lead us by the hand, moving forward step-by-step with humility and commitment.

Knoosuke Matsushita[1]

Businessmen go down with their businesses because they like the old way so well they cannot bring themselves to change. One sees them all about—men who did not know that yesterday is past, and who woke up this morning with their last year's ideas.

Henry Ford[2]

After reading and studying the concepts, examples, and illustrations in Chapter 3, readers should be able:

1   To identify and understand three mindsets—ethnocentric, polycentric, and geocentric—common to leaders and their followers working in foreign national cultures. They will understand the weaknesses of the ethnocentric and polycentric, and why the geocentric is the most effective mindset.

2   To understand how MNEs limit investment risk until they learn the characteristics of a foreign competitive business environment. MNEs become willing to advance from less risky export strategies, to licensing or franchising, to joint venture, to wholly owned entry strategies, as learning reduces perceptions of risk and uncertainty.

3   To understand three approaches—anticipatory, reactive, and crisis—to handling changes in an MNE's competitive environment.

4   To understand four genetically based human temperaments and leadership styles—Tactical, Logistical, Diplomatic, and Strategic—that predict individual strengths and weaknesses in relation to change and learning.

5   To understand the characteristic leadership and learning styles, based on temperament, found in the national cultures of the most important trading nations.

INTRODUCTION

This chapter considers both how multinational corporations (MNC) or enterprises (MNE),[3] and the individuals that lead these organizations, learn in the contexts of performance and change. An MNE is a company that does business in two or more countries. The purpose of such a commercial enterprise is to achieve a financial return, or profitability, for its shareholders while providing a variety of benefits for all its stakeholders, including suppliers, customers, employees, and even the public at large. It seeks to achieve profitability by developing an intended strategy for taking advantage of the bases of competitive advantage in its industry versus its competitors. The strategy is, however, the easiest part. The real challenge is organizing internal capabilities—management, systems, and resources—to support the strategy. MNEs must also learn how foreign market conditions differ such that existing home-market strategies may be appropriately adapted. New internal capabilities may be required to deal with new competitive factors and uncertainties.

The challenges faced by MNEs in new national markets are multiple. First, a new national market is filled with uncertainties[4] for a new entrant. Political, economic, social, and technological differences in an unfamiliar cultural landscape affect the nature of competition in unfamiliar ways, creating uncertainty.[5]

Sadly, leaders' mindsets[6] affect their capacity to learn in ways that reduce uncertainty. *Ethnocentric* mindsets deny the existence of uncertainty and the need to learn, expecting that existing strategies will be effective in new markets. When Target Corporation, the second most successful American retailer after Walmart, entered Canada in 2015, it adopted the attitude that it did not need to understand Canadian market dynamics. It offered lesser product selection at higher prices than in the US, and was forced to withdraw after a year with massive financial losses. *Polycentric* mindsets believe that the strategies of the home market will not work in the same ways in a new and unfamiliar foreign market, and that the strategy must take into account only the competitive dynamics and local practices of that foreign market. The most successful mindset for learning is the *geocentric*. With the geocentric mindset, leaders understand that their greatest success is the combining of what is already known from home markets with what is being learned about success in the new foreign market. Hyundai is an excellent recent example of the geocentric, learning by trial and error the styling and product accessory assortment expectations of North American car buyers, and the Japanese methods for producing reliability. These have been combined with competent low-cost Korean manufacturing. Hyundai cars have become very popular in North America, with better accessories and reliability at a lower price than many American car equivalents.

Another learning process by which MNEs increase their success in foreign markets over time is encapsulated by the *theory of internationalization*.[7] This theory is based on the observation that MNE management generally responds very conservatively to market uncertainty, and tries to avoid financial risk until uncertainty is reduced through learning. When an MNE first plans its entry into a new foreign market it is likely to first enter using an *export* strategy. Export is the least risky export strategy. For example, products may be advertised on the internet (or print advertising), and only exported upon sale and receipt of the payment. The exporter risks nothing except the cost of the website, or the advertisement. Or product inventory is shipped to a local market distributor who sells it. Mitsubishi used to sell its automobiles through Chrysler Corporation, branded as Dodge or Chrysler cars, before feeling confident enough to develop its own wholly owned North American manufacturing, sales, and distribution system. One problem with export is that profitability tends to be low. Low profitability is an incentive to learn how to do better.

When companies' leaders believe they have developed some understanding of a foreign market by exporting, they become willing to take somewhat greater risks. *Licensing* and *franchising* become options. Both involve licensing products or services to companies or individuals that will invest their own capital to produce and/or sell products or services locally. Licensing and franchising are often used by MNEs that do not have the financial resources or interest in developing a particular foreign national market. Profitability is better than exporting, but still relatively low.

Alternatively, an MNE that does have the resources and interest in developing a new market to its fullest potential may progress to a *joint venture*. The MNE usually partners with a local firm that has the knowledge the MNE seeks. The local firm only agrees to the joint venture because the MNE has knowledge it seeks. Usually the MNE offers a superior product, hoping to obtain competent local market knowledge from its partner. Over 50 percent of international joint ventures fail because the venture partners do not have positive and trustworthy relationships. Serious effort is needed to find potentially positive relationships before a joint venture is considered.

The most profitable and risky form of foreign market entry is *wholly owned*, either through (1) *acquisition* or (2) *greenfield*, where a new subsidiary is built from scratch. This is the riskiest option because the MNE has invested all the financial, human, and operational resources, and because it must rely solely on what it has learned in order to be successful. It is the most profitable (or unprofitable), because profits are not shared with distributors, licensees, franchisees, or joint-venture partners.

Unfortunately for MNEs, even a foreign market strategy that has proven itself successful may begin to fail over time because competitive business environments constantly change and MNEs have to learn to adapt. For example, the 2015 Paris Accord on global warming and climate change has changed public opinion about the desirability of developing LNG (liquid natural gas) in northern British Columbia in Canada, or the building of oil sands pipelines in Canada and the US. The successes of Tesla's electric cars and Toyota's hybrid cars are beginning to reshape the strategies of global automobile companies due to the evidence of global climate change.

Crossan et al.[8] have observed three ways that MNEs learn to adapt to change. The most successful learning companies engage in *anticipatory change*. The company's products are still successful and profitability is still good, but the company sees that in the future this may cease to be the case and begins to turn in new directions. Toyota began to emphasize hybrid cars more than ten years ago—before climate change became an important issue for the public—and now it has already developed better hybrid technology than most competitors. With *reactive change*, a company begins to respond only when its profitability begins to fall. With *crisis change*, a company has denied the need for change until profitability is gone and bankruptcy looms as a real threat. Blackberry, formerly RIM, has been struggling with crisis change for the last five years, recently ending its in-house production of smartphones in 2016.

At the same time, the internal capabilities of MNEs are also constantly changing, or need to change to achieve new capabilities for new strategies for both old and new products/services. New corporate leaders may come with different skillsets, values, and management styles, enabling them to learn in ways that previous leaders were unable. Alan Mulally, president and CEO of Ford Motor Company through 2015, was the first CEO of Ford whose background was not in automobiles, having saved Boeing from bankruptcy. Mulally did the "unthinkable, eliminating prestigious but unprofitable brands (Jaguar, Land Rover, Saab, Hummer), reorganizing management to achieve greater cooperation, and cutting costs by globalizing the same car lines across international markets."[9]

When organizations learn, or need to do so, we call it *organizational learning.*[10] Weick defined learning as "sense-making."[11] Learning means figuring out how to make use of relevant knowledge that is continuously being revised and updated. We assume that for organizations, and individuals, there is rarely a "right" answer for achieving effectiveness in unfamiliar cultural environments, nor is "the" answer even known. There are, however, better and worse answers.

Some have argued that the question of "who" learns is the great myth in organizational learning.[12] Organizations don't really learn. Organizations are composed of individual people. There is no such thing as an organization. The term is just a shorthand for groups of individuals working together in a division of labor. From this point of view, learning simply refers to the processes of thinking and remembering that take place in any given individual's mind.

The antithetical argument is that, in addition to individual learning, people appear to learn differently when they are learning in groups.

> People appear to think in conjunction or partnership with others and with the help of culturally provided tools and implements. . . . In other words, it is not just the "person-solo" who learns, but the "person-plus," the whole system of interrelated factors.[13]

Salomon and Perkins[14] took the view, adopted by this chapter, that "solo" and "plus" represented separate forms of learning but that they should also be viewed as being interdependent and in dynamic interaction. The divisions of labor within organizations produce jointly shared kinds of know-how that an individual could not access on his/her own.

Because organizational and individual learning are so interdependent, it may seem to you that it is not always easy to differentiate between them. If we refer to the mindset of an organization as it sees its international operations, is it the organization that sees itself that way, or a majority of the senior management team, or just one powerful leader who runs the company the way she/he sees fit? Personality research has shown that the character of the organization and the way it functions may stem from the preferences of the leader and/or his/her senior managers.[15] Bridges identifies 16 different organizational personalities, based on the Myers–Briggs Type Indicator,[16] that have different strengths and weaknesses, and that are more or less effective depending on the situation.[17]

In the same spirit of psychological inquiry, Keirsey[18] identified four genetically based personality temperaments that were characteristic of humans-as-species in any culture, which affected how individuals responded to change, and what kinds of learning they were more or less likely to undertake. Keirsey applied his theory of temperament to business leadership and four leadership styles–*Tactical, Logistical, Diplomatic,* and *Strategic*–that responded to change differently, and had different learning priorities based on different competencies. Using Massey's[19] identification of the national character[20] of over 100 national cultures, we may predict the strengths and weaknesses of managers in different cultures in reacting to change and the need for learning.

ASPECTS OF ORGANIZATIONAL LEARNING

We have chosen to classify learning into two categories. *Organizational learning* refers to situations in which new capacities are learned by organizations that positively (or negatively) influence their performance in foreign markets. *Individual learning* refers to how individual leaders and their subordinates learn, and even what they are most likely to learn, and want to learn, according to cross-cultural personality and information-processing research.

Dixon[21] defined organizational learning as: "the intentional use of learning processes at the individual, group, and system level to continuously transform the organization in a direction that is increasingly satisfying to its stakeholders."[22] This assumes that:[23]

1   There are many possible right answers in the sense that there may be many ways to reach the same goal. As long as a solution is competitive in the environment and the organization has, or can get the capabilities to do it, it remains a possibility.
2   People who are concerned about and/or affected by a problem are capable of developing useful knowledge to find a solution.
3   Learning occurs in the context of work, often by adapting existing practices, and results from intentional efforts.

Organizations increase their collective competence through the learning achieved by individual leaders and followers. Knowledge gained through individual learning becomes reified throughout organizations. Learning results in more effective MNE strategies based on better understanding of a market's competitive dynamics, and more effective systems, policies, and procedures. Managers and employees are hired, based on relevant learning, whose capabilities mirror learned requirements, and who remain in place when key individuals have left.

We have chosen to group three topics under organizational learning. First, there are both effective and ineffective mindsets for doing business in foreign markets. Second, learning about foreign markets reduces uncertainty and increases the willingness of MNEs to attempt more risky but also more potentially profitable entry strategies. Third, MNEs respond in three ways to environmental change, depending on how perceptive their learning about their competitive environment has been.

MANAGEMENT MINDSETS AND LEARNING

The leaders and management teams of MNEs have mindsets about how they see themselves, their companies, and how business should be done in international markets. These mindsets, or attitudes, strongly influence the MNEs' strategies, the organization of their internal capabilities, and what kinds of learning the MNEs are likely to achieve, if any. A mindset becomes the intentional basis for an overall international strategy. The strategy becomes the basis for identifying and organizing the management abilities, organizational systems, and resources needed to be successful. The mindset becomes part of the administrative heritage[24] of the MNE and, as such, is very difficult to change because all the managers and personnel have been hired to enact it, and the internal capabilities are organized to suit it. Both N. V. Philips and Matsushita Electric (Panasonic) struggled for decades to change their administrative heritage mindsets, with very limited success.[25]

The idea of mindsets seems to have developed from the view in International Strategy that any MNE will be committed to one of two basic strategies–*global efficiency* or *local responsiveness*–and that the choice will depend on the nature of the industry. Some industries compete on the same basis around the world, so global efficiency is especially important. Customers around the world buy airplanes, computers, automobiles, smartphones, and so on, with the same purchasing criteria regardless of their nation or culture. Therefore, any MNE competing in such a global industry should use a *global strategy* because a similar value equation for global products works with customers everywhere.

By contrast, some industries are very dependent on local and cultural criteria for whether their products or services will sell, and what value equation must be developed to influence customers to buy. Here, local responsiveness becomes critical. These observations would apply to any foodstuffs industry, as well as cosmetics, and, lately, green industries. For example, the province of British Columbia in Canada forbids the burning of LNG to produce electricity because it produces too much greenhouse gas (GHG). However, it encourages the production and export of LNG to sell to China, where it would displace coal burning, resulting in reduced GHGs. Therefore, MNEs competing in this industry would need to use a *local responsiveness* strategy.

Of course, there are some industries traditionally perceived as requiring either global efficiency or local responsiveness, where combinations of both basic strategies have proven successful. Part of Toyota's success in becoming the top-selling automobile company in the world has been its ability to focus its production directly at different segments of the car-buying public. Short production runs of many differently equipped cars, rather than huge runs of less differentiated cars intended for any conceivable customer, allow for both cost efficiency and greater responsiveness.

Perlmutter[26] originated the concept of MNE mindsets–*ethnocentric*, *polycentric*, and *geocentric*. He also argued that MNE mindsets evolved over time from ethnocentric to geocentric, as companies learned better ways to be successful in foreign markets. The ethnocentric mindset generally resulted in a global efficiency strategy. The polycentric was always locally responsive. The geocentric tried to simultaneously achieve both global efficiency and local responsiveness.

Bartlett and Ghoshal,[27] and Bartlett and Beamish[28] refined the concept, arguing that there were four mentalities (or mindsets)–*international*, *multinational*, *global*, and *transnational*. They argued, however, that any movement between mindsets was difficult because each formed a difficult-to-change administrative heritage. Their international and global mentalities were both very similar to Perlmutter's ethnocentric mindset, and based on the

EXHIBIT 3.1 COMPARING PERLMUTTER'S THREE MINDSETS

Strategy and organization	Ethnocentric	Polycentric	Geocentric
Overall strategy	Global	Locally responsive	Global and locally responsive
Decision-making authority	High in headquarters	Relatively low in headquarters	Collaborative between headquarters and subsidiaries
Organizational control	Headquarters controls. Home-country standards applied to all persons and performance	Subsidiary managers control own operations. Headquarters apply overall financial controls	Headquarters and subsidiaries collaborate to find universal and locally applied standards
Organizational complexity	Headquarters full function and complex. Simple at subsidiary level	Subsidiaries full function and operationally independent	Headquarters and subsidiaries increasingly complex and interdependent
Communication and information flow	High volume to subsidiaries: orders, commands, advice, inspections	Little to and from subsidiaries. Little between subsidiaries	Both ways and between subsidiaries, whose managers are on top management team
Perpetuation (recruiting, staffing, development)	Recruit and develop home-country people for positions everywhere	Develop local people for key positions in their own country	Develop local people everywhere for key positions everywhere

Source: Perlmutter, H. V. "The Tortuous Evolution of Multinational Enterprises," *Columbia Journal of World Business*, Vol. 1, 1969, pp. 9–18.

idea of global efficiency. The multinational mentality was similar to the polycentric, and the transnational to the geocentric. Exhibit 3.1 provides points of comparison between Perlmutter's three mindsets.

Ethnocentric mindsets: the absence of learning

Learning would be limited, if it occurred at all, if an MNE's leaders had an ethnocentric mindset. Perlmutter imagines the attitude of home-country managers about their subsidiaries as follows:[29]

We, the home nationals of X company, are superior to, more trustworthy and more reliable than any foreigners in headquarters or subsidiaries. We will be willing to build facilities in your country if you acknowledge our inherent superiority and accept our methods and conditions for doing the job.

This attitude results in "home-made" task and performance criteria being applied to all subsidiary personnel. As well, home-country managers expect that any strategies and products that have been successful in the home country will also succeed in any subsidiary located in any other country. These expectations result in a communication process in which subsidiary managers receive a huge volume of advice, counsel, and directives from the home office about how things should be done. There are many inspections to make sure the locals are doing things the "right" way. This does not offend the subsidiary managers because all of them are home-country managers that have been prepared for their role, and who see their career progression as being promoted back to headquarters.

In one study of Canadian software manufacturers doing business in the US,[30] this attitude was commonly found among the least successful companies with the lowest performance in the US. In one very low-performance company based in Vancouver, Canada, the CEO reported that Americans were incapable of understanding an effective selling process, even for selling in the US. All American salespeople were brought to Vancouver to be taught effective Canadian sales techniques, and any that insisted on using non-approved American techniques were disciplined or fired. Meanwhile, in the top-performing companies, the attitude was quite different. The best salespeople for selling software to Americans were considered to be experienced American software salespersons. In these top-performing companies, American salespeople were hired and expected to rely on their own experience without interference from their Canadian headquarters managers.

It might seem odd to suggest that this is not an uncommon attitude among American MNEs and their leaders. Yet it is common enough for Americans, among others, to observe that much of the best management literature and textbooks are produced in the US, along with much of the organizational and management behavior research. Most American business school rating organizations rate American business schools as the world's best, and even many of the best foreign schools much lower.

It is easy for many Americans to have the attitude that the management of international business organizations is based on universal principles developed from American practices. And it is easy to believe that this attitude is shared around the world. Go to any major bookstore worldwide and ask the clerk to show you the management section. In China, Hong Kong, Singapore, Kuala Lumpur, Seoul, and so on, it is always the same. There is a huge selection of the latest American books on business and management. If you ask "Are there any locally produced books?" the answer is either amazement at such a strange question, or one is led to a dark corner in the back where there are a few local books on management on a single shelf.

However, researchers in the US should not assume that American management techniques are necessarily the best, even for American managers or for managers of other countries. American management techniques are based on American values and assumptions (for example, that we can influence and control the future to a high degree). Managers from other countries do not necessarily have such values and assumptions—at least they may not place as much emphasis or importance on them. Some Japanese, Chinese, and Malaysian managers and business professors have argued that this expectation of the universality of American business values represents a colonial or imperialistic attitude.[31] The idea is that when the colonial troops went home, control was maintained with the expectation that American ideas and practices were the best. Many in Asia seem to want to be the best American managers they can be. They will never be as effective Americans as Americans are themselves, and this will give American managers a competitive edge.

Exhibit 3.2 identifies many US values related to business practices. The second column suggests examples of how the American cultural values might influence management practices. The third column offers possible alternative values that are often more effective when applied appropriately locally. The fourth column suggests where the alternative values might be more effectively applied than the American ones in the first column.

EXHIBIT 3.2 AMERICAN VALUES AND POSSIBLE ALTERNATIVES

Aspects of US culture[a]	Management functions affected	Alternative aspect in other cultures	Where alternative more effective
The individual can influence the future (where there is a will, there is a way)	Planning and scheduling	Life follows a preordained course, and human action is determined by the will of God or nature	Islam acknowledges the supreme will of God; Indian culture acknowledges predestination
The individual can change and improve the environment	Organizational environment; morale; productivity	People are intended to adjust to the physical environment rather than trying to alter it	First Nations (Canada); Aboriginal populations worldwide
An individual should be realistic in his/her aspirations	Goal setting; career development	Ideals are to be pursued regardless of what is realistic	Entrepreneurs and their organizations in any nation
We must work hard to accomplish our objectives (Puritan and Protestant ethic)	Motivation and reward systems	Hard work is not the only prerequisite for success. Wisdom, luck, time and relationships as well	Common enough attitude among workers outside Northern Europe and North America
Commitments should be honored (people will do what they say and in time)	Negotiating and bargaining; deadlines	A commitment may be superseded by a conflicting request. An agreement may only signify intention	Contracts and MOUs (memoranda of understanding) in China, Japan, for example

	Aspects of US culture[a]	Management functions affected	Alternative aspect in other cultures	Where alternative more effective
E X H I B I T 3.2	One should effectively use one's time (time is money, which can be saved or wasted)	Long- and short-range planning	Schedules are important but only in relation to other priorities	High relationship cultures. Slow messaging, polychronic cultures (see Chapter 4)
	A primary obligation of an employee is to the organization	Loyalty; commitment; motivation	The individual employee has a primary obligation to family and friends	China, Taiwan, overseas Chinese
	The employer or employee can terminate the relationship	Motivation; company commitment; downsizing; succession planning	Employment is lifetime; the value of seniority	Japanese twentieth-century big business culture offered "lifetime" employment
	The best qualified persons should be given the available positions	Ethics; employment; recruiting, selection, promotions, rewards	Family, friendship and other considerations should determine employment practices	China, for instance
	A person can be removed if he/she does not perform well	Promotion; retention	The removal of a person from a position causes great loss of prestige/face, and will rarely be done	Confucian societies; bureaucracies based on seniority
	All levels of management are open to qualified individuals (a clerk can rise to the presidency)	Employment practices; promotion	Education or family ties are primary vehicles for mobility	India (castes); Britain or anywhere else ascriptive values trump achievement values
	Decision-making should be based on facts and not intuition	Decision-making; market research	The wisdom of the leadership is essential, and questioning it shows lack of confidence	First Nations (Canada); India (castes)
	Data should be accurate	Record keeping; accounting; finance	Accurate data are not always valued or possible by Western standards	Third World
	Each person is expected to have and express their opinion; conflicts handled by discussing points of disagreement	Communications; negotiations; handling conflicts	Open conflicts cause loss of face. Discuss areas of agreement. Assume opposites complement	Asia

Aspects of US culture[a]	Management functions affected	Alternative aspect in other cultures	Where alternative more effective
A decision-maker is expected to consult persons who can contribute relevant information	Decision-making; leadership; management style	Decisions should be made by those in authority. Subordinates do not expect consultation	Russia, for instance
Employees will work hard to improve their position in the company	Selection; promotion; management by objectives	Personal ambition is discouraged	Asia (especially females)
Competition stimulates high performance	Career development; marketing	Competition leads to imbalances; disharmony; favoring Western vs. local companies	Government monopolies and marketing boards in Canada; chaebols in Korea
A person is expected to do whatever is necessary to get the job done	Assignment of tasks; performance; deadlines; organizational effectiveness	Kinds of work are accorded high or low status. Some work may be below one's dignity or position	India (castes), for instance
Change is considered an improvement and a dynamic reality	Planning; change management; morale; organizational development	Tradition is revered and the power of the leaders is based on maintenance of a stable structure	Confucian societies in Asia
What works is important	Communication; technology; planning; quality control	Symbols and the process are more important than the end point	First Nations (Canada); Aboriginal societies anywhere
Persons and systems are evaluated	Punishments; rewards; performance appraisal; accountability	Persons are evaluated in ways that do not embarrass or cause loss of face	China; Britain (anywhere ascription trumps achievement as a value)

Note: [a] "Aspect" here refers to a belief, value, attitude, or assumption that is part of culture in that it is shared by a large number of persons in that culture.

EXHIBIT 3.2

It should be easy to see that having an ethnocentric mindset is not conducive to learning how to be successful in foreign markets. The mindset is not open to the possibility that the existing strategy may not be successful. Success is simply assumed. When American managers, or American wannabees, hold fast to the aspects enumerated on the left side of Exhibit 3.2, assuming them to reflect universal management practices, they become less effective where those aspects do not apply, and the performance of their companies is reduced.

Polycentric mindsets: learning but not integrating

An organization that adopted a polycentric mindset would place a high premium on having local managers that know how to do business in other nations. It would, however, fail to integrate learning between subsidiaries, or between its subsidiaries and home-market best practices. It would assume that anything learned about one foreign market would not apply to any other foreign market. Learning would be local, but apply only within each subsidiary individually. Perlmutter imagined the attitude of home-country managers about their subsidiaries in the following way:[32]

> Let the Romans do it their way. We really don't understand what is going on there, but we have confidence in them. As long as they earn a profit, we want to remain in the background.

The key assumptions with this mindset are that foreign cultures are different, non-natives will have difficulty understanding the culture and being effective, and that local people will know what works best for them. A subsidiary located in a foreign culture should therefore be as local and as locally responsive as possible. Coordination and control across the MNE is achieved with good overall financial controls, but the home office cannot and will not direct local managers in how to be operationally successful.

While the MNE does learn to adapt its products and activities to local markets, the learning is not integrated into a company-wide competitive advantage. Each subsidiary functions as an independent entity and the knowledge learned in one is assumed to apply only to that one. Also, each subsidiary is run essentially as a quasi-independent company, and subsidiary managers jealously guard their independence, both from headquarters and also from other subsidiaries. Nor is the learning collated and integrated in the home-country headquarters, because it is assumed not to be useful for other subsidiaries, or for the overall company.

Geocentric mindsets: worldwide innovation and learning

Organizations and leaders adopting a geocentric mindset will achieve the most effective and performance-enhancing learning. The goal of a geocentric mindset is to integrate both headquarters and subsidiary learning in order to find the best practices for each, and also to identify where practices and products developed in one worldwide location can be applied or adapted to other locations. Geocentric MNEs seek to simultaneously achieve global efficiency and local adaptation. Perlmutter[33] suggested that geocentric managers say to themselves the following sorts of things:

> Where in the world shall we raise money, build our plant, conduct R&D, and get and launch new ideas to serve our present and future customers. . . . Where in the world can I get the help to serve my customers best in this country? Where in the world can I export products developed in this country—products which meet worldwide standards as opposed to purely local standards.

And in contradistinction to the polycentric mindset, the geocentric leader says:

> We aim not to be just a good local company, but the best local company in terms of the quality of management and the worldwide (not local) standards we establish in domestic and export production. If we were only as good as local companies, we would deserve to be nationalized.

The geocentric mindset seeks the best managers and personnel, regardless of nationality, to deal with the MNE's problems anywhere in its operations. Its ultimate goal is to create an integrated worldwide strategy enacted by the integrated capabilities of both headquarters and all subsidiaries. The subsidiaries are considered neither colonies (ethnocentric), nor independent city-states (polycentric), but as parts of a whole that is focused simultaneously on the MNE's worldwide and local objectives. This attitude is intended to produce a collaborative and cooperative effort on the parts of both headquarters and all subsidiaries to establish worldwide standards, and permissible local standards variations. It is applied to key allocation decisions on new products, new plants, and new R&D centers.

One benefit of a geocentric mindset is that subsidiaries do not fight, each hoping to become a fully functional independent business. Allocation decisions for producing different elements of a product value chain (R&D, sourcing, manufacturing, marketing, sales, service) may be made more rationally, locating each in the most cost, tax, or politically safest location. Microsoft, for example, was able to satisfy Chinese government pressure for local R&D as well as manufacturing by developing a major high-technology R&D center in Beijing in addition to their other worldwide locations.[34] In doing so for political reasons, they discovered that Chinese R&D engineers were well-trained, highly motivated, and cost significantly less than equivalent American personnel. In return, Microsoft received greater access to the Chinese microcomputer market.

By contrast, Blackberry, having an ethnocentric mindset, resisted[35] transferring any value chain activities out of Canada, let alone to China, despite the Chinese demands for local manufacturing as a condition for market entry. Of course, Blackberry's negotiations to enter China in a big way failed. Research has shown that Canadian and American companies have been more successful in China when they are willing to transfer value chain activities directly to China.[36] This was generally only possible with a geocentric mindset. In the same way, American auto manufacturers have moved much of their manufacturing to Mexico to reduce costs. Honda developed an R&D center for the US, staffed by American designers. This center envisioned the Honda Element, a big success with American car buyers but never popular in Japan. And, many airline companies have moved their customer service functions to India to reduce costs.

Learning and the theory of internationalization

Learning to enter and successfully build a business presence in a new foreign market can be a very uncertain and time-consuming process for any company, including established MNEs. There are so many potential sources of uncertainty in an unfamiliar foreign market: political, economic, social, technological, and cultural. Companies want to limit their exposure to unknown risks until they have learned to understand and assess all relevant uncertainties. It is very costly for MNEs to find and hire well-informed and experienced local human resources as a means of reducing uncertainty. It is expensive and time-consuming to find and build trust-based relationships with potential joint-venture partnerships with successful local companies as a way of learning how to do business in a new local market. Greenfields (starting your own subsidiary from scratch) and acquisitions require huge investments and are therefore very risky, especially if you are unfamiliar with local business conditions. The problems small- and medium-sized enterprises (SMEs) face are magnified by their relative lack of resources.

The Uppsala theory of internationalization predicts that MNEs will intensify their activities in a foreign market, learning and initiating new entry strategies that typically improve their performance outcomes,[37] as they learn about the market and reduce their uncertainties about it.[38] As companies learn more about a foreign market they become more willing to use entry strategies that entail more risk to their resources but also have the potential for higher returns. An entry strategy is defined as an institutional arrangement making possible the entry of a firm's products or services, or technology, human resources, or management into a foreign nation.[39]

The theory argues that MNEs choose their entry strategies based on the amount of information they have about a foreign market. If decision-makers have little or no relevant information, or are unconfident about the information they have, then they are uncertain about their ability to analyze the nature of competitive advantage and little confidence about their ability to predict the future course of the market.[40] Uncertainty is defined as the difference between the information decision-makers currently have and the information needed to be successful in a market.[41] Uncertainty causes decision-makers to be unsure about whether what they have learned from their previous experience in other national markets will be applicable to a new market, and whether their organization of internal capabilities will be effective.

This learning theory observes that decision-makers will have a maximum level of market risk they are willing to accept when entering a new foreign market for the first time.[42] Risk is understood as the perceived level of possible threat to the financial security of the company if the entry fails and the resources committed to the entry are lost. When a company makes a first entry, perceived market uncertainty is usually high because decision-makers usually have little direct knowledge about market conditions. A large commitment of resources is unlikely because such a commitment would raise total market risk beyond an acceptable threshold.[43] Resources are defined as dedicated assets—a manufacturing plant, a sales and service office, or local managers or employees—that could not be redeployed without a significant cost. An exception would be a very large and well-resourced MNE that had hired competent local market experts and was not making an entry costly enough to threaten overall financial survival. Microsoft's wholly owned entry into Beijing, opening an R&D center, would be such a case,[44] but Microsoft had started in China with exporting, as predicted by the theory.

Typically, at an initial stage when uncertainty is at its maximum, MNEs *export* their products to a new foreign market using an agent or distributor. An export strategy is preferred because the MNE puts as little of its resources at risk as possible. Usually only a small stock of product is provided to the distributor, with more available when sales are made. Even less risky is a direct mail or website approach in which the MNE contacts potential customers by mail, email, or web-based ads, and the product is shipped directly upon order and prepayment. Export strategies would include: (1) direct mail or website sales; (2) distribution through a home-market distributor that sells in the foreign market as well; (3) distribution through a distributor located in the foreign market; and (4) selling in the foreign market using salespersons based in the home market that sell by email, or Skype, or that travel to foreign market customers for face-to-face meetings.

Export strategies tend not to be particularly profitable because only relatively small numbers of sales are made. The MNE is simply dabbling in the new market, hoping to learn about the buying preferences of customers, whether its products are competitive, and whether the new market could be a profitable source of sales. Distributors provide very little push for individual products. If a customer shows no interest in a particular product, the distributor offers other possibilities. An exporting company should understand that one of the goals of many distributors is to prevent or retard the ability of the exporters to learn about the foreign market because that knowledge represents the competitive edge of the distributor. If the MNE understood its customers and the market, its uncertainty would be reduced and it would be confident about bypassing the distributor.

Distributors can be expensive. Kevin O'Leary,[45] of *The Dragon's Den* fame on Canadian TV, was the CEO of Softkey, which began as a software distributor. Softkey offered to invest money to promote a small software developer's product in the US. If sales were achieved, Softkey would recover its initial marketing investment and then charge about 25 percent of the value of future sales. Softkey became so successful as a software marketing firm that one CEO of another software company reported that Softkey could charge in fees as much as 70 percent of the value of the sales it generated.

As decision-makers learn more about a foreign market, perceived uncertainty is reduced, and a greater willingness develops to make bigger financial commitments while still retaining the original threshold of maximum acceptable market risk. The second stage of internationalization usually involves either *licensing or franchising*. These strategies tend to have better financial pay-offs than exporting, but still suffer from the need to pay a substantial proportion of the overall profit to the local market representatives. The MNE has learned that there is a market for its product but is either unwilling to take the risk of direct investment, or regards the market as either too small or incidental to its main strategic interests. The MNE signs a long-term contract with a local market company that will produce, sell, and distribute the MNE's products or services in its market.[46] The contractual agreement transfers product knowledge or management know-how to the local company. The local company will usually be expected to transfer any technological innovations it produces to the MNE, and should also be required to produce minimum levels of sales to maintain its contractual position.

With a licensing strategy, the local licensee receives the right to use specific licensor patents, industrial know-how, or trademarks for a period of time in exchange for a royalty—an annual sum or a percentage of gross or net sales. With a franchising strategy, the franchisee receives help in management skills, marketing, and organizing, in addition to the use of patents and trademarks, and industrial know-how. The franchisee typically pays an initial fee, and a percentage for supplies received, and total sales. The franchisor may help select a competitive location, supply the fixtures, help in recruiting employees, and provide a manual that offers direction on running a successful franchise operation. Most franchisors expect franchisees to obtain all their supplies from the franchisor. Seven-Eleven is an exception in this regard. Its franchisees are expected to purchase a percentage of their supplies from the franchisor, which also offers incentives to increase that percentage.

Alternatively, an MNE may, as a second internationalization stage, seek a strategic collaboration in the form of *alliances or joint ventures* with a local firm. MNEs considering strategic collaborations have learned enough to know that they are interested in expanding within a market. Usually there is some gap in their knowledge that they hope to learn through a joint venture. A typical joint-venture strategy is for an MNE to offer its more advanced technology to a local partner in exchange for learning how to market and sell in that market.

Depending on the level of goodwill, a race to learn may take place. The danger for the MNE is that the local partner will learn its advanced technology before the MNE learns the local market, thereby creating a potential global competitor. The MNE loses when its local partner dissolves the joint venture. It has lost control of its technology but has not yet learned how to be successful in the local market. The danger for the local partner is that the MNE will learn how to market and sell in its local market, and not need the local partner, before the latter learns the technology.

The Indian joint venture between Honda Motor Company and the Hero Group is instructive in this regard.[47] The two combined to produce the Hero-Honda joint venture, the most successful motorcycle manufacturing and sales company in India in the 1990s. Honda provided the motorcycle technology while Hero provided the local marketing and sales. After ten years, Honda learned to set up its own sales and distribution system, while Hero had simply relied on Honda's technology and not set up its own R&D. Honda continued to support Hero, but the latter became dependent on Honda's goodwill.

Selecting a compatible joint-venture partner is the best protection against these kinds of competitive outcomes. The partners must ensure that they have:

1   *Complementarity*. Initially, this was the case for Honda and Hero. Honda had world-competitive motorcycle technology while Hero was very successful at marketing and selling in India. This changed, however, as Honda learned and Hero didn't.
2   *Convergence of goals*. Initially, this was true for Honda and Hero. Honda was a global MNE interested in India only to keep up with its global competitors that already had Indian joint ventures. Hero was only interested in the Indian market and did not pose a global threat to Honda.
3   *Commitment*. Both partners must believe that they may trust each other, recognizing that cooperation builds trust, as do reliability, competence, and personal relationship over time. Hero communicated a lack of commitment to Honda over time by trying to sign agreements with Honda's global competitors.
4   *Compatibility*. This is achieved through asymmetrical skills that produce clear and non-overlapping responsibilities. Choi and Beamish[48] argued that Koreans and Americans were so culturally different that they could not successfully work together in joint ventures. If, however, their roles were asymmetrical and non-overlapping, then Korean–American joint ventures could be very successful. In the case of Hero and Honda, compatibility was lost when Honda understood Indian marketing practices.

Research has shown that the most profitable foreign market strategies are *wholly owned* (WO),[49] and this supports the need for learning.[50] Exhibit 3.3 summarizes the levels of market risk, required resource commitment, and potential profitability of a variety of entry strategies. The very high potential profitability of WO strategies is balanced by very high potential for losses if what an MNE has learned is insufficient.

MNEs are comfortable implementing WO strategies (greenfield and acquisition) when they have fully learned the political, economic, social, and technological differences (PEST) in a local market compared with their home markets. They have developed the marketing and sales expertise for the local market, either because their personnel have developed the required tacit knowledge through joint ventures and/or alliances, or because experienced local or expatriate personnel have been hired. *Greenfield* is the setting up of a WO operation from the ground up. Dell Computer Corporation has been very successful in Latin America through its greenfield operations there.[51] *Acquisition* is the acquiring of a successful local firm through which the MNE plans to operate. Daimler-Benz faced crisis-level problems when it acquired the unsuccessful Chrysler, and is reputed to have paid a billion dollars to Fiat to take Chrysler off its hands.

EXHIBIT 3.3 RELATIVE ATTRACTIVENESS OF FOREIGN MARKET ENTRY STRATEGIES

Foreign market entry mode	Market risk	Resource commitment	Potential profitability
Export: direct mail, website	Low	Low	Low
Export: agent or distributor	Low	Low	Low
Licensing; franchising	Moderate	Moderate	Low to moderate
Minority joint venture (owns less than 50 percent)	High	Moderate	Moderate
50/50 joint venture	High	Moderate	Moderate
Majority joint venture (owns more than 50 percent)	High	Moderate to high	Moderate
Wholly owned subsidiary: acquisition	High	High	High
Wholly owned subsidiary: greenfield	High	Very high	Very high

Sources: Erramilli, M. K. and Rao, C. P. "Choice of Foreign Market Entry Modes by Service Firms: Role of Market Knowledge," *Management International Review*, Vol. 30, 1990, pp. 135–150. Root, F. R. *Entry Strategies for International Markets*. San Francisco, CA: Jossey-Bass, 1998.

ENVIRONMENTAL CHANGE AND ITS LEARNING EFFECTS

A company usually becomes an MNE to find greater competitive advantage within more globalized industry environments than it enjoyed in its own national domestic environment. An international market may provide a more *secure supply* of raw materials. For example, Canada has become a larger supplier of oil to the US than any individual Middle Eastern country, and an attractive location for American oil and gas investment, because it enjoys far greater political stability.

An international market may provide *new markets* for products or services. Most MNEs that enter a new international market do so on the basis of having a technological or R&D advantage over the existing domestic competitors.[52] They have a better, more advanced, or more desirable product or service that can be sold for a premium that more than offsets the increased costs of doing business abroad. MNEs usually intend to achieve higher levels of profitability in international markets because of the greater risk than domestic markets. Mercedes, for example, only sells its luxury auto models worldwide, even though it is not an exclusively luxury brand in Germany.

In addition, and especially before the global recession of 2008, MNEs sought *low-cost factors of production* to reduce the cost of manufactured products. These were then primarily shipped back to the markets of more developed nations. China, for example, initially began to develop its economy after 1979 by attracting foreign investment that was enticed by low labor costs, inexpensive land, and low taxes. China's domestic consumer market was not attractive to MNEs at that time because most people were poor and couldn't afford the products they were producing. With the onset of the 2008 global recession and the debt crisis in many G8 countries, the markets in developed countries became less able to purchase the products produced abroad. MNEs have learned that the emerging markets themselves are a better opportunity for the sale of their locally produced products[53] as local standards of living rose. Since the early 2000s, for example, average wages in China have risen fourfold. There are now as many in China with middleclass incomes as the entire US population.

According to Crossan et al.,[54] all companies, including MNEs, face three kinds of change conditions that negatively affect their performance and that require them to learn new ways of doing business. *Crisis change* is a situation in which a company's performance has declined substantially either because of poor products and/or services, a poor competitive strategy, or an inability to drive the strategy because of inconsistency between strategy and the company's internal capabilities. There is an imminent threat of bankruptcy. In this situation, the company's strategic capabilities are low but the willingness to change is high because "the writing is on the wall."

As of 2016, Blackberry (formerly RIM) is in the midst of crisis change that has lasted a number of years. After dominating the business smartphone market as recently as 2009, it fell behind Apple, Samsung, and Google in product development. In 2012, big client businesses, part of their installed base, began to discard their Blackberries and switch to these competitors. In 2016, Blackberry announced that it would no longer build smartphones but concentrate entirely on developing and selling software. Yet the crisis continues because Blackberry hasn't turned a quarterly profit in years and is slowly burning through its last cash reserves.

Companies can learn new "tricks" and survive crisis change situations, but their odds of success have been estimated at only 50/50, the same as flipping a coin. When General Motors and Chrysler entered bankruptcy and were sustained by government loans in 2009, both were able to find new ways to compete. In 2012, Chrysler became the top-selling automobile brand in Canada and has retained that position. General Motors briefly regained its status as the top-selling brand in the world in 2011, when Toyota production was stalled by a major earthquake and tsunami in northeastern Japan. The point, however, is that there are many warnings that change is necessary. The crisis develops because a company has not seen it coming, and learned earlier what to do instead.

Reactive change is usually the stage at which companies realize that they need to change before a crisis can develop. Products and/or services are beginning to lose competitive advantage. Sales and profits are off former highs. Managers begin to realize that the company is on a downslope and the readiness for change begins to develop.

This was the situation at Ford Motor Company[55] when Bill Ford Jr., Henry Ford's great grandson, took over as CEO in 2001, promising that the money-losing Ford would make a

$7 billion profit within five years. Ford quality had become so questionable that many former customers refused ever to consider buying another Ford. Meanwhile, the company was stuck with high labor costs because of unions that resisted efforts to achieve wage levels consistent with the Japanese competition, and any efforts to increase factory productivity. Ford had too many inefficient plants for the number of vehicles they could sell, and managers that were not above sabotaging each other's efforts to try to advance their own careers. At the same time, high gasoline costs were scaring customers away from the big pickups and SUVs that generated most of Ford's profits.

For a while, Bill Ford was successful. He strengthened Ford's alliance with the Japanese Mazda, and used Mazda and Swedish Volvo technology as the basis for new Ford cars of higher quality. He began development of a hybrid car. Yet his efforts failed when the fuel crisis of 2006 led to the collapse of Ford's truck and SUV sales. In the third quarter of 2006 alone, Ford posted a nearly $6 billion loss, Ford's worst quarter in 14 years. When Alan Mulally took over as CEO, he inherited a crisis change situation. Given that even iconic companies can fail to respond effectively to the need for reactive change, there must be earlier opportunities to learn to respond to the need for change.

Anticipatory change is the awareness that a company's strategy has reached its potential limits to growth. Performance is still rising but at a slower rate. Resistance to the possibility of change is likely to be higher than in reactive or crisis situations. The general feeling may be that growth has slowed because of macro-economic factors and not because the company's competitive position has eroded. Or senior managers may simply be swept away by their feelings of success and invincibility, and not be watching closely enough.

Richmond Engineering,[56] a Vancouver, British Columbia, based telephone and street-light pole manufacturing SME with annual sales of C$24 million, provides a good example of anticipatory change. By 1984, it had reached its limits of growth. Richmond was the market leader in pole manufacturing and sales in western Canada, but because of the costs of transportation it was not feasible to sell in either eastern Canada or the western US. Having hit their maximum growth potential in their home market, the CEO, a very strong woman entrepreneur, began to look for joint-venture opportunities in China. Her goal was to manufacture in China at significantly lower costs than in Canada and to supply the quickly expanding China market.

Richmond employed an agent in Hong Kong between 1984 and 1989. In 1987, a joint-venture agreement was being negotiated to produce Richmond poles with Hong Kong financing in Shenzhen, but this deal fell apart after Tiananmen Square in 1989. Between 1989 and 1991, Richmond assessed dozens of offers from China before finding a real possibility in the Beijing area. By 1993, a joint-venture agreement was in place and by 1999 the joint venture was selling poles in China and Abu Dhabi, as well as selling a turnkey manufacturing plant in China.

The lesson here about learning to respond to the need for change is that it is best to do so earlier rather than later. Exhibit 3.4 offers some shorthand comparisons between the three stages of need for change.

EXHIBIT 3.4 COMPARISON OF CRISIS, REACTIVE, AND ANTICIPATORY CHANGE SITUATIONS

	Crisis	Reactive	Anticipatory
Situation			
Performance	Critically low	Lower than before	Slower but still growing
Time pressure	High	Medium	Low
Resistance	Low	Mixed to high	High
Concerns			
Strategic	Rapid change to avoid business failure	Temporary glitch or changed conditions?	Plan still works well
Classification	Urgent change as soon as possible	Normal change: reassess strategic plan	Standard change: take advantage of opportunities
Leadership	Reactive	Reactive	Proactive

Source: Crossan, M. M., Rouse, M. J., Fry, J. N., and Killing, J. P. *Strategic Analysis and Action*, 7th edn. Toronto, ON: Pearson Prentice Hall, 2009, p. 217.

E
X
H
I
B
I
T

3.4

Effects of change and declining performance

Companies' learning behavior is generally driven by their market performance. Market success is critical. The best managers want to work at the best and most successful companies. If a company's performance starts to go downhill, good personnel may begin to leave in search of better opportunities. Banks and financial institutions either do not want to lend to companies doing poorly, or the rates they charge become higher and higher as the company's credit rating declines. The value of a publicly traded company's stock also reflects investors' perceptions of how successful the company is. And the compensation and incentive packages of senior executives are often tied into share price. The stock options senior managers receive as incentives will not have as good value if the share price declines. There are many measures of how a company is performing. Some of these are identified in Exhibit 3.5.

Measures of profitability are made more complex because of the possible effects of inflation or levels of competition within an industry. We are not as used to considering the effects of inflation because G8 interest rates have been so low for so many years and inflation has not been more than 1–3 percent for a long time. If, however, a company's sales and/or profits were rising at 5 percent annually, but inflation was running at 10 percent per annum, or the company's competitors were growing at the same 10 percent per year, then the position of the company would be declining in inflation-adjusted dollars by 5 percent per year.

**E
X
H
I
B
I
T

3.5**

EXHIBIT 3.5 MEASURES OF FIRM PERFORMANCE

Performance outcomes	Outputs	Inputs
Sales results, profit margins	Financial	People (satisfaction, retention, quality of work life)
Return on assets (ROA), income (ROI), equity (ROE)	Productivity, efficiency and quality	Technology (information and data, reliability, satisfaction)
Objectives defined in strategic plan and achieved or surpassed	Activity ratios (asset and inventory turnover)	Fixed assets (security, utilization, quality)
Customer results: satisfaction, quality, timeliness	Management effectiveness and innovation	

Source: adapted from http://en.wikipedia.org/wiki/File:Performance_Reference_Model.jpg.

Environmental changes requiring organizational learning

In addition to learning (or not learning) from the performance of their international operations, MNE leaders must also learn to adapt to a variety of environmental changes. Global leaders with foresight scan for information about their competitive environment, local and worldwide, that may cause changes in strategies, policies, and technologies. They analyze and anticipate trends that influence their companies' futures. Some positive forces of change drive us to increase or decrease the workforce, or to be more aware or responsive to community needs. Over a decade ago, Moran and Riesenberger[57] described 12 environmental forces impacting organizations and influencing change that are still evident today. Some proactive environmental forces are as follows:

1   *Global sourcing*–organizations are seeking nondomestic sources of raw materials because of cost and quality.

2   *New and evolving markets*–these are providing unique growth opportunities.

3   *Economies of scale*–today's global marketplace requires different approaches, resulting in competitive advantages in price and quality.

4   Movement toward *homogeneous demand*–globalization is resulting in similar products being required worldwide.

5   *Lowered transportation costs*–world transportation costs of many products have fallen significantly because of innovations.

6   Reduced government *tariffs and taxes*–the protectionist tendencies of many governments are declining, as evidenced by the North American Free Trade Agreement (NAFTA) and the European Union policies and agreements.

7   *Telecommunications*–falling prices as a result of privatization, and new technologies are impacting globalization. Digital communications, the internet, and wireless communications have vastly expanded this effect.

8   *Homogeneous technical standards*–the International Organization for Standardization (ISO) has been successful in developing global standards, including ISO 9000 (quality management), ISO 14000 (environmental management), ISO 26000 (social responsibility), and six other ISO standards.

Some reactive forces, present in the global environment, are as follows:

1   *Competition*–new competitive threats are regularly experienced by organizations.

2   *Risk of volatile exchange rates*–the constant fluctuation of exchange rates in many countries impacts profits.

3   *Customers are becoming more global consumers*–globalization is impacting customers in ways that increase "local content" in subsidiary-produced goods.

4   *Global technological change*–technological improvements coming from many areas of the world require organizations to adjust their strategies to survive.

INDIVIDUAL LEARNING

It would be wrongheaded to claim that none of the above discussions of organizational learning applied to individual learning as well. For example, a person reading about the differences between ethnocentric, polycentric, and geocentric mindsets might learn to prefer the geocentric for its nonjudgmental attitudes about cultures. This section, however, is intended to outline some of the major differences between how people from different cultures react to change, what they prefer to learn in response to change, and how their competencies may differ on average.

When we work together in joint ventures, for example, or when headquarters managers are trying to teach subsidiary managers new ways of organizing, or vice versa, learning may fail because learning styles vary from country to country. For example, in North American business education, it is common to discuss points of disagreement, argue over them, and eventually come to some agreement or consensus. This approach generally fails in China, where it is not the custom to discuss points of disagreement in case somebody suffers a loss of face. Once one's face has been lost, one feels disrespected and unwilling to cooperate further, both immediately and in future with those responsible. Instead, the Chinese prefer to consider all the points they agree on until the areas of potential disagreement largely disappear into the overall agreement. And whereas Euro-North Americans tend to think dualistically such that there is always a preferred alternative and a discredited one, the Chinese tend to believe that opposites are complementary and may be combined in a yin–yang fashion. Even the meanings of the concepts we learn may differ from culture to culture.

In the US, "consensus" means we all end up agreeing. In Japan it means that this time "we" will agree with "you" but next time you will remember it is your turn to agree with us.

We all have a set of highly organized constructs around which we organize our "private" worlds. Literally, we construct a mental system for putting order, as we perceive it, into our life spaces. This intellectual synthesis relates to our images of self, family, role, organization, nation, and universe. Such constructs then become psychological anchors or reference points for our mental functioning and well-being. Our unique construct systems exert a pushing/pulling effect on all other ideas and experiences we encounter. We assign meaning almost automatically to the multiple sensations and perceptions that bombard us daily.

Human interaction is dynamic, however, and so pressures for change build up for individuals and in institutions. For example, when a manager from Grand Rapids, Michigan, is transferred for a three-year assignment to Riyadh, Saudi Arabia, or Bangalore, India, that person is challenged to change many of his/her understandings about life and people. The same may be said for the corporate culture when a company attempts to transplant operations from Paris, France, to the Middle East or Asia. These forces for change can be avoided, resisted, or incorporated into the person's perceptual field. If the latter happens, then change becomes a catalyst for restructuring our constructs, giving us an opportunity for growth. In other words, individuals and institutions can adapt and develop.

When leaders do not prepare their followers for necessary and inevitable change, the consequences can be disastrous. For example, many national, educational, political, and religious systems suffer from "culture lag." That is, as the human mainstream has moved ahead to a new stage of development, this particular community is locked into a past mindset. In 2016, the conservative political party in Canada formally acknowledged the legality of same-sex marriage even though it had already been legal in Canada for more than ten years. They were just catching up with what the majority of Canadians believed to be reality.

In the Middle East, ultra-traditional religious views and practices diminish the role of women, deterring development of female potential and positive contributions. In Africa, the tribal ruling system has broken down, and the instability has led to a series of military coups and local despots, along with social chaos and ethnic killings. In the US, open-door policies for visitors, foreigners, and immigrants are being undermined by fears of terrorism, forcing additional regulation of immigration and travel requirements, as well as security practices.

When a society or a system is imprisoned by its past traditions, attitudes, and beliefs, it may produce unsavory results. Many perceive themselves as oppressed, and so they resort to rioting, fire bombings, and even the taking of innocent lives—witness tensions in the US about illegal immigration, and the "Black Lives Matter" movement, the continuing Arab–Israeli violence in Israel and the Palestinian Authority, and the "Idle-No-More" Aboriginal movement in Canada demanding an immediate end to historic grievances. In Europe there have been riots by and about immigrants, and protests over Islamic hijabs and "burkini" bathing suits in France, not to mention the banning of hijabs at universities in Istanbul—an Islamic country. All these events, and many others worldwide, show the negative results when people divide themselves into factions that do not understand each other's mindsets by which they understand their own situations.

In today's changing business cultures as well, people are also challenged to alter the way they perceive or think about their work and how it is to be performed. The shifting context of the work environment has been described as the new work culture.[58]

Temperament, learning, and change

In Chapter 2 we discussed the effects of personality on communication styles using the Jungian theory of psychological types.[59] In Chapter 11 we apply the same Jungian personality model to problem-solving. Keirsey[60] developed his own model of personality temperament as an outgrowth of Jung's theory. He argued that his four genetically based temperaments, and the leadership styles he developed from them—*Tactical*, *Logistical*, *Diplomatic*, and *Strategic*—had consistently existed in human populations for thousands of years, and had originally been independently described by Hippocrates, Plato, and Aristotle in Ancient Greece. Plato, for example, had named the temperaments Iconic, Pistic, Noetic, and Dianoetic.[61]

According to Keirsey, each temperament produces a different style of leadership with different competencies for learning, and different reactions to change. Because the temperaments are heritable, they represent behavioral defaults. Keirsey's model is an especially valuable learning tool for students of management, thanks to the internet, because of the ease with which you may determine your temperament and leadership style. Any student may access a free personality test on the internet.[62] These tests provide nominal-level assessments for each of four bipolar scales used to determine an individual's temperament. For example:

1   Extraversion (E) versus Introversion (I): You will receive either "E" or "I" depending on which one you scored higher on, simply by answering the test questions.
2   Sensing (S) versus iNtuiting (N): You will receive either "S" or "N."
3   Thinking (T) versus Feeling (F): You will receive either "T" or "F."
4   Judging (J) versus Perceiving (P): You will receive either "J" or "F."

These self-assessment tests produce 16 four-letter personality styles (ISTJ, ISFJ, ESTJ, ESFJ, ISTP, ISFP, ESTP, ESFP, INFJ, INFP, ENFP, ENFJ, INTP, INTJ, ENTP, ENTJ). If your four-letter personality assessment contains "S" and "P," then as an SP your temperament is *Tactical*. If your four-letter personality assessment contains "S" and "J," then as an SJ your temperament is *Logistical*. If your four-letter personality assessment contains "N" and "F," then as an NF your temperament is *Diplomatic*. If your four-letter personality assessment contains "N" and "T," then as an NT your temperament is *Strategic*. Exhibit 3.6 indicates the strengths and weaknesses of the four leadership styles, based on temperament, in relation to handling change and learning.

Tacticians (SP), Diplomats (NF), and Strategists (NT) support different kinds of strategic and organizational change more easily than Logicians (SJ), whose most comfortable role is systems maintenance. Strategists have the widest intellectual vision for change, and they are the most innovative systems builders, but their weakness is that they are concerned more with strategic and organizational systems than the people who work for the organization. Diplomats are the reverse, with their greatest concern being the training, development, and empowerment of people to the level of their greatest potentiality. Tacticians are at their strongest dealing with unplanned change, seeing potential trouble earlier, putting out unexpected "fires" by changing systems, structures, and job descriptions on the basis of what they know works, or what has worked for other organizations in the past. By contrast, Logicians are good at making organizations run smoothly by building interlocking policies and procedures that prevent the need for "firefighting," and that do not encourage a need for gratuitous or faddish change for its own sake. The four temperaments are described in Exhibit 3.6.

EXHIBIT 3.6 FOUR TEMPERAMENT-BASED LEADERSHIP STYLES, CHANGE AND LEARNING

Characteristic style	Tactical (SP)	Logistical (SJ)	Diplomatic (NF)	Strategic (NT)
Handles change	Welcomes and seeks change. May react negatively to changes initiated by others. Supports unplanned crisis-based change.	Prefers stability and preserves status quo. May not be responsive to changing needs. Supports change based on facts.	Supports enhancing quality of work life by meeting individual needs of employees and clients. Supports change based on human values.	Architects of change with focus on designing improved systems. Early adopter of new ideas. Supports change based on efficiency.
Managerial strengths	Troubleshooting and firefighting; finds breakdowns and errors to fix expeditiously; great strength in environmental scanning.	Builds/runs effective bureaucracy; efficient meetings, well-ordered agenda. Maintains stable system. Understands organizational values. Honors policies' intent.	Personal style. Develops capabilities of others. Strong commitment to staff. Offers enthusiasm, listening, and approval. Good with unstructured meetings.	Theoretical orientation; leading-edge strategic and organizational thinking; creative systems design; maximizes output while minimizing inputs.

Characteristic style	Tactical (SP)	Logistical (SJ)	Diplomatic (NF)	Strategic (NT)
Managerial weakness	Avoids theory; does not like unfamiliar solutions; immediate problems preempt attention.	Preserves procedures including less effective rules and regulations. Engages in anger and blaming. Sees others as "good" or "bad." Creates tense relationships.	May play favorites. May support "underdog" and guilt-load opponents. May be overhelpful. Spends too much time helping others and gets behind and stressed out.	Object- but not people-oriented; others find him/her cold, distant, and unappreciative. Escalates standards for self and others. Does not honor status/ seniority.
Deals with colleagues	Easily responds; open minded, adaptable, patient, flexible; changes easily as new facts and situations emerge.	Fails to speak in positive ways. May use sarcasm and sharp criticism intended to be helpful. Annoyed if others eschew standard operating procedures.	Relates well and is popular. Enjoys being sociable and being caught up with others' problems. Democratic style offers delegation, culture of personal initiative.	Easily tracks thought processes of others. Responsive to new ideas. Gets bored easily and may withdraw. Will stand against crowd for what she/he believes.
Team contributions	Spurs action with verbal planning and decision-making; spots problems early.	Builds/maintains effective formal systems. Competent execution of strategic plans.	Personalized people-oriented point of view. "Sells" organization to clients. Gaood public relations. Strong values.	Strong support for planned change. Offers theoretical structure. Offers usable options.

Source: Keirsey, D. and Bates, M. *Please Understand Me: Character & Temperament Types.* Del Mar, CA: Prometheus Nemesis Book Company, 1984, pp. 129–155.

In a nutshell, Tacticians are known for their effective entrepreneurial/intrapreneurial attitudes, especially their quick environmental scanning for opportunities for improvement, and their fast implementation of these opportunities as soon as possible. Logicians are especially good at organizing and running practical formal organizations with clear reporting relationships that run smoothly, but not good at initiating change. Diplomats are especially good at building informal relationships based on cooperation, shared goals, mutual benefits, constructive controversy handling, and trust. Strategists are best at designing systems intended to produce new organizational systems achieving maximum efficiency and effectiveness, and they are the most innovative in developing the leading-edge organizations that will ultimately be managed by others. It is also worth noting that Tacticians and Logicians are the most practical in their skillsets, while Diplomats and Strategists are the most abstract. In addition, Logicians and Diplomats are more altruistic in their concern for the comfort and success of others, while Tacticians and Strategists are more self-interested in putting their satisfactions ahead of that of others.

Temperament and national culture

Some nations and cultures are more important for international business. Almost 95 percent of international trade (exports + imports) is currently conducted by 20 nations. These are indicated in Exhibit 3.7. Most of us will find that our international business-related careers mainly involve doing business with managers and companies from these nations. However,

EXHIBIT 3.7 BIGGEST TRADING NATIONS (WORLD TOTAL = $27,567 BILLION)

Rank	Nation	Total international trade (B$)	% value of world trade	Cumulative value (B$)
1	USA	3,825.0	13.9	3,825.0
2	China[a]	3,561.0	12.9	7,386.0
3	Germany	2,882.0	10.5	10,268.0
4	Japan	1,595.5	5.8	11,863.5
5	France	1,263.0	4.6	13,126.5
6	United Kingdom	1,150.3	4.2	14,276.8
7	Netherlands	1,091.0	4.0	15,367.8
8	South Korea	1,084.0	3.9	16,451.8
9	Italy	1,050.1	3.8	17,501.9
-	Hong Kong	944.8	3.4	18,446.7
10	Canada	910.2	3.3	19,356.9
11	Russia	843.4	3.1	20,200.3
12	Singapore	818.8	3.0	21,019.1
13	India	792.3	2.9	21,811.4
14	Spain	715.2	2.6	22,526.6
15	Mexico	678.2	2.5	23,204.8
16	Belgium	664.4	2.4	23,869.2
17	Taiwan	623.7	2.3	24,492.9
18	Switzerland	607.9	2.2	25,100.8
19	Australia	502.3	1.8	25,603.1
20	Brazil	470.4	1.7	26,073.5
	Total Top 20		94.8%	

Source: CIA, *The World Factbook, 2013*. www.cia.gov/library/publications/the-world-factbook (retrieved September 16, 2016).

Note: [a] China + Hong Kong = 16.2 percent of world trade. Hong Kong has been part of China since 1997 but is often treated as a separate entity.

these nations do business throughout the world and there is no guarantee where you will be assigned, or with whom you will have to conduct business.

With our globally interdependent economy, it is essential that we appreciate and understand the perspectives and goals of our world trade partners. This is especially true when these trade partners are trying to work together for certain agreed-upon objectives. We recognize that we are most comfortable communicating with those who are the most similar to us. This comfort level tends to decrease as dissimilarity increases.

Research has demonstrated that communication openness tends to be a precursor to different group members' response to conflict, which can impact a diverse group's performance.[63] Reasons cited[64] include that members prefer to communicate and are more open with others who are most similar to themselves, and perceived dissimilarity tends to negatively impact communication. People are often unaware when misunderstandings occur or "errors" are committed while working with persons from different cultures. A cross-cultural *faux pas* results when we fail to recognize that persons of other cultural backgrounds have certain goals, customs, thought patterns, and/or values different from our own. This is also true when national cultures have a greater or lesser openness to change, or different kinds of change. It is also true when individuals from national cultures other than our own have been inclined to learn based on different interests than our own, and propose solutions to change problems quite different from those that we would ourselves favor.

Massey[65] conducted a study to identify the personality types most characteristic of over 100 national cultures. His study was discussed in detail in Chapter 2 on intercultural communications. His findings make it possible to identify predominant Keirsey leadership styles—Tactical, Logistical, Diplomatic, and Strategic—based on temperament for the world's 20 top trading nations. These results are presented in Exhibit 3.8.

The largest group of national cultures are predominantly Logistical (SJ) in their orientations toward change and learning. This group includes both North American nations (US and Canada), and the largest group of European nations (Germany, UK, Netherlands, and Switzerland), plus Japan, South Korea, Singapore, and Australia. It includes all English-speaking nations (US, UK, Canada, and Australia), especially significant because research shows that upwards of 75 percent of undergraduate and MBA students in both the US and Canada in recent years are Logistical in temperament,[66] suggesting this is the current style orientation of American and Canadian managers. The same has been found true of South Korean business students.[67] It would be easy for English-speaking business students, and practicing managers—the main groups reading *Managing Cultural Differences*—to assume that Logistical thinking about change was the normal orientation worldwide.

Consider, based on Exhibit 3.7, that the Logistical temperament is mainly concerned with getting existing organizations to run smoothly through bureaucratic processes like interlocking policies and procedures. Logicians are not interested, unlike Strategists, in faddish change, regardless of whether it appears innovative or not. Nor are Logicians, unlike Tacticians, the best at handling unplanned change intended to solve immediate and unexpected problems. Nor are Logicians, unlike Diplomats, particularly good at building trust-based informal

EXHIBIT 3.8 TEMPERAMENT BY NATIONAL CULTURE FOR THE TOP 20 TRADING NATIONS

Rank	National Culture	Tactical (SP)	Logistical (SJ)	Diplomatic (NF)	Strategic (NT)	No data
1.	US		Yes			
2.	China	Yes				
3.	Germany		Yes			
4.	Japan		Yes			
5.	France				Yes	
6.	United Kingdom (England)		Yes			
7.	Netherlands		Yes			
8.	South Korea		Yes			
9.	Italy			Yes		
10.	Canada (English, not French)		Yes			
11.	Russia			Yes		
12.	Singapore		Yes			
13.	India			Yes		
14.	Spain			Yes		
15.	Mexico	Yes				
16.	Belgium	Yes				
17.	Taiwan					No data
18.	Switzerland		Yes			
19.	Australia		Yes			
20.	Brazil			Yes		

Source: adapted from Massey, B. *Where in the World Do I Belong?* USA: Jetlag Press, 2006.

relations or democratically based organization cultures. Basically, Logicians tend to be traditional thinkers that support tried-and-true solutions known to have worked in the past.

The second largest group of national cultures is Diplomatic in orientation (Italy, Russia, India, Spain, and Brazil). Following Exhibit 3.7, we would assume that their approach to change would be building more effective people-oriented personal relationships, rather than the impersonal bureaucratic fixes favored by Logicians. Diplomats are very concerned with the comfort and development of personnel to solve change problems and could be expected to reject procedural solutions that treated personnel as objects rather than people. Diplomats would also find the Logistical approach to helping through criticism difficult to bear. It's not that Logicians do not mean to be helpful in offering criticism, but the Diplomatic temperament is well-known to be "thin-skinned" and to take criticism personally, even when it is not intended that way. It would be fair to conclude that Logicians (SJ) would experience these difficulties working in countries whose national character is predominantly Diplomatic (NF).

The third largest group of national cultures is Tactical in orientation (China, Mexico, and Belgium). We would expect that individuals representing these cultures would be very entrepreneurial in their orientation—very quick to identify and grasp opportunities in their external competitive environments without the need to create the bureaucracies favored by Logicians to support organizational reach, or the trust-based interpersonal relationships favored by Diplomats to persuade and motivate personnel to take an interest. Tacticians are also very capable of adjusting their positions and organizations to solve problems often before other temperaments notice. Tactician organizations may change faster, though in traditional directions, than Logicians can comfortably keep up.

Only France was characteristically Strategic in orientation. Strategists are very theoretical and innovative, and quickly lose interest if others do not share their enthusiasm. The Strategic temperament is not supportive of Logistical bureaucratic solutions if they are inefficient. Nor are they particularly good at building and maintaining cooperative informal relationships that Diplomats favor because they tend to regard less innovative people as less competent or less interesting, and say so. Nor do Strategists favor the traditionally proven enhancements favored by Tacticians. Therefore, Tacticians, Logicians, and Diplomats will all be challenged to success- fully engage Strategists, with the danger that Strategists tend to withdraw from high-conflict situations that demand too much of their time for too little positive benefit.

In an ideal world, however, the best learning in the face of change is a problem-solving team composed of all four temperaments. Strategists are the innovators who envision the strategic and organizational solutions most likely to achieve the best results for the lowest resource costs. Logicians are the best able to translate the Strategists' vision into a working formal organization that is effectively interdependent in its organization to produce products or services. Diplomats are best able to build human systems, personal relationships, and organization cultures that obtain the best results possible from all managers and employees. Tacticians are the best for identifying operational problems and fixing them before they become serious. If all four temperaments understand each other's strengths and weak- nesses, they will be better able to learn to work effectively together without allowing minor annoyances related to style to sabotage their willingness to cooperate.

CONCLUSIONS

Global leaders should not only be sources of innovation, but also be skilled in using change strategies and methods. Agents of change may apply their efforts to alter personal, organi- zational, and national cultural goals. Operating globally in diverse cultures and circum- stances necessitates appropriate adaptation of organizational objectives, management procedures, corporate processes, and technologies. Global leaders must learn to be as knowledgeable as possible wherever they are located, even if it means creative circumven- tion of local constraints. Innovators may respect the established system while working to bend or beat it to make it more responsive to satisfying human need.

In this chapter we have presented the idea that all global leaders must be, first and foremost, learners. The geocentric mindset is particularly open to learning from every direction and encourages others to have the same attitude. By contrast, the ethnocentric mindset is not open to learning, and the polycentric mindset does not assimilate, collate, and integrate learning to find additional uses for it. Learning is essential for companies to develop the confidence to employ the most potentially profitable WO strategies for operating in foreign markets. Greater openness to learning also increases the probability that MNEs will adapt to changing market conditions before their financial performance is negatively impacted.

At the same time, global leaders and their followers are predisposed by their national genetic heritages to greater (Tactical, Diplomatic, and Strategic) or lesser (Logistical) openness to required change, and have greater or lesser facility for learning specific content related to adapting to change. We do not see these habitual predilections as deterministic but as opportunities for training and development. If the main English-speaking trading nations are all predominantly logistical in orientation, and therefore more bureaucratic in orientation, and less open to change, then to be forewarned is to be forearmed. If you determine that you are a Logician, then you should presumably be more open to the views of Tacticians, Diplomats, and Strategists, and not at all dismissive. Each of the learning styles has a different view related to change, and offers different skills for dealing with it. Each is able to help the other so that all become more effective if they work together in cooperation.

MIND STRETCHING

1   Is the "Westernization of the World" happening as a function of globalization? Are different cultures "converging" in the sense of becoming more alike? Why or why not?

2   Have we lost our "curiosity" about other people and nations? Curiosity has been demonstrated to be an important trait of skillful global leaders.

3   If you could be a person from a culture other than your own, what culture would that be? Why?

4   If you were the manager responsible for a company entering into a new foreign market, what do you think you would need to know? How would you find out? How much risk would you be willing to take at the beginning of your career, depending on your success?

5   If you were working as an expatriate in another culture, do you think you would have an ethnocentric, polycentric, or geocentric mindset? Support your view with evidence from the way you behave in the present with people that you know.

6   Calculate your learning style (SP, SJ, NF, or NT).[68] Divide into homogeneous groups of Tacticians (SP), Logicians (SJ), Diplomats (NF), and Strategists (NT). Use Exhibit 3.6 to determine what percentage of the descriptors for your temperament are characteristic of all the people in your group. What percentage are characteristic of the majority of members in your group?[69] Or, form heterogeneous groups with two or more temperaments present. How do the different temperaments bother or annoy each other in relation to getting work done?

NOTES

1   Matsushita, K. *The Path: Find Fulfillment Through Prosperity from Japan's Father of Management*. New York: McGraw-Hill, 2010, pp. 21–22, 7. Matsushita was the founder of Panasonic.

2   Hoffman, B. G. *American Icon: Alan Mulally and the Fight to Save Ford Motor Company*. New York: Crown Business, 2012.

3   Salomon, G. *Distributed Cognitions: Psychological and Educational Considerations*. Cambridge: Cambridge University Press, 1993, p. xiii.

4   Courtney, H., Kirkland, J., and Viguerie, P. "Strategy Under Uncertainty," in H. Merchant (ed.), *Competing in Emerging Markets: Cases and Readings*. New York: Routledge, 2008, pp. 168–184.

5   This is the PEST model of uncertainty. See Crossan, M. M., Rouse, M. J., Rowe, W. G., and Maurer, C. C. *Strategic Analysis and Action*, 9th edn. Toronto, ON: Pearson, 2016, p. 63.

6   Perlmutter, H. V. "The Tortuous Evolution of Multinational Enterprises," *Columbia Journal of World Business*, Vol. 1, 1969, pp. 9–18.

7   Root, F. R. *Entry Strategies for International Markets*. San Francisco, CA: Jossey-Bass, 1998.

8   Crossan et al., *Strategic Analysis and Action*.

9   Hoffman, *American Icon*, p. xvi.

10 Weick, K. E. *Making Sense of the Organization, Volume 2: The Impermanent Organization*. Chichester: Wiley, 2012.

11 Ibid.

12 Prange, C. "Organizational Learning: Desperately Seeking Theory," in M. Easterby-Smith, L. Araujo, and J. Burgoyne (eds.), *Organizational Learning and the Learning Organization*. London: Sage, 1999.

13 Ibid., p. xvi.

14 Salomon, G. and Perkins, D. N. "Individual and Social Aspects of Learning," *Review of Research in Education*, Vol. 23, 1998, pp. 1–24.

15 Bridges, W. *The Character of Organizations: Using Jungian Type in Organizational Development*. Boston, MA: Nicholas Brealey Publishing, 2000.

16 Bayne, R. *Psychological Types at Work: An MBTI Perspective*. London: Thompson Learning, 2004.

17 Bridges, *The Character of Organizations*.

18 Keirsey, D. *Personology*. Del Mar, CA: Prometheus Nemesis Book Company, 2010.

19 Massey, B. *Where in the World Do I Belong?* USA: Jetlag Press, 2006.

20 Inkeles, A. *National Character: A Psycho-Social Perspective*. New Brunswick, NJ: Transaction Publishers, 2015.

21 Dixon, N. *The Organizational Learning Cycle: How We Can Learn Collectively*. London: McGraw-Hill, 1994.

22 Ibid., p. 5.

23 Ibid., p. 2.

24 Bartlett, C. A. and Ghoshal, S. *Managing Across Borders: The Transnational Solution*. Boston, MA: Harvard Business School, 1991.

25 Bartlett, C. A. "Philips versus Matsushita: Competing Strategic and Organizational Choices," in C. A. Bartlett and P. W. Beamish (eds.), *Transnational Management: Text, Cases, and Readings in Cross-Border Management*, 6th edn. New York: McGraw-Hill, 2011, pp. 331–347.

26 Perlmutter, "The Tortuous Evolution of Multinational Enterprises."

27 Bartlett and Ghoshal, *Managing Across Borders*.

28 Bartlett, C. A. and Beamish, P. W. (eds.). *Transnational Management: Text, Cases, and Readings in Cross-Border Management,* 6th edn. New York: McGraw-Hill, 2011.

29 Perlmutter, "The Tortuous Evolution of Multinational Enterprises."

30 Abramson, N. R. "Configuration, Coordination, Learning and Foreign Market Entry: A Study of Canadian Software Companies Entering the United States." London, ON: University of Western Ontario doctoral thesis, 1992.

31 See, for example, Panitch, L. *American Empire and the Political Economy of Global Finance*. Basingstoke: Palgrave Macmillan, 2009.

32 Perlmutter, "The Tortuous Evolution of Multinational Enterprises."

33 Ibid.

34 Buderi, R. and Huang, G. T. *Guanxi: Microsoft and Bill Gates' Plan to Win the Road Ahead*. London: Random House, 2007.

35 White, R. and Beamish, P.W. "Research in Motion: Managing Explosive Growth," in C. A. Bartlett and P. W. Beamish (eds.), *Transnational Management: Text, Cases, and Readings in Cross-Border Management*, 6th edn. New York: McGraw-Hill, 2011, pp. 68–82.

36 Abramson, N. R. and Ai, J. X. "Canadian Companies Doing Business in China: Key Success Factors," *Management International Review*, Vol. 39, No. 1, 1999, pp. 7–35.

37 Hornell, E. and Vahlne, J. E. *Multinationals: The Swedish Case*. London: Croom Helm, 1986.

38 Blomstermo, A. and Sharma, D. D. *Learning in the Internationalization Process of Firms*. Northampton, MA: Edward Elgar, 2003.

39 Root, *Entry Strategies for International Markets*.

40 Johanson, J. and Vahlne, J. E. "The Internationalization Process of the Firm: A Model of Knowledge Development and Increasing Foreign Market Commitments," *Journal of International Business Studies*, Vol. 8, 1977, pp. 23–33.

41 Galbraith, J. *Designing Complex Organizations*. Reading, MA: Addison-Wesley, 1973.

42 Erramilli, M. K. and Rao, C. P. "Choice of Foreign Market Entry Modes by Service Firms: Role of Market Knowledge," *Management International Review*, Vol. 30, 1990, pp. 135–150.

43 Mascarenhas, B. "The Coordination of Manufacturing Interdependence in Multinational Companies," *Journal of International Business Studies*, Vol. 16, 1984, pp. 91–106.

44 Buderi and Huang, *Guanxi*.

45 O'Leary, K. *Cold Hard Truth: On Business, Money & Life*. Toronto, ON: Doubleday Canada, 2011.

46 Root, *Entry Strategies for International Markets*.

47 Ramaswamy, K. and Sankhe, R. "Hero Honda Motors (India) Ltd.: Is It Honda that Made It a Hero?" in H. Merchant (ed.), *Competing in Emerging Markets: Cases and Readings*. New York: Routledge, 2008, pp. 72–92.

48 Choi, C. B. and Beamish, P. W. "Split Management Control and International Joint Venture Performance," *Journal of International Business Studies*, Vol. 35, 2004, pp. 201–215.

49 Root, *Entry Strategies for International Markets*.

50 Ibid.

51 Nelson, R. "Dell's Dilemma in Brazil: Negotiating at the State Level," in H. Merchant (ed.), *Competing in Emerging Markets: Cases and Readings*. New York: Routledge, 2008, pp. 1–17.

52 Root, *Entry Strategies for International Markets*.

53 Smick, D. *The World Is Curved: Hidden Dangers to the Global Economy*. New York: Portfolio, 2009.

54 Crossan et al., *Strategic Analysis and Action*.

55 Hoffman, *American Icon*.

56 Abramson, N. R. "Building Effective Business Relationships in China: The Case of Richmond Engineering," in A. E. Safarian and P. W. Beamish (eds.), *North American Firms in East Asia*. Toronto, ON: University of Toronto Press, 1999, pp. 119–145. The name of the company is disguised at the request of the company.

57 Moran, R. T. and Riesenberger, J. R. *The Global Challenge: Building New Worldwide Enterprises*. London: McGraw-Hill, 1994; cited in Harris, P. R. *Managing the Knowledge Culture*. Amherst, MA: HRD Press, 2005.

58 Harris, P. R. *The Work Culture Handbook*. Mumbai: Jaico Publishing, 2003.

59 Jung, C. G. *Psychological Types*. Princeton, NJ: Princeton University Press, 1976.

60 Keirsey, *Personology*. See also Keirsey, D. *Please Understand Me II: Temperament, Character, Intelligence*. Del Mar, CA: Prometheus Nemesis Book Company, 1998.

61 Keirsey, *Personology*, p. 10.
62 The Keirsey Temperament Sorter (KTS-II) is available for free on the internet at www.Keirsey.com (retrieved September 16, 2016). I ask my students to Google "personality test" and take the Free Personality Test at www.16personalities.com (retrieved September 16, 2016) as a basis for in-class discussion.
63 Ayoko, O. B. "Communication Openess, Conflict Events, and Reactions to Conflict in Culturally Diverse Workgroups," *Cross-Cultural Management*, Vol. 14, No. 2, 2007, pp. 105–124.
64 Ibid.
65 Massey, *Where in the World Do I Belong?*
66 Abramson, N. R. "A Longitudinal Study of Psychological Temperament in American and Canadian Business Students: Implications for Managers' Emergent Consensus Strategies," unpublished.
67 Abramson, N. R. and Keating, R. J. "Knowledge Management Through the Lens of the Cognitive Theory of Strategy: American, Chinese and Thai Decision-Making Capabilities," *Journal of Global Business*, Vol. 17, No. 34, 2006, pp. 27–42.
68 See Note 61.
69 We find in our classes that between 35 and 100 percent are characteristic of all or most members of a temperament group.

4 NEGOTIATING LONG TERM FOR MUTUAL BENEFIT

In game theory or economic theory, a zero-sum negotiation occurs when one participant's benefit (gain) or loss is balanced by the losses or benefits (gains) of the other participant. The result is zero. One gains 100, and the other loses 100, or vice-versa.

A non-zero-sum negotiation occurs when the gains or losses of the participants in a negotiation are either less than or more than zero.

Skillful negotiators build trust and negotiate for mutual long-term benefit of all.[1]

Negotiating is not a theoretical activity. It is a face-to-face activity, kind of like a dance in which partners influence each other. Behaving as an effective negotiator involves great skill. A good example of a skillful negotiator is Abraham Lincoln,[2] the 16th president of the United States. The skills he demonstrated in discussions leading to the Emancipation Declaration demonstrate the importance of the skills of "resilience, forbearance, emotional intelligence, thoughtful listening, and the consideration of all sides of an argument," as well as "staying true to a larger mission."

Another author[3] writes: "Classically trained negotiators take a win-at-all-costs approach based on concealment, camouflage, and deception." This appears to be the negotiating perspective of Donald Trump, the US Republican presidential candidate in 2016. He presented himself to the American public as one who "would make a deal," including making Mexico pay for a wall along the border with Mexico and the US.

After reading and studying concepts/examples and illustrations in Chapter 4, the reader should:

1   Understand the importance of approaching international negotiating relation-ships with the perspective of building a future together as partners.
2   Be convinced that learning as much as possible about your negotiating partners is a benefit for all.
3   Be able to use the framework for international business negotiations for mutual benefit.
4   Become a more skillful negotiator.

LEARNING OBJECTIVES

Selected aspects of the following appeared in a book entitled *Getting Your Yen's Worth* by Robert Moran.[4] It was updated and modified in 2017, given the many changes in Japanese society and business culture. However, deeper aspects of all cultural change enter slowly, and Japan is no exception.

We recommend that all individuals negotiating with potential partners for any reason have a thorough understanding of their negotiating counterparts. The example is Japan, but our advice applies in all global negotiating experiences. Please read the following.

JAPANESE PATTERNS OF BEHAVIOR

In order to successfully build business partnerships with Japanese businessmen, or now increasingly Japanese businesswomen, it is important to understand, recognize, and respond appropriately to Japanese patterns of behavior. The following are several key aspects.

1   An important feature of Japanese behavior is the way in which emotions are handled. Howard Van Zandt,[5] in his article "How to Negotiate in Japan," gives this example of the different role of emotions in a business relationship:

> Recently, a friend came to my office bringing a small potted Chinese bamboo. He explained that in his garden was a large bamboo which had had a baby. He carefully nourished the little one until it was big enough to put in a pot and bring to me. He advised me on its care.

2   Japanese negotiators are also quite skillful in concealing negative emotions. Professor Chie Nakane of Tokyo University, after studying behavior patterns of Europeans, Indians, and Americans, notes that the emotional expression of Japanese is comparable

to that of Italians. One difference, she remarks, is that while the Italian's display of emotions may have nothing whatever to do with anyone in particular, the Japanese expression of emotion is decidedly directed toward or against a specific cause or individual. Negative feelings of Japanese are often difficult for non-Japanese to detect.

3   Japanese negotiators also dislike power displays. In negotiations, the Japanese are very capable of, and prefer, conciliation, as opposed to alienation. Differences are settled in a manner so that no one "loses face."

4   Japanese also prefer to work in groups rather than alone, and are likely to attribute negotiation success to working together. An outsider may say "*I* did it," whereas a Japanese would say "*We* did it."

5   The system of decision-making in Japan is one based on consensus. A formalized proposal is passed both upward and horizontally in the hierarchy. The success of this system, however, is that as authority is distributed among the lower tiers of the hierarchy, everyone contributes to the decisions.

6   The trait of not directly saying "no" is one that confuses most Westerners. According to Professor Nakane:[6]

> Expression of "no" is virtually never used outside of completely reciprocal relationships, and from superior to inferior. You rarely receive a "no" from a Japanese.

Learning verbal cues for "no" in the Japanese language takes outsiders a long time. When a Japanese is feeling pressured to give an answer, he may draw breath through his teeth and say "sah" (no meaning), or a slightly less ambiguous response: "It is very difficult." In both cases, the negotiator probably means "no."

7   Negative questions also cause misunderstandings for negotiators. For example:

> Foreigner: "Do you want to play golf this weekend?"
> Japanese: "Yes, I want to play golf this weekend."
> Japanese: "Yes, I don't want to play golf this weekend."

For a Japanese, "yes" does not always mean "yes," and "no" does not always mean "no." "Yes" may simply mean "I understand the question."

8   Close friends are very important in order for Japanese to feel secure. There are, however, varying degrees of friendship. Professor Nakane states:

> The relative strength of the human bond tends to increase in proportion to the length and intensity of actual contact. The reason the newcomer in any Japanese group is placed at the very bottom of the hierarchy is that he has the shortest period of contact. This is a primary condition of the seniority system, which dominates Japan. Therefore, the placement of an individual in a social group is governed by the length of the individual's contact with the group. In other words, the actual contact itself becomes the individual's private social capital.

A day in the life of a Japanese negotiator[7]

The ability to walk in the shoes of another is called empathy. Before reading about the education, training, and negotiating strategies used by Japanese negotiators, read the following passages from the diary of a Japanese to give you a "feel" for your negotiating counterparts.

MARCH

My alarm clock rang at seven as usual. I am sleepy. Every night, I come home too late, especially last night at two in the morning. I drank a lot with my customer. Although drinking with the customer is a part of my job, I have to be on time for work the next morning.

It is Friday today. Nothing special for the Japanese businessman. My company has a five-day-week program, but last year I only took six days of Saturdays for my holidays.

I did not have enough time to eat breakfast this morning. I stayed in bed too long. More and more businessmen eat breakfast at a station-stall rather than at home. We just eat one bean-jam bun and drink a bottle of milk. In winter, we can see a long line in front of the soba-ya at the station.

APRIL

Sunday is my day for rest. I used to be in bed until 11 or noon. Japanese breakfast style has been changing. TV commercials say "Put tomato juice on the breakfast table" and "Before breakfast, let's drink vegetable juice."

After napping, I took a walk. On the way, I stopped by Pachinko Parlor. One time I played for eight hours, and during this period, I did not eat anything. We businessmen concentrate on shooting the balls in order to forget our anxieties at work.

After talking a walk, I went to a golf driving range, but I had to wait for two hours. So I gave up practicing today. We need reservations a week in advance to secure a place on the driving range.

MAY

This afternoon, I made a business call to the president of a major client with my two bosses. At that time, I remembered the business etiquette that I learned in the training period.

When we are served tea, the order of drinking is the president first, the director, bucho, kacho, and then myself. When we leave the room, we have to put the lid on the teacup.

Around ten o'clock in the evening, I was at Narita International Airport. The president's daughter was going abroad. I was standing at the customs entrance with a flower basket because my client's favorite subject of conversation is his daughter's achievements.

In my business diary, the birthdays of my clients, their wives, and even their children are listed.

JUNE

I am very surprised to see many older employees who are working, but are losing their positions. They are *madogiwa-zoku* (meaning "people sitting next to the window"). These people are assigned to very boring and unconstructive jobs and forced to work all day facing the window without any hope of promotion.

JULY

This morning, the personnel changes in our company were announced. We are often moved around not only all over Japan but abroad. My manager was promoted to our Sapporo office. Although he has to move alone because of his children's education and other problems such as housing and taking care of parents, he cannot refuse this assignment. If he refuses it, his life with the company will not be happy.

AUGUST

I plan to take a summer vacation. Last summer, I took four days. Nearly 80 percent of *kacho* said they cannot forget work during vacation, and they become worried about work if their vacation exceeds three days.

SEPTEMBER

Today, I went to play golf with my customers at Utsuno-miya Country Club. I had to get up at 3:30 a.m., although last night I went to bed at 1:00 a.m. First of all, I picked my boss up, then went to my client's house. On the way to the golf course, we are talking about many things, even business matters.

We bet chocolates on the game. One chocolate is worth ¥500. I would not be allowed to win the game, or play it stupidly, because they are clients. Sometimes, we play 19 holes. If I won the golf game, I would be expected to lose the mahjongg. If I lost the golf game, I should lose the mahjongg, too.

OCTOBER

I had to install our products for a customer who owns fashion boutiques in Tokyo. This owner is a so-called career woman.

NOVEMBER

It was fun to drink with my colleagues in the small shops. Our topics when drinking are always about our bosses. Last night, we were talking about just one of our bosses.

My friend: "That manager makes me mad."
Me: "He is not good at his job, he is always kissing his boss' ass."
My friend: "He likes to chase skirts, too. He has no business holding that job."
Me: "I cannot stand to work for someone like that."
My friend: "That's right, that's right, let's get drunk."

Suddenly, our boss appeared.

Boss: "Good evening. May I join you?"
My friend: "Oh, Kacho-san, what a pleasure to see you, please join us, we are just saying how happy we are to have you as our boss."
Me: "You are always so good to us."
Boss: "Do you think so? As a matter of fact, the present director is incompetent; all he is good for is bullshitting."
My friend: "That's right, he is impotent and bold."

The Japanese education system

An objective of Japanese education is to prepare students to become exemplary citizens and model workers in any company. This education begins in the home, where the child learns the essence of Japanese culture. At an early age, he learns the importance of courtesy, consideration, and self-discipline. These attributes carry over into all aspects of life, from family life to school to the working world.

The top companies in Japan select their employees from the best universities, and competition for admittance to these schools is fierce. Students are admitted on the basis of their scores on an entrance examination. Much of the educational system at the primary, middle, and high school levels is geared to preparing students for college entrance examinations.

Preparation for the exams begins with enrolling the child in the best possible elementary school. Students attend supplementary schools (on Saturdays or after school) while they are in elementary or secondary school to better prepare themselves for the entrance examinations to the best and most prestigious high schools. Due to its educational system, Japan has a competent and well-educated workforce.

Japanese company selection process

Most large companies in Japan offer lifetime employment to many of their employees. Barring serious long-term economic depression, these employees expect never to be laid off. If a company dissolves or merges with another company, the employees expect that new jobs will be offered.

Japanese management emphasizes the long-term results of its policies. By keeping employees for life and involving them in the plans and decisions of the company, management feels employees will develop a sense of loyalty for the company and take pride in their work.

Japanese companies also provide a sense of belonging to their employees. Life revolves around the company. Company gymnasiums, swimming pools, and sports facilities are provided by many companies for use during the exercise period or after-work hours, and the immediate effect of exercising is that the employee has energy and stamina to work productively.

Promotion

Promotion and salary increases are mainly determined by the number of years in the company. However, education, productiveness, and cooperation are also considered. Top management positions are awarded to those with the greatest ability, the broadest experience, and the longest years of service. Older workers typically hold top management positions.

During the training period, the company becomes the worker's life. Often, new employees live in company dormitories. Japanese workers internalize the company ideology—the company is their home away from home, so they accept the present psychic investment in anticipation of future capital appreciation. From the Japanese point of view, there are two reasons for the strong loyal-worker attitude of the Japanese worker: (1) to show appreciation for this lifetime employment status; and (2) they want to move up in the company. Japanese are trained to work in a group or as a team. As a result, the Japanese are dedicated and loyal to other members of a Japanese team, no matter what happens. This loyalty provides the foundation for future relationships. Japanese employees are trained to depend on each other, and especially upon their seniors, since they can act as mentors.

Group effort takes on great importance. In Japan, one rarely accomplishes anything by oneself. It may be that one person initiates the action or does the majority of the work, but it is necessary to involve others so that the overall feeling of group effort and achievement is shared.

Decision-making

Ringi seido or consensus in decision-making is the style in Japan, and is used by many of the large firms, as well as many small- and medium-sized firms.

All decisions are thoroughly reviewed and discussed by each relevant department that might be affected. A form, called the *ringi-sho*, is circulated for the appropriate seal of approval. Reluctant persons will be allowed to question the initiator, which takes time and patience, as explanations and agreements may have to be repeated for each new group. The Japanese refer to this system as "bottom-up" planning. While the review process may take a lot of time from a Western perspective, once consensus is reached the implementation stage is rapid and efficient.

Understanding the *ringi* is crucial to successful negotiations in Japan because it is the "filter" through which a Japanese negotiator's ideas must pass. The negotiator may not have the authority to make decisions beyond those granted by the group.

While the use of the *ringi-sho* is widespread, it is not used for every transaction. A company will usually set a financial limit above which a *ringi-sho* is required but below which approvals for business decisions can be made by various individuals within the organization.

To understand the importance of "culture" when negotiating with individuals in today's global world, dealing with conflicts, having a high degree of emotional intelligence, and being able to "profile" accurately one's negotiating counterparts are significant ingredients in negotiating success. It is also important for negotiators to develop a "partnership mindset" as each approaches a negotiation to achieve long-term mutual benefits.

This chapter is intended to be conceptual and immediately useful, whether negotiating at home or abroad, and to persuade readers that skillful global negotiating is a necessary learned skill in today's business world.

There is a significant increase in business travel to and from the US, China, India, Russia, Brazil, and many other countries. Globalization has resulted in increased business travel to many countries in order to buy, sell, form mergers or acquisitions, build relationships, and for many other activities. Most of these business relationships will involve some form of negotiation.

Today's leaders seek business ventures in the global arena, crisscrossing the world to negotiate and bargain. Many claim the success rate of mergers and acquisitions to be less than 50 percent for successful integration, although little hard data are available, but state that these mergers typically fail to achieve the targeted results.

Appreciating the complexities of labor negotiations in one's home country or negotiating a contract in a foreign country has made leaders understand the competency and skill needed to effectively work out these partnerships to mutual benefit.

In the twenty-first century, global leaders increasingly do their negotiating *electronically*, by telephone, fax, email, and video conferencing. One of the most powerful communication tools for this purpose is the internet. It offers quick and easy negotiation opportunities with manufacturers, suppliers, customers, and even government regulators. But it also requires more openness, transparency, and trust.

LEARNING OBJECTIVES

THREE EXAMPLES OF "CULTURAL BAGGAGE"

A US example

Graham and Herberger[8] describe a combination of characteristics typical of American negotiators. They are part of the cultural baggage such nationals bring to the negotiating table and, according to Graham and Herberger, typify the American "John Wayne" style of negotiating.

"I can go it alone."	Many US executives seem to believe they can handle any negotiating situation by themselves, and they are outnumbered in most negotiating situations.
"Just call me John."	Americans value informality and equality in human relations. They try to make people feel comfortable by playing down status distinctions.
"Pardon my French."	Americans aren't very talented at speaking foreign languages.
"Check with the home office."	American negotiators get upset when, halfway through a negotiation, the other side says "I'll have to check with the home office." The implication is that the decision-makers are not present.
"Get to the point."	American negotiators prefer to come directly to the point, getting to the heart of the matter quickly.
"Lay your cards on the table."	Americans expect honest information at the bargaining table.
"Don't just sit there, speak up."	Americans don't deal well with silence during negotiations.
"Don't take no for an answer."	Persistence is highly valued by Americans, and is part of the deeply ingrained competitive spirit that manifests itself in every aspect of American life.
"One thing at a time."	Americans usually attack a complex negotiation task sequentially; that is, they separate the issues and settle them one at a time.
"A deal is a deal."	When Americans make an agreement and give their word, they expect to honor the agreement no matter the circumstances.
"I am what I am."	Few Americans take pride in changing their minds, even in difficult circumstances.

These comments on American negotiators may appear to be harsh. They are not intended to isolate Americans as lacking in global negotiating skills. In today's marketplace, other nationalities can learn, as well as Americans, how to negotiate more effectively and skillfully.

A European example

A German-Swiss buyer of goods is visiting a Chinese entrepreneur, trying to close a contract. The Chinese sits inscrutably while the Swiss expounds his detailed proposal. The

Swiss finishes his speech, a bit nervous at receiving so little feedback. Finally, the Chinese speaks: "This is not good for us." And then: "Let me take you for dinner."[9]

According to the German-Swiss, the relationship may be in trouble, but the Chinese, in fact, may be keenly interested and wants to strengthen the relationship with a social event.

In Exhibit 4.1, Acuff[10] is not complimentary in his report card on American negotiators' skills.

We hope, as our horizons are widened by the global experience, that we are getting better at understanding the national character of our negotiating counterparts, confronting cultural stereotypes, and putting the negotiating process into a cultural context.

An example from any country: a case of failure[11]

This person is a successful businessperson who is much admired by colleagues for the ability to negotiate difficult deals. Frank, open, and uncompromising manner has earned this person a great deal of respect at the bargaining table. Last year, this person was sent by his corporation to Japan to negotiate an important contract. This person was confident of success, as both sides had already agreed on many important points.

The contract did not get signed, and this person believed that Japanese business culture is the most frustrating one ever encountered.

EXHIBIT 4.1 THE US NEGOTIATOR'S GLOBAL REPORT CARD

Competency	Grade
Preparation	B–
Synergistic approach (win–win)	D
Cultural IQ	D
Adapting the negotiating process to the host country environment	D
Patience	D
Listening	D
Linguistic abilities	F
Using language that is simple and accessible	C
High aspirations	B+
Personal integrity	A–
Building solid relationships	D

Source: Adapted from Acuff, F. L. *How to Negotiate with Anyone Anywhere around the World.* New York: Amacom, 1993, Exhibit 8.1, p. 192.

EXHIBIT 4.1

NEGOTIATING ACROSS CULTURES

Negotiation is a process in which two or more entities come together to discuss common and conflicting interests in order to reach an agreement of mutual benefit. In international business negotiations, the negotiation process differs from culture to culture in language, cultural conditioning, negotiating styles, approaches to problem-solving, and building trust, among many other factors.

National character

Studies of national character call attention to both the patterns of personality that negotiators tend to exhibit and the collective concerns that give a nation a distinctive outlook in international relationships. Foreign negotiators concerned with international image may be preoccupied with discussions of their national heritage, identity, and language. Cultural attitudes, such as ethnocentrism or xenophobia, may influence the tone of the argument.

Foreign negotiators often display many different styles of logic and reasoning. They frequently find that discussions are impeded because the two sides seem to be pursuing different paths of logic. Negotiation breakdown may result from the way issues are conceptualized, the way evidence and new information are used, or the way one point seems to lead to the next.

During the discussions, the foreign counterpart may pay more attention to some arguments than to others. Greater weight may be given to legal precedence, expert opinion, technical data, amity, or reciprocal advantage. A good international negotiator will discover what is persuasive to the foreign counterpart and use that method of persuasion.

Negotiators may place different values on agreements and hold different assumptions about the way contracts should be honored. The negotiator must find out what steps the counterpart intends to take in implementing the agreement. A signature on a piece of paper or a handshake may signify friendship rather than the closing of a contract.

Cross-cultural noise

Noise consists of background distractions that have nothing to do with the substance of the foreign negotiator's message. Factors such as gestures, personal proximity, and office surroundings may unintentionally interfere with communication. The danger of misinterpretation of messages necessitates analysis of various contextual factors.

Interpreters and translators

There are limitations in translating certain ideas, concepts, meanings, and nuances. Subjective meaning may not come across through words alone. Gestures, tone of voice, cadence, and double entendres are all meant to transmit a message. Yet these are not included in a translation.

Sometimes a negotiator will try to communicate a concept or idea that does not exist in the counterpart's culture. For example, the American and English concept of "fair play" seems to have no exact equivalent in any other language. How, then, can an English national expect "fair play" from a foreign counterpart?

Interpreters and translators may have difficulty transmitting the logic of key arguments. This is especially true in discussions of abstract concepts such as planning and international strategy. The parties may think they have come to an agreement when, in fact, they have entirely different intentions and understandings.

Fisher's five-part framework provides scholars and consultants with a launching pad for both theory building and practical applications. Two working papers, "Assess, Don't Assume, Part 1: Etiquette and Material Culture in Negotiation" and "Assess, Part II: Cross-Border Differences in Decision-making, Governance, and Political Economy," are also excellent in identifying the cultural variables in global negotiations.[12]

In Chapter 2 we covered some of the complexities in communicating effectively across geographical and cultural boundaries. Consider, however, the following Anglo−EU translation guide of phrases that are routinely used in face-to-face negotiations and could easily lead to misunderstandings.

ANGLO−EU TRANSLATION GUIDE

What the British say	What the British might mean	What others might understand
I hear what you say	I disagree and do not want to discuss it further	He accepts my point of view
With the greatest respect...	I think you are an idiot	He is listening to me
That's not bad	That's good	That's poor
That is a very brave proposal	You are insane	He thinks I have courage
Quite good	A bit disappointing	Quite good
I would suggest...	Do it or be prepared to justify yourself	Think about the idea, but do what you like
Oh, incidentally/by the way	The primary purpose of our discussion is...	That is not very important
I was a bit disappointed that	I am annoyed that	It doesn't really matter
Very interesting	That is clearly nonsense	They are impressed
I'll bear it in mind	I've forgotten it already	They will probably do it

I'm sure it's my fault	It's your fault	Why do they think it was their fault?
You must come for dinner	It's not an invitation, I'm just being polite	I will get an invitation soon
I almost agree	I don't agree at all	He's not far from agreement
I only have a few minor comments	Please rewrite completely	He has found a few typos
Could we consider some other options?	I don't like your idea	They have not yet decided

Source: www.scribd.com/doc/55551980/Anglo-EU-Translation-Guide.

ASSUMPTIONS AND NEGOTIATING

When people communicate, they make certain assumptions about the other's process of perceiving, judging, thinking, and reasoning patterns. These assumptions are made without realization. Correct assumptions facilitate communication, but incorrect assumptions lead to misunderstandings, and miscommunication often results.

The most common assumption is projective cognitive similarity; that is, one assumes that the other perceives, judges, thinks, and reasons the same way he or she does. Persons from the same culture, but with a different education, age, background, and experience, often have difficulty communicating. American managers experience greater difficulties communicating with managers from other cultures than with managers from their own culture. However, in some contexts, American managers share more interests with other members of the world managerial subculture than with their own workers or union leaders. The effects of our cultural conditioning are so pervasive that people whose experience has been limited to the rules of one culture can have difficulty understanding communication based on another set of rules.

To create cultural synergistic solutions to management problems and international negotiating, US managers must identify and understand what is American about America, what common cultural traits are shared by Americans, and what values and assumptions form their foundation.

Awareness of cultural influences is essential for transferring concepts, technology, or ideas. Depending on the cultures, there may be an overlap of values in a specific area and, therefore, the problems related to transferring ideas will be minimal. However, in some instances, the gap will be significant and cause serious problems. According to Graham,[13] there are four problems in international business negotiations: (1) language, (2) nonverbal behavior, (3) values, and (4) thinking and decision-making.

The problems increase in importance and complexity because of their subtle nature. For instance, it is easy to ascertain the language differences between the French and Brazilians.

The solution is either state-of-the-art translating headsets or interpreting/translating teams to accommodate each side. The problem is obvious and relatively easy to address.

Cultural differences concerning nonverbal behavior are often not so obvious; we are not as aware of these behaviors. In face-to-face negotiations, we give and receive nonverbal behavioral cues. Some argue that these cues are the critical messages of a negotiation. The nonverbal signals from our counterparts can be so subtle that we may feel a sense of discomfort but may not know exactly why. For example, when a Japanese negotiator fails to make eye contact, it may produce a sense of unease in the foreigner, but it may simply be shyness on the part of the Japanese. Often, nonverbal intercultural friction affects business negotiations, but goes undefined and more often uncorrected.

Laver and Trudgill, in Scheu-Lottgen and Hernandez-Campoy, also point out that, during conversations, one must act almost as a detective, not only considering the words and speech but also attempting to establish, from an array of clues, the state of mind and the profile and perspective of the other's identity.[14]

The difference in values is even more obscure and harder to understand. For example, Americans value objectivity, competitiveness, equity, and punctuality, and often presume that other cultures hold the same values in high esteem. Regarding punctuality, Graham states, "Everyone else in the world knows no negotiation tactic is more useful with Americans. Nobody places more value on time. Nobody has less patience when things slow down."[15]

Generally, during a complex negotiation, Westerners divide the large tasks up into smaller ones. One can move through the smaller tasks, finishing one and moving on to the next, sensing accomplishment along the way. Issues are resolved at each step in the process, and the final agreement is the sum of the sequence. However, in Eastern thinking all issues are discussed, often with no apparent order, and concessions, when made, occur at the conclusion of negotiations. The Western approach is sequential and the Eastern is holistic—the two are worlds apart. Therefore, American negotiators have difficulty measuring progress during negotiations with the Japanese, and the differences in the thinking and decision-making processes can result in blunders. For the Japanese, the long-term goal is a mutually beneficial ongoing business relationship.

FRAMEWORK FOR INTERNATIONAL BUSINESS NEGOTIATIONS

A successful negotiation is a "win–win situation" in which both parties gain. Many factors affect a negotiation's outcome.

There are varied negotiation postures, bases from which to negotiate. One framework by Weiss and Stripp[16] maintains that there are 12 variables in every international negotiation that impact the negotiation, and can therefore significantly influence the outcome, either positively or negatively.

■ *Basic conception of negotiation process.* There are two opposing approaches to the concept of negotiation: strategic and synergistic. In the strategic model, resources are perceived as limited. The sides are competitive and, as a result of bargaining, one side is perceived as getting a larger portion of the pie. In the synergistic model, resources are unlimited. Each party wants to cooperate so that all can have what they want. Counterparts look for alternative ways to obtain the desired results.

■ *Negotiator selection criteria.* These criteria include negotiating experience, seniority, political affiliation, gender, ethnic ties, kinship, technical knowledge, and personal attributes (e.g., affability, loyalty, and trustworthiness). Each culture has preferences and biases regarding selection.

■ *Significance of type of issue.* Defining the issues in negotiation is critical. Generally, substantive issues focus on control and use of resources (space, power, property). Relationship-based issues center on the ongoing nature of mutual or reciprocal interests. The negotiation should not hinder relationships and future negotiations.

■ *Concern with protocol.* Protocol is the accepted practices of social behavior and interaction. Rules of protocol can be formal or informal. Americans are generally less formal than Germans, for example.

■ *Complexity of language.* Complexity refers to the degree of reliance on nonverbal cues to convey and interpret intentions and information in dialogue. These cues include distance (space), eye contact, gestures, and silence. There are high- and low-context communications. Cultures that are high context in communication (China) are fast and efficient communicators, and information is in the physical context or preprogrammed in the person. Low-context communication, in contrast, is information conveyed by the words, without shared meaning implied. The US has a low-context culture.

■ *Nature of persuasive arguments.* One way or another, negotiation involves attempts to influence the other party. Counterparts can use an emotional or logical approach.

■ *Role of individuals' aspirations.* The emphasis negotiators place on their individual goals and need for recognition may also vary. In some cases, the position of a negotiator may reflect personal goals to a greater extent than corporate goals. In contrast, a negotiator may want to prove he or she is a hard bargainer and compromise the goals of the corporation.

■ *Bases of trust.* Every negotiator, at some point, must face the critical issue of trust. One must eventually trust one's counterparts; otherwise, resolution would be impossible. Trust can be based on the written laws of a particular country, or it can be based on friendship and mutual respect and esteem.

■ *Risk-taking propensity.* Negotiators can be perceived as either "cautious" (low risk-takers), or "adventurous" (high risk-takers). If a negotiator selects a solution that has lower rewards but higher probability of success, he or she is not a risk-taker. If the negotiator chooses higher rewards but a lower probability of success, then he or she is "adventurous" and a risk-taker.

■   *Value of time.* Each culture has a different way of perceiving and acting on time. Monochronic cultures emphasize making agendas and being on time for appointments, generally seeing time as a quantity to be scheduled. Polychronic cultures stress the involvement of people rather than preset schedules. The future cannot be firm, so planning takes on little consequence.

■   *Decision-making system.* Broadly understood, decision-making systems can be "authoritative" or "consensual." In authoritative decision-making, an individual makes the decision without consulting with his or her superiors. However, senior executives may overturn the decision. In consensual decision-making, negotiators do not have the authority to make decisions unless they consult their superiors.

■   *Form of satisfactory agreement.* Generally, there are two broad forms of agreement. One is the written contract that covers possible contingencies. The other is the broad oral agreement that binds the negotiating parties through the quality of their relationship.

Negotiation insights for India, China, Brazil, South Korea, Germany, and Russia[17]

Can statements that are mostly accurate be made about a group of people or a "culture"? Is there a "national character" of a people, that is, a system of beliefs, attitudes, and values that are dominant in a country or nation as a result of common experiences?

In the definition of national character, there are three assumptions: (1) all people belonging to a certain culture are alike in some respects; (2) they are somewhat different from other cultures in the same respects; and (3) the characteristics ascribed to them are in some way related to the fact that they are citizens of a given country.

During negotiations, however, all anyone can observe is human behavior. We see what people do. What are the determinants of human behavior? We believe one has to consider three factors: culture (a national character); personality (no two people from the same culture are exactly alike); and context (where does the behavior take place—in New York? São Paulo? Tokyo? Jeddah?).

What follows is a summary of aspects of Chinese, Brazilian, German, and Russian "national character." Remember that "personality" and "context" are also determinants of behavior.

Framework applied to Chinese negotiators

1   Basic concept of the negotiation process
   ■   Intelligence gathering
   ■   Statements emphasizing "friendship"
   ■   Hard bargaining

2 Negotiator selection criteria
   - ■ Technical expertise
   - ■ In times of turbulence/change political reliability
3 Significance of type of issue
   - ■ Relationship-based issues receive attention
   - ■ Connections (*guanxi*) important
4 Concern with protocol
   - ■ High concern with proper etiquette
   - ■ Use "home court" as advantage
5 Complexity of language
   - ■ Very high-context with implicit and unstated desires and approaches
6 Nature of persuasive arguments
   - ■ "No compromising" to establish economic value
7 Role of individuals' aspirations
   - ■ Individual aspirations are resurfacing but "standing out" is unusual
8 Bases of trust
   - ■ Past record is important
9 Risk-taking propensity
   - ■ High avoidance of risk-taking resulting in meticulous and tough negotiating tactics and strategy
10 Value of time
   - ■ Long view of time, and masters at the art of stalling
11 Decision-making system
   - ■ Appearance of participative decision-making, but in reality is an authoritative system with higher levels always controlling
12 Form of satisfactory agreement
   - ■ Carefully worded contracts, but legal infrastructure lacking

Framework applied to Brazilian negotiators

1 Basic concept of the negotiation process
   - ■ Verbal facility, harmony, and eloquence are valued
   - ■ Negotiating is often a long process
   - ■ Establishing trust is critical to success
2 Negotiator selection criteria
   - ■ Seniority is important
   - ■ Oratory skills, social and political connections, and academic training are significant
3 Significance of type of issue
   - ■ Early in the discussion, building relationships is important

4 Concern with protocol
- Formal in social hierarchy and ceremony
- Dress is important

5 Complexity of language
- Less direct and high-context

6 Nature of persuasive arguments
- Inference, indirection, but with common sense

7 Role of individuals' aspirations
- Brazilians are individualistic, and outshining one's colleagues is acceptable

8 Bases of trust
- Trust is built slowly

9 Risk-taking propensity
- Basically low on risk-taking

10 Value of time
- Not hurried . . . a more polychronic approach to schedules

11 Decision-making system
- Bureaucratic and hierarchical

12 Form of satisfactory agreement
- A handshake and words of honor are followed by details that are formalized by lawyers

Framework applied to German negotiators

1 Basic concept of the negotiation process
- Direct, explicit, analytical, and logical

2 Negotiator selection criteria
- Excellent technical knowledge and strong educational background

3 Significance of type of issue
- Get right down to business
- Honest and straightforward

4 Concern with protocol
- Serious, controlled, and disciplined

5 Complexity of language
- Low-context—frank and realistic

6 Nature of persuasive arguments
- Careful research, orderly and persuasive presentation

7 Role of individual aspirations
- Strong sense of duty and company loyalty

8 Bases of trust
- Convince with competence and performance, facts, and actions

9 Risk-taking propensity
- ■ Avoid risk by sticking to what is known

10 Value of time
- ■ Being "on time" is always important

11 Decision-making system
- ■ Top down

12 Form of satisfactory agreement
- ■ Written and binding documents

Framework applied to Russian negotiators

1 Basic concept of the negotiation process
- ■ A competitive process where one side "wins"

2 Negotiator selection criteria
- ■ Professional negotiators are selected on the basis of specialization

3 Significance of type of issue
- ■ Hard bargaining, personal relationships play only a small role

4 Concern with protocol
- ■ Rules and protocol should be known and followed

5 Complexity of language
- ■ Low-context and direct

6 Nature of persuasive arguments
- ■ Delaying negotiations and wearing down their counterparts is often a style

7 Role of individual aspirations
- ■ Individualistic in contrast with the recent past

8 Bases of trust
- ■ "Caution" is important

9 Risk-taking propensity
- ■ High risk-takers
- ■ Corruption endemic

10 Value of time
- ■ Long and demanding

11 Decision-making system
- ■ Very hierarchical

12 Form of satisfactory agreement
- ■ Contracts are cleverly written, and details are often omitted

Having an awareness of the above will assist negotiators from any country when negotiating with Japanese in Japan or anywhere. But remember, in Chapter 1 we discussed the importance of considering culture, personality, and context in understanding the behavior of anyone.

Figure 4.1

Figure 4.2

Figure 4.3

Figure 4.4

Figure 4.5

Figure 4.6

Without this awareness, the previous cartoons might explain the reactions of some "gaijin" or foreigners about Japanese negotiating behavior.

CONFLICT RESOLUTION AND NEGOTIATIONS

By definition, all successful negotiations involve at least some resolution of conflicts. Unsuccessful negotiation involves at least one conflict, large or small, that has not been resolved.

Like leadership and power, conflict is a fascinating subject for research and discussion in organizations. Traditionally, the social scientists who have studied conflict have been keenly aware of its destructive element, which is observed in wars, strikes, family disruption, and disharmony. We will identify some themes reflecting the US viewpoint with regard to conflict, and suggest ways that other cultures resolve disputes. As Rensis Likert stated many years ago, "The strategies and principles used by a society and all its institutions for dealing with disagreements reflect the basic values and philosophy in that society."[18]

What is conflict? Like the word culture, there is no single agreed-upon definition. Thomas[19] states: "Conflict is the process that begins when one party perceives that the other has frustrated, or is about to frustrate, some concern of his." This frustration may result from actions that range from intellectual disagreement to physical violence. Another definition of "conflict" holds that it results when two or more persons or things attempt to occupy the same space at the same time. The management of conflict is a major issue at the personal and organizational levels, and all negotiations involve a resolution of conflicting interests and needs.

Most US negotiators view conflict as a healthy, natural, and inevitable part of relationships and negotiations. This constructive approach to conflict views the positive attributes in any conflict situation. The belief that conflict is constructive requires that problems be addressed directly, and that people can be motivated to search for solutions to these problems. Constructive disagreement may in fact be an integral part of American organizations. Stewart states:

> When faced with a problem, Americans like to get to its source. This means facing the facts, meeting the problem head on, putting the cards on the table, and getting information straight from the horse's mouth. It is also desirable to face people directly, to confront them intentionally.[20]

However, conflict in organizations is perceived to have disadvantages when there are wide differences in viewpoints or perspectives and these are carried to the extreme. In this case, conflict is perceived as destructive, as the conflict creates a high level of stress for the individuals involved, which in turn affects their ability to perform. This undermines the cooperative dimension necessary in work groups, and results in time and energy being devoted to finding resolutions, which could otherwise have been spent on organizational objectives. Such a situation also thwarts the decision-making process. Conflict resolution should be viewed as a win–win situation.

With the change in emphasis from the elimination of conflict to the management of conflict, Thomas[21] identified two models of conflict between social units. The process model appears as follows:

$$\text{Frustration} \rightarrow \text{Conceptualization} \rightarrow \text{Behavior} \rightarrow \text{Outcome} \rightarrow \text{Frustration}$$
$$\uparrow \qquad\qquad \uparrow$$
$$\text{Others' reactions}$$

The frustration of one party leads to a conceptualization of the situation, to some behavior, to the reaction of the other party, and then to agreement or the lack of agreement. In the latter case, the conflict episode is continued with further frustration, a new conceptualization, etc. The process model is concerned with the influence of an event (e.g., the conceptualization of the problems). The structural model attempts to understand conflict by studying how underlying conditions shape events. "The structural model is concerned with identifying the pressures and constraints which bear upon the parties' behavior; for example, social pressures, personal predispositions, established negotiation procedures and rules, incentives, and so on."[22] The structural model attempts to predict the effect of these conditions on the behavior of the individuals involved in conflict. Thomas maintains that the two models complement each other.

Thomas and Kilmann suggest a two-dimensional scheme, with one dimension being the cooperative–uncooperative striving to satisfy the other's concern, and the second being the degree to which one assertively pursues one's own concerns.[23] In Exhibit 4.2, the assertive style (4) is competitive and represents a desire to satisfy one's concern at the expense of the other. The cooperative style (2) attempts to satisfy the other but not one's own concern. A compromising style (3) is a preference for moderate but incomplete satisfaction of both parties. Labor-management disputes in the US characterize this style. A collaborative style (5) attempts to fully satisfy the concerns of both parties and is most synergistic. The avoidance style (1) is an indifference to the concerns of either party. The cooperative style as opposed to uncooperative is an Eastern mode of resolving conflict, and the assertive mode is more Western.

The effective global manager must achieve a synergistic solution, diagnosing conflict accurately and determining a strategy for managing the conflict.

EXHIBIT 4.2 A TWO-DIMENSIONAL SCHEMATIC SHOWING VARIOUS STYLES OF CONFLICT RESOLUTION

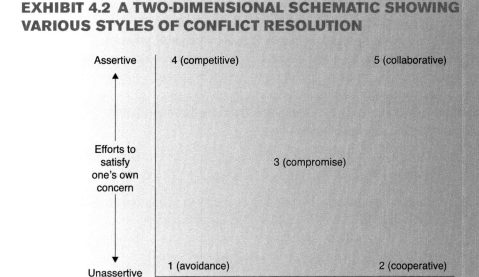

Source: Kilmann, R. H. and Thomas, K. W. "A Forced-Choice Measure of Conflict-Handling Behavior: The 'Mode' Instrument." Los Angeles Graduate School of Management, Working Paper, 1973, p.7.

Conflict management in the Arab world

In the Arab world, the role of the mediator is important in resolving conflict. Thus, "the greater the prestige of the mediator, and the deeper the respect he commands, the better the chances that his efforts at mediating a dispute will be successful."[24] Some highly regarded families and groups carry ascribed status as mediators. The mediator must be impartial and beyond pressures, including monetary ones, from either side in the dispute. The mediator will often promote compromise by appealing to the wishes of other respected parties; for example, "Do it for the sake of . . . your father/brother." The ethical force of such an argument ("for the sake of") has three underlying assumptions, all of which remain unspoken but nonetheless understood by the disputants:

1   Each individual is obligated by ties of kinship to act in a manner that his kinsmen find gratifying.
2   The kinsmen, especially the older ones, are interested in the settlement of any conflict involving their kin group because every conflict represents a potential danger to the honor of the family.
3   By modifying one's position, the disputant can manifest generosity which, in turn, redounds to the honor of kin and Bedouin values.

Conflict management in Japan

"To understand typical behavioral responses to conflict situations in Japan requires a basic understanding of the history and cultural environment of Japan."[25] Accordingly, it is necessary to first ascertain the key psychological and cultural variables that affect Japanese conflict management phenomena, and then to determine how they interrelate with each other to create various deviations within a larger cultural norm. The Japanese conflict management system includes both institutionalized conflict management structures and behavioral conflict management techniques.

Styles of handling conflict in Japan

Five styles of handling conflict are used in Japan: avoiding, compromising, obliging, integrating, and dominating. Of these five styles, the Japanese prefer the avoiding style. In numerous examples of Japanese managers' responses to the statement "Organizations would be better off if conflict could be eliminated," Japanese agree very strongly.

AVOIDING

On a behavioral level, the Japanese commonly employ a number of techniques to avoid conflict. Many of these techniques are not uncommon in cultures around the world, but they provide particular insight into Japanese conflict management.

One of their most effective techniques is sometimes referred to as triadic management. To avoid confrontation between two people, the Japanese often create a triad with another outside individual to manage the situation. Conflict between the two parties may be communicated through the third party in an indirect manner. The third party may take a more active role as an arbiter in situations where there is an apparent stalemate. In such a situation, the third party, who is respected by both of the other individuals, may provide a breakthrough by presenting her- or himself as the person on whose behalf the other two parties are to resolve the conflict. She or he urges the conflicting parties to relent so that she or he can "save face" (*kao*), with an implicit threat that she or he will take offense if her or his intervention is not heeded. To prevent humiliation to the arbiter, both parties may comply, even though they might prefer to remain in conflict with each other. Although this triadic management technique is by no means unique to Japan, it is utilized extensively, and provides one of the greatest vehicles for conflict management within the culture. Those skilled in global negotiations often use this method in Japan.

COMPROMISING

A variant of triadic management, known as displacement, can often manifest itself in a variety of ways. Usually, the displacement will take place in the form of an offended individual attempting to convey his or her anger or resentment to a third party, who is in a far more favorable position to transfer the feelings of the injured party to the injuring party in a manner that is less conflicting.

OBLIGING

Another technique often utilized to avoid direct confrontation is commonly referred to as conflict acceptance. Instead of rejecting or correcting an undesirable state of affairs, the individual persuades her- or himself or is advised by someone else to accept the situation. This somewhat fatalistic or deterministic approach is rooted in the strong Buddhist influence on the culture throughout the history of Japan.

INTEGRATING

Another, less-utilized technique employed to avoid direct confrontation may be referred to as self-aggression or self-confrontation. In this technique, one party expresses a grievance against another by exaggerated compliance.

DOMINATING

This style of conflict resolution is contrary to the very nature of the Japanese character and, consequently, is used only rarely.

Interpreters and translators during negotiations

The importance of an interpreter in business negotiations cannot be overemphasized. It is the interpreter who can assist with the accurate communication of ideas between the two teams. A linguistic interpreter can also be a cultural interpreter, letting the negotiators know of actual or potential cultural misunderstandings. It is advisable to remember the following points concerning the use of interpreters:

- Brief the interpreter in advance about the subject. Select an interpreter knowledgeable about the product or subject.
- Speak clearly and slowly.
- Avoid little-known words.
- Explain the major idea in two or three different ways, as the point may be lost if discussed only once.
- Avoid talking for more than a minute or two without giving the interpreter a chance to speak.
- While talking, allow the interpreter time to make notes about what is being said.
- Do not lose confidence if the interpreter uses a dictionary.

- Permit the interpreter to spend as much time as necessary in clarifying points whose meanings are obscure.
- Do not interrupt the interpreter as he or she translates, to avoid misunderstandings.
- Avoid long sentences, double negatives, or the use of negative wordings when a positive form could be used.
- Avoid superfluous words. Your point may be lost if wrapped up in generalities.
- Try to be expressive, and use gestures to support your verbal messages.
- During meetings, write out the main points discussed. In this way, both parties can double-check their understanding.
- After meetings, confirm in writing what has been agreed.
- Do not expect an interpreter to work for over two hours without a rest.
- Consider using two interpreters if negotiation is to last an entire day or into the evening, so that when one tires, the other can take over.
- Don't be concerned if a speaker talks for five minutes and the interpreter covers it in half a minute.
- Be understanding if the interpreter makes a mistake.
- Ask the interpreter for advice if there are problems.

Successful negotiation procedures

Negotiations bring together two parties, each with an expectation of the outcome. On examination, the two parties evaluate their leverage, authority, and tactics. To close a negotiation that was the best possible deal for both sides means that, most likely, neither side feels cheated or duped and that a spirit of fairness pervaded the negotiation. When international negotiations take place, the cultural differences and implications can spin the negotiation in unanticipated directions. Weiss has established five steps for analyzing and developing a culturally responsive strategy for international negotiations.[26]

1   *Study your own culture's negotiation script.* When we are in our home culture, we behave almost automatically. Studying observations about their home culture by outsiders as well as their own self-examinations will enable a negotiator to construct an accurate national profile. What does your side bring to the party?

2   *Learn the negotiation script of your counterpart.* A first-time negotiator should build a profile of his or her counterparts from the ground up. An experienced negotiator should review and research his or her counterparts, adding new information. Beware of cultural biases. What does this party bring to the negotiations?

3   *Consider the relationship and circumstance.* Whether you are the buyer or the seller in a negotiation will affect the relationship, and an adjustment of strategy will have to occur. Any previous negotiating relationship with a counterpart, as well as his or her home culture and its familiarity with yours, will also affect the outcome. What is the context of the relationship?

4   *Predict the counterpart's approach.* If your counterpart's approach is similar to yours, or you perhaps can influence the selection of the approach, these deliberations will preview the possible interactions during preparation for the negotiation. Generally, approaches will be complementary or conflicting.

5   *Choose your strategy.* After completing the first four steps, the selection of the strategy must be feasible, given the cross-cultural dimensions of the negotiations and the counterpart's approach, be appropriate to the relationship, and, hopefully, be a win–win for both parties.

Wederspahn suggests that human resource development programs within global corporations should include an International Negotiations Workshop with a cultural overview of the counterpart party in negotiations.[27] The model is based on the high-/low-context approach to culture discussed elsewhere in this book. *Position-based negotiation* is based on the win–lose paradigm–the more one party receives, the more the other has to give up in the pursuit of self-interest and maximizing advantage. The main focus is on position–advancing, defending, and rationalizing it. Concessions made should be compensated by corresponding gains. Objective and impersonal data should be used to justify one's demands and trade-offs. Tactics include overstating demands, multiple fallback positions, pressure and dramatic displays, hidden agendas, bluffing, and keeping one's opponents off balance. In contrast, *interest-based negotiation* assumes that a mutually advantageous agreement is possible and desirable; expectations are for collaboration that is win–win and that brings benefits to both parties. This approach looks to long-term payoffs in the relationship, so that there is mutual openness and information sharing to better understand each other's needs, constraints, and aspirations. Trust-building includes visits to each other's facilities, establishing explicit and objective standards of fairness, designing systems to share gain/risk, giving and receiving help from one another, as well as socializing and creating a common strategy and culture.

THE PRICE OF FAILED NEGOTIATIONS

War is a conflict in the extreme, and often results when diplomacy and negotiations have failed. Recent research on post-traumatic stress disorder (PTSD) has suggested that serious conflict, such as war or occupation, can produce years of traumatic experiences, especially for many who have engaged in the extreme conflict. David Berceli, a trauma therapist and expert on Arab–American relations, has written on this in personal communication with Robert Moran (Exhibit 4.3).

EXHIBIT 4.3 WAR FORGES A NEW ERA IN CORPORATE ARAB/ AMERICAN RELATIONSHIPS

In the United States, "Roughly 3.6 days of work impairment per month associated with Post-Traumatic Stress Disorder (PTSD)[a] translates into an annual productivity loss in excess of $3 billion."[b] These figures and subsequent loss in productivity increase dramatically in countries throughout the world that have been ravaged by war, political violence, or sectarian armed conflict. As a result of recent events in the Middle East, international corporations operating there need to seriously consider the staggering toll that emotional pain and suffering will have on the functional and productive capacity of their employees. "There is no avoiding the traumatic aftermath of war; it reaches into every segment of society."[c] Work impairment due to secondary comorbid disorders of PTSD such as anxiety, depression, irritability, disturbed sleep, and elevated mood disorders all damage the cognitive and interpersonal skills of employees. This has a staggering impact on the social structure and eventually the economy of any corporation or society. As a result of this reality, whether they want to or not, corporations operating in war-torn countries of the Middle East will be forced to implement programs and procedures to deal with the systemic consequences of the trauma their employees have experienced...

As the average duration of each trauma episode is reported to be more than seven years, "the typical person with PTSD has a duration of active symptoms for more than two decades. The process of healing, therefore, will have to be measured in terms of generations rather than years."[d] Beginning with the rebuilding of Iraq, corporate social responsibility and financial profitability should be seen as inseparable ideologies because of the severe and systemic trauma experienced by the Iraqi people. With some simple but strategic trauma behavior modifications, over time corporations will be able to break down antagonism and build alliances across opposing sides. They will be able to use the trauma of their employees as a common opportunity for gain. If they know what they are doing, they can use these opportunities to "reduce contentious behaviors and increase conciliation."[e]

Notes: [a] PTSD is the re-experiencing of disrupting emotions or behaviors following the initial trauma.

[b] This report is from the Department of Health Care Policy, Kessler R. Harvard Medical School, Boston, MA. It can be found in the *Journal of Clinical Psychiatry*, 2000, Vol. 61 (Suppl. 5), pp. 4–12.

[c] Levine, P. *We Are All Neighbors*. Boulder, CO: Foundation for Human Enrichment, 2002, p. 3.

[d] Department of Health Care Policy.

[e] Baldwin, D. "Innovation, Controversy and Consensus in Traumatology," *The International Electronic Journal of Innovations in the Study of the Traumatization Process and Methods for Reducing or Eliminating Related Human Suffering*, Vol. 3, No. 1, Article 3.

Emotional intelligence and negotiations

Everyone knows the meaning of IQ (intelligence quotient) and the importance of technical skills and intelligence to perform many job responsibilities. Some in an organization are referred to as "techies." Many also have personal experience with individuals who are very intelligent and have good technical skills but have failed in a leadership position.

Coleman[28] researched about 200 global companies, and found that the traditional attributes associated with leadership—intelligence, vision, toughness, etc.—are insufficient. He states that effective leaders must have a higher degree of emotional intelligence as well. According to Coleman, there are five components of emotional intelligence:

1   Self-awareness or the ability to recognize and understand one's moods and emotions, as well as their effect on others. This is characterized by self-confidence and a realistic assessment.
2   Self-regulation or the ability to control or redirect disruptive impulses and moods and the propensity to suspend judgment. This is characterized by trustworthiness, integrity, and a comfort with ambiguity.
3   Motivation or the ability to work for reasons that go beyond money or status. This is characterized by a strong drive to achieve optimism even in the face of failure.
4   Empathy or the ability to understand the emotional makeup of other people. This is characterized by expertise in building and retaining talent.
5   Social skills or proficiency in managing relationships and building networks. This is characterized by skills in leading change and expertise in building and leading teams.

Negotiators who are bilingual also appear to have a number of advantages over monolingual negotiators. For children, it has been demonstrated that multilingual exposure improves cognitive skills and social abilities. It can be that these advantages and others continue through life for bilingual or multilingual persons.

Climate change negotiations have a history of being contentious and struggling to find any meaningful agreement. In her paper,[29] Susan Biniaz identified a number of language-based tools negotiators have used to resolve differences that sometimes are as "subtle as a shift in the placement of a comma."

CONCLUSIONS

Roger Fisher,[30] the negotiating guru, in an interview about emotions and negotiations, stated: "I don't have people criticizing me for talking about emotions . . . no one says it's a soft, fuzzy side." In short, keeping your feelings hidden, saying "don't become emotional" during a heated argument, may become obsolete.

This perspective is supported by Fromm,[31] who wrote:

Emotions provide important information to us and to the other side. If we are able to express our emotions in a constructive way and at an appropriate time in the negotiation, rather than destroying or hurting the negotiation process, it can greatly enhance it.

Emotional intelligence contributes to a skillful negotiator's toolbox. The instruments and questionnaire to measure one's emotional intelligence or emotional competence are easily available and recommended to all global negotiators.

MIND STRETCHING

1   As a negotiator, list your strengths and your weaknesses. Write an action plan to become a more skillful negotiator.

2   Become an astute observer of human behavior. As you observe the behavior of others in different situations, what are the determinants? Culture? Personality? Context?

3   How can you increase your styles of resolving conflicts when negotiating across cultures?

4   Apply the concepts in this chapter to any global dispute. Why are there as many unresolved issues?

5   Do our global business and political leaders have a high degree of observable emotional intelligence?

NOTES

1   Moran, R. Stated in a session to executives on negotiation across cultures, February 2010.
2   *New York Times*, January 27, 2013.
3   Walch, Karen. "Seize the Sky: Discovering the Secrets of Negotiation Power," *Thunderbird Magazine*, Fall 2012.
4   Moran, R. *Getting Your Yen's Worth*. Houston, TX: Gulf Publishing Company, 1989. Sixth printing.
5   Van Zandt, H. F. "How to Negotiate in Japan," *HBR*, November/December 1970.
6   Nakane, C. *Japanese Society*. Berkeley, CA: University of California Press, 1970.
7   Taken from the actual diary of a Japanese negotiator and used with permission.
8   Graham, J. and Herberger, R. "Negotiating Abroad: Don't Shoot from the Hip," *Harvard Business Review*, July/August 1983.
9   Dierdorff, D. (ed.). *The Sage Handbook of Intercultural Competence*. Thousand Oaks, CA: Sage, 2009.
10   Acuff, F. L. *How to Negotiate with Anyone, Anywhere Around the World*. New York: Amacom, 1993.
11   Based on the actual experience of a US company in Japan.
12   "Assess, Don't Assume, Part 1: Etiquette and Material Culture in Negotiation" and "Assess, Part II: Cross-Border Differences in Decision-making, Governance, and Political Economy." HBR Working Paper 10-048 and Working Paper 10-050, 20.
13   Graham, J. "*Vis-à-Vis*: International Business Negotiations," in P. Ghauri and J. C. Usunier (eds.), *International Business Negotiations*. Oxford: Pergamon, 1996.
14   Scheu-Lottgen, U. D. and Hernandez-Campoy, J. M. "An Analysis of Sociocultural Miscommunication: English, Spanish and German," *International Journal of Intercultural Relations*, Vol. 22, No. 4, 1998.
15   Graham, "*Vis-à-Vis*."
16   Weiss, S. and Stripp, W. *Negotiating with Foreign Business Persons*. New York University, Graduate School of Business Administration, Monograph #89–9, 1985.

17 Moran, R. T. and Harris, P. R. *Managing Cultural Synergy*. Houston, TX: Gulf Publishing Company, 1982. Material updated in 2006.

18 Likert, R. and Likert, J. G. *New Ways of Managing Conflict*. New York: McGraw-Hill, 1976.

19 Thomas, K. W. "Conflict and Conflict Management." University of California Working Paper 74–3, 1974.

20 Stewart, E. C. *American Cultural Patterns: A Cross-Cultural Perspective*. LaGrange Park, IL: Intercultural Network, 1979.

21 Thomas, "Conflict and Conflict Management."

22 Ibid.

23 Kilmann, R. H. and Thomas, K. W. "A Forced-Choice Measure of Conflict Handling Behavior: The 'Mode' Instrument." Los Angeles Graduate School of Management, Working Paper, 1973, pp. 12–73.

24 Patai, R. *The Arab Mind*. New York: Charles Scribner & Sons, 1976. Moran, R. T., Allen, J., Wichmann, R., Ando, T., and Sasano, M. "Japan," in A. Rahim and A. Blum (eds.), *Global Perspectives on Organizational Conflict*. London: Praeger, 1994. Material updated in 2006, pp. 18ff.

25 Weiss, S. E. "Negotiating with 'Romans': Part 2," *Sloan Management Review*, Spring, 1994.

26 Ibid.

27 Wederspahn, G. M. "The Fine Art of International Negotiation," *HR News/Society for Human Resource Management*, January, 1993, pp. C6–7.

28 Coleman, D. "Inside the Mind of the Leader," *Harvard Business Review*, January, 2006.

29 Biniaz, S. "Comma But Differentiated Responsibilities: Punctuation and 30 Other Ways Negotiators Have Resolved Issues in the International Climate Change Regime." Sabin Center for Climate Change Law, 2016.

30 www.news.harvard.edu/gazette/2005/10.13/03-reason.html.

31 Fromm, D. "Dealing with Your Emotions in Negotiations," *The Negotiation Magazine*, November, 2005.

5 WOMEN LEADERS IN GLOBAL BUSINESS

Dear Ms. Moran:

Thank you for your email.

We do not carry women's pilot shirts. I did check online and found a website that lists this item: www.mypilot-store.com.

Please let me know if I can be of further assistance.

Sincerely,
Customer Service

Dear Customer Service,

Thanks for your response; it is appreciated. I was able to do a search and was initially excited to find "girls are pilots, too" websites, only to be disappointed in finding they sell pink tank tops with "I love my pilot" written on them, with a link to "dogs are pilots, too" (selling stuffed animals).

After further searching, I was able to find one that sells proper professional women's pilot shirts. The search was a bit of a disappointment (in more ways than one), but if I ever need aviation cookware, I know where to find it online now. I guess one has to have a sense of humor . . .

May I suggest you (being one of the most popular pilot supply websites) sell women's pilot shirts?

Thank you, Rebecca,
Pilot in Tanzania, East Africa

After reading and studying concepts/examples and illustrations in Chapter 5, all should:

1   Be more aware of some of the many challenges women experience as they work in an environment previously or presently dominated by men.
2   Be keenly aware of the unique challenges of women in a number of countries around the world.
3   Find a few more ways to continue your journey as a woman in a male-dominated work world.
4   Commit to mentoring other women who might find value in your advice.

About 6 percent of pilots worldwide are women—see also "The female pilot" box.

THE "FEMALE" PILOT

"A lady pilot! You go, girl!" is the reaction that I mostly get. But it hasn't always been so complimentary. "Are you a pilot? You're way too young to be a pilot. I'd have to see your license." Actually, I think that was meant as a compliment as well.

Apparently, I am not a pilot. I'm a "female pilot," just as a man isn't a nurse but a "male nurse." Despite being in a profession with mostly male colleagues, many of my passengers are very happy to see a "female pilot." I suppose those Westerners who may have an issue with my gender are aware of their bias and keep it to themselves.

But not everyone hides it. The advantage of being an American is that most people think that we don't speak any other language and, therefore, they are at liberty to speak about us within earshot. Being of slightly playful character, I do not always initially reveal the languages I speak.

I had just joined a new company and was on a training flight with another pilot. The Captain, Sarah, and I stood at the foot of the aircraft stairs and greeted the five young and boisterous French passengers. Sarah, several years younger than I, is a highly qualified, very experienced, beautiful, blond American pilot. As Sarah and I introduced ourselves and gave the security briefing from the cockpit, one of the French men said nervously and sarcastically to his friends: "Deux jeunes filles pilotes—j'ai confiance."

"Everything is okay back there?" I asked in English to the man. "Yes" he said.

Sarah landed at our destination. Not able to feel the moment of touch-down, it was what we call a greaser—a perfectly smooth landing. I turned around to the passengers and said in French, "Deux jeunes filles pilotes—pas trop mal, eh?"

As the young Frenchman's face went white, his friends burst into laughter.

Source: Rebecca Moran, Tanzania, 2012.

IN ITALY THE FEMALE DOCTOR IS "MISS"

If I asked you to mentally visualize a doctor, the vast majority would think of a man. Perhaps old, white-haired, or young and cool, with a white coat or green surgical gown, and stethoscopes around the neck. Don't worry—this prejudice comes from really far away.

In the most ancient civilizations, the practice of medicine was absolutely prohibited to women. In Athens, in the fourth century BC, a young woman named Agnodice had to disguise herself as a man in order to practice gynecologist work, revealing her sexual identity only to her patients. She soon became rather popular because she was very skilled, so her male colleagues insinuated that "he" seduced the patients. To avoid the death penalty, in court she dropped her robe and revealed the deceit; but, unfortunately, she was accused of unlawful practice of the medical profession.

The history of women in medicine is full of stories like this. The real turning point was some British students, including Elizabeth Garret Anderson, who took the entrance test to Medicine Hospital of London in 1861, which only she passed. But she was expelled from the English university and completed her medical studies in other countries, and then returned to the UK and founded the London School of Medicine for Women, which the English Medical Association was forced to recognize.

Today, in Italy, students of medicine are mostly girls. In 1999, when I started university, there were 180 students and 75 percent were female. The reason is maybe because women are often more organized in the study, or perhaps because the long training (in Italy, university of medicine lasts six years; and then to be a specialist, you have to go through another five years of residency) discourages boys who are less stubborn and often less motivated. Maybe it is because the female nature is more suitable for assistance and care.

Women doctors now represent 40 percent of total doctors; but under 30 years of age 63 percent are women, but only 14 percent have managerial positions (1,272 vs. 10,154 men). Also, nowadays in the medical profession, maternity is still seen as an obstacle, and we often work exhausting shifts, including nights and weekends.

> Despite all this, we continue to study, visit, operate, and work, taking care of people, but we are still aware that in the hallway, next to a male colleague, a passing patient will approach him with "Doctor" and us with "Miss," especially if you are a surgeon, as I obstinately am.
>
> Source: Dr. Chiara Mariani, Surgeon, Pisa, Italy.

In April 2013, it was estimated that the world's population was about seven billion, with about half female and half male.[1] The five largest countries in the world by population are: China (1,354,040,000), India (1,210,000,000), the US (314,573,000), Indonesia (238,000,000), and Brazil (194,000,000). The proportion of women relative to men, both working in employed positions, varies globally, and ranges from 20 percent in Arab countries like Bahrain, Iraq, Qatar, Oman, Saudi Arabia, and the United Arab Emirates, to 50 percent in countries like Cambodia, Ghana, and Latvia, to much higher in the US, Canada, and many European countries.[2] Worldwide, more men than women are found in the upper echelons of government and business, and it is these leaders who hold the greatest influence in shaping their country's policies and corporate HR management structures and behaviors.[3]

Historically and currently, there remains a significant gap in female representation, compensation in the upper echelons of the global workforce, as well as having the same rights as men in all aspects.

ARE WOMEN THE ANSWER TO PROBLEMS OF CULTURE CLASH?

A number of years ago, one of the authors (Moran) wrote an article for his column in the global management magazine, *International Management*, which was published in Europe, Africa, Asia-Pacific, Latin America, and in Arabic for Arab speakers in the Middle East. This is an abridged and updated version for the tenth edition of our book.

In a column in the magazine *International Management*, a woman wrote that a professional woman cannot have the best of both worlds—private and business. She also recommends that the ambitious woman "postpone having children."

Postponing children assumes she has a husband or partner who can't or won't do much at home. Women not only can do well in business, they make superior international executives because they can outperform men on the international scene, and have the necessary global leadership skills for the following reasons:

1   They tend to approach relationships and negotiations from a "win–win" strategy that results in success for both sides rather than the sports-oriented, win–lose approach of many men.

2   Women tend to be more formal, show more respect, and take more care in establishing relationships than men. (A Japanese manager told me of a recent offensive experience in Australia when an Australian counterpart was calling him "Naka" within five minutes because his name was too long. Few women would be so insensitive or presumptuous.)

3   Women tend to be better listeners and more sympathetic than men and, therefore, can tune in to the needs and expectations of their foreign counterparts.

4   Women graduating with MBAs or other advanced degrees are as interested as men in international careers, and have the necessary skills to do well. Given equal opportunity, women and men have about the same amount of skill and aptitude for verbal and mathematical reasoning, scientific interests, managerial abilities, and everything else.

There are other reasons. Of course, not all women are better than all men. But women, in general, have the qualities that work well overseas. In light of this, it is paradoxical that so few women have risen to international management positions.

The following from recent books or widely respected newspapers in the US are examples that show that women have a long way to go before they can be considered equal to men in law or society. The reason they are not equal is because men have the power.

■ From the book, *On Saudi Arabia*, by Karen Elliott House:[4] According to Wahhabi Islam, men must obey Allah and women must obey men. "Fortunately for men, Allah is distant, but unfortunately for women, men are omnipresent," writes House. However, this is changing, even in Saudi Arabia, as we shall see later in this chapter.

■ Hans Kung, a well-known Catholic priest and long-time colleague and friend of the pope emeritus, wrote the following under the title "A Vatican Spring" in the *New York Times*:[5] "A recent poll in Germany shows 85 percent of Catholics in favor of letting priests marry and 75 percent in favor of ordaining women."

■ In *The Economist*:[6] "In India, rape has long been depressingly common. . . . The UN's human-rights chief calls rape in India a national problem . . . sexual violence in villages, though little reported, keeps girls and women indoors after dark."

■ Nicholas Kristof wrote in the *New York Times*:[7] "Gender violence is one of the world's most common human-rights abuses. Women worldwide ages 15 through 44 are more likely to die or be maimed by male violence than because of cancer, malaria, and traffic accidents combined."

■ Sohrab Ahmari, in the *Wall Street Journal*,[8] wrote about a Saudi woman who was driving a car: "Members of the Committee for the Promotion of Virtue and the Prevention of Vice, the Saudi morality police, surrounded the car. 'Girl,' screamed one. 'Get out, we don't allow women to drive.' She asked, 'Sir, what law did I break?' 'You didn't break any laws,' they said. 'You violated our . . . custom.'"

- Alissa Rubin, in the *New York Times*,[9] wrote: "A father who borrowed $2,500.00 to pay for hospital expenses for his wife and cannot repay the loan will be forced to have their 6-year-old daughter leave her family home forever to be married to the lender's 17-year-old son."
- The National Partnership for Women and Families analysis of census data showed the pay gap between men and women in the US is still significant. Women earn 77 cents for every 1 dollar paid to full-time working men.[10]
- During the 2016 US presidential campaign, footage emerged in which Donald Trump was seen and heard saying that he was able to grope and kiss women at will. He subsequently reported this was just "men's locker room talk." However, a number of women have subsequently claimed that contact with Trump was not only locker room talk.

And on, and on, and on. Similar examples can be found in the newspapers of any society if the press is free.

We believe that culture counts. Culture provides guidance, and some cultures have rigid rules for expected female and male roles, and, as such, provides the values and the subsequent expected behavioral norms for men and women within each culture.[11] Gender norms vary across cultures, and can influence how women combine the expected roles of a female leader with the general role expectations of their culture.[12] Culture sets the expected norms and values of gender-related behaviors, and there are many differences within nations and cultures with how these play out.[13]

While culture can set the standard for expected behaviors, this does not mean that all men and all women will automatically respond to these cultural norms accordingly. For example, Egyptian women collectively stood up for their rights and were not required to wear a veil from the 1920s and were able to vote in 1956; however, in 2009 a survey done in Egypt of 15,000 youths revealed that 67 percent of female respondents still believed that a woman deserves to be beaten by her husband if she speaks to another man.[14] In another example, a global study of 62 women with families and prominent leadership work-related positions found that "the American women leaders pride themselves on never missing their children's school play or soccer games; mothers in Hong Kong put more emphasis in helping their children with their school work; the Chinese mothers across the different societies emphasize family dinners, describing how they eat with their children before they go to their business dinners or go back to work in the office at night."[15]

From an organizational perspective, we contend that companies that use and build on an increasingly diverse workforce that include women will have a competitive advantage. While the number of international businesswomen has grown over the years, this number has not increased at a rate consistent with the number of women in

LEARNING OBJECTIVES

the workforce of their respective countries. Globalization has transformed worldwide organizational culture and the workforce, and this has created an increased need for enhanced workforce collaboration and support. Since national corporations have expanded to global corporations, companies have had to respond to an increasingly diverse workplace of varying ethnicities, nationalities, and languages.

Over the last 50 years, an increasing number of professional women have entered and remained in the global workforce. For all workforce professionals to perform to their potential, they need support, training, and mentoring. Often, for women and minorities, the challenge can go well beyond this. If women comprise less than 20 percent of the directors in highly developed countries, progress for women is still far from accomplished.

In this chapter we address some of the opportunities and challenges faced by women as global businesspeople. Our first objective is to raise awareness about the status and challenges and opportunities of women in global organizations. The second objective is to suggest some ideas about women as global leaders and specific issues women may confront in managing cultural differences.

CURRENT STATUS OF GLOBAL WOMEN MANAGERS

Although globally women have considerably increased their presence in all industries, Exhibits 5.1 and 5.2 are researched examples illustrating that progress is yet to be made.

Meyerson and Fletcher[16] wrote of an outdated, but prevalent, practice of women still tending to be responsible for the "softer" aspects of work, while corporate culture is predisposed to highly value the traits of toughness, aggressiveness, and decisiveness—all stereotypically associated with men. Nevertheless, this isn't to say that men are to blame and that all men benefit because corporate culture is primarily male-dominated.

Many organizations are working hard to leverage workforce diversity and gender equality so that all people can succeed. The key to making concrete changes in organizations is their leadership, which must have a keen interest in recruiting and *retaining* a diverse workforce while promoting qualified women. Unfortunately, statistics demonstrate that companies are falling short of the goal of gender equity in the workplace. Meyerson and Fletcher stated that

> Women at the highest levels of business are still rare. They comprise only 10 percent of senior managers in *Fortune* 500 companies; less than 4 percent of the uppermost ranks of CEO, president, vice president, and COO; and less than 3 percent of top corporate earners.[17]

EXHIBIT 5.1 STATUS OF GLOBAL WOMEN EXECUTIVE OFFICERS, 2016, AN UPDATE

- There were women on the board of every FTSE100 company in the UK. Women comprised 26 percent of the boards.
- However, the percentage of women on the FTSE100 boards in executive directorship is 9.7 percent.
- In the United States, women on boards of the S&P500 is 19.9 percent.
- In India, women hold 7.7 percent of board seats.
- Globally, women hold 12 percent of board seats.
- In Norway, women hold 37 percent of board seats, which is close to Norway's goal of 40 percent.

Source: Young, G. "Women, Naturally Better Leaders for the 21st Century." White Paper, 2016.

EXHIBIT 5.1

Likewise, tied to the challenge of leveraging a diverse workforce with equal opportunity and compensation, the statistics for women of minority ethnicities are even worse: "Although women of color make up 23 percent of the U. S. women's workforce, they account for only 14 percent of women in managerial roles. African-American women comprise only 6 percent of the women in managerial roles."[18]

In 2010, *The Economist*[19] published an article discussing the position of women in the workplace. This is not intended to be compared to their article published in 2005; the purpose is to look at working women relative to men worldwide:

- There is an increase in the number of women in the workplace; women in the US and in Spain now make up 49.9 percent of all workers, and in the US women earn almost 60 percent of all university degrees.
- The unemployment rates for men in Japan and in Italy are more than 20 percent higher for women, and even though women's employment has risen significantly in the last decade, it is still well below that of men, and more than 20 percent below that of Denmark and Sweden.
- Women, on average, still earn significantly less than men, and are underrepresented at the top of organizations.
- Women are often still forced to choose between motherhood and careers, and, as a response, in Switzerland, more than 40 percent of women are childless or delay having children for so long that they are prime candidates for fertility treatment.

E
X
H
I
B
I
T

5.2

EXHIBIT 5.2 SELECT SURVEY RESULTS OF THE CORPORATE GENDER GAP REPORT, 2010

A select group of over 3,000 companies responded to this survey of about 25 questions in each of the 30 member countries of the OECD (Organization for Economic Cooperation and Development) and Brazil, China, Russia, and India. In each economy, a minimum of 20 completed surveys of 100 companies were completed. The following are some selected results.

Female employees (%)	India	23	Female employees were found to be concentrated in entry-level to mid-level positions.
	Japan	24	
	Turkey	26	
	Austria	29	
	Finland	44	
	Canada	46	
	Spain	48	
	US	52	
Average number of women holding the CEO position (%)	Italy	11	Among the following survey respondents—Belgium, Canada, Czech Republic, France, India, Greece, Mexico, Netherlands, Switzerland, the US, and UK—there were no female CEOs.
	Brazil	11	
	Norway	12	
	Turkey	12	
	Finland	13	
Corporate measurement and target setting	Of the sample, 64 percent of the companies surveyed did not set any specific targets, quotas, or affirmative goals.		72 percent of the companies surveyed did not monitor salary gaps between women and men or implement counteractive procedures.
Maternity leave practices	13 percent of surveyed companies offered no maternity leave.		India, Mexico, and the US offered the minimum leave time, and 33 percent of companies in Mexico offered less than the minimum leave time.

Source: Tesfachew, T., Zahidi, S., and Ibarra, H. "Measuring the Corporate Gender Gap," in S. Zahidi and H. Ibarra (eds.), *The Corporate Gender Gap Report 2010*. Geneva: World Economic Forum, 2010.

www.weforum.org/pdf/gendergap/corporate2010.pdf (retrieved April 27, 2010).

However,

■ Finland and Hungary provide up to three years of paid leave for women, and Germany has introduced a parent salary to encourage mothers to stay home for a time while keeping their careers.

- More than 90 percent of organizations in Germany and Sweden allow for flexible working, dividing the work week in new ways to allow for improved work–family balance.
- In paid family leave, the US trails most of the globe.[20]

According to a report by the BBC, 75 percent of women work in the five lowest paid sectors; women hold less than 10 percent of top positions in FTSE100 companies, the police, the judiciary, and trade unions.[21] Retired women have on average a little over half the income of retired men. Barriers to women's entry into senior management, otherwise known as the "glass ceiling," exist across the globe, and it is worse in some areas of the world than in others. An article on the most influential women in business highlighted that it is easier to find ethnic British and Chinese women in positions of power, but much more difficult to find Korean or German women at the same level.[22] And although women represent 43 percent of the European workforce, they are still largely underrepresented in top management—in the UK, women represent slightly over 30 percent of managers and senior executives.[23]

One of the best examples of a society that promotes gender equality is Norway.[24] Here, 80 percent of Norwegian women work outside of the home, and half of the current government ministers are women. Scandinavian countries have the highest level of female employment in the world, and the fewest social problems, as the state has been closely involved in promoting gender equality. For example, Norway has used quota threats to increase female representation; the result is that about 40 percent of the legislators are now women.[25] In 2002, a law was instated requiring that 40 percent of all company board members be women, and gave until 2006 for companies to comply.[26]

Yet, while representation has increased, the expected link between women and performance in the board room was found to still be questionable. This is possibly because of the fact that the boards chiefly supervise and give advice to executives and top managers who are mostly men. Global representation in the board room and among executives and top managers still has a long way to go: "In the United States, roughly 15 percent of the board members of the *Fortune* 500 companies are women, while at the top of Asian companies, women remain scarce: in China and India, they hold roughly 5 percent of board seats, and in Japan, just 1.4 percent." While "women represent 27–32 percent of managers in Nordic countries, against 34 percent to 43 percent in Australia, Britain, Canada, and the United States, where maternity leave is more limited."[27]

Creating opportunities for female representation in the global workplace is only part of the matter. Biases or stereotypes are beliefs that influence behavior, and, often, these beliefs can lead to unequal treatment and representation. Stereotypes often hinder—although women and men are equal in their managerial abilities and overall ability to succeed—the promotion of women to senior positions.

What would you do? Ask five women and five men their opinion. My hunch is there would be differences between men and women.

In January 2016, Iranian President Hassan Rouhani and President Francois Hollande of France were scheduled to have a luncheon. President Rouhani insisted that no wine be served at lunch. President Hollande canceled the luncheon. What would you recommend? The host is French, the guests are Iranian.

GLOBAL CULTURAL STEREOTYPES ABOUT WOMEN LEADERS

Psychological research has found that there are two types of sexist ideologies; one, benevolent sexism, is rooted in the belief that the gender differences are complementary and that women should be protected and taken care of; the other, hostile sexism, is rooted in the belief that women are inferior to men.[28] These sexist ideologies are rooted in each culture's stereotypic views about how women "should" behave. When women behave differently from prescribed stereotypes, often there are penalties that are administered.[29] "For example, women who are viewed as self-promoting or as 'acting like men' . . . are judged as deficient in social skills, are less liked and socially accepted, and receive fewer recommendations for employment."[30]

From Asia to the Americas to Europe, some of the unfortunate and disturbing *global stereotypes* include, but are not limited to, the following.

Women's behavior at work

■ Women are fundamentally different and too "soft" to handle hard-nosed managerial decisions. Women cannot be aggressive enough, and will therefore lose business or do not have the competitive edge needed to win.

■ Contrary to the stereotype that women are too "soft," when women behave in accordance with the behaviors expected of their male counterparts, then the stereotype changes to the following: women overcompensate when in male environments, and become too masculine when managing, alienating employees and often alarming clients.

■ Yet in China, especially after the Cultural Revolution, women are expected to behave more aggressively.

■ Women lack quantitative skills, and therefore cannot hold technical positions or understand the numbers required in a profit-and-loss environment. Women possess "soft" skills such as communication and team building.

Women and mothers

■ Women are not as dedicated or as committed as their male counterparts, and therefore are not "executive material."

■ Once a woman becomes a mother, her priorities change completely and she can no longer be counted on as before. Women often opt to quit working and become full-time mothers. How can a company promote someone who they know will ultimately leave? Companies cannot afford to have women coming and going whenever they wish.

Women in an international context

■ Women are not interested in an international career, and therefore should not be considered for international positions. In addition, women can't handle the cultural differences that occur outside their home country.

■ When companies send women abroad, their image will be less credible in male-dominated societies.

Women interacting within their working environment

■ Other men won't take the woman manager seriously. Interestingly, many Japanese managers tell us they see "foreign" first and being a woman next.

■ Because of current sexual harassment laws, nothing can be said to women without it getting blown out of proportion, and the result is that all interaction becomes suspect.

■ Women cause problems by looking for love in the workplace, and this will disrupt the workplace and ultimately lead to greater problems.

■ There aren't enough qualified women to promote. No matter how hard the company has tried, there just aren't any women with the exact qualifications they are looking for.

Such stereotypes are extremely counterproductive in the workplace. Blind stereotypes inhibit women and men from working effectively together, and inhibit women from working to their potential because they are active in keeping women "in their place." Overall, whether they are benevolent or hostile forms of sexism, they inhibit the advancement of women in business around the world, and obscure women's skills.[31]

Stereotypes can hinder the advancement of women

Quite often, these stereotypes go unnoticed by both men and women as they are so deeply rooted within a culture. Other times, even when aware of these stereotypes, some women might choose to behave according to the stereotype in order to avoid dealing with strong attitudinal obstructions while at work. There are a variety of global issues that confront women in the workplace. A few are highlighted to gain a greater understanding of the obstacles women must still overcome.

■ *Women are more likely to be pigeonholed into less-challenging positions than men.* Women are often tracked into separate, and less promising, career paths. As upper-management positions require broad and varied experience among other skills and talents, as well as a sense of responsibility, many potential male executives are "pipelined" through certain high-visibility and high-responsibility areas such as marketing, finance, and production.[32] These are often referred to as "line" positions, in preparation for upper-management promotion. Women

> tend to be in supporting, 'staff' function areas—personnel/human resources, communications, public relations, and customer relations. Movement between these positions and 'line' positions is rare in most major companies. Furthermore, career ladders in staff functions are generally shorter than those in line functions, offering fewer possibilities to gain varied experience.[33]

This is a stereotype that can be found across the globe; women are seen as more "human" and therefore better suited for a specific type of job, such as human resources, communications, public relations, and marketing. Management, especially in the areas of finance and information services, continues to often be seen as a job better suited for men.

This stereotype could be linked to the global expectation of a woman's role as mother or primary caretaker in the family. This common stereotype is as follows: If a woman's focus is on bearing children, she would subsequently be taking time off, and could not be considered an effective front-line executive. In Chile, a woman's marital status can be an important consideration during the hiring process; it is generally featured at the top of a resume with other essentials such as name, address, and phone number, along with a photograph. A young, married woman with no children can be considered a "risky investment" because the perception is that she will soon have children, leave her job, and the company will have to pay for pregnancy expenses. Although times may be changing in Chile, it is still generally expected that women will relinquish their career aspirations and stay at home when children arrive. For some women, this can begin immediately after marriage.

During the 1980s, in the US, the "mommy track" was designed to facilitate having children and maintaining a professional life. Nevertheless, many women who choose to have children still maintain high career aspirations and get stuck in less-challenging or -demanding jobs. While this stereotype tends to be focused upon the role of women, it is also evolving into a parental stereotype, as a number of male partners and husbands of working women are staying home to care for children.[34]

■ *Significant pay gaps exist between women and men in the same position.* Despite considerable progress and a variety of laws designed to prevent wage discrimination, women are still earning less than their male counterparts for the same job.[35] The BBC reported that, according to the Equal Opportunities Commission, there is a 19 percent pay gap between men and women in the UK.[36]

■ *Exclusive corporate cultures.* One influential factor still affecting women's advancement in business, and this is true in many areas across the globe, is that most of today's existing work environments were designed by men. Women, functioning in sometimes a more male-oriented corporate culture, are often under pressure to adapt or transform their styles of working. This, however, is slowly changing. In Japan, for example, women face a challenge to adapt to the expectation that management requires mixing work and play, often by drinking and bar-hopping until the late hours. Women colleagues are nowadays invited to join in with such social activities, although a married woman with a family might find it very difficult to meet, on a consistent basis, such a time commitment. In some South American countries, strong, unspoken norms exist about what is appropriate or inappropriate for a woman to do, regardless of career position; as such, higher-level female executives can be excluded from after-work activities and/or can exclude themselves in fear of the backlash from breaching these norms.

In some American corporate environments, younger generations of women have almost eradicated the "male only" designated corporate culture by joining in, and instigating, happy hours, golf games, and softball tournaments. In some cases, these women have even redefined the culture itself by adding new twists like cultural outings or joining in on the "male only" outings.

■ *Limited access to information, contacts, and high-level networking opportunities.* While the term "old boys' network" was coined long ago, in many companies the institution itself is thriving. The "old boys' network" refers primarily to a group of white male executives who have an informal yet somewhat exclusive club that manifests itself in the upper echelons of management. Women and people of color are generally not included. Communication within these exclusive informal networks can perpetuate gender stereotyping and bias through jokes, stories, and slurs. Whether it is on the golf course, hunting, having late-night drinks, or in the men's room, women can often be excluded from this high-level interaction, when it is often these informal networks that can improve chances of promotion and success.

According to *The Economist*, few women are able to reach the higher management levels because of exclusion from informal networks, which across the globe can include late-night boozing and a common tradition for sales teams to take potential clients to strip clubs.[37] Executives and upper-level managers like to hire who they know, and the more contact with an individual the better. Unfortunately for women, many of the "bonding" experiences take place in venues that are not necessarily women-friendly. In Israel, women are almost completely excluded from the senior ranks of the military. This exclusion from what is considered by many in the corporate world as an invaluable learning experience for managing large organizations limits women as choices for future senior executives.[38]

As a result, women often are not informed of advancement opportunities, are not as visible as male colleagues, and are not given additional opportunities to prove their credibility for promotion. According to Wernick,[39]

> Managers and executives look for "signals" from those they will select to advance. Those signals found to be most significant indicate credibility and provide increased access to visibility to decision-makers. Access to information, which is critical to advancement, is often limited to selected groups or individuals within the managerial ranks or workplace.

This can be exacerbated when the company does not have a formal executive development program or tracking program that explicitly monitors promotions and pay increases for employees.

■ *Fewer women participate in executive development programs, employer-sponsored training programs, or "fast-track" programs.* As evidenced through a variety of studies, women are often not given as many opportunities as their male colleagues for education, training, or special high-profile programs. This could emanate from the stereotype that women will eventually leave their jobs to have children, so why invest the money in enhancing their skills when a man would be a better "investment" opportunity? Without proper corporate intervention to increase women's participation in such programs and opportunities, the result would be that women remain in their positions with little to no overall growth.

What about leadership skills? Differences between men and women?

What does good research tell us? Between 2006 and 2013, Leadership, a research organization in the UK, undertook some original research[40] using accepted 360° assessment instruments. Data were collected from 155 individuals, of whom 64 were women and 91 men. All were based at the time in the UK and were drawn across the public, private, and not-for-profit sectors.

The survey comprised 92 statements of behavior, and respondents were asked to rate to which level they observe the behavior along a five-point scale, from never or almost never (1) to always (5). Comparing the mean Difference Index scores of men against women showed that women fared better than men in 15 of 19 capabilities. Exhibit 5.3 shows the results.

Organizations need to develop a strong commitment to promote women to leadership positions and include women on positions in replacement tables. Many women have excellent leadership skills.

EXHIBIT 5.3 DIFFERENCE INDEX SCORES

Men scored better than women in:

- emotional self-control
- self-confidence
- accurate self-assessment
- adaptability (not statistically significant).

Women scored better than men in:

- emotional self-awareness
- achievement orientation
- optimism
- transparency
- initiative
- empathy
- organizational awareness
- service orientation
- developing others
- inspirational leadership
- influence
- change catalyst
- conflict management
- building bonds
- teamwork and collaboration
- communications
- trustworthiness
- conscientiousness.

BALANCING WORK AND FAMILY

THE PLIGHT OF A WORKING MOTHER

Two years ago, while at our summer cottage in northern Ontario, Canada, I took some old, what we call junk, to the local dump. While there, I scrounged around and found some good "junk" that I brought back to our cottage.

I was thrilled with a couple of my new treasures, and sent this email to our five adult children: "Tell us about an interesting day this week. I just returned from the dump with some treasures that were interesting to me."

Ben emailed: "I woke up in a sleeping bag on the sand in the Sinai, after a night under the stars. Had tea made by a Bedouin, then drove to Mt. Sinai, visited St Catherine's monastery, and saw the burning bush—still alive. After many Army checkpoints, made it to the airport, when I had a Greek salad and checked my email before (now) boarding a flight to Istanbul."

Rebecca's email came next: "I woke up at 5 a.m., pressed my snooze button once, made a take-away breakfast of tea and oatmeal, and headed to the airport when I flew with a trainee pilot of over eight hours, at the end of which our flaps failed (no problem), then the standby backup flap motor failed (also really no problem, but it was interesting), then came home to a yummy home-made pizza and Eli fell asleep without crying, the biggest 'wow' of the day."

Finally, Molly, our daughter with three young children, sent this email: "I picked the kids up from daycare, and Martha fell on the way to the car. She skinned her knee a little and started to cry and yell and scream at the top of her lungs … 'Mommy, mommy, I can't walk, my blood, my blood, scream, scream, I don't like this … scream, scream' as if she was about to die. Then I picked up Henry and put him in the car. Then he started to cry because he wanted to get in the car by himself. Then Charlotte started to cry, and I don't know why … maybe because her brother and sister were crying. So all three were crying at the top of their lungs. It lasted the entire way home, which was only five minutes, thank goodness, but at that moment I wish I was either at the dump, in the Sinai, or on a plane with failed flaps … anywhere but in the car with three screaming children."

A WORKING MOM

I am 38 years old, work full-time, and have three children under 6 years old. I knew once I started to have children that I wanted to continue to work, but I did not know if it would be possible after the second. I have found that working for a company that is supportive of working mothers made all the difference. The company I work for has an on-site daycare, run by Bright Horizons. After my second child was born, I went back to work when he was 12 weeks old. I was able to visit and nurse him during the day. I now have a third child and, again, went back to work when she was 12 weeks old and was also able to make daily visits. While some companies might think this is not being productive, I found that not having to worry during the day and do a few personal feedings helped me be extremely efficient at work.

I know a lot of women do not want to make the choice between family and career. Unfortunately, sometimes you need to if the company you work for is not supportive. A change I would want to make for working moms in the US is additional time for maternity leave. While the current FMLA entitlement is 12 work weeks of leave in a 12-month period for the birth of a child, I think adding four more weeks for a total of 16 weeks would encourage more moms to go back to work, should that be their choice.

Source: Molly Hyland, New Hampshire, US, 2013.

Balancing life outside of work and life at work is a major concern of most working professionals. It is also a major concern for working couples who, when working equally together, balance work and family to the benefit of both partners. Here we define balancing work and family "as the degree to which an individual is able to simultaneously balance the temporal, emotional, and behavioral demands of both paid work and family responsibilities."[41] Though, in the past, women were required to make a clear choice as to whether they wanted to have a career or a family, today a professional career and motherhood are no longer considered mutually exclusive, as the concept of fatherhood has also evolved.

Nevertheless, working mothers who are not married to men who partake equally in the family responsibilities tend to have to juggle two full-time jobs. When national cultural norms still promote a more traditional model of "parenthood," the work–family balance debate is relegated as an issue that women face. Even though, in some cases, this can conceal a male belief that household- and child-related work are primarily women's responsibilities,[42] it is also an issue that men face in an effort to find work–family balance.

A series of women were interviewed who were either middle or senior managers and who had recently become new mothers,[43] and all of the women interviewed stated that motherhood had given them a new perspective on their work, and that this was, in general, very positive. They also felt that motherhood had given them a new sense of confidence, enabling them to let their personalities become apparent in the workplace. Planning was critical to juggle the daily demands of family and work.

Nevertheless, many women, particularly in Europe and Asia, choose to take a break from professional work once they begin a family. Furthermore, more research should be done to look at how men balance work and family as well, for as long as the stereotype that caring for children and the home is an expected female role is encouraged worldwide, and relevant research tends to focus on women's attitudes toward work–family balance, this stereotype is reinforced.

Challenges faced with trying to balance work and family

It is certainly a strain to balance one's personal and professional responsibilities. In the US, for example, there is still a lingering belief that it is the woman's responsibility to take care of children. Separating work and family into two different domains tends to be found in current Western thinking, and it supports a popular myth that women can choose one or the other, but having both is extremely difficult—when, in reality, women have almost always worked and had families, and only the context has shifted and changed over the years.[44] In the US, many American businesses are addressing the bottom-line implications of employees' need for affordable and high-quality child and elder care. Wiley Harris of GE Capital Services states that "Every employee is important to our company's health, and when employees are distracted by family issues, we lose productivity."[45] The Family and Medical Leave Act of 1993 in the US was a response to concerns from men and women about being able to care for family members at critical life stages without the risk of job loss. Even with its enactment, the US continues to compare poorly with other developed countries such as France, Sweden, Canada, and Finland, where family care is institutionalized.

Research on work–family balance

Lately, research on work–family balance started to include things like "positive spillover, balance, interface, mutual facilitation," and can incorporate an international perspective.[46] For example, in Chinese society, where work and family are seen as interdependent,[47] and roles tend to be more nebulous, work is seen as having a long-term benefit for the family. Furthermore, the Maoist ideology of gender equality and the one-child-per-family *policy* have greatly contributed to women's promotion and motivation in the workplace, with them no longer having to focus on finding daycare.[48] However, Chinese Confucian principles of governance and morality still result in women being seen by some as less than men.[49] That being said, however, Chen et al.'s study[50] found that Chinese women's work motivation was just as high as that of Chinese men, and managerial motivation was found to be positively related to the hierarchical job level. Among their findings was that intrinsic motivation, standing out from the group, and exercising power might be factors that enable women to supersede negative work-related prejudices about work–family dynamics that could hamper job advancement.

In Europe, a study[51] of managers from 20 different EU countries analyzed the intersection of, and among, the following three variables: (1) the degree of each country's national gender equality; (2) the degree of organizational support for work–family balance; and (3) individual qualities, such as individual managers' work–family balance characteristics. This study noted correctly that a country's national gender equality and context are very relevant. Work–family balance can be supported by national government regulations and programs, such as Sweden's policy on subsidized childcare programs and required parental leave.

Furthermore, it was found that organizations are more likely to follow through if their external environment enforces compliance, thus reflecting the relationship between national context and organizational practice. This study underscored how important national context is to gender equality in the areas of parents being able to have work–life balance; and women's life expectancy, education, and standard of living. Overall, parents who have positive work–family balance tend to be more satisfied with their job, are more committed to their organization, and are more satisfied with their family dynamics as well.[52]

In many European countries, states provide childcare support and have national programs to facilitate work–family balance; in the US, the individual employers are expected to be the principal purveyor of family assistance, even though they often feel it is not their responsibility but the family's.[53] However, these programs of the employers are successful only if top management are committed to their implementation.[54] A very recent study[55] of US personnel analyzed supervisors' perceptions of family–work conflict and the ability to balance expectations of both, through investigating two aspects of promotability: (1) the manager's perceptions of the promotability of their employees; and (2) employee statements of whether they had been nominated for promotion or not. They[56] found that managers had the propensity to pigeonhole women as the gender that experienced more work–family conflict, even after the researchers controlled for family responsibilities and the women's own perceptions of work–family balance. The main contribution of this study is the finding that even though women's work–family conflict may impact their career progress, the perceptions of their work–family conflict that their superiors may have can also influence their career advancement, and these perceptions can unwittingly create the "glass ceiling" effect.

THE GLASS CEILING

The "glass ceiling" refers to barriers to reaching the upper echelons of organizations. These barriers to the advancement of women and minorities are often very subtle. For example, a very interesting study[57] in 2008 looked at HR personnel records of a *Fortune* 500 company from 1967 to 1993, drawing a random sample of more than 5,000 managers of both genders. After dividing the sample into four work levels (entry, middle, upper-middle, and upper), the analysis revealed that women tended to be hired at lower levels and lower salaries than their male complement, and were more likely to be located in support positions. The result was that women were less likely to be on the path to the top of the organization, and even by 1993, while 40 percent of the women hired were in entry-level positions, in the higher echelons they were only 20 percent of middle managers, and 10 percent of the upper-middle and upper levels.

Other research[58] has found that there are subtleties that influence the "glass ceiling" barriers, which consist of gender stereotypes, a deficiency of opportunities for women to acquire the necessary work experience and knowledge to excel, a scarcity of top management dedication to initiatives for gender equality and equal opportunity, and a male wealth stereotype that men deserve greater salaries than women.[59]

Exhibit 5.4 presents the findings of research about women and wages worldwide. It provides us with one way to understand the impact of female worker wage proportion relative to men, with *special attention* to merit pay and strikes, on payment within and across organizations and occupations. This interesting study concluded that many employees are underpaid relative to their country's level of wealth, and points toward sociopsychological forces that impact economic compensation.

EXHIBIT 5.4 A STUDY OF WOMEN AND WAGES WORLDWIDE

■ 59 countries that had estimates for wages from a World Economic Forum Global Competitive Report were included in the study. The survey measured the perceptions of 3,934 government officials and senior business leaders working in these 59 countries.

■ The factors used to determine the objective size of the gender contrast (the national proportion of working women) included the country's:

- overall male/female ratio (0.52 in Qatar $< x <$ 1.19 in Latvia);
- fertility rate (1.2 in Italy $< x <$ 7.6 in Yemen);
- economic growth rate (?0.09 in Georgia $< x <$ 0.09 in China);
- socioeconomic necessity of families having a dual income; and
- war and emigration.

Findings

1 Workers in countries with larger proportions of working women *were found to be underpaid.*

2 Neither payroll taxes, merit pay, nor strikes could substitute working women as the main predictor of underpayment; *however*, they did appear to account partially, in a curvilinear fashion, for *this* underpayment.

3 Both previous results appeared to be driven by the following economic and sociopsychological forces:

a. The proportion of working women is a demographic and sociopsychological factor.

b. Underpayment across countries with little merit pay or strikes can be tied to men's higher status relative to women.

c. Underpayment across countries where merit pay or strikes are more common can be better tied to the absence of salient gender contrasts.

Source: Van de Vliert, E. and Van der Vegt, G. "Women and Wages Worldwide: How the National Proportion of Working Women Brings Underpayment into the Organization," *Organization Studies*, Vol. 25, No. 6, 2004, pp. 969–986.

COMPANY INITIATIVES TO BREAK THE GLASS CEILING

Most companies have put into place specific programs to assist in breaking down barriers impeding a woman's progression. Many include a combination of flexible work arrangements, mentoring, women's support groups, and leadership development. Various companies have also developed support and structures designed to advance women.

Quality management models: audits

Even though a lot of research, conferences, meetings, and workshops have been conducted in the area of gender and diversity, and there are an increasing number of qualified and career-oriented women in industry, there appears to still be limited progress within industry in Europe. This is because, in Europe, resistance is found through low commitment by top managers, weak gender or diversity marketing campaigns, and no incentives or systemic planned methods to improve the diversity and gender policy.[60] In order to improve processes such that women in corporations become a source of productivity and high performance, audits help to provide documented, systemic examination of this topic, and can assist industry to improve its gender-related policies. Rather than looking simply at the number of men or women involved in an industry, audits help to examine the contributions of different areas and groups within that industry. Audits help to provide instruments to verify management and information on the efficiency of a company's performance, and provide mechanisms to display how strategic decisions play out, as well as a benchmark to compare with other companies.[61]

A tracking system

Accenture was the winner of the "2003 Catalyst Award for Innovative Programs to Help Women Advance in the Workplace." Accenture developed a global "Great Place to Work for Women" initiative, and uses a variety of innovative processes such as geographic scorecards, global surveys, and performance appraisals to guarantee that company leadership remains accountable for the initiative's results. Joe Forehand, Accenture's chairman and CEO, states:

> Empowerment without opportunity is useless. At Accenture, we've focused on fostering a more inclusive work environment. Our Great Place to Work for Women program is one way we're enabling women to take charge of their careers and move into broader leadership roles.[62]

A support structure: mentoring programs

IBM, 3M, and many other companies have women's networks in place to help promote women's careers. Apparently, one-third of all *Fortune* 100 companies have such networks aimed at developing skills, building careers, and supporting women. Research has demonstrated that mentoring is a critical part of career success. Mentoring is defined as

> a cooperative and nurturing relationship between a more experienced businessperson and a less experienced person who wants to learn about a particular business and gain valuable insight into some of the unspoken subtleties of doing business.[63]

Many experts claim that it is beneficial to have more than one mentor present within an organization, and that these mentors should be at different levels. Mentoring comes into play at crucial points in an individual's career and can be an effective source of advice and encouragement.

Men and women seem to view mentoring in different ways.[64] It is often more difficult for women than men to find appropriate mentors. Many websites have popped up in the past few years offering women the opportunity to network with each other in a nontraditional setting. The US Small Business Administration has set up a specific program, open to all women, specifically focused on helping women entrepreneurs and those considering becoming entrepreneurs.

Work still to be done

Although women have achieved significant advances since entering the workplace, much remains to be done for women to be considered as qualified and talented as men. Companies need to take more responsibilities and initiatives to fully integrate women into their environments at all levels of the corporate hierarchy. Companies that champion diversity champion women. Some issues to consider include the following:

- *Increasing the flow of information and educating women about current issues*. It is only with concrete facts and information about women's position in the workplace that any calibration of gains can be measured. Catalyst,[65] a nonprofit organization focused on women's issues in the workplace, has taken a wonderful role in initiating this process. When women appreciate where they have been and understand the issues that confront them, they can see and decide where the future lies.
- *Demonstrating* CEO *commitment*. As the corporate leader, the CEO has the most significant influence on the direction and vision of the firm. It is through her or his direction that a "persistent campaign of incremental changes that discover and destroy the deeply embedded roots of discrimination" will occur.[66]
- *Closing the pay gap*. A true merit system distinguishes individuals on the basis of their effort and skills, and rewards each person for his or her work, regardless of gender. Men and women work equally hard in the same positions; their pay should reflect this equality.
- *Increasing recruitment, providing training opportunities, and placing women in high-profile positions*. Companies should step-up their efforts to recruit and train qualified women, and ensure that more women get access to "line" positions versus being immediately segmented into "staff" positions.

  Recruiting the right potential very much depends on the individual employer attractiveness. Besides challenging projects and job security, equality and family-friendly policy belong to the most important motivation factors. This means that

... for a company, it is a must to implement gender mainstreaming activities within the concept of high-qualified diversity management.[67]

What it's really like to work in Hollywood (if you are not a straight, white man)[68]

The statistics tell a story. Women and minorities are underrepresented in front of and behind the camera.

The following are quotes from Hollywood folks interviewed for the article.

I didn't speak Spanish [growing up]. I'm ninth generation. I mean, I'm as American as apple pie. I'm very proud of my heritage. But I remember moving to L. A. and auditioning and not being Latin enough for certain roles. Some white male casting director was dictating what it meant to be Latin. He decided I needed an accent. He decided I should [have] darker-colored skin. The gatekeepers are not usually people of color, so they don't understand you should be looking for way more colors of the rainbow within that one ethnicity.

Eva Longoria, star, director, producer, *Telenovela*

I never saw people like me on television in the States (after working in Shanghai). It was very difficult [to get representation in the 1980s]. Someone told me the Bessie Loo Agency represented all the Asians–James Hong was there, Beulah Quo. There were a couple of people playing butlers, maids. [The agent] probably thought I was telling fairy tales when I told him I won best actress in China.

Joan Chen, actress, *Twin Peaks*, *Marco Polo*

I remember my first meeting with the producers on "Erin Brockovich," before Steven Soderbergh came onto it, and saying, "This scene where she's shimmying down a well in a micromini? I can't do that." [They said], "But that's really what happened." And I go, "I know, but once you make it a movie, you have to re-examine, what's the function of this scene?" I didn't feel I was being fully understood. People assumed it was about my sense of modesty. And you just think, "No, you're not hearing what I'm saying." Steven and I were very in sync on how we wanted to portray her–the sexiness as well as the soul–and I didn't have to wear a micromini shimmying down a well.

Julia Roberts, actress, *Money Monster*

We once had a meeting with a guy. I won't say the company. [She and I were] dressed to the nines. We talked about sports, politics, everything, and this man had the nerve to say, "When is your manager going to get here?" because he expected some middle-aged white guy. I [charged] him 10 times more than I was going to.

Shakim Comere, manager of Queen Latifah and producing partner

If [a script doesn't specify, a role is] presumed to be white and male. For "Deep Impact," Mimi Leder, the director, wanted to cast Morgan as the president, and somebody at the studio said, "We're not making a science-fiction movie; you can't have Morgan Freeman play the president." But she really fought for it.

> Lori McReary, producing partner with Morgan Freeman, president, Producers Guild of America

[On *Carrie*], I got half my salary. It's happened twice. I have a quote, and they said, "We'll give you half. Take it or leave it." They know, if you like something, you are willing to take less money. And that's not great for you, or women, but it's still better—every movie I make, it still matters. At the end of the year, they're like, how many [of the top 100] movies were made by women in the system, and that year it was two. Me and "Frozen."

> Kimberly Peirce

I can't tell you how many arguments I have on sets where the filmmakers want my wardrobe to be different, and I'll say, "Why don't you have [the male co-star] take his shirt off?" With love scenes, the camera angle is from the man's point of view. All of that absolutely infuriates me.

> Jurnee Smollett-Bell, actress, *Underground*

My very first audition ever, I was about 16, and the casting director [for a commercial] said, "Can you do it again but sound more Latino?" I had no idea what she was talking about. "You mean you want me to speak in Spanish?" She's like, "No. Do it in English but just sound more Latino." I genuinely didn't realize until later that she was asking me to speak English with a broken accent. It confused me, because I thought, I am Latino, so isn't this what a Latino sounds like? From the get-go of my career, I thought, there's a certain box or a certain way that you're seen, which I didn't feel growing up.

> America Ferrera

WOMEN AND OVERSEAS, EXPATRIATE ASSIGNMENTS

Women's representation in the global arena has grown (albeit slowly) to 17 percent of the expatriate population, though in some industry sections the percentage is considerably higher.[69] Although the percentage of women expatriates is rising, many companies fail to send women overseas, in particular to areas of the world where the demarcation between male and female roles is clearly defined. Global women managers often talk about the "double-take" or stares they receive in Asia, South America, or the Middle East when they are first introduced. For example, in Latin America, women report having been mistaken for the wife or the secretary during important high-level business meetings and social events.

However, most women who were sent abroad say that the first reaction of surprise is quickly replaced by professionalism and respect.

The expatriate glass ceiling (the glass border)

In multinational companies, a foreign assignment is often the stepping stone to a higher-level management position. A recent study[70] found that employees who exhibited greater personal agency and had fewer family obligations were more willing to go on expatriate assignments, search for expatriate jobs, and leave their home countries. This same study found that women with partners and/or children were most restrained in their willingness to expatriate. Even with willingness to expatriate, there is still a strong disparity between the number of male and female managers, not only in home-country operations, but also in expatriate assignments.[71] This expatriate "glass ceiling" has three implications: (1) there is a greater challenge to filling expatriate assignments as, nowadays, men often opt out because of family and dual-career concerns; (2) a lack of diversity of the top management group can lead to homogeneity, and thus weaker leadership decision-making; and (3) if lower-level women feel that the opportunity is limited, they may be less motivated to compete for higher-level jobs.[72]

Breaking the glass border to succeed in an expatriate assignment

From 2000 on, women's participation in international assignments has been on the rise; data from Europe, Australia, and the US have found a rise of 16.5 percent of women in expatriate assignments between 2000 and 2005.[73] Nevertheless, there is an underrepresentation of women on international assignments.

> These barriers are informed, predicated, and reinforced by organizational and societal conventions, including the lack of women mentors and role models, the weakness of female organizational networking, and lack of social support that influence promotion to, and acceptance at, the top.[74]

Breaking this ceiling requires concerted corporate programs, as well as determined efforts by women, to actively engage in self-promotion and networking.

Three strategies are recommended[75] to assist women to advance toward top-level positions and into foreign assignments. (1) *Preassignment strategies*: It is recommended that women be proactive agents of change in their own career, and recognize their cultural values that might influence their behavior. Companies should reevaluate and change policies and procedures related to selection, training, and repatriation of female expatriates. They should improve the training of the selection's decision-makers as well, to avoid anti-women bias, while assisting couples who have dual careers to collectively manage both their careers so that a woman can take an international assignment. (2) *On-assignment strategies*: It is recommended for women to proactively find a mentor and take advantage of reverse learning and hindsight. Companies should match assignments to assist with the expatriate adjustment, and continue training and mentoring programs. (3) *Post-assignment strategies*: It is recommended for women to volunteer to be a mentor. Doing so, they also take responsibility to manage their own career. Companies should have women who were on assignments internationally become mentors for future female expatriates.

When many women have been nominated for an international business assignment in what the company thought would be a hostile culture, most of these women have succeeded with flying colors. Why? Because expatriate women are not expected to behave according to the same social guidelines as natives of that particular culture, and women can be "especially adept at cross-cultural management skills because they use behavior patterns emphasizing sensitivity, communication skills, community, and relationships. This personal orientation is valuable in globalization."[76] Women are often seen as foreigners first, and thus can be beholden to different rules of conduct than the local women. Here are some words of advice for women to help lay the groundwork:[77]

1   *Establish credibility.* Have strong support from senior management in the organization, and make sure that your expertise is communicated to the destination location.
2   *Have a higher-ranking person* who knows the people in the culture with whom you will be working, and talk openly about your credentials.
3   *Present yourself* as sincere, professional, and confident.
4   *Act reserved* with male colleagues (and formal).
5   *Wear tasteful, conservative clothing*, especially in male hierarchical cultures.
6   *Express your opinions* politely, diplomatically, and tactfully.

The difficulties that women may encounter when working on a foreign assignment depend to a certain extent on the social and economic context of the country in which they are conducting business, and on the individuals with whom they come into contact. Both the woman international manager and the company she represents can take steps to minimize any negative aspects.

■   *Companies and managers should lay the groundwork.* Do not surprise a client. While this recommendation is not only specific to a foreign assignment, before any meeting, regardless of the gender of the participants, it is important to provide adequate information about the agenda and who will be present.
■   *Practice what is preached.* If a corporation empowers women managers and treats them equally and seriously in business dealings abroad, it should ensure that women are also treated equally and fairly in the organization. Success begins at home.
■   *Consider both women and men for international positions.* Do not rely on the assumption that women will not want to accept the position.
■   *Provide proper cross-cultural training and preparation courses.* Training is vital to all managers to be successful abroad. Specific assistance should also include what to

expect from male superiors, peers, clients, and subordinates, and how to handle uncomfortable situations, such as discrimination.

■ *Be realistic.* Women managers abroad suffer from the same culture shock as men. It is important to keep expectations reasonable, build trust, and create professional relationships.

HOW HAVE SEVERAL SPECIFIC WOMEN SUCCEEDED? ARE THEY GOING ABOUT BUSINESS DIFFERENTLY?

Selected women managers' views

The August 5, 1996, edition of *Fortune* ran an article titled "Women, Sex, and Power." Contrary to what the title might suggest, the article focused on seven women who are the best of the best in their fields of business. Among these were Charlotte Beers (Ogilvy & Mather) and Jill Barad (Mattel). These women are part of the new female elite who are changing the way women reach the top. The following recommendations are still relevant today:

■ *Have confidence in yourself.* In the past, many women felt obliged to hide their femininity so as to be seen as managers first and women second. Many women in today's business world no longer view their sexuality as a hindrance. Despite the fact that the office is often still male-dominated, they are no longer attempting to become more male-like or androgynous in order to be promoted.

■ *Survive and overcome difficult working conditions.* Most women, especially of older generations, have had to face discrimination from men and women alike. Charlotte Beers remembers: "Early in my career, during my first week at J. Walter Thomson in Chicago, I had a secretary who asked the company for a transfer. She told me, 'No offense, but I want to work for a man who's going to move ahead.'" The story goes that two years later, the secretary, impressed by Beers' stellar career path, asked to come back, and Beers, who liked her honesty, accepted.[78] Many successful businesswomen have had to overcome adverse working conditions and have been able to build their careers during these tough moments.

■ *Do things differently.* Many women are successful by incorporating aspects of their personality into their work or by daring to do things differently. In the end, many of them drastically change the way business in their field is done. Linda Marcelli, of Merrill Lynch, started selling stocks by setting up personal meetings instead of cold calling. Anita Roddick was an international hit with her "Body Shop" that brought environmental consciousness to a new level.

■ *Have your own leadership style—neither "feminine" nor "masculine."* Women are often described as having a more "open" approach to management, relying on consensus building as opposed to the old style of command and control. Recent research demonstrates that women and men executives in similar positions demonstrate more similar behaviors than dissimilar. This research has shown that "Women who have made it into senior positions are in most respects indistinguishable from the men in equivalent positions. In fact, the similarities between women and men far outweigh the differences between women and men as groups."[79]

Many women are concerned that the debate as to whether men and women exhibit different leadership styles continues to perpetuate typical stereotypes of women as "soft" managers. As Adler and Izraeli point out, managers (male and female) in the US have tended to identify stereotypically "masculine" (aggressive) characteristics as managerial and stereotypically "feminine" (cooperative and communicative) characteristics as unmanagerial.[80]

More and more companies are assertively trying to advance women's issues. "Woman-friendly" companies have been proven to provide a more beneficial environment to both *men* and *women*.[81]

Changes for women–even in Saudi Arabia

In the February 2016 issue of *National Geographic*,[82] some of the many changes for women in Saudi Arabia are highlighted with text and pictures.

Consider the following statistics:

1   In 1999, 30 percent of school-age girls attended. In 2014, 99 percent of girls attend.
2   In 1994, 89,448 men were enrolled in a Bachelor's degree program and 68,959 women were enrolled. In 2014, 581,136 men versus 624,322 women were enrolled.
3   In 2015, women comprised 22 percent of the labor market.

This is progress for women, but still there is significant gender segregation, and there is much women cannot do: they may not drive a car; a woman cannot have any physical contact with a man who is not her husband, her father, her uncle, or her brother; and women must wear an abaya, the ankle-length fully covering garment. The religious police are not always obvious, but they are present.

Women in Saudi Arabia cannot vote, nor can they in Vatican City, but in Saudi Arabia they will soon. The struggle for Saudi Arabia is for women to be truly modern and at the same time truly Saudi. They are making progress, but slowly.

CONCLUSIONS

Careful observation reveals a rapidly increasing number of countries and companies moving away, for the first time, from their historical men-only pattern of senior leadership. The question is no longer "is the pattern changing?" but rather "which companies will take advantage of the trend, and which will fall behind?" Which companies and countries will lead in recognizing and understanding the talents that women bring to leadership, and which will limit their potential by clinging to historic men-only patterns?[83]

Depending on the country, different societal forces have contributed to increasing female presence in high-level positions within corporations. Women in the US have benefited from affirmative action and equal opportunity laws that hold employers accountable for promoting women. In Germany, women are becoming increasingly present in the political arena. Nevertheless, despite recent progress in most countries, women's advancement in the business arena has been steady but slow. As we move further into the twenty-first century, companies will need to increasingly reflect this diversity in all levels of their workforce.

The problem of how to get women into those positions of great importance throughout the enterprise still remains. Numerous barriers still exist for women across the globe. Women have made incredible advances, yet one of their next great challenges will be to assure proportional representation in senior management positions. A strong business imperative can be made that companies who do not address the needs of their women employees (as well as employees of minority cultures) in terms of recruiting, promotion, and career development will suffer the following long-term consequences:

■ not being viewed as an employer of choice;
■ undervaluing top performers; therefore, not using employees' full potential; and
■ losing a competitive edge.

In today's competitive world, ignoring the potential of the greatest (in number and in potential) group of your workforce is more than just an oversight—it is extremely costly.

We end this chapter with a recommendation to read *Lean In* by Sheryl Sandberg.[84] She has, in her book, both valuable information on the place of women in the political and business world and the challenges for both women and men in the roles of men and women today and in the future.

She states:

Of the 195 independent countries in the world, only 17 are led by women.
Of the Fortune 500 CEOs, only 21 are women.
A truly equal world would be one where women ran half our countries and companies and men ran half our homes.

MIND STRETCHING

The most important determinant of a country's competitiveness is its human talent—the skills, education, and productivity of its workforce. Women account for one-half of the potential talent base throughout the world and, therefore, over time, a nation's competitiveness depends significantly on whether and how it educates and utilizes its female talent.[85]

1   What are the expectations of the role of women in your culture?
2   What are the stereotypes about women that are believed and communicated in your culture?
3   What is your personal view of men and women's role:
    ■   in relationships?
    ■   in family?
    ■   in business?
    ■   in politics?
4   How do your personal views of men and your personal views of women influence how you relate to, communicate with, and interact with men and women in each of the above contexts?
5   What are the specific issues women may experience in business in specific countries in North America, Central America, South America, Europe, Asia, the Middle East, and Africa?
6   What are some methods to address negative gender stereotypes, and redefine them such that they are changed into positives?
7   How does religion influence the expected role of men and women?

NOTES

1   www.cia.gov/library/publications/the-world-factbook/geos/xx.html# People (retrieved February 4, 2010).
2   Van de Vliert, E. and Van der Vegt, G. "Women and Wages Worldwide: How the National Proportion of Working Women Brings Underpayment into the Organization," *Organization Studies*, Vol. 25, No. 6, 2004, pp. 969–986.
3   Ibid.
4   House, K. E. *On Saudi Arabia*. New York: Alfred A. Knox, 2012.
5   Kung, H. "A Vatican Spring," *New York Times*, February 28, 2013.
6   "Rape and Murder in Delhi," *The Economist*, January 5, 2013.
7   Kristof, N. D. "Is Delhi So Different from Steubenville?" *New York Times*, January 13, 2013.
8   Ahamari, S. "The Woman Who Dared to Drive," *Wall Street Journal*, March 2, 2013.
9   Rubin, A. "Painful Payment for Afghan Debt of 'Alissa Rubin,'" *New York Times*, April 1, 2013.
10 *USA Today*, April 30, 2013.
11 Halpern, D. and Cheung, F. *Women at the Top: Powerful Leaders Tell Us How to Combine Work and Family*. Malden, MA: Wiley-Blackwell, 2008.
12 Ibid.
13 Ibid.
14 "Arab Women Rights, Some Say They Don't Want Them," *The Economist*, March 27, 2010, p. 53.
15 Ibid., p. 171.

16 Meyerson, D. E. and Fletcher, J. K. "A Modest Manifesto for Shattering the Glass Ceiling," in S. A. Hewlett and C. B. Luce (eds.), *Harvard Business Review on Women in Business*. Boston, MA: Harvard Business School Press, 2005, pp. 69–94.

17 Ibid., p. 70.

18 Ibid., p. 94.

19 "Female Power," *The Economist*, January, 2, 2010, pp. 49–51.

20 Renard, T. S. *New York Times*, February 23, 2013.

21 "Britons 'Accept' Pay Sexism," *BBC News*, February 28, 2006, www.newsvote.bbc.co.uk/1/hi/business/3038394.stm.

22 "Most Powerful Women in Business, the Power 50: Why Are Some Women More Successful in Some Countries Than in Others?" *Fortune*, September 27, 2002.

23 www.AdvancingWomen2003.org.

24 Clark, N. "Getting Women into Boardrooms, by Law," *The International Herald Tribune*, Thursday, January 28, 2010, p. 1.

25 "We Did It!" *The Economist*, January 2, 2010, p. 7.

26 Clark, "Getting Women into Boardrooms."

27 Ibid., p. 9.

28 Halpern and Cheung, *Women at the Top.*

29 Tyler, J. and McCullough, J. "Violating Prescriptive Stereotypes on Job Resumes: A Self-Presentational Perspective," *Management Communication Quarterly*, Vol. 23, No. 2, 2009, pp. 272–287.

30 Ibid., p. 273.

31 Mihail, D. "Gender-Based Stereotypes in the Workplace: The Case of Greece," *Equal Opportunities International*, Vol. 25, No. 5, 2006, pp. 373–388.

32 Glanton, E. "Pay Gap Endures at Highest Levels," *AP News*, womenconnect.com, November 10, 1998.

33 Glass Ceiling Commission. "Good Business: Making Full Use of the Nation's Human Capital," The Glass Ceiling Fact-Finding Report, 1995.

34 "She Works, He Doesn't," *Newsweek*, May 12, 2003.

35 Catalyst 2002 Census of Women Corporate Officers and Top Earners of the *Fortune* 500.

36 "Britons 'Accept' Pay Sexism."

37 "The Conundrum of the 'Glass Ceiling,'" *The Economist*, July 23, 2005, pp. 63–65.

38 Adler, N. and Izraeli, D. "Where in the World Are the Women Executives?" *Business Quarterly*, London, 1994.

39 Wernick, E. "Preparedness, Career Advancement, and the 'Glass Ceiling,'" Glass Ceiling Commission, May 1994.

40 Young, G. "Women, Naturally Better Leaders for the 21st Century," White Paper, 2016.

41 Lyness, K. and Kropf, M. "The Relationships of National Gender Equality and Organizational Support with Work–Family Balance: A Study of European Managers," *Human Relations*, Vol. 58, No. 1, 2005, pp. 33–60.

42 Yegisu, C. "Can Men Stomach Marrying Wealthier Women?" *Daily News and Economic Review*, Istanbul, January 23–24, 2010, p. 10.

43 Tanton, M. *Women in Management: A Developing Presence*, London: Routledge, 1994, p. 82.

44 Halpern and Cheung, *Women at the Top*, p. 176.

45 www.pathfinder.com/ParentTime/workfamily/workcare.html.

46 Halpern and Cheung, *Women at the Top*, p. 176.

47 Ibid.

48 Chen, C., Yu, K., and Miner, J. "Motivation to Manage: A Study of Women in Chinese State-Owned Enterprises," *Journal of Applied Behavioral Science*, Vol. 33, No. 2, 1997, pp. 160–173.

49 Ibid.

50 Ibid.

51 Lyness and Kropf, "The Relationships of National Gender Equality."
52 Carlson, D., Grzywacz, J., and Zivnuska, S. "Is Work–Family Balance More than Conflict and Enrichment," *Human Relations*, Vol. 62, No. 10, 2009, pp. 1459–1486.
53 Halpern and Cheung, *Women at the Top*.
54 Ibid.
55 Hoobler, J., Wayne, S., and Lemmon, G. "Bosses' Perceptions of Family–Work Conflict and Women's Promotability: 'Glass Ceiling' Effects," *Academy of Management Journal*, Vol. 52, No. 5, 2009, pp. 939–957.
56 Ibid.
57 Wyld, D. "How Do Women Fare When the Promotion Rules Change?" *Academy of Management Perspectives*, Vol. 22, No. 4, 2008, pp. 83–85.
58 Bell, M., McLaughlin, M., and Sequeira, J. "Discrimination, Harassment, and the 'Glass Ceiling': Women Executives as Change Agents," *Journal of Business Ethics*, Vol. 37, 2002, pp. 65–76.
59 Williams, M., Paluck, E., and Spencer-Rodgers, J. "The Masculinity of Money: Automatic Stereotypes Predict Gender Differences in Estimated Salaries," *Psychology of Women Quarterly*, Vol. 34, 2010, pp. 7–20.
60 Domsch, M. "Quality Management in Gender and Diversity: The Role of Auditing," In European Commission, *Women in Science and Technology: The Business Perspective*. Brussels: European Communities, 2006, pp. 37–47.
61 Ibid.
62 Catalyst 2002 Census of Women Corporate Officers and Top Earners of the *Fortune* 500.
63 www.advancingwomen.com.
64 Karsten, M. F. *Management and Gender: Issues and Attitudes*. Westport, CT: Praeger Publishers, 1994.
65 Catalyst 2002 Census of Women Corporate Officers and Top Earners of the *Fortune* 500.
66 Meyerson, D. E. and Fletcher, J. K. "A Modest Manifesto for Shattering the 'Glass Ceiling,'" *Harvard Business Review on Women in Business*, January/February, 2005, p. 70.
67 Domsch, "Quality Management in Gender and Diversity."
68 *New York Times*, February 28, 2016. Arts and Leisure, pp. 14–18.
69 Solomon, C. M. *Women Managers in the Global Workplace: Success Through Intercultural Understanding*. Arlington, VA: Mobility, 2006.
70 Tharenou, P. "Disruptive Decisions to Leave Home: Gender and Family Differences in Expatriation Choices," *Organizational Behavior and Human Decision Processes*, Vol. 105, 2008, pp. 183–200.
71 Inch, G., McIntyre, N., and Napier, N. "The Expatriate 'Glass Ceiling': The Second Layer of Glass," *Journal of Business Ethics*, Vol. 83, 2008, pp. 19–28.
72 Ibid.
73 Altman, Y. and Shortland, S. "Women and International Assignments: Taking Stock–A 25-Year Review," *Human Resource Management*, Vol. 47, No. 2, 2008, pp. 199–216.
74 Ibid., p. 207.
75 Inch et al., "The Expatriate 'Glass Ceiling.'"
76 Adler, N. J. *Organizational Behavior*, 3rd edn. Cincinnati, OH: South-Western Publishing, 1997, pp. 308–309.
77 Adler, N. J. *International Dimensions of Organizational Behavior*, 4th edn. New York: South-Western Publishing/Thomson Learning, 2002.
78 "Women, Sex and Power," *Fortune*, August 5, 1996.
79 Wajcman, J. *Managing Like a Man*. University Park, PA: Pennsylvania State University Press, 1998.
80 Adler, N. J. and Izraeli, D. J. (eds.). *Women in Management Worldwide*. London: M.E. Sharpe, 1988, pp. 20–24.
81 Wilkof, M. V. "Is Your Company and Its Culture Women-Friendly?" *Journal for Quality and Participation*, Vol. 18, No. 3, p. 66.

82 Gorney, C. *National Geographic*, February 2016.

83 Adler, *International Dimensions of Organizational Behavior*, pp. 173–174.

84 Sandberg, S. *Lean In: Women, Work, and the Will to Lead*. New York: Knopf Publishing Group, 2013.

85 Tesfachew, T., Zahidi, S., and Ibarra, H. "Measuring the Corporate Gender Gap," in S. Zahidi and H. Ibarra (eds.), *The Corporate Gender Gap Report 2010*. Geneva: World Economic Forum, 2010. www.weforum.org/pdf/gendergap/ corporate2010.pdf (retrieved April 27, 2010).

6 MOTIVATING THE GLOBAL WORKFORCE
The case for diversity and inclusion

Diversity in the world is a basic characteristic of human society, and also the key condition for a lively and dynamic world as we see today.

Hu Jintao[1]

It is not competition that is the most frequent and important factor in the ability to survive and evolve; rather it is cooperation and mutual aid. . . . [There is] an ongoing tension between what is good for the individual and what is good for others and society.

David W. Johnson[2]

After reading and studying the concepts, examples, and illustrations in Chapter 6, readers should be able to understand and appreciate:

1   Greater levels of problem-solving and decision-making diversity improve perform-ance outcomes by increasing amounts of relevant information.

2   The many sources of diversity include cultural, business functional, geographical areas, sex, gender identity, and hierarchical level, as well as others. Recently, immigration has become a controversial source of diversity, especially in the European Union. Immigration has always been a source of diversity in the US and Canada.

3   Diversity is only a source of improved problem-solving performance when it is tightly and successfully integrated.

4   Bartlett and Ghoshal[3] have identified three integration mechanisms—legitimizing, information coordination, and shared vision—that integrate diversity and improve the foreign market performance of MNEs.

5   Johnson[4] and others have demonstrated that cooperative goal interdependence, producing constructive controversy within problem-solving groups, is the most effective means of integrating problem-solving diversity.

6   Cooperative goal interdependence may produce concurrence seeking, rather than constructive controversy. Concurrence seeking is a less effective mecha-nism for integrating diversity.

7   Readers will learn to identify the characteristics of both, and how to deliberately build cooperative goal interdependence and constructive controversy.

INTRODUCTION

Most executives state that the effective utilization of the talents of all employees is the orga-nization's greatest asset. This has been viewed as more challenging for multinational enter-prises (MNEs) with an increasing multicultural workforce. "In recent years, diversity management has been considered both an issue of employment relations and an issue for all sections of the organization, from financing and accounting to customer relations and from strategy to marketing."[5] To unleash the talent and potential of this changing workforce, companies and governments are assessing their organizational systems to capitalize on the benefits of a diverse workforce and clientele.

In the field of knowledge management, it has been widely acknowledged that having greater relevant problem-solving and decision-making differentiation, or diversity, is a competitive advantage. This is especially the case for highly complex and uncertain international business competitive environments.[6] Diversity in the forms of culture, age, gender, race/ethnicity, nationality, personality, values, and attitudes[7] provide greater awareness of, and openness to, potentially relevant information. This additional information generally produces better decisions in complex environments than those achieved by more homogeneous decision-makers.[8]

The main issue for achieving these problem-solving advantages is that diversity must be strongly integrated within work groups. Diversity increases the forces of divergence and disagreement, potentially resulting in greater levels of conflict and lower social integration. People tend to be more attracted to working with others who share similar values and attitudes, and tend to be less attracted to those they regard as outsiders, that is, different from themselves in important ways.[9] Under conditions of conflict, groups tend to break apart along their lines of diversity and compete for primacy unless they are strongly integrated. Bartlett and Beamish argued that the task of integrating diverse capabilities across an MNE was a more important one than developing a corporate strategy based on taking advantage of that diversity.[10]

The purpose of this chapter is threefold. First, it makes the case for why cultural diversity is an important competitive advantage for business organizations. Second, it reviews the potential sources of useful diversity. Third, and most importantly, it discusses the critical question of how to integrate cultural diversity so as to achieve diversity's benefits, because without effective integration, homogeneity may result in better outcomes. The evidence supports the management adage: "Differentiation + Integration = Performance (D + I = P)." However, even within effective integration mechanisms, there are better and worse. Having cooperative goals within a diverse group is essential for effective integration, but diverse perspectives must be able to challenge each other, and even come into conflict, in order to learn from each other. "Constructive controversy," allowing and facilitating diverse perspectives to debate, is more effective than "concurrence seeking" in which conflict is disallowed and groups tend to settle on majority positions without exploring minority perspectives.[11]

In this context, global leadership itself is considered as a powerful integrator of differentiation and diversity. Ethical, visionary, and even situational leadership are all organizational processes intended to facilitate the greatest expression of the maximum potential of each employee. Leadership integrates human resources into a common purpose despite their differences.

CULTURAL DIVERSITY COMPETITIVE ADVANTAGES

Knowledge management has been considered a potential source of competitive advantage in international business and comparative management since the times of Lawrence and Lorsch.[12] They observed that increasing amounts of problem-solving and decision-making differentiation helped MNEs to "bridge unavoidable differences among cultures."

Later, Lawrence and Dyer[13] argued that the environmental uncertainty characteristic of international markets produced high levels of information complexity so that it was more difficult to plan an effective course of action than in domestic markets. As information complexity increased, the amount of information needed to make informed decisions also increased. The most effective response that an MNE could make was to increase its problem-solving and decision-making diversity, thereby increasing the capacity to learn (see Chapter 3).

MNEs could increase diversity by including, in its decision-making, managers tasked with global, regional, local, product, and functional roles. Headquarters' managers would have the global perspective of the entire company. In American MNEs especially, it is common even for headquarters' managers to represent cultural diversity because the top jobs go to the most competent employees, often from subsidiaries, regardless of nationality. By contrast, in Japanese MNEs, Japanese managers almost always hold the top jobs at headquarters. Subsidiary managers could be counted on for regional and local views, and might also represent differing cross-cultural perspectives depending on their nationality. Local managers would understand the political, economic, social, and technological differences that would represent sources of uncertainty for managers from headquarters.[14] Product managers would represent their product-related perspectives. Bringing together the often-antithetical functional views of marketers and operations managers, for example, could provide more creative corporate decisions. Marketing is usually focused on customer needs and is usually organized as a profit center. Operations is usually focused on operational efficiency and is usually organized as a cost center.

Greater diversity produces diverse perspectives and access to different kinds of information for decision-making.[15] Groups with more diverse views tend to produce more ideas and proposed solutions, and have greater resources for problem-solving.[16] Even psychological diversity is important for improved decision-making. Management consultants commonly train senior management teams in business and organized religion using the Myers–Briggs Type Indicator,[17] or Human Dynamics.[18]

The more that various kinds of diversity are allowed to participate in problem-solving, the more differentiated the information available to influence the eventual decision, and the less the uncertainty. The goal of maximizing diversity of perspectives within decision-making teams is to ensure that the best and most comprehensive information is used to set the corporate strategies intended to maximize MNE performance.

Bartlett and Ghoshal[19] observed that increased decision-making diversity would only become a competitive advantage for MNEs if the diversity could be integrated into the MNE's decision-making processes: "The ability to link and leverage knowledge is increasingly the factor that differentiates the winners from the losers."

Bartlett and Ghoshal argued, however, that the key problem was not obtaining greater decision-making diversity, but ensuring that it received a hearing and was included in the problem-solving process. Newly included diversity was usually a minority perspective intentionally added to preexisting decision-making groups that were already used to dominating decision outcomes themselves. The new diverse perspectives had to be legitimated, and the greatest barriers to this were "ingrained management mentalities" and "established informal relationships"[20] ratified by the sense of administrative heritage that decisions had always been made a certain way by certain decision-makers.

It was not enough that minority perspectives existed on a management team because these perspectives could be excluded from the decision-making process by an organization's dominant perspectives, and the rule of the majority. Derrida,[21] the French existential philosopher, noted that there was generally a democratic principle in play that could predict the probable impact of different perspectives on decision-making outcomes. Perspectives that constituted a democratic majority would dominate decisions because the majority's more similar views would discount the discordant views of minorities.

If no single perspective formed a democratic majority, then compromises were more likely among the bigger pluralities. Even here, a small minority was likely to be ignored or excluded unless it was sufficiently large to form a majority with a large plurality. An organization could only ensure that minority cultural diversity usefully participated in decision-making if special integrative efforts were made to ensure their inclusion.

Buckley and Carter[22] defined knowledge as the antithesis of uncertainty. Uncertainty—for example having to deal with an unfamiliar national culture—makes decision-makers unsure about which actions to undertake to achieve desired outcomes. Greater knowledge in advance of decision-making should lead to reduced uncertainty about which actions will be effective. The problem with knowledge, however, is that it is not clear whether an assertion is really knowledge, or only someone's belief, until after it has been applied and an outcome has emerged. At the time the decision is being made, knowledge appears to be just someone's belief based on incomplete information—a prediction—rather than a demonstrably true belief.[23] According to Buckley and Carter, the key factor affecting performance was the quality of the judgment of those responsible for choosing which beliefs the firm would act on and which not.

Kogut and Zander[24] divided knowledge into what they called "explicit" and "tacit." *Explicit* knowledge was defined as easy to write down and therefore easy to teach because it was not complex and was easy to state in the form of general principles. It would include the kinds of theories and action principles commonly taught in business education and found in textbooks.

By contrast, *tacit* or implicit knowledge was based on having relevant experience and understanding what would or would not work in practice. This tacit knowledge is difficult to write down or teach because it is complex and often situational. Its value is often contingent on the ability of decision-makers to see its value and make it work in new applications. Kogut and Zander[25] argued that it was this practical and applied tacit knowledge that most positively affected MNE performance if it could be successfully transferred into the decision process. Because tacit knowledge was difficult to state and teach, the individuals with it needed to be included in the decision process. Li and Shenkar[26] later added to the definition of tacit knowledge that it was experiential, idiosyncratic, and rooted in action–therefore difficult to communicate or learn except through direct experience. However, it was also of great value strategically because it was unique and difficult for competitors to acquire.[27]

For example,[28] global marketers generally believe that there are a number of global marketing practices that are effective in any global marketplace. These practices are taught as explicit knowledge to all marketers. In a study of Canadian SMEs doing business in Malaysia and Singapore, it was found that some of these practices were useful for building high-performance relationships, but others were useless in that locale. In fact, there were two local relationship-building practices that were even more important. A Western marketer would never know about these two local practices until she/he observed them in action, and they became part of his/her tacit understanding about how to market in this region. The only way to obtain this tacit knowledge expertise would be to include experienced Southeast Asian marketers in one's planning, but most Western companies did not believing in the universal principles (see Chapter 15).

Diversity and work team performance

Current research supports the view that heterogeneous work teams (more diversity) achieve better results and greater productivity than homogeneous teams (less or no diversity).[29] While some studies have reported performance gains attributed to cultural diversity in work teams, others have reported the opposite finding.

Attempting to resolve the question definitively, Stahl et al.[30] conducted a major meta-analysis of 108 previous empirical studies, including 10,632 work teams. They concluded that there was no significant relationship between greater cultural diversity and higher performance. However, the reasons given by Stahl et al. as to why the culturally diverse work teams generally did not achieve higher performance was because their integration was insufficient. The study reported that the more diverse teams had greater levels of conflict and lower social integration than the more homogeneous groups, but according to theory, greater conflict and lower social integration are signs of lower integration. This seemed to represent a conceptual flaw, suggesting that further research would be advisable using more effectively integrated work teams.

Stahl et al.[31] did find that work groups with higher levels of cultural diversity did, however, achieve significantly higher creativity in their problem-solving. Group members generally felt significantly higher levels of satisfaction that their personal needs had been adequately fulfilled. Creativity could be considered potentially a competitive advantage in itself since standard solutions would also be more predictable and easier for competitors to counter. Exhibit 6.1 provides monitoring activities that global organizational leaders may utilize to effectively assist the improvement of performance for all their employees.

We know that diversity management is directly linked to team functioning, and can either improve or upset team performance.[32] As organizations rely on teams to accomplish a vast number of tasks, the question of how teams should be composed and managed has

EXHIBIT 6.1 EXAMPLES OF INDICATORS THAT COMPANIES CAN USE TO MONITOR EMPLOYEE PERFORMANCE

- Implementing employee surveys to evaluate employee attitudes and degrees of satisfaction, and identify areas in need of improvement.
- Ongoing discussions with employee networks and their resource groups.
- Workforce profiling to summarize nationalities, religions, gender, languages, and age to understand demographics and understand where there might be an underrepresentation.
- Setting up a database of employee skills to monitor employee development and progression.
- Providing for diverse perspectives in standard business performance reviews, and provisions for equal pay evaluations.
- Examining the complaints registered with regard to bullying, harassment, and the nature with which, the speed by which, and how solutions are found.
- Examining business costs due to absenteeism, lateness, and illness.
- Monitoring employee responses in exit interviews and organizing comments by gender and ethnicity to determine if there are patterns.

Source: adapted from European Commission, "The Business Case for Diversity: Good Practices in the Workplace." Luxemburg Office for Official Publications of the European Communities, 2005. http://ec.europa.eu/social/BlobServlet?docID=1428&langID =en (retrieved April 14, 2010).

come under greater scrutiny.[33] The composition of teams should take into account the salience of diversity in a team, and the levels of interdependence and longevity that a team will have to deal with,[34] along with the reward structure associated with team output. For example, Homan et al.[35] reported that a high degree of diversity in both high-performing and low-performing teams influenced performance. The reward structure greatly influenced the highest performing teams, while the teams in which diversity was most salient and had the lowest level of openness also were the lowest performing teams.

Exhibit 6.2 provides a list of the knowledge, skills, and abilities that all individuals can learn to help improve their own performance when working with individuals from a different culture.

In another study of cross-national cognitive diversity differences,[36] it was found that American management samples had somewhat higher cognitive diversity than Chinese samples, and much higher diversity than Thai samples. The study argued that perhaps this greater cognitive diversity was one reason why Americans and Chinese were more successful as international traders than the Thai. The Americans and Chinese might be better able to handle a greater range of potentially relevant information, and find more creative and innovative strategies and practices.

Globalization is shaping our world today. Globalization has the effect of bringing cultural diversity into direct contact, magnifying the need for tacit understandings of how to

EXHIBIT 6.2 SOME KEY INDIVIDUAL COMPETENCIES RELATED TO PERFORMANCE

Barrett encourages individuals and teams who are working within the global arena to cultivate the following competencies. Some of these are tacit and learned through experience. Others are explicitly learned through education and training. Most can be developed with effort.

Knowledge to cultivate

- Learn about other nations' histories, cultures, national systems, values, customs, and the many ethnic groups that live within these nations.
- Learn how different systems, organizations, groups, and individuals discover how to work together through understanding change, management practices, and philosophies.
- Learn about group development and group dynamics to understand how groups interact.
- Learn to understand how the macro-levels (nation, organization) and micro-levels (group, individual) of interaction are co-created.

Abilities to cultivate

- Learn how to be at ease with the unfamiliar.
- Learn how to think like people who are remarkably different from yourself. This helps discourage ethnocentrism.
- Learn how to *learn*, and be open to continuous learning and to rapidly adapting to new situations.
- Learn how to cultivate meaningful relationships with people very different from yourself both culturally and personally, based upon respect, cooperation, trust, shared goals, and constructive ways of handling conflict.
- Learn how to manage your stress, and learn to see difficulties as opportunities to *learn*.
- Learn to be aware of yourself; learn to accept feedback, both positive and negative.
- Learn to focus on improving yourself; learn to take personal responsibility rather than blaming others for your own limitations or difficulties.

Source: adapted from Barrett, G. "Cultivating Global Teams: Diversity Management Square (DM2)", in C. Mann and K. Gotz (eds.), *Borderless Business: Managing the Far-Flung Enterprise*. Westport, CT: Praeger, 2006, pp. 275–294,

proceed in a greater number of cultural contexts even in your home-country markets. Advances in telecommunications, mass transportation, technology, and changes in the global political arena have led to the emergence of a global, information-oriented culture. The internet and email mean that you may be dealing with people from around the world without realizing, at any moment.

With the expansion of globalization, awareness of the global complexities involved in cross-cultural interactions has become more necessary. Globalization has greatly increased interaction at the macro-level, as exemplified by the expansion of technology through business. At the micro-level, it is exemplified by the individual use of laptops, cellular phones, and the internet to communicate anywhere at any time. While it can be said that at the macro-level there is a form of global culture around the use of technology, communication advances, and the practice of business, at the micro-level the experiences, values, perceptions, and behaviors of individuals vary within and across national and ethnic cultures. We need to include those with local knowledge in our decision-making to make sure our decisions make sense in local contexts.

Capitalizing on human diversity

As a concept, diversity has different meanings and applications, depending on where you are in the world. Within our information society, it is important to recognize that increasing globalism enormously impacts the workforce worldwide. For leading-edge organizations, this denotes the creation of an organizational cultural norm to embrace diversity to maximize the potential of personnel, especially through cohesive work teams.[37]

Research[38] has demonstrated that as the length of time increases when diverse group members work together, the negative effects of *surface-level diversity* (i.e., age, gender, sex, and ethnicity) decrease. In other words, as you get to know your teammates, you relate to them more as they are, and less as they might appear to be as stereotypes. Furthermore, in this research, the effects of *deep-level diversity* (attitudes, beliefs, values) were positive because they led, through discussion, to increased information about each group member. These deep-level diversity characteristics at the group level meant that, over time, the richness of information exchange was augmented. This produced a more profound mutual understanding and greater satisfaction among members.

For global managers, the challenge is to find innovative ways to improve human commitment and performance at work. Since so many people aim to achieve their full potential through their work and career, the new work culture fosters values such as empowerment and character development. Success is gauged not so much in terms of organizational status as in the quality of work life. There is very strong empirical confirmation that successful diversity management and a resulting improvement in organizational performance are positively correlated.[39]

SOURCES OF GLOBAL DIVERSITY

All in all, diversity is related to the vast range of differences that requires attention to facilitate living and working together effectively. Human diversity has been popularly understood to refer to differences of color, ethnic origin, gender, sexual or religious preferences, age, and disabilities. In academic research, diversity has been characterized as either surface-level or deep-level diversity.[40] Surface-level includes demographic characteristics such as sex, age, race/ethnicity, and nationality. Deep-level refers to differences between individuals' psychological characteristics such as personality types, cognitive preferences, values, attitudes, gender identity, background socialization, social class, problem-solving strategies, ability levels, skillsets, and level in the organizational hierarchy, as well as personal cultural background. Personality preferences distributions have been found to vary culture[41] and work-related values.[42]

Other definitions of organizational diversity recognize a wider range of characteristics. According to American Express Financial Advisors,[43] they include: race, gender, age, physical ability, physical appearance, nationality, cultural heritage, personal background, functional experience, position in the organization, mental and physical challenges, family responsibilities, sexual orientation, military experience, educational background, style differences, economic status, thinking patterns, political backgrounds, city/state/region of residence, IQ level, smoking preference, weight, marital status, nontraditional job, religion, white collar, language, blue collar, and height.

Migration/immigration as a source of diversity

Historically and currently, the movement of people from one locale to another has encouraged the formation of our diversity. Evolutionists believe that the modern human race evolved in eastern Africa and migrated over thousands of years to Europe in one direction, and across Asia in the other direction. Groups of Asians migrated across a land bridge at what is now the Bering Sea to become Aboriginal First Nations and populate the Americas. Races evolved later in response to local conditions.

In the late 1990s, Allan Wilson and his colleagues used mtDNA to determine human ancestry. By comparing mtDNA and Y chromosomes from people of diverse populations, they were able to map human migration originating in Africa many years ago.[44] "Migration has helped to create humans, drove us to conquer a planet, shaped our societies, and promises to reshape them again. . . . If they [people] had not moved and intermingled as they did, they probably would have evolved into a different species."[45] AncestryDNA[46] currently offers any person the opportunity to assess their personal ancestry and ethnic mix. By sending in a DNA sample and the fee, an individual can determine which parts of Europe, Asia, Africa, the Americas, etc. their DNA is from and in what percentages. Research has shown that while humans-as-species all have personalities composed of the same psychological variables,[47] the distributions of these variables vary by national culture[48] because of differences in national gene pools.[49] These psychological differences mean that immigration and migration produce diversity in individual preferences for problem-solving (see Chapter 11) and communications styles (see Chapter 2) based on differences in national character.[50]

There are many sources of immigration and migration in today's world. It is estimated[51] that there were 21.3 million refugees, worldwide, in 2015, including 4.9 million from Syria, 2.7

EXHIBIT 6.3 ROOT CAUSES OF IMMIGRATION

Principal "push" factors	Principal "pull" factors
War and civil strife, including religious conflicts	Substantial immigration markets and channels opened up to the West
Economic decline, rising poverty and unemployment	Family reunion, economic safety
Population pressures; burgeoning numbers of unemployed young people	Freedom from fear of violence, persecution, hunger, and/or poverty
Political instability	Political freedom
Large-scale natural disasters and ecological degradation	Economic opportunity
Human rights violations	Education
Denial of education and healthcare for selected minorities including women; other persecutions	Maintaining ethnic identity

Source: adapted from Stalker, P. "The Work of Strangers: A Survey of International Migration," in W. R. Bohning and M. L. Schloeter (eds.), *Aids in Place of Migration*. Geneva: International Labour Office, 1994.

million from Afghanistan, and 1.3 million from Somalia. The country hosting the largest number of refugees was Turkey (2.5 million); these refugees have produced the EU refugee crisis, crossing by boat to Greece and hoping to walk through the Balkan nations to reach Germany. By 2016, Germany had received over one million refugees with mixed results, while the UK was threatening to leave the European Union, in part over migration-related issues.

It was estimated that there were about 214 million international migrant workers and their families worldwide, and an estimated 20–30 million of them were unauthorized, having illegally entered their countries of choice. The US Department of Homeland Security estimated that there were 11.4 million "unauthorized immigrants" in the US in 2012. Estimates suggest the number peaked at 12 million in 2007 and had declined by 2016 to 11 million.[52] This was a major issue in the 2016 US election.

Exhibit 6.3 summarizes the dual impact of the ongoing push and pull of immigration. When people leave their homes, generally there is a "push" factor from the country of origin, and a "pull" factor to the destination country.

INTEGRATING DIVERSITY

The benefits of diversity in terms of greater collective access to relevant information, more creative solutions, and reduced negative conflict, can only be achieved when problem-solving and decision-making groups are tightly integrated. There is a general human "similarity-attraction" tendency[53] for people to prefer to work with, and cooperate with, others whom they perceive as similar to themselves in values, beliefs, and attitudes. Less similar individuals tend to be perceived as outsiders.[54] As a result, there is a naturally greater tendency for more diverse decision-making groups to have greater levels of intra-group controversy and conflict.

In addition, MNE decision-making groups are under considerable external stress and time pressure because they are tasked with understanding a complex, uncertain, and relatively unfamiliar international environment. Usually strategic planning is undertaken because the firm's performance is less than expected or, worse, has begun to decline due to changes in the competitive environment. Decisions are needed quickly to reverse the performance declines.

Lau and Murnighan[55] observed the tendency under external pressures for diverse groups to fracture along the fault-lines of their diversity into opposing subgroups. Their analogy was that of an "earthquake" where the "fault-lines" were split apart. If the disagreements or conflicts seemed to be too great, the members of the subgroups believed that the differences were irreconcilable.[56]

Three coordination mechanisms

Bartlett and Ghoshal[57] argued that three coordination mechanisms could be used to integrate diverse teams effectively enough to prevent these kinds of internal conflicts and divisions. First, diverse perspectives had to be *legitimized* by creating a balance between multiple perspectives. *Legitimizing diversity* required three steps:[58]

Building legitimacy: An underrepresented group could be given more legitimacy in the eyes of other more influential groups by transferring into it high-status personnel. Bringing in new people of higher status was necessary because the status and credibility of those already in the underrepresented group had already been established negatively in others' minds.

Providing access: Managers representing the underrepresented perspectives and/or capabilities needed to be seen as supporting, and be supported by, the MNE's objectives, interests, and priorities. The emergent group needed to be plugged into the company's information system, and the information system modified to facilitate the group's particular needs for receiving and transmitting information. This encouraged the development of new channels of communication. It created information linkages across management groups, and encouraged information sharing and joint decision-making based on access to the same information.

Ensuring influence: The managers in the underrepresented group needed organizational clout to ensure their ability to influence decisions. The group needed to receive an allocation of resources: financial (budget), operational (authority over, and responsibility for physical sites, locations, or other operational resources), and/or human (groups of personnel). Control over resources empowered the emergent group in its negotiations with established management groups. Established groups needed to win the cooperation and support of the emergent group to achieve their own ends. This latter step of ensuring influence is the most important step. It requires that senior management support the re-allocation of resources and influence, and deal with any resistance to the change.

Bartlett and Ghoshal's[59] second coordination mechanism, *information coordination*, was intended to manage information complexity by developing flexible informal coordination. Highly diverse management teams would be better able to collect relevant information for their decision-making through the use of informal and group information coordination mechanisms. Teams that relied only on formal information coordination were likely to obtain less information and be less effective.

Informal information coordination was based on the creation of relationships between managers representing diverse perspectives that were outside the boundaries of formal working relationships. Group information coordination was based on the use of task forces, joint problem-solving teams, and committees. Formal information coordination was based on policies, procedures, and information systems that defined what information was required and should be collected.

MNEs may use training and development workshops as a means of building informal coordination. Managers are gathered, apparently to learn a new technique or process. They have, however, been carefully selected as individuals who should be able to call on each other to solve commonly faced problems or situations. The real hope of such programs is that the participants will build informal relationships both during the training, and during the downtime between training sessions. Later, these individuals may be assigned to committees and/or task forces to further develop and strengthen their informal relationships.

Informal and group coordination mechanisms were more likely to improve information gathering and decision-making because the important information needed was likely to be geographically dispersed and situation-specific. It was likely to be tacit (based on personal experience), and not explicit (written down somewhere). Senior management generally does not know exactly what information is, or will become, critical for its planning processes. If it did know, the information could be collected formally through reporting procedures.

Bartlett and Ghoshal's[60] third coordination mechanism, *shared vision*, was intended to motivate all MNE managers to cooperate, share information, listen to others' contributions, and use all available information in decision-making. Shared vision consisted of a process for uniting the entire organization with "a common understanding of, identification with, and commitment to the organization's objectives, priorities, and values."[61] All individuals and units in the organization must be inculcated with a common vision of organizational goals.

Genuine commitment to these goals was achieved by creating genuine functional, sequential, and goal interdependence between managers at headquarters, subsidiaries, functions, line, staff, etc. This interdependence ensured that managers must cooperate to achieve their individual and collective goals. Integration, collaboration, and cooperation became self-enforcing processes because each organizational unit was connected to other units by shared goals and rewards. Each had to cooperate with those it was connected with so that all linked units could achieve their jointly held performance goals. Rewards were similarly linked so that units could not achieve performance rewards if other associated units did not achieve their requisite performance.

Allan Mulally, the "man who saved Ford," provided an interesting example of shared vision.[62] By creating a shared vision of Ford as a geocentric company ("One Ford"—see Chapter 3), Ford was transformed. In just five years, Ford went from a perennial money loser with a history of poor automobile quality, to become the top American car company in the eyes of American car buyers. By focusing on "One Ford," division vice presidents had to stop competing with each other for primacy, R&D was shared between automobile divisions, and the company was able to design models that could sell worldwide rather than just in specific geographic markets. Mulally's vision brought all of Ford's resources together in cooperation, rather than being divided against each other in competition.

Integration through cooperative interdependence

Humankind seems always to organize itself around one of three principles.[63] With cooperation, people are organized to work together toward jointly shared goals. With competition, people compete with each other for goal attainment, with only the victors achieving the goals and rewards. With individualistic goal attainment, people neither cooperate nor compete, but work separately for the goals they have individually in mind.

Social interdependence theory has identified four types of human resource coordination intended to stimulate cooperation. These seem strongly related to Bartlett and Ghoshal's *shared vision* coordination mechanism.[64] This has identified a number of coordination variables that create interdependence between individuals and organizational units, based on shared goals that make cooperation and collaboration self-enforcing if the goals are to be attained.

1   *Task interdependence*—refers to the way the workflow is arranged between individuals and units.[65] A subordinate form is *sequential interdependence* where work must proceed along a fixed course, like an assembly line, with each subsequent job dependent on the one before having been completed.
2   *Role interdependence*—refers to the position in the hierarchy of authority of individuals and units. This has been operationalized mainly in studies of leadership style.[66]
3   *Knowledge interdependence*—refers to the differentiated expertise of individuals and units that must be combined to achieve an outcome.[67]
4   *Goal interdependence*—refers to the ways individual employees and organizational units are organized to achieve corporate goals and outcomes. Goal interdependence, also known as *social interdependence*, produces relatively stable self-sustaining patterns of interaction.[68]

According to social interdependence theory, social interdependence exists when an individual must rely on others for his/her goal attainment.[69] The type of interdependence that exists in a work group determines how individual members work and interact with each other. Cooperative interdependence, or cooperation, exists when individuals understand that they can only achieve their goals if those they are cooperating with do the same. Competitive interdependence, or competition, exists when individuals understand that they can only reach their goals if those they are competing with fail to do so. Individualistic interdependence, neither cooperation nor competition, exists when individuals understand that they may reach their goals regardless of whether other individuals, related or not, reach theirs. An example of a cooperative interdependent situation would be a group assignment in a class in which all students in the group will receive the same grade. A competitive interdependent situation would exist in a class in which final grades were to be bell-curved and only a limited number of students could achieve an A, regardless of their scores on individual assignments. An individualistic interdependent situation would exist for students when a class was not bell-curved and they received exactly the average of their scores on all the assignments regardless of others' grades, or for graduate students completing individual graduation theses.

There are a number of points of similarity between goal interdependence theory and Bartlett and Ghoshal's coordination mechanisms (see Exhibit 6.4). The theory of goal interdependence identifies that individuals working within conditions of cooperation and shared goals will achieve higher performance than individuals competing against each other to

EXHIBIT 6.4 COMPARING BARTLETT AND GHOSHAL'S THEORY OF COORDINATION WITH THE THEORY OF GOAL INTERDEPENDENCE

Bartlett and Ghoshal[70]	Goal interdependence[71]
If human resources are coordinated using genuine interdependence based on shared goals, then cooperation will result in higher foreign market performance.	If cooperative goal interdependence exists, then coordination will be based on shared goals, leading to higher individual and organizational performance.
Informal and group coordination mechanisms will contribute to higher foreign market performance.	Cooperative goal interdependence leads to increased development of informal and group information-processing mechanisms.
Decision-making groups with greater diversity of perspectives results in higher foreign market performance.	Cooperative goal interdependence facilitates the development of learning groups with greater cultural diversity of perspectives.
Use of the three coordination mechanisms results in a transnational (geocentric) corporation with higher foreign market performance.	Cooperative goal interdependence facilitates and produces higher individual, group, and organizational performance.

achieve goals. This is similar to Bartlett and Ghoshal's observation that individuals linked by a shared vision of organizational goals will have higher performance than in organizations in which individuals are expected to compete with each other for their goal attainment.

In the cooperative goal condition, an individual's own work contributes both to his/her own goal attainment and that of others in his/her work team or organization. The degree of this correlation of individuals' goals may range from partial to total.[72] Individuals and units recognize this linkage and realize that they can only attain their goals if the linked others do so as well.[73]

The motivation produced by cooperative goal interdependence is also similar to that produced by shared vision. Managers sharing their company's shared vision understand their company's strategy, identify with its strategic goals, and are committed to its success.[74] Even managers that may privately disagree cooperate out of self-interest because those that do not "buy in" do not fit with senior management plans and risk their positions. Managers coordinated using cooperative goal interdependence may also cooperate out of self-interest.[75] It is also possible, however, that an organization that has an administrative heritage of applying cooperative interdependence over a long period of time will have attracted managers and employees who prefer to cooperate out of altruism, or commitment to the public good of the organization, regardless of self-interest (see Chapter 9). Organizational cultures tend to attract employees who feel more comfortable with the conditions of those cultures.[76]

Competitive goal interdependence exists when organizational members are expected to compete with each other for goal attainment. This condition may exist when individuals or units must compete with each other for budget, when multiple work teams are charged with finding solutions to the same set of problems, or simply when individuals compete for influence or prestige in the hopes of material advancement within an organization. Competitive goal interdependence is similar to Bartlett and Ghoshal's[77] concern with the negative performance effects of inter-unit rivalries. A win–lose situation is created as one individual or unit progresses while another related individual or unit fails.[78]

Individualistic goal interdependence exists when the goals of individuals or units in an organization are not linked either positively or negatively so that goal achievement is unrelated to the achievements of others.[79] In this case, individuals' and units' self-interest is to minimize interaction since it is irrelevant to task and goal achievement.[80] A request for help may be received from an independent individual or unit, but helping will not contribute to the goal attainment of the helper, and may detract in terms of time lost.

The goal interdependence literature has identified five variables that may be used to predict whether an organization is characterized by cooperative goal interdependence or not. These include:

1 *Goal structure*: Individuals and units within an organization will have a subjective perception or expectation as to whether they are more likely to be rewarded for cooperating, or not cooperating, to achieve organizational goals. Rewards for non-

cooperation indicate that goals are not jointly held across individuals or units. A goal is defined as a desired future state of being. A goal structure is defined as the most probable relationship between defined work goals and the pattern of working relationships most likely to achieve those goals in a particular organizational setting.[81]

2   *Control systems*: The leadership or supervisory style and reward systems of an organization reinforce the subjective perceptions of individuals and groups about whether they are expected to work toward cooperatively shared goals or not. Supervisory systems may encourage the expectation of cooperation by encouraging individuals to consult with superiors or co-workers in the setting of work goals, use shared decision-making, participate in objective and impartial performance appraisal systems, or give/receive frequent and helpful work-related feedback. The more common these kinds of systems, the more cooperative the work relationships are perceived to be. Reward systems may facilitate cooperative goal interdependence by offering group rewards for group success, inducing information sharing and mutual assistance.[82] By contrast, control systems that place individuals and groups in competition for limited resources, honors, or promotions, and that offer rewards by defining winners and losers, reinforce perceptions of competitive goal interdependence.

3   *Interaction patterns*: Cooperative interaction patterns tend to be marked with empathy, willingness to freely share information and advice, delegation of authority and responsibility, and positive feelings. Competitive and individualistic interaction patterns tend to lack interpersonal empathy, information sharing, delegation, and positive feelings.

4   *Trust*: Trust is the willingness to accept the possibility of a potentially very large downside to achieve a relatively small upside because of confidence that the downside will not occur. Commercial flight is an example. Trust is usually a function of demonstrations of long-term reliability, competence, and often, positive personal relationship. The possibility of cooperative goal interdependence is influenced by the willingness to trust between individuals and groups. If one cannot trust those one is working with, then collaboration or cooperation is unlikely.[83]

5   *Time*: It takes more time to build trusting relationships. Trust builds from mistrust, to neutrality, to cooperation, before becoming trust. Task groups with relatively short assigned time frames do not allow for the demonstration of the dependability, honesty, competence, and likeability needed for trust to develop,[84] unless the group is composed of individuals having a longer history of working together.

Goal interdependence theory predicts that cooperative goal interdependence will be characterized by goal structures perceived to be cooperative, control systems that reinforce cooperative behavior, cooperative interaction patterns, trust, and the allocation of enough time for task completion to allow trust to develop between individuals and units. Competitive or individualistic goal interdependence—and less integration of diverse views—will develop when individuals or units perceive goal structures to be non-cooperative, and/or when control systems are not strong enough to reinforce cooperative behavior. Non-cooperative interaction patterns, and the lack of trust, or too short a time allocation for trust to develop, also harm the possibility of cooperative goal interdependence.

Cooperative goal interdependence facilitates the development of informal and group information coordination mechanisms. Individuals and groups are willing to share information and assist each other because it is in their interest to maximize joint effectiveness.[85] The shared information is trusted because the individuals are cooperating to help each other pursue their self-interest on a collective basis. The information sharing is reinforced by positive interpersonal feelings that develop because everyone is on the same side.[86]

With competitive or individualistic goal interdependence, individuals and groups are less likely to share information informally.[87] Individuals or groups may attempt to mislead or obstruct others by providing inaccurate information, or may regard with suspicion—for the same reasons—information received from others.[88] Friendliness between individuals and groups is impaired by direct competition for the same outcomes. Dislike tends to develop for those seen, or suspected, to have actively frustrated one's own goal attainment.

A meta-analysis[89] of 31 studies (and 107 results) conducted between 1944 and 1982 found that cooperative interdependence resulted in significantly greater interpersonal attraction between ethically and racially diverse persons. Competitive or individualistic goal interdependence, in comparison, reduced attraction. A meta-analysis combines the results of a number of studies and determines the average effect, or effect size, across all the studies. The finding was judged to be reliable, meaning that in a future similar study it could be hypothesized with confidence that this result would occur again. Other studies also support this finding. For example:

- Cooperative goal interdependence was found to reduce preexisting prejudice and negative attitudes about others. Prejudice was not reduced by competitive or individualistic goal interdependence, or simple proximity.[90]
- Cooperative interdependence was significantly related to an increased willingness to help individuals of a different culture. This willingness was associated with a greater expectation that those culturally diverse individuals liked or cared about them.[91]
- Cooperative goal interdependence was related to the development of a shared group identity between individuals of different cultures. Individuals developed attitudes they shared in common and developed greater empathy with each other.[92]
- Cooperative goal interdependence resulted in an increased willingness for culturally diverse individuals to spend free time together. Individuals initiated a higher frequency of intercultural contacts and counted more culturally diverse individuals as their friends.[93]
- Cooperative goal interdependence was related to an integrative conflict resolution process called *constructive controversy*, defined as a rational process that facilitates the open expression of diverse minority positions even when they conflict with majority views. Recent research has demonstrated that constructive controversy

handling may be *the sparkplug* making cooperative goal interdependence the most effective mechanism for both integrating diversity and improving performance outcomes, and is discussed in the next section.[94]

A second meta-analysis provided strong empirical support for these observations.[95] This meta-analysis included 122 studies and 286 separate findings on the relationship between goal interdependence and learning outcomes. All the studies were North American and all had been conducted prior to 1981. The principal finding was that both learning and performance were significantly higher for groups organized around cooperative goal interdependence.

The study reported three moderators of the relationship that increased the effects of cooperative goal interdependence. The first was type of *task*. Cooperative interdependence was particularly related to increased performance for complex tasks requiring coordinated work, effective information exchange, division of labor within groups, and effective interpersonal communications. The second moderator was *accountability*. Individuals or group members needed to be visibly accountable in quantifiable terms to avoid the possibility of free riding, or desertion. The third moderator was group *size*. The effects of cooperative goal interdependence were more pronounced in small groups than large; for example a small management decision-making team.

Integration through constructive controversy

The most recent research[96] related to cooperative goal interdependence has demonstrated that constructive controversy, or the way conflict is handled within cooperatively structured groups, is *the key variable* for achieving the most productive results from diversity. Cooperative interdependence integrates, and constructive controversy elicits the maximal problem-solving advantages from the diverse perspectives.

Constructive controversy involves the willingness to discuss the advantages and disadvantages of proposed actions, intending to synthesize potentially new and creative solutions. This might be considered a form of dialectical reasoning in which various solutions are compared and contrasted in the hopes that each might offer improvements to the other. A first solution, called a thesis, is proposed. A second solution, called an antithesis, is proposed to counter and critique the thesis. The goal is to find a synthesis that incorporates the strong points of both the thesis and antithesis, while eliminating the perceived weaknesses of both. Participants representing diverse perspectives use arguments and counterarguments attempting to refute each other's points of view, hoping to resolve their conflicting assessments.

Having cooperative goals does not mean that individuals or groups should not be in conflict. Sincere cooperation may result in much conflict[97] and dissent.[98] Dissent means differing in opinion or conclusion from the majority and tends to result in arguments between majority and minority viewpoints. The question becomes how these inevitable conflicts should be handled to increase the effectiveness of diverse perspectives in contributing to the majority view. *Concurrency seeking* will result when individuals and groups feel uncomfortable with conflict and seek to limit it. *Constructive controversy* will result if individuals and groups are willing to risk conflict, confident that their commitment to shared goals will maintain integration. Exhibit 6.5 summarizes the similarities and differences between constructive controversy and concurrency seeking.

With constructive controversy, it is considered preferable that to make the effective use of diversity, different perspectives will disagree, criticize, and attempt to refute each other's analyses and conclusions. They may even get angry; some shouting for attention, some reduced to tears. What holds them together is that they are arguing about what they perceive to be the best and most effective means of achieving the goals to which they are all committed. They disagree, even perhaps demonstrably, because they have different perspectives, are attuned to different kinds of relevant information, and are committed to finding the best collective solution with the best outcomes for the whole group.

EXHIBIT 6.5 COMPARING CONSTRUCTIVE CONTROVERSY AND CONCURRENCE SEEKING

Characteristics	Constructive controversy	Concurrence seeking
Initial recommendation	Collecting and organizing information to derive conclusions	Collecting and organizing information to derive conclusions
Discussion process	Presenting views, offering rationales, advocating preferences, elaborating information	Presenting views, offering rationales, advocating preferences, elaborating information
Dialectical uncertainty	Challenge from dissenting viewpoints creates conceptual conflict and uncertainty about own views	Challenge from dissenting viewpoints creates conceptual conflict and uncertainty about own views
Response to conflict and uncertainty	Conflict resolution motivates search for new information and perspectives	Fear about conflict limits information search thereby strengthening adherence to own point of view
Revised recommendation	Synthesis and integration of conflicting views	Speedy acceptance of dominant view
Probable outcomes	Maximal participation of diverse viewpoints, higher solution creativity, stronger relationships	Minority viewpoints are not included, lower solution creativity, relationship dissatisfaction unexpressed

Source: Johnson, D. W. *Constructive Controversy: Theory, Research, Practice.* Cambridge: Cambridge University Press, 2015.

A constructive controversy process is structured and establishes a number of guide-lines. These include:

1   *Cooperative context*: The group must come to a consensus. If the performance of the group is being evaluated, members will receive the same group evaluation. There are behavioral norms required in a cooperative context as well. The group is seeking the best-informed judgment or solution. No one is winning his/her own view at the expense of others. Criticisms are directed at ideas and not at individual people. Members have to listen to others' positions, and eventually advo-cate them by formally switching sides, even if they do not agree with those positions. Members have to allow themselves, and be allowed by others, to change their minds when persuaded logically or rationally. There is no "flip-flopping," only learning.

2   *Constructive controversy process*: All members will research and prepare their own positions from the point of view of their own specialized knowledge. Each will:
    a.   present and advocate the position they have prepared.
    b.   analyze and critically evaluate the positions of other members while rebutting criticisms of their own positions. This forces members to develop and clarify their original positions in the face of challenges from others with different points of view.
    c.   reverse perspectives, assuming other members' positions as others assume theirs, to communicate that they are able to see the issue from all points of view. This discourages members from closed-minded adherence to their own points of view, and ignoring or avoiding information that would disconfirm elements of their positions.
    d.   synthesize and integrate members' perspectives and specialized information into a joint solution that all members can accept. This creates information inter-dependence by demonstrating how information is complementary. It encour-ages cooperative information exchange while discouraging competitive feelings of competence threat.

3   Specific roles may be assigned to group members. A person assigned a "devil's advo-cate" role may be more able to direct challenges or criticisms of other members' posi-tions without seeming to be making personal attacks. A person assigned a "synthesizer" role may receive more room to speculate about novel combinations of ideas derived from a number of members' positions.

Conflict creates positives related both to process and outcome.[99] It may stimulate individual members' interest, reduce disinterest and boredom, and hold interest and atten-tion. It may promote cognitive, analytical, or even ethical development by causing individuals to think more deeply about what they or others believe. It may stimulate individuals to offer information the group may not otherwise have accessed, leading to more complete testing of analysis and solutions. The main issue with conflict in constructive controversy is how to prevent it from being destructive to group integration.

The important aspect of concurrence seeking that must be emphasized is that it is also based on cooperative goal interdependence. It is a less effective form for integrating diversity based on the fear that conflict either signals individualistic interdependence, or will create it because discomfort with conflict will cause members to psychologically or physically leave the group. Individuals who believe that cooperation means, by definition, getting along and always being "nice," are more likely to end up with concurrence seeking. This may produce better results than individualistic or competitive interdependent problem-solving, but will eliminate much of the potential advantage of minority viewpoint diverse perspectives.

Concurrence seeking exists when individuals' ideas, information, opinions, or conclusions are apparently incompatible and discussion is limited or curtailed to avoid disagreement, argument, and/or conflict. Realistic appraisal of contrary views is avoided in favor of the need to demonstrate cooperation by premature agreement.[100] A majority viewpoint becomes apparent and those with minority perspectives are pressured, often nonverbally, by the majority to conform. Participants quickly compromise or assent, never disagreeing or raising awkward questions, to avoid open disagreement and maintain group harmony and apparent cooperation. If dissenters continue to press their minority views, they may be labeled as not being team players, disliked, and out-voted.[101] They may be functionally ostracized as punishment and not included, or have little influence in future group decision-making. Majorities seek to strengthen their majority positions by seeking only confirmatory information. This tends to eliminate divergent minority view-points. A false consensus emerges with all members ostensibly agreeing while, privately, some members may disagree and feel excluded by the process. Harmony is equated with loyalty.

Research has consistently demonstrated the superiority of constructive controversy over concurrence seeking, as well as competitive and individualistic forms of problem-solving, for integrating cultural diversity, bringing people together, and producing better problem-solving. For example:

- Constructive controversy was found to promote greater liking, and increased the quality of interpersonal relationships between managers and their subordinates across cultural boundaries.[102]
- Individuals engaged in constructive controversy tended to be more open-minded to information and thought from a variety of positions other than their own. When the context was competitive, individuals were more close-minded and less willing to make concessions, having a defensive adherence to their own initial positions.[103]
- Constructive controversy tended to produce in individuals a more accurate and complete understanding of others' cognitive perspectives.[104] These understandings

enhanced individuals' abilities to find beneficial agreements under conditions of conflict.[105]

■   Individuals that engaged in constructive controversy liked the decision-making process better than individuals engaged in concurrence seeking.[106]

■   Individuals engaged in constructive controversy demonstrated greater concern of international justice issues,[107] and higher levels of ethical motivation, judgment, and character.[108]

It may appear to some observers that constructive controversy is very American in its emphasis on confrontation of viewpoints and may not be successful in cultures that value interpersonal harmony and preservation of others' "face" (see Chapter 14) or respect. Tjosvold's research has demonstrated that constructive controversy is an effective high-performance integrator even in China, where the value placed on harmony and face are paramount.[109]

Constructive controversy is actually quite the opposite of Western European dualistic thinking where there is a "right" answer and a "wrong" answer and the debate is about which is which. Constructive controversy is, in fact, closer to Western dialectical problem-solving, or to the Chinese view that opposites are complementary. Through detailed discussions that include advocates of different viewpoints, switching sides to advocate each other's views while arguing against their own, positions that might have initially seemed contradictory begin to merge as points of agreement between sides emerge through synthesis. Therefore, a process seeming ostensibly very Western in its reliance on conflict and identifying points of disagreement is stood on its head as the points of agreement emerge through synthesis of apparent opposites.

Leadership as an integrator

Global leadership has two main purposes. The first is to set the strategy for an MNE to compete in both the global business environment as well as in each local environment in which the MNE competes (see Chapter 11). The second purpose of global leadership is to integrate the worldwide internal capabilities of the MNE so that it may effectively pursue and implement its strategy. Leadership style is a function of senior management's preferences. It affects organizational systems and structure, organizational culture, as well as the selection and management of the MNE's human resources.

Over the years there have been many approaches to understanding what leadership is and how it functions.[110] In the first half of the twentieth century, *trait* theories were developed in an attempt to find the intellectual, psychological, social, or physical characteristics that were consistent with leadership success. Even today, Jungian psychologists categorize leadership styles in terms of their underlying personality preferences for information processing.

Keirsey,[111] for example, derived four basic leadership styles (see Chapter 3 in relation to learning) from Jungian psychological theory, each with characteristic strengths and weaknesses. Keirsey argued that leaders were not consciously aware of these predilections because the preferences were habitual and possibly genetically based.

The *logistical* leader (Sensing/Judging, or SJ) was particularly skilled at building complex formal organizations and is often a valued manager in MNEs. The *strategic* leader (iNtuiting/Thinking, or NT) was particularly skilled at developing innovative and efficient organizations, and is especially valued in senior management. The *diplomatic* leader (iNtuiting/Feeling, or NF) was particularly skilled at building interpersonal relationships based on cooperation, trust, and shared goals. The *tactical* leader (Sensing/Perceiving, or SP) was particularly skillful at identifying opportunities and finding the means to grasp them quickly, but uncomfortable with formal organization. Tactical leaders were often entrepreneurs. Freudian psychologists also developed trait theories about how leadership was impacted by personal psychological characteristics.[112]

In the latter half of the twentieth century, *behavioral* theories of leadership emerged.[113] Leaders were understood to manage between two principle variables in their efforts to motivate staff to get work done in an efficient or an effective fashion. *Task orientation* (TO) was the focus on getting tasks done, and organizing workers efficiently. TO involved initiating and structuring the roles, tasks, goals, supervision, and checkpoints intended to facilitate task achievement. *Relationship orientation* (RO) involved building positive and personal relationships with one's staff that would influence and motivate them to get the tasks done. RO involved demonstrating consideration for staff by being cooperative, building trust, and mutual respect, showing understanding for others' feelings, and building personal relationships.

Blake and Mouton[114] used these two dimensions to create a *situational* leadership grid containing five leadership styles: (1) high TO/low RO; (2) high TO/high RO; (3) low

EXHIBIT 6.6 REDDIN'S LEADERSHIP GRID

Related leader	Integrated leader	
Low TO	High TO	
High RO	High RO	
Separated leader	**Dedicated leader**	
Low TO	High TO	
Low RO	Low RO	

Source: Adapted from Reddin, W. J. *Managerial Effectiveness*. London: McGraw-Hill, 1970.

E X H I B I T 6.6

TO/high RO; (4) low TO/low RO; and (5) medium TO and RO. Reddin[115] used the task and relationship dimensions to create a leadership grid containing four leadership styles. Reddin's grid is illustrated in Exhibit 6.6.

Dedicated leaders dominated their staff by giving many verbal instructions, evaluating performance, and assigning rewards and punishments, all without feeling the need to build personal relationships with their staff. *Integrated* leaders negotiated goals and organized work while providing high levels of socioemotional support for their staff. *Related* leaders built personal relationships with staff and counted on their staff to be motivated by the positive relationships to get the work done. *Separated* leaders relied on policies, procedures, and rules to define how work should be done, and offered little task guidance or relational support.

Blake and Mouton[116] argued that the Integrated leadership style was the best one because leaders had to achieve requisite task performance, and also build and maintain good working relationships with their staff. By contrast, Reddin,[117] Fiedler,[118] and Hersey and Blanchard[119] all agreed that all four leadership styles could be effective or ineffective, depending on whether or not they were applied in situationally correct ways.

This idea of *situational leadership* has become a standard for understanding leadership effectiveness. It has been suggested that situational leadership is the ideal pattern, or archetype, for Western conceptions of leadership effectiveness. Even in Judaic and Christian Bible stories, dating back thousands of years, God led Abraham using what could be considered situational leadership.[120]

Hersey and Blanchard observed that the most appropriate leadership style depended on the *maturity* level of the staff persons being led and managed. Maturity was defined as a function of motivation level, willingness/ability to set goals and accept responsibility, relevant education level, and relevant experience. A manager would be more successful managing his/her employee based on the employee's level of maturity. A follower with low maturity should be led with a more directive Dedicated style. Relatively unmotivated, uneducated employees with little relevant experience would fit this bill.

Business students, in contrast, are motivated or they wouldn't be in class or in school. Most of them are quite able to set goals and generally take responsibility for completing assignments. On the other hand, they are in the middle of their relevant education, and many have limited relevant business experience. It would be appropriate to assume them to have medium maturity and use an Integrated leadership style. A professor using an Integrated leadership style would set work goals, negotiate what constituted good output and goal achievement, and build positive relationships, hoping to encourage motivation and commitment.

Professional employees—senior managers, experienced lawyers, accountants, and professors, for example—would be considered to have high maturity. They know the tasks they are responsible for, have an established track record for doing them, and are trained to achieve them. It would be appropriate to expect to manage them with a low TO leadership style. The question would be whether you needed to build positive relationships (RO) with them or not. This would depend on your personal style—whether you were happier building relationships with staff or not. However, highly skilled professional workers should function well when managed with either a Related or a Separated leadership style. If they do not, you should reevaluate your assessment of their maturity level and alter your leadership style as needed.

In the context of international business, it is also evident that some styles of situational leadership better fit certain MNE mindsets. In Chapter 3 we discussed *ethnocentric*, *polycentric*, and *geocentric* mindsets. These mindsets governed how MNEs organized their worldwide operations, defining appropriate relationships between headquarters and subsidiaries.

The hallmark of the ethnocentric mindset (and the very similar international and global mentalities) was that headquarters controlled all the operations of its subsidiaries, requiring the subsidiaries to conform to the MNE's home-country standards. Headquarters provided a steady stream of instructions, and inspections by headquarters personnel. Subsidiary personnel were not valued for their expertise or experience in a local market. Under these conditions, a Dedicated leadership style might be considered the most situationally appropriate. High TO is required to ensure that a subsidiary is always on track with headquarters' expectations. High RO is not required, and perhaps not even advisable, because the leaders from the headquarters do not value the expertise or experience of local employees except insofar as they conform to expectations. Since no highly educated, experienced, and motivated local personnel would want to work in such a repressive organizational culture, the maturity of those that do work there might not be very high.

In Chapter 3 we argued that this ethnocentric mindset was not an effective way to manage an MNE. The point here, however, is that it creates an internal organization culture in which the leadership style most likely to be perceived as effective would be Dedicated. A subsidiary leader who adopted a high RO leadership style would be seen at headquarters as behaving inappropriately, and if his/her local employees were not mature in their attitudes might be unable to achieve assigned performance goals because of his/her lack of emphasis on TO.

The hallmark of the geocentric mindset was to integrate the cultural and functional diversity that existed within all headquarters and subsidiary units, to produce the best possible performance outcomes. Headquarters and subsidiaries would be expected to collaborate at all levels so that any innovations discovered in any location may be adapted or applied to any other location, where it could add to the performance of the overall company. Here, both high TO and high RO are appropriate—an Integrated leadership style. This would foster the greatest commitment to the overarching vision of the MNE, and the strongest relationships to facilitate informal coordination of information, and strong relationships to integrate the diversity. Of course, even if the overall leadership style was Integrated, relatively immature (possibly new) individual employees should still be managed in a Dedicated style. Very mature professional staff would be best motivated with either Related or Separated leadership. It is best to manage employees individually based on their individual maturity, rather than trying to apply the same standards to everyone. Leadership is not "one-size-fits-all."

CONCLUSIONS

Cultural diversity, as well as diversity in its other forms, is one of the most vital assets any MNE possesses in its efforts to solve problems and make decisions that promise high performance worldwide. With tight integration based on cooperative goal interdependence and constructive controversy, greater diversity seems to generally result in higher performance outcomes despite some evidence to the contrary.

The key to making diversity a competitive advantage is strong and tight integration. Underrepresented minority diversity representatives must be empowered by being recognized by senior management. They must be given authority over budget and operational resources so that other groups must engage and cooperate with them. Information must be coordinated informally to ensure that as much data as possible will be available when needed. All the elements of diversity must be united by a common corporate vision, usually represented by a geocentric mindset, organized by leaders who adopt situationally appropriate Integrated leadership styles.

The integrating vision must translate into cooperative goal interdependence in which individuals and units are committed to pursuing the same goals, and receive collective rewards so individuals are not incentivized to defect and compete for individual goals and rewards. It is important also to remember that cooperative goal interdependence may result in either constructive controversy or concurrency seeking, depending on whether group members are capable of handling the conflict inherent in genuine cooperation. Constructive controversy is far more successful than concurrency seeking in obtaining the value that diversity may provide for effective decision-making. Competitive and individualistic goal interdependence are both much less successful in integrating diversity.

The following statements, from Bassi and Russ-Eft,[121] are helpful in considering the value of diversity and how to achieve its maximal benefit for organizational decision-making.

1   People who are part of the minority culture do not want to be simply tolerated. No one wants that. They want to be valued. If they are valued, they can be more effective.
2   Few will admit to feelings or expressions of racism or cultural intolerance in any organization or society, but we all need to learn how to work with one another more effectively and sensitively.
3   When power is shared, people are able to devote tremendous energy to the work at hand.
4   Human beings are the most important asset of any organization. They are the only sustainable competitive advantage for the future.
5   Diversity is to be cherished, for it enriches life and advances the actualization of human potential.

MIND STRETCHING

1   In what ways does a multicultural workforce impact an organization's productivity?

2   Why is it important to take a systems approach to improve employee performance within global organizations?

3   Provide an example of a cross-cultural organizational experience that you were involved in that was difficult for you. How was it difficult? How would you improve the situation?

4   What kinds of diversity are you aware of in your classroom? Does everyone seem to have the right and the willingness to be able to speak his/her mind? Is there anything, or any micro-messages, that discourage this ability on anyone's part? How could the expression of diversity be improved?

5   When you work in a small group, which integrators do you use to ensure team effectiveness? Which could you use that you do not currently? Can you see yourselves switching points of view and arguing against whichever points you have been arguing for? Do you think it would be easier to come to agreement if everyone did this?

6   Do you believe your organization or educational institution values diversity? Explain why or why not, and give specific examples. Apply the principles for creating constructive controversy to small groups discussing this question.

NOTES

1   Quoted at www.brainyquote.com/quotes/keywords/diversity.html (retrieved January 13, 2013).

2   Johnson, D. W. *Constructive Controversy: Theory, Research, Practice.* Cambridge: Cambridge University Press, 2015.

3   Bartlett, C. A. and Ghoshal, S. *Managing Across Borders: The Transnational Solution.* Boston, MA: Harvard Business School, 1989.

4   Johnson, *Constructive Controversy.*

5   Ozbilgin, M. "Global Diversity Management," in P. Smith, M. Peterson, and D. Thomas (eds.), *The Handbook of Cross-Cultural Management Research.* Los Angeles, CA: Sage, 2008, pp. 379–396. Quote taken from pp. 395–396.

6   Bartlett and Ghoshal, *Managing Across Borders.*

7   Stahl, G. K., Maznevski, M. L., Voigt, A., and Jonsen, K. "Unraveling the Effects of Cultural Diversity in Teams: A Meta-Analysis of Research on Multicultural Work Groups," *Journal of International Business Studies,* Vol. 41, No. 4, 2010, pp. 690–709.

8   Lawrence, P. R. and Dyer, D. *Renewing American Industry.* New York: Free Press, 1983.

9   Stahl et al., "Unraveling the Effects of Cultural Diversity in Teams."

10 Bartlett, C. A. and Beamish, P. W. *Transnational Management: Text, Cases, and Readings in Cross-Border Management,* 6th edn. New York: McGraw-Hill, 2011.

11 Johnson, *Constructive Controversy.*

12 Lawrence, P. R. and Lorsch, J. W. *Organization and Environment.* Boston, MA: Harvard Business School, 1967.

13 Lawrence and Dyer, *Renewing American Industry.*

14 Crossan, M. M., Rouse, M. J., Rowe, W. G., and Maurer, C. C. *Strategic Analysis and Action*, 9th edn. Toronto, ON: Pearson, 2016.

15 Johnson, D. W. and Johnson, F. *Joining Together: Group Theory and Group Skills*, 11th edn. Boston, MA: Allyn & Bacon, 2013.

16 Ibid.

17 See www.psychometrics.com for trainer certification programs (retrieved December 14, 2016).

18 See www.humandynamics.com (retrieved December 14, 2016).

19 Bartlett and Ghoshal, *Managing Across Borders.*

20 Ibid., p. 143.

21 Derrida, J. *The Other Heading: Reflections on Today's Europe.* Indianapolis, IN: Indiana University Press, 1990.

22 Buckley, P. J. and Carter, M. J. "A Formal Analysis of Knowledge Combination in Multinational Enterprises," *Journal of International Business Studies*, Vol. 35, 2004, pp. 371–384.

23 Fransman, M. "Information, Knowledge, Vision, and Theories of the Firm," in G. Dosi, D. J. Teece, and J. Chytry (eds.), *Technology, Organization and Competitiveness: Perspectives on Industrial and Corporate Change.* Oxford: Oxford University Press, 1998.

24 Kogut, B. and Zander, U. "Knowledge of the Firm and the Evolutionary Theory of the Multinational Corporation," *Journal of International Business Studies*, Vol. 24, 1993, pp. 625–645.

25 Ibid.

26 Li, J. and Shenkar, O. "Knowledge Search and Governance Choice: International Joint Ventures in the People's Republic of China," *Management International Review*, Vol. 43, 2003, pp. 91–109.

27 Barney, J. "Firm Resources and Sustained Competitive Advantage," *Journal of Management*, Vol. 12, 1991, pp. 99–120.

28 Abramson, N. R. "Building Business Relationships Using Western Marketing Practices in East Asia," in M. A. Abdullah and M. I. B. Bakar (eds.), *Small and Medium Enterprises in Asian Pacific Countries.* Huntington, NY: NOVA, 2000, pp. 3–27.

29 See Johnson, D. W. and Johnson, R. T. *Cooperation and Competition: Theory and Research.* Edina, MN: Interaction Book Company, 1989. Johnson, D. W. and Johnson, R. T. "Energizing Learning: The Instructional Power of Conflict," *Educational Researcher*, Vol. 38, No. 1, 2009, pp. 37–51.

30 Stahl et al., "Unraveling the Effects of Cultural Diversity in Teams."

31 Ibid.

32 Homan, A., Hollenbeck, J., Humphrey, S., Knippenberg, D., Ilgen, D., and Van Kleef, G. "Facing Differences with an Open Mind: Openness to Experience, Salience of Intragroup Differences, and Performance of Diverse Workgroups," *Academy of Management Journal*, Vol. 51, No. 6, 2008, pp. 1204–1222.

33 Kearney, E., Gebert, D., and Voehpel, S. "When and How Diversity Benefits Teams: The Importance of Team Members' Need for Cognition," *Academy of Management Journal*, Vol. 52, No. 3, 2009, pp. 581–598.

34 Joshi, A. and Roh, H. "The Role of Context in Work Team Diversity Research: A Meta-Analytic Review," *Academy of Management Journal*, Vol. 52, No. 3, 2009, pp. 533–627.

35 Homan et al., "Facing Differences with an Open Mind."

36 Abramson, N. R. and Keating, R. J. "Knowledge Management Through the Lens of the Cognitive Theory of Strategy: American, Chinese, and Thai Decision-Making Capabilities," *Journal of Global Business*, Vol. 17, No. 34, pp. 27–42.

37 Gardenswartz, L. and Rowe, A. *Managing Diversity: A Complete Desk Reference.* San Diego, CA: Pfeiffer, 1993.

38 Harrison, D., Price, K., and Bell, M. "Beyond Relational Demography: Time and the Effects of Surface- and Deep-Level Diversity on Work Group Cohesion," *Academy of Management Journal*, Vol. 41, No. 1, 1998, pp. 96–107.

39 Ozbilgin, M. "Global Diversity Management," in P. Smith, M. Peterson, and D. Thomas (eds.), *The Handbook of Cross-Cultural Management Research*. Los Angeles, CA: Sage, 2008, pp. 379–396.

40 Stahl et al., "Unraveling the Effects of Cultural Diversity in Teams."

41 For example: Abramson and Keating, "Knowledge Management Through the Lens of the Cognitive Theory of Strategy."

42 House, R. J., Hanges, P. W., Javidan, M., Dorfman, P., and Gupta, V. (eds.). *Culture, Leadership, and Organizations: The GLOBE Study of 62 Societies*. Beverley Hills, CA: Sage, 2004.

43 American Express Financial Advisors. "Diversity: Report to Benchmark Partners," in B. Abramms and G. F. Simons (eds.), *Cultural Diversity Sourcebook*. Amherst, MA: ODT, 1996.

44 Parfit, M. "Human Migration," *National Geographic*, October, 1998, pp. 11–14.

45 Ibid.

46 AncestryDNA at www.dna.ancestry.ca (retrieved September 2, 2016).

47 See: Buss, D. M. *Evolutionary Psychology: The New Science of the Mind*, 3rd edn. Boston, MA: Pearson, 2008; De Vos, G. A. and De Vos, E. S. *Basic Dimensions in Conscious Thought: The Self and Socialization of Human Concerns*, Volume 1. Oxford: Rowman & Littlefield, 2004.

48 Massey, B. *Where in the World Do I Belong?* USA: Jetlag Press, 2006.

49 McCrae, R. R. and Costa, P. T. Jr. *Personality in Adulthood: A Five-Factor Theory Perspective*. New York: Guilford Press, 2003.

50 Inkeles, A. *National Character: A Psycho-Social Perspective*. New Brunswick, NJ: Transaction Publishers, 2015.

51 UNHCR: The UN Refugee Agency, "Figures at a Glance," www.unhcr.org (retrieved September 2, 2016).

52 https://en.m.wikipedia.org/wiki/illegal-immigration-to-the-United-States (retrieved September 2, 2016).

53 Stahl et al., "Unraveling the Effects of Cultural Diversity in Teams."

54 Tajfel, H. "Social Psychology of Intergroup Relations," *Annual Review of Psychology*, Vol. 33, 1982, pp. 1–39.

55 Lau, D. C. and Murnighan, J. K. "Interactions within Groups and Subgroups: The Effects of Demographic Faultlines," *Academy of Management Journal*, Vol. 48, No. 4, 2005, pp. 645–659.

56 Dyck, B. and Starke, F. A. "The Formation of Breakaway Organizations: Observations and a Process Model," *Administrative Science Quarterly*, Vol. 44, 1999, pp. 792–822.

57 Bartlett, C. A. and Ghoshal, S. "Managing Across Borders: New Strategic Requirements," *Sloan Management Review*, summer, 1987, pp. 7–17.

58 Bartlett and Ghoshal, *Managing Across Borders*.

59 Bartlett and Ghoshal, "Managing Across Borders."

60 Bartlett and Ghoshal, *Managing Across Borders*.

61 Ibid.

62 Hoffman, B. G. *American Icon: Alan Mulally and the Fight to Save Ford Motor Company*. New York: Crown Business, 2013.

63 Johnson, *Constructive Controversy*.

64 Bartlett and Ghoshal, *Managing Across Borders*.

65 Thompson, J. D. *Organizations in Action*. New York: McGraw-Hill, 1967.

66 Mohr, L. B. "Organizational Technology and Organizational Structure," *Administrative Science Quarterly*, Vol. 16, 1971, pp. 444–459.

67 Van de Ven, A. H., Delbecq, A. L. and Koenig, R. "Determinants of Coordination Modes within Organizations," *American Sociological Review*, Vol. 41, 1976, pp. 322–338.

68 Deutsch, M. *Distributive Justice: A Social Psychological Perspective*. New Haven, CT: Yale University Press, 1985. Also see Tjosvold, D. "The Dynamics of Interdependence in Organizations," *Human Relations*, Vol. 37, 1986, pp. 517–540.

69 Johnson, D. W. and Johnson, R. T. "New Developments in Social Interdependence Theory," *Genetic, Social, and General Psychology Monographs*, Vol. 131, No. 4, 2005, pp. 285–358.

70 Bartlett and Ghoshal, *Managing Across Borders*.

71 Johnson, D. W., Johnson, R. T. and Maruyama, G. "Interdependence and Interpersonal Attraction among Heterogeneous and Homogeneous Individuals: A Theoretical Formulation and a Meta-Analysis of the Research," *Review of Educational Research*, Vol. 53, 1983, pp. 5–54.

72 Deutsch, *Distributive Justice*.

73 Tjosvold, D. and Chia, L. C. "Conflict Between Managers and Workers: The Role of Cooperation and Competition," *The Journal of Social Psychology*, Vol. 129, 1988, pp. 235–247.

74 Bartlett and Ghoshal, "Managing Across Borders."

75 Deutsch, *Distributive Justice*.

76 Lawrence and Lorsch, *Organization and Environment*.

77 Bartlett and Ghoshal, "Managing Across Borders: New Organizational Responses," *Sloan Management Review*, fall, 1987, pp. 43–54.

78 Tjosvold, D. "Cooperation Theory and Organizations," *Human Relations*, Vol. 37, 1984, pp. 743–767.

79 Johnson, R. T., Johnson, D. W., and Stanne, M. B. "Effects of Cooperative, Competitive and Individualistic Goal Structures on Computer-Assisted Instruction," *Journal of Educational Psychology*, Vol. 77, 1985, pp. 668–677.

80 Tjosvold, D. "Cooperative and Competitive Dynamics Within and Between Organizational Units," *Human Relations*, Vol. 41, 1988, pp. 425–436.

81 Johnson, D. W. and Johnson, R. T. "Cooperative, Competitive and Individualistic Learning," *Journal of Research and Development in Education*, Vol. 12, 1978, pp. 3–15.

82 Tjosvold, D. "Interdependence and Power Between Managers and Employees: A Study of the Leader Relationship," *Journal of Management*, Vol. 15, 1989, pp. 49–62.

83 Young, L. C. and Wilkinson, I. F. "The Role of Trust and Cooperation in Marketing Channels," *European Journal of Marketing*, Vol. 23, 1989, pp. 109–122.

84 Swan, J. E., Trawick, I. F., and Silva, D. W. "How Industrial Salespeople Gain Customer Trust," *Industrial Marketing Management*, Vol. 14, 1985, pp. 203–211.

85 Tjosvold, "Interdependence and Power Between Managers and Employees."

86 Tjosvold, D. "Dynamics Within Participation: An Experimental Investigation," *Group and Organization Studies*, Vol. 10, 1985, pp. 260–277.

87 Deutsch, M. "Theory of Cooperation and Competition," *Human Relations*, Vol. 2, 1949, pp. 129–152. Deutsch, M. "An Experimental Study of the Effects of Cooperation and Competition Upon the Group Process," *Human Relations*, Vol. 2, 1949, pp. 199–231.

88 Tjosvold, "Cooperation Theory and Organizations."

89 Johnson et al., "Interdependence and Interpersonal Attraction among Heterogeneous and Homogeneous Individuals."

90 Scott, R. *National Comparisons of Racial Attitudes of Segregated and Desegregated Students*. Baltimore, MD: John Hopkins University Press, 1979.

91 Johnson, D. W. and Johnson, R. T. "Effects of Cooperative, Competitive and Individualistic Learning Experiences on Interethnic Interaction and Friendships," *Journal of Social Psychology*, Vol. 118, 1982, pp. 47–58.

92 Johnson et al., "Interdependence and Interpersonal Attraction among Heterogeneous and Homogeneous Individuals." Johnson and Johnson, "Effects of Cooperative, Competitive and Individualistic Learning Experiences on Interethnic Interaction and Friendships."

93 Johnson, D. W. and Johnson, R. T. "Effects of Cooperative and Individualistic Learning Experiences on Interethnic Interaction," *Journal of Interethnic Interaction*, Vol. 73, 1981, pp. 444–449.

94 Johnson, *Constructive Controversy*.

95 Johnson, D. W., Maruyama, G., Johnson, R., Nelson, D., and Skon, L. "Effects of Cooperative, Competitive and Individualistic Goal Structures on Achievement: A Meta-Analysis," *Psychological Bulletin*, Vol. 89, 1981, pp. 47–62.

96 Johnson, *Constructive Controversy*.

97 Johnson, D. W. and Johnson, R. T. *Creative Controversy: Intellectual Challenge in the Classroom*, 4th edn. Edina, MN: Interaction Book Company, 2007.

98 Johnson and Johnson, *Joining Together*.

99 Ibid.

100 Johnson and Johnson, *Creative Controversy*.

101 Freeze, M. and Fay, D. "Personal Initiative (PI): An Active Performance Concept for Work in the 21st Century," *Research in Organizational Behavior*, Vol. 23, 2001, pp. 133–187. Collins, J. C. and Porras, J. I. *Built to Last: Successful Habits of Visionary Companies*. New York: Harper Collins Publisher, 1994.

102 Chen, Y. F. and Tjosvold, D. "Participative Leadership by American and Chinese Managers in China: The Role of Relationships," *Journal of Management Studies*, Vol. 43, pp. 1727–1752.

103 Johnson, D. W., Johnson, R.T., and Scott, L. "The Effects of Cooperative and Individualized Instruction on Student Attitudes and Achievement," *Journal of Social Psychology*, Vol. 104, 1978, pp. 207–216.

104 Johnson, D. W. and Johnson, R. T. "Energizing Learning: The Instructional Power of Conflict," *Educational Researcher*, Vol. 38, No. 1, 2009, pp. 37–51.

105 Galinsky, A. D., Maddux, W. W., Gilin, D., and White, J. B. "Why It Pays to Get Inside the Head of Your Opponent: The Differential Effects of Perspective Taking and Empathy in Negotiations," *Psychological Science*, Vol. 19, No. 1, 2008, pp. 378–384.

106 Ibid.

107 Snell, R. S., Tjosvold, D., and Su, F. "Resolving Ethical Conflicts at Work Through Cooperative Goals and Constructive Controversy in the People's Republic of China," *Asia Pacific Journal of Management*, Vol. 23, 2006, pp. 319–343.

108 Tichy, M., Johnson, D. W., Johnson, R. T., and Roseth, C. "The Impact of Constructive Controversy on Moral Development," *Journal of Applied Social Psychology*, Vol. 40, No. 4, 2010, pp. 765–787.

109 See, for example, Tjosvold, D., Hui, C., and Sun, H. "Can Chinese Discuss Conflicts Openly? Field and Experimental Studies of Face Dynamics in China," *Group Decision and Negotiation*, Vol. 13, 2004, pp. 351–373. Tjosvold, D., Law, K. S., and Sun, H. "Collectivistic and Individualistic Values: Their Effects on Group Dynamics and Productivity in China," *Group Decision and Negotiation*, Vol. 12, 2003, pp. 243–263; Tjosvold, D. and Su, F. S. "Managing Anger and Annoyance in Organizations in China: The Role of Constructive Controversy," *Group and Organization Management*, Vol. 32, No. 3, 2007, pp. 260–289.

110 Abramson, N. R. "The Leadership Archetype: A Jungian Analysis of Similarities between Modern Leadership Theory and the Abraham Myth in the Judaic-Christian Tradition," *Journal of Business Ethics*, Vol. 72, 2007, pp. 115–129.

111 Keirsey, D. *Please Understand Me* II: *Temperament, Character, Intelligence*. Del Mar, CA: Prometheus Nemesis, 1998.

112 See Zaleznik, A. *Executive's Guide to Motivating People: How Freudian Theory Can Turn Good Executives into Better Leaders*. Chicago, IL: Bonus Books, 1990. Also see Kets de Vries, M. *The Leadership Mystique: A User's Manual for the Human Enterprise*. London: Prentice Hall, 2001.

113 Abramson, "The Leadership Archetype."

114 Blake, R. R. and Mouton, J. S. *The Managerial Grid: Key Orientations for Achieving Production*. Houston, TX: Gulf Publishing, 1964.

115 Reddin, W. J. *Managerial Effectiveness*. London: McGraw-Hill, 1970.

116 Blake and Mouton, *The Managerial Grid*.

117 Reddin, *Managerial Effectiveness*.

118 Fiedler, F. E. *Leadership Experience and Leadership Performance*. Alexandria, VA: US Army Research Institute for the Behavioral and Social Sciences, 1994.

119 Hersey, P. and Blanchard, K. H. *Management of Organizational Behavior: Utilizing Human Resources*. Englewood Cliffs, NJ: Prentice-Hall, 1993.

120 Abramson, "The Leadership Archetype."

121 Bassi, L. J. and Russ-Eft, D. (eds.). *What Works: Assessment, Development, and Measurement*. Alexandria, VA: American Society for Training and Development, 1997.

7 LESSONS FOR GLOBAL LEADERS

The motivation for writing this chapter came from an experience several years ago. Since 1976, I have been a faculty in an MBA program at Thunderbird School of Global Management in Arizona. My teaching continued until recently. During my time at Thunderbird, I participated as a faculty member in a significant number of executive education programs, ranging from two days in length to two weeks, with middle to senior managers and executives of global companies.

In many, but not all, of our programs, besides asking participants to complete a comprehensive evaluation at the end of the program, we did a follow-up evaluation, especially if the program was held on a regular basis, such as once per year or even more frequently. I was the "academic director" of a two-week program for a rather large diverse global company. Approximately six months after a program and five months before the next program, we had compiled all evaluations, and had some suggestions for changes and improvements based on our analysis of a long program evaluation form completed by all participants. I arranged for a follow-up one-hour discussion with six participants in the past program to listen to their suggestions for the future.

In the telephone conversation, when I came to a highly rated faculty, I asked if the subject he spoke on was very relevant for their responsibilities, and all said "yes." "Should I invite him to return for the next program?" All enthusiastically said "yes."

Then I asked them to share with me one idea they remember from his presentation. *No one could remember anything from his presentation*, but "it was great."

Why couldn't anyone remember anything? *We know that most students, after 24 hours in a class, only remember about 10 percent of what was discussed*, and many remember less.

L
E
A
R
N
I
N
G

O
B
J
E
C
T
I
V
E
S

After reading and studying concepts/examples and illustrations in Chapter 7, readers should:

1   Have identified at least two or three leadership behaviors that are relevant to their responsibilities, and commit to enhance several leadership behaviors over the next several months.
2   Understand one's behavior as a leader is more important than words, promises, or theory.
3   Commit to "shadowing" the most competent global leader in their enterprise and observing their behavior in different circumstances.

In this chapter you will read about Sir Ernest Shackleton, as a leader of an adventure, research on the skills of effective negotiators, the CEO skills of Sir Winston Churchill, and a commencement speech made by Steve Jobs at Stanford University in 2005.

Some ideas on "leadership competencies"

An article appeared in a recent issue of *The Economist*[1] shortly after the death of Andy Grove, who joined Intel as its first employee in 1968. The one-page description, whose lead-in title was "The Man Who Put Intel Inside," was extremely complimentary. Andy Grove's "genius was an organization-builder and manager rather than an innovator." The article wrote that he believed in "creative confrontation" (which sometimes meant screaming matches).

For anyone reading this and wondering what the behaviors of creative confrontation were, they might be a bit puzzled. What follows are some ideas on competencies.

In the not too distant past, there was significant interest in trying to identify personality traits that were associated with job performance and skill. Research did not show much correlation between personality traits and skill on the job. Nor did academic aptitude or knowledge content tests predict success in life or job performance. In the US, researchers discovered that scores on written exams for applicants to the Foreign Service in the US demonstrated that the higher the individual scored on the tests, the worse he or she did as a diplomat.[2]

LESSON ONE: SIR ERNEST SHACKLETON

Nothing ever goes exactly as planned.

Anonymous

Sir Ernest Shackleton, 1874–1922.

The story[3]

After the Norwegian Roald Amundsen reached the South Pole in advance of the British Expedition under Robert Scott by a few days, there was another Antarctic challenge; namely, crossing of the South polar continent from sea to sea, a distance of approximately 1,180 miles.

Ernest Shackleton failed in the goal to cross from sea to sea, but the story of his attempt has examples of high adventure, strenuous days, great determination, and supreme loyalty when he and his crew were caught in the polar ice for nearly two years. The map in Exhibit 7.1 shows the key dates and locations. The trip had significant geographic and scientific goals, including whether the chain of mountains from the Ross Sea to the Pole extends across the continent.

- Shackleton received almost 5,000 applications for men who wanted to join the expedition.
- The *Endurance*, Shackleton's ship, sailed from London on August 1, 1914.
- The *Endurance* left Argentina in October 1914 and headed for Vahsel Bay, where they expected to land and begin their preparations for the journey to the Pole. Their British colleagues on the ship *Aurora* were to find land on the opposite side of Antarctica. The two teams were to meet at the South Pole.
- About one mile from shore, the *Endurance* was caught in the ice on January 18, 1915.
- The *Endurance* and crew were in ice floes of the Weddell Sea until October 27, 1915, when the crew abandoned ship because of a major leak.
- On November 21, 1915, the *Endurance* sank to the bottom of the Weddell Sea.
- The crew was on the ice until April 9, 1916, when they found open water and headed for Elephant Island (to the crew's knowledge, no one had set foot on the island before).
- The three lifeboats arrived on Elephant Island.
- Shackleton and five men left on the Caird lifeboat (seven meters long) for South Georgia.

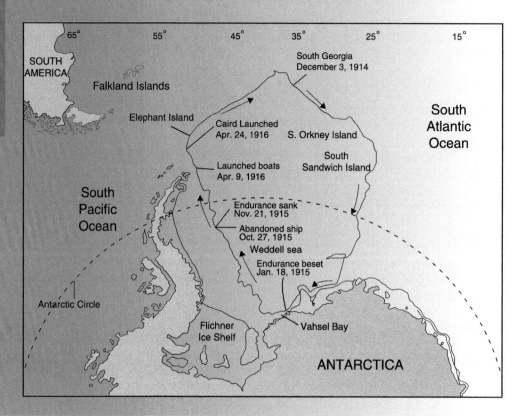

EXHIBIT 7.1 MAP OF SHACKLETON'S JOURNEY

- On May 20, 1916, Shackleton and five companions arrived at the whaling station in South Georgia.
- On August 30, 1916, Shackleton and Chilean sailors arrived on Elephant Island to take all back to Chile for a celebratory stop on their way home.

Aspects of Shackleton's leadership

In the best leadership book we have ever read, *Shackleton's Way: Leadership Lessons from the Great Antarctic Explorer*,[4] the authors Morrell and Capparell analyze the diaries of Shackleton and the crew and ask: How did Shackleton lead, what did he do? Leadership is not theoretical–leadership is behavior.

The following are some behaviors Morrell and Capparell identified that we believe are particularly relevant to leaders of global projects.

SHACKLETON'S WAY OF DEVELOPING LEADERSHIP SKILLS

- Broaden your cultural and social horizons beyond your usual experiences.
- Find a way to turn setbacks and failures to you advantage.
- Be bold in vision and careful in planning.

SHACKLETON'S WAY OF SELECTING AND ORGANIZING A CREW

- Start with a solid core of talent you know from past experience.
- Your No. 2 is your most important person.
- Work with those who share your vision.
- Surround yourself with cheerful, optimistic people.
- Hire those with the talents and expertise you lack.
- Look for hidden skills of team members.

SHACKLETON'S WAY OF FORGING A UNITED AND LOYAL TEAM

- Always keep the door open to all.
- Be fair and impartial.
- Lead by example.
- Have regular meetings to build *esprit de corps* (group loyalty).

SHACKLETON'S WAY OF DEVELOPING INDIVIDUAL TALENT

- Make sure each person has challenging and important work.
- Give consistent feedback on performance.
- Reward the individual as well as the group.

SHACKLETON'S WAY OF GETTING THE GROUP THROUGH A CRISIS

- Get rid of unnecessary middle layers of authority.
- Keep your malcontents close to you.
- Ask for advice and information from a variety of sources.
- Confront rumors and negative behavior immediately.

SHACKLETON'S WAY OF FORMING GROUPS FOR THE TOUGHEST TASKS

- Make sure you have some highly skilled individuals who can handle tough challenges.
- Empower the team leaders so they have the authority to handle their own team.
- Do not be afraid to change your mind when you see your plan is not working.

SHACKLETON'S WAY OF FINDING THE DETERMINATION TO MOVE FORWARD

■   Go-for-broke risks become more acceptable as options narrow.

■   Let your team inspire you.

■   Celebrate even small successes.

Most participants in executive education programs who hear the story of Shackleton remember, use, and find benefit using different leadership skills as they are relevant to their specific situations. But the ones that seem to get the most "traction" and are remembered and are used are the following:

■   Keep the malcontents close.

■   Learn the hidden talents of team members.

■   Celebrate small successes.

Three explorers

Robert Scott, an English naval officer, became the leader of the Discovery Expedition to the South Pole. With two other men, he did not reach the South Pole, nearly starved for lack of provisions, and nearly froze, but they made it back to their ship and returned to England. In a subsequent exploration in 1911, Scott and five members of his team made it to the South Pole. But Amundsen had already planted the Norwegian flag on the Pole. They froze to death on their return. Their bodies were found a year later.

Roald Amundsen, with a team of expert skiers and 52 of the best sled dogs available, said "The outcome of the expedition depends on them [the dogs]," headed for the South Pole and on December 14, 1911, reached it.

A member of Scott's team, Apsley Cherry-Garrard,[5] after returning from Antarctica, wrote: "For a joint scientific and geographical piece of organization, give me Scott . . . for a dash to the Pole and nothing else, Amundsen, and if I am in the devil of a hole and want to get out of it, give me Shackleton every time."

LESSON TWO: BUILDING PARTNERSHIP FOR MATERIAL BENEFIT

Let us not be blind to our differences—but let us also direct attention to our common interests.

John F. Kennedy

In Chapter 4 on the topic of negotiating long-term for mutual benefit, we covered the "cultural aspects" of negotiating when our partners are from different cultures. In reality, in the widest sense, we negotiate with others rather frequently. Businesspeople negotiate with colleagues outside their organization, such as with suppliers, and within their organization, such as when negotiations take place with different departments. Many books have been written on the topic.

But do the books, articles, or speeches by negotiating "gurus" differentiate between the behaviors of "skilled negotiators" and "average negotiators"?

The following is a summary of a research project that analyzed actual negotiations.[6] The researchers' methods allowed them to differentiate between skilled negotiators and average negotiators by using behavioral analysis techniques as they observed the negotiations and recorded the discussion. They identified "successful" negotiators as those who:

■   were rated as effective by both sides;
■   had a "track record" of significant success; and
■   had a low incidence of "implementation" failures.

A total of 48 negotiators who met all three success criteria were studied. They included union representatives (17), management representatives (12), contract negotiators (10), and others (9).

The 48 successful negotiators were studied over a total of 102 separate negotiating sessions. In the following description, the successful negotiators are called the "skilled" group. In comparison, the negotiators who either failed to meet the criteria or about whom no criterion data were available were called the "average" group.

During the planning process

Negotiation training emphasizes the importance of planning.

■   *Planning time.* No significant difference was found between the total planning time of skilled and average negotiators prior to actual negotiation.
■   *Exploration of options.* The skilled negotiator considers a wider range of outcomes or options for action than does the average negotiator.
■   *Common ground.* The research showed that the skilled negotiators gave more than three times as much attention to common-ground areas as did average negotiators.
■   *Long term or short term?* With the average negotiator, approximately one comment in 25 met the criterion of long-term consideration; namely, a comment that involved any factor extending beyond the immediate implementation of the issue under negotiation.
■   *Setting limits.* The researchers asked negotiators about their objectives, and recorded whether their replies referred to single-point objectives (e.g., "We aim to settle at 83") or to a defined range (e.g., "We hope to get 85, but we would settle for a minimum of 77"). Skilled negotiators were significantly more likely to set upper and lower limits–to

plan in terms of range. Average negotiators, in contrast, were more likely to plan their objectives around a fixed point.

■ *Sequence and issue planning*. The term "planning" frequently refers to a process of sequencing—putting a number of events, points, or potential occurrences into a time sequence. Critical path analysis and other forms of network planning are examples.

Typical sequence plan used by average negotiators:

A then B then C then D Issues are linked.

Typical issue plan used by skilled negotiators:

Issues are independent and not linked by sequence.

The clear advantage of issue planning over sequence planning is flexibility.

Face-to-face behavior

Skilled negotiators show marked differences in their face-to-face behavior, compared with average negotiators. They use certain types of behavior significantly more frequently, while they tend to avoid other types.

■ *Irritators*. Certain words and phrases that are commonly used during negotiation have negligible value in persuading the other party, but do cause irritation. Probably the most frequent example of these is the term "generous offer" used by a negotiator to describe his or her proposal.

■ *Counterproposals*. During negotiation, one party frequently puts forward a proposal, and the other party immediately responds with a counterproposal. Researchers found that skilled negotiators made immediate counterproposals much less frequently than average negotiators.

■ *Argument dilution*. This way of thinking predisposes us to believe that there is some special merit in quantity. Having five reasons for doing something is considered more persuasive than having only one reason. One may feel that the more he or she can put on his or her scale, the more likely it is to tip the balance of an argument in his or her favor. The researchers found that the opposite was true. The skilled negotiator used fewer reasons to back up each of his or her arguments.

■ *Reviewing the negotiation*. The researchers asked negotiators how likely they were to spend time reviewing the negotiation afterward. Over two-thirds of the skilled negotiators claimed that they always set aside some time after a negotiation to review it and consider what they had learned. Just under half of average negotiators, in contrast, made the same claim.

The "skillful negotiators" during the planning phase of negotiating and during the face-to-face interactions behaved differently than the "average negotiators." These behaviors can be learned or enhanced as a global leader.

LESSON THREE: WINSTON CHURCHILL, AS CEO

> I also hope that I sometimes suggested to the lion the right place to use his claws.
> Winston Churchill on the occasion of his 80th birthday

A history briefing of Sir Winston Churchill[7]

- Born to a British father and an American mother, on November 30, 1874, and died January 24, 1965.
- Churchill arrived in Africa as a young man and spent many years there.
- Was enrolled at Sandhurst, Britain's Royal Military college.
- Winston's father was "harsh" and his mother was "cool" toward him.
- In his early education, he developed a love of and facility with the English language.
- When he graduated from Harrow, a prestigious British school, he joined the military.
- He became a war correspondent.
- He fought for the British in South Africa.
- Returning to England, he won a seat in Parliament in 1900.
- He served in World War I between 1914 and 1918.
- In 1930, he withdrew from the liberal Labor Party government and worked against a bill designed to give India the status of a self-governing dominion.
- In September 1939, Hitler invaded Poland.
- Churchill became Prime Minister of England in May 1940 and was a remarkable war leader.
- In July 1945, the people failed to reelect him in the general election, but he was returned to office in 1951.
- He was awarded the Nobel Prize for Literature.

Sir Winston Churchill is viewed by many as one of the great leaders of the twentieth century. Following are some of his leadership traits as summarized from the book, *Winston Churchill CEO.*

ONE

I pass with relief from the tossing sea of Cause and Theory to the firmer ground of Result and Fact.

Churchill 1898

Effective leadership is never a matter of imposing ideas on people, but rather of connecting ideas, values, and goals to the members of the enterprise and to the realities of the environment.

TWO

It is better to be an actor than a critic.

Churchill 1989

Problems are invitations to action, as taking ownership of a problem gives one a stake in the enterprise.

THREE

You will make all kinds of mistakes.

A leader who undertakes a high-risk decision without much hope for success is clearly headed to failure.

FOUR

Change is the master key. A man can wear out a particular part of the mind by continually using it.

What happens to leadership in the absence of curiosity? Britain's King George III showed no curiosity about the nature of the discontent in the American colonies; hence, revolution and eventually a new country, the US.

FIVE

One ought to be just before one is generous.

Churchill 1947

The exercise of power and not justice is tyranny.

SIX

> Nothing is more dangerous ... than to live in the temperamental atmosphere of a Gallup Poll, always feeling one's pulse and taking one's temperature.
>
> Churchill 1941

The reason humans are afraid of rocking the boat is that it makes everyone uncomfortable. But, that is the point of rocking the boat.

SEVEN

> I cannot forecast to you the action of Russia. It is a riddle wrapped in a mystery inside an enigma.
>
> Churchill 1939

People and organizations act from the perspective of their own self-interest.

EIGHT

> I have nothing to offer but blood, toil, tears, and sweat.
>
> Churchill 1940

To be a great leader is to accept responsibility and to possess authority. You can choose to be either a politician or a leader.

NINE

> Now this is not the end. It is not even the beginning of the end. But it is, perhaps, the end of the beginning.
>
> Churchill 1942

Churchill never let his passion become dogma, but he remained flexible as fresh insights altered priorities.

FRAMEWORK: LEADERSHIP SKILLS TO MAKE GLOBALIZATION SUCCEED

> We all have the capacity to inspire and empower others. But we must first be willing to devote ourselves to our personal growth and development as leaders.[8]

Read the example of when one person with leadership responsibilities "worked" on his personal growth and development.

PERSONAL GROWTH AND DEVELOPMENT

The first example I can think of was when I was in Japan as a young man. I arrived in Japan by ship in 1964 as a Catholic priest. It didn't take a long time to meet missionaries and others who didn't like being in Japan, who didn't speak Japanese at all or not well, and who were counting the days till they could go home to North America or Europe.

I also met and worked with people who loved Japan, spoke Japanese well, and considered Japan their home. I engaged regularly with them and observed their behavior and positiveness. I never worked harder in my life than I did in Japan to learn a difficult language well. And I almost always associated with others who loved being in Japan.

My mom and dad were chemically dependent—my father on alcohol and my mother on prescription drugs. As a graduate student with two young children in the mid-1970s, I learned that I "was a child of parents who were chemically dependent." I also read research that demonstrated persuasively that I had to understand how being a child of an alcoholic could influence how I was parenting my two children then and three other children within the next four years. All seven of us spent time attending courses, workshops with professionals.

When I finished my graduate studies, I was employed by a university. I wanted to be a professor who influenced his students. To do this, I attended lectures of the best professors rated by students and watched how they conducted their classes. They were my models, and in time I asked them to come to a class when I was teaching and they gave me feedback. Sometimes it was positive, sometimes it wasn't.

Toward the end of my professional career, I was elected by my peers to be chairman of the department. I watched the behavior of the teachers in our academic institution. I tried to behave as the best of them by speaking clearly, being transparent, understanding strategy, listening to all, judging fairly, but mostly by being committed to students.

In a retirement note sent by one of my colleagues, he wrote: "In all my interactions with you or at departmental meetings, I never experienced you to speak out of both sides of your mouth."

Source: Moran, R. Notes of a talk given in London, England, March 2013.

Since the 1960s, leadership scholars have conducted more than 1,000 studies in an attempt to determine the definitive styles, characteristics, or personality traits of great leaders. None of the studies have produced a clear profile of an ideal leader.[9]

Leadership remains a hot topic among bestselling business books. Some world leaders share their insight into leadership and performance in a political context.

Jimmy Carter, 39th president of the United States, commented about leadership in conflict resolution: "All too often, conflicts and wars arise when we fail to consider the views of others or to communicate with them about differences between us."[10] The Carter Center Principles for Peacemakers (see www.cartercenter.org/peace) amplifies their vision of what a global leader should do, which provides useful guidance for corporate executives:

- Strive to have the international community and all sides in any conflict agree to the basic premise that military force should be used only as a last resort.
- Study the history and causes of the dispute thoroughly.
- Seek help from other mediators, especially those who know the region and are known and respected there.
- Be prepared to go back and forth between adversaries who cannot or will not confront each other.
- Be willing to deal with the key people in any dispute, even if they have been isolated or condemned by other parties or organizations.
- Insist that human rights be protected, that international law be honored.
- Tell the truth, even when it may not contribute to a quick agreement.
- Never despair, even when the situation seems hopeless.

Mikhail Gorbachev, former President of the Soviet Union, observed this on leadership:

The world is becoming ever more integrated. . . . The real leaders of today are capable of integrating the interests of their countries and peoples into the interests of the entire world community. . . . [A] leader combines a political and a moral authority.[11]

Desmond Tutu, the South African Archbishop who received the Nobel Peace Prize in 1984, writes:

The authentic leader has a solidarity with those he or she is leading . . . The good leader is one who is affirming of others, nurturing their best selves, coaxing them to become the best they are capable of becoming . . . [has] the capacity to read the signs of the times . . . knows when to make concessions.[12]

L. D. Schaeffer, then-CEO of Blue Cross of California, described leadership not as a "state, but as a journey, requiring different styles that are determined in part by the demands of the marketplace."[13]

Meena Surie Wilson,[14] in her book on corporate India, states clearly: "Aspiring leaders must learn continuously, which is why there is so much power in learning to learn from experience." This applies to political and business leaders.

The challenge of measuring effectiveness and predicting global performance

In an earlier survey[15] of over 100 executives of global organizations, we found that along a continuum of 0–100 percent, over 60 percent agreed that "global managers are made, not born," and 72 percent agreed that "in global organizations, a new kind of leader is required."

Many business school professors and executives of global organizations know what the key positions are in organizations, but most are less successful in predicting who will be a star performer in that position. And when star performers are identified, they find it difficult to articulate what makes them the best.

Wilson Learning Corporation[16] has developed a global competency model based on an examination of the literature and interviews with organizations in the airline, high-tech, telecommunications, and consumer goods industries. They have identified the following themes related to global leadership:

- understanding the business from a global perspective;
- assimilating and acting on large amounts of complex or ambiguous information;
- driving change based on global strategy;
- commitment to learning;
- effective cross-cultural communication; and
- establishing personal connections readily across cultural boundaries.

Moran and Riesenberger[17] developed a straightforward model of globalization related to performance based on research and experience. The framework is presented in Exhibit 7.2. External factors such as the economies of scale, global sourcing opportunities, exchange rate exposure risks, and other factors present increasing opportunities for organizations to become global.

As a result, the vision, mission, and structure of the organization change. However, to benefit from organizations becoming "global," new and different leadership competencies are required. When the competencies possessed by the leaders are marginal, the benefits are minimal. When leaders possess these competencies to a high degree, the benefits are significant. "Making It Overseas," a *Harvard Business Review* article,[18] suggests similar skills continue to be required today.

EXHIBIT 7.2 MORAN/RIESENBERGER FRAMEWORK

External forces

■ Economies of scale	■ Homogeneous technical standards	■ Competition from international competitors
■ New and evolving markets	■ New and evolving markets	
■ Global sourcing opportunities	■ Global sourcing opportunities	■ New and evolving markets
■ Reduced tariffs/ customs barriers, and tax advantages in many countries	■ Reduced tariffs/customs barriers and tax advantages in many countries	■ Global sourcing opportunities
		■ Reduced tariffs/ customs barriers and tax advantages in many countries

Globalization

Vision	*Strategy*	*Structure*
↑	↑ ↑	↑

Competencies required to make it work

Attitudes	**Leadership**	**Interaction Leadership**	**Cultural Leadership**
■ Possesses a global mindset	■ Facilitates organizational change	■ Negotiates and approaches conflicts in a collaborative mode	■ Understands their own culture, values, and assumptions
■ Has the ability to work as equals with persons of diverse background	■ Creates learning systems	■ Manages skillfully the foreign deployment cycle	■ Accurately profiles organizational culture and national culture of others
■ Has a long-term orientation	■ Motivates employees to excellence	■ Leads and participates effectively in multicultural teams	■ Avoids cultural mistakes and behaves in a manner that demonstrates knowledge and respect for the way of conducting business in other countries

Source: Moran, R. T. and Riesenberger, J. R. *The Global Challenge: Building the New Worldwide Enterprise.* New York: McGraw-Hill, 1994.

DESCRIPTION OF COMPETENCIES

Leadership attitudes

Possess a global mindset. In the play *South Pacific*, Rogers and Hammerstein wrote:[19]

You've got to be taught to hate and fear
You've got to be taught from year to year,
It's got to be drummed in your dear little ear,
You've got to be carefully taught.
You've got to be taught to be afraid
Of peoples whose eyes are oddly made,
And people whose skin is a different shade,
You've got to be carefully taught.
You've got to be taught before it's too late,
Before you are six or seven or eight,
To hate all the people your relatives hate,
You've got to be carefully taught.
You've got to be carefully taught.

The lyrics state eloquently what we have known for a long time: namely, a fundamental vehicle for learning has always been, and will continue to be, other humans. At birth, infants are completely dependent on others for survival. In maturing and throughout the socialization process, children learn that the gratification of needs is, to a large extent, dependent on demonstrating "appropriate" behavior. In groups, whether family, business, or other, individual social needs become suggestive to the influence of others, especially those in authority.

Attitudes are learned, and therefore can be unlearned. A *global mindset* is an attitude; it is not knowledge or information. We learn to be ethnocentric, and we can learn to be global in our perspective.

Global mindsets

Stephen Rhinesmith postulates that a "global mindset" is a requirement of a global leader who will guide institutions and organizations into the future. He defines a mindset as:

a predisposition to see the world in a particular way that sets boundaries and provides explanations for why things are the way they are, while at the same time establishing guidance for ways in which we should behave. In other words, a mindset is a filter through which we look at the world.[20]

Rhinesmith states that people with global mindsets approach the world in a number of particular ways. Specifically, they:

1   Look for the "big picture"; that is, they look for multiple possibilities for any event or occurrence—they aren't satisfied with the obvious.

2   Understand that the rapidly changing, interdependent world in which we are living is indeed complex, and that working in these environments where conflicts need to be managed skillfully is the norm rather than the exception.

3   Are "process-oriented"; in our experience, this is the most important dimension, and the one that is most lacking in individuals who are not globally oriented. Many individuals are unable to understand or are unwilling to learn to "process"; namely, to reflect on the "how" as opposed to the "what."

4   Consider diversity as a resource and know how to work effectively in multicultural teams; an ability to collaborate instead of competing is also integral to the person with a global mindset.

5   Are not uncomfortable with change or ambiguity.

6   Are open to new experiences.

With globalization, contact between persons from different cultures increases. What happens when this occurs? Do individuals become more global or more ethnocentric?

Following a review of the literature on intergroup contact, Amir[21] concluded that the direction of attitude change, following contact with people who are different, depends largely on the conditions under which the contact has taken place. He indicates that there are "favorable" conditions, which reduce prejudice, and "unfavorable" ones, which may increase prejudice.

The favorable condition of "equal status" as a factor in reducing prejudice was reported by Allport.[22] He pointed out that, for contact between groups to be an element in reducing prejudice, it must be based on equal status contact between majority and minority groups in the pursuit of common goals. Organizations that are globalizing must have common goals.

Works as an equal with persons from diverse backgrounds

The ascendance of people from minority groups to leadership positions offers the organization an opportunity to explore new ideas and approaches. Companies that find new, innovative approaches are the ones that are experiencing success today—not the ones that have maintained the status quo. Tom Peters, coauthor of *In Search of Excellence*, declares: "Gone are the days of women succeeding by learning to play men's games. Instead, the time has come for men on the move to learn to play women's games."[23]

Has a long-term orientation

There are many reasons why companies have not been successful in competing in the global marketplace. One of these reasons is "short-termism." Dick Ferry, president and cofounder of Korn/Ferry, addresses this issue:

Corporate America may talk, on an intellectual level, about what it'll take to succeed in the twenty-first century, but when it gets right down to decision-making, all that matters is the next quarterly earnings report.

That's what's driving much of the system. With that mindset, everything else becomes secondary to the ability to deliver the next quarterly earnings push-up. We're on a treadmill. The reward system in this country is geared to the short term.[24]

Why do our foreign competitors take a long view? In Germany and Japan, "cross-ownership" is the norm. *Stakeholders* (customers, suppliers, and banks) are closely involved in the operations of the business.

The short-term view also has other implications. For total quality management to work, organizations must take a long-term view and exercise patience. Few dispute the importance of total quality. However, several recent studies on total quality management have questioned the short-term "quick-fix" mentality of individuals who do not recognize the need for long-term approaches in the implementation of total quality management.

The orientation to short-termism is almost an addiction, and is present in most corporations. Long-term orientation is a critical competency to make globalization work.

The global leader facilitating change

Most global leaders believe managing organizational change is a serious challenge. This was true in the 1990s when the *Harvard Business Review* World Leadership Survey of approximately 12,000 global managers from 25 countries[25] concluded that change is a part of corporate life.

Percy Barnevik, the former CEO of Asea Brown Boveri (ABB) Ltd., puts it this way:

I try to make people accept that change is a way of life. I often got the question from Swiss and Germans: "Mr. Barnevik, aren't you happy now? Can't we relax a bit?" They see new targets as a threat or an inconvenience. But I say, you must get used to the idea that we are changing all the time.[26]

Why do most change initiatives fail to reach their full potential? Steve Gambrell and Craig Stevens[27] suggest there are three phases of organizational change: what occurs before, during, and after changes. They believe that for the change process to be successful, an organized plan is necessary throughout each phase of the change process. Part of this action plan includes understanding motivations for resistance, differences in employee/management perceptions, and the importance of ongoing communication.

Gambrell and Stevens state that to maximize the chances of positive outcome, it is important that the following skills of leaders are developed:

- unbiased open-mindedness;
- good strategic planning abilities;
- good team-building skills; and
- effective communications skills.

Global leaders need these skills to effectively facilitate and lead organizational change.

Creates learning systems

Peter Senge said it best in his book *The Fifth Discipline*: "The organizations that will truly excel in the future will be the organizations that discover how to tap people's commitment and capacity to learn at *all* levels in an organization."[28] The case study is an example of a nonlearning organization in a global context.[29]

CASE STUDY

Several long conversations I've had recently with a European executive have made me acutely aware of two major cross-cultural organizational problems. The first is the inability of many companies to make use of new expertise developed by individuals in the firm. The second is the rather serious reentry problems experienced by many expatriates following a successful international experience.

My friend is 51 years old. He has worked for one of the largest chemical companies in Europe for more than 25 years. He joined the company as a young chemical engineer, completed his apprenticeship, and accepted a position as a sales representative in Australia. He lived there until his return to Europe five years ago.

After his first five years in Australia, he was appointed president of a small subsidiary. Though the European parent company has a policy of job rotation every three years, no replacements were available, so he was happy to stay on in Australia, working for various subsidiary companies.

By the end of his Australia stint, he was a member of many of the most important boards in the country. By all obvious measures, he was a success. The companies he managed flourished, and several of them were sold at considerable profit. Yet, during his long spell in Australia, he never once had a performance appraisal, and never knew clearly how his work was viewed by his superiors in Europe.

When he was eventually replaced in Australia by another European, he was brought home and given a job that he has found to be neither satisfying nor challenging. He has specific responsibilities related to overseas assignments in one country. Ironically, his immediate boss has never lived outside his native country.

This executive's case highlights the tragic inability of many large organizations to handle their people well, and to integrate their individual learning into the organization.

C A S E   S T U D Y

What is most surprising to me is the executive's claim that since his return, he has never been consulted about Australia by anyone in his company.

He knows the country well—his company has large investments there, not all of them going so well today. He believes that his replacement is not doing well, and that two or three of the Europeans assigned there should be reassigned. The trouble is that all are "being propped up," he says, by someone in the European headquarters.

But the real problem, as this case illustrates, is what to do with these people when they eventually return to Europe or their home country.

In creating learning systems, the leader must be the teacher. Senge believes that

leaders of learning organizations must do more than just formulate strategies to exploit emerging trends. They must be able to help people understand the systemic forces that shape change. It is not enough to intuitively grasp these forces.

Leaders must help others see the bigger picture, and cannot just impose their strategies and vision. Concurrently, and perhaps most importantly, leaders must "foster learning" continually for all employees.

Source: Senge, P. M. *The Fifth Discipline*. New York: Doubleday Currency, 1990.

Motivates employees to excellence

George Land and Beth Jarman address the challenge of getting a large organization to pull its employees together to work toward a common goal.[30] They recommend following the principles of "Future Pull." The task will then become easier, and should result in greater trust and loyalty of the employees. Future Pull has several components:

1   *Know your purpose and vision.* A vision is the bigger picture. In other words, what is the company's ultimate goal and purpose for its employees? This should relate to the employees and not to the product.

2   *Commit to achieve your vision and purpose.* "Actions speak louder than words." The leader and members of top management must be committed to the vision, and must reinforce it on a daily basis with their actions.

3   *Abundance is nature's natural state.* When the vision is embraced and the employees have been empowered, it follows that the rewards will also be there.

4   *Make the world a better place by living according to shared values.* Team building is almost always a key component. Expand the vision externally to customers—not just employees.

In global companies, the complexity of motivating employees to excellence is increased. To whom do they give their allegiance? Robert Reich asks, "Who is them?"[31] He defines "them" as the growing group of global managers. Their allegiance is not to any particular nation or culture, but to the success of their company. Motivating employees to excellence is a task of the leaders of global organizations.

Negotiates and approaches conflicts in a collaborative mode

To make globalization work, we need to negotiate and approach conflicts collaboratively. Skillful international business negotiators *know* more than, and *behave* (act) differently from, nonskillful negotiators.

This leadership skill is covered in detail in Chapter 4.

Manages skillfully the foreign deployment cycle

The necessity to prepare for global assignments and a successful global deployment process is demonstrated by research on Canadian technical advisers by the Canadian International Development Agency. The book *Cross-Cultural Effectiveness*[32] established an important interaction between overseas effectiveness and overseas satisfaction.

In terms of overseas effectiveness, the study found that 65 percent of the technical advisers were neither effective nor ineffective, 20 percent were highly effective, and 10 percent were very ineffective. However, no matter how effective or ineffective they were, 75 percent were satisfied, 10 percent were neutral, and 15 percent were highly dissatisfied with their assignments.

This competency is covered in detail in Chapter 8.

Leads and participates effectively in multicultural teams

My worst experiences at Thunderbird were the project teams I had to participate in.
Recent Master of International Management Graduate

The teams I was a member of were the best learning experiences I've ever had.
Another Recent Master of International Management Graduate

Every morning in Africa, when a gazelle wakes up, it knows that it must run faster than the fastest lion or it will be killed. Every morning when a lion wakes up, it knows that it must run faster than the slowest gazelle or it will starve.

Moral: It doesn't matter whether you are a lion or a gazelle. When the sun comes up, you had better be running.

"High performance teams," "teamwork," "worldwide global product teams," and other words expressing similar ideas are commonplace in management literature today. Stories of teams producing remarkable accomplishments are well-known. Well-functioning teams can increase productivity and creativity.

However, functioning skillfully in a team is a learned skill. We have covered aspects of effective teams in the first part of this chapter.

Understands their own culture, values, and assumptions

Know thyself.

Socrates

Global managers from one country have to work and negotiate with their global counterparts regularly. A common requirement is that they must each be able to communicate effectively and work with individuals who have been socialized in a different cultural environment, and whose customs, values, lifestyles, beliefs, management practices, and other important aspects of their personal and professional lives are different.

A European executive during a personal conversation said: "I can't think of any situation in my 25 years of international experience when international business was made easier because people from more than one country were participating." A global manager must be aware of the many beliefs and values that underlie his or her own country's business practices, management techniques, and strategies.

"The journey to authentic leadership begins with understanding the story of your life."[33] When the 75 members of the Stanford Graduate School of Business Advisory Council were asked to recommend the most important capability for leaders to develop, their answer was nearly unanimous: Self-awareness. Meena Wilson[34] wrote: "Self-awareness is sensing our impact on others, which is trickier to grasp."

Accurately profiles the organizational culture and national culture of others

Corporate culture is the way of life of an organization. The best recent book on the subject is John Kotter and James Heskett's *Corporate Culture and Performance*. From their studies of many large organizations, they conclude that:[35]

1   Corporate culture can have a significant impact on a firm's long-term economic performance.
2   Corporate culture will probably be an even more important factor in determining the success or failure of firms in the next decade.
3   Corporate cultures that inhibit strong long-term financial performance are not rare; they develop easily, even in firms that are full of reasonable and intelligent people.

4   Although tough to change, corporate cultures can be made more performance-enhancing.

Hofstede's research on aspects of national culture is covered in Chapter 1.

Avoids cultural mistakes and behaves in a manner that demonstrates knowledge of and respect for other countries

Many years ago, Jack Condon and Fathi Yousef wrote:

> Many people believe that the language of gestures is universal. Many people believe that one picture is worth a thousand words, the implication being that what we see is ever so much clearer than what is said. Many people believe that communication means speaking, and that misunderstandings only occur with speaking. Many people believe that smiling and frowning and clapping are purely natural expressions. Many people believe that the world is flat.[36]

Mark Dankberg[37] summarized a quality every global business leader should possess: "Empathy—the ability to understand whoever it is you are dealing with."

It is important to state loudly and clearly that it is our experience, supported by long discussions with many global managers, as well as research, that *not only American globals make mistakes; Japanese, French, German, Swedes, Chinese, Mexicans, and globals from all other countries also make cultural errors.*

FINAL LESSON: FROM STEVE JOBS

Everyone knows something about Steve Jobs. He died as a young man of pancreatic cancer. Some may not have viewed or read[38] his commencement address at Stanford University in June 2005 when he was CEO of Apple Computers and Pixar Animation Studios.

Watch the 14-minute video. You can Google his speech or read a copy. It is worth your time.

From the speech, our concluding leadership lessons from Steve Jobs are:

1   "Trust in something—your gut, destiny, life, karma . . . connect the dots looking backward." "Find something you love."
2   "Getting fired from Apple was the best thing that ever happened to me." "I still loved what it did." "I decided to start over."
3   "When I was 17, I read a quote that went something like: If you live each day as if it was your last, someday you'll certainly be right." "Stay hungry, stay foolish."

MIND STRETCHING

1   Why do some global leaders believe that making a good speech that is cheered makes them effective global leaders?
2   Are people born to be global leaders or are the skills/behaviors learned?
3   Have you ever kept a journal for 30 days or more covering a short description of each leadership opportunity you were presented with and debriefing yourself the next day?

NOTES

1   "The Man Who Put Intel Inside," *The Economist,* March 26, 2016.
2   Russ-Ef, D. and Bassi, L. J. *What Works: Assessment, Development, and Measurement.* Alexandria, VA: ASTD, 1997.
3   Shackleton, Sir E. *South: The Story of Shackleton's Last Expedition 1914–17.* New York: Macmillan, 1920.
4   Morrell, M. and Capparell, S. *Shackleton's Way: Leadership Lessons from the Great Antarctic Explorer.* London: Viking Penguin Publishing, 2001.
5   Cherry-Garrard, A. *The Worst Journey in the World.* London: self-published, 1920.
6   "Behavior of Successful Negotiators," Huthwaite Research Group Report, 1976, 1982.
7   Data, quotes, and brief explanations are taken from Axelrod, A. *25 Lessons for Bold Business Leaders, Winston Churchill CEO.* New York: Sterling Publishing, 2009.
8   George, B., Sims, P., McLean, A. N., and Mayer, D. "Discovering Your Authentic Leadership," *Harvard Business Review*, February, 2007.
9   Ibid.
10 Carter, J. "Searching for Peace," in *Essays on Leadership.* Washington, DC: Carnegie Commission on Preventing Deadly Conflict, 1998, pp. 26, 36–36.
11 Gorbachev, M. "On Non-Violent Leadership," in *Essays on Leadership.* Washington, DC: Carnegie Commission on Preventing Deadly Conflict, 1998, pp. 64–65.
12 Tutu, D. "Leadership," in *Essays on Leadership.* Washington, DC: Carnegie Commission on Preventing Deadly Conflict, 1998, pp. 70–71.
13 Schaeffer, L. D. "The Leadership Journey," *Harvard Business Review*, October, 2002.
14 Wilson, M. S. *Developing Tomorrow's Leaders Today.* New Delhi: Jossey-Bass, 2010.
15 Moran, R. T. and Riesenberger, J. R. *The Global Challenge: Building the New World Enterprise.* New York: McGraw-Hill, 1994. And more strongly supported in interviews by Robert Moran in 2009 and 2010.
16 Leimbach, M. and Muller, A. *Winning the War for Talent: Global Leadership Competencies.* Wilson Learning Corporation, Version 1.0, 2001.
17 Moran and Riesenberger, *The Global Challenge.* And more strongly supported in interviews by Robert Moran in 2009 and 2010.
18 Javidan, M., Teagarden, M., and Bowen, D. "Making It Overseas: Developing the Skills You Need to Succeed as an International Leader," *Harvard Business Review*, April, 2010.
19 "You've Got to Be Taught," from the play *South Pacific*, music by Richard Rogers, lyrics by Oscar Hammerstein II, 1949.
20 Rhinesmith, S. *A Manager's Guide to Globalization.* Homewood, IL: Business One Irwin, 1993.
21 Amir, Y. "Contact Hypotheses in Ethnic Relation," *Psychological Bulletin*, Vol. 71, 1969, pp. 319–342.

22 Allport, G. *The Nature of Prejudice*. Reading, MA: Addison-Wesley, 1954.

23 Peters, T. and Waterman, R. *In Search of Excellence*. New York: Harper Row, 1982.

24 Quoted by Bennis, W. *On Becoming a Leader*. Reading, MA: Addison-Wesley, 1989, p. 23.

25 Kantor, R. "Transcending Business Boundaries: 12,000 World Managers View Change," *Harvard Business Review*, May/June, 1991.

26 Barnevik, P. "Mr. Barnevik, Aren't You Happy Now?" *Business Week*, September 27, 1993, p. 128.

27 Gambrell, S. W. and Stevens, C. A. "Moving through the Three Phases of Organizational Change," *International Management*, July–August, 1992, pp. 4–6.

28 Senge, P. M. *The Fifth Discipline*. New York: Doubleday Currency, 1990.

29 Moran, R. T. "Cross-Cultural Contact," *International Management*, January, 1988, modified 2010.

30 Land, G. and Jarman, B. "Future Pull," *The Futurist*, July–August, 1992, pp. 25–27.

31 Reich, R. B. "Who is Them?" *Harvard Business Review*, March–April, 1991, pp. 77–88.

32 Kealy, D. J. *Cross-Cultural Effectiveness: A Study of Canadian Technical Advisors Overseas*. Quebec: Canadian International Development Agency, 1990.

33 George et al. "Discovering Your Authentic Leadership."

34 Wilson, *Developing Tomorrow's Leaders Today*.

35 Kotter, J. P. and Heskett, J. L. *Corporate Culture and Performance*. New York: Free Press, 1992.

36 Condon, J. and Yousef, F. *An Introduction to Intercultural Communication*. Indianapolis, IN: Bobbs-Merrill, 1988.

37 Wibbeke, E. S. and McArthur, S. *Global Business Leadership*, 2nd edn. Abingdon: Routledge, 2013.

38 Steve Jobs' Stanford Commencement Speech, 2005; can be easily found via Google.

8 TEAMS
Colocated or virtual

Multinational organizations have a special role not only in building cross-cultural bridges, but in innovating synergies through their practical knowledge of putting together human and natural resources with the knowhow of managing both in the most effective ways.[1]

Linda Zhou, Alice Wei Zhao, Lori Ying, Angela Yu-Yun Yeung, Lynnelle Lin Ye, Kevin Young Xu, Benjamin Chang Sun, Jane Yoonhae Suh, Katheryn Cheng Shi, Sunanda Sharma, Sarine Gayaneh Shahmirian, Arjun Ranganath Puranik, Raman Venkat Nelakant, Akhil Mathew, Paul Masih Das, David Chienyun Liu, Elisa Bisi Lin, Yifan Li, Lanair Amaad Lett, Ruoyi Jiang, Otana Agape Jakpor, Peter Danming Hu, Yale Wang Fan, Yuval Yaacov Calev, Levent Alpoge, John Vincenzo Capodilupo, and Namrata Anand.[2]

I have been a participant or a leader of many global teams. The biggest challenge is to create alignment and commitment among members.

> A senior scientist working for a major global European pharmaceutical company

Teams work best if their members have a strong common culture.

> *The Economist*, March 19, 2016, p. 71

Study groups have become a rite of passage at M.B.A. programs, a way for students to practice working in teams and a reflection of the increasing demand for employees who can adroitly navigate group dynamics.

> Charles Duhigg, *New York Times Magazine*, February 28, 2016

After reading and studying concepts/examples and illustrations in Chapter 8, readers should:

1   Know how to identify a team they either lead or are a member of along the path of a working group to a high-performing team.
2   Be able to increase the performance of any team they are members of by using concepts/ideas/suggestions in this chapter.
3   Believe in the importance of facilitating global teams that result in synergy.

Synergy is a difficult word to understand, and even more challenging to implement. It implies a belief that we can learn from others and others can learn from us. On global teams, it implies every member has the potential to contribute. On global teams, it means the collective contribution of the team far exceeds the sum of the individual contributions of each team member.

Fareed Zakaria said it well: "If, on the one hand, we come together and work on common problems of humanity, imagine the opportunities it would create for everyone."[3] Cultural synergy is a dynamic approach to managing cultural diversity in a variety of contexts.

Cultural synergy builds on common ground, transcending mere awareness of difference, to form multifaceted strategic alliances and partnerships. In this manner, people who represent disparate perspectives and needs find ways through working together to seek a solution where all parties are content with the outcome and therefore together succeed.

Synergy comes from the Greek word meaning *working together*. This powerful concept:

1   represents a dynamic process;
2   involves adapting and learning;
3   involves joint action in which the total effect is greater than the sum of effects when acting independently;
4   creates an integrated solution;
5   does not signify compromise, yet in true synergy nothing is given up or lost; and
6   develops the potential of members by facilitating the release of team energies.

Synergy is a cooperative or combined action, and occurs when diverse or disparate individuals or groups collaborate for a common cause. The objective is to increase effectiveness by sharing perceptions and experiences, insights, and knowledge.

Synergy begins between colleagues, then extends to their organizations, and finally involves countries. The differences in the world's people can lead to mutual growth and accomplishment that is more than the single contribution of each party. As people, we can go beyond awareness of our own cultural heritage to produce something greater through synergistic actions. The sharing of dissimilar perceptions and cultural backgrounds can be used to enhance problem-solving and improve decision-making. Using information and technology to promote cooperation among disparate elements in human systems creates something better than existed by separate endeavors.

Some cultures are synergistic and inclined toward cooperation, while others tend toward individualism and competition. The late anthropologist Ruth Benedict studied this phenomenon. Her research was amplified by groundbreaking humanistic psychologist Abraham Maslow. A summary of their characterizations of high-synergy and low-synergy societies is presented in Exhibit 8.1.

E X H I B I T 8.1

EXHIBIT 8.1 CHARACTERIZATIONS OF HIGH-SYNERGY AND LOW-SYNERGY SOCIETIES

High-synergy society	Low-synergy society
▪ Emphasis is on cooperation for mutual advantage.	▪ Uncooperative, very competitive culture; enhances rugged individualistic and "dog-eat-dog" attitudes.
▪ Conspicuous for a nonaggressive social order.	▪ Aggressive and antagonistic behavior toward one another, leading to either psychological or physical violence toward the other.
▪ Social institutions promote individual and group development.	▪ Social arrangements self-centered; collaboration is not reinforced as desired behavior.
▪ Society idealizes win–win situation.	▪ Society adheres to win–lose approach.
▪ Leadership fosters sharing wealth and advantage for the common good. Cooperatives are encouraged, and poverty is fought.	▪ Leadership encourages private or individual gain and advantage, especially by the power elite; poverty is tolerated, even ignored.
▪ Society seeks to use community resources and talents for the common wealth, and encourages development of human potential of all citizenry.	▪ Society permits exploitation of poor and minorities, and tolerates the siphoning of its wealth by the privileged few; develops power elites and leaves the powerless undeveloped.
▪ Open system of secure people who tend to be benevolent, helpful, friendly, and generous; its heroes are altruistic and philanthropic.	▪ Closed system with insecure people who tend toward suspiciousness, ruthlessness, and clannishness; idealizes the "strong man" concerned with greed and acquisition.

High-synergy society	Low-synergy society
■ Belief system, religion, or philosophy is comforting and life is consoling; emphasis is on the god of love; power is to be used for the benefit of the whole community; individuals/groups are helped to work out hurt and humiliations.	■ Belief system is frightening, punishing, terrifying; members are psychologically beaten or humiliated by the strong; power is for personal profit; emphasis is on the god of vengeance; hatreds go deep and "blood feuds" abound; violence is the means for compensation for hurt and humiliation.
■ Generally, the citizenry is psychologically healthy, and mutual reciprocity is evident in relationships; open to change; low rate of crime and mental illness.	■ Generally, the citizenry tend to be defensive, jealous; mass paranoia and hostility; fears change and advocates status quo; high rate of crime and mental illness.

E X H I B I T 8.1

Source: Ruth Benedict, Anthropologist; Abraham Maslow, Psychologist.

HIGH-PERFORMING TEAMS

Virtually every working person is on some team or group who agree on a goal or task and are assigned or volunteer to work with others to successfully accomplish the task. Most agree that all teams go through the four states of forming, storming, norming, and performing. Exhibit 8.2 is a useful way of linking the performance of a team along the path to becoming a high-performing team over time.

RATING THE PERFORMANCE OF YOUR GLOBAL TEAMS

In seminars and workshops the authors have conducted since the 1990s, we often ask participants to rate the performance of teams they participate in, using the scale in Exhibit 8.3.

We have found there are very few ratings of 1 or 2 and very few of 9 or 10. When the average of groups of 30 or more who participate on many different teams is calculated, the score is almost never above 7, indicating clearly that most teams never reach the high-performing team of Exhibit 8.2. What follows suggests some of the reasons.

UNDERSTANDING TEAM STRATEGY

The dictionary defines a *team* as a number of persons associated in some joint action, while *teamwork* is described as a cooperative or coordinated effort by persons working together.

EXHIBIT 8.2 TYPICAL PHASES ON THE PATH TO BECOMING A HIGH-PERFORMING TEAM

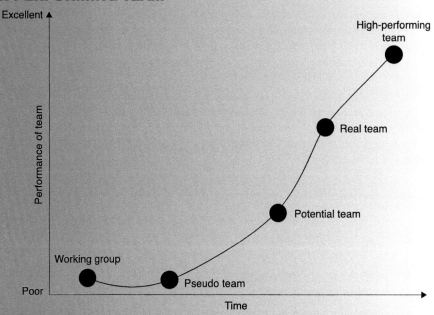

Working group: A working group is a collection of individuals each doing his or her best.

Pseudo team: They call themselves a team, but they are really still a collection of individuals.

Potential team: They are at the beginning of committing to a common purpose and holding one another accountable.

Real team: A real team consists of people with skills who are committed to a shared purpose, goals, and work practices.

High-performing team: These teams go beyond real teams in the level of commitment members have to the organization, to each other, and to the tasks of the team.

Source: Katzenback, J. R. and Smith, D. K. *Wisdom of Teams*. New York: Harper Business, 2003.

EXHIBIT 8.3 TEAM PERFORMANCE

Poor performance									Excellent performance
1	2	3	4	5	6	7	8	9	10

Teams are collections of people who must rely on group collaboration if each member is to experience the optimum of success and goal achievement.

Changing technology and markets have stimulated the team approach to management, because temporary groups can function across organizational divisions and better cope with diversity of membership. Multicultural and multifunctional teams are becoming commonplace. Furthermore, the complexity of society and the human systems devised to meet new and continuing needs require a pooling of resources and talents. Inflation, resource scarcity, reduced personnel levels, budget cuts, and similar constraints have underscored the demands for better coordination and synergy in the use of "brainpower."

In effect, the team management model alters organizational culture. The term used currently is *self-managed teams*, which contribute to employee empowerment and problem-solving. Such work units evolve their own unique *team culture*. As noted previously, high-technology corporations excel with project teams consisting of a variety of skilled specialists from management information systems, accounting, and new technologies. With the team approach, obsolete business separations give way to synergistic, functional arrangements among those employed in manufacturing, marketing, and administration; line and staff activities overlap and often merge.

TEAM BUILDING FOR SUCCESS AND SYNERGY

Many executives make provisions for team building or training within their organizations by qualified internal or external consultants. In such human-relations training, leaders seek to cultivate a *team environment* that facilitates the group's performance. However, these guidelines might be questioned in whole or in part by readers from other national or cultural backgrounds. In essence, in team building, members learn:

■ tolerance of ambiguity, uncertainty, and seeming lack of structure;
■ to take interest in each member's achievement, as well as the group's;
■ the ability to give and accept feedback in a nondefensive manner;
■ openness to change, innovation, group consensus, team decision-making, and creative problem-solving;
■ to create a team atmosphere that is informal, relaxed, comfortable, and non-judgmental;
■ the capacity to establish intense, short-term member relations, and to disconnect for the next project;
■ to keep group communication on target and schedule, while permitting disagreement and valuing effective listening;
■ to urge a spirit of constructive criticism, and authentic, nonevaluative feedback;
■ to encourage members to express feelings and to be concerned about group morale/maintenance;

- to clarify roles, relationships, assignments, and responsibilities;
- to share leadership functions within a group and to use total member resources;
- to pause periodically from task pursuits to reexamine and reevaluate team progress and communications;
- to foster trust, confidence, and commitment within the group;
- sensitivity to the team's linking function with other work units;
- to foster a norm that members will be supportive and respectful of one another, and realistic in their expectations of each other;
- to promote an approach that is goal-directed, seeks group participation, divides the labor fairly, and synchronizes effort;
- to set high performance standards for the group; and
- to cultivate listening skills.

Since each team experience is different, uniqueness and flexibility should be encouraged. Yet, at the same time, coordination and integration of team effort with other units and the whole enterprise are essential if the sum is to be greater than its parts. When team cultures contain the elements previously outlined and are reflective of the whole organizational environment, then they become closely knit and productive. The more team participation is provided and employees are included in team decision-making, the healthier and more relevant is that human system.

IMPROVING PERFORMANCE THROUGH TEAM CULTURE

Just like the organization in general, we might have an image of the team as a smaller "energy exchange system." When the group functions well, human psychic and physical energy is used effectively. Team interaction is an energy exchange. As the group seeks to achieve its goals, members energize or motivate themselves and one another by example. Team planning and changes become projections on energy use and its alteration. Every aspect of the group process can be analyzed in terms of this human energy paradigm. The key issue, then, is how the team manages its energies most productively and avoids underutilizing or even wasting the group energies. There are ways that members can analyze their functions and performance in projects, task forces, or product teams.

Team behavior can be examined from the viewpoint of task functions, which initiate, give, or seek information, clarify or elaborate on member ideas, and summarize or synthesize. It can also be seen from the angle of group maintenance or morale building, such as encouraging, expressing group feeling, harmonizing, and compromising. It is the last element that builds group cohesion and camaraderie.

Such periodic behavioral review and data gathering can be useful to improve the group's effectiveness. Not only can the information help a member to change his or her team behavior, but when such findings are combined into a visual profile, they offer a diagnosis of team health from time to time. It is recommended that teams pause on occasion for such self-examination. Sometimes a third-person facilitator, such as an internal or external consultant, can be most helpful in this analysis of team culture and progress. When the group's assessment is summarized, the team can then view its implications for more effective use of member energies.

Team participation is an intensive learning experience. When members voluntarily involve themselves and fully participate, personal and professional growth are fostered. The team is like a laboratory of the larger organizational world in which it operates. Although a temporary experience, it is an opportunity for individual and team development. Each participant shares self and insights from the basis of unique life and organizational experiences. Synergy occurs when the members listen to each other and enter into the private worlds of the others. Total team perception and wisdom then become more than the sum of the parts.

If the organization's culture emphasizes employee participation through team management, the group micro-cultures are likely to reflect that system's macro-culture. Thus, collaborative management should be evident not only within an individual team, but in intergroup relations. There is an implicit assumption that the team culture exerts a significant influence on an individual member's behavior. As a team member, one functions beyond the individual level, becoming representative of the group "persona." Those who serve in two or more interlocking groups are expected to act as linking pins in the accomplishment of the organizational mission through these separate but interdependent entities.

Everything that anthropologists would examine in the culture of people in a national or organizational group can be analyzed in the miniature environment of the team. These can range from the group's beliefs and attitudes, to procedures and practices, to priorities and technologies. The team atmosphere, task orientation or processes, communication patterns, role clarification or negotiation, conflict resolution, decision-making, action planning, intragroup and intergroup relations, can all be scrutinized for better diagnosis of the group's dynamics. When a global manager or consultant engages in such analysis, the team can become more effective in the use of its energies.

GLOBAL TEAMS

Social scientists are conducting research on what people can do in small multinational groups to facilitate a meaningful experience and productive outcome. One exciting example of this occurred at the East–West Center in Honolulu, Hawaii.

At its Culture Learning Institute, Dr. Kathleen K. Wilson spearheaded an investigation with 15 other distinguished colleagues on the factors influencing the management of International Cooperative Research and Development (ICRD) projects. Their ICRD findings have implications for any professional seeking to improve human performance and collaboration. Although the researchers examined project team effectiveness among internationals, their insights can be extrapolated to other forms of inter- and intragroup behavior, whether it is a matrix organization, product team, taskforce, or any work unit.

The contexts in which international cooperative groups operate may vary, but there are similar factors present that affect performance. These external factors affect the environment within the project itself, and include such diverse elements as political, organizational, and cultural aspects, the size and scope of the endeavor, the disciplinary background of team members, and their individual characteristics, research, and development policies and problems. A summary of factors that foster or hinder professional synergy is given in Exhibit 8.4. Certainly, the exhaustive list of situations that influence a project's effectiveness points to the need for strategies to manage the many cultural differences existing between and among professionals attempting to work together. One can apply these observations to real-time group situations, such as teams functioning:

■ within the United Nations or UNESCO, the World Health Organization, World Bank, or International Monetary Fund;
■ within a global corporation that spans many countries and includes multinational membership;
■ within the International Space Station, both on the ground and in orbit, with its sponsorship of some 16 nations; and
■ within the European Union as it moved from 15 members to include 10 more from Central and Eastern Europe.

The East–West Center's research on international cooperation projects offers some criteria that can be used in recruiting, selecting, and assessing professionals. *Team member characteristics* that foster group synergy are also implied in Exhibit 8.2. Such benchmarks can be helpful in interviewing potential team members, choosing collaborators, and setting goals for self-improvement in organizational relations.

Finally, these ICRD researchers offered some indications for ensuring synergy within global teams. First, they established these criteria for evaluating international project effectiveness and management competence:

1 individual team member satisfaction;
2 group satisfaction and morale;
3 work progress relative to intended goal statements;
4 social and cultural impact of the endeavor on people.

Second, the East–West Center's researchers also identified interpersonal skills that influence a professional group's situation and accomplishments. These international team competencies and capacities are summarized in Exhibit 8.5.

Charles Duhigg, in his article in the *New York Times Magazine*,[4] reported on some findings from teams in Silicon Valley where "software engineers are encouraged to work together, in part because studies show that groups tend to innovate faster." The *Harvard Business Review* reported that the time managers and employees spend on team activities has also significantly increased.

EXHIBIT 8.4 HUMAN FACTORS THAT FOSTER OR HINDER PROFESSIONAL SYNERGY WITHIN A PROJECT

- How project business is planned;
- consideration of other problem-solving viewpoints;
- how the work should be organized;
- approach to R&D tasks;
- definition of R&D problems;
- ambiguity resolution and problem formulation;
- methods and procedures;
- decision-making relative to recurring problems;
- allocation of resources to team members;
- accountability procedures relative to resource use;
- timing and sequencing approaches;
- determining objectives for an R&D effort;
- affiliation and liaison with external groups and degree of formality in their work relations;
- quantity and type of project human resources;
- qualifications, recruitment, and selection of new members;
- new member orientation and training on the project;
- management of responsibilities;
- underutilization of workers relative to skill competencies;
- motivating behavior and reward expectations;
- coordination of long-/short-term members;
- agreement on degree of innovation required;
- experience with cooperation, especially relative to international R&D tasks;
- official language(s) to use on projects;
- method of reporting everyone's involvement in the project;
- coping with internal demands and visitors;
- meeting face-to-face or having to resort to other forms of more impersonal communication;
- involvement in making viewpoints known;
- power differences because of institution resources brought to the project;
- prestige, risk-taking, tolerance of uncertainty, and perceptions;
- project leadership and/or organizational policies changing unexpectedly;
- quality of work presented in evaluation methods;
- what constituted success in project work, and what to do when members fail to meet group expectations;
- clarification of roles in the relationships.

EXHIBIT 8.5 SELF-MANAGEMENT COMPETENCIES AND EFFECTIVE TEAM MEMBERS

Self-management competencies permit the project member to:

- recognize other members' participation in ways they find rewarding;
- avoid unnecessary conflicts among other team members, as well as resolve unavoidable ones to mutual satisfaction;
- integrate different team members' skills to achieve project goals;
- negotiate acceptable working arrangements with other team members and their organizations;
- regard others' feelings and exercise tactfulness;
- develop equitable benefits for other team members;
- accept suggestions/feedback to improve his or her participation;
- provide useful specific suggestions and appropriate feedback;
- facilitate positive interaction among culturally different members, whether in terms of macro-differences (national/political), or micro-differences (discipline or training);
- gain acceptance because of empathy expressed and sensitivity to end users;
- encourage dissemination of project outcomes throughout its life;
- recognize national/international differences in problem statements and procedures, so as to create appropriate project organizational responses;
- anticipate and plan for probable difficulties in project implementation;
- recognize discrete functions, coordinating discrete tasks with overall project goals; and
- coordinate transitions among different kinds of activities within the project.

The effective team member has the capacity for:

- flexibility and openness to change and others' viewpoints;
- exercising patience, perseverance, and professional security;
- thinking in multidimensional terms and considering different sides of issues;
- dealing with ambiguity, role shifts, and differences in personal and professional styles or social and political systems;
- managing stress and tension well, while scheduling tasks systematically;
- cross-cultural communication and demonstrating sensitivity to language problems among colleagues;
- anticipating consequences of one's own behavior;
- dealing with unfamiliar situations and lifestyle changes;
- dealing well with different organizational structures and policies;
- gathering useful information related to future projects.

Duhigg also reported on how Google began to focus on how to build the "perfect team" as Google top management believed that "building the best teams meant combining the best people." An initiative in Google code named Project Aristotle tried to figure out why some Google teams "stumbled while others soared." This is a summary of what Google did and what they learned.

1 The Project Aristotle team began by reviewing many studies of how teams worked. When researchers used what they learned from the studies and applied it to teams in Google, they failed to find "patterns" and it didn't seem to matter what the mix was of specific personality types, skills, or backgrounds.

2 Individual group norms, even though the norms may be different from group to group, seem to be important. The Aristotle team conclusions on this point were "undeniable, and influencing group norms were keys to improving Google's teams." But what norms did the successful teams share?

What emerged is "how the teammates treated one another." This factor raised the "collective intelligence" of the team.

The researchers also noticed two behaviors that all good teams seemed to share. First, all team members spoke about the same amount; and second, all team members had high "average social sensibility," meaning they were skilled at interpreting how others were reacting based largely on nonverbal signals. As a result, members of the team felt safe in "risk-taking."

One of the Google researchers concluded: "And I had research telling me it was O.K. to follow my gut. So that's what I did."

MEETING WHEN TEAMS ARE VIRTUAL

In today's global world, it is not unusual to have important meetings of team members when two are located in Switzerland, two in the US (one on the East Coast and one on the West Coast), one in Brazil, one in China, and one in Japan. They work for a pharmaceutical company and all have a PhD in chemistry or biology.

Just setting up the meeting is a major task due to the many time-zone differences. A good list of learnings and suggestions is provided by David Mittleman, Robert Briggs, and Jay Nunamaker.[5]

Meetings with virtual (geographically distributed) teams

Lesson 1: It is hard to follow what is happening during a virtual meeting.

■ Distribute an explicit pre-meeting plan including specific times for involvement (takes into account multitasking and focuses attention when needed).

■ Clearly communicate the transition from one meeting stage to the next.

Lesson 2: People don't get feedback when working over a distance.

■ Seek feedback from, and give feedback to, different team members. Engage the quiet ones.

Lesson 3: People forget who is attending the meeting.

■ Develop a practice of feeding back participants' names when communicating. "Brigitte, I understand your concern. . . ."
■ Do a periodic poll to see who is still part of the meeting.

Lesson 4: It is harder to build a team when we are not face-to-face.

■ Develop and communicate an unambiguous vision and set of goals for the team.
■ Have face-to-face kick-off meetings, when possible.

Lesson 5: It is tough to sort out email communications.

■ Develop a set of email rules and hold the team accountable for following them. For example:
  – answer requests within 24 hours;
  – send group mail only when all recipients need it;
  – reread from the recipients' perspective before sending emails.

Lesson 6: It is harder to reach agreement over a distance.

■ Agree on structured decision-making processes up front. Who will be responsible for what decisions, and how will differences in opinion be resolved?

Lesson 7: Small empathetic gestures go a long way with those who usually suffer the most with time-zone differences.

■ Gestures such as switching the late-night or very early morning burden periodically builds significant appreciation among distributed team members.

TEAM LEADERS OR MEMBERS AS INFLUENCERS OF OTHERS ON A TEAM

A challenge global leaders experience today is how to influence across cultures and functions the individuals with whom they work and their global partners. Aware of the cultural influences on the personalities, motivations, and values of their counterparts, skillful leaders are able to influence others, whether it is by giving orders and directions to individuals under their authority or by "influencing with authority." Leaders know what they want to accomplish, but how to achieve it and who are the key people they need to influence to succeed are routine unknowns.

According to Cohen and Bradford,[6] the following points are key in successfully influencing others:

- Assume any individual, even an adversary, can be an ally.
- Be clear what you want.
- Understand the "cultures" of all those to be influenced.
- Identify your own and others' currencies.
- Build the relationships and develop partners.
- Use formal and informal influencing skills.

Exhibit 8.6 shows a model of influence without authority.

All leaders have some power, which is the ability to influence others, inside or outside of an organization or enterprise, whether it is a business, government agency, or a nation, to do what you want them to do when you want them to do it. The total power of any individual is a combination of formal power or power associated with position, plus informal power, which is personal and a function of one's skills, expertise, and credibility.

EXHIBIT 8.6 COHEN/BRADFORD MODEL OF INFLUENCE WITHOUT AUTHORITY

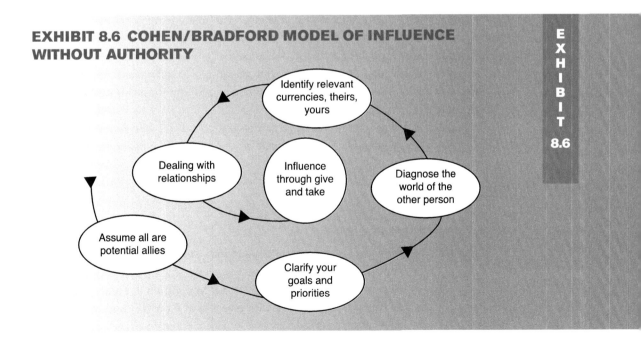

EXHIBIT 8.6

Verma[7] states that there are eight sources of power.

- *Legitimate power*–derives from position or status.
- *Persuasive*–derives from personal skills and ability in winning others' cooperation.
- *Contact/network*–derives from who we know and our connections.
- *Information*–derives from the information we have and knowledge of how organizations work.
- *Expertise*–derives from knowledge.
- *Referent*–derives from our reputation in an organization.
- *Coercive*–derives from our ability to punish.
- *Reward*–derives from our ability to reward.

HIGH-PERFORMING GLOBAL LEADERSHIP

To ensure top performance, the global leader continually updates and broadens his or her understanding of culture and its impact on our lives. Although there may be few management theories that can be universally applied across all cultures, there are many principles and practices of leadership that can be adapted to various countries. Despite the cultural differences in managerial approaches, it is possible to produce cultural synergy in the pragmatic operations of management.

Elashmawi and Harris,[8] in their research into global joint ventures, focused on clashes within multicultural work environments, such as establishing a plant overseas. These offshore enterprises require the hiring, training, and management of local in-country personnel of differing cultural and technical backgrounds. Elashmawi and Harris identified cultural clashes arising from language and nonverbal communication, time and space orientation, decision-making and information systems, conduct of meetings and training, as well as motivation. On the other hand, Hampden-Turner and Trompenaars[9] urge transforming conflicting values into complementary values.

Technology transfer in the twenty-first century has seen accelerated growth in *outsourcing/insourcing/nearsourcing*, especially in the fields of information technology and services.

TEAMS AND EMPOWERMENT

The concept of empowerment refers to altering management style and transforming organizational arrangements from hierarchical to more participatory–sharing authority and responsibility with workers in a variety of ways. It is expressed through an Integrated leadership style that works to include all potentially relevant diversity in an MNE, and integrate it to achieve the best possible result, both globally and locally.

To *empower* means that leaders give individual members more freedom to act, thereby allowing them to demonstrate their capabilities. Inclusion, rather than exclusion, particularly with regard to women and minorities, becomes the organizational norm, based on the competence of the individual. This approach is more open and decentralized.

This form of team management is spreading across Asia and Europe. The Japanese, who are culturally group-oriented, use consensus decision-making that sacrifices implementation speed in *favor* of giving all relevant employees input. Meanwhile, in some countries in Asia and Eastern Europe, empowerment is manifesting itself in political restructuring from authoritarianism to democracy and free enterprise. Managers are freed from government or party controls and are able to involve their co-workers in the process of reshaping factories, cooperatives, and businesses. As globalization bridges the gap between national economies and peoples, empowerment does the same between management and labor. Kouzes and Posner[10] state that there is one clear and consistent message about empowerment: "feeling powerful—literally feeling 'able'—comes from a deep sense of being in control of our own lives."

When we feel we can determine our own destiny, and we have the assurance that the resources and individuals needed to support us are available, we can persist in our efforts. Conversely, when others control an individual, he/she may comply, or passively resist, but not excel. Leadership through empowerment enhances the individual's self-confidence and personal effectiveness. Kouzes and Posner[11] have identified *five* fundamental strategies for empowering others.

Ensure self-leadership by putting people in control of their lives. When leaders share power and control with others, they demonstrate trust and respect in others' abilities. They, in essence, make a covenant with them that is reciprocal and mutually beneficial. Individuals who can influence their leaders are more attached to them and committed to the organization. In the Integrated style of leadership, negotiating goals is an example of both high TO and empowerment. For lower maturity employees, some freedom may be granted and frequent checks made to ensure responsibility is being taken. This is a means of incrementally developing greater maturity in employees.

Provide choice. Providing individuals with options and discretion in the day-to-day operation of their jobs increases creativity and flexibility, as one is freed from the standard set of rules and procedures. Jobs that are broadly designed and defined encourage this. However, this is not an option that may be provided to low-maturity employees who do not have the experience or commitment to warranty the trust.

Develop competence. Leaders must invest in developing individuals' skills and competencies—maturity,[12] in other words. Giving employees opportunities to grow in their area of expertise, as well as in general business knowledge, enables them to act in the best interest of the corporation and the customer.

Assign critical tasks. Usually, those with the most power or authority address the most critical organizational problems. However, in innovative corporations, research and development, for example, is brought to the factory floor. Empowerment encourages involvement and responsibility regarding tasks that employees can own and make excellent critical judgments about.

Offer visible support. Leaders who want to empower are highly visible and make conscientious efforts to have employees gain recognition and validation. Making connections and building strong networks and relationships is empowering. A leader should also introduce employees to others in the corporation or community who may help them along their career path. Individuals take responsibility for their own career development, while leaders create a work environment that encourages others to achieve their human potential.

Leaders who share power help to build trust and shared responsibility. Employees view improvements and communication as a two-way street, with the leader being as influenced by his or her workforce as the workforce is by management. Each is committed to effectively doing their part.

With a multicultural workforce and customer base, leadership must provide the vision, motivation, and reasons for commitment. For contemporary organizations and their workers, knowledge and innovation lead to global marketplace success.

INTERCULTURAL, CULTURAL, INTERETHNIC, AND ANY COUPLE RELATIONSHIP AS A TEAM

In 2008, in the US, more than 14 percent of new marriages were[13] between persons who belonged to different ethnic groups. Today, the percentage is probably higher. In other countries, it is probably very low and in others even higher.

But couple relationships have some of the issues of an organizational team and some unique issues.

A peculiarity of people working in a global world is the high number of bicultural marriages. What could be more natural? These relationships develop because more and more people are leaving their home country to study or work. Nature does the rest. But just as a large percentage of international joint ventures don't last beyond five years, some intercultural marriages don't work out either. Not much is written about this sensitive subject, but it is getting common enough to suggest some readers may find the following of interest.

What are some of the major challenges of these relationships? Based on interviews with many partners of bicultural marriages, we believe the central issue is the ability of the couple to cope with differences in values and attitudes toward such matters as male–female roles, finances, religious differences, and child-rearing practices.

Cultures set their own behavioral norms, which determine what is right and wrong, what is to be done or avoided. Acceptable standards may range from the work ethic or pleasure to tough discipline or permissiveness for children; from rigid submission of the wife to her husband, to women's liberation.

All marriage partners struggle to come to terms with each other's values. In intercultural marriages, this struggle is intensified and becomes the root of many troubles due to the lack of a common cultural link that has shaped the partner's values. Imagine how the values may differ in a marriage between a Christian and a Muslim.

Issues of sexuality are sensitive in intercultural marriages. Someone once observed that a couple could take four sets of grandparents to bed with them. Hence, misunderstandings are bound to arise over different concepts about virginity, birth control, the number of children, marital fidelity, and sexual practices.

Money is the source of many problems in any marriage—more so in intercultural ones. The usual bones of contention are who makes the money and who decides how much is spent, how much is saved, and for what purpose. In some cultures, women have complete control of domestic finances; in others, women have no say at all.

Many people are unaware of the importance of religion in their lives until they start living with someone who doesn't share similar beliefs. Many intercultural marriage partners are of different religions. But even if the partners follow the same religion, conflicts arise over different doctrinal practices. Degrees of orthodoxy and observances of religious holidays frequently cause problems.

When children and in-laws are involved, the "battle lines" encircle some of these issues, and the pressure on the relationship is tremendous.

"We were all right until the children came," adds the partner of a bicultural relationship. Then the questions of name, the role of grandparents, language teaching, discipline, and rewards all come to the fore. Parenting is the real test to determine the strength of a bicultural marriage.

For an intercultural marriage to work, the partners need a common goal. Each must have a strong concept of self and be fully committed to the marriage. Each must be flexible and learn how to reduce or eliminate "invaders" that threaten the stability of the relationship.

The key ingredient is genuine interest and enthusiasm for the other's culture. This will ensure long-term shared interests, as each partner progressively taps the other's storehouse of knowledge.

For when there are language differences between the couple and they wish their children to be multilingual, the following is some of what we know.

As the American language expert, journalist, and satirist H. L. Mencken once wrote, "If English was good enough for Jesus Christ, it's good enough for me." The ultimate cynic, Mencken was summing up the ethnocentric, not to say arrogant, attitude of some English-speakers toward foreign languages.

A student tells the story of the difficult choice he and his wife faced regarding which language to use in their expanding household. Should they bring up their children in his language (French) or his wife's (Japanese)? The Japanese grandparents were eager to know the answer. "We told them that I intended to speak to the children in French, my wife in Japanese, and that they would probably learn English later on with playmates," the student recalled. The grandparents were concerned, however, that the mother and father would be overloading the children to such an extent that "they would learn nothing."

Soon after the first child was born, the French grandmother flew in from France. Once again, the inevitable question was posed. While looking at the baby, the grandmother sighed and said, "Poor little guy!"

As it turned out, the parents are doing it "naturally," with the two mother tongues coexisting in the household.

Parents are in a position of authority when it comes to this decision, and their judgment should be carefully considered. Will the child attend school in the country's dominant language? Will its grandparents be able to communicate with the child? Is there a need to be fluent in a lingua franca (English) or a culturally prestigious language such as French?

Internationally minded parents deal with the problem in a variety of ways. The Franco-Japanese family perhaps unconsciously adopted the technique of the late French linguist Maurice Gramont. He called it "*une personne, une langue*," encouraging parents to talk to the child in their native language, ensuring instinctive fluency.

Often, parents use one language in the home and the other outside. Some families use one language with the child initially and then, at a specific age (between ages three and five, for example), introduce the other language. Others use two languages interchangeably, allowing such factors as topic, situation, person, and place to dictate the choice of language.

But all of these approaches assume that the parents and the children will have the determination to pursue their noble goal.

Francois Crosjean, in the book *Life With Two Languages: An Introduction to Bilingualism*, cites the example of a French boy named Cyril who moved with his parents to the US. Cyril attended an English-language daycare center, brought home English-speaking friends, and watched television. Native-born friends of his parents often came to dinner.

Soon, Cyril realized that his parents spoke quite good English, and there was no other reason to speak French. Gradually, he started speaking English to his parents and ceased to be actively bilingual. Cyril's parents could have isolated him from the English environment, but they either did not think it was natural or did not have the time and energy to do so.

Perhaps the basic payoff for the strain and trauma of family-generated bilingualism is that we are destined to live in a highly interdependent, global community. Those who can communicate will lead the way. To speak more than one language is no longer a luxury, it is becoming a necessity.

CONCLUSIONS

After explaining the concept of cultural synergy, this chapter provided a contrast of societies that could be characterized as having high or low synergy, as well as organizational culture that reflects high and low synergy.

Within organizations, the research insights reported here centered on behaviors and practices that contribute to synergy and success among teams, particularly in terms of international projects. Global leaders actively create a better future through synergistic efforts with fellow professionals. Global leaders seek to be effective bridge-builders between the cultural realities or worlds of both past and future.

MIND STRETCHING

1   Synergy is a goal, but why is it so difficult for global teams to become high-performing teams?
2   Give examples of teams you have been on that are not very productive and some that are very productive. What role did the leader play and what skills may or may not have been displayed?
3   Do you know how to diagnose a team's effectiveness?
4   In what ways is a marriage like a team at Google?
5   How is a bicultural marriage different from a monocultural marriage?

NOTES

1   Freeman, O. L. "'Foreword' by former president of Business International Corporation, Governor of Minnesota, and US Secretary of Agriculture," in R. T. Moran and P. R. Harris (eds.), *Managing Cultural Synergy*. Houston, TX: Gulf Publishing, 1982.
2   Friedman, T. "America's Real Dream Team," *New York Times*, March 22, 2010, listing the majority of high school finalists in the 2010 Intel Science Talent Search.
3   Katzenback, J. R. and Smith, D. K. *Wisdom of Teams*. New York: Harper Business, 2003.
4   Duhigg, C. *New York Times Magazine*, February 28, 2016.
5   Mittleman, D. D., Briggs, R. O., and Nunamaker, J. F. "Best Practices in Facilitating Virtual Meetings: Some Notes from Initial Experiences," *Group Facilitation: A Research and Applications Journal*, Vol. 2, 2000, pp. 1–11.
6   Cohen, A. R. and Bradford, D. L. *Influence Without Authority*. Hoboken, NJ: Wiley, 2005.
7   Verma, V. K. *Managing the Project Team*. Newton Square, PA: PMI Publications, 1997.
8   Elashmawi, F. and Harris, P. R. *Multicultural Management 2000: Essential Skills for Global Business Success*. Houston, TX: Gulf Professional Publishing, 1998. Also refer to Elashmawi, F. (ed.). *Competing Globally: Mastering Multicultural Management and Negotiations*. Burlington, MA: Elsevier/Butterworth-Heinemann, 2001.
9   Hampden-Turner, C. M. and Trompenaars, F. *Building Cross-Cultural Competence: How to Create Wealth from Conflicting Values*. New Haven, CT: Yale University Press, 2002.
10 Kouzes, J. M. and Posner, B. Z. *The Leadership Challenge*. San Francisco, CA: Jossey-Bass, 1995.
11 Ibid.
12 Hershey, P. and Blanchard, K. H. *Management of Organizational Behavior: Utilizing Human Resources*. Englewood Cliffs, NJ: Prentice-Hall, 1988.
13 Gaines, S. O., Clark, E. M., and Afful, S. E. "Interethnic Marriage in the United States," *Journal of Social Issues*, Vol. 71, No. 4, 2015, p. 647.

9 GLOBAL BUSINESS ETHICS
Building personal ethics to achieve trust and relationship

When you observe goodness in others, then inspect yourself, desirous of culti-vating it. When you observe badness in others, then examine yourself, fearful of discovering it. If you find goodness in your person, then commend yourself, desirous of holding firm to it. If you find badness in your person, then reproach yourself, regarding it as calamity.

Xunzi[1]

I am confident that it is both possible and worthwhile to attempt a new secular approach to universal ethics. My confidence comes from my conviction that all of us, all human beings, are basically inclined or disposed toward what we perceive to be good. . . . We all appreciate the kindness of others. . . . We all prefer the love of others to their hatred . . . others' generosity to their meanness.

Dalai Lama[2]

The true test of the spiritual maturity of a civilization, then, is not really the level of its moral behavior, but the way it responds to moral misbehavior. . . . How rigorously do we hold people accountable for their misdeeds, and how actively do we encourage people to make amends for their errors?

Louis E. Newman[3]

After reading and studying the concepts, examples, and illustrations in Chapter 9, readers should be able to understand and appreciate:

1   Scientific evolutionary psychology research has confirmed that the minds of humans-as-species have evolved to favor two strategic approaches to ethics—self-interest and altruism—as ecological niches, each increasing evolutionary fitness depending on environmental circumstances.

2   Sociological research has identified that human cultures may be divided primarily into two groupings of national cultures. Sensate cultures, common in Euro-North American nations, are generally organized around ethics of self-interest and reject "supersensory" values (ideals that are beyond the human senses to observe). Ideational cultures, more common elsewhere, are generally organized around ethics of altruism and ideal supersensory values.

3   Major religious ethical systems (Christian, Muslim, Hindu, Buddhist) as well as Asian (Confucianism) and Western (Kantian, Kierkegaardian) philosophical systems tend to represent Ideational ethical systems, and are organized around the competition between values of self-interest and altruism. They tend to be governed by supersensory values such as "God" (Christianity, Islam, Hinduism, Judaism), "Sage" (Confucianism), "Nirvana" (Buddhism), and "public good" (Kantian philosophy).

4   Ideational ethical systems, religious and secular, agree that altruism and cooperation represent superior ethics to self-interest and competition. Sensate ethics does not agree.

5   Global business ethics are primarily Sensate and governed by self-interest. Global business is generally governed by values of pleasure-seeking, utility, efficiency, effectiveness, and profitability.

6   Ideational religious and secular ethical systems agree that self-interest is "evil," altruism is "good," and that humans can learn to become good by learning and practicing altruistic values (or remain good through practice as in Mencian Confucianism).

7   These differences in ethical values between Ideational and Sensate cultures increase the probability that relationships between Ideational and Sensate parties may be damaged or broken by value conflicts. Relationship damage is also likely between Sensate individuals or groupings because of competition for dominance.

8   Under these circumstances, it is useful to have a process for mending damaged or broken relationships. In a situation in which one party is aggrieved and another party is perceived to have caused harm, reconciliation is possible if the harm-doer repents, encouraging the aggrieved party to forgive. A seven-stage repentance

process is outlined. From the Sensate point of view, reconciliation is more efficient than building new relationships. From the Ideational point of view, repentance, forgiveness, and reconciliation represent an altruistic process. Reconciliation will succeed if the harm-doer's behavior changes and the offense is not repeated.

INTRODUCTION

The subject of this chapter is ethics, applied to global leaders and their subordinates doing business and building successful cross-cultural trust-based business relationships around the world. An ethic is a set of principles defining right conduct for a social group, a culture, or a nation.[4] Ethics is the study of the nature of morals and the moral choices deemed correct by those professing a specific ethic.[5] The main sources of worldwide ethical thinking are religion, and ethical or moral philosophy. Evolutionary psychology (EP) has scientifically confirmed the ethical dichotomy between altruism and self-interest almost inevitably addressed by both religious and philosophical ethics. Sorokin[6] observed that, sociologically speaking, there were two main types of ethical systems: Sensate (more self-interest) and Ideational (more altruistic). We assume, with Kierkegaard, that self-interest and altruism are alternate ethical systems.[7] This chapter has followed Sorokin's dichotomy, considering a number of worldwide Ideational ethical systems in terms of how they interface with the relationship-building practices of the Sensate ethics of Western business and its globalization agenda. Interestingly, the Dalai Lama has proposed a new secular ethics, based on altruism but not upon any specific religious system,[8] suggesting it as the basis for a more ethical approach to building effective cross-cultural business relationships.

The purpose of this chapter is to acquaint and prepare readers for a number of predominant ethical systems likely to be encountered. Given the major differences between Sensate and Ideational ethics, it is all too easy even for well-informed businesspeople to offend individuals from other cultures, or to be offended themselves, given the vagaries of intercultural communications (see Chapter 2), and cultural value differences. A second purpose is to recommend a process for repairing and reconciling relationships inadvertently damaged by ethical differences.

Exhibit 9.1 suggests the relative importance of the world's most prevalent ethical systems, both religious and philosophical. It is based on a 2011 world population of seven billion. Of course, it is simplistic to imply that any of these world religions are monolithic in their ethical views. Christianity is divided into Protestant, Roman Catholic, and Orthodox groupings, as well as many smaller subgroupings. Many who claim to be "Christian" do not apply Christian ethics to their actions and this undoubtedly applies to others from other ethical systems as well. Confucianism is divided between the Xunzi school in China, and the

EXHIBIT 9.1 MAIN WORLD RELIGIONS AND NUMBER OF ADHERENTS (2011)[9]

Religion	Percentage of world population	Number of adherents (billions)
Christian	31.5	2.21
Islam	23.2	1.62
Atheist/unaffiliated	16.3	1.14
Hindu	15.0	1.05
Buddhist	7.1	0.50
Folk	5.9	0.41
Other	0.8	0.06
Jewish	0.2	0.01
Total	100.0	7.00

Mencius school predominant in Japan, Korea, and Southeast Asia. Buddhism has three main groupings. Judaism is divided between Orthodox, Conservative, and Liberal, and the three groups disagree vigorously over correct ethics, as will attest any who have been in Jerusalem on a Sabbath. Philosophical ethics is divided into many schemes, presumably found under "atheist/unaffiliated" or "other."

In addition, there is some confusion between religious and philosophical ethics. The majority religion in China is supposedly Buddhist, but the majority of Chinese are strongly influenced by Confucian ethical philosophy, argued by some to be a religion.[10] Japan is a Confucian culture, but many Japanese are syncretists, espousing Shinto and Buddhism. South Korea is the same, though more likely Christian or Buddhist. Pellissier[11] argued that there were, in 2011, 1.5 billion Confucians worldwide, and that Confucianism was the dominant ethical practice in China, Korea, Japan, Taiwan, and Singapore. It was also strongly represented in Thailand, Indonesia, Malaysia, Brunei, the Philippines, and Vietnam due to large populations of overseas Chinese. Confucianism is as important, worldwide, as Islam or even Christianity.

In addition, global business has its own ethics—generally more secular—and globalization has brought its values and ethics to businesspeople worldwide. One cannot assume that because one is doing business in China, for example, that one's Chinese counterparts will represent Confucian or Buddhist values. They may be Christians, or Communists. They may have taken business degrees in North America or Europe and have adopted Western secular values. They may be like Japanese expatriates who are reported to switch between Western and Japanese relational values depending on whether they are working in the West or Japan.[12] It is important to remember that this chapter presents ideal types of ethical systems, in the terms by which they present themselves. The discussion in this chapter may guide by offering clues about how a person from such-and-such a place may see ethics, and if they seem to have this-or-that ethical value, then these other values are often connected as well. The goal is, however, always to learn specifically about the persons you are dealing with and not to rely on stereotypes.

The scope of this chapter has been to take an evolutionary psychological and socio-logical approach to ethics. Both have observed that the main worldwide ethical debate has always been between those favoring self-interest, and those advocating altruism. Most world ethical systems have tended to favor altruism, but global business is often perceived as very self-interested. The conflict between the two has produced much angst, and soured relationships against the trust and cooperation needed to successfully do business. Confucianism and Buddhism were surveyed because of their strong influence, especially in Asia, and their commitment to altruism as the basis for ethics. Western Judeo-Christian and Western secular ethics were considered mainly because of their literatures for repairing relationships damaged by disagreements over differing ethical beliefs. Note that Islamic business ethics are covered in Chapter 12, and Hindu beliefs briefly in Chapter 15.

ETHICS AND EVOLUTIONARY PSYCHOLOGY

Darwin believed, as part of his theory of evolution, that the properties of human minds and mental behavioral strategies had evolved through natural selection, as well as brain sizes and physical attributes.[13] He[14] argued that random mutations occurred in individuals of a species that produced behavioral variations in response to the environment. If a mutation was advantageous, then representative individuals were more "fit" and had higher survival and reproductive rates. If the mutation was contained within the organism's genetic make-up, over time it would become part of the make-up of the entire species so that the species would become better adapted to its environment.[15]

A mental property or strategic response to a recurrent dangerous situation that offered a competitive advantage for individual survival would be "selected for" if it increased human psychological fitness over time.[16] Greater fitness increased the probability that individuals possessing the adaptation would procreate more successfully than those without.[17] For example, a human walking through an Indian jungle spies an adult tiger eyeing him/her for lunch. There is no time to think. The human must go with his/her immediate unreflective choice. She/he may run, freeze, play dead, or climb the nearby tree. The human who runs is lost—tigers are faster. Freezing or playing dead may work with grizzly bears on another conti-nent, but in India tigers are unimpressed. Climbing the tree is the right choice because older tigers are heavy and don't climb well. Lucky it wasn't a leopard! The climber lives to repro-duce and pass on his/her genes. The others are less likely to procreate, having been eaten. Eventually, this climbing strategy will have been "selected for" and become characteristic of all the humans-as-species.

Evolutionary Psychology has been defined as the analysis of biologically based mental mechanisms characteristic of humans as a species, developed through an evolutionary process of adaptation[18] that influences human behavior. These mental mechanisms have been understood to be human universals that influence behavior in consistent ways[19] and that are culturally and historically invariant.[20] They function as stereotypical information-processing preferences that result in typical sets of action.[21]

Psychological information-processing devices are understood to have evolved because they solved specific problems related to human survival, and were preserved in the human genetic code.[22] An evolved psychological mechanism that influenced a strategic orientation advantageous to an environment would emerge over time as a dominant information-processing and decision-making predisposition. It would operate as an unconscious and habitual biological imperative[23] that influenced individual conscious strategizing in specific directions

Strategy content was indisputably related to two universal aspects of the human environment: competition and cooperation. On the one hand, strategy aided competition, serving self-interest, within a social dominance system. Dominance hierarchy is defined as a set of hierarchical relationships that allow some individuals within a group to reliably gain greater access than others to key resources that contribute to survival and reproduction.[24] Dominance hierarchies have been a universal and recurrent feature of human environments,[25] and EP research has identified two self-interest based strategies, dominance-seeking and submission, that have evolved as adaptations, increasing individuals' situational competitive fitness. In any situation, one individual is dominant because she/he would win an all-out fight. Less powerful individuals submit to this dominant individual.

Individuals recognize, however, that it is generally best to avoid all-out fights for dominance.[26] All-out fighting to defend or achieve rank is a foolish strategy because either or both parties could be injured.[27] A cognitive assessment ability has evolved, allowing evaluation of one's own fighting abilities relative to the abilities of others. Dominants and submissives have evolved the self-interested capacity to assess and predict, in advance, who would win, and to declare the winner without suffering the potential costs of fighting. For humans, this assessment would include apparent fighting abilities, position-power, track record, and the ability to recruit powerful allies. The dominant individual achieves better access to key resources. The submissive individual loses access to, or pays a higher price for, key resources, but dreams of a time when the dominant individual can be more successfully challenged.[28] Trickery also evolved in the form of bluffing, because the assessment of dominance was subjective.[29] The trickster might bluff that she/he was more powerful when she/he was not hoping to put others off their guard.

On the other hand, altruistic strategies also evolved to facilitate cooperation within social organization, another universal feature of human environments.[30] In order to compete in external environments, people needed to be efficiently organized, and cooperation achieved this. Considerable EP research has addressed the evolution of cooperation.

EP research has defined altruism as willingness to reduce one's own individual competitive position and environmental fitness by making costly sacrifices of resources that benefit those for whom the sacrifices are made. Since Darwin, natural selection has been viewed as a competitive and self-interested process through which individuals with greater adaptive fitness benefit at the expense of those less fit. It was considered a puzzle that altruism could even evolve, given that altruistic acts reduced the giver's fitness by transferring resources to less advantaged recipients.[31] Yet altruism has evolved both in humans and nonhuman animals. It was evident in hunter-gatherer societies thought to be representative of prehistoric human communities,[32] among primates,[33] and even among vampire bats.[34]

Evolutionary psychology research has identified two forms of altruism. Reciprocal or limited altruism constituted the delivery of benefits from one individual to another, in the short term, predicated on the expectation of receiving equivalent benefits, reciprocated in the long term.[35] The reciprocal altruist trusted that these future benefits would be received.[36]

Costly signaling, or unlimited altruism, by contrast, did not require reciprocation. It signaled to the recipient that the giver was an excellent and trustworthy candidate for a long-term alliance.[37] The costly signaler engaged in an act of friendship[38] and friends usually helped out friends in need.

It may be inferred from the EP literature that there was competition between individuals preferring self-interest strategies and those preferring altruism, because altruists also faced the problem of trickery and cheating.[39] Self-interested individuals pretended to be altruists, trying to appear trustworthy so as to receive benefits or help that they had no intention of later reciprocating.[40] In response, altruists evolved specific psychological mechanisms for detecting cheaters, including the ability to recognize the names and faces of individuals for as long as 34 years,[41] and remembering the history of their interactions—particularly whether someone was a cooperator or a cheater.[42] In response, self-interested cheaters co-evolved adaptations to avoid being detected as cheaters, usually taking the form of either "defection"[43] or "free riding."[44]

A fundamental premise of EP theory has been that a successful psychological adaptation that enhanced strategic environmental fitness would become characteristic of the entire species over evolutionary history.[45] Different rates of survival and reproduction would ensure universality over time. This expectation seemed not to apply in the struggle between self-interest and altruism. Neither seemed imminently likely to become universal at the other's expense. Either dominance-seeking or altruism strategies provided offsetting adaptive values such that neither could become universal at the expense of the other, or one was a more recent adaptation and an insufficient evolutionary period has passed to allow one to replace the other.

Nettle[46] argued in the context of personality that a universal human personality had not emerged through evolutionary history as personality dimensions had differential tradeoffs between fitness costs and benefits. Self-interest, for example, might confer greater adaptive fitness in some kinds of situations—like autocracy—while producing costs in other situations—like democracy—that made altruism of greater adaptive value.[47] MacDonald[48] proposed that personality dimensions represented a continuum of viable alternative strategies for maximizing fitness across a range of recurrent problems related to survival. Altruism and self-interest were consequently in competition with each other and each had a greater probability of prevailing depending on the situation. Each could be considered an alternative strategic niche.[49] Natural selection favored mechanisms that caused individuals to seek niches in which competition was less severe so strategic niches had adaptive advantage.[50]

Considerable research has shown that while the same personality variables are characteristic of humans-as-species in all human cultures studied, the distributions of these personality variables differs significantly from culture to culture.[51] If *self-interest* and *altruism* represent potentially equally successful evolutionary niches, then it would not be surprising to find more self-interested national cultures, as well as more altruistic national cultures. In fact, there are more individualistic cultures, and more collectivist cultures.[52] The more individualistic cultures, including Northern European and North American (US and Canada), emphasize individual needs and accomplishments, and individuals as independent actors responsible for their own success or failure.[53] In more collectivist cultures, including many Asian and Latin American, people are more concerned with cooperation than competition, and value collective achievements more than individual ones.[54] The individualistic cultures value individual self-interest and a competitive process for determining individual success. The collectivist cultures value altruistic cooperation as a means for collective achievement. It is not surprising that individualist cultures have different bases for judging actions as ethical or not that differ from more collectivist cultures.

Ethics in Sensate versus Ideational cultures

Sorokin[55] observed that cultures could be classified according to patterns of uniformity in their worldviews. He identified two main organizing worldviews, plus one that was a combination of the other two. Each had its own mentality, system of truth and knowledge, philosophy, mores, codes of conduct, and predominant types of social relationships.

Sorokin called "Sensate"[56] northern European and North American (US and Canada) cultures that primarily espoused individualistic and self-interested values in the twentieth century.[57] Sensate cultures were so named because for them the only reality was that which could be directly witnessed through individuals' organs of sensory perception. Various Asian and Latin American cultures, in contrast, tended to prefer collectivistic and altruistic extrasensory values; Sorokin classified these as "Ideational." People from Ideational cultures generally believed that sensory reality was illusory, and that beneath it was an extra- or supersensory reality. We also find this belief in Platonic and Husserlian philosophy, where there are believed to be many sensory appearances of deeper underlying truths.[58] Sorokin also identified a third group of cultures called "Idealistic"–these supported mixtures of the Sensate and Ideational in a variety of mixtures.

Every culture has its own set of ethical values because an ethical orientation is a universal component of any cultural mindset. To a large extent, the value specificity of any culture is uniquely its own. However, there are organizing principles for ethicality that are held in common within either Sensate or Ideational cultures that are different between Sensate and Ideational. Of course, discrepancy must be allowed for between the predominant ethical ideals of a culture and the real behavior of its members. When Kant[59] demands that all individuals behave according to a "categorical imperative" such that no action is acceptable that would do much harm if everyone did it, he is opposing individual self-interest that undermines the public good. If everyone believed lying was routinely acceptable behavior, trust in others would become untenable. Some people do lie, intending to take advantage of others' trust, and Kant called them "evil." Sorokin also offers the qualification that Sensate and Ideational are "ideal types" and that no culture is ever exactly one or the other, just more one than the other. Exhibit 9.2 lists characteristics defining and distinguishing Ideational and Sensate cultures as categories.

Ideational ethics may be considered an ethics of absolute principles. The supreme objective in life is realization of its highest value. The central intent of the Ideational ethical system, regardless of the specific nature and values of its host culture, is to bring its members into unity with what is perceived as absolute and perfect values. These absolutes may be understood to emanate from an all-powerful being like God, or could be supersensory absolute values like Plato's ideal forms. The commands of the God, or the value-expectations, are considered absolute in the sense that persons wanting to achieve the ideals of the society have to obey. These expectations usually have to do with the self-development of the individual toward achieving the perceived perfection (Buddhist Nirvana, for example) or achieving certain standards of interpersonal relationships (Christian "love your neighbor as yourself"). They apply to everyone, and the value of any individual in society

EXHIBIT 9.2 ETHICAL CHARACTERISTICS OF IDEATIONAL AND SENSATE CULTURES

Ideational dominants	Sensate dominants
Idealism	Materialism
Sociological universalism	Sociological singularism
Ethics of absolute principles—usually altruistic and collectivistic in its concern for all members of society	Ethics of happiness (hedonism, utilitarianism, eudemonism)—usually self-interested and individualistic in its concern with the successful
Static character of life with a slow rate of change	Dynamic character of social life with a rapid rate of change
"Scripture" as the main form of literature	Secular realism and naturalism in literature, with sensualism and sexualism
Theocratic power	Secular power
"Expiation" as the basic principle of punishment	Punishment as re-education, possibly with elimination of socially dangerous

Source: Sorokin, P. Social and Cultural Dynamics. Boston, MA: Porter Sargent, 1970, p. 15.

depends on the extent to which the values are imminent and manifest in his/her life. These behavioral injunctions are not concerned with increasing happiness, pleasure, or utility. Values of relativity and expediency are their antithesis.

Sensate ethics may be considered an ethics of happiness. The central intent of a Sensate ethical system, regardless of the specific nature and values of its host culture, is to increase the sum total of sensory happiness, pleasure, and utility for individuals in a culture. Sensate material happiness is the sole standard because Sensate cultures accept no super-sensory reality, and supersensory rewards, like being "good," are not perceived to have physical reality. Such a system must be based on relativistic values because the emphasis on materialism, and its improvement to increase satisfaction, means that sensate conditions are constantly changing. As the sensory environment changes, ethical rules also have to change. For example, Canadian society is only just beginning to address new laws to protect individuals' privacy on the internet. These laws were unnecessary only a few years ago before it became easy to send a person's uncensored photographs to varieties of user groups without the person's permission. So, Sensate ethical systems are both relativistic, rely on expediency, and are changeable over time.

Globalization has largely been driven by Sensate cultures intent upon increasing universal happiness by improving standards of living. Worldwide trade organizations and agreements have similarly been driven by Sensate cultures intent on achieving uniform standards for trade throughout the world. There is great uncertainty in international trade as businesspeople from different cultures may not understand each other's cultural expectations and behaviors. It produces utility for them when all the trading nations agree to follow the same rules and standards, and apply the same evaluative ethics, because it makes their representatives' actions more predictable, thereby reducing uncertainty.

Sensate ethics has been based on six action principles, or value-expectations.[60] These represent the dominant characteristics of the Sensate mentality in many cultures around the world.

1. *Utilitarian*: Sensate ethics demands that everything be materially useful. If a product or service is useful, then it is good. If it is not useful, or costs more than can be charged for it, then it is not good.
2. *Hedonism*: Sensate ethics demands that every experience, product, or service provide individual enjoyment. Businesses, NGOs, and governments encourage the finding of happiness from the procurement and enjoyment of products and services. Anything that does not provide sensate pleasure is apt to be regarded as worthless.
3. *Profitability*: Sensate ethics allows almost any activity or event to be made into a profit-making business. By contrast, Ideational Islamic cultures prohibit involvement in "halal" industries believed to be immoral (see Chapter 12).
4. *Leadership*: The money-makers are Sensate heroes. Bill Gates is a world-leading philanthropist, having become rich at Microsoft. Donald Trump is a very successful businessman and politician.

5   *Relativism*: Sensate ethics believes that all values are only relatively true, depending on the situation, the culture, and/or interest group. Everyone is entitled to believe what she/he likes because there are no absolutes.

6   *Rule of force*: When there are no absolute moral standards, there is only influence, position authority, power, or coercion to persuade others to comply with Sensate cultural or political demands. Rewards are offered for conformity to Sensate social expectations, but punishments are available for those insufficiently motivated by rewards.

The problem for the application of Sensate ethics in managing cultural differences is that globalization has not achieved a worldwide convergence of cultural values. Many national cultures are either primarily or largely Ideational. China proclaimed itself a Confucian nation at the 2008 Beijing Olympic Games Opening Ceremony, and its president, Xi Jinping, has cracked down on corruption even among powerful Communist leaders. Confucianism is an Ideational culture, as will be seen. Highly religious cultures like Iran or Saudi Arabia tend to be Ideational because they recognize transcendental supersensory beings or ideals. Hinduism and Buddhism hold that sensory reality is a veil hiding the true supersensory reality being striven for. Though many nominal Christians have Senate ethical views as members of Christendom, devout Christians recognize a divine being whose expectations shape the Christian life. As such, Christians also hold to an Ideational ethics, and believe that sensory reality is an illusion; "for now we see only a reflection as in a mirror; then [after death–author] we shall see face to face."[61] Islam, and Judaism, are the same in recognizing a supreme being, and defining sin and hubris as placing one's self-interest ahead of one's God's expectations about how one will live one's life.

Referencing Exhibit 9.1, it is evident that most of the world's population could be committed to Ideational, as opposed to Sensate ethics. It cannot be known what percentage of Christians, Muslims, Hindus, Buddhists, Jews, and other religionists are devout in their personal beliefs in supersensory realities. Together, however, there is a chance that 83.7 percent of the humans anyone meets, excluding the "atheist and unaffiliated" category, could be committed to supersensory values and Ideational ethics.

Given the antithetical differences in worldviews, Sensate businesspeople representing globalization are bound to experience difficulties in Ideational cultures if they do not understand and make allowance for the views of their Ideational counterparts. It is important that Western businesspeople understand that the most important Sensate values–utility and pleasure–are values least appreciated and pursued by Ideational cultures. Exhibit 9.3 observes that American values are changing from Ideational to Sensate.

EXHIBIT 9.3 WHAT ARE AMERICA'S VALUES IN 2016?

Are they the values of an earlier time—say those inscribed on the Statue of Liberty that welcomed the immigrants who came to New York harbor hoping to build a new and better life? "Give me your tired, your poor, your huddled masses, yearning to breathe free, the wretched refuse of your teeming shore." These values have come under siege in many parts of the US. Some politicians have lately impugned immigrants as being like criminals and terrorists, exploiting American generosity while breaking American laws.

If American values are the old beliefs in individuality, and the ability of any American to build a good life for his/her family through hard work, many Americans seem to have lost faith, telling pollsters that the nation is going in the wrong direction. Many now say that the middle class is becoming poor, and the poor will never become rich no matter how hard they work.

Search Google for "American values" and you will find that Americans have grown very worried about the economy, jobs, and healthcare. Are these really values?

Many Americans mention "freedom" as a key value. Freedom of religion, speech, sexual orientation, and opportunity. Many are concerned about "equality," including lately between races ("Black Lives Matter!"), and gender (LGBTQ). Many would count free enterprise, the Constitution, and individual responsibility as important values.

The majority of Americans say they believe in God but not as many attend church as in past generations. There seems to be a conflict for many between "freedom of religion" and sexual or gender equality. A lot of people feel that some values they hold are being threatened by circumstances.

A guide prepared for foreign students coming to study in the US says that Americans are informal but private people. They believe everyone is created equal. They value being on time. They believe in formal authority but are not deferential, and expect to be able to say what they think. They believe in the importance of family values, but encourage family members to be independent.

One thing most Americans agree on is that the US is a great country that defends "human rights" almost anywhere in the world that these rights are threatened. These days, different groups of Americans have different views about many of the values that used to stand for all Americans all the time.

Source: McParland, K. "America's Values Aren't Trumps," *Vancouver Sun*, August 18, 2016, p. NP8.

IDEATIONAL ETHICS: CONFUCIANISM IN CHINA

Confucianism is the dominant ethical philosophy, religion, or way-of-life for 1.5 billion people worldwide, or approximately 21.4 percent of the world's human population, including China and Japan, the second and third largest world economies by 2016 GDP nominal ranking.[62] While similar, Chinese and Japanese Confucianism are not identical. The focus here is on the Chinese version since China's economy is now more than twice the size of Japan's, and growing more rapidly. All forms of Confucianism represent Ideational worldviews. The supersensory value is not a god or a supernatural being, but a set of action-oriented values that comprise the fully ethical "sage" or "Confucian individual." Anyone may seek to pursue the path of the sage, progressing in stages from unconscious to conscious self-interest, to the "junzi" who is able to control his/her natural feelings of self-interest in favor of altruistic values of benevolence toward others, righteousness or right ethical relationships with others, and fidelity, meaning the ability to build long-term trust-based relationships. Only Confucius, the originary Confucian scholar, was acknowledged to have achieved the "sage" stage at which altruism became natural, and self-interest ceased to be an issue.

Confucianism, like various religious traditions and Kant's[63] philosophy of the categorical imperative, observed that people were either "evil" or ethical. Confucian definitions of ethical behavior emphasized altruistic values, while "evil" behavior was defined in terms of self-interest. At the simplest level of analysis, there were three great Confucian philosophers—Confucius (551–479 BCE), Mencius (fourth century BCE), and Xunzi (298–238 BCE)—from whom Confucianism was derived. Hagen[64] has suggested that if Confucius was the "Socrates" of Chinese (Confucian) philosophy, then Mencius could be considered its "Plato" and Xunzi its "Aristotle." Mencius and Xunzi, like Plato and Aristotle, defined the two principal opposite directions that subsequent thinkers flowed. Yet both Mencius and Xunzi agreed that the three greatest ethical values were "benevolence," "righteousness," and "fidelity," and that the majority of people who did not sincerely practice these values were "evil." Benevolence was defined as a central concern for the well-being of others.[65] Righteousness meant commitment to a set of ethical standards that brought order and peacefulness to social relations by delineating proper social roles.[66] Fidelity meant applying benevolence and righteousness to one's relations with others at all times, and in all situations regardless of circumstances. Pursuing one's self-interest ahead of these values was considered unethical even though the majority of people did so.

Scholars argue that the foundations of modern Chinese Confucianism are derived from Xunzi, while Japanese, Korean, and most other varieties flow from Mencius. The Confucian foundations of Chinese business ethics have become an important subject because of a key difference between Xunzi's and Mencius' teachings. Xunzi believed that human nature was naturally evil and people's ethics should be tested. Mencius believed human nature was good and that people could be generally trusted.

Confucianism was always an important aspect of the Chinese social system. Ackerman[67] et al. called Confucianism the fundamental Chinese philosophy influencing Chinese political, social, and economic practice. Yan and Sorenson[68] observed that Confucian values were vital to Chinese culture and the philosophical basis for all levels of human interaction. Confucian ethics played a pivotal role in guiding Chinese thought and behavior.[69] Its principles were embedded in Chinese minds and considered omnipresent and relevant to every aspect of business life.[70] Woods and Lamond[71] regarded Confucian ethics as the basis for Chinese business ethics that guided the individual self-regulated practice of Chinese managers.

Analyses of Confucianism have been used to understand Chinese business practices in a number of contexts, including business ethics,[72] ethical self-regulation,[73] leadership,[74] cross-cultural negotiations,[75] and marketing.[76] *Guanxi*, or interpersonal connections,[77] has been of considerable interest in the literature as a product of Confucian values,[78] a major key success factor for doing business in China,[79] and as the basis for business relationships between Chinese and Western businesspeople.[80]

The discussion of the Confucian roots of Chinese business ethics and their implications for Westerners is of particular importance for two reasons. First, Confucianism was deliberately revived in China, after its partial suppression during the Cultural Revolution, through the authority of the Chinese government and academia, as a basis for ethical behavior.[81] Kissinger[82] observed that former President Hu Jintao and Premier Wen Jiabo had returned to traditional wisdom, were overseeing a revival in Confucian studies in the school system, and had sanctioned the media celebration of Confucius, including proclaiming China a Confucian state. In January 2011, China marked the complete rehabilitation of Confucius by erecting his statue in Tiananmen Square. It became apparent that the Chinese had intentionally decided to place a much higher value on the importance of Confucian values in everyday life.

Second, various researchers had observed that the Chinese were very committed to Confucianism as the basis for their interactions with Westerners. Chan[83] reported that Confucian ethics were understood by Chinese to diverge from Western ethics in significant ways that were responsible for the meteoric success of East Asian economies in the 1980s and 1990s. Hoivik[84] observed that the Chinese did not easily accept foreign ethical standards. Yan and Sorenson[85] observed that the Chinese believed that Confucianism provided a set of social norms or guidelines for proper business-related behavior. When these social norms were violated, normative conflict occurred. Any individual committed to Confucianism was expected to assertively correct the norm violation. This need to correct foreigners was intended to take precedence over both self-interest and concern for the foreigner, resulting in potentially assertive and non-cooperative behavior. These reactions seemed predictable given Carlin and Strong's[86] assertion that there were serious validity problems for Westerners who asserted that Western ethical frameworks were universally applicable to non-Western ethical contexts. Lu[87] observed that business ethics in China needed to be developed from a Chinese and not a Western perspective. Westerners could not effectively enter into ethics-based relationships with Chinese unless they understood how Chinese Confucian ethics were understood by the Chinese and adapted to Chinese expectations.

If Westerners were required to understand and adapt to Chinese Confucian precepts, then they were handicapped by a misunderstanding in the Western literature. Westerners have always believed that Chinese Confucianism was derived from Confucius and Mencius, when there is evidence that the Chinese Communist Party deliberately favored Xunzi. Xunzi's philosophy dominated Confucianism in the Qin (221–208 BCE) and Han (206 BCE– 220 CE) dynasties, but fell out of favor. By the time of the neo-Confucian sage Zhu Xi (1130–1200 CE), Xunzi's writings had disappeared.[88] There is considerable evidence that Xunzi Confucianism was revived in China in the nineteenth century. Late Qing Dynasty

Confucian scholar-officials, or literati, believed that Xunzi's philosophy was more useful than that of Confucius/Mencius in addressing the economic woes China experienced at that time. Xunzi was perceived to have been more progressive and his views fitted the problems China was experiencing better than the Confucian/Mencian views.[89]

Xunzi Confucianism

Xunzi had insisted that the value of ideas and principles lay solely in whether they had a useful social purpose. In arguing that human desires must be restrained, he recognized that the critical social problem creating strife, disorder, and poverty was the struggle for resources. Xunzi argued that the problem of scarcity of resources was a direct result of State acceptance of Mencian views that economic development was less important than ethical purity. The goal of the State should be to establish ritual order based on appropriate rules of conduct, producing a situation in which all people could satisfy their appropriate needs based on their place in the hierarchy.

Xunzi considered modest profit a virtue[90] and encouraged both economic development and international trade. By contrast, Confucius[91] had argued that virtue was more important than economic gain, and that one should value truth ahead of food, comfort or adequate housing. Mencius[92] warned against the corruption he believed inherent in wealth creation. Chinese nineteenth- and twentieth-century social reformers, including Mao Zedong and Deng Xiaoping, interpreted these Confucian and Mencian views as supporting the imperial social order.

In addition, Xunzi rejected ascribed status. He argued that one's rank should depend on one's individual merit. By contrast, Confucius/Mencius accepted the principle of ascribed status, seemingly supporting the status quo. Mencius qualified his views, saying that leaders had to behave virtuously or they could be overthrown. This view was anathema for the high power-distance Chinese culture, and emperors in previous times had redacted it from Mencius' work at times. The Communists also banned Mencius during the Cultural Revolution. As a result of these differences, Confucius/Mencius has been perceived in modern Communist China to support the old imperial order of society, and not to support political, social, and economic reform.

Twohey[93] contended that Xunzi's views became key principles for the reform movement that evolved into the Communist State. At the same time, the Confucius/Mencius school was rejected as supporting the old order.[94] Further, the Japanese had endorsed and enforced Confucius/Mencius Confucianism during the war of Chinese conquest (1932–1945), leading to its further subsequent rejection by the Chinese after World War II.

When Confucianism was suppressed in China during the Cultural Revolution (1966–1976), only Confucius and Mencius were suppressed and their writings banned, while Xunzi was "praised because he advocated that man exercises control over nature by bringing his subjective initiative into play."[95] In 1950, after the People's Republic was established, Xunzi Confucianism was implicitly endorsed by the State when a concordance of Xunzi's writings was published in Beijing.[96]

By the early 1960s, Xunzi was being described in China as the greatest materialist in ancient China, while attacks mounted against scholars attempting to modernize Confucius' work.[97] Yang Rongguo, a Chinese philosopher involved in the "Criticize Confucius" campaign, argued that Xunzi was a progressive thinker because he held that the purpose of ritual (Li) was to satisfy the desires of the people and meet their expectations.[98] This made Xunzi a "liberator" of the oppressed classes. At the same time, Yang condemned Confucius and Mencius because of their desire to promote ritual (Li) that upheld the positions of the "old slave aristocracy."[99] Yang's interpretation became so popular that during the anti-Confucian campaign (1973–1974), it was officially adopted as "correct" doctrine, and it became dangerous to criticize Xunzi in public.[100]

Bell observed that Xunzi Confucianism had done "more to shape the actual politics of East Asian societies than anyone else" (p. 39).[101] He also argued that in contemporary China, Xunzi was the basis for social practices intended to limit and civilize human desires. These practices specified different treatment for different people, depending on the level or stage of moral enlightenment each had achieved. The most ethical treatment was reserved for the most exemplary, and punishments reserved for those that declined to cooperate with the ritual expectations. This view has been expressed in recent Chinese analyses of State organization and power.[102] Therefore, it is fair to conclude that Xunzi Confucianism is the basis of ethics and business ethics in China today.

Xunzi and the problem of evil

Xunzi argued[103] that people were born with a "fondness for profit" which, if maintained, would lead to "struggle and contention" and the loss of "yielding and deference." People were born with feelings of superiority and dislike that would lead to cruelty and the loss of "loyalty and trustworthiness." People were born with bodily desires that would lead to "lasciviousness" and the loss of social order. If people did not learn to control their bad, or evil, dispositions, then struggle, competitiveness, and violence would become the basis for their social action. People had to learn to control their self-interest in favor of altruistic concern for the needs of others. This could only happen through the transforming influence of ethically minded teachers, good models, and deliberate efforts to practice ritualistic altruism-building behavior. Xunzi encouraged Confucians to test the ethics of strangers by offering them unethical opportunities and observing the result.

It was a concern for foreigners coming to China to do business if the initial expectation under the dominant Chinese ethical philosophy generally assumed that foreigners were bad or evil in intent. It was a greater concern if "fondness for profit" confirmed those evil intentions because Western business is generally concerned with achieving shareholder profits in all business transactions if possible. It explained why, when foreign MNCs were first entering China with the "Open Door Policy" initiated by Deng Xiao-ping in the later twentieth century, Chinese negotiators generally proposed deals in which foreign profits were to be in the long term rather than the short term.[104] Xunzi had written that "if the gentleman can avoid harming *yi*, or 'righteous,' because of desire for profit, then for him there will be no source from which dishonor and disgrace might come upon him."[105]

If "bodily desires" and lasciviousness connoted evil intent, Western foreigners were disadvantaged in coming from a highly materialistic culture that promoted "free love" and lately free internet pornography. Lasciviousness means the expression of lust, lechery, and exciting sexual desires. And, of course, Western business takes pride in its competitiveness, and most businesspeople continuously struggle to "get ahead." Xunzi Confucianism also condemned these preferences as signs of being inwardly unethical.

In the context of cross-cultural business relationships,[106] Xunzi made the following comparisons about those who behaved badly, and those who behaved well.

> If your bearing is reverent and respectful and your heart is loyal and trustworthy, if your method is ritual and *yi* and your disposition is concern for others, then you may wander across the whole world, and even if you become trapped among barbarians, no one will fail to value you. . . .
>
> If you show scrupulousness, honesty, integrity, trustworthiness, self-control, and meticulousness, then you may wander across the whole world, and even if you become trapped among barbarians, no one will fail to employ you. . . .
>
> If your bearing is arrogant and obtuse and your heart is stubborn and deceitful . . . your truest essence is polluted and corrupt, then you may wander across the whole world, and even if you reach every corner of it, no one will fail to consider you base. . . .
>
> If you are grasping and will not yield in pleasant matters, if you are perverse and dishonest, if you are not meticulous in work, then you may wander across the whole world, and even if you reach every corner of it, no one will fail to reject you.[107]

Stages in becoming ethical

Confucius divided humankind into two ethical categories: junzi and petty.[108] The junzi was an individual who was in the process of learning to put altruism for others ahead of personal self-interest though she/he was always tempted. For the junzi, morality was the supreme value that she/he tried her/his best to strive for with courage, inner calm, and self-confidence. Morality functioned as a kind of inner restraint that prevented one making mistakes. Ideally, when the junzi met someone morally superior to her/himself, she/he strived to become equal. When she/he met another less moral, she/he examined her/himself, reflecting on her/his own comparable failings and working to improve upon past behavior. By contrast, the petty woman/man was without interest in ethics or morality, greedy for immediate gain, and sought loopholes in agreements to obtain small advantages and trivial favors.

Xunzi maintained the typology between morally striving junzi, or Superior Person, and the morally uninterested petty woman/man. The good person was "correct, ordered, peaceful, and controlled," while the bad person was "deviant, dangerous, unruly, and chaotic."[109] Xunzi offered the example of two brothers. As petty men, they would compete against each other for their own profit at the other's expense. As junzi, they would be willing to sacrifice their collective self-interest for the betterment of others.

> Suppose there were brothers who had some property to divide, and that they followed the fondness for benefit and desire for gain in their inborn dispositions and nature. If they were to do so, then the brothers would conflict and contend with each other for it. However, let them be transformed by the proper form and order contained in ritual and *yi*. If so, then they would even give it over to their countrymen.[110]

EXHIBIT 9.4 XUNZI CONFUCIAN SPHERES OF MORAL REASONING

Stage	Xunzi Confucian stages
Unconsciously self-interested	**Common:** Ruled by desires and feelings. Follows established customs. Desires wealth and possessions, riches and profit as the highest goal. Lacks correct moral feeling. Conventional ethics: support parents = enlightenment.
Consciously self-interested	**Ordinary Confucian:** Ruled by desires and feelings considered "evil" by public morality. Crooked and selfish but hope others see one as public-spirited. Engage in foolishness but hope others see one as acting correctly. Ignorant but hope to be seen as wise. Pretend to be ethical in order to cheat stupid people. Satisfied if security needs fulfilled.
Ethical	**Superior Person (junzi):** Desires and feelings under control. Restrains selfishness to be public-spirited but with difficulty. Restrains emotions to act correctly but with difficulty. Scholarly learning of *Ren*, *Yi*, and *Li*. Understands knowledge is incomplete and admits it. Does not cheat others; fears the law; dares not be remiss or proud.
Ideal	**Great Confucian or Sage:** Desires and feelings under control. Distinguishes wrong from right like black from white. Adjusts to all principles and situations effortlessly. Completely at ease with *Ren*, *Yi*, and *Li*. Speech and actions correspond.

Source: Hutton, E. L. *Xunzi: The Complete Text*. Princeton, NJ: Princeton University Press, 2014.

Xunzi did, however, refine Confucius' two categories, junzi and petty, into four categories (see Exhibit 9.4). The petty category was divided into "Common" and "Ordinary Confucian."[111] The difference between the two was that while both were entirely self-interested, the Ordinary Confucian had become aware that his/her intentions were self-interested and could be regarded as exploitative or even evil by others. She/he had learned to hide these motives in order to better take advantage of situations and others by trying to be seen as ethical.

According to Xunzi, the Ordinary Confucians were more highly developed ethically because they had become more self-aware of their self-interest and understood that their values were at odds with societal norms and the public good. Otherwise they would not be so concerned to disguise themselves with false impressions. Xunzi observed that they seemed to recognize the "evil" in their actions—"crookedness," "selfishness," "foulness"— because they sought to hide these behaviors. When Xunzi proposed that Confucians test the ethics of foreigners and strangers by offering dubious opportunities, it was to ferret out these ethical pretenders.

Similarly, Xunzi divided Confucius' junzi category into the Superior Person (junzi) and the Great Confucian or Sage. This was intended to show that even good people struggled with temptation in order to maintain their ethical and moral enlightenment. A Superior Person generally practiced habitually proper behaviors of benevolence and justice, but struggled to control his/her desires and emotions. If he/she did not succeed in maintaining self-control, then regression to the Ordinary stage was possible. Xunzi believed that the Superior Person was finely balanced between *yin* (evil) and *yang* (good).[112]

Junzi negotiations with strangers

To avoid regressing to the self-interested Ordinary stage, the Superior Person needed to be very careful in his/her dealings with those from the Common and Ordinary stages. The problem was complicated because the Ordinary Confucian was adept at hiding their true self-interested intentions behind an ethical façade.

The problem was also complicated because the defining characteristic of the Superior Person was dispositional and there was no formalized code or rulebook to follow.[113] Benevolence was an attitude in relation to others, much like the Christian command "to love your neighbor as yourself" that did not specify who your neighbor was nor what actions constituted love. Righteousness meant focusing on what was just, fitting, or appropriate, but did not specify how. Xunzi offered clues. He warned that the Superior Person's conduct should be above reproach. If one was interpreted as favoring profit over benevolence and justice, that was very damaging for one's reputation as a Superior Person.[114]

Yet, a Superior Person could be deceived if she/he were not careful and this risked his/her status as junzi. The danger was that an Ordinary Confucian (or self-interested foreigner) could trick him/her into accepting a relationship or benefits perceived to be improper. Xunzi recommended that the Superior Person test the enlightenment of the other before revealing him/herself as the truly ethical person she/he was.[115] The Superior Person was advised to maintain his/her distance and hide his/her true disposition, while looking closely and evaluating the stranger or foreigner until it was clear that he/she was dealing with another enlightened being.[116] Keenan writes that in the context of relationship building,

> [If someone] is trying to communicate a complex need or desire to you, if your own desires, your own ego, and your own needs fill your mind while you attempt to listen, you are not likely to hear an unfiltered version of what that person is saying. But if you are as serene as a quiet pond, you are more likely to reflect, mirror-like, the reality opposite you.[117]

Xunzi taught that the Superior Person could use apparently unethical tactics to test another's enlightenment. The goal was to tempt a false Superior Person (Ordinary stage) to reveal him/herself by offering a deal that proved to them that you yourself were not ethically enlightened. The false Superior Person would interpret that the supposed counterpart placed self-interest ahead of virtue, and reveal his/her true motives. Xunzi stated:

> Benevolent, righteous, and virtuous acts are ordinarily safe methods of action; however, it is possible that they may be dangerous. Filthiness, lying and cheating, assault and robbery are ordinarily dangerous methods of action; however, it is possible that they may be safe.[118]

The danger in this approach was that the Superior Person would have to offer or ask for an inducement—a gift or favor, for example—to see if the counterpart would actually take or give it. The goal was to ferret out deceivers with false ethics.

Though the Superior Person was ethically forbidden to actually give or take the favor or gift, simply asking or offering could convince an ethical Western counterpart that the Chinese Superior Person was, in fact, unethical. Xunzi[119] stated bluntly that the Superior Person could not, and would not, accept gifts or favors, even having asked for them as a testing strategy. If any counterpart, Chinese or foreign, was revealed as a false Superior Person by these tactics, then Xunzi recommended that the relationship be ended immediately as evil. If the Superior Person was not the boss and unable to terminate the relationship, she/he could seek to have it assigned to a Chinese Common or Ordinary stage counterpart who would feel freer to pursue ethically dubious relationships as opportunities arose.

The Westerner, no matter his/her rank, was owed no explanation because principles of harmony forbade it as a loss of "face" for both. However, a Western counterpart, asked for or offered an unethical advantage as a Confucian strategy, would not know his/her Chinese counterpart's actual intent, and likely assume it was a genuinely unethical offer or request.

IDEATIONAL ETHICS: BUDDHISM

There are other Ideational ethical systems that do not automatically condemn Sensate value systems despite sharing the Confucian preference for altruism over self-interest. Buddhist Ideational ethics, as represented by the Dalai Lama, Tibetan Buddhists' supreme authority, share with Confucianism the goal of personal ethical development in the direction of achieving a supersensory higher morality while seeking not to condemn others for their perceived ethical failings.

The Dalai Lama, the titular leader of Tibetan Buddhism, argues that one must restrain oneself from self-interested criticism and action, accept suffering, practice virtue in relationships, and meet others with compassion.[120] Altruistic behavior is understood to encourage more positive interpersonal relationships regardless of the ethics of one's counterpart. There is no sense, as with Xunzi, that the ethical person's ethics will be threatened by exposure to less ethical counterparts as long as the ethical Buddhist behaves with altruism. And for the Buddhist,[121] "reconciliation" is a key altruistic goal when relationships have been injured by self-interested competitiveness, aggression, hostility, or violence. Reconciliation implies that a broken relationship is repaired through a process of mutual repentance and forgiveness, restoring the possibility of the relationship again.[122]

Buddhist ethical practices

There are three major schools of Buddhism. Mahayana Buddhism is the largest with 360 million followers; it is commonly practiced in East Asia and includes over half of all worldwide Buddhists. The second largest school is Theravada (150 million followers), with most of its members in Southeast Asia. The third and smallest school is Vajrayana (18 million followers), found mostly in Tibet, Mongolia, and Russia. Thanks to the Dalai Lama, however, Vajrayana is the best-known school and has seven million non-Asian adherents. Buddhism is extremely influential as an ethical system in China, Thailand, Cambodia, and Japan (see Exhibit 9.5).

Buddhism is an Ideational ethical system whose supersensory goal is "enlightenment" or Nirvana. Adherents believe (as do Hindus) that they will be reincarnated over and over until all ethical conundrums have been solved or mastered through learning practical ethical action. At that point, their individual essences merge into unity—Nirvana—and reincarnation ceases. Mahayana is known as "big boat" Buddhism because a person who has already achieved enlightenment may decline Nirvana and choose to return to the world to help others also achieve enlightenment through his/her teachings. Buddha was such a person, and Tibetan Buddhists believe the Dalai Lama is too. By contrast, Theravada is "little boat" Buddhism. On the "little boat" only one person may cross the river into enlightenment, based on his/her own self-awareness, self-discipline, and knowledge.[123] Theravada is a non-theistic ethical system while Mahayana devotees may acknowledge deities.[124] This discussion focuses on the teachings of the Dalai Lama.[125]

EXHIBIT 9.5 TEN LARGEST BUDDHIST NATIONAL POPULATIONS

Country	Number of Buddhists (millions)	Percentage of population	Percentage of worldwide Buddhists
China	244.1	18.2	46.4
Thailand	64.4	93.2	12.2
Japan	45.8	36.2	9.4
Myanmar	38.4	87.9	7.3
Sri Lanka	14.5	69.3	2.8
Vietnam	14.4	16.4	2.7
Cambodia	13.7	96.9	2.9
South Korea	11.1	22.9	2.1
India	9.3	0.8	1.8
Malaysia	5.0	17.7	1.0
TOTAL	499.5	18.1 (AV)	94.9

Source: "Buddhism by Country," www.wikipedia.com (retrieved August 18, 2016).

Buddhism teaches that the individual setting out on the road to enlightenment must learn to become more compassionate, patient, contented, self-disciplined, kind, generous, and forgiving in his/her thoughts and behavior. She/he must be able to discern in his/her behavior whether his/her actions are in the direction of these altruistic goals. This means understanding what constitutes negative emotions and behavior so as to restrain them. This in turn requires "mind training"[126] to learn to remain calm and in control, regardless of circumstances.

Mind training, or mindfulness, is accomplished in three stages or levels:

1   an ethic of restraint;
2   an ethic of virtue;
3   an ethic of altruism.

To ultimately achieve enlightenment, the committed Buddhist believes that she/he must apply all three ethics to all aspects of her/his life, including all thoughts and actions.

First, the *ethic of restraint* means deliberately learning not to do harm to others, either actual or potential. Non-violence is a critical value. From a business perspective, simply formulating a competitive strategy intended to create advantage by doing harm to competitors, or a marketing value statement that creates an inaccurate impression of a product or service, could be considered a potential harm. This ethic of restraint, however, may explain the unwillingness of some Chinese, Japanese, and Southeast Asian business counterparts to directly refuse offers and opportunities offered by Western businesspeople (see Chapters 14 and 15).

Those who intend to do others no harm must learn to enhance their personal values and to act only positively in relation to others. They need a "toolkit" that includes "heedfulness, mindfulness, and introspective awareness."[127] *Heedfulness* is defined as an attitude of attentive cautiousness. One must contemplate the meaning of actions and not rush impulsively and headlong into them. *Mindfulness* means becoming aware of one's own habitual patterns of feelings, thoughts, and behaviors so as to be able to eliminate those that could result in potential or actual harm to others. This involves recalling and assessing past actions to try to avoid the hypocrisy of inconsistency between beliefs and actions. *Introspective awareness* means honestly observing oneself as one acts—monitoring oneself—to correct negative behavior as, or immediately after, it occurs.

One must retain a balance between self-respect and consideration for others. One must maintain one's sense of personal integrity as a person committed to these values, while also remaining open to others' opinions, especially if they offer criticisms of one's thinking or actions.

Second, the *ethic of virtue* means actively trying to do good. If one has succeeded in refraining from doing harm to others through heedfulness, mindfulness, and introspective self-awareness, then one can proceed to this stage of altruistic action. The Dalai Lama describes this in the following way.

> We can benefit others through our actions by being warm and generous toward them, by being charitable, and by helping those in need. Therefore, when misfortune befalls others, or they make mistakes, rather than responding with ridicule or blame, we must reach out and help them. Benefiting others through our speech includes praising others, listening to their problems, and offering them advice and encouragement. . . . It is useful to cultivate an attitude of sympathetic joy in others' achievements and good fortune . . . a powerful antidote to envy.[128]

Third, the *ethic of altruism* means genuinely dedicating all of one's intentionality to the welfare of others. The Dalai Lama calls this "the highest form of ethical practice," seen by many as "the main avenue to liberation or to unity with God."[129] It simply requires serving others rather than oneself. It is a clear insistence that altruism is of higher value than self-interest.

A new non-religious secular ethics

If altruistic values—kindness, support, generosity, and forgiveness—are part of the evolved mind of humans-as-species, and globalization and international business promote cooperation between nations and individuals, then could an altruistic secular ethics be within reach?[130] The Dalai Lama asks this question and answers: "Yes!" Historically, altruistic Ideational ethics has been the province of world religions, but religions have historically competed with each other for members and influence while promoting altruism within themselves for their own members. No religion has universal appeal, and no ethics based on a single religion will appeal to more than a fraction of humankind. To the extent that major world religions and the religiously unaffiliated (see Exhibit 9.1) espouse similar altruistic values, it is possible to conceive of a grand and inclusive secular Ideational approach to universal ethics.

> We all appreciate the kindness of others. We are all, by nature, oriented to the basic human values of love and compassion. We all prefer the love of others to their hatred. We all prefer others' generosity to their meanness. And who among us does not prefer tolerance, respect, and forgiveness of our failings to bigotry, disrespect, and resentment?[131]

The Dalai Lama proposes universal values as the basis for a universal secular Ideational ethics. Regardless of whether they are universally held, these values are a reasonable starting point for building and maintaining trust-based cross-cultural business relationships.

The sharp differences in value commitments between Sensate and Ideational cultures, based on the conflict between self-interest and altruism, means that relationships between Sensate and Ideational individuals are always in danger of damage or breakage. Relationships become unexpectedly broken due to unforeseen consequences from fundamentally different worldviews and mindsets that govern individual behavior through habitual unintentional patterns of action. This is the reality of a world governed by two great antithetical ethical systems. Any worldwide ethical synthesis must take account of these two contrary ethical worldviews. Realistically, it cannot discount one in favor of the other, no matter how appealing the result.

Western Euro-North American businesspersons, and their supporters, tend to represent self-interested Sensate ethical values. The most important values in Sensate ethical systems are pleasure, efficiency, effectiveness, and profitability. Business is almost universally interested in attracting customers to products and services that will improve customers' perceived quality of life (more pleasure and less pain). Business does its best to organize its inputs efficiently to reduce its costs, and effectively to support its competitive strategic plans. Growing market share, cost control, and effective strategic plans are the guarantors of greater profitability. Ideational individuals and organizations, meanwhile, are focused on values other than utility and profitability. Conflicts are bound to arise when idealism faces off against pragmatism.

It is all too easy for international businesspersons to suddenly find themselves in apparently intractable value conflicts, and damaged or broken relationships, because of the difference between Sensate and Ideational values. It should be the goal of both sides to repair these relationships, working to repair trust and cooperation, rather than engaging in "win–lose" conflicts in which one side wins and the other mobilizes its legal appeals, or even resorts to violence. When the Dalai Lama says that forgiveness and reconciliation are the keys to solving these relationship conflicts, he is addressing these issues.

Take forgiveness. Two levels here. One level: forgiveness means you shouldn't develop feelings of revenge. Because revenge harms the other person, therefore it is a form of violence. With violence, there is usually counter-violence. This generates even more violence—the problem never goes away. . . . Another level: forgiveness means you should not try to develop feelings of anger toward your enemy. Anger doesn't solve the problem. Anger only brings uncomfortable feelings to yourself. Anger destroys your own peace of mind. . . . I think that's the main reason why we should forgive.[132]

However, unilateral forgiving is only one step on the road to reconciliation of damaged or broken relationships. Reconciliation has usually been seen, for millennia of human history, as a two-way street in which the person who feels she/he has been harmed must forgive, and the person perceived as the harm-doer must repent.[133]

WESTERN JUDEO-CHRISTIAN VIEWS ON RECONCILIATION

The Judeo-Christian ethical tradition has presented much thought over millennia about how broken relationships could be mended and reconciled. Both Judaism and Christianity believed in a personal God whose relationships with humanity were broken because of "sin." Sin was defined as humans exercising their free-will to act independently and oppose God's preferences. However, a Western counterpart, asked for or offered an unethical advantage, would not know his/her Chinese counterpart's actual intent, and likely assume it was a genuinely unethical offer or request. Kierkegaard defined as the worst kind of evil and hubris the person who believed that his/her values transcended God's, and in his/her own mind took God's place.[134]

Even when we take God out of the equation for building and maintaining human relationships, the problem of "sin," in the sense of the clash between individuals' free wills and values, remains. When two individuals, or entities, seek to build a relationship for business together, but discover significant value conflicts, relational conflict results. The goal for both is to achieve a working relationship by finding an acceptable consensus or compromise. If a cooperative relationship can be established, then over time trust may be built through demonstrations of long-term reliability, competence, and fair dealing. Conflicts over goals or values, depending on their severity, produce competition as opposed to cooperation, and either damage or break the intended relationship.

Western cultures' dualistic thinking compounds the problem of competing points of view because of the belief that when there are competing answers, one is right and the other must be wrong. Worse, Western businesspersons are trained to confront areas of disagreement to determine which view is correct.[135] The problem may be less severe in Eastern cultures, where opposites are more likely to be viewed as complementary and the focus is on finding areas of agreement. Chinese conflict management involves emphasizing and expanding areas of agreement until differences become insignificant.

Considerable research has shown that individuals or groups committed to achieving cooperative goals achieve significantly higher performance than those that compete, or withdraw and individualistically go their own ways (see Chapter 6).[136] By choosing to judge and condemn another individual or group for free-will beliefs different from one's own, by refusing to seek to cooperate, the one judging injures his/her own outcomes as well. By making decisions based on one's own perspective without considering alternative points of view, relationships become damaged or broken, and cooperation is lost.[137] Since it seems natural for humankind to reflexively and unstrategically discount each other's values and viewpoints, relationships are often damaged and must either be repaired, or much work will be required to replace them.

Reconciliation through forgiveness and repentance

A damaged relationship cannot be repaired, nor two parties reconciled, without forgiveness of the perceived harm-doer by the party that feels it has been harmed. Forgiveness is not, however, sufficient in itself to produce reconciliation. Forgiveness is not forgetting the offense or the negative feelings it has produced, nor understanding why the other party behaved as they did, nor offering mercy in the form of compassion for the position of the party perceived as the harm-doer.[138] Without forgiveness by the party that feels aggrieved, however, the relationship will sour into resentment, which will likely develop into bitterness, malice, and even hatred and the desire for revenge.[139] Distrust and resentment develop from the fear of the party perceiving injury that, if the harm-doer does not understand, then the injury may be repeated. This uncertainty and fear means that trust will be irrevocably lost.

What forgiveness does mean is that the party perceiving itself to be harmed releases the perceived harm-doer from the debt owed for the injury, absolving him/her of the penalty of the damaged relationship.[140] Forgiveness is an alternative to retribution[141]—making the harm-doer pay—but in order to be so, the perceived harm-doer has to confess and repent, and the party experiencing the harm has to agree that it will not receive compensation for what has been lost. Forgiveness means that the harm-receiver's need for justice will be *satisfied* by confession, repentance, and eventual reconciliation. If the harm-receiver insists on compensation, or refuses to forgive because of the perceived seriousness of the offense, then the relationship cannot be reconciled and trust never restored "because the offender will never be able to do enough to satisfy the harm-receiver's need for compensation or repayment for the damage caused."[142]

Desmond Tutu, as chairman of the South Africa Truth and Reconciliation Commission, used this process to reconcile "whites" and "blacks" in South Africa after the end of Apartheid. People who had committed race-related atrocities were allowed to confess their actions publicly to the TRC and received forgiveness in the sense that they were not prosecuted nor were they liable for compensation claims. Those who did not confess and repent were prosecuted. Tutu reported that he believed that this process averted a race war of retribution in South Africa.[143]

Repentance is accomplished in seven steps: culpability, remorse, confession, apology, restitution, soul-searching, and change of intention and behavior toward the aggrieved.[144] The beginning of the process is for the perceived harm-doer to acknowledge to him/herself, but more importantly to the aggrieved, that she/he/it (an individual or a company) has done something hurtful to the harm-receiver. This can be difficult since there is a natural human desire to evade responsibility and blame. This need to not be at fault leads to the common non-apology that "we" are sorry "if" you are the "kind of person" who would be offended by such-and-such. This kind of apology tries to push the blame back onto the aggrieved party by suggesting she/he/it is the unreasonable party.

The goal, however, of repentance is to restore a damaged or broken relationship caused by some injury or conflict. Reconciliation requires renewed trust or at least willingness to cooperate long enough to see whether there can be trust. Trust requires trustworthiness, and so the first step is simply acknowledgment that something has been said or done that has produced offense. Repentance is only possible if the party perceived as the harm-doer is willing to acknowledge culpability, and take responsibility for it.

The next stage is more emotional than rational. It involves feeling remorse or regret for the actions that caused blame. It is natural for an altruistic person to feel remorse if she/he intended to be cooperative and was perceived to be competitive and only self-interested. It is just as natural for a self-interested person to feel remorse if only because it is inefficient to have invested time and effort in building a relationship that may have been lost, resulting in loss of effectiveness and lower performance outcomes. It is important, either way, for remorse to be visible to the aggrieved party. Judges routinely impose heavier sentences on convicted persons who have expressed no remorse for their crimes.

Confession means detailing the specific behaviors that the perceived harm-doer understands to have caused the offense. This feels risky when communicated directly to the aggrieved party. There may be anger or further accusation. The aggrieved may identify other actions they found offensive. However, the aggrieved party also sees that the perceived harm-doer understands exactly what the problem has been.

Apology always seeks forgiveness. Forgiveness is usually a function of whether the apology is judged to be sincere. Sincerity is generally a function of whether the perceived harm-doer is willing to accept responsibility without reservation, and express remorse. In some cultures, like Canadian and Japanese, apology is a normal practice. In others, greater defensiveness is a norm.

Sometimes an offense is so severe that the aggrieved party demands restitution. In simple terms, something broken should be repaired or replaced. Something stolen should be returned. Trust violated must be regained through long-term reliability. Apologies are a beginning, but only actions demonstrate that a commitment is real. A harm-doer seeking forgiveness may offer a better price or better terms. When the working conditions of Chinese factory workers assembling Apple smartphones were exposed in the worldwide press, Apple agreed to regularly monitor the working conditions of its suppliers, requiring their compliance with standards for nondiscriminatory hiring, and the elimination of overtime beyond sixty hours per week.[145]

In the final steps of soul-searching and change of intention and behavior, the focus for the harm-doer shifts from past to future. Full reconciliation of the relationship may only be achieved when the aggrieved party is willing to trust that the harm perceived to have been experienced will not recur. Usually reconciliation is tentative at first until the harm-doer demonstrates reliably that they are both thinking and acting differently. The ultimate test for both the original harm-doer and aggrieved party is whether the former can resist the temptation to commit the same offense in the same circumstances.

There are mixed views on whether the repentance process is sufficient to justify forgiveness in all cases. Wiesenthal argued that in the case of the Nazi persecution of the Jews, and the Holocaust, it was not possible for him to forgive.[146] Wiesenthal posed this question to a number of respondents to create a symposium discussion. Desmond Tutu said that he had learned about forgiveness from Nelson Mandela, South Africa's first black president, who had been imprisoned for many years. Mandela had invited his white jailor to his presidential inauguration. He said:

> I could tell of others, both black and white and less well-known, who if asked, "What would you have done?" would have done the same—they would have forgiven amazingly, unbelievably. . . . It is clear that if we look only to retributive justice, then we could just as well close up shop. Forgiveness is not some nebulous thing. It is practical politics. Without forgiveness, there is no future.[147]

The Dalai Lama also participated, arguing that he would forgive even people who committed atrocities—but he would not forget, to ensure that there was no repetition in the future. It was all too easy to become angry and "self-righteously condemn" others as enemies, but it was not "the Buddhist way."[148] Volf,[149] who did not participate in the symposium, argued that as a Croat it was very difficult for him to forgive the Serbians who committed "ethnic cleansing" against Croats in the Yugoslavian Civil War. However, as a Christian theologian he felt obligated to do his best to find a way to reconciliation.

Scheler,[150] a Christian and later a secular philosopher, argued that through sincere repentance, a penitent could change his/her past, and essentially become a different person than she/he was before.

> The *sense* and *worth* of the whole of our life still to come, at every moment of our life, [is] within the scope of our *freedom* of action. We are the disposers merely of our future; there is also no part of our past life which—while its component natural reality is of course less freely alterable than the future—might not still be genuinely altered in its *meaning* and *worth*, through entering our life's total significance as a constituent of the self-revision which is always possible.[151]

The acts that damaged or broke the relationship would remain the same because they were in the past. The significance of the acts, understood now as negative, would be changed through acceptance of culpability, remorse, confession, apology, possible restitution, and the proof of sincerity in altered current intentions and actions.

Under these circumstances, there is a Rabbinic debate about the responsibility of the party that perceives that it was harmed.[152] The majority has argued that the repentant harm-doer is not forgiven, regardless of his/her/its sincerity, until the harm-receiver truly forgives. The minority, however, has argued that a person who has so successfully changed his/her thinking and actions through repentance "is no longer the same person" and deserves forgiveness and reconciliation.[153] To refuse to forgive a harm-doer who has so thoroughly reformed him/herself through sincere repentance is itself a "sin" requiring forgiveness in turn.[154] Refusing forgiveness, having received sincere repentance, turns the aggrieved into the harm-doer, and the harm-doer into the victim. Therefore, repentance for harm done places an ethical expectation on the aggrieved party to forgive, and give the relationship another chance. A businessperson may repent (or forgive) out of altruism or self-interest, but either way the goal is a trustworthy relationship and a renewed ability to work together.

CONCLUSIONS

Both Eastern and Western religious and secular ethics have identified the same two bases for human ethical thinking: altruism and self-interest. Evolutionary psychology has confirmed that the human mind evolved in response to recurrent situations in the human environment in these two directions, and that each could be considered an ecological niche that conferred greater selective "fitness." Some people are more predisposed in favor of altruism, while others are more predisposed in favor of self-interest. At the same time, sociological analysis has proposed that some cultures, called Sensate, are more self-interested. Others, called Ideational, are more altruistic. Western Euro-North American cultures tend to be more Sensate in their commitment to values of greater pleasure and utility. Global business tends to be more Sensate in its commitment to these values as well as efficiency, effectiveness, and profitability. Asian, African, and Latin American cultures have tended to be more Ideational in their commitment to supersensory values, including "God," "gods," and ideal values like benevolence, righteousness, and fidelity.

This chapter has taken the position that the major challenge of international ethics was to build trustworthy relationships even when relatively Sensate businesspeople have to work with Ideational counterparts. Value conflicts between the two have great potential for damaging their relationships. A reconciliation process was proposed for repairing these damaged and broken relationships. In Jewish, Christian, and secular philosophy, this reconciliation of damaged or broken relationships is achieved through a process of repentance and forgiveness.

MIND STRETCHING

1   Immanuel Kant offered the following case for discussion in his classes. Suppose you are a business owner and know that your relatively new start-up business will definitely go bankrupt without a capital infusion, and will probably go bankrupt with additional capital. Do you approach investors to ask them to invest in your business? Do you ask your family (the major source for small start-ups)? Do you approach banks or investment capitalists? Do you provide fully accurate audited statements of your firm's performance, or not? What do your answers say about your personal ethics?

2   Some business writers have argued that globalization has caused value convergence across a variety of cultures. Would you say that the cultures you are familiar with have become more self-interested and Sensate over time? Or more altruistic and Ideational? What's your evidence?

3   Google "personality test," and select www.16personalities.com/free-personality-test (retrieved August 22, 2016). This is a version of the MBTI personality test. If you score "SJ" or "NF" as part of your four-letter outcome, you are probably more predisposed in favor of altruism. If you score "SP" or "NT" you are probably more predisposed in favor of self-interest. Do these results make sense to you in the way you relate to other people? Or not? Think of some examples to justify your assessment of yourself.

NOTES

1   Hutton, E. L. *Xunzi: The Complete Text*. Princeton, NJ: Princeton University, 2016, p. 9.

2   Dalai Lama. *Beyond Religion: Ethics for a Whole World*. Toronto, ON: McClelland & Stewart Ltd., 2011, p. xiv.

3   Newman, L. E. *Repentance: The Meaning & Practice of Teshuvah*. Woodstock, VT: Jewish Lights Publishing, 2010, pp. 205–206.

4   *The American Heritage Dictionary of the English Language*, 4th edn. Boston, MA: Houghton Mifflin Company, 2000, p. 611.

5   Ibid.

6   Sorokin, P. *Social and Cultural Dynamics: A Study of Change in Major Systems of Art, Truth, Ethics, Law and Social Relationships*, abridged edition. Boston, MA: Porter Sargent Publisher, 1970.

7   Kierkegaard, S. *Either/Or: A Fragment of Life*. London: Penguin Books, 1992.

8   Dalai Lama. *Beyond Religion: Ethics for a Whole World*. London: Rider, 2013.

9   Wikipedia. "List of Religious Populations," https://en.m.wikipedia.org/wiki/List-of-religious-populations (retrieved August 10, 2016).

10 Sun, A. *Confucianism as a World Religion: Contested Histories and Contemporary Realities*. Princeton, NJ: Princeton University Press, 2016.

11 Pellissier, H. "Why is 'Confucian Culture' So Wildly Successful?" Institute for Ethics and Emerging Technologies, 2011. http://ieet.org/index.php/IEET/more/pellissier20110829 (retrieved August 7, 2016).

12 March, R. M. *The Japanese Negotiator: Subtlety and Strategy Beyond Western Logic*. Tokyo: Kodansha International, 1990.

13 Tooby, J. and Cosmides, L. "The Psychological Foundations of Culture," in J. H. Barkow, L. Cosmides, and J. Tooby, *The Adapted Mind: Evolutionary Psychology and the Generation of Culture*. New York: Oxford University Press, 1995, pp. 19–136.

14 Darwin, C. *The Origin of Species*. New York: Penguin Books, 1985.

15 Saad, G. "Applying Evolutionary Psychology in Understanding the Representation of Women in Advertising," *Psychology & Marketing*, Vol. 21, 2004, pp. 593–612.

16 DiClemente, D. F. and Hantula, D. A. "Optimal Foraging Online: Increasing Sensitivity to Delay," *Psychology & Marketing*, Vol. 20, 2003, pp. 785–809.

17 Cosmides, L. and Tooby, J. "Cognitive Adaptations for Social Exchange," in J. H. Barkow, L. Cosmides, and J. Tooby, *The Adapted Mind: Evolutionary Psychology and the Generation of Culture*. New York: Oxford University Press, 1995, pp. 163–228.

18 Buss, D. M. *Evolutionary Psychology: The New Science of the Mind*, 3rd edn. Boston, MA: Pearson Education, 2008.

19 Brown, D. E. *Human Universals*. Boston, MA: McGraw-Hill, 1991.

20 Saad, "Applying Evolutionary Psychology in Understanding the Representation of Women in Advertising."

21 Hantula, D. A. "Guest Editorial: Evolutionary Psychology and Consumption," *Psychology & Marketing*, Vol. 20, 2003, pp. 757–763.

22 Buss, *Evolutionary Psychology*. Also see Slama, M. E. "Book Review: David M. Buss, Evolutionary Psychology: The New Science of the Mind (Second Edition)," *Psychology & Marketing*, Vol. 22, 2005, pp. 931–935.

23 Scheler, M. *Man's Place in Nature*, New York: Noonday Press, 1974.

24 Cummins, D. D. "Social Norms and Other Minds: The Evolutionary Roots of Higher Cognition," in D. D. Cummins and C. Allen (eds.), *The Evolution of the Mind*. New York: Oxford University Press, 1998, pp. 30–50.

25 Brown, *Human Universals*.

26 Pinker, S. *How the Mind Works*. New York: Norton Publishing, 1997.

27 Buss, *Evolutionary Psychology*.

28 Pinker, *How the Mind Works*.

29 Buss, *Evolutionary Psychology*.

30 Brown, *Human Universals*; Buss, *Evolutionary Psychology*.

31 Cosmides and Tooby, "Cognitive Adaptations for Social Exchange."

32 Cashdan, E. "Hunters and Gatherers: Economic Behavior in Bands," in S. Plattner (ed.), *Economic Anthropology*. Stanford, CA: Stanford University Press, 1989, pp. 21–48.

33 de Waal, F. *Chimpanzee Politics: Sex and Power Among the Apes*. Baltimore, MD: Johns Hopkins University Press, 1982.

34 Wilkinson, G. W. "Reciprocal Food Sharing in the Vampire Bat," *Nature*, Vol. 308, 1982, pp. 181–184.

35 Axelrod, R. *The Evolution of Cooperation*. New York: Basic Books, 1984.

36 Cosmides and Tooby, "Cognitive Adaptations for Social Exchange."

37 Gintes, H., Smith, E., and Bowles, S. "Costly Signaling and Cooperation," *Journal of Theoretical Biology*, Vol. 213, 2001, pp. 103–119. Grafen, A. "Biological Signals as Handicaps," *Journal of Theoretical Biology*, Vol. 144, 1990, pp. 517–546.

38 Tooby, J. and Cosmides, L. "Friendship and the Banker's Paradox: Other Pathways to the Evolution of Adaptations for Altruism," *Proceedings of the British Academy*, Vol. 88, 1996, pp. 119–143.

39 Buss, *Evolutionary Psychology*.

40 Cosmides and Tooby, "Cognitive Adaptations for Social Exchange."

41 Bahrick, H. P., Bahrick, P. O., and Wittlinger, R. P. "Fifty Years of Memory for Names and Faces: A Cross-Sectional Approach," *Journal of Experimental Psychology*, Vol. 104, 1975, pp. 54–75.

42 Cosmides and Tooby, "Cognitive Adaptations for Social Exchange."

43 Maynard Smith, J. and Price, G. "The Logic of Animal Conflict," *Nature*, Vol. 246, pp. 15–18.

44 Shinada, M. and Yamagishi, T. "Punishing Free Riders: Direct and Indirect Promotion of Cooperation," *Evolution and Human Behavior*, Vol. 28, No. 5, 2007, pp. 330–339.

45 Tooby and Cosmides, "The Psychological Foundations of Culture."

46 Nettle, D. "The Evolution of Personality Variation in Humans and Other Animals," *American Psychologist*, Vol. 61, No. 6, 2006, pp. 622–631.

47 Nettle, D. "An Evolutionary Approach to the Extroversion Continuum," *Evolution and Human Behavior*, Vol. 26, No. 4, 2005, pp. 363–373.

48 MacDonald, K. "Evolution, the Five-Factor Model, and Levels of Personality," *Journal of Personality*, Vol. 63, 1995, pp. 525–568.

49 Maynard Smith, J. *Evolution and the Theory of Games*. Cambridge: Cambridge University Press. Wilson, D. S. "Adaptive Genetic Variation and Human Evolutionary Psychology," *Ethology and Sociobiology*, Vol. 15, 1994, pp. 219–235.

50 Buss, *Evolutionary Psychology*.

51 For example, see McCrae, R. R. and Costa, P. T. Jr. *Personality in Adulthood: A Five-Factor Theory Perspective*, 2nd edn. New York: Guilford Press, 2003. Seagal, S. and Horne, D. *Human Dynamics: A New Framework for Understanding People and Realizing the Potential in Our Organizations*. Waltham, MA: Pegasus Communications, 1992.

52 Triandis, H. C. "Individualism–Collectivism and Personality," *Journal of Personality*, Vol. 69, 2001, pp. 907–924.

53 Burger, J. M. *Personality*, 6th edn. Singapore: Wadsworth/Thompson Learning, 2004.

54 Ibid.

55 Sorokin, *Social and Cultural Dynamics*.

56 Brown, H. O. *The Sensate Culture: Western Civilization Between Chaos and Transformation*. Dallas, TX: Word Publishing.

57 Part of Sorokin's thesis, beyond the scope here, was that Western culture had changed in its central organizing principle, from Ideational in its early history, to primarily Sensate after 1880 CE. With globalization, Asian cultures have become more Sensate and less Ideational since the latter half of the twentieth century, due to the influence of Western Sensate values, economic opportunities, and trade treaties.

58 For Plato, see Bostock, D. "Plato," in Honderich, T. (ed.), *The Philosophers: Introducing Great Western Thinkers*. Oxford: Oxford University Press, 1999, pp. 14–21. For phenomenology, see Inwood, M. J. "Husserl," in Honderich, T. (ed.), *The Philosophers: Introducing Great Western Thinkers*. Oxford: Oxford University Press, 1999, pp. 210–215.

59 Sullivan, R. J. *An Introduction to Kant's Ethics*. Cambridge: Cambridge University Press, 1995, p. 133.

60 Sorokin, *Social and Cultural Dynamics*, pp. 426–428.

61 1 Corinthians 13: 12a.

62 Top 101 News. "Top 10 Largest Economies in the World," www.top101news.com (retrieved August 10, 2016).

63 Sullivan, R. J. *Immanuel Kant's Moral Theory*. Cambridge: Cambridge University Press, 1997.

64 Hagen, K. *The Philosophy of Xunzi: A Reconstruction*. Chicago, IL: Open Court, 2007.

65 Hutton, *Xunzi: The Complete Text*.

66 Ibid.

67 Ackerman, D., Hu, J. and Wei, L. "Confucius, Cars, and the Big Business: Impact of Government Involvement in Business on Consumer Perceptions Under Confucianism," *Journal of Business Ethics*, Vol. 88, 2009, pp. 473–482.

68 Yan, J. and Sorenson, R. L. "The Influence of Confucian Ideology on Conflict in Chinese Family Business," *Journal of International Cross Cultural Management*, Vol. 4, No. 1, 2004, pp. 5–17.

69 Zhang, H., Cone, M. H., Everett, A. M., and Elkin, G. "Aesthetic Leadership in Chinese Business: A Philosophic Perspective," *Journal of Business Ethics*, Vol. 101, 2011, pp. 475–491.

70 Fam, K.-S., Yang, Z., and Hyman, M. "Confucian/Chopsticks Marketing," *Journal of Business Ethics*, Vol. 88, 2009, pp. 393–397.

71 Woods, P. R. and Lamond, D. A. "What Would Confucius Do? Confucian Ethics and Self-Regulation in Management," *Journal of Business Ethics Online*, 2011, DOI: 10.1007/s10551-011-011-0838-5.

72 Hoivik, H. V. W. "East Meets West: Tacit Messages About Business Ethics in Stories Told by Chinese Managers," *Journal of Business Ethics*, Vol. 74, 2007, pp. 457–469. Ip, P. K. "The Challenge of Developing a Business Ethics in China," *Journal of Business Ethics*, Vol. 88, 2009, pp. 211–224. Provis, C. "Virtuous Decision Making for Business Ethics," *Journal of Business Ethics*, Vol. 91, 2010, pp. 3–16.

73 Woods and Lamond, "What Would Confucius Do?"

74 Zhang et al., "Aesthetic Leadership in Chinese Business."

75 Deverge, M. "Negotiating with the Chinese," *Euro-Asian Business Review*, Vol. 5, No. 1, 1986, pp. 34–36.

76 Ackerman et al., "Confucius, Cars, and the Big Business"; Fam et al. "Confucian/Chopsticks Marketing"; Zhu, Y. "Confucian Ethics Exhibited in the Discourse of Chinese Business and Marketing Communication," *Journal of Business Ethics*, Vol. 88, 2009, pp. 517–528.

77 Fan, Y. "Guanxi's Consequences: Personal Gains at Social Cost," *Journal of Business Ethics*, Vol. 38, 2002, pp. 371–380.

78 Wong, M. "Guanxi Management as Complex Adaptive Systems: A Case Study of Taiwanese FDI in China," *Journal of Business Ethics*, Vol. 91, 2010, pp. 419–432.

79 Lovett, S. L., Simmons, L., and Kali, R. "Guanxi Versus the Market: Ethics and Efficiency," *Journal of International Business Studies*, Vol. 30, No. 2, 1999, pp. 231–247.

80 Ip, P. K. "Is Confucianism Good for Business Ethics in China?" *Journal of Business Ethics*, Vol. 88, 2009, pp. 463–476. Lin, L.-H. "Cultural and Organizational Antecedents of Guanxi: The Chinese Cases," *Journal of Business Ethics*, Vol. 99, pp. 441–451. Warden, C. A. and Chan, J. F. "Chinese Negotiators' Subjective Variations in Intercultural Negotiations," *Journal of Business Ethics*, Vol. 88, 2009, pp. 529–537.

81 Bell, D. *China's New Confucianism: Politics and Everyday Life in a Changing Society*. Princeton, NJ: Princeton University Press, 2008.

82 Kissinger, H. *On China*. Toronto, ON: Allen Lane, 2011.

83 Chan, G. K. Y. "The Relevance and Value of Confucianism in Contemporary Business Ethics," *Journal of Business Ethics*, Vol. 77, 2008, pp. 347–360.

84 Hoivik, "East Meets West."

85 Yan and Sorenson, "The Influence of Confucian Ideology on Conflict in Chinese Family Business."

86 Carlin, W. B. and Strong, K. C. "A Critique of Western Philosophical Ethics: Multidisciplinary Alternatives for Framing Ethical Dilemmas," *Journal of Business Ethics*, Vol. 14, 1995, pp. 387–396.

87 Lu, X. "Business Ethics in China," *Journal of Business Ethics*, Vol. 16, 1997, pp. 1509–1518.

88 Plaks, A. *Ta Hsueh and Chung Yung: The Highest Order of Cultivation and On the Practice of the Mean*. London: Penguin Books, 2003.

89 Dubs, H. H. *The Works of Hsuntze*. Taipei, ROC: Ch'eng-Wen Publishing, 1973.

90 Ibid., p. 53.

91 Confucius, *The Analects*. London: Alfred A. Knopf, 2000.

92 Mencius, *Mencius*. London: Penguin Books, 2004.

93 Twohey, M. *Authority and Welfare in China: Modern Debates in Historical Perspective*. Basingstoke: Macmillan, 1999.

94 Levenson, J. R. "The Place of Confucianism in Communist China," *The China Quarterly*, Vol. 12, 1962, pp. 1–18.

95 Goldman, M. "China's Anti-Confucian Campaign, 1973–74," *The China Quarterly*, Vol. 63, 1975, pp. 435–462; quoted pp. 446–447.

96 Xunzi, *Xunzi Yinde*. Beijing: Harvard-Yenching Institute Sinological Index Series Supplement No. 22, 1950.

97 Twohey, *Authority and Welfare in China*.

98 Yang cited in Louie, K. *Inheriting Tradition: Interpretations of the Classical Philosophers in Communist China, 1949–1966*. Oxford: Oxford University Press, 1986.

99 Ibid., p. 173.

100 Ibid., p. 174.

101 Bell, *China's New Confucianism*, p. 39.

102 Yan, X. *Ancient Chinese Thought, Modern Chinese Power*. Princeton, NJ: Princeton University Press, 2011.

103 Hutton, *Xunzi: The Complete Text*.

104 Abramson, N. R. "Do the Chinese Seek Relationship? A Psychological Analysis of Chinese–American Business Negotiations Using the Jungian Typology," *Journal of Global Business*, Vol. 16, 2005, pp. 7–22.

105 Hutton, *Xunzi: The Complete Text*, pp. 330–331.

106 Xunzi was the only founding Confucian philosopher who supported international trade, and wrote specifically about business relationships with "barbarians," as the Chinese called people from outside China.

107 Ibid., pp. 12–13 passim.

108 Yu, D. *Confucius from the Heart: Ancient Wisdom for Today's World*. London: Macmillan, 2009.

109 Hutton, *Xunzi: The Complete Text*, p. 252.

110 Ibid., p. 251.

111 Dubs, *The Works of Hsuntze*.

112 Xunzi's idea of moral/ethical stages of development is very similar to Kierkegaard's theory of progressive spheres of moral reasoning. See Roberts, D. *Kirkegaard's Analysis of Radical Evil*. London: Continuum, 2006.

113 Hagen, *The Philosophy of Xunzi*.

114 Dubs, *The Works of Hsuntze*.

115 Ibid.

116 Yu, *Confucius from the Heart*.

117 Keenan, B. C., *Neo-Confucian Self-Cultivation*. Honolulu: University of Hawaii Press, 2011.

118 Dubs, *The Works of Hsuntze*, pp. 59–60.

119 Ibid.

120 Dalai Lama, *Ethics for the New Millennium*. New York: Riverhead Books, 2001.

121 Dalai Lama. *Beyond Religion*, p. 197.

122 Abramson, N. R. and Senyshyn, Y. "Effective Punishment Through Forgiveness: Rediscovering Kierkegaard's Knight of Faith in the Abraham Story," *Organization Studies*, Vol. 31, No. 5, 2010, pp. 55–581.

123 Anon. "What Are the Differences between Mahayana and Theravada Buddhism?" https://groups.google.com/forum, December 2, 2006 (retrieved August 19, 2016).

124 Oinopaponton. "Differences Between Mahayana and Theravada Buddhism?" www.ask.metafilter.com, July 14, 2009 (retrieved August 19, 2016).

125 Dalai Lama. *Beyond Religion*. Dalai Lama and Chan, V. *The Wisdom of Forgiveness: Intimate Conversations and Journeys*. New York: Riverhead Books, 2005.

126 Dalai Lama. *Beyond Religion*, p. 101.

127 Ibid., p. 107.

128 Ibid., p. 111.

129 Ibid.

130 Ibid.

131 Ibid., p. xiv.

132 Dalai Lama and Chan, *The Wisdom of Forgiveness*, pp. 234–235.

133 Abramson, N. R. and Senyshyn, Y. "Punishment and Forgiveness: A Phenomenological Analysis of Archetypal Leadership Patterns and the Implications for Educational Practice," *Interchange*, Vol. 40, No. 4, 2009, pp. 373–402.

134 Roberts, D. *Kierkegaard's Analysis of Radical Evil*. London: Continuum, 2006.

135 Lawrence, P. R. and Lorsch, J. W. *Organization and Environment*. Boston, MA: Harvard Business Review Press, 2010.

136 Coleman, P. and Deutsch, M. *Morton Deutsch: Major Texts in Peace Psychology*. New York: Springer, 2015. Coleman, P., Marcus, E., and Deutsch, M. *The Handbook of Conflict Resolution*. San Francisco, CA: Jossey-Bass, 2014. Deutsch, M. *The Resolution of Conflict: Constructive and Destructive Processes*. New Haven, CT: Yale University Press, 1973. Johnson, D. W. *Constructive Controversy: Theory, Research, Practice*. Cambridge: Cambridge University Press, 2015.

137 Johnson, *Constructive Controversy*.

138 Cecrle, R. J. *Balancing the Scales of Justice with Forgiveness and Repentance*. LaVergne, TN: Xulon Press, 2007.

139 Grisvold, C. L. *Forgiveness: A Philosophical Exploration*. Cambridge: Cambridge University Press, 2007.

140 Peli, P. H. *On Repentance in the Thought and Oral Discourses of Rabbi Joseph B. Soloveitchik*. Jerusalem: Oroth Publishing House, 1980.

141 Tutu, D. M. *No Future Without Forgiveness*. New York: Doubleday Random House, 1999.

142 Cecrle, *Balancing the Scales of Justice with Forgiveness and Repentance*, p. 109.

143 Ibid. A fuller discussion is also to be found in Abramson and Senyshyn, "Effective Punishment Through Forgiveness."

144 Newman, L. E. *Repentance: The Meaning & Practice of Teshuvah*. Woodstock, VT: Jewish Lights Publishing, 2010.

145 Kan, M. "Low Wages, Long Hours Persist at iPhone Factory, Says Labor Group," October 22, 2015, www.cnet.com (retrieved August 22, 2016).

146 Wiesenthal, S. *The Sunflower: On the Possibilities and Limits of Forgiveness*. New York: Schocken Books, 1998.

147 Desmond Tutu in *The Sunflower: On the Possibilities and Limits of Forgiveness*, pp. 267–268.

148 Dalai Lama in *The Sunflower: On the Possibilities and Limits of Forgiveness*, pp. 129–130.

149 Volf, M. *Exclusion and Embrace*. Oxford: Abingdon Press, 2016.

150 Scheler, M. *On the Eternal in Man*. London: Transaction Publishers, 2009.

151 Ibid., p. 40.

152 Newman, *Repentance*.

153 Ibid., p. 82.

154 Mishneh Torah, "Laws of Repentance," 2: 9–10, in Newman, *Repentance*, p. 93.

10 MANAGING GLOBAL TRANSITIONS AND RELOCATIONS

We need to throw our hats far away to make retrieving them interesting.

French saying

A tourist is someone who travels to see things that are different and then complains when they are not the same.

Anonymous

It is impossible to live among a foreign people and not become changed by them.

Viet Thang Nguyen[1]

L
E
A
R
N
I
N
G

O
B
J
E
C
T
I
V
E
S

After reading and studying concepts/examples and illustrations in Chapter 10, readers should:

1   Know the meaning of "culture shock," "reentry," "role shock," and other issues related to global relocation challenges.
2   Understand the foreign deployment process and the importance of selecting individuals based on their skills and training so they will succeed.
3   Be able to empathize with an individual who has just returned from an overseas assignment who has told you "nobody in this company seems to care."
4   Believe that we all have stereotypes, but we can adjust them based on our experiences in another country.
5   Smile when you hear people say: "We did Rome in three days, then spent two days in Paris."

The number of leisure travelers and passport-holders for most countries has increased over the past five years, as has the number of business travelers from many countries.

This chapter has several objectives: first, to understand the challenges inherent in transitional experiences and relocations; second, to examine ways for fostering acculturation when abroad, especially through training in business etiquette and protocols for living and working skillfully in a different environment. We will begin with four examples.

OUR FAMILY MOVES BACK TO FRANCE

- Married in 1995 to Sebastien
- Two years in France (Paris)
- Four years in the US (Arizona, Texas, Chicago)
- Nine years in France (Paris)—with the birth of Heloise (now 13) and Theodore (now 10)
- Seven years in the US (Chicago)
- Currently in France (Lyon)

And here we go again. . . . After seven very happy years in Chicago, we decided as a family—after lots of discussion and weighing of pros and cons—to once again uproot and move back to France, to a country we knew well and loved, but this time to a new city. Why, and why again? We are a multicultural family (French, American, and Canadian), and thought an additional move would expose our children and ourselves to new experiences and therefore be another real growth opportunity . . . .

This move entailed for the first time Sebastien quitting a job he loved; Heloise and Theodore leaving the school and friends they loved at the French Lycee of Chicago; and for me, working full-time as the head of Global HR at our corporate headquarters in Lyon.

After rediscovering how stressful an international relocation can be (we clearly erased that part from our memories!), we are now five months into the experience and, despite some ups and downs, so far, so good.

So what has this new experience highlighted?

- Starting anew in a new environment forces each of us to home in on some adaptation skills we hadn't had to use for a while.
- Even though Sebastien is French, and we had all lived in France and the children were half French. . . . coming back and being full-time in the French culture brought to the surface certain cultural differences, about different approaches to time, sociability, notions of hierarchy, and social formalisms.

So here are some things to perhaps think about for any family considering an international assignment:

- If you have children, talk to them about the projected move openly and early on. This helped us, of course, get a sense for Heloise and Theodore's concerns, but also helped them feel like they had input into the upcoming big change. In the end, they were very excited about the move rather than nervous about the unknown.
- It's very difficult to quickly get a feel for schools and places to live. We found getting connected to friends of friends or contacts, and getting input from as many sources as possible, helped us get a real feel for what would be best for us.
- Check in and check in again. Everyone adapts differently and has their ups and downs at different moments. We found our two children—one started off strong and the other less so—had different feelings about the move and at different times.
- We realized we all had to be patient with each other as our readaptation to France was not on the same schedule.

After five months in France, their birth country, some quotes from Heloise and Theodore:

- I am happy to be back in France.
- I Facetime many of my friends in Chicago, and it is free.
- I was scared at first because I didn't know anyone in my new class.
- I am ahead in English but behind in Math, Spanish, and German.
- An international experience for any kid will allow them to learn another language and experience a new culture.

SAGA OF MY BRAZILIAN ADVENTURE

The adventure was finally started. The airplane landed smoothly in Guarulhos Airport in São Paulo, Brazil, early in the morning on January 2, 2004. This was to be about the last smooth experience I would have for a long while.

Many times, I wondered how I was so lucky to have found my way into the position I was in. Here I was, a person from the rural Midwestern US, being charged with upgrading the breadth and depth of a major multinational company's corn-breeding organization in Brazil. I was to do this from a base in central Brazil, right on the frontier of the Cerrados, the vast Brazilian savannah. This must have been what it was like when my grandfather emigrated from Europe to southwest Minnesota about 100 years ago. He was moving to the land of Crazy Horse, the famous Sioux Indian Chief, big sky, and horse races by the pool hall. I was moving to the land of Rondon, Amazonia, big-time agricultural entrepreneurs, and the best football (soccer) in the world.

At Customs, I immediately noticed things were different. People from the US were being segregated into a separate line. This had never happened before. Fortunately, I was at the head of the line, since there were only a few people on the flight from the US, and only a very small group of them were US citizens. As I walked up to the tables, I noticed they were manned by the federal police, and the tables were in addition to the customary immigration booths that one passes through to enter the country. It all seemed rather haphazard, but very police-like.

As I handed the tall, brasiliera in a federal police uniform my passport, I inquired:

"What is going on?"
"What do you think of your president?" she growled.
"What is the right response?"

She gave me an attractive smile and eased off. She then explained "that some judge in Mato Grosso" had ordered her to come to the airport and provide the same scrutiny to the incoming people from the US as the US was giving to the brasilieros. This was done at the last minute, and only for political reasons.

She then proceeded to fingerprint me, all ten fingers dipped into ink and pressed onto a card. I then had numbers somehow arranged onto a card, maybe it was my passport number, and held this against my chest while the other policeman "photographed" me. Both were a source of amusement, as I was the first one for them, and they were somewhat shocked at the process once they actually did it, especially for an *ianqui* who, they learned, enjoyed their country.

Finally, I was appropriately documented and allowed to go to the other line for the normal immigration, behind all the other foreigners on my flight and another much fuller flight. Eventually, I passed through immigration and went to retrieve my luggage.

I was coming into the country with only what I was carrying, so I was traveling heavy. After filling my luggage cart with the four bags I was carrying, two quite large and heavy, plus my carry-on bag and briefcase, I headed out the door. Finally!

No sooner had I passed through the door than a very smartly dressed man with a perfect haircut and smile came up to me and asked me if I was an American. I indicated I was, and only then noticed the person with the television camera coming up. He introduced himself as working for a television station in São Paulo, and he asked if he could interview me regarding my thoughts on the revised immigration procedure for US citizens.

My immediate thought was, "This is trouble." I had some experience with the press in the past and had an inherent distrust of their appetite for controversy. I politely responded: "No, but I am sure there are others that would be happy to respond to your questions."

With that I turned away and began to make my way through the crowded airport. Guarulhos is one of the few airports that I travel to that can be crowded on January 2.

I must have looked like a beleaguered American with lots of heavy baggage, tired from 18 hours of traveling, needing to change clothes, wanting to brush my teeth, needing a cup of coffee, and working my way through the crowd. Before I went 20 feet, the television reporter again asked for an interview, only this time the man with the camera appeared to have it running. Again, I politely declined.

By the time I reached the center of the main hallway in the airport, the crowd thinned, but once again, my shadow—the television news personality—was there to ask for an interview. This time, I reconsidered. I decided he was not going to go away, and I did not want to be cast as the ugly American. The best approach was to give him a brief interview, and then I would be able to have some peace.

> "How did you feel about the new immigration procedures, fingerprinting, and photographing of everyone from the United States?"
> "I like Brazil so much that it is worth the effort."

A noticeably perplexed look began to appear on his face.

> "Was the line long, and did you have to wait a long time?"
> "Yes, the line was long, but so was the other line."

By this time, the interviewer realized this would be a rather boring interview, so he stopped asking questions and thanked me for my time.

I was sure I had escaped unscathed and went on to my destination, Brasilia, which required another six hours of travel time.

Two weeks later, I traveled back to São Paulo to participate in a week-long Portuguese immersion course. No sooner had I been introduced to my first professor than she recognized me from television. She was shocked.

Apparently, the news program had found a US citizen who was sufficiently angry that they obtained the desired emotion. They ran my interview along with the other one as a measure of the range in response.

About this time, widely publicized reports began to appear of an incident involving a pilot of a US commercial airline. Apparently, the pilot became angry with the delays on entering the country; flight crews normally do not have to stand in line with all the passengers; they receive preferential treatment at immigration. He very publicly insulted the federal police. He was arrested and fined a considerable amount of money.[2]

MY FIRST TRULY GLOBAL EXPERIENCE

I was the Learning and Development Program Manager for a global executive development course with modules taking place in Brazil, China, India, the US, and UK over an 18-month period. The modules became mini-projects with temporary virtual work teams established, working together for short, intensive periods of time, and then disbanding. My goal was to quickly establish trust and rapport, an environment in which you can individually give your best and speak up with your ideas or concerns.

I have undertaken the role of program manager on significant but predominately UK/ Europe-based change programs. I felt confident in terms of the development process; however, I soon learned the complexities and significance of working across cultures.

Our first overseas module in São Paulo, Brazil, was a challenge—first, I had difficulty understanding the spoken English of our Brazilian team members and, more importantly, their way of working. I had to check myself when I started the telephone calls—I wanted to get straight into the tasks, updates, and issues, and I quickly learned that our colleagues would prefer an informal start, with a general chat over how we are doing, the weather, our family, etc. A crucial step in building relationships and a good lesson learned.

Our second overseas module took place in Georgia, US, supported by a very focused, dynamic, and experienced events team. Our calls would start: "Hi, how are you? Great, thanks. Right, where are we up to?" Our working was efficient and we established some very strong working relationships. During a lessons-learned conference call I chaired at the end of the hugely successful module, I was provided with a list of items that had not gone well and should be put right next time. This was a significant difference from our Brazilian colleagues and meant I needed to shift my style to be more direct, clear, concise, and resilient to ensure we maintained rapport.

Our third module took place in Shanghai, China. I was taken aback by a lack of challenge, discussion, or ideas that were offered to counter my suggestions. I actually found it unnerving to not receive any obvious feedback such as I had experienced with the US. I wanted a "sense of certainty" and I wasn't able to achieve this to the extent I required. I learned that our Chinese colleagues are not direct in their communication style and that I should look for more subtle messages.

Our fourth and final overseas module took place in India. I started this module in a similar way as the others, working collaboratively, and happy to lead as and when required. I did notice early on that some decisions were made without my involvement. Having learned more about the Indian culture, attitudes toward women, and respect for seniority, I took an opportunity to share my background with our Indian colleagues, and adapt my style to become more assertive and decisive in our discussions. However, I knew there was a line—to try too hard would flip from collaboration to compliance—and I didn't want that. The contrast from my colleagues was dramatic; I was now referred to for decisions, with greater involvement and transparency.

This global experience has had a profound effect on me personally and professionally. The opportunity to travel and learn from our overseas colleagues and delegates has left a lasting effect on me, for which I am truly grateful.[3]

BEING NORMAL IN MY "PERSONAL" CULTURE[4]

I was raised in a big family that had elements of individual freedom "to be a kid" while following a tight scheme of family discipline. The freedom included being released, unsupervised, with my seven brothers, almost on a daily basis to explore the desert surroundings. This is where I learned the double life of (1) being curious and having fun with a bundle of kids, as well as (2) listening to my elders and "following the crowd/conforming."

I went happily along in my childhood and young adult life collecting my "normal labels," like a nicely decorated Girl Scout sash. When I tried real hard, I got good grades and I was able to attend "the best schools." I performed well and did what was "expected" of me. I was normal. My personal culture (value, ideals, etc.) were a mix of what I experienced myself and what was taught to me.

Getting older, the expectations people had for me started to feel uncomfortable. It started when I needed to defend my choice of undergraduate degree: biology. Why was I studying biology and *not* becoming a doctor? I was in no way interested in medicine, but had a *curiosity* as to why clouds formed and how fish guts worked. I wanted to understand the natural science part of the world. This was what seemed to be the beginning of picking and choosing what parts of my culture fit me best and what parts just weren't "me." Choosing for myself, it was perceived by others that I was not following the path that was expected of me.

After graduating, I continued in the *normal* expected trajectory of getting a "good and promising job." After three years, by "applying myself," I competed for and was offered a prestigious job that included work in environmental law. This new job would be comfortable, it would advance me, and it would keep me in the world of "making it/being normal," and . . . I panicked. This was not entirely "me." I saw my life flash in front of me, with me as the passenger and not the driver.

So, I pushed the eject button and jettisoned myself out of that world, out of the watchful eye of the culture that was comfortable. I made it a bit easier by physically removing myself far away.

I moved to Africa.

There, I could challenge myself, disown the labels that did not suit me, and attempt to discover what *it* was that forms me. What was left that I valued once removed from the "normal" life? It became easier to understand my personal culture/identity by experiencing/ encountering it in another culture, outside my own culture. This is where my curiosity and need to engage with others worked nicely. I could pick, choose, reject, and/or adapt ideas and values, and connect with other people and their ideals and values. I didn't need to change; I just needed to understand myself better.

I could see my culture from the outside while fully submerged/surrounded by an entirely different culture. I found many similarities, many conflicting ideas, and some new and interesting twists about how other people thought and acted.

Nowadays, I continue to be surprised and find comfort in the uncomfortable; and I have a normal life. I have learned to not be threatened by another culture nor mesmerized by it. I didn't "go native" and abandon the values and ideals I felt were mine. I found that people were curious about my culture, and I about theirs. By being open, intrigued, and curious, both parties enjoyed finding the silly idiosyncrasies of each other's culture. I have found the possibilities in the impossibilities.

CURIOSITY, REFLECTION, TOLERANCE, ATTITUDE, FLEXIBILITY

Constraints: Labels, identities, external culture (nonpersonal culture), expectations that do not fit with your personal culture.

Liberations: Curiosity, exploration, interest, engagement, selecting values from the other cultures (including the culture you were raised in) that fit with your personal culture.

UPROOTED CHILDHOODS

In a wonderful book of memories of growing up global, *Uprooted Childhoods*,[5] the memories of several well-known authors who were born in one country and grew up in different countries were chronicled. They were, in many ways, nomadic children. The following quotations seem relevant to the subject in this chapter.

- From Isabel Allende, author, who experienced a nomadic childhood: "The contrast between the puritanism of my school, where work was exalted and neither bodily impurities nor lightning flash of imagination allowed, and the creative idleness and enveloping sensuality of those both branded my soul."
- From Pat Conroy, author and son of a Marine Corps fighter pilot: "Our lives were desperate and sad," "I moved more than 20 times, and I attended 11 schools in 12 years," "Home is a foreign word in my vocabulary."

- From Faith Eidse, author: "During my first 18 years, I moved 18 times," "I grew up not knowing what I would be. . . . I felt pressure to fit in . . . but there was a constant tearing inside . . . of not belonging."
- From Nina Sichel, author: "For them, home is a real place, and for me, it is a shifting definition."
- From Peter Ruppert, author: "History and language also shape us."
- From Carlos Fuentes, author: "The shock of alienation and the shock of recognition are sometimes one and the same."

In December 2012, the UN World Tourism Barometer stated that someone became the one billionth (1,000,000,000) tourist, setting a new record for world travel.[6]

Culture impacts identity: "culture shock"

Most business and leisure travelers feel comfortable in predictable environments. Sojourners or travelers for short- or long-term presence in a new environment are enjoying their travel and are more successful in the business assignments and are able to react and behave in new and often unpredictable situations with little visible discomfort or irritation. Discomfort leads to frustration and negative feelings and stereotyping.

National stereotypes: how far can you trust them?

Can we trust the well-known stereotypes of other people? Here is an example.

Many years ago, I was giving a speech to a group of 50 Japanese bankers, many of whom were visiting the US for the first time. Toward the end of my talk, I illustrated a management concept with an example from our youngest child. At the conclusion of my talk, a banker raised his hand and asked the following question: "Where did your child sleep?"

I told him that our youngest child slept in a room called the nursery. "I think we Japanese love our children more than you Americans love your children," he responded. "I have two children aged three and six. My three-year-old sleeps in the same room with me and my wife on the *tatami* mat floor. Whenever she wakes up at night, my wife gets up right away and attends to her needs. Perhaps that is why old people are in old-age homes in the United States—because you separate them as children."

In my opinion, the fact that our child and many other children may not sleep with their parents has *nothing* to do with love. On the other hand, it is a practice that influences the characteristics we develop as adults. In the West, we bring up our children to be independent and individual. In Japan, children are encouraged to be dependent and group-oriented. The place where they sleep plays a role in this process. Consider the following statements.

The concept of national character or the basic personality of a culture was developed by two anthropologists, Drs. Abram Kardiner and Ralph Linton, who proposed:

1   Because early experiences exert a lasting effect on personality, similar early experiences tend to produce similar personality configurations.

2   Child-rearing practices of a society are culturally patterned and tend to be similar (although not identical) for the various families within the culture. An example is the place where young children sleep at home.

3   These practices differ from culture to culture.

There is a wealth of evidence that has been provided by anthropologists, sociologists, psychologists, and others to support these claims. As a result, it follows that:

- members of any culture have many elements of early experience in common;
- they also have many personality traits in common; and
- since the early experience of individuals differs from one culture to another, the personality characteristics and values differ from culture to culture.

> "Sicilians either belong to the Mafia or a relative does."
> "The problem with this country is that the Jews control everything. Worst of all, they're cheap and sneaky."
> "Blacks are lazy and think they've got everything coming to them."
> "The French are nationalistic and dislike all foreigners."
> "The Japanese are hard-working and intelligent, but they're also sly."

These statements are stereotypes and contain "pictures in our heads" that are exaggerated beliefs and oversimplifications. Stereotypes often originate from the experiences of others and are used to complete the pictures in our heads about unknown situations.

A 1986 survey by the Stockholm School of Economics and a US organization found, in terms of teamwork and communication when working with Americans, both Swedes and Americans believe that the Swedish strengths as managers are that they are used to and seek consensus, that they are good listeners and loyal. But, they rely heavily on the team for initiatives, communicate too infrequently, avoid competition with others in the company, avoid conflicts and taking sides, are not direct, and fear confrontation.

Long-term perspective

Regarding business strategy, the same study found that Swedes and Americans believe the Swedes take a long-term perspective, see the importance of company values, and care for quality.

Gunnila Masreliez-Steen, a Swedish management consultant with experience in many Swedish organizations, describes Swedish businesspeople at home and abroad as

> concerned about people. This concern shows in their history, laws, and how managers function. Swedes have to take a long-term perspective, so it is important to know that your people will be loyal.

For example, because terminations of employment are very restricted, a manager must learn to work with his people. Abroad, however, Swedes use technical subjects almost exclusively as a way of getting to know their counterparts. Social discussions are rather rare and this is a liability.

Abroad, the Swedish negotiator is also often perceived as "cold" when discussing areas outside the technical. But he possesses another quality I would add—a strong desire to learn in all areas.

We all have some stereotypes in one form or another and may become "ethnocentric" in perspective.

The *Random House Dictionary* defines ethnocentrism as "belief in the inherent superiority of one's own group and culture; it may be accompanied by feelings of contempt for those others who do not belong; it views and measures alien cultures and groups in terms of one's own culture."

Ideally, through successful transitions, we become more global in perspective and less ethnocentric. When this is coupled with a formal study of the language and culture of a people, we gain new insights into ways of improving our interactions and becoming aware of the influence of our culture on our behavior. We then have the possibility of understanding that our culture itself can create obstacles in cross-cultural interactions. These obstacles are compounded when ethnocentrism is extreme.

Ethnocentrism also exists in organizations. It might be seen, for example, in those that place only home-country personnel in important positions in their worldwide operations. These people are paid more in the belief that they are more competent, intelligent, and reliable. Lack of ethnocentrism is seen in organizations when superiority and competence are not equated with nationality.

The attitude of nonethnocentrism in people is probably related to the complex psychosocial development of a tolerant and strong personality. Such personalities are capable of multidimensional thinking, are comfortable with ambiguity, and have high self-esteem.

Nonethnocentric organizations have similar characteristics. In the village of Supai in Northern Arizona, where about 300 Indians have lived in peace for several hundred years, there is a sign over the counter in the café that reads: "Do not judge another man until you have walked one mile in his moccasins." This is a description of empathy.

In the research of criteria relevant to overseas experience, empathy has been found in all studies to be an important quality for both adjustment and success. Ethnocentrism and empathy are opposites. If one believes in the superiority of one's group and culture and has feelings of contempt toward others, it is impossible to walk in their shoes.

The ability to express empathy varies. Some people show an interest in others clearly—others are unable to project even a superficial interest.

Here are two good measures to determine empathy. First, can you work well with people whose values and way of doing things are different from yours? Second, when working with people from different cultures, do you believe and behave in such a way that you are concerned only with end results and not people's feelings or reactions?

The transitional experience is significant in that it may alter our sense of identity. Fearn,[7] writing on the subject of philosophy, makes the point that all humans are faced with three critical questions: (1) *Who am I?* (mind and body); (2) *What do I know?* (language and knowledge); (3) *What should I do?* (morals and meaning of life). Major turning points in our lives often force us to rethink our answers to these inquiries, which affect our self-perception and the image we project to others.

All transitions influence one's sense of identity—some strengthen this sense of self, while others may threaten that identity or even change it. That is why we should deal with this matter before departure overseas. When we go outside our home culture into a foreign culture, we may, for example, experience an identity crisis abroad. As a result, personal development occurs when we redefine our answers to the above questions, thereby expanding our perceptual field.

Perhaps the most important lesson for the cross-cultural sojourner is to understand one's cultural baggage.

RELOCATION CHALLENGES

When we relocate within our own country or abroad, we may be subject to culture shock. Although scholars have only researched this phenomenon since the 1960s or so, its impact on people has been written about in works of fiction as early as 1862, including Tolstoy in *The Cossacks*. Jack London, in a 1900 story, described what it felt like to be a "foreigner," but in a literary, not scientific, way. London describes what a sojourner should expect:

> He must be prepared to forget many of the things he learned, and to acquire such customs as are inherent with existence in the new land; he must abandon the old ideals and the old gods, and oftentimes he must reverse the very code by which his conduct has hitherto been shaped. . . . The pressures of the altered environment are almost unbearable, and they chafe in body and spirit under the new restrictions which are not understood. This chafing is bound to act and react, producing diverse evils and leading to various misfortunes.[8]

Essentially, culture shock, as described by London, is our psychological reaction to a totally unfamiliar or alien environment, which often occurs with any major transitional experience.[9] Culture shock is neither good nor bad, necessary nor unnecessary. It is a reality that many people face when in strange and unexpected situations that makes it difficult for automatic coping, as we do in our home culture. Oberg referred to culture shock as a generalized trauma one experiences in a new and different culture because of having to learn and cope with a vast array of new cultural cues and expectations, while discovering that your old ones probably do not fit or work. More precisely, he notes:

Culture shock is precipitated by the anxiety that results from losing all our familiar signs and symbols of social intercourse. These signs or cues include the thousand and one ways in which we orient ourselves to the situations of daily life—how to give orders, how to make purchases, when and when not to respond. Now these cues, which may be words, gestures, facial expressions, customs, or norms, are acquired by all of us in the course of growing up, and are as much a part of our culture as the language we speak, or the beliefs we accept. All of us depend for our peace of mind and efficiency on hundreds of these cues, most of which we are not consciously aware of.[10]

EXHIBIT 10.1 THE FOREIGN DEPLOYMENT PROCESS: SELECTION/ PREPARATION/SUPPORT/REENTRY BEST PRACTICES

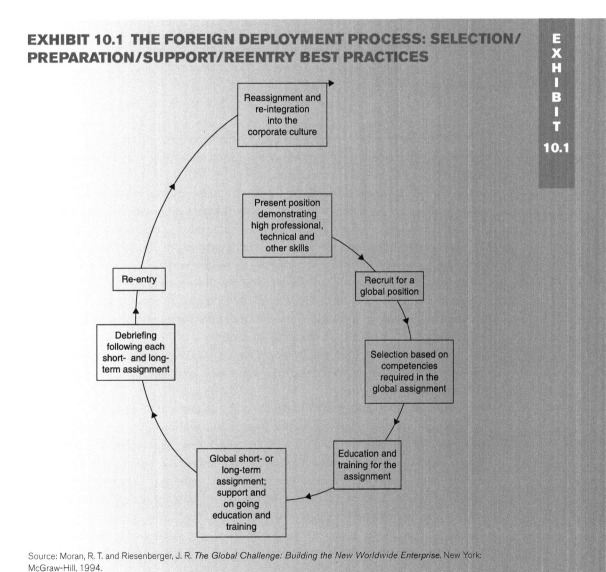

Source: Moran, R. T. and Riesenberger, J. R. *The Global Challenge: Building the New Worldwide Enterprise.* New York: McGraw-Hill, 1994.

Myriad forms of culture shock

A new form of this trauma, growing exponentially throughout the world, is *future shock*, of which Alvin Toffler warned in his 1970 book of that title, and again in a 1980 volume, *The Third Wave*. Essentially, this mass culture shock is being experienced by whole groups and nations because of the inability to transition rapidly from a previous stage of human development (e.g., agricultural or industrial) into our present Information Society, or knowledge culture. The technological, scientific, and knowledge advances have been so large and so accelerated that many people cannot cope with the pace of these changes. They opt-out or are bypassed by the mainstream of civilizations; many end up in an underclass position in modern society. Furthermore, today, countries and institutions—such as religious, educational, and political systems—are resisting modernization, suffering from culture lag, and living in the past, unable to cope with present and future challenges. For institutions, the same phenomenon is referred to as *organization shock*.

According to Klopf,[11] there are six stages of culture shock resulting from relocation.

1   The *preliminary stage* involves preparation for the experience. During this stage, anticipation and excitement build as one packs, makes reservations, and plans for departure with many unrealistic expectations.

2   Arrival at the destination marks the *spectator stage*, during which there are many strange sights and different people. All of this newness produces fascination with the culture. This honeymoon stage may last from a few days to six months.

3   The *participation stage* occurs when the individual must do the hard work of living in the culture and learning about it, especially its language. The honeymoon has ended. The sights have been visited and, now, coping with everyday life must occur.

4   When problems begin to arise that are difficult to handle, usually the *shock stage* sets in. Irritability, lethargy, depression, and loneliness are symptoms. One must find ways to confront and adjust to the differences in culture.

5   If the individual reaches the *adjustment stage*, identification with the host culture has progressed satisfactorily. Relationships with locals develop, along with a sense of belonging and acceptance.

6   For individuals living permanently in a culture, the adjustment stage finishes the transition period—one may assimilate or become bicultural in mindset. For those who are temporarily living in a host culture, the return to the home culture introduces the *reentry stage*. Culture shock in reverse may set in, with individuals again going through the above five stages, but this time in their native land. A sense of discomfort, disorientation, and even frustration may be experienced, often up to six or maybe more months.

The pace at which one advances through these stages is different for each individual. For those who are experienced in international travel, it may quicken and perhaps lessen the trauma.

However, for the *long-term expatriate* exposed to a very different culture from one's own, physical and psychological concerns may be real or imagined. Those experiencing culture shock manifest the obvious symptoms, such as excessive anxiety over cleanliness and sanitary conditions, feeling that what is new and strange may be "dirty." This may be seen with reference to water, food, dishes, and bedding, or evident in unreasonable fear of servants and shopkeepers because of disease they might bear. Other indications of such traumatic behavior are feelings of helplessness and confusion, growing dependence on long-term residents of one's own nationality, constant irritations over delays and minor frustrations, and undue worry about being cheated, robbed, or injured. Some may exhibit symptoms of mild hypochondria, expressing apprehension about minor pains, skin eruptions, and other ailments, real or imagined—it may even get to the point of actual psychosomatic illnesses. Often, individuals experiencing culture shock postpone learning the local language and customs, dwelling instead on their loneliness and longing for home, to be with one's own, and to talk to people who "make sense." However, persons who seek international assignments as a means of escaping "back-home problems" with career, marriage, or substance abuse will probably only exacerbate personal problems that would be better resolved in their home culture.

Osland[12] uses the concept of "learning to live with paradox" instead of emphasizing the shock that may come from experiences in an alien society. Such paradox occurs when we have to hold ideas in mind that are seemingly opposite to the home perspectives. Osland calls this the "road of trials" when we are confronted with obstacles and tests on our way to "normally" perceiving and functioning. To deal with such paradoxes more effectively, she proposes we learn from expatriates who have gone before us, which can begin before departure and continue on-site.

To facilitate acculturation, organizations responsible for sending others abroad should be careful in their recruitment and selection of individuals for international assignments. Surveys have shown that those who adjust and work well outside their own culture are usually well-integrated personalities, with qualities such as *flexibility*, *personal stability*, *social maturity*, and *social inventiveness*. Such candidates for overseas work are not given to unrealistic expectations, irrational concepts of self or others, nor do they have tendencies toward excessive depression, discouragement, criticism, or hostility. Global corporations, government agencies, and international organizations that sponsor people abroad have a responsibility to prevent or reduce culture shock among their representatives. It is not only necessary for individual acculturation, but is more cost-effective, while promoting out-of-country productivity and improving client or customer relations with host nationals. This will be discussed further in the section on deployment systems.

One should also be realistic about the difficulties that may be experienced when living abroad. Intestinal disorders and exotic diseases are real, and may not always be avoided by inoculations or new antibiotics. In some countries, water, power, transportation, and housing shortages are facts, and one may be seriously inconvenienced in terms of physical comfort.

Political instability, ethnic feuds, and social breakdown may make an assignment unacceptable. Adjustment may also be slowed because of not knowing the local language, or in trying to cope with strange climates and customs. But we are born with the ability to learn, to adapt, to survive, to enjoy. After all, human beings do create culture, so the shocks caused by such differences are not unbearable or without value. The intercultural experience can be more satisfying, contributing much to personal and professional satisfaction. One can discover friends everywhere. The expatriate experience has always meant accepting risk implicit in living and traveling beyond our own borders.

As NGOs increase in number and influence, *global humanitarians* are more prevalent. But today, their service abroad on behalf of others may often place them in "harm's way." Civil strife may cause them to shut down operations, or they may face kidnapping, bodily harm, and even death.

Role shock

The phenomenon and process of culture shock have applications to other life crises. For instance, there is also role shock. Each of us chooses, is assigned, or is conditioned to a variety of roles in society and its institutions—man or woman, family member, son or daughter, parent or child, husband or wife (single/married/divorced), teacher or engineer, manager or union organizer, amateur or professional. In these positions, people have expectations of us, as we do of their varied positions. These role opportunities or constraints often differ in another culture. A woman, for instance, may do in one culture what is forbidden in another. In some societies, senior citizens are revered, and in others ignored. In some cultures, the youth regard teachers with awe, while others treat them as inferiors or "buddies."

Role perception is subject to change according to time, place, and circumstances. But since the mid-twentieth century, our defined roles have changed at an accelerating rate. In the past, our roles were fairly stable, clear, and predictable. Today, our roles are fuzzy, more unpredictable, and fluid. The person who has a particular understanding of what a manager is and does may be upset when he or she finally achieves that role, only to discover it to be altered considerably! Our traditional views of such functions are suddenly obsolete. All this role uncertainty can be very disconcerting; the resulting shock to our psyche may be severe and long-lasting. Role shock can lead to an identity crisis, especially if one's sense of self and life are tightly linked to a career or work role. Consider the trauma an older person experiences when suddenly there is a reduction in the workforce, and unemployment lines are long, while jobs are scarce. Furthermore, a cross-cultural assignment can accentuate role shock. Many individuals sent abroad find themselves adjusting to totally different role requirements than back home.

Role shock may be apparent as a result of organizational mergers or acquisition, or of reorganization or redesign of a system. The outcome may cause a person's position to be combined with others, downsized, or even lost. In the past decade, many middle managers were simply eliminated in corporations trying to cope with new economic conditions. Even when one retains his or her post within a newly acquired company, the organization and its culture may perceive "your role" in an entirely different way. Role transformation or elimination may come from new technologies, new research, new markets, or new crises.

In a new role, a global manager may be asked to make speeches to global audiences. Imagine the scene. He has been in the country about six months and has been asked to give a 30-minute talk to a group of employees on what's new in the corporate headquarters.

He begins his speech with a joke. It falls flat, so he tells another story. Undaunted by his failure to get any reaction from the audience, he plunges into his talk. It is little more than an unstructured compilation of what is new, linked by flimsy themes. He breezes through the points that he makes, relying on anecdotal evidence to illustrate their practical application.

He sits down to polite applause. "It didn't go down particularly well with this audience," is the courteous feedback the speaker is given by the organizers. Why?

Speakers in the US customarily open with a joke to "break the ice." This practice is frowned upon in Japan. Generally, good speakers in Japan begin in a humble vein and show their respect for the audience by honoring them in some small way.

One European began a speech in Japan this way:

> If I were an American and you were an American audience, I would probably begin my speech with a joke. If I were Japanese speaking to a Japanese audience, I would probably begin with an apology. Since I am neither American nor Japanese, I will begin with an apology for not telling a joke.

The Japanese audience laughed. The speaker make a good first impression and showed that he knew a little about Japan.

Wearing conservative suits while making speeches or presentations in Japan is also very important. Japanese audiences also look for sincerity in speakers.

When giving speeches or presentations in France, perhaps more than in many other countries, a foreign speaker has to prove himself. Opinions should always be supported with data and facts.

The use of gestures, facial expressions, and lively body movements are characteristic of effective speakers in France. However, the excessive use of aggressive, hard-sell techniques could turn-off listeners and result in a loss of respect for the speaker. French audiences are best won over by gentle persuasion.

The types of questions audiences of different cultures ask can often be predicted. German audiences, for example, tend to focus on technical questions; hence, figures given during a presentation must be exact. Americans favor practical questions to explore how things work in practice. Swedish audiences seem to pose more theoretical questions that seek to define the implications of strategies mentioned during the presentation.

Reentry home issues

"I hadn't lived in the US since 2003, when the *New York Times* moved me to Beijing as a foreign correspondent, along with my wife and two kids. We assumed we would move back home soon enough, but it never happened. We lived for six years in China and New Delhi, where my beat was South Asia. By the time we settled in Rome in 2013, we had drifted into the category of American expatriates. When we saw our countrymen around the city—big, friendly tourists, a bit loud—my kids referred to them as 'the Americans.'"[13]

When expatriates return from foreign deployment, they face another form of reverse culture shock. Reentry research and its impact on the individual and the organization has been largely neglected.[14]

Having objectively perceived his or her culture from abroad, one can have a more severe and sustained jolt through reentry into a home culture. The intercultural experience widens perceptions and broadens constructs, so the person is less myopic in the homeland and more cosmopolitan. Some returning "expats," or those returning from long service overseas, feel a subtle downgrading and loss of prestige and benefits. Others bemoan the loss of household help and social contacts, as well as other "perks." This is especially evident with members of the military who come home after a lengthy deployment in other parts of the world. Many feel uncomfortable for six months or more in their native land, frustrated with their organization and bored with their "narrow-minded" colleagues who never left home. Some returnees seem out of touch with what has happened in their country or corporation during their absence, and no longer seem to fit into the domestic organization.

The coming-home phenomenon described here can be temporary and less intense if the expatriate is helped by a professional reorientation program. For some, culture and reentry shocks may be the catalysts for major choices and transitions, such as a new locale and new relationships, pursuit of additional education or training, a change in job or career, and generally an improved lifestyle. While some expatriates never make the necessary readjustments, living as strangers in their home cultures, for the majority the intercultural experience is very positive, a turning point toward an enriched quality of life.

ONE FAMILY'S EXPERIENCE AFTER LIVING IN EUROPE AND RETURNING HOME

"Nobody, I mean nobody, asked me anything about France," said a young American woman after returning from two years in France.

The incident illustrates the mixed feelings of persons returning home after a prolonged experience living overseas. Until recently, the reintegration of an expatriate into his/her home society was viewed as a fairly simple process of renewal, and it was the least-considered facet of foreign assignments. Now, more and more organizations and researchers are giving the deserved attention to the problems that arise during the transitional period from living abroad to settling down back at home. Companies are finding that returning expatriates confronted with the inevitable changes that have taken place during their foreign postings often go through a period of uncertainty as intense as the cultural shock experienced when they initially settled abroad.

Especially vulnerable to reentry shock are persons who have taken a keen interest in the host culture. For them, an extended period abroad can be a profound experience, prompting a reexamination of their lives, values, and attitudes.

The policy of many organizations is to send "fast-track" managers overseas for international experience. After a few years, they return to the home office with a more cosmopolitan viewpoint. However, much of their knowledge of business realities abroad is squandered, because companies rarely have programs to exploit it.

Accustomed to higher salaries, big expense accounts, bonuses, servants, and other overseas benefits, returning expatriates are often discontented with the lowered expectations and compensation at home. For some, there is a marked change in lifestyles; they no longer have the social privileges, contacts, and perks that often come with foreign assignments. They may return to the life of a middle manager in suburbia and miss their former movement in prestigious circles and involvement with high-level government officials.

MESSAGE FOR THE EXECUTIVES OF GLOBAL ORGANIZATIONS

Mr. Hans is 51 years old. He has worked for one of the largest chemical companies in Europe for more than 25 years. He joined the company as a young chemical engineer, completed his apprenticeship, and accepted a position as a sales representative in Australia. He lived there until his return to Europe five years ago.

After his first five years in Australia, he was appointed president of a small subsidiary. Though the European parent company has a policy of job rotation every three years, no replacements were available, so he was happy to stay on in Australia working for various subsidiary companies.

By the end of his Australian stint, he was a member of many of the most important boards in the country. By all obvious measures, he was a success. The companies he managed flourished, and several of them were sold at considerable profit. Yet during his long spell in Australia, he never once had a performance appraisal and never knew clearly how his work was viewed by his superiors in Europe.

When he was eventually replaced in Australia by another European, he was brought home and given a job that he has found to be neither satisfying nor challenging. Ironically, his immediate boss has never lived outside his native country.

The executive's case highlights the tragic inability of many large organizations to handle their people well and to integrate their individual learning into the organization. What is most surprising to me is the executive's claim that, since his return in 2012, he has never been consulted about Australia by anyone in his company. He knows the country well—his company has large investments there, not all of them going so well today. He believes that his replacement is not doing well and that two or three of the Europeans assigned there should be reassigned. The trouble is that all are "being propped up," he says, by someone in the European headquarters.

But the real problem, as this case illustrates, is what to do with these people when they eventually return to Europe.

Optimizing individual employee and organizational needs has long been a management problem. Developing and maintaining relevant competencies within a work setting has been equally challenging.

The executive's many years of successful service in Australia show that he has learned from his experience. The pity is that his organization has not benefited from the experience, as the barriers for organizational learning appear to be too high. His learning is not being integrated in the organization or being passed on. It would appear in such cases that each person fails or succeeds by a trial-and-error method.

Recently, a group of 20 expatriates were asked if they had been "debriefed" after their experience overseas. All answered no. What a loss!

CROSS-BORDER GLOBAL TRAVEL

Today, global travel for short or long periods is common. Such travel may be for pleasure, professional development, education, business, or military service. Humans have the capacity to move their bodies and/or their brains. The latter is evident in unmanned, automated space missions to the far corners of the universe. Electronic travel may range from telephone, radio, and television, to computer exchanges via the internet in the form of email, websites, chat rooms, podcasts, blogs, and wikis. In all cases, cross-cultural sensitivity and skills can facilitate global communications.

In today's global village, the number of people living in another country for lengthy periods is increasing. Virtually everyone comes into contact with individuals who speak a different language or who were reared in another culture. In this twenty-first century, cultural homogeneity and isolation exist in very few places—heterogeneity, or diversity, is the reality everywhere. Within our shrinking world, everyone, from executives to entertainers, soldiers to humanitarian volunteers, needs skills in managing both cultural differences and synergy.[15] Furthermore, we are transitioning into an emerging *knowledge culture* that offers new applications for such competencies. Richard Lewis suggests that it is a risk-taking, electronic culture that: (1) encourages entrepreneurialism, Western-style individualism, and rapid decision cycles; (2) responds quickly and flexibly to end-user needs; (3) allows for greater customization of brands and services; and (4) communicates interactively for "communities of families and friends."[16]

Embarking on a "hero's journey" is the way the late anthropologist Joseph Campbell describes the challenge of living outside one's culture, while Osland reports on adventures abroad as "hero's tales."[17]

Furthermore, we have not even to risk the adventure alone, for the heroes of all time have gone before us. The labyrinth is thoroughly known. We have only to follow the thread of the hero path, and where we have thought to find an abomination, we shall find a god. And where we have thought to slay another, we shall slay ourselves. Where we had thought to travel outward, we will come to the center of our own existence. And where we had thought to be alone, we will be one with the world.

COPING WITH TRANSITIONAL CHALLENGES

Early researchers in cross-cultural studies were concerned primarily with what happened when a person transitioned from their home culture to a host culture. Today, interdependence between nations has facilitated the cross-border flow of people, ideas, and information. But we have a broader view of *transition trauma* associated with life's turning points, be they relocation or other personal and professional challenges. The trauma may simply be triggered by multiple career assignments or opportunities, whether experienced domestically or internationally. In addition to the ordinary lifestyle transitions that everyone faces, contemporaries must cope with rapid alterations in their work, environments, and cultures.

Increasingly, we interact with people who are very different from us, or in situations that are unfamiliar. Even when we share a common nationality, we may have to deal with citizens who are indeed "foreign" to us in their thinking, attitudes, vocabulary, and background. Individuals may face challenges within their environment due to their upbringing or local cultural conditioning. These challenges present opportunities either for growth or disruption. Such turning points in life may range from married couples who divorce; to families who move from one geographic area to another, whether at home or abroad; to those who have major alterations in careers, jobs, or roles; to personally confronting issues of serious illness or even death. To get a sense of transitional experiences that can cause culture shock, consider the scenarios shown in Exhibit 10.2.

All of the incidents in Exhibit 10.2 are *real, transitional experiences*. Each is an example of a life challenge that can be perceived as either devastating or a new chance. Having in-depth, intercultural encounters can be stimulating or psychologically disturbing, depending on your preparation and approach to them. Acculturation, or the process of adjustment to new experiences or living environment, takes time, possibly months and even years, while one learns new skills for responding and adapting to the unfamiliar. The extent of the trauma depends on the situation, such as whether one lives abroad among the native population or in a protected compound, be it a military, diplomatic, corporate, or religious enclave. The experience of coping with global diversity can be renewing or debilitating. When we are strangers in a place where the traditions and customs are foreign and unexpected, we may lose our balance and become unsure of ourselves. The same thing can happen within our own society when change happens so rapidly that the old traditions, the cues we live by, are suddenly undermined and irrelevant, threatening our sense of self.

EXHIBIT 10.2 UN STUDY CITES VALUE OF GLOBAL MIGRATION

A recent UN study reported a surge in global migration at the turn of this century that is keeping populations from declining in Europe, as well as stimulating economic growth in North America by increased foreign income and workers.

Majority to minority culture

Your company transfers you and your family to a section of your country where you feel like an alien. From the Northeast, you come to this Sunbelt state that is so different and unique. Your boss suggests you enroll at the local university to take a course entitled "Living Texas" to introduce you to the myths and mannerisms of Texans.

Transitions in the global marketplace

You are a North American marketing consultant for a global high-technology company. Because of your expertise, you are much in demand, traveling beyond your home culture on short assignments. Your professional activities take you to a variety of host cultures. Typically, you are there for one to two weeks, consulting with local executives, many of whom are quite different in their approach to you as a woman. Most of your clients are men from cultures as diverse as Indonesia, Malaysia, Mexico, India, Hungary, and Russia.

Technology transfer

You are an engineer from a highly industrialized nation. Your overseas assignments are mainly to less-developed countries. You realize that the indigenous population is not ready for sophisticated technologies. To help them in their transition to modern economies, rather than sell them expensive equipment that they cannot afford or maintain, you prefer to design appropriate machines that pump water, cook food, and meet their real and practical needs.

Adjusting to new immigrants

You live in east San Diego near a local Somali community and have been a leader, helping new arrivals to acculturate. You have been notified that some 10,000 more Somali Bantu refugees are being relocated to the US with your government's assistance. Two hundred of these tribal people, descendants of slaves, are coming to "America's Finest City."

Deployment for war and peacekeeping

As a US Marine sergeant, you are a veteran of the Iraq War. You were one of those marines who went off to fight in the last decade and returned forever changed by your brief, intense experience with death and privation. You came back a driven and changed man, worrying if your marriage would also become a casualty.

Immigration or movement from one area to another has been part of the human story for thousands of years. Eugene Tartakovsky's book entitled *Immigration and Policies, Challenges and Impact* gives viewpoints on key issues of immigration and studies using a variety of methodologies on many topics, such as the psychological theories of pre-migration moti-vating immigration policies of selected countries toward immigrants and the challenging adjustment issues of immigrants. It is hard to even imagine the difficulties of many who crossed the Mediterranean or crossed the narrower waters from Turkey to Greece in search of being safe in a different land for themselves and their families. Helping immigrant and refugee individuals and families stay or regain mental, physical, and emotional health as they face the challenges of integration is an important responsibility for all immigrant-receiving countries.

Source: Tartakovsky, E. (ed.). *Immigration and Policies, Challenges and Impact.* Hauppauge: Novo Science Publishers, 2013.

Transitional experiences offer two alternatives—to cope or to "cop out." One can learn to comprehend, survive in, and grow through immersion in a different culture. The positive result can be increased self-development. Whenever we leave home for the unfamiliar, it involves basic changes in habits, relationships, and sources of satisfaction. Inherent in cultural change is the opportunity to leave behind, perhaps temporarily, one set of relation-ships and living patterns and to enrich one's life by experimenting with new ones. Implicit in the personal conflict and discontinuity produced by such experiences is the possible tran-scendence from environment or family support to self-support. Intercultural situations of psychological, social, or cultural stress also stimulate us to review and redefine our lives—to see our own country and people in a new perspective. Or, we may reject the changes or new culture and lose a possible growth opportunity.[18]

FOSTERING ACCULTURATION STRATEGIES

After the initial phases of culture shock pass, with hope, acculturation begins. Anyone who has gone from home to live, work, or study in a foreign country must learn about and adapt to another quite distinct cultural environment. As early as the 1930s, *acculturation* was being formally researched by scholars. The definition developed then is just as valid today—when groups of individuals having different cultures come into continuous first-hand contact with subsequent changes in the original cultural patterns of either or both groups.[19]

Most obviously, one must assimilate to fulfill practical needs for survival and accommodation in strange situations, like finding grocery stores, doctors, schools, banks, etc. Integration into a different society produces more personal changes, as one moves beyond the familiar patterns and institutions of the old, while attempting to absorb and understand the new. Value systems and attitudes also undergo alteration in this process. Furthermore, there may be biological changes as one adjusts to a different climate, bacteria and viruses, or unknown food and plant life. Also, social changes occur as the visitor seeks to find and form new relationships and friendships. All of these happenings may result in stress or tension.

Sociologists point out that stable, healthy family relationships can make the difference between success and failure in the foreign assignment. Families who interact in mutually supportive ways can be their own resource for acculturation into another environment. As ambassadors of your native culture, do endeavor to establish wholesome intercultural relations with the local people. Such behavior not only contributes to creating a favorable image of your own country, but facilitates your adjustment as well. Extending culture shock can be a hindrance to forming friendships and effective business relations abroad. Travelers abroad have to reach out and create a friendly, positive impression, lest we be perceived as arrogant and imperious.

The following ten recommendations will help to deflate the stress and tension overseas, while advancing successful acculturation:

- *Be culturally prepared*. Forewarned is forearmed. Individual or group study and training are necessary to understand cultural factors and cultural specifics. Public libraries and the internet provide a variety of resource material. Also, the public health service will advise about required inoculations, dietary choices, and other sanitary data. Before departure, the person scheduled for overseas service can experiment with the food in restaurants representative of the second culture. Furthermore, one might establish contact in his or her homeland with foreign émigrés, students, or visitors from the area to which he or she is going. A helpful approach is to seek out your own *cultural mentor*—a wise friend or counselor who has lived in the host country, or who is there upon arrival. The expatriate's mentor is capable of guidance, encouragement, and help in mastering the intricacies of a new culture. Sometimes your organizational sponsor abroad may link you to such a resource or even provide a *cultural coach*.

- *Learn local communication complexities*. Study the language of the place to which one is assigned. At least, learn some of the basics that will help in exchanging greetings and shopping. In addition, advance your communication skills in the host culture, as recommended in Chapter 2. Published guides can be helpful in learning expected courtesies and customs.

■ *Interact with the host nationals.* Meeting with people from the country you are going to is helpful. There are many such foreign nationals within your own organization or local community who may provide introductions to relatives and friends abroad, as well as useful information regarding their native culture and its unique customs. If one lives overseas within a corporate or military colony, avoid the "compound mentality." Be immersed in the host culture. Whenever feasible, join in the artistic and community functions, the carnivals and rites, the international fraternal or professional associations. Offer to teach students or businesspeople one's language in exchange for knowledge of their language; share skills from skiing to tennis, from the performing to the intellectual arts—all means for making friends worldwide.

■ *Be creative and experimental.* Innovating abroad may mean taking risks to get around barriers of bureaucracy and communication to lessen social distance. This principle extends from experimenting with the local food to keeping a diary as an escape to record one's adventures and frustrations. Tours, hobbies, and a variety of cultural pursuits can produce positive results. One needs to be existential and open to the daily opportunities that will be presented. Consider preparing a newsletter for the "folks back home" in which you share your cross-cultural adventures and insights, either by regular or electronic mail.

■ *Be culturally sensitive.* Be aware of the special customs and traditions that, if followed by a visitor, will make one more acceptable. Recognize that in some cultures, such as in Asia and the Middle East, saving face and not giving offense is considered quite important. Certainly, avoid stereotyping the natives and criticizing their local practices and procedures, while using the standard of one's own country for comparison. Americans are dynamic and pragmatic, generally liking to organize things "better," so it may be a challenge for them to relax and adjust to a different rhythm of the place and people they are visiting.

■ *Recognize complexities in host cultures.* Counteract the tendency to make quick, simplistic assessments of situations. Most complex societies comprise different ethnic or religious groups, stratified into social classes or castes, differentiated by regions or geographical factors, separated into rural and urban settlements. Each of these may have distinct subcultural characteristics over which is superimposed an official language, national institutions, and peculiar customs or history that tie a people together. Avoid pat generalizations and quick assumptions. Instead, be tentative when drawing conclusions, realizing one's point of contact is a limited sample within a multifaceted society.

■ *Understand oneself as a culture bearer.* When going abroad, each person takes his or her own culture, conditioning, and distortions. Thus, one views everything in the host culture through the unique filter of his or her own cultural background. For example, if one is raised in democratic traditions, it may be unsettling to live in a society that values the authority of the head male in the family and extends this reverence to national leaders. But with locals, quiet conversations and behavior may persuade others to appreciate your cultural perspectives.

- *Be patient, understanding, and accepting of self and hosts.* In an unfamiliar environment, one must be more tolerant and flexible. An attitude of healthy curiosity, a willingness to bear inconveniences, and patience when answers or solutions are not forthcoming or difficult to obtain are valuable ways to maintain mental balance. Such patience may also extend to other compatriots who struggle with cultural adjustment.

- *Be realistic in expectations.* Avoid overestimating oneself, your hosts, or the cross-cultural experience. Disappointments can be lessened if one scales down expectations. This applies to everything from airline schedules to renting rooms. Global managers, especially, must be careful in new cultures not to set unreasonable work expectations for themselves or others until both are acclimatized.

- *Accept the challenge of intercultural experiences.* Anticipate, savor, and confront the psychological challenge of adapting and changing as a result of a new cross-cultural opportunity. Be prepared to alter one's habits, attitudes, values, tastes, relationships, or sources of satisfaction. Such flexibility can become a means for personal growth, and the transnational experience can be more fulfilling. Of course, a deep interest and commitment to your work—professionalism—can be marvelous therapy in intercultural situations, countering isolation and strangeness when living outside your home culture.

Deployment systems

When an organization is sending people out of the country as its representatives, it has an obligation to ensure that such persons are adequately selected, prepared, and supported, as well as assisted when they return to the homeland. The sponsors need to have a *system* for relocating their personnel or members. Behavioral scientists have been investigating the whole phenomenon of people exchanges, especially for those who live and work in isolated and confined environments (ICE).[20] The latter experience may range from offshore oil rigs and polar research stations to undersea submarines, orbiting space stations, or a lunar base. The following describes the four major components in a relocation or deployment system, whether terrestrial or in space. The extent to which these guidelines are followed depends on the length of the assignment.

The *Sage Handbook of Intercultural Competence*[21] has many chapters that are especially relevant for anyone who wishes to explore this topic in more detail (especially chapters 1, 3, 6, 14, 28, and 29).

STAGE 1: PERSONNEL AND PROGRAM ASSESSMENT

The first major component in a relocation or foreign deployment system involves assessing individual candidates for service abroad or in ICE, and later evaluating their on-site performance. In addition, the sponsor should periodically and objectively evaluate its relocation services and training, including transfer and reentry process.

■ *Predeparture assessment*—from the perspective of the sponsoring organization's responsibilities, a complete foreign deployment evaluation system needs to do the following:

  – Ascertain the adaptability of key personnel for foreign service, including their ability to deal with the host nationals effectively.

  – Develop a psychological profile for the candidate—summarize a psychological evaluation of the candidate's skills in human relations within an intercultural context, as well as determine the candidate's ability to cope with changes and differences, and the candidate's susceptibility to severe culture shock.

  – Identify specific physical and intellectual barriers to successful adjustment in the foreign environment, if possible, to correct any deficiencies before departure.

  – Highlight any specific technical or management factors that need strengthening before the cross-cultural assignment.

  – Seek out any personal or family problems that would undermine employee effectiveness abroad.

  – Develop a performance review plan for the individual when abroad, as well as assessment of the support services to be rendered.

  – Adapt the above evaluation process to foreign nationals brought on assignment into domestic operations.

  – Involve expatriate employees who have returned from foreign sites or host country nationals in predeparture training of émigrés.

  – Provide instruments for data gathering about the candidates' attitudes and competencies regarding change, intercultural knowledge and relations, and communication skills. These may involve commercial or homemade questionnaires, inventories, checklists, and culture shock tests.

  – Use assessment and training simulations, case studies, and critical incidents that approximate life abroad.

  – Employ a reality check on individual expectations regarding the foreign post, as to living conditions, job requirements, opportunities, and incongruities.

■ *On-site assessment*—when the individual is sent overseas, the continuing performance review might further investigate the following:

  – The actual tasks or activities the expatriate engages in, and the person's ability to accomplish them.

  – The people with whom the individual interacts—his/her ability to deal with the indigenous or local population.

  – The extent to which the official posting requires social interactions with host and third-country nationals, as well as expatriates from other organizations—capacity of the sojourner to deal with such a variety of human relationships.

  – The work duties required, whether by an individual or team collaboration, especially with persons outside the company.

  – The language skills required (English or a foreign language), and the capacity of that employee to meet them.

- The individual's outlook abroad, whether provincial or cosmopolitan. Has that person demonstrated interest in the local culture and its manifestations? Has the organization's representative made satisfactory progress in the foreign culture?
- The expatriate's self-reporting—his/her sense of how the international experience is affecting personal and family life, including impact of absence from the homeland while on foreign assignment (i.e., influence on personal life and that of dependents, as well as on career development and life plans).
- The overall rating of the individual's performance and adjustment in the foreign assignment and its society.

■ *Continuing system improvements*—findings and insights obtained from both the predeparture and on-site assessment programs should be viewed as feedback to further improve the relocation system for the next group of candidates. For example, a survey of employees on foreign assignment or of expatriates who have returned may reveal special needs and problems that the organization's foreign deployment system is, or is not, addressing satisfactorily.

The selection systems of organizations vary, but some use the following techniques:

- Within the HRD division or department, establish an assessment center that has the responsibility for recruitment and selection of overseas personnel.
- Outsource for services by contracting an external relocation resource, such as intercultural consultants and/or an international executive/management/technical search firm.
- Set up a selection review board made up of an organization's own employees or members, qualified volunteers who have served abroad, especially in the target culture; include company specialists in corporate health and personnel services.
- Limit selection for overseas assignments to expatriates who have previously demonstrated their effectiveness abroad, whether within the organization or hired from outside.

■ *Selection criteria*—overall, seek candidates for overseas service who are capable of empathy, openness, persistence, sensitivity to intercultural factors, respect for others, role flexibility, tolerance for ambiguity, and who possess two-way communication skills. Research indicates that possession of these characteristics is correlated to adaptation and effectiveness outside an individual's home culture.

STAGE 2: PERSONNEL ORIENTATION AND TRAINING

The second component in a foreign deployment system is some type of self- or group-learning experience or training about culture generally, as well as specifics about the target area's culture. This can be accomplished electronically or in live sessions with PowerPoint briefings. The general content can include learning modules on cross-cultural communications and change, understanding culture and its influence on behavior, culture shock and cross-cultural relations, improving organizational relations, and intercultural effectiveness. To increase cultural awareness and skills, several alternative methods are available.

An increasingly popular means of cross-cultural learning is electronic, especially by means of computers and television. To supplement or replace formal group instruction, individualized learning packages can be provided for the employee and his/her family. Such programmed learning and media systems can educate on cultural differences in general, as well as on the specific country to be visited. This type of learning can occur in a company learning center or at home with one's family. It might also serve as preparation for classroom instruction.

Culture-specific briefing programs can be developed for a particular geographical region or country, such as those provided in Chapters 12–18. For example, the Middle East could be a subject of study, with particular emphasis on Egypt, Saudi Arabia, and Turkey, or even Israel/Palestine, Iraq, and Iran. A learning program of 12 or more hours can be designed with a self-instruction manual for individual study, or the materials used for group training. Obviously, no relocation orientation is complete without adequate language and technical training. However, the focus here is on cultural training and preparation.

Current thinking on this second stage of foreign deployment leads us to these recommendations for dividing the preparation for service abroad into four phases. In other words, the predeparture program would involve the following components. The time and scope of each activity would again depend on whether it was a long- or short-term assignment out of country.

Phase 1: general culture/area orientation

1   Become aware of the factors that make a culture unique and the characteristics of the home culture that most influence employee behavior abroad.
2   Seek local cross-cultural experience, and engage in intercultural communication with minority cultures within the homeland so as to sensitize oneself to cultural differences.
3   Foster more global attitudes and tolerance within the candidate family, while counteracting prejudice and ethnocentrism. For example, cook national dishes of other countries, attend cultural weeks or exhibits of foreign or ethnic groups, or invite a foreigner to your home.

Phase 2: language orientation

1   Undertake formal training in the language of the host country.
2   Supplement classroom experience with self-learning in the language, by listening to the foreign tongue via audio/video media or radio; by watching television and films or using the internet; by reading newspapers, magazines, or books in the new language; by speaking to others who have this language proficiency.

3   Build a 500-word survival vocabulary in the target language.

4   Develop specialized vocabularies for the job, marketplace, etc.

5   Practice the language at every opportunity, especially with family members.

6   Seek further education in the language upon arrival in the host country.

Phase 3: culture-specific orientation

1   Learn and gather data about cultural specifics of the host country.

2   Understand and prepare to counteract "culture shock."

3   Check out specific company policies about the assigned country. These policies are related to allowances for transportation, housing, education, expense accounts, and provisions for salaries, taxes, and other fringe benefits, including medical service and emergency leave.

4   Obtain necessary transfer documents (passports, visas, etc.), and learn customs, policies, and regulations, as well as currency restrictions, for entry and exit to the host country.

5   Interview, in person or electronically, fellow employees who have returned from the host country. Get practical information about banking, shopping, currency, climate, mail, and law enforcement.

6   Read travel books and other information about the country and culture.

Phase 4: job environment/organization orientation

1   Obtain information about the overseas job environment and organization.

2   Be aware of the government's customs, restrictions, and attitudes regarding business, and your local corporation or project.

3   Arrange for necessary technical training to assure high performance abroad; seek a local mentor or coach.

Relocation strategies should encompass the staff engaged in recruiting, selecting, and training; the employee and dependents assigned abroad; as well as the host culture managers who are responsible for expatriate personnel in the new environment. The focus should be on the opportunities afforded by the international assignment for personal growth, professional exchange and development, and the effective representation of country and corporation.

STAGE 3: SUPPORT SERVICE: ON-SITE SUPPORT AND MONITORING

Once employees have been recruited, selected, trained, and transported abroad, the organizational responsibility to personnel should be to:

1   facilitate their integration into a different work environment and host culture;

2   evaluate their needs and performance abroad; and

3   encourage morale and career development, especially through homeland communications.

As a follow-up to the predeparture training and after the employee or family arrives in the host country, some type of on-site orientation and briefing should be arranged. Back home, there might have been a lack of readiness to listen to details about the job and new community. Now that the expatriates are faced with the daily realities of life abroad, they may have many questions. Periodically, the newcomers should be provided opportunities to come together socially and share as a group.

The in-country orientation should be pragmatic and meet the needs of the expatriate family. It should demonstrate that the organization cares about its people. It should aid the employee and his or her family to resolve immediate living problems; to meet the challenge of the host culture and the opportunities it offers for travel, personal growth, and intercultural exchange; to reduce the culture shock and to grow from that experience; and to provide communication links to the local community and the home organization. Much of this can be accomplished in a systematic, informal, friendly group setting, or even electronically.

STAGE 4: REACCULTURATION–REENTRY PROGRAM

The last component in the foreign deployment system involves reintegrating the expatriate into the home society and domestic organization. The person or family who has been abroad for some time will discover when they return that the homeland and the organizational cultures will have changed. The reentry process begins overseas with the psychological withdrawal the expatriate faces with returning home. Upon return, reentry shock may occur for six months or more, as the person struggles to readjust to the lifestyle and tempo of the changed home and organizational cultures. In addition to the challenge of reestablishing home and family life is the issue of reassignment in the parent company or agency.

For many expatriates, the last stage of the culture shock process is a time of crises and trauma. Such personnel may experience mild or severe *reentry shock*. The experience abroad for those who are sensitive and who become involved in the host culture is profound. It causes many people to reexamine their lives, values, attitudes, to assess how they became what they are. It is a turning point, prompting lifestyle changes when they get back. The reentry process becomes the opportunity to carry out these aspirations. Individuals may not be satisfied to return to old neighborhoods, old friends, or the same job or company affiliation. Many wish to apply their new self-insights and to seek new ways of personal growth. The organization that sent them abroad in the first place should be empathetic to this reality and be prepared to deal with it, including by providing severance benefit packages or even outplacement services. The relocation system is incomplete unless it helps returning employees to fit comfortably into their home culture and organization. Closing the deployment loop may involve group coun-seling with personnel specialists, psychologists, and former expatriates. Always consider expatriates coming back from an overseas assignment as a valuable resource. The corpora-tion can learn much from their cross-cultural experience.

An example of the reentry complexity is described by Chang,[22] demonstrating how the interaction between mothers and their children changed when the student returned. The research demonstrated that the mothers' confusion about their children's cultural identity resulted in confusion about their motherhood identity. One of the coauthors of this book remembers overhearing his mother on the telephone with one of her friends after he returned from working overseas for five years: "I don't know what happened to Bob when he was in China." However, I wasn't in China; I was in Japan.

BUSINESS ETIQUETTE AND PROTOCOL ABROAD

Cooperation in world trade and commerce is considered by many to be humanity's best chance to maintain global peace and prosperity. Training in managing change, interpersonal skills, cultural difference, and creating synergy can improve not only human relations, but the "bottom line."

Webster's Dictionary defines protocol as *a code prescribing adherence to correct etiquette and procedures*. While modern management, the internet, and mass communica-tions are forming new protocols for the global marketplace, we still cannot ignore the local expectations for business and professional activities. Nelson[23] advises these basic proto-cols be observed:

1   Remember and pronounce people's names correctly.
2   Use appropriate rank and titles when required.
3   Know the local variables of time and punctuality.
4   Create the right impression with suitable dress.
5   Practice behavior that demonstrates concern for others, tact and discretion, and knowledge of what constitutes good manners and ethics locally.
6   Communicate with intercultural sensitivity, verbally and nonverbally, whether in person, electronically, or in writing or printing.
7   Give and receive gifts and favors appropriate to local traditions.
8   Enjoy social events while being conscious of local customs relative to food and drink, such as prohibitions, the use of utensils, dining out and entertaining, and seating arrangements.

According to Lewis,[24] a *psychological contract* is forged between the individual and the institution that employs that person. This represents unwritten, unexpressed needs and expectations on the part of both parties. For an employee or member, it is a highly subjective perspective, and is the glue that binds that person to the organization. In the disappearing industrial work culture, the psychological contract focused on job security in return for loyalty and hard work. Currently, the emphasis is for employees to give their organizational support in return for compensation, plus opportunities to learn and acquire new skills. Employability, rather than stability, is the centerpiece of the contract. And the contract varies somewhat when personnel are posted outside their homelands.

For expatriate workers, the employer has more influence in terms of provisions for housing, education, welfare, recreation, and social events. Because of this, perceived contractual violations may provoke intense reactions from employees overseas. This dissatisfaction may be expressed in a variety of ways from negative communications and damage to company reputation, to misconduct, hostility, and even sabotage. Continued exposure abroad to a stressful environment may cause alterations in sleeping patterns, high anxiety, neurotic defense mechanisms, and other manifestations of culture shock.

ASSESSMENT INSTRUMENTS[25]

Most global leaders have received feedback from completing a variety of questionnaires and instruments designed to measure skills and attitudes, such as linguistic ability, which is easy to access, and global mindset attitudes,[26] which are very difficult to measure.

Over the years, we have found the following instruments to be valuable from the list of Fantini in *The Sage Handbook of Intercultural Competence*.[27]

- Assessment of Intercultural Competence (AIC)
  Measures: Intercultural competence, including language proficiency.
  Description: This questionnaire, designed in a YOGA format ("Your Objectives, Guidelines, and Assessment") is used for self-assessment and assessment by peers and teachers. The tool monitors the development of the intercultural competence of sojourners (and hosts) over time, providing valid and reliable indicators.
- Cross-Cultural Adaptability Inventory (CCAI)
  Measures: Individual potential for cross-cultural adaptability.
  Description: A culture-general instrument designed to assess individual potential for cross-cultural adaptability.
- Cross-Cultural Assessor (CCA)
  Measures: Individual understanding of self and others.
  Description: This tool is designed to improve people's understanding of themselves and others, as well as to promote positive attitudes toward cultural difference.
- Cultural Orientations Indicator® (COI®)
  Measures: Cultural preferences.

> *Description*: A web-based cross-cultural assessment tool that allows individuals to assess their personal cultural preferences and compare them with generalized profiles of other cultures.

- Global Literacy Survey

    Measures: World knowledge.

    Description: A self-test used to measure the degree of knowledge young Americans have about the world.

- Global Team Process Questionnaire™ (GTPQ)

    Measures: Effectiveness of global teams.

    Description: A proprietary instrument designed to help global teams improve their effectiveness and productivity.

- GlobeSmart

    Measures: Effectiveness of global teams.

    Description: A web-based tool that investigates how to conduct business effectively in 35 countries.

ACADEMIC STUDIES ON "ACCULTURATION"

For anyone interested in issues of acculturation and what the research tells us, we recommend the following studies, all published in *The International Journal of Intercultural Relations*:[28]

- "Perceptions of Social Strategies in Intercultural Relations: The Case of Ethiopian Immigrants in Israel," Anat Korem and Gabriel Horenczyk.
- "Perceived Organizational Support: A Meaningful Contribution to Expatriate Development Professionals' Well-Being," Nicola F. de Paul and Lynette H. Bikos.
- "Cultural Distance and Emotional Problems Among Immigrant and Refugee Youth in Canada: Findings from the New Canadian Child and Youth Study," Morton Beiser, Sofia Puente-Duran, and Feng Hou.
- "Acculturation and Overseas Assignments: A Review and Research Agenda," Miguel Gonzalez-Loureiro, Timothy Kiessling, and Marina Dabic.
- "Pioneers Across War Zones: The Lived Acculturation Expressions of U. S. Female Military Expatriates," Kelly Fisher, Kate Hutchings, and Luisa Helena Pinto.

CONCLUSIONS

Life is filled with changes and challenges, some of which can be turned into opportunities for personal and professional growth.[29] Some happen by going abroad into another culture, or even in making the passage from an industrial to a knowledge work environment. The trauma experienced in this adjustment process can take many forms, whether it is called culture or reentry shock, role or organization shock, or even future shock. Essentially, cross-cultural transitions threaten our sense of identity. Such transitions force us to rethink and reevaluate the way we read meaning into our private worlds. They are opportunities to learn and develop, causing a transformation in our behavior and lifestyle, as well as in our management or leadership.

Organizations can reduce such shocks to their personnel by coaching, counseling, and training. The stress and anxiety that may result need not lead to severe disorientation, depression, and unhealthy behavior. These can be countered by increasing awareness and information that provides more enjoyable intercultural experiences.

When considered in the context of sending employees overseas on assignment, the return on organizational investment in cross-cultural preparation and continuing support services can be considerable. We recommend that sponsoring multinational corporations or agencies institute a foreign deployment *system*. This approach to relocation activities will not only reduce premature return costs and much unhappiness among expatriates and overseas customers, but it can improve performance, productivity, and profitability in the world market. Furthermore, observing and practicing both national and international protocol facilitates human performance and cooperation, especially in development projects. Such counsel becomes even more meaningful in the context of technology transfer, whether within a nation or across borders.

MIND STRETCHING

1   Explain the concept of the transitional experience and its many manifestations. Apply these insights to the university graduate going into the world of work, or civilian and military personnel assigned overseas.

2   Why are so many workers leaving their culture of origin to work abroad, despite the many difficulties encountered? What are the responsibilities of communities and organizations in facilitating the acculturation of foreign newcomers?

3   Why does a relocation assignment pose a challenge to one's sense of identity?

4   What are culture and reentry shock? How can these phenomena be avoided or limited?

5   What is your understanding of being "global"?

6   Why should world-class corporations have a foreign deployment system? Overall, what does such a system entail?

NOTES

1   Viet Thang Nguyen, *The Sympathizer*. New York: Grove Press, 2015, p. 216.
2   Shoper, J. April 18, 2006, email to Robert Moran. Used with permission.

3 Green, K. March 28, 2013, email to Robert Moran. Used with permission.

4 Terhell, P. McCauley, February 1, 2013, email to Robert Moran. Used with permission.

5 Sichel, E. F. and Sichel, N. (eds.). *Uprooted Childhoods: Memories of Growing Up Global*. Boston, MA: Nicholas Brealey/Intercultural Press, 2001, 2004.

6 *Hemispheres Magazine*, April 2013.

7 Fearn, N. *Philosophy: The Latest Answers to the Oldest Questions*. New York: Atlanta Books, 2005.

8 Lewis, T. and Jungman, R. (eds.). *On Being Foreign: Culture Shock in Short Fiction*. Yarmouth: Intercultural Press, 1986. Kols, L. R. *Survival Kit for Intercultural Living*. Palo Alto, CA: Nicholas Brealey, 2011. Storti, C. *The Art of Coming Home*. Boston, MA: Nicholas Brealey/Intercultural Press, 1986, 2001.

9 Furnham, A. and Bochner, S. *Culture Shock: Psychological Reactions to an Unfamiliar Environment*. New York: Methuen, 1986.

10 Oberg, K. *Culture Shock and the Problem of Adjustment to New Cultural Environments*. Washington, DC: Foreign Service Institute, 1958. Storti, *The Art of Crossing Cultures*; Sichel and Sichel, *Uprooted Childhoods*.

11 Klopf, D. W. *Intercultural Encounters*, 3rd edn. Englewood, CO: Morton Publishing Company, 1995. Also refer to Gundling, E. *Working Global Smart: 12 People Skills for Doing Business Across Borders*. Palo Alto, CA: Nicholas Brealey, 2010; Ember, C. R. (ed.). *Cultures of the World*. New York: Macmillan, 1999.

12 Osland, J. S. "The Hero's Adventure: The Overseas Experience of Expatriate Business People," unpublished doctoral dissertation, Case Western University, 1990. Available through University Microfilms International, 300 N. Zeeb Road, Ann Arbor, MI 48106. Also refer to Dr. Eileen Sheridan-Wibbeke's more recent doctoral dissertation on this subject in 2005 at the University of Phoenix Online.

13 Excerpt read by the author during 2016 on an airplane.

14 Szkudlarek, B. "Reentry: A Review of the Literature," *International Journal of Intercultural Relations*, Vol. 34, 2010, pp. 1–21.

15 Peterson, B. *Cultural Intelligence: A Guide to Working with People from Other Cultures*. Palo Alto, CA: Nicholas Brealey, 2004. Storti, C. *Figuring Foreigners Out*. Boston, MA: Nicholas Brealey/Intercultural Press, 1999.

16 Lewis, R. D. *The Cultural Imperative: Global Trends in the 21st Century*. Boston, MA: Nicholas Brealey, 2002, p. 228. See also Lewis, R. D. *When Cultures Collide: Managing Successfully Across Cultures*. Boston, MA: Nicholas Brealey, 2000.

17 Campbell, J. *Hero with a Thousand Faces*. Princeton, NJ: Princeton University Press, 1968. Osland, J. S. *The Adventure of Working Abroad: Hero Tales from the Global Frontier*. San Francisco, CA: Jossey-Bass, 1995. Hofstede, G. J., Peterson, P. B., and Hofstede, G. *Exploring Culture: Exercises, Stories, and Synthetic Cultures*. Boston, MA: Nicholas Brealey/Intercultural Press, 2002.

18 Spencer, S. A. and Adams, J. D. *Life Changes: Growing Through Personal Transition*. San Luis Obispo, CA: Impact, 1990. Bridges, W. *Transitions: Make Sense of Life's Changes*. Cambridge, MA: Da Capo Press, 2004. Biracress, T. and Biracress, N. *Over Fifty: Resource Book for the Better Half of Your Life*. New York: HarperPerennial, 1991. Cort-VanArsdale, D. *Transitions: A Woman's Guide to Successful Retirement*. New York: HarperPerennial, 1992.

19 Berry, J. W. "Psychology of Acculturation," in R. W. Brislin (ed.), *Applied Cross-Cultural Psychology*. Newbury Park, CA: Sage, 1990. Laroche, L. *Managing Cultural Diversity in Technical Professions*. Burlington, MA: Elsevier/Butterworth-Heinemann, 2002.

20 Relative to *deployment systems*, refer to Haines, S. G. *The Manager's Pocket Guide to Systems Thinking and Learning*. Amherst, MA: HRD Press, 2004. Also contact the Society for Human Performance in Extreme Environments for information and publications (email: Society@HPPE.org or website www.hpee.org). Relative to a *space deployment system*, see Harrison, A. A. *Spacefaring: The Human Dimension*. Berkeley, CA: University of California Press, 2001. Harris, P. R. *Launch Out: A Science-Based Novel about Lunar Industrialization*. Haverford, PA: Infinity Publishing, 2003. Freeman,

M. *Challenges of Human Space Exploration*. London: Springer, 2000; Harris, P. R. *Living and Working in Space: Human Behavior, Culture, and Organization*. Chichester: Wiley, 1996.

21 Deardorff, D. K. (ed.). *The Sage Handbook of Intercultural Competence*. Newbury Park, CA: Sage, 2009.

22 Chang, Y. "A Qualitative Study of Temporary Reentry from Significant Others' Perspective," *International Journal of Intercultural Relations*, Vol. 33, 2009, pp. 259–263.

23 Nelson, C. A. *Protocol for Profit: A Manager's Guide to Competing Worldwide*. London: International Thomas Business Press, 1998. Olafsson, G. *When in Rome or Rio or Riyadh: Cultural Q&A's for Successful Business Behavior Around the World*. Palo Alto, CA: Nicholas Brealey, 2004; Mole, J. *Mind Your Manners: Managing Business Cultures in the New Global Europe*. Boston, MA: Nicholas Brealey/Intercultural Press, 2004.

24 Lewis, K. G. "Breakdown: A Psychological Contract for Expatriates," *European Business Review*, Vol. 97, No. 6, 1997, pp. 279–293. Also refer to Rampersad, H. K. *Total Performance Scorecard: Redefining Management to Achieve Performance with Integrity*. Burlington, MA: Elsevier/Butterworth-Heinemann, 2003.

25 Deardorff, *The Sage Handbook of Intercultural Competence*.

26 Javidan, M., Teagarden, M., and Bowen, D. "Making It Overseas: Developing the Skills You Need to Succeed as an International Leader," *Harvard Business Review*, April, 2010.

27 Deardorff, *The Sage Handbook of Intercultural Competence*.

28 *The International Journal of Intercultural Relations*, Vol. 49, 2015.

29 Sheehy, G. *New Passages, Mapping Your Life Across Time*. New York: Random House, 1995.

11 INTERNATIONAL STRATEGY IN A GLOBAL BUSINESS ENVIRONMENT

You've got to trust the process . . . Do you have a point of view about the future? Check. Is it still the right vision today? Check. Do you have a comprehensive plan to deliver that? Check. If you get skilled and motivated people working together through this process, you're going to figure it out. But you've got to trust it. The leader's job is to remind people of that vision, make sure they stick to the process, and keep them working together. Working together *always* works.

Alan Mulally[1]

Today the greatest failing of businesspeople, politicians, and diplomats is that their narrow view of others cannot discern the cultural differences of people. They see the world in only one or two dimensions.

Michihiro Matsumoto[2]

An army which can cause men to submit without fighting is the best; one that wins a hundred victories in a hundred battles is mediocre; and the one that uses deep moats and high fortifications for its own defense is the lowest . . . The ultimate goal of strategy is to restore the system to a relatively stable condition so that the fruits of victory can be enjoyed. On many occasions, focusing too much on winning battles and wars brings unintended and undesirable consequences that are beyond our strategic capacity to repair. This is the principal reason why Sun Tzu always insists on the need to win wars on the moral and mental levels, while attempting to avoid the physical level.

Derek M. C. Yuen[3]

The real voyage of discovery consists not in seeing new lands but seeing with new eyes.

Marcel Proust[4]

LEARNING OBJECTIVES

After reading and studying the concepts, examples, and illustrations in Chapter 11, readers should be able to understand and appreciate:

1. The traditional Western contingency discourse strategic planning process including *external* analysis (*industry analysis*, identification of *KSFs*, *competitive analysis*, strategic alternatives), *internal* analysis (internal capabilities *gaps* related to *leadership*, *organization* systems, *resources*), and *execution* of the plan.
2. Japanese strategic planning intended to identify and exploit weaknesses, targeting the counterpart individuals tasked with strategic planning and implementation, as opposed to general strategic plans at the larger company and industry level of analysis.
3. The Western sociocognitive discourse of strategic planning that alerts individuals, using Jungian personality theory, to their personal problem-solving habitual dispositions that may be targeted by Japanese and other counterparts intending to achieve competitive advantage against you.
4. Chinese strategic planning intended to achieve competitive advantage without apparent "warlike" competition through the exercise of soft power, and strategies intended to facilitate the defeat of strong opponents by their weaker opponents.

INTRODUCTION

Strategy is the concrete plan by which an MNE (multinational enterprise) intends to compete successfully in its marketplaces. Originally a military concept, Clausewitz[5] defined strategy as the plan for a campaign intended to achieve intended goals or objectives. In business, however, the strategy includes the objective analysis intended to identify an MNE's goals, and the plan for organizing the company's internal capabilities so they are consistent with and support the strategy. Moltke's[6] definition of strategy as "the practical adaptation of the means placed at a general's disposal to the attainment of the object in view" is a better definition for business. The goal of an intended strategy is to achieve a competitive advantage in an industry or market against an MNE's competitors that will be reflected in strong positive financial performance results. In a new and innovative market, strategies may expand market size and all competitors benefit from the growth. In mature industries where growth is limited, companies compete and expand by taking market share from their competitors.

According to Rouleau and Seguin,[7] Western strategic thinking is quite diverse, with four types of strategic discourse. Mintzberg et al.[8] observed ten schools of strategic management theory. In practice, however, the theoretical orientation most frequently taught in Western business schools is the contingency discourse[9] or positioning school[10] approach of strategic management's "holy father" Michael Porter.[11] Many have followed in Porter's footsteps, occasionally reaching beyond him to improve upon his tried-and-true conventional wisdom.[12]

In a nutshell, the Western conception of strategy, received from Porter, divides an MNE's "world" into external and internal portions. The external orientation includes the *external business environment* in which the company competes for market share and profitability. It also includes a corporate *vision* for how the company could more successfully compete, and a proposed *strategy* for doing so. The strategy results from an *industry analysis* of the bases of competitive advantage in the MNE's industry and/or the intended geographical marketplace, as well as a *competitive analysis* intended to identify the MNE's strengths and weaknesses versus its direct competitors. The strategy is developed to take advantages of opportunities and ameliorate threats on the *key success factors* (KSFs) most related to achieving advantage. An opportunity is a situation in which the MNE is stronger than its direct competitors on an important KSF. A threat is the reverse, where the MNE is weaker.

The internal orientation includes an analysis of the *internal capabilities* of the MNE, both as they exist and as they need to be enhanced in order to support the proposed strategy. It considers *leadership* capability and preference, *organization* systems, and human, operational, and financial *resources*. If the internal analysis demonstrates that one or more *gaps* exist in needed key capabilities but cannot be efficiently filled, then the strategy is not workable. When the internal capabilities are *consistent* with those required for the strategy, then an operational *plan* is developed to implement it. Efficient *execution* is understood to be the key to success. Inconsistency between internal capabilities and strategy will, however, doom the execution of any plan.

Porter's strategy paradigm may be considered a "direct" and "first strike,"–as opposed to "indirect" and "counter-strike"–model of strategic action. Strategic planners, usually conceptualized as the CEO and senior management team, or analysts responsible to them, scan the external competitive environment searching for opportunities to directly attack their companies' markets and financial results through the application of their corporate vision. Through building requisite KSFs and finding competitors without these competitive strengths, a target is found. A plan is developed through strategic planning to enhance performance outcomes at competitors' expense. The model assumes that the stronger and better-prepared company will overcome the weaker and unprepared opponent. Strategy implementation is like a "war." The CEO and his/her team "builds up and maintains his[/her] strength and weakens that of his[/her] opponent, avoids battle at his[/her] disadvantage and maneuvers to achieve superiority at the focal points where [she/]he chooses to give battle."[13]

There are, however, limitations regarding Porter's model. First, direct strategies have rarely been successful in military history. Liddell Hart charted the course of 30 wars, covering 280 campaigns, and in only six cases was a decisive result procured from "a plan of direct strategic approach."[14] In military affairs, indirect strategies have been far more successful because elastic defensive strategies are generally stronger[15] than offensive strategies when the defenders know the intent. The most effective indirect strategies lure or surprise the opponent into making a mistake by "dislocation of the opponent's mind and dispositions."[16]

Second, Rouleau and Seguin observe that the contingency discourse is too deterministic in its operational assumptions. It assumes that certain types of organizational or product/service changes will produce higher performance. The positive or negative effects of individual decision-makers or employees are, however, discounted because the *level of analysis* is generally the individual company, or its organizational units. Decision-makers are assumed to be rational entities all behaving in identical ways and assuming each has identical information. An individual decision-maker could not be lured or surprised, as Hart suggests, because at the company level of analysis, individuals are not part of the planning equation.

In the same way, competing companies in the external environment are deterministically following their own strategic plans without consideration of their likely responses to a direct strategic maneuver against them. So, competitors are, in theory, generally taken unawares. This latter observation points to a related criticism that contingency strategic planning produces a synchronic, rather than a diachronic, view of a competitive environment. The analysis produces a picture thought to be of the situation at a single point in time, like a snapshot. It must be repeated over and over if the effects of competitors' responses are to be observed, but it is generally only repeated at fixed intervals, or whenever company performance has weakened.

Third, contingency discourse assumes operational stability of the external environment including political, social, economic, and technological stability. The effect of the strategic plan can be reliably predicted because it is assumed that there are no other significant changes going on in the competitive environment at the same time. This would be a reasonable assumption under conditions of political and social stability generally found in OECD (Organization for Economic Cooperation and Development) countries like the US, Canada, EU countries, Japan, etc. It might not be true for high-uncertainty countries like Iran, Russia, and even China, where capricious changes in political and legal systems are quite possible or probable. Interestingly, in the recent US election, one major party candidate proposed abolishing NAFTA (the North American Free Trade Agreement), threatening major international business environmental uncertainty related to American markets.

Finally, and perhaps most importantly, contingency discourse appears to mistake itself as *the* universal theory for strategic planning, as opposed to a Western theory based on Western cultural assumptions not universally accepted in non-Western cultures. Nor does it usually understand itself as only one of four Western discourses that might be usefully combined to form a unified theory more competitive with competing strategic planning theories from, for example, Japan or China. Japanese strategic thinking is a case in point as to how an improved strategic planning theory may be created by combining Western contingency discourse with homegrown Japanese strategy. While Japanese business students learn their Porter, they also study Musashi's *Book of Five Rings*.[17] Musashi was a famous seventeenth-century warrior whose book teaches strategic and tactical principles. Musashi's *level of analysis* is the individual strategist, and Japanese strategists learn to aim their strategies at the weaknesses of those individuals who compose and execute their competitors' strategies. They follow the Sun Tzu[18] adage that the general who knows him/herself and his/her enemy will always be victorious, while knowing only oneself will result in victory only half the time.

Fortunately, the Western "sociocognitive" discourse[19] may be used to address this deficiency. It offers methods for determining the strengths and weaknesses of individuals, as opposed to competing companies, and through self-assessment you may guard yourself from your own weaknesses as well. This represents a useful addition to contingency discourse.

Chinese strategic thinking is also an interesting case in point because it may be based on strategic assumptions that are indirect and counter-striking (as opposed to direct and first-striking), and have no Western counterpart. Yuen[20] has argued that while Western theory operates at a purely strategic level in its intentions to win the competitive battles between companies, Chinese theory begins at a "grand" strategic level. Liddell Hart[21] describes "grand strategy" and its lack in Western theorizing in the following way:

> While the horizon of strategy is bounded by the war, grand strategy looks beyond the war to the subsequent peace. It should not only combine the various instruments, but so regulate their use as to avoid damage to the future state of peace—for its security and prosperity. The sorry state of peace, for both sides, that has followed most wars can be traced to the fact that, unlike strategy, the realm of grand strategy is for the most part *terra incognita*—still awaiting exploration, and understanding.

Yuen[22] observes that Chinese strategic thinking, exemplified in Sun Tzu and Lao Tzu,[23] is adept at achieving competitive advantage and improved performance outcomes without the competitive battle between rivals assumed by contingency theory, under conditions of peaceful coexistence. This is achieved through the application of "soft power" strategies,[24] developed in Chinese strategic manuals almost 2,500 years ago, as opposed to Nye's[25] Western introduction of the idea in 2012. In addition, Yuen observes that Lao Tzu's *Tao De Ching* is specifically geared to offer strategies by which weaker opponents may defeat stronger adversaries—the opposite expectation from Porter and contingency discourse.

THE STRATEGIC PLANNING PROCESS

The *Double Diamond* model of strategy provides a useful overview of all the elements involved in strategic planning and how they interact (see Exhibit 11.1).

On the left diamond of the Double Diamond model, we have *external analysis* functions. Global leadership has a *vision* for what the MNE intends to accomplish. The competitive industry *environment* that the MNE competes in must be analyzed in order to determine the sources of competitive advantage, or KSFs. A *strategy* will be proposed based on the MNE's strengths and weaknesses on the KSFs in relation to its direct competitors. Where

EXHIBIT 11.1 DOUBLE DIAMOND STRATEGY MODEL

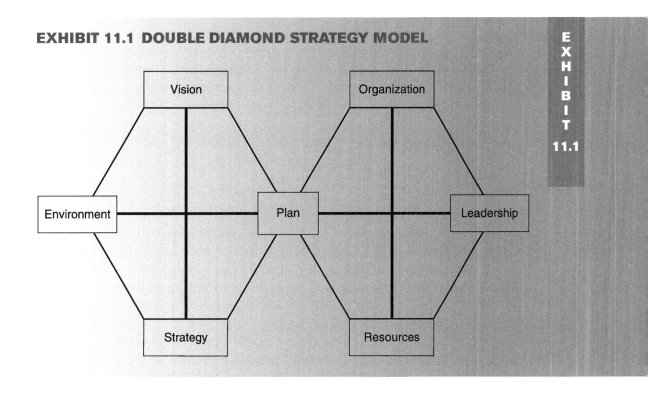

the MNE is stronger on a KSF, there is a potential opportunity. Where the MNE is weaker, there is a competitive threat that must be ameliorated.

On the right diamond, we have *internal analysis* functions. A strategy has been proposed by the external analysis. The question is whether the MNE has, or can efficiently obtain, the internal capabilities needed to effectively implement it. A plan is worthless if it cannot be executed.[26] Usually the question of how to organize the company's capabilities to execute the proposed strategy is more challenging than finding an appropriate strategic plan.[27] We must consider three categories of internal capabilities. *Resources* are easily divided into *human*, *operational*, and financial categories, and there may be interaction effects (e.g., poor finances = less human/operational capabilities). *Organization* capabilities are often considered in the categories of *structure*, *systems*, and *organization culture*. *Leadership* is the third critical internal capability. It includes management preferences and goals, relevant experience, mindset (see Chapter 3 on learning), and ethical orientation (see Chapter 9 on ethics). Later in the chapter, we will argue in our discussion of *sociocognitive strategic discourse* that it also includes individual differences in personality that affect decision-making through differential identification of information considered key to making effective decisions. If the internal capabilities are consistent with the requirements of the strategy, then an efficient step-by-step plan is formulated, with checkpoints to ensure provisional success, as part of an effective execution process.

External analysis

A strategic plan is constructed based on the interaction between management's vision of what their company should achieve, and the bases of competitive advantage in each industry that the company competes. The *vision* is important because it is the guiding philosophy and the performance expectations. The *competitive environment* is important because it is real (as opposed to "perceived")—real competitors are doing their best to develop better products, services, and organizations to gain market share and profitability at each other's expense.

Vision

The vision is the guiding philosophy of the organization. This vision is usually expressed as one or more overarching goals that encompass the intentionality of the leadership. It determines, for example, what products/services a company intends to produce, where it wants to establish markets, what its mindset is (ethnocentric, polycentric, geocentric—see Chapter 3), or whether a company will behave ethically or opportunistically. *Ben and Jerry*, the quality ice-cream company, has always been known to place a high premium on ethicality because this was the value of its founders.

The vision may be expressed as a *mission statement* made available to all employees—like the wallet cards provided at Ford Motor Company[28]—stating what the company expects of itself and employees. Ford's *One Ford, One Team, One Plan, One Goal* mission statement refers to managers' resolve to focus solely on the Ford marquee (selling off Jaguar, Land Rover, etc.), to work with a geocentric cooperative plan across all international divisions, with the single-minded goal of newly exciting and profitable worldwide products.

Industry analysis

Industry analysis is the first step of analyzing the competitive environment on the way to formulating a strategy to operationalize corporate vision. Porter[29] observed that the competitive dynamics of any industry could be analyzed in terms of five forces that determined the bases of competitive advantage. A KSF would be any characteristic way in which any company could reduce the power of any of these forces as limiting factors for a company's success. These KSFs would be true for any company that competed in that industry. Porter's Five Forces follow.[30]

1   *Barriers to entry*, or conversely the *threat of new entrants*. New entrants bring new capacity, new resources, and the desire to gain market share at others' expense. The threat of new entrants depends on the strength of barriers to entry that are present or that companies can develop to defend their positions. If barriers are high, the threat of new entrants will be low. In the smartphone industry, a KSF could be the ability to manufacture in an emerging market to achieve high product quality at a low

price—iPhones are manufactured in China; Galaxies in South Korea. Blackberry phones generally cost more to produce because they were manufactured in Canada or the US. Exhibit 11.2 indicates criteria related to entry barriers. Any of its items could represent a KSF if it significantly affected the ability of new entrants to enter, or allowed existing firms to block new entrants.[31]

2   *Buyer power.* Customers have product and service expectations. If companies in an industry face a small number of concentrated buyers that purchase in large volumes, or even if many individual customers are psychologically organized to expect the same product values, then buyers may have considerable power. KSFs for reducing customer power usually entail having just the product features or cache that most customers want. Because of the cache of Apple products, Apple can charge more and customers have so far not minded. If a company does not have the most desirable product characteristics, charging a lower price may be a compensating KSF. Buyer power criteria are found in Exhibit 11.3.[32]

3   *Supplier power.* A supplier may exert power over an industry if it controls supply, and can raise prices without the fear of backward integration by its customers. Backward integration means the customers set up their own supplier. In the 1990s, Intel was the only leading-edge chip-maker for personal computers because of its advanced technological capabilities, and had tremendous pricing power. Intel now has competitors and no longer dominates the chip market. A KSF would be to have multiple suppliers each able to replace the others. Then, the power of individual suppliers is reduced. Supplier power criteria are found in Exhibit 11.4.[33]

4   *Substitutes power.* Substitutes are products or services from other industries that may be used for the same or similar function as those in the industry being analyzed. They place a ceiling on the prices that can be charged, and may even eventually result in an older industry being replaced by a newer one. Over the last decade, cellphones (formerly a substitute for landlines) have been replaced by smartphones (originally a substitute). Now smartphones are the predominant product, cellphones a niche product for older customers and Third World countries. A substitute for the smartphone (and the notebook computer) is the tablet. Since tablets were released, notebook and laptop sales have declined because they have expensive features many customers do not need. Substitutes power criteria are found in Exhibit 11.5.[34]

5   *Rivalry.* Rivalry occurs either because some competitors feel the pressure of competition, or see opportunities to improve their position, or have the size, scope, and/or reach to take advantage of other companies' lesser capabilities. "Firms are mutually dependent,"[35] so a rise in the fortunes of one may come at the expense of others unless the whole market is growing rapidly. The competitive dynamics in the other four forces feed into rivalry, so for example, KSFs that satisfy customers may represent rivalry opportunities if one company can achieve them, and other companies cannot. Size, however, is often a KSF here. Larger automobile companies like Toyota and GM are able to produce different cars in a full range of prices, sizes, and capabilities.

A small company like Subaru has the capabilities to compete only in the small automobile and SUV all-wheel-drive segments. Rivalry criteria are found in Exhibit 11.6.[36]

Most industries would have between three and eight KSFs identified through industry analysis. Too few and it would be hard to identify specific opportunities for individual companies that were not shared by all companies. Too many, and it would be hard to develop a cohesive plan for taking advantage of so many opportunities, or ameliorating so many threats.

We could gauge the relative importance, or ranking, of the KSFs by how many times the same KSF was identified in different forces. For example, *low price* is undoubtedly a KSF in the consumer products industry and Walmart has been a champion in that industry. Walmart's customers value the low prices for reasonably good quality (customer power). Having such low prices makes it hard for small, medium, and even large companies to compete (barriers to entry). Walmart sources many products from small Chinese and other Asian suppliers whose prices are low, and who are easily replaced so Walmart can demand low prices (supplier power). Walmart's size as a giant MNE means that it can compete against smaller competitors on price, and even sell some products at a loss to gain or keep market share (rivalry). The same KSF appears in four of five forces (not substitutes) and is therefore very important in this industry—for Walmart and all its competitors.

EXHIBIT 11.2 ENTRY BARRIER CRITERIA

EXHIBIT 11.2

Economies of scale or scope
Proprietary product (or service) differences
Brand identity
Switching costs
Capital requirements
Access to distribution
Absolute cost advantages

- Proprietary learning curve
- Access to necessary inputs
- Proprietary low-cost product design

Government policy

- Home base government (e.g., tax policy, anti-corruption, etc.)
- Local government

Nongovernmental organization policy
Expected retaliation

Source: Porter, M. *Competitive Strategy: Techniques for Analyzing Industries and Competitors.* New York: Free Press, 1980.

EXHIBIT 11.3 BUYER POWER CRITERIA

Bargaining leverage

- Buyer concentration versus firm concentration
- Buyer volume
- Buyer switching costs relative to firm switching costs
- Buyer information
- Ability to backward integrate
- Substitute products.

Price sensitivity

- Price divided by total purchases
- Product differences
- Brand identity
- Impact on quality and/or performance
- Buyer profitability
- Incentives for purchase

Source: Porter, M. *Competitive Strategy: Techniques for Analyzing Industries and Competitors.* New York: Free Press, 1980.

EXHIBIT 11.3

EXHIBIT 11.4 SUPPLIER POWER CRITERIA

Differentiation of inputs
Switching costs of suppliers, and firms being supplied
Potential substitute inputs
Supplier concentration
Importance of volume to the supplier
Cost relative to total customer purchases
Impacts of cost on price leader or differentiation strategies
Threat of forward or backward integration

Source: Porter, M. *Competitive Strategy: Techniques for Analyzing Industries and Competitors.* New York: Free Press, 1980.

EXHIBIT 11.4

An analyst would consider which of the criteria in Exhibits 11.2–11.6 applied in the industry being analyzed, and would discuss only those that did apply. The analyst would be concerned with which forces exerted a strong or weak power over the industry's competitive dynamics. For forces exerting a strong power, the most important criteria for having that effect would be considered KSFs.

E
X
H
I
B
I
T

11.5

EXHIBIT 11.5 SUBSTITUTES POWER CRITERIA

Relative price performance of substitutes
Relative product or service performance of substitutes
Switching costs
Buyer propensity to substitute
Disruptive technology potential: a simpler product eliminating unnecessary features

Source: Porter, M. *Competitive Strategy: Techniques for Analyzing Industries and Competitors.* New York: Free Press, 1980.

E
X
H
I
B
I
T

11.6

EXHIBIT 11.6 RIVALRY CRITERIA

Company size
Industry growth (more rivalry in slower-growth industries)
Fixed costs versus value added
Cyclicality or intermittent over-capacity
Product differences
Brand identity
Switching costs
Information complexity
Diversity of competitors
Mindset (ethnocentric, polycentric, geocentric)
Exit barriers

Source: Porter, M. *Competitive Strategy: Techniques for Analyzing Industries and Competitors.* New York: Free Press, 1980.

Please note as well that some aspects of a force could be strong while other aspects are weak. For example, in a high-technology industry, R&D technologist workers who supply their labor could be disproportionately important as suppliers. By contrast, suppliers of physical components might have low power. It would be better to say that the R&D personnel suppliers had high power and the others low power, than to average everything out and say that overall supplier power was medium.

In addition, it is often appropriate to segment different classes of customers under buyer power. High-, medium-, and low-end customers may be moved by different purchase criteria and have more or less power as buyer groups. Low-end customers are more often compelled to seek price leader lower-priced options. High-end customers are more likely to find differentiated products with more features and higher cost more appealing and be willing and able to pay. Higher-end customers are more likely to be early adopters of new and innovative products, and therefore have more power in newly emerging high-technology industries.

Competitive analysis

The purpose of competitive analysis is to determine how a specific company of interest is doing against its direct competitors on the KSFs identified in the industry analysis. This shifts the level of analysis from the industry to the company. We want to know for each KSF whether our company is doing better or worse than our direct competitors. If our company has an advantage on a KSF, it is an opportunity for our strategy. If our competitors have an advantage on a KSF, it is a threat we need to find means to counter. We know the competitor will be looking for ways to take advantage of our weakness.

The usual approach is to rate our company against our competitors on the KSFs to see where our opportunities (or threats) lie. Exhibit 11.7 offers an illustrative example. There are three competitors, including the market leader, in addition to our company. There are three KSFs: low cost, delivery speed, and quality. We have scored each company based on how well they do on each KSF, with one point for the lowest score, and three points for the highest. Our company scores low on cost and quality, but best on delivery speed. Our company is also lowest in total points. We intuit that quality is less important than low cost because the market leader has the lowest costs but scores low on quality—the same as our company. We interpret from our competitive analysis that our company needs to have lower cost. If we can equal the cost of the market leader, then we would have an overall advantage, given better delivery speed. If we were able to equal the prices of the market leader, our total score of "6" would be the best of the lot.

EXHIBIT 11.7 COMPETITIVE ANALYSIS

KSFs	Our company	Market leader	Competitor #2	Competitor #3
Low cost (/3)	1	3	1	1
Delivery (/3)	2	1	1	0.5
Quality (/3)	1	1	3	3
Total score	4	5	5	4.5

Strategy

Porter[37] argued that there were only three strategies (see Exhibit 11.8). A company could seek to be the *price leader* in its industry by achieving the lowest costs and prices for its

EXHIBIT 11.8 THREE GENERIC STRATEGIES

	Uniqueness perceived by customer	Low-cost position
Industry-wide target	Differentiation strategy	Overall cost leadership
Segment target only	Focus strategy	Focus strategy

Source: Porter, M. E. *Competitive Strategy*. New York: Free Press, 1998, p. 39.

E X H I B I T

11.8

customers. The goal of the *cost leadership* strategy is to produce a competitive product at the lowest cost to customers. It is important to note that only one company can be the absolute cost leader and it is likely to be the company with the lowest production, selling, and administrative costs. However, other companies may also compete on price by having relatively low prices.

By contrast, a *differentiation* strategy is intended to offer additional features that customers want, and are willing to pay more for. Customers pay more because they perceive the product or service either as unique or better fitting their needs. For example, BMW produces relatively expensive cars for a well-heeled segment that values driving dynamics, the latest technology, and the image of being seen to be successful. By contrast, a poorer person's BMW could be a Mazda ("zoom zoom") or VW GTI. These cars have similarly impressive driving dynamics but are cheaper and lack the BMW cache. When a company uses a differentiation strategy to target a particular buyer segment, it is called a *focus* strategy, which usually aims at the specific needs or desires of that segment. Subaru's all-wheel-drive focus concentrates on customers facing difficult weather or terrain.

We should, however, regard Porter's three strategies with some skepticism. According to Bartlett and Beamish,[38] MNEs with geocentric mindsets (see Chapter 3) are able to simultaneously achieve cost leadership and differentiation. Hyundai has become legendary in the automobile industry for having lower prices and higher levels of features than its North American, Japanese, or European competitors. Its *Genesis* luxury sedan was rated higher in 2013 in quality and equal in reliability to Cadillac's *CTS*, and Mercedes *E350* while costing $7,000 less than the former and $11,500 less than the latter. Lately, Genesis has become its own luxury brand, in the same way that Lincolns may be Fords, all dressed up and a bit more, or Infinitis are Nissans underneath the extras.

We should also be aware that the Chinese teach their business students using both Sun Tzu,[39] and the 36 stratagems of Ancient China (also see Chapter 14).[40] The Japanese teach their business students the *Book of Five Rings*[41] that contains additional non-Western strategies. The point is that these Chinese and Japanese business students are being equipped with strategic ideas that Western students do not hear about. Westerners learn three. Chinese and Japanese learn many more that you never hear about in the West, so you cannot prepare for them.

Internal analysis

The right diamond of the Double Diamond model (see Exhibit 11.1) is concerned with assessing whether the internal resources of the company are capable, or could efficiently be made capable, for implementing the strategic plan. Efficiency is generally a function of whether the company has the financial capability to develop or acquire the needed capabilities. Any gap in required capabilities—resources, organizational systems, or leadership—that cannot be filled means the proposed strategy will have to be revised.

Resources and implementation

Resources include human, operational, and financial resources. The basic idea for ensuring that resources are, or can be made, consistent with the strategic plan is simple enough. We consider *not* the entire scope of resources existing in the MNE, but only those required for the proposed strategy. When we see that a particular resource is inadequate for the required tasks, we are identifying a critical resource *gap*.[42] We assess the cost of filling the resource gap. If the total resource costs are less than the profitability estimated from the strategy, then the analysis may proceed. Exhibit 11.9 offers a list of resources that could be considered. Exhibit 11.10 offers a possible template for reporting resources gaps and solutions. It may also be used for organization and leadership gaps.

EXHIBIT 11.9 POTENTIALLY NECESSARY RESOURCES

E
X
H
I
B
I
T

11.9

Human

- Potential; depth, experience; skills; flexibility of management; professional staff and workforce
- Commitment, loyalty, morale
- Union and association relationships

Operational

- Facilities; locations; geographical coverage
- Access to low-cost inputs/factors of production; distribution of product value chain (R&D, sourcing, manufacturing, marketing, sales, service) to low-cost locations
- Supplier relationships

E
X
H
I
B
I
T

11.9

- Plant costs, capacity, efficiency, and flexibility
- Proprietary processes, information technology, and know-how
- Expertise in relevant product and process development
- Scalability of facilities, personnel efforts
- Technology/marketing partnerships and agreements
- Logistics reliability and efficiency
- Quality or cost reputation; customer relationships
- Marketing sales force and distribution capabilities.

Financial

- Performance, scale, cash flow, assets, cash
- Capacity to raise capital; cost of capital
- Shareholder expectations; market assessments
- Banking and investor relations
- Resilience to cyclical or unanticipated market downturns.

Source: adapted from Crossan, M. M., et al. *Strategic Analysis and Action*, 7th edn. Toronto, ON: Pearson Prentice-Hall, 2009, p. 108.

E
X
H
I
B
I
T

11.10

EXHIBIT 11.10 GAP ANALYSIS PROTOCOL

Resource category	Required resources	Available resources	Major gaps	Gap-closing solution and cost
Human				
Operational				
Financial				
Other				

Source: adapted from Crossan, M. M., et al. *Strategic Analysis and Action*, 7th edn. Toronto, ON: Pearson Prentice-Hall, 2009, p. 118.

Organization and implementation

Organizational capabilities should be considered in terms of structure, systems, and organization culture. They should be assessed in the same manner as resources described above. Exhibit 11.11 offers a list of potential organization-related capabilities to consider.

EXHIBIT 11.11 POTENTIALLY NECESSARY ORGANIZATION CAPABILITIES

Structural

- Authoritarian versus democratic decision-making
- Ethnocentric (HQ dominates subsidiaries); polycentric (portfolio of subsidiaries independent of HQ except financial controls); geocentric (HQ and subsidiaries pool authority and learning)
- Geographic divisions versus functional areas versus matrix management

Systems

- Control; reporting; decision-making; information technology (IT); recruitment; hiring; performance appraisal; compensation; inventory—there are many

Organizational culture

- Authoritarian versus democratic; flexibility; resistance to change; bureaucratic; entrepreneurial
- Innovative: capacity to support strategies based on new ideas—through new markets, products/services, processes, technologies
- Productivity: capacity to support strategies based on cost efficiency and price
- Speed: capacity to support speed to market, speed of R&D, speed to satisfy new or existing customer needs
- Cross-cultural effectiveness: ability to support cooperation between employees from different cultures; ability to attract and retain local market employees in subsidiaries and at headquarters. Cultural diversity as a competitive advantage
- Interdependence and cooperation (or not) between functional areas (marketing and operations) or geographical units (headquarters and subsidiaries)

Source: adapted from Bartlett, C. A. and Beamish, P. W. *Transnational Management*, 6th edn. New York: McGraw-Hill, 2011. Also Crossan, M. M., et al. *Strategic Analysis and Action*, 7th edn. Toronto, ON: Pearson Prentice-Hall, 2009, p. 159.

Leadership and implementation

The leadership of the company influences both the planning process through its vision, and also the implementation through its actions. In addition to the leaders or senior management team, mid-level managers and lower-level supervisors may facilitate or retard the achievement of the strategic plan. They may actively support the plan, offer only lip service in support, or even resist its implementation. Leadership influences the implementation in many ways, including their *management preferences* and *capabilities, leadership style,* and *ethical orientations.*

Management preferences, capabilities, and style

Management preferences are based on personal attributes, education and learning, and experience derived from job contexts. These characteristics influence how leaders and managers perceive business situations, evaluate options, and select goals and actions. While management preferences influence the strategic planning process through the vision of company leaders, here we are concerned with the preferences of all levels of management as they affect actions intended to achieve implementation.

The question related to management preferences is similar to the one posed for resources and organization. Will management preferences support the proposed plan, or are there preference gaps that will need to be filled if the plan is to succeed? And as before, if management preferences cannot be made consistent with the proposed plan, then the plan will fail and will have to be revised.

We dealt with the question of leadership style in Chapter 6. We discussed leadership as an integration mechanism for increasing the cohesion of organizations. Leaders must be sensitive to the maturity of their employees. According to Hersey and Blanchard,[43] for example, employees with lower education, motivation, and willingness to set goals for themselves and take responsibility are less mature and should be led with a more autocratic style. As maturity increases, greater levels of democratic leadership may be added to the mix. We also discussed leader mindsets in Chapter 3. Leaders must attempt to avoid an ethnocentric mindset, assuming that local-country colleagues are incompetent compared to home-country colleagues, since such a mindset risks inappropriate authoritarian leadership with mature employees, and poor outcomes.

Managerial ethics

Ethics were considered in detail in Chapter 9. Leaders are more likely to have loyal followers if they are loyal to their followers as well, and generally this means behaving altruistically in regard to the needs and expectations of their employees. Abramson[44] argued that it was the responsibility of the ethical leader to be loyal to his/her employees regardless of their loyalty to him/her.

Leadership should be aware, however, that practices that may represent corruption, bribery, and illegal practices in their home countries may be perceived differently abroad. Truth and honesty are noble ideals, but they are also relative. As managers operate globally, they must be aware of the relativism in each culture regarding acceptance of a tip, favor, bribe, incentive, etc. Different criteria and values between Eastern and Western cultures, for example, determine what is acceptable or appropriate. In developing countries where people struggle to survive, bribes and corruption, especially in the public sector, are endemic to the system. In industrialized countries, the practice is often more sophisticated, less visible, but prevalent. In 2012–2013, two mayors of Montreal, Canada's second largest city, were forced to resign amid allegations from a public inquiry that they accepted bribes in the form of political contributions to award public construction projects.[45]

In China, small gifts and favors associated with guanxi relationships are considered normal business practice (see Chapter 14). For American businesspeople, these gifts and favors represent corrupt practices,[46] though it may be that individual instances may or may not represent corrupt intentions.[47] It is, however, possible that we Westerners apply different standards to the Chinese than ourselves. It is a common practice for North American businesses to buy season tickets for boxes at professional football or baseball stadiums. The tickets are available so that a company's more favored clients or customers may attend with company representatives. If this were being done in China, would Westerners consider it a corrupt practice? The perception of bribery, for example, is culturally relative and one's conscience is "culturally conditioned."[48]

Our view is that the need to decide whether certain actions are always ethical, or always not ethical represents a Western cultural propensity for dualistic thinking. Dualism is essentially the need to choose between apparent opposites because if one is right, the alternatives must be wrong. Insisting on choosing is actually the imposition of a Western cultural value that may be foreign to particular societies' alternate cultural beliefs. By contrast, the Chinese view of opposites is that they are complementary in the same way that the principle of passivity (yin) and activity (yang) complement because both may apply simultaneously to a person's actions; sometimes she/he takes action and sometimes she/he does not, both as part of the same activity.

The important principle is that leaders will achieve greater commitment from their followers through behavior perceived to be ethical. Self-interested leadership too often ends up badly for the interests of less influential subordinates, and the most competent followers have the greatest ability to leave in search of a company with leadership more to their liking. In today's global marketplace, there is a positive trend toward good corporate citizenship and business ethics. Thus, global leaders at all levels of management are concerned that neither the organization nor its personnel engage in behavior that harms society.

Distributive justice implies that performance and promotion are based on merit, not influence; benefits are distributed in return for helping the organization achieve its goals. In too many corporate scandals, managers acted as if they were accountable to nobody. Procedural justice means that the processes through which decisions are made are both fair and transparent. Interpersonal justice means that people are treated with politeness, dignity, and respect by authorities implementing procedures and making decisions. Informational justice means that explanations are given and information conveyed about why procedures were implemented in certain ways, or why outcomes were distributed in certain ways. All of these forms of organizational justice[49] are considered goals to be achieved by business ethics.

Thus, the movement toward corporate social responsibility (CSR)—that is, good management and accountability for the benefit of stakeholders and society—is a positive thing. It means that ethical behavior, like ordinary decency and distributed justice, are adhered to by organizational leaders[50] even in emerging markets where employees are hired, and factories set up to take advantage of low cost factors. When a clothing factory, or sweatshop, collapsed in Dhaka in April 2013, killing 1,100 workers, the corporate response was swift. The factory had been producing Joe Fresh brand clothes for Loblaw Inc. Loblaw senior officials immediately flew to Dhaka, promising compensation for the workers' families, and pledged never again to accept suppliers unless their work sites were safe.

Implementing the plan

Many years ago the magazine *Canadian Business* surveyed senior executives and HR managers to produce a "report card" for MBA business graduates they had hired. While the MBAs received an "A" for their abilities in strategic analysis, they received an "F" for their abilities to implement, or execute, their strategic plans. This was equally true for the graduates of the "best" business schools. Yet according to Bossidy and Charan,[51] executing plans is a leader's most important function, and poor execution skills are "*the* great unaddressed issue in the business world today."[52]

Perhaps the problem is that getting managers to execute tasks that they may be unenthusiastic about, not trained for, or that interrupt their normal routines, is meticulous and overly repetitive work. It requires patient and helpful supervision, plus a lot of checking to make sure tasks are being accomplished correctly and on time. Eventually, resisters must be confronted and angry words may be spoken as part of unpleasant corrective situations. And it's just not sexy or innovative enough for ambitious followers who want to be noticed and promoted by their bosses. So the plan fails, and a new plan must be devised to make up for lost time. And this plan is often devised by a new group of managers who replaced the ones who were not committed to the last plan.

Yet implementation is not that hard. It just requires doing things in proper order, and constantly checking to make sure that what you think is getting done is actually getting done. What you need is a flowchart for planning the most cost-efficient implementation of related activities, and you need to determine and get agreement about who is responsible for what, and by when. Exhibit 11.12 describes an example of plan implementation through flowcharting at a Canadian junior gold-surveying company.

EXHIBIT 11.12 IMPLEMENTATION FLOWCHARTING AT A JUNIOR GOLD-SURVEYING COMPANY

I was invited to consult with the management of the XY junior gold-survey company for the implementation of its new strategic plan. Its business was to survey new potential mine sites, selling those with promising potential to senior gold companies for future development. The initial survey had to be done by airplane to quickly eliminate unpromising sites. The problem was that the availability of air survey equipment was extremely limited; many junior golds were competing to lease it, and the surveys were to be done in the Canadian Arctic during the very short summer between June and September. The previous summer, XY had been able to survey only a fraction of its properties, and it was negatively impacting company finances. The plan called for the acquisition of XY's own survey equipment. Management was ready to do this despite its expense, because without it, XY would run out of money. The equipment was easily available, though expensive.

"If you have the air survey equipment," I asked, "Is that all you need?" "No," was the answer. In addition to the survey equipment, XY needed the airplane, the pilot, a trained operator to use the equipment, and a hanger to store the plane near the exploration sites. In addition, it was autumn and the current survey season had already been lost. Surveying could not commence till the following June or July. It would take a month to order the survey equipment but then it would sit around for months unused. The plane and pilot were equally easy since they could be retained by contract for the summer, but it had to be the right kind of plane, and an experienced pilot—and these were in high demand during the Arctic summers. The greatest lag time was to train an XY equipment operator, and to build the hanger in the right location. Both would take months.

The most efficient execution of the plan was to coordinate all actions so they culminated together the next June, in time for some inflight testing before the surveying commenced. If the plane and pilot were in high demand, they should be booked immediately. If they were already unavailable, XY might need their own. If training the operator and building the hanger took six months each, those tasks should commence in November. The equipment could be booked to arrive, and be paid for, in May. XY was saved the major expense of the survey equipment until it was actually needed.

JAPANESE STRATEGIC THEORY

Several of the greatest weaknesses of the Western contingency theory of strategic management are revealed when it is compared to the Japanese strategic theories developed by Musashi Miyamoto.[53] Japanese strategy is also direct and first-strike oriented, but is aimed not at the competitive environment nor the direct competitor companies. It is aimed directly at the individual strategists who create and execute the competitors' strategies.

Musashi reveals two questionable interlinked assumptions common to the Western contingency strategic discourse. First, what is assumed to be an objective analysis of the competitive environment is actually the strategists' subjective impression of that objective reality. Individual analysts accumulate this subjective impression from the objective external environment but have cognitive biases that affect the identification and valuation of information considered relevant to its construction.[54] A strategy may be aimed against these cognitive biases by attempting to manipulate or distort the strategist's understanding of what she/he perceives as the objective environment.

Second, the cognitive biases of individuals are not constants, but vary from strategist to strategist. A strategist who studies the cognitive biases of his/her individual counterpart opponents may gain valuable insights of competitive advantage for his/her company. Western strategists schooled in contingency strategic discourse are simply unequipped to deal with this individual level of strategic analysis because they have learned only to consider the industry and company levels of analysis. Contingency theory assumes that all individuals are more-or-less the same—rational and interchangeable in the sense that everyone would behave similarly given the same information.[55] Musashi argues this is entirely false.

Third, most Western strategists are trained in using Porter and the contingency strategic discourse and become expert in its application. This form of analysis has become the foundation for most Western strategic planning. Most Western strategists routinely follow the path from industry analysis, to competitive analysis, to strategy development using KSFs, and then evaluating whether a firm's internal capabilities will support the strategy. It is predictable. Musashi teaches how to take advantage of predictability and to throw it off course with unexpected behavior that causes opponents to lose their presence of mind.

In contrast, Japanese managers are well prepared to deal with Western strategic planning and execution. Musashi was a famous seventeenth-century Japanese swordfighter and duelist. His strategic theories were developed on the basis of a career of one-on-one duels, often to the death, and make no mention of organizing armies or states in the way that Chinese strategists like Sun Tzu did. Japanese strategic theory relies on Western theory for the organization of corporate internal capabilities and resources, as well as the analysis of competitive advantage. Many Japanese managers have either received their management educations in the West, or trained at Japanese institutions that teach Western management theory as a means of preparing their students to work and compete in Western countries. They have simply added the individual level of analysis, taught by Musashi, to Western strategic theories and practice.

Musashi taught[56] that the most critical aspect of the external environment was the individual opponent that you faced. He did not mean company versus company in the context of industry-wide KSFs, but the individual strategist's direct counterpart(s) assembling the strategic plans of their direct competitors. He recommended acute observation to identify the strengths and weaknesses in individual counterparts' characters, attitudes, and behaviors. He suggested that even the smallest details could be important and that it was often these that tripped people up and brought failure, because often senior managers delegated the analyses to undependable or poorly trained subordinates. He argued that through observation you could find weaknesses in opponents that not even they were aware of. For example, an opponent might always and habitually proceed using a predictable set of analytical procedures—for example, Crossan et al.'s "diamond drill" or "series of procedural steps"[57] for testing the likelihood a strategy would be successful. Musashi observed that when opponents routinely followed the same habitual steps, they were often mentally coasting, relatively unfocused, and not actively trying to do their best.

Regarding strategies, Musashi taught that one should avoid using the same strategy and tactics over and over. It is Western conventional wisdom that the best specific methods and/or processes should be developed, and as "best practices" they are repeatedly applied, over and over, in each new situation. The problem with "traditional forms"[58] was that they blinded the strategist with the illusion that all the important variables were covered. They became barriers preventing one from seeing the realities of particular engagements with individuals whose strengths, weaknesses, and predilections differed from one to another. Letting go of a style, however, having already become expert in its use, is difficult. There is a tendency for experts to stop their training when they have reached a master skill level, rather than aiming for continuous improvement. De Mente[59] reported:

> One of Musashi's primary goals in traveling around the country and meeting other samurai in duels and demonstration bouts was to observe and learn their different styles of fighting. The more familiar he became with the variety of fighting tactics, the less likely he was to see a style he hadn't seen before or didn't know how to defeat. Musashi made it his practice to never depend on a particular form, even those he had perfected. His approach was to change to any style that would give him an advantage over his opponent.

The danger in repeating the same analytical procedures or executing actions over and over was that repetition made the strategist predictable to his/her opponent. If an opponent were psychologically committed through his/her training and expertise to just one form or process—the contingency strategic discourse, for example—she/he would be inflexible and slow to adapt to unfamiliar strategies or tactics. She/he would not quickly grasp that an opponent was doing something different and unexpected. Yet Mintzberg et al.[60] identified ten Western schools of strategic analysis most of which are never taught in most business strategy courses, nine of which (excluding Porter's positioning school) could be used to throw a Porter acolyte off his/her best game.

The goal in being flexible in your strategy was to thwart the opponent's predictable actions, forcing him/her onto unfamiliar ground where she/he was more likely to make mistakes. By being able to predict your opponent's moves, you could get inside his/her head, anticipating his/her actions, taking measures to interfere with his/her plans. If you could interrupt your opponent's focus so that she/he lost the rhythm and sequence of actions, then she/he became vulnerable. When that happened, you should not allow her/him to withdraw, or relent or compromise yourself, but press harder to crush her/his spirit to ensure she/he would never again want to mess with you.

The acute observation needed to see what your opponent was thinking and how she/he was organizing his/her actions came from clearing the mind through Zen meditation. Musashi recommended meditation for that purpose, and it is a common practice among Japanese businesspeople to do so for 15–20 minutes each day. Zen meditation improved the ability to think more clearly, and function more effectively. It taught a person that the primary obstacle to enlightenment was one's own ego—the selfish and glorified sense of self. Reducing one's sense of self-importance allowed the objective and unemotional observation of the opponent, and his/her actions. Without the illusion of egotistical self-importance or selfish ambitions as distractions, the "empty mind" could more spontaneously react to circumstances, and subconscious intuition could direct one's actions. Zen teaches that in this mental state, accomplishing a task is as easy as thinking it.[61]

The sociocognitive strategic discourse

The sociocognitive strategic discourse,[62] or cognitive school of strategy,[63] is the only Western strategic discourse that encourages consideration of the perceptual and cognitive biases used by individual analysts and implementers in building and executing strategies. "Objective" reality is considered to be socially and psychologically constructed.[64] It is "selectively perceived, cognitively rearranged, or interpersonally negotiated."[65] Individuals possess "multiple realities"[66] when they possess different cognitive biases, causing them to select different sets of information about the objective situation as important or unimportant. We would argue with Mintzberg et al.[67] that there definitely is an objective external environment within which companies must compete, but that strategists, because of their individual cognitive differences, obtain different interpretations of it and what to do about it.

If Japanese strategic theory teaches us that our cognitive biases are visible in our actions and may be used to predict our thinking, planning, and action, then the sociocognitive discourse is helpful in exposing to ourselves what these cognitive biases are and their effects. It does not, in itself, answer the problem of becoming predictable by overusing the analytical sequences of Porter and the contingency discourse. It does, however, offer a second form of strategic analysis, and it allows us to look at our individual competitor opponents in the same way that Musashi has taught Japanese strategists to look at us.

Following Mintzberg et al.'s example,[68] we have chosen to use Jungian personality theory to identify four introverted problem-solving preferences that humans use to select the information they regard as relevant, to judge its relative importance for problem-solving, and to discard information considered unimportant or irrelevant to their concerns. In Chapter 2, in the context of intercultural communication, we discussed the Jungian theory of personality types[69] in detail. It is based on two attitudes ("extraverted" and "introverted"), two information-gathering functions ("sensing" and "intuiting"), and two information-evaluating functions ("thinking" and "feeling"). Discussion was presented in Chapter 2 indicating that these two attitudes and four functions are characteristic of all humans-as-species regardless of their cultural affiliation, as genetically based behavioral preferences. Jungian personality types may also be used to identify the psychological "national character"[70] predominant in the problem-solving of individuals from particular national cultures, thanks to Massey's work,[71] also described in Chapter 2. In Chapter 2 we discussed four extraverted communication styles that affected intercultural and cross-national communications. In this chapter, we present four introverted problem-solving styles: (1) Introverted Feeling (Fi); Introverted Sensing (Si); Introverted Thinking (Ti); and Introverted iNtuiting (Ni). In Chapters 12 (Middle East), 14 (East Asia), 15 (South and Southeast Asia, and Australia), and 18 (Canada and the US), we will combine the problem-solving and communications styles to produce full Jungian national characters for the nations under discussion. These will be used to consider their effects on cross-national interactions.

The importance of these four problem-solving personality-based preferences is three-fold. First, as genetically based behavioral preferences,[72] they become habitual patterns of preferred behavior of which individuals are unaware because they are applied to every problem-solving situation. They seem so natural because of life-long repetition that individuals may believe that everyone is the same. Second, each problem-solving preference produces a characteristic sequence of behavior marking an individual's problem-solving. The behavior pattern is typical to that psychological preference, but different from the problem-solving styles. Third, these behavioral preferences are visible to others schooled in seeing them. When Musashi teaches that through acute observation you may observe the strengths and weaknesses of your strategic opponent, you may achieve the same results in this way, to achieve competitive advantage against strategic opponents.

Beebe[73] has offered simple three-word descriptions of the four Jungian introverted problem-solving styles (see Exhibit 11.13). For example, Si, the most common style for English-speaking and Western European national characters, appears to others to be primarily focused on implementation, but is intended by Si problem-solvers to be verifying in advance that implementation is possible. Notice that this describes Porter's contingency strategic theory. Porter's purpose is clearly implementation of effective action. Before implementation, the conditions in the competitive environment must be verified, and then the ability of the internal capabilities to support the strategic action. An expert contingency strategist who was adept at applying Porter's analysis could fully account for all his/her analysis, strategic recommendations, and action plan. Si is fixated on the objective characteristics of the external and internal situations. However, Fi problem-solvers, predominant in many other national cultures, are focused more on judging potential actions and appraising overall goals based on values that they regard as non-negotiable. They are much less interested in objective situations as they currently exist, than on creating the objective circumstances that will support their values.

EXHIBIT 11.13 FOUR JUNGIAN PROBLEM-SOLVING STYLES

Personality type	As it appears to others	As it is intended	At its most developed
Introverted Sensing (**Si**)	Implementing	Verifying	Accounting
Introverted iNtuiting (**Ni**)	Imagining	Knowing	Divining
Introverted Thinking (**Ti**)	Naming	Defining	Understanding
Introverted Feeling (**Fi**)	Judging	Appraising	Establishing the value

Source: Beebe, J. *Energies and Patterns in Psychological Type: The Reservoir of Consciousness.* London: Routledge, 2016.

The four problem-solving attitude-function preferences are described in more detail as follows:[74]

- *Introverted Feeling (Fi)*: Fi individuals base their decision-making on their feelings and their belief that their actions will support strongly held personal values. These values may or may not conform to their society's values, but if not, Fi individuals will resist peer pressure and maintain their own value-commitments. They seek harmony and order, influencing others through their actions more than their words. Because their feelings are introverted and not externalized, they may appear unemotional, or indifferent, and responding to strangers without friendship or interpersonal warmth. Others may see Fi individuals as quiet, inaccessible, and hard to get to know. However, they are flexible, modest, nonjudgmental, and forgiving, tending to mediate conflict by affirming the value of all sides.

- *Introverted Sensing (Si)*: Si individuals work quietly, systematically, and in-depth to achieve useful results. They deal in facts and details in a careful and orderly fashion, even reporting a photographic memory for details. Si individuals are thorough and conscientious, but discount any data that is not sensory. They distrust imaginative people that are less accurate with facts (Fi, Ti, and Ni). They value efficiency and cost-effectiveness. Others may see them as calm and passive, as if not reacting to events going on around them. They might seem difficult to get to know because they tend to hold their thoughts and feelings within themselves.

- *Introverted Thinking (Ti)*: Ti individuals live in a Socratic world where every assumption and statement may be questioned as to its accuracy and truth. They are more interested in ordering and evaluating ideas than facts and data, and theories or conceptual parameters must be ordered and clarified before data may be considered and evaluated. Ti individuals tend to value new ideas and generalizing theoretical explanations more highly than facts, which may be considered mere arbitrary appearances of underlying ideal truths. Others may see them as difficult, inconsiderate, arrogant, and even anti-social because they prefer to argue what they regard as the correct view in a self-interested way regardless of the feelings of others. Because Ti individuals have quick and insightful minds, they may regard those who do not accept their analysis as stupid and may not shy away from saying so.

■ *Introverted iNtuiting (Ni)*: Ni individuals think in terms of images and metaphors that are difficult to communicate and that are not shared with others until well-developed. They are imaginative, combining disparate ideas into new systems, strategies, and theories. They have a facility for simplifying complex problems by finding and rearranging essential elements, while remain unconfused by situational appearances. They appear to others as quiet, distant, daydreaming, and somewhat absent-minded nonconformists who do not communicate well or in expected directions.

The easiest method by which to calculate your own Jungian problem-solving style is to use one of the free Jungian, MBTI, or Keirsey personality instruments.[75] Exhibit 2.8 (see Chapter 2) gives the 16 four-letter MBTI or Keirsey personality types that these instruments would calculate as yours and their equivalent Jungian attitude-functions. Referring to Exhibit 2.8, it does not matter for the purpose of our discussion in this chapter whether your problem-solving preference is "dominant" or "auxiliary" (see Chapter 2 for discussion of this point). Introverted problem-solving styles (Fi, Si, Ti, Ni) are the basis of individual problem-solving either way. For comparative purposes, one study[76] showed that on a worldwide basis, Si was the most common style, with 46.4 percent of the sample. Fi was second most common at 29.8 percent, followed by Ti at 16.2 percent, and Ni at 7.9 percent.

Beyond using these descriptions of the four problem-solving preferences to observe individual competitors to identify their strengths, weaknesses, and the kinds of difficulties you might expect to face, we are also able to predict the problem-solving style most characteristic in nations as part of their national character.[77] Massey[78] conducted a qualitative worldwide study to determine the psychological type most common in over 100 nations. This study and its method is discussed in detail in Chapter 2. On the other hand, you should not believe that because a problem-solving style is predominant in a national culture, that you will see only that one. All four problem-solving styles are characteristic of human populations. All four are likely to be encountered in every nation, though in differing distributions. Massey's study prepares you for probabilities, but it is not an oracle.

Exhibit 11.14 indicates the most characteristic problem-solving preferences for the most important international trading nations (bolded) accounting for almost 95 percent of world trade. These are the nations most international business executives are likely to encounter. A number of other nations are included that are mentioned in other chapters of this book.

It is interesting to observe that there are, with a few notable exceptions, *two main human and international approaches to problem-solving* characteristic of these national characters. These are *Si and Fi*. On the Si side are found the notable internal business

EXHIBIT 11.14 SI, FI, TI, NI INTROVERTED NATIONAL ATTITUDE-FUNCTION PROBLEM-SOLVING PREFERENCES

Geographic area	Introverted Sensing (Si)	Introverted Feeling (Fi)	Introverted Thinking (Ti)	Introverted iNtuition (Ni)
North America	US, Canada (Anglophone)	None	None	Canada (Francophone)
Latin America	None	Mexico, Brazil	Argentina	None
East Asia	Japan, South Korea, Taiwan	China	None	None
South and Southeast Asia	Australia, Singapore, Malaysia, Vietnam	India, Indonesia	None	None
Middle East	Iran	Saudi Arabia, Turkey	Iraq, Israel	None
Europe	Germany, United Kingdom, Netherlands	Russia, Italy, Spain, Dutch Belgium, Switzerland	None	France, Belgium (French)
Africa	Nigeria	South Africa, Tanzania	None	None

Source: Massey, B. *Where in the World Do I Belong?* USA: Jetlag Press, 2006.

powerhouses of the US, Japan, Germany, and the UK, as well as secondary but still important economies such as Canada (English), South Korea, and Singapore. On the Fi side are other important international powerhouse economies such as China and India, as well as secondary but important emerging markets such as Mexico, Brazil, Saudi Arabia, and Russia. We would hypothesize that individuals from countries within the same clusters would experience less stress dealing with each other because of the shared approach to problem-solving processes.

On the other hand, Si problem-solvers dealing with Fi counterparts, and vice versa, would experience more difficulties and stress. For example, Si American negotiators would experience less interactional stress communicating and negotiating with Si Japanese counterparts than Fi Chinese counterparts because the evaluation criteria are so different. Chinese negotiators would conceptualize their problem-solving in terms of personal values and feelings, while Americans would be more likely to focus impersonally on what they understood as the facts.

France is an interesting exception to the observation that all the major international business economies are either Si or Fi. Its cultural preference for Ni decision-making suggests that French negotiators would experience greater dissonance than other international traders in international negotiations because it has the only national character with that problem-solving preference. Also interesting is that the only other "nation" with this Ni cultural decision-making preference is the Francophone (French) province of Quebec in Canada. Should Quebec ever vote for independence from the rest of Canada (there have been two such referendums), Quebec trade representatives might experience greater than average stress negotiating independent international trade deals.

It is best to illustrate the potential difficulties between problem-solving preferences by offering examples. Since the most common difficulty would be expected between individuals from predominantly Si and Fi nations, we will start there. It is also interesting to consider in less detail the problems that Ni and Ti may experience and create for the other preferences, though in less detail. Differences between these problem-solving preferences may put great stress on interaction between representative problem-solvers. This is because what is considered normal process by one preference is discounted by the counter-expectations of normalcy for another preference.

1   *Si (United States, Japan, Germany, United Kingdom) versus Fi (China, India, Russia, Saudi Arabia) decision-making*:
    a.   Si decision-makers decide on the basis of objective facts observed from sensory data while discounting the value of any data or information that is extrasensory (values and theories). Fi decision-makers decide on the basis of their feelings about their counterparts, and whether they feel that their strongly held personal or social values are being upheld.
    b.   Si decision-makers have an extremely accurate perception and memory for sensory data—a photographic memory—including everything said in discussions and how their counterparts looked. They distrust more imaginative people who are less accurate in their perception of data. Fi decision-makers will uphold their value-commitments regardless of contrary evidence, and prefer commitments to concrete actions over long discussions.
    c.   Fi decision-makers may appear to others to be unemotional and indifferent, with few offers of friendship or interpersonal warmth. Si decision-makers are also challenged to build friendly relationships because they discount contrary decision criteria and do not easily communicate their feelings.
    d.   Fi decision-makers value interpersonal harmony and forgiveness, and are generally nonjudgmental and altruistic in outlook. Si decision-makers value efficiency and cost-effectiveness, and tend to be more self-interested in achieving their own, and their organizations' objectives. Fi decision-makers will fight if compromise is apparently impossible.
2   *Ni (France) versus Si or Fi*:
    a.   Ni decision-makers are very theoretically oriented, thinking in terms of images and metaphors, and imaginatively combining apparently disparate ideas into

new systems, strategies, and working theories. Si decision-makers distrust imaginative counterparts, and discount extrasensory theoretical observations divorced from specific sensory information. Fi decision-makers are more concerned with upholding their values than seeing them redefined or reshaped.

3   *Ti (Israel, Iraq, Argentina) versus Si, Fi, Ni:*

    a.   Ti decision-makers question every assumption, seeking the true and essential state of affairs. They will question the validity of Fi values, and the validity of Si data. Ni creativity may be questioned because if this new and untested possibility may be envisioned, how is it better than this other new and untested possibility. When Ti believes it knows "the truth" it will argue without compromise.

Through self-assessment and careful observation of one's counterparts at competing companies, a strategist may derive useful knowledge from this application of the sociocognitive strategic discourse that may add to individual or corporate competitiveness. By applying more than one strategic discourse—contingency and sociocognitive—a strategist may avoid predictability.

CHINESE STRATEGIC THEORY

The argument has been made recently that Chinese strategic theory is more advanced than either Japanese or Western.[79] While Western theory is stronger on competitive strategies and the use of technology as companies and nations vie against each other, Chinese theory operates at the level of "grand strategy,"[80] looking beyond strategic competition or warfare between companies to what the subsequent peace will look like and achieve.[81] Competitive situations without clear positive outcomes are avoided, but through the exercise of soft power, competitive gains may be achieved without overt conflict. Soft power is defined[82] as attracting and persuading others to want the outcomes you are pursuing through co-optation rather than coercion. Allies are co-opted, or brought into cooperation by invitation and their willingness to adopt ideas for their own use, because Chinese companies present themselves as living up to their political and/or ethical values, and their policies as both legitimate and having moral authority.[83] Sun Tzu taught that moral authority would be evidenced when Chinese leaders focused on six leadership criteria:[84]

1   building character rather than image;

2   leading with actions rather than words;

3   sharing employee trials and hardships rather than just successes;

4   motivating emotionally and not just materially;

5   assigning clear missions to followers; and

6   focusing on strategy ahead of organization.

Chinese business strategies are indirect, as opposed to direct as in the cases of the West and Japan. This appears an advantage given Liddell Hart's finding that over 25 centuries, direct strategies were used successfully very infrequently, and the indirect strategy produced the most hopeful economic outcomes.[85] Liddell Hart quoted Lenin, who said:[86]

> The soundest strategy in war is to postpone operations until the moral disintegration of the enemy renders the delivery of the mortal blow both possible and easy. . . . The soundest strategy in any campaign is to postpone battle and the soundest tactics to postpone attack, until the moral dislocation of the enemy renders the delivery of a decisive blow practicable.

At the same time, Chinese strategists have recognized for more than two millennia that a stronger power may force a weaker opponent to defend itself. Strategies were developed based on Taoist principles to help the weaker opponents win out. Chinese strategies tend to focus on counter-punching, as opposed to the first-strike preferences of Western and Japanese strategies, because "the defensive is the stronger form of strategy as well as the more economical."[87]

It is a curious and disconcerting possibility for Westerners to consider the possibility that non-Western theories have become (or always were) more advanced than their own after centuries of Western technological superiority. It is even more unsettling considering that Chinese strategic theory is based in large part on the works of Sun Tzu[88] and Lao Tzu,[89] who both lived and wrote more than 2,300 years ago. In large part, the problem for the West in understanding Chinese strategy has been caused by mistranslations of Sun Tzu and other comparable works. Yuen[90] observes that Sun Tzu's work is not significantly different from that of Clausewitz,[91] a nineteenth-century Prussian general, but has been misunderstood because the Chinese language employs logical principles differing from formal Western logic. As a result, Western attempts at translation have seemed to violate "the military and strategic 'common sense' of the West and many major tenets of Western strategic logic."[92]

It is an interesting illustration of the problems inherent in *managing cultural differences* that the West has consistently misunderstood Chinese strategic intent because the Chinese logic system is fundamentally different from that of the West. It demonstrates the falsity of the belief that because any text may be translated into English, we will then know what those in another culture actually think. Chinese strategic thought generally does not rely on the means–ends rational model employed in its Western counterpart. English translations of Sun Tzu have tended to interpret it using the means–ends model, reducing the book to a series of aphorisms stating that if you do this, then that will be the result. In fact, Sun Tzu is grand strategy because of an holistic perspective that employs all means of influence–soft power, for example–and not merely competitive and military elements. It considers economic costs of conflict in detail, and fully integrates the value of diplomacy, politics, and being both ethical, and perceived as ethical.[93] Therefore, Chinese strategy "places a much higher premium on brain power than on sheer force and technology."[94]

Chinese logic is dialectical (thesis + antithesis = synthesis), and works through pairs of opposites like yin/yang (or receptive/energetic, or defensive/offensive). Contradictions between opposites allow more intricate and delicate understanding of interrelationships between objects or processes, and integration of apparent opposites. In the case of strategy, the yin/yang principle of defense/offense allows the two concepts to interact "at once interconnected, interpenetrating, and interdependent in an uninterrupted manner."[95] Chinese logic rejects the Western logical assumption that "A" and "not A" are always different. It also rejects the Western assumption that a proposition cannot simultaneously be both true and false.

Chinese strategies that the West has interpreted as primarily defensive are in fact both defensive and offensive depending on the situational dynamics, flowing together depending upon opportunity, in the form of a water strategy.[96] The strength of water is its flexibility. It represents the most nonconfrontational form of interaction, because it conforms itself instantly and without effort to whatever shape or terrain it encounters, and moves in the direction of least resistance. When a gap appears in a competitor's strategy, the water strategy immediately and effortlessly switches into offense and flows into and through that gap.[97] De Bono has suggested that the strategic competition between Asia and the West is between "water logic" and "rock logic"—complete flexibility versus absolute resiliency.[98] When Chinese MNEs appear to Westerners to employ defensive and nonaggressive strategies that avoid overt competition and conflict, they may be doing so as part of a competitive offensive strategy, catching their Western competitors unawares.

Recent global events may illustrate this grand strategic approach that is simultaneously offensive and defensive. While China claimed the Sendaku Islands from Japan, and Japan and its American allies organized the defense, the Chinese simultaneously built artificial islands in the South China Sea as land-based aircraft carriers. By late 2016, the dust had not completely settled, but the Chinese seemed to have firm control over the South China Sea despite international protests. By late 2016, the Philippines had given up their protests and declared that they would reduce their ties with the US, to seek better relations with China. It seemed an example of the Chinese strategy of "look to the East to strike to the West"[99]—or south in this case. China seemed to have gained control of the South China Sea without conflict, and begun to pry the Philippines from its American orbit.

When pressed into immediate competition and conflict against their intended interests, the Chinese have strategies intended to support and sustain the weaker party. In another example of Western misunderstanding of Chinese texts, Sawyer[100] argued that Lao Tzu's *Tao Te Ching*,[101] usually understood as Taoist philosophy, was originally an ancient strategy manual based on Sun Tzu. It is based on the Taoist principle that when a quality achieves its highest and most powerful expression, it also reaches a "tipping point" where it begins to irrevocably retreat into its opposite form.[102] The text makes three sets of strategic recommendations based on deceiving a powerful foe.[103]

- ■ Set 1:
  - – Warfare is the Way (Tao) of deception.
  - – Thus although [you are] capable, display incapability to them.
  - – When committed to employing your forces, feign inactivity.
  - – When [your objective] is nearby, make it appear as if distant;
  - – When far away, create the illusion of being nearby.
- ■ Set 2:
  - – Display profits to entice them.
  - – Create disorder [in their forces] and take them.
  - – If they are substantial, prepare for them;
  - – If they are strong, avoid them.
- ■ Set 3:
  - – If they are angry, perturb them.
  - – Be deferential to foster their arrogance [If they are humble, encourage their arrogance.]
  - – If they are rested, force them to exert themselves.
  - – If they are united, cause them to be separated.

This is a long-term, indirect, water strategy intended to create weaknesses. It ultimately intends that the powerful enemy will be worn down, as a hurricane blows down a mighty tree while tall grass bends and is unaffected. The power of a powerful enemy will be magnified until it reaches beyond its point of maximum attainable power, seen as the tipping point. In set 1, the goal is to make oneself appear incompetent and disorganized when one is not. In set 2, the goal is to entice, while organizing and avoiding their power. In set 3, the goal is to make the enemy angry, and arrogant, while tiring them out, separating them from their allies, and sowing dissention among them to destroy their unity. Certainly the examples of the Roman, Ottoman, and British Empires, as well as General Motors, Motorola, Yahoo, and many formerly great companies, show that great powers may dissolve without a deciding battle ever having been fought.

CONCLUSIONS

Bourgeois et al.[104] offers some handy rules of thumb for how to generally decide what your plan should be after you have analyzed the external environment and considered the internal capabilities that are either available or obtainable. These are summarized in Exhibit 11.15.

An MNE with strong opportunities in its external environment and the internal capabilities needed to make its plan succeed should be pursuing a *growth* strategy. If the same company has internal capability gaps that prevent its plan from succeeding, it should *address those weaknesses* before attempting to take advantage of opportunities with a growth strategy.

E X H I B I T 11.15

EXHIBIT 11.15 RULES OF THUMB FOR STRATEGIC PLANNING

	Weak internal capabilities	Strong internal capabilities
Good external opportunities	Fix strategic weaknesses	Grow
Major external threats	Divestiture	Diversification

Source: Bourgeois, L. J. III, Duhaime, I. M., and Stimpert, J. L. *Strategic Management Concise: A Managerial Perspective.* Fort Worth, TX: Harcourt College, 2000.

If an MNE has strong internal capabilities but its industry is not attractive and there are threats to its current levels of performance, then it should consider *diversification* into a related industry with better prospects. On the other hand, if an MNE is faced with both serious external threats and weak internal capabilities, it should consider *divestiture*. While such a simple rule of thumb does not tell you the plan, it points in helpful directions.

Strategic planners would be well advised not to put all their eggs in Porter's contingency discourse basket. If most Western strategic plans are undergirded by Porter, then your competitors will know what you are planning because they view the competitive environment in similar ways. Your plans will be predictable, and not just to the Japanese. It is a helpful path to strategic advantage to spend some time analyzing the strengths and weaknesses of your counterparts (and yourself) who are devising their strategies against your company, and maybe pinpointing you. And watch out for companies, not just Chinese, whose competitive positions seem to improve without apparent effort. They are probably using strategies you have never considered, and best you learn before they do it to you and your company.

MIND STRETCHING

1   Porter would argue that every strategic decision-maker facing the same industry and competitive analysis, and internal capabilities, would produce the same strategy. We argue that because managers may be Si (Introverted Sensing), Fi (Introverted Feeling), Ti (Introverted Thinking) or Ni (Introverted iNtuiting) in their problem-solving preferences, that this would not be true. What do you think? Which one are you? Do you problem-solve in exactly the same way as your friends or fellow students?

2   Take one of the free internet-based MBTI or Keirsey personality tests. Use Exhibit 2.8 in Chapter 2 to determine whether your problem-solving preference is Si, Fi, Ti, or Ni. Work in a small group where everyone has the same preference. Do the descriptions make sense for how you all problem-solve? To what extent?

3 Now work in a small group where people have different problem-solving preferences. If you look closely at how other people organize their thinking, and discuss problem-solving, can you guess what other peoples' preferences, strengths, and weaknesses might be? Musashi says maybe you could.

4 Pick a company that you like in an industry you have familiarity with. Look at the Chinese strategies for helping a smaller competitor defeat a larger one. Could you design a strategy for your company, Porter style, that could make use of these Chinese ideas?

NOTES

1 Hoffman, B. G. *American Icon: Alan Mulally and the Fight to Save Ford Motor Company*. New York: Crown Business, 2012.

2 Michihiro Matsumoto in de Mente, L. *Samurai Strategies: 42 Martial Secrets from Musashi's Book of Five Rings*. Tokyo: Tuttle Publishing, 2008.

3 Yuen, D. M. C. *Deciphering Sun Tzu: How to Read The Art of War*. Oxford: Oxford University Press, 2014.

4 Proust, M. *In Search of Lost Time*. New York: Modern Library, 2012.

5 Clausewitz, C. von, *On War*. Oxford: Oxford University Press, 2008.

6 Helmuth von Moltke the Younger, quoted in Liddell Hart, B. H. *Strategy*, 2nd rev. edn. New York: Meridian (Penguin), 1991.

7 Rouleau, L. and Seguin, F. "Strategy and Organization Theories: Common Forms of Discourse," *Journal of Management Studies*, Vol. 32, No. 1, 1995, pp. 101–117.

8 Mintzberg, H., Ahlstrand, B., and Lampel, J. *Strategy Safari: A Guided Tour Through the Wilds of Strategic Management*. New York: The Free Press, 1998.

9 Rouleau and Seguin "Strategy and Organization Theories.".

10 Mintzberg et al., *Strategy Safari*.

11 Porter, M. E. *Competitive Strategy: Creating and Sustaining Superior Performance*. New York: The Free Press, 1980.

12 For example, Crossan, M. M., Rouse, M. J., Rowe, W. G., and Maurer, C. C. *Strategic Analysis and Action*, 9th edn. Toronto, ON: Pearson, 2016.

13 Sun, H. C. *The Wiles of War: 36 Military Strategies from Ancient China*. Beijing: Foreign Languages Press, 1993, p. iii.

14 Liddell Hart, *Strategy*, p. 144.

15 Clausewitz, *On War*.

16 Liddell Hart, *Strategy*, p. 147.

17 Musashi, M. *The Book of Five Rings*. Boston, MA: Shambhala Library, 2003.

18 Wusun, L. *Sun Zi: The Art of War, Sun Bin: The Art of War; Two Chinese Military Classics in One Volume*. Beijing: People's China Publishing House, 1995.

19 Rouleau and Seguin, "Strategy and Organization Theories."

20 Yuen, *Deciphering Sun Tzu*.

21 Liddell Hart, *Strategy*, p. 322.

22 Ibid.

23 Sawyer, R. D. *The Tao of War*. New York: Basic Books, 2009.

24 Nye, J. S. Jr. *Soft Power: The Means to Success in World Politics*. New York: Public Affairs, 2009.

25 Ibid.

26 Crossan et al., *Strategic Analysis and Action.*

27 Bartlett, C. A. and Beamish, P. W. *Transnational Management: Text, Cases, and Readings in Cross-Border Management*, 6th edn. New York: McGraw-Hill, 2011.

28 Hoffman, *American Icon.*

29 Porter, M. E. *Competitive Advantage: Creating and Sustaining Superior Performance.* Toronto: Simon & Schuster Canada Inc., 2008.

30 Ibid.

31 Ibid.

32 Ibid.

33 Ibid.

34 Ibid.

35 Ibid., p. 17.

36 Ibid.

37 Ibid.

38 Bartlett and Beamish, *Transnational Management.*

39 Sun Tzu. *The Art of War.* New York: Dover, 2002.

40 Yuan, G. *Lure the Tiger Out of the Mountains: How to Apply the 36 Stratagems of Ancient China to the Modern World.* New York: Touchstone Books, 1992.

41 Musashi, *The Book of Five Rings.*

42 Crossan et al., *Strategic Analysis and Action.*

43 Hersey, P. and Blanchard, K. H. *Management of Organizational Behavior: Utilizing Human Resources.* Englewood Cliffs, NJ: Prentice-Hall, 1993.

44 Abramson, N. R. "The Leadership Archetype: A Jungian Analysis of Similarities Between Modern Leadership Theory and the Abraham Myth in the Judaic-Christian Tradition," *Journal of Business Ethics*, Vol. 72, 2006, pp. 115–129.

45 Austen, I. "Montreal Mayor Resigns After Bribery Arrest," *New York Times*, June 18, 2013, www.nytimes.com/2013/06/10/world (retrieved April 10, 2017).

46 Su, C., Singy, M. J., and Littlefield, J. E. "Is Guanxi Orientation Bad, Ethically Speaking? A Study of Chinese Enterprises," *Journal of Business Ethics*, Vol. 44, 2003, pp. 303–312.

47 Dunfee, T. W. and Warren, D. E. "Is Guanxi Ethical? A Normative Analysis of Doing Business in China," *Journal of Business Ethics*, Vol. 32, 2001, pp. 191–204.

48 Lane, H. W., Maznevski, M., DiStefano, J. J. and Dietz, J. *International Management Behavior: Leading with a Global Mindset*, 6th edn. New York: Wiley, 2009.

49 Cropanzano, R. and Ambrose, M. L. *The Oxford Handbook of Justice in the Workplace.* Oxford: Oxford University Press, 2015.

50 Beniff, M. and Southwick, K. *Compassionate Capitalism: Can Corporations Make Doing Good an Integral Part of Doing Well?* London: Career Press, 2004.

51 Bossidy, L. and Charan, R. *Execution: The Discipline of Getting Things Done.* New York: Crown Business, 2002.

52 Ibid., p. 5.

53 Musashi, *The Book of Five Rings.*

54 Bazerman, M. *Judgment in Managerial Decision Making*, 4th edn. New York: Wiley, 1998.

55 Rouleau and Seguin, "Strategy and Organization Theories."

56 See de Mente, L. *Samurai Strategies: 42 Martial Secrets from Musashi's Book of Five Rings.* Tokyo: Tuttle Publishing, 2008. Also see Musashi, *Book of Five Rings.*

57 Crossan, M. M., Rouse, M. J., Fry, J. N., and Killing, J. P. *Strategic Analysis and Action*, 7th edn. Toronto, ON: Pearson Prentice-Hall, 2009, p. 80.

58 Porter could be regarded as representing a traditional form of analysis since his theories were published in 1980, more than 35 years ago.

59 de Mente, *Samurai Strategies*.

60 Mintzberg et al., *Strategy Safari*.

61 Ibid.

62 Rouleau and Seguin, "Strategy and Organization Theories."

63 Mintzberg et al., *Strategy Safari*.

64 Berger, P. L. and Luckmann, T. *The Social Construction of Reality: A Treatise in the Sociology of Knowledge*. Garden City, NY: Anchor Doubleday & Company, 1967.

65 Rouleau and Seguin, "Strategy and Organization Theories."

66 Ibid.

67 Mintzberg et al., *Strategy Safari*

68 Ibid., pp. 154–155. Mintzberg et al. used the Myers Briggs Type Indicator (MBTI), while we have used the older Jungian theory that the MBTI was derived from.

69 See Jung, C. G. *Psychological Types*. Princeton, NJ: Princeton University Press, 1976.

70 Inkeles, A. *National Character: A Psycho-Social Perspective*. New Brunswick, NJ: Transaction Publishers, 2015.

71 Massey, B. *Where in the World Do I Belong?* USA: Jetlag Press, 2006.

72 See Berger, J. M. *Personality*, 6th edn. Belmont, CA: Thompson Wadsworth, 2004, for discussion of personality dimensions as genetically based.

73 Beebe, J. *Energies and Patterns in Psychological Type: The Reservoir of Consciousness*. London: Routledge, 2016.

74 See Abramson, N. R. "Do the Chinese Seek Relationship? A Psychological Analysis of Chinese–American Business Negotiations Using the Jungian Typology," *Journal of Global Business*, Vol. 16, No. 31, 2006, pp. 7–22. Also Thompson, H. L. *Jung's Function-Attitudes Explained*. Watkinsville, GA: Wormhole Publishing, 1996. Also, Sharp, D. *Personality Types: Jung's Model of Typology*. Toronto, ON: Inner City Books, 1987.

75 The Keirsey Temperament Sorter (KTS-II) is available for free on the internet at www.Keirsey.com (retrieved September 16, 2016). I ask my students to Google "personality test" and take the free personality test at www.16personalities.com (retrieved September 16, 2016) as a basis for in-class discussion.

76 Career Testing and Career Direction, "How Rare Is Your Personality Type?" www.careerplanner.com (retrieved September 16, 2016).

77 Inkeles, *National Character*.

78 Massey, *Where in the World Do I Belong?*

79 Yuen, *Deciphering Sun Tzu*.

80 Ibid.

81 Liddell Hart, *Strategy*.

82 Nye, *Soft Power*.

83 Ibid.

84 McNeilly, M. R. *Sun Tzu and the Art of Business: Six Strategic Principles for Managers*, rev. edn. Oxford: Oxford University Press, 2012, p. 155.

85 Liddell Hart, *Strategy*.

86 Ibid., p. 147.

87 Ibid., p. 146.

88 Yuen, *Deciphering Sun Tzu*. For the most popular English translation of Sun Tzu, see Sawyer, R. D. *The Seven Military Classics of Ancient China Including The Art of War*. Boulder, CO: Westview Press, 1993.

89 Sawyer, *The Tao of War*.

90 Yuen, *Deciphering Sun Tzu*.

91 Clausewitz, *On War*.

92 Yuen, *Deciphering Sun Tzu*, Kindle version, hence no page numbers.

93 See Qiao, L. and Wang, X. *Unrestricted Warfare*. Beijing: PLA Literature and Arts Publishing House, 1999.

94 Yuen, *Deciphering Sun Tzu*.

95 Ibid.

96 Ibid.

97 de Mente, *Samurai Strategies*.

98 de Bono, E. *Lateral Thinking: A Textbook of Creativity*. New York: Penguin Books, 2009.

99 Yuan, *Lure the Tiger Out of the Mountains*.

100 Sawyer, *The Tao of War*.

101 Mitchell, S. *Tao Te Ching: A New English Version*. New York: HarperCollins Publishers, 2009.

102 Yuen, *Deciphering Sun Tzu*, chapter 3.

103 Quoted from Ibid.

104 Bourgeois, L. J. III, Duhaime, I. M., and Stimpert, J. L. *Strategic Management Concise: A Managerial Perspective*. Fort Worth, TX: Harcourt College, 2001.

12 DOING BUSINESS IN THE MIDDLE EAST

The Orient and Islam have a kind of extra-real, phenomenologically reduced status that puts them out of reach of everyone except the Western expert. From the beginning of Western speculation about the Orient, the one thing the Orient could not do was to represent itself. Evidence of the Orient was credible only after it had passed through and been made firm by the refining fire of the Orientalist's work.

E. W. Said[1]

This is about the revival of the spirit of doing business the Islam way. . . . Muslims must start thinking globally. . . . [to] prevent a total "westernization" of the globe. . . . Islam is the only faith that has an economic system that is well defined and that has proven its efficacy and strength. We have to go back to this system . . . in order to give strength to the Islamic world.

K. Mahmood[2]

After reading and studying the concepts, examples, and illustrations in Chapter 12, readers should be able to understand and appreciate:

1　Islamic expectations about ethical business practices—while not all Muslims are devout, Western business ethics are often divergent and devout Muslims may regard divergent beliefs and behaviors as religiously "evil" as opposed to simply culturally diverse.

2　Middle Eastern practice, especially in Arab culture, favors close personal business relationships based on trust as a precondition to doing business. Western businesspeople should be prepared to build closer relationships than is usual in the West.

3　The Extraverted Thinking (Te) communication preferences (see Chapter 2) found in the US, UK, Australia, Germany, and France are not the norm for any Middle Eastern nation. In Turkey, Israel, and Iraq, Extraverted Sensing (Se) is the norm. In Saudi Arabia, Extraverted iNtuiting (Ne) is the norm. In Iran (and Canada), Extraverted Feeling (Fe) is the norm. This profound difference in communication preferences may lead to many difficulties.

4　The Introverted Sensing (Si) problem-solving style (see Chapter 11) usual in the West is not the norm for any Middle Eastern nation except Iran. Turkey and Saudi Arabia are Introverted Feeling (Fi). Israel and Iraq are Introverted Thinking (Ti). Westerners will have difficulty understanding the problem-solving basis for decision-making, and vice versa.

5　Cultural practices related to business and building effective business relations for Turkey, Egypt, Saudi Arabia, and Iran, with capsule summaries for Israel and Iraq, are provided. It is a goal that readers understand cultural conditions related to business in these countries.

INTRODUCTION

The Middle East has been a meeting point and battleground for competing civilizations for thousands of years. The region is marked by the intersection of three continents—Europe, Asia, and Africa. It stretches from Turkey and Egypt in the northwest and southwest to Saudi Arabia and the United Arab Emirates (UAE) in the south, to Iran and Afghanistan in the east. It is the home of humanities' first stone temple, Gobekli Tepe in present-day Turkey, dated to approximately 9600 BCE, 6,600 years before England's ancient Stonehenge.[3] Three of the world's greatest religions—Judaism, Christianity, and Islam—were founded there and all three claim Jerusalem as their holy city. Known as the Fertile Crescent, it was the heartland of the ancient civilizations of Sumer, Babylonia, Assyria, and Persia along the Tigris and Euphrates rivers in present-day Iraq, and pharaonic Egypt along the Nile.

By 323 BCE, Alexander the Great had conquered ancient Persia, and over the centuries Romans, Parthians, Ottomans, British, and French contested for dominance. In the twentieth century it was the battleground for Israel, Palestine, and the Arab states opposing Israel's existence. Osama bin Laden, leader of Al Qaeda, and responsible for the "9–11" (September 11, 2001) terror attacks on New York and Washington DC, was from Saudi Arabia. The US fought wars in Afghanistan and Iraq as a result. War-torn Syria, with its present-day refugees flooding into Europe and beyond, is a Middle Eastern country, as is the terror group or "caliphate" known variously as ISIL, ISIS, or Daesh. Today, the leading regional powers of Saudi Arabia (Sunni Muslim) and Iran (Shiite Muslim) uneasily face each other over primacy.

The Middle East is nonetheless a promising opportunity for Western business. According to the Global Intelligence Monitor,[4] four of the world's most promising emerging markets are Turkey (#9), Saudi Arabia (#18), the UAE (#21), and Egypt (#22). All the nations with the exception of Israel are Muslim in religion. Many are Arab, though not Turkey or Iran. The purpose of this chapter is to facilitate the entry and long-term prospects of Western business by revealing cultural differences that require a "heads-up" to avoid making interactional mistakes that local businesspeople will find egregious even in a foreign business associate.

The chapter is organized into two distinct parts. First, there are commonalities that exist across clusters of Middle Eastern national cultures that will be experienced as distinct cultural differences by businesspeople from English-speaking cultures (US, UK, Canada, and Australia), and the European Union or EU (e.g., Germany and France). Islam has strong expectations about appropriate business ethics and behavior. Arab culture conducts business in certain ways. In most Middle Eastern cultures, business relationships are closer, communications more indirect, and negotiations more competitive than the norms for Westerners. In Chapter 2 we discussed Jungian extraverted psychological attitude-functions[5] as part of national character[6] that affects predominant communication styles in individual national cultures. In Chapter 11, we discussed Jungian introverted psychological attitude-functions that affected individual problem-solving strategies that again differ by national character in terms of their most preferred styles. The interesting aspect of these psychological predilections for communicating and problem-solving is that for the most part the preferences of Middle Eastern national cultures are entirely different from those of Western cultures. This results in our prediction that there is much potential for cross-cultural conflict. The different approaches to problem-solving and different expectations regarding appropriate communications magnifies the difficulty of reaching agreements.

Second, the chapter provides more detailed consideration of the national cultures of Turkey, Egypt, Saudi Arabia, and Iran, and capsule summaries for Israel and Iraq. These are judged to be areas of greatest interest for Western business, and where there is the most difference.

COMMONALITIES ACROSS MIDDLE EASTERN CULTURES

The influence of Islam on business

Since the seventh century CE, Islam has been the principal integrator among the peoples of the Middle East—a *way of life*, not just a religion. *Islam* is an Arabic word that means surrender or submission to Allah or God. Non-Arabs, such as the Turks and Iraqis, are linked to their Muslim brothers and sisters throughout the world through their religion of Islam.[7]

Islam began in 570 CE with the birth of Muhammad the Prophet in Mecca. In the century following the Prophet's death in 632 CE, zealous Bedouin forces swept out of the Arabian peninsula to impose Islam on vast areas stretching from Spain to the borders of China. The holy book of Islam is the Qur'an (Koran) containing the discourses Allah revealed to his Prophet Muhammad. The main divisions of Islam include the Sunni Muslims in Algeria, Turkey, and Saudi Arabia, and the Shia Muslims in Iran and Iraq. No Middle East visitor, business, military, or governmental, can hope to comprehend its peoples without understanding the powerful religious and cultural force of Islam. Its primary tenets are summarized in Exhibit 12.1.

EXHIBIT 12.1 PILLARS OF ISLAMIC BELIEF

Profession of Faith (Shahadah)—open proclamation of submission that "there is no God but Allah and Muhammad is the messenger of God." At mosques this is chanted five times each day.

Prayer (Salah)—at prescribed hours, worship or ritual prayer five times daily, individually if not preferably in groups. The bowing or kneeling for this is toward Mecca; the Muslim doing this must be pure, hence newly washed and not dirty. Friday is the traditional day of rest, when the congregational prayers of men at midday should ordinarily be performed in the mosque.

Almsgiving (Zakah)—the Qur'an teaches that all believers must give to the needy, and today this is normally a personal act ranging from 2 to 10 percent of one's yearly income.

Fasting (Sawm)—throughout the 30-day lunar month of Ramadan, a Muslim abstains from food and drink, while practicing continence in other respects, from dawn to sunset; in some Muslim countries, such as Saudi Arabia, the obligation is legally enforced.

Pilgrimage (Haj)—at least once in a lifetime, if one is able, a Muslim is expected to perform this act of piety by going to Mecca as a pilgrim during the month of Haj; merit is great for those who go there and perform the rites and ceremonies for 8–13 days.

Some Muslims believe in a sixth pillar, *Holy War* or *Al-Jihad*, offering the reward of salvation. This effort to promote Islamic doctrine among non-Muslims is not necessarily done through warfare as in past ages. All observant Muslims are expected to practice hospitality toward strangers, even "infidels."

To appreciate Islam's worldwide cultural influence, consider the many other countries in which the world's 1.5 billion Muslims are influential. Parts of Europe have large Muslim populations, including Albania, Bosnia, France, Spain, and Russia. There are large Muslim communities in both the US and Canada. In Asia, entire nations are predominantly Muslim (e.g., Bangladesh, Pakistan, Malaysia, and Indonesia). In Africa as well, there are Islamic nations (e.g., Gambia, Morocco, and northern Nigeria). In the twenty-first century, Indonesia is the largest Muslim nation, and Malaysia is known as the model Islamic economic state.[8] Our discussions of Muslim business ethics and practices would apply to Muslims everywhere.

Islamic business versus Western business[9]

Islam views different aspects of worldly life as interrelated parts that should be integrated into a person's spiritual life. Business is one of these interrelated parts.[10] "*Divine guidance*" is a fundamental component of the Islamic economic system. While Western business separates religion from economic activity, Islam establishes a certain set of divine rules on the economic activities of its adherents in an attempt to control individual ethics. This divinity aspect of economic activity of a Muslim businessperson sets him/her apart from a Western businessperson whose main criterion in his/her involvement in business is to maximize benefit and self-interest.

One of the well-known differences between the Western and Islamic systems lies in the financing sphere of economics. Like contemporary economics, the Islamic economic system recognizes both debt and equity financing. Unlike contemporary economics, the Islamic economic system forbids a lender to charge a predetermined rate of interest irrespective of the economic circumstances of the borrowers. Thus, "interest" is prohibited.

Instead, Islam supports "musharakah." In these contracts, both the entrepreneur and the investor supply capital to a joint venture. Profits and losses are borne by both partners based on a predetermined ratio to be negotiated, but the ratio does not necessarily coincide with the relative financing inputs. Islam also supports "mudarabah," which is a partnership agreement in which a partner (the investor) allocates money to the other party (the entrepreneur) who is in charge of business activities and management. For a mudarabah partnership, it is necessary to determine the proportion of profit going to each party.

Islamic financing is an industry supported by Western business for Islamic investments. The UK is the leading Western country where government policies fully support Islamic products in the banking sector. There are five financial institutions that are fully Sharia compliant, more than in any other Western country. Also, Malaysia, Singapore, and China have recently made significant investments in the Islamic finance industry. In 2010, Islamic financial investments were largest in Iran ($388 billion), Saudi Arabia ($151 billion), and Malaysia ($133 billion).

Islamic management practices

Ahmad and Gazdar[11] maintain that the Qur'an, and its commentaries, define a set of management practices recommended for Islamic business and management for over 1,000 years. They provide guidance on economics, ethics, social organization, and management. Islamic management experts believe that modern Western management practices are slowly converging with these established Islamic principles.

These Qur'an-based principles of management are understood in Muslim cultures to be divine revelations, and entirely free from any practical shortcomings. This is as opposed to Western practices that are open to constant revision on the basis of new research, and where there may be little agreement as to what the "ideal" practices should be.

Ahmad and Gazdar[12] argue that Islam has encouraged all those who engage in business to adopt 40 management principles as a set of consistent guidelines to be applied within all Islamic countries. They observed that Western businesses that have been successful in Islamic countries–Citigroup, Deutsche Bank, HSBC, and Lloyds TSB in the financial sector, for example–have adopted these principles.

Islam tends to promote altruistic rather than self-interested management practices (see Chapter 9). It focuses its attention more on the individual people who manage or are managed, and less on management methodologies. This is because Islam believes that it is the individual people that guide and apply these management methodologies through their motivations, enthusiasm, desires, and emotions. Sixteen "best practices" are related to the qualities of a good manager (see Exhibit 12.2).

It is important for non-Muslims to recognize that some typical and everyday Western business practices contravene these 16 Islamic principles of management. Work is not an act of worship for most secular Westerners. Lawyers may be employed, and court battles fought, after contracts are signed in disputes about what the contracts actually meant in

EXHIBIT 12.2 QUALITIES OF A GOOD MANAGER AS DEFINED BY ISLAM

Qualities	Operationalization
Work as an act of worship	Islam defines taking care of one's family as a duty. Working is therefore an act of worship of God, and must be done in a spirit of commitment and sincerity.
Fulfill all contracts	Islam requires contractual obligations to be fulfilled. Not doing so, or subsequently arguing about terms, is sinful and unlawful. This will ensure justice and fair dealings.
Keeping promises	This is mentioned many times in the Qur'an ("Fulfill promises because you will be held accountable for promises"–Chapter 17, Verse 34).

Qualities	Operationalization
Loyalty to employer	The manager is always loyal to the employer because he/she is under contract. Company secrets are protected from competitors or ex-employees with grudges.
No kickbacks	A manager neither offers nor receives kickbacks, including gifts or business expenses. Islamic practice is to avoid gray areas between clearly lawful or unlawful.
Do not fight for leadership	People who fight or maneuver to be appointed leaders are disqualified as unsuitable. One registers interest through one's career plan, but must be recognized by others simply from the quality of his/her work.
Build trust	Honesty, integrity, reliability, safeguarding confidences, and commitment to justice are required behaviors so that a manager will be clearly trustworthy.
Always be truthful	"There is no charity more beloved to God than speaking the truth" (Bayhagi, www.almoltaga.ps/english/archive/index.php/t−1182.html). It is acknowledged that this is a challenge for salespeople.
Be optimistic	Even if a manager violates an Islamic principle, he/she should be optimistic because sins will be erased if they are sincerely repented and followed up with good deeds.
Admit mistakes; learn from them	Not admitting mistakes is to defy humankind's imperfect nature. Acknowledge at once. Inform superiors so correction is possible. Show sensitivity to those injured. Apologize. Accept responsibility. Develop a superior-reviewed plan of action.
Avoid pride	Pride is defined as "disdaining what is true, and despising people" (Sunan Abu Dawud, Book 27, Hadith 4081). Never conceal the truth or look down on others. Pride results in discrimination against others.
Time management	Control internet time wastage. It leads to a 40 percent productivity loss. Avoid using office time for non-business activities.
Seek and share knowledge	This increases personal and team effectiveness.
Manage anger	Islam advises managers not to become angry, and never to make judgments while angry.
Aim for excellence	Since work is an act of worship, it should be a worthy gift to God.
Be just	Justice and fair dealing is an obligation (Qur'an, chapter 16, verse 90). This includes distributive and procedural justice. Subordinates will be angry if treated unjustly.

Source: Ahmad, S. and Gazdar, M. *40 Islamic Principles for Successful Management*. London: HotHive Publications, 2009.

EXHIBIT 12.2

practice. Promises are more likely to be kept if they are written into contracts. Western managers maneuver for leadership positions, perhaps "shamelessly" in the eyes of Islamic counterparts. Truth is not always spoken, so as to maintain an advantage. Pride is often evident in the clothes, jewelry, and automobiles managers prefer to be seen with. The point is that Westerners may offend Islamic counterparts unintentionally through their normal everyday management and behavioral styles. Westerners doing business with devout Muslims must be sensitive to Muslim management expectations. Nor is it clear who is devout, or not, when Islam is simply the cultural way of life.

The principles in Exhibit 12.2 are reasonably self-explanatory and many are not unlike many Western practices. Confronting evil may need some explanation. A manager who deviates from any of these management principles, including foreigners and non-Muslims, could be accused of "evil" and censured. The Prophet Muhammad stated that the best response to evil was to confront it and take steps to establish justice in its place. Second best, if one did not have the power or authority to confront, was to speak out against evil. Third best was to silently condemn and resist, passively or actively. Westerners may unknowingly be silently resisted based on behaviors considered entirely normal in the West.

Islamic leadership

Islamic leadership[13] is similar to Western leadership in resting on either personal power or positional authority. Where it begins to differ is in its definition of the two primary roles that a leader may fulfill in his/her organization. The *servant-leader* sees him/herself as the servant of his/her followers, seeking the welfare of followers and guiding them toward the good.[14] As Greenleaf[15] put it:

> The servant-leader is a servant first . . . it begins with the natural feeling that one wants to serve, to serve *first*. . . . The best test, and the most difficult to administer, is: Do those served grow as persons? Do they, *while being served*, become healthier, wiser, freer, more autonomous, more likely themselves to become servants? *And*, what is the effect on the least privileged in society; will they benefit, or, at least, not be further deprived?

The second legitimate primary role of an Islamic leader is as *guardian-leader*. The Prophet Muhammad defined this sense of leadership as the one who protected his/her community against tyranny and oppression. She/he encouraged awareness of the requirements of Allah and Islam, protecting him/herself against sin (*taqwa*), and promoting justice. Abu Hurairah,[16] an Islamic commentator, wrote:

> The Prophet of Allah (peace be upon him) said: "A commander (of the Muslims) is a shield for them. They fight behind him and they are protected by him (from tyrants and aggressors). If he enjoins fear of Allah, the Exalted and Glorious, and dispenses

justice, there will be a (great) reward for him; and if he enjoins otherwise, it rebounds on him."

The point to note about both Muslim leadership roles is that they require the leader to set aside his/her self-interest in favor of social goods. This is a major difference between Western and Islamic leadership values. The basis of modern Western economic theory, derived from the philosopher Adam Smith, has been that it was possible to derive the best economic benefits for everyone in a society when individuals consistently acted in their own self-interest. The self-interests of all the people in an organization or society created a self-regulating mechanism in the marketplace, or "invisible hand," ensuring an equitable distribution of social benefits. By contrast, the Islamic view is that self-interest is a social evil that must be confronted and discarded in favor of social values as defined by the Qur'an and its commentators. The Chinese Confucian philosophers Mencius and Xunzi also held this view that self-interest was evil (see Chapter 9).

The evident conflicts between Islamic and Western business values and practices may result in Islamic businesspersons feeling uncomfortable doing business with Westerners or even refusing to be recruited as managers in Western enterprises. Exhibit 12.3 describes such a case of a devoutly Islamic Turkish MBA student who decided after completing her MBA in Canada that she could never practice as a Western manager because of value conflicts between her Islamic faith and what she had been taught in her Western MBA program.

Arab culture

For Westerners, another key to a better understanding of the contemporary Middle East is Arab culture. Over 20 Arab countries may be identified as members of the League of Arab States, including Saudi Arabia, Egypt, Syria, Jordan, the Palestinian Authority, the UAE, and Yemen. There are significant cultural minorities in some countries, such as the Egyptian Coptic Christians, who are 10 percent of Egypt's population.

Here are five key distinguishing characteristics of Arab culture:

1 *Arab language*. For Arabs, Arabic is sacred because it was the means by which God revealed the Qur'an to Muhammad. Classical Arabic is used not only by religious scholars, but also the educated and the media. There are many forms of more common colloquial Arabic as well.

2 *Arab values*. In traditional societies, the paramount virtues are considered to be dignity, honor, reputation, family, and courteous and harmonious communications. A shared honor code frequently dictates certain behaviors, especially to preserve the family's reputation. Gender roles differ substantially from the West in Arab societies, which are often ultra-conservative, with women wearing hijab or niqab (veils) in public. The Qur'an does not say that women must be veiled, only that they must be modest

E
X
H
I
B
I
T

12.3

EXHIBIT 12.3 EFFECTS OF VALUE CONFLICTS BETWEEN WESTERN BUSINESS AND ISLAM

A case study of a Muslim MBA business student

It was my first week at the university, as a first-year business student, and I was looking forward to the first lecture with the professor of microeconomics. I remember that I was puzzled by his answer, referring to conventional economics theory, to his own question with regard to the definition of an "Economic Man." He said that "Economic Man" is described as a rational individual who intends to maximize his utility. Based on the "self-interest" principle of economics, if every individual acts in the best interest of him/herself, total and equitable welfare will be maintained in the society. I thought that it would not be possible to maintain welfare in a society where everyone acted in the best interest of him/herself and concluded that the self-interest principle was completely in contrast to the brotherhood concept of Islam which enjoins every Muslim to look after his/her Muslim brothers and sisters.

Furthermore, even someone with a basic knowledge of the Islamic principles would know that we, Muslims, are prohibited to become involved in "haram"[17] business areas, or trade "haram" goods, or earn our living through "haram" means. I would be considered "irrational" in the eyes of a Western businessperson in a situation where I did not take advantage of an opportunity to make a large profit by declining to get involved in haram professions such as contributing to the production or consumption of alcoholic beverages.

Having a business career was a meaningful profession in my eyes because the Prophet Muhammad was involved in trade and he acquired fame as an honest merchant in his society at the time when the Qur'an was being revealed to him. Given that the fundamental principles underlying conventional Western economic theory are in conflict with my religious values, I lost my motivation to function as a businesswoman.

Source: Mrs. Zeynep Kara; formerly an accounting executive at KPMG, Vancouver, Canada branch, and now an instructor at Columbia College, Vancouver, Canada, writing about her experience in the Beedie School of Business MBA program.

in appearance by covering their arms and hair, which are considered sensual. Foreigners at all costs should avoid causing an Arab to lose face, or be disrespected, in relation to these values.

3 *Arab personal distance.* Arabs seek close personal relationships, preferably without great distance or intermediaries. This cultural difference also extends to an Arab facing or not facing another person; to view another peripherally is impolite, so to sit or stand back-to-back is rude. Although Arabs may be very involved when interacting with friends, they may not seek a close distance in conversations with strangers or casual acquaintances. Yet, they are generally a warm and expressive people, both verbally and nonverbally.

4   *Arab sociability and equality.* Cordiality is at the core of this culture. The first business meeting is devoted to getting acquainted, with little regard for schedule or appointments. The traditional greeting is to place one's right hand on the chest near the heart as an indication of sincerity and warmth, though modern Arabs may precede this with a long, limp handshake. There are Islamic taboos against eating pork, drinking alcohol, gambling, and prostitution.

5   *Arab women.* The Arab patriarchal culture places the male in the dominant role, while protecting and respecting the female. In an Arab household, for example, the man is overtly the head, with a strong role and influence. The mother is often the authority "behind the scenes" on family matters. Honorable female behavior implies being loving mothers and daughters, acting in modest and respectful ways, including running efficient and generous households. Publicly, the woman defers to her husband, but privately she may be more assertive. During an interview, Dr. Fatima Mernissi stated: "The whole Muslim system is based on the assumption that the woman is a powerful and dangerous being."[18]

In some Arab countries, women enjoy equality with men, while in others there are severe limitations on their role. In more traditional Arab communities, where mullahs control marriage laws, men are allowed to marry more than one woman, including foreigners. Women may marry only one husband, excluding foreigners. Husbands may divorce without stating a cause, whereas a wife must specify grounds to the satisfaction of the court, and in a courtroom it takes the testimony of two females to equal one male.

There is great diversity within the Arab world on the status of women. Contrast a woman's role in Saudi Arabia, where she cannot drive a car by herself or attend a mixed-gender university or workplace, with that in the Muslim country of Brunei in Southeast Asia. There, women outnumber men at universities, drive automobiles, hold senior offices in both the public and private sectors, and can even serve as ambassadors and airline pilots. Some Muslim women are protesting and working against stifling morality toward greater emancipation for their gender.[19] However, foreign females visiting Arab countries must exercise great sensitivity to what is acceptable or unacceptable in local situations.

Jungian personality types, national character and communication styles

In Chapter 2 we discussed four extraverted attitude-functions that impact communications style preferences, based on Jungian personality theory,[20] that are genetically based and characteristic of all humans-as-species,[21] and part of a nation's national character. National character is defined as a set of psychological dispositions built into the personalities of the individuals that make up a society.[22] In this case, national cultures are characterized by psychological predispositions favoring a specific communication style that differs among Middle Eastern nations, and between Middle Eastern and Western nations. It is not that everyone in a national culture favors just one communication style, but one style is predominant, or most probable to be encountered in each nation.

Thanks to Massey's[23] study of over 100 national cultures, also discussed in Chapter 2, we are able to identify and compare the predominant communication style preference for many national cultures. Exhibit 12.4 identifies the attitude-function communication predilections of eight Middle Eastern nations, plus five referent Western English-speaking and EU nations. Western referent nations are starred (*). Data were not available for Egypt, one of the countries covered in this chapter.

The observation that jumps out immediately is that, with the exception of Canada and Iran, the Western referent nations habitually prefer an entirely different communication style than all the Middle Eastern nations for which we have data. There are bound to be communications difficulties between the two sides, laced with incredulity and frustration. These are genetically based preferences so novice Westerners (and novice Middle Easterners) will assume that almost everybody communicates in much the same way as in their home nation until they discover that this is not the case when they come to the Middle East or deal with Westerners for the first time. We should add, however, that you will always find some people in every culture using all four communication styles. These differences in national preference are just the ones most common.

In the following sections we discuss the differences in communication styles between Se (Iraq, Israel, Turkey) and Te (the Western nations except Canada), and the differences between Ne (Saudi Arabia) and Te. The difference between Fe (Iran, Canada) and Te are discussed in detail in Chapter 18 in the context of Canada and the US, and we refer you there for explanation.

EXHIBIT 12.4 JUNGIAN COMMUNICATION STYLE PREFERENCES FOR MIDDLE EASTERN AND WESTERN NATIONS

Jungian attitude-function	Predominant national preference
Extraverted Sensing (Se)	Iraq Israel Turkey
Extraverted Feeling (Fe)	Iran *Canada
Extraverted Thinking (Te)	*Australia *Germany *UK *USA
Extraverted iNtuiting (Ne)	Saudi Arabia

Source: National preferences derived from Massey, B. *Where in the World Do I Belong?* USA: Jetlag Press, 2006.

Iraq, Israel and Turkey (Se) versus the West (Te)

Se is the communication style predominant in Iraq, Israel, and Turkey. It may be the preferred communication style throughout much of the Middle East, including Yemen and Cyprus. None of our Western referent nations share this preference. With the exception of Canada, the other referent nations all prefer the Te communications style.

The strength of Se is its extraordinary realism and its memory for objective facts. It perceives and remembers virtually all factual data it encounters in and about its external environment, including minute details often missed by others. In discussions, it seeks the specifics and details about every proposal placed on the negotiating table. It is likely to have extremely accurate recall of every trial balloon, offer, and proposal made by its negotiation counterparts; likely more accurately than the recall of its counterparts. On the other hand, it has little interest in complex theoretical explanations, and will not agree to be bound by others' interpretive rules, preferring its own realistic and data-specific interpretations. It may appear disorganized but fully commands all factual elements.

The strength (and weakness) of Te is that while its interpretations are always driven by objective data, facts, or generally accepted ideas, it is generally guided by a theoretical ruling principle that it believes to be right—for example, free trade, fair trade, capitalism, free speech, etc. This ruling principle is perceived to be an objective reality or an objectively oriented intellectual formula that should dictate the behavior of both Te and its counterparts. Te tends to regard objects, people, and processes in black-and-white terms (good or bad) depending on their agreement with the ruling principle, and judge themselves and others with "shoulds" and "oughts." Te understands itself to be logical in its thought processes and is quick to provide its rationale for its proposals and behaviors. Te is driven to plan, organize, direct, and control all aspects of its external environment. It has a strong need for early closure, and forward movement, and does not like to revisit issues thought already to be decided. Te has a strong memory for data, intellectual knowledge, principles, and rules, but may force data into its preferred models, and even discard data that contradicts its ruling principles. Friends may experience Te as "tyrannous" or controlling, but these feelings only develop with personal involvement.

Te and Se will experience predictable communications problems.

1   Te will want to organize and control the interpretation of data, and the negotiation process, according to its guiding principles and rules. Se will reject theoretical guiding principles, and Te rules of conduct. Se will seek to establish its own rules that are limited to the data and not guided or controlled by theoretical principles.
2   Se will have a more accurate memory of actual data and discussions, including Te presentations, trial balloons, and offers. Se will reject Te preference for cause/effect explanations, and Te preference for feeding data into preexisting interpretive schemes. Se will regard Te handling of information as sloppy.

3   Te will regard Se as "bad" when its guiding principles are rejected, and disorganized in its presentations when Te interpretive schemes are ignored or rejected.

In a stressful negotiation, Se will become suspicious of Te motives and engage in officious data-driven hair-splitting. Te will take Se criticism very personally, "hating" the implied rejection, and express themselves with at times uncontrolled emotions.

Saudi Arabia (Ne) versus the West (Te)

Ne is the predominant communication style preference for Saudi Arabia, Jordan, and Afghanistan. It is also quite different from the Te communication style preferences of our Western referent nations, with the exception of Canada, as described in the previous section. The differences between Ne and Te (described above) produce a whole set of different communications problems for Westerners in Saudi Arabia than would be encountered in Turkey or Israel, for example.

The strength of Ne is quite different from both Te and Se. Ne comprehends theoretical complexity easily and is adept at "reading between the lines," intuiting underlying intentions, or seeing the true situation beneath a series of appearances, incidents, or proposals. It is good at flexibly changing directions and compromising to adapt to its external environment. Ne is creative in seeing possibilities, not apparent to others, inherent in objective situations. As a result, Ne engages in constant search for the widest range of possible alternatives, often proposing creative possibilities that have not been envisioned or considered by others. On the other hand, the enthusiasm for ideas and/or projects quickly tapers off into boredom as new possibilities emerge. Ne's focus is on ideas rather than persons. Counterparts perceive Ne to jump back and forth unsystematically between divergent possibilities. There is little expectation of time efficiency. Worst, perhaps, is that Ne memory is not strong in recalling objective data, though it does recall its intuitive interpretations, is subject to information overload, and may remember inaccurately that something was done when they had only considered doing it.

There will be predictable communications issues between Western Te and Saudi (and Jordanian) Ne:

1   Ne rejects Te logic, data, and guiding principles. Ne reads "between the lines," ferreting out Te's real motives and goals that lie, unstated, behind their proposals. Ne proposes alternatives and/or solutions Te has not considered that may violate Te's logic and guiding principles.
2   Te conventionality bores Ne, resulting in inefficient follow-up. Ne unconventionality unsettles Te. Ne will "revisit" issues that Te has regarded as decided and closed.

In a stressful negotiation, Ne feels physically ill, and may experience hypochondria. Te takes perceived criticism personally and may respond with uncontrolled emotional outbursts.

Jungian personality types, national character, and problem-solving styles

In Chapter 11 we discussed four introverted attitude-functions that affect problem-solving style preferences, based on Jungian personality theory,[24] are genetically based[25] and also a characteristic of national character.[26] As with the communication styles just discussed, all humans have one of four of these problem-solving styles, and the predominant style varies by national culture[27] due to distribution differences in national gene pools.[28] Exhibit 12.5 identifies the problem-solving style preferences of the same eight Middle Eastern nations, plus five referent Western English-speaking and EU nations. Western referent nations are starred (*). Data were not available for Egypt, which is also discussed in greater detail later in this chapter.

The main differences in approaches to problem-solving that Western businesspeople will experience in the Middle East are between the Si style that is characteristic of all five referent Western countries, and the Fi style predominant in Saudi Arabia and Turkey, or the Ti style predominant in Iraq and Israel. These comparisons are made in the next two sections. Note that Iran shares its predominant Si problem-solving style with the Western nations. Westerners should have no difficulty understanding Iranian problem-solving approaches once they have acclimatized to Islamic cultural differences and the Iranian Fe communications style (see Chapter 18 for discussion of Fe in the context of Canada).

EXHIBIT 12.5 JUNGIAN PROBLEM-SOLVING STYLE PREFERENCES FOR MIDDLE EASTERN AND WESTERN NATIONS

Jungian attitude-function	Predominant national preference
Introverted Sensing (Si)	Iran *Australia *Canada *Germany *UK *US
Introverted Feeling (Fi)	Saudi Arabia Turkey
Introverted Thinking (Ti)	Iraq Israel

Source: National preferences derived from Massey, B. *Where in the World Do I Belong?* USA: Jetlag Press, 2006.

All Western referent nations (Si) versus Saudi Arabia and Turkey (Fi)

Si is the predominant problem-solving national style preference for our Western referent nations. Westerners doing business in these Middle Eastern nations should expect to encounter problem-solving approaches quite different from what could reasonably be expected in most Western countries. The biggest difference is that while Western Si problem-solving is based on objective information and logic, Fi evaluates on the basis of values that Si tends to regard as extrasensory, and largely irrelevant. Fi, however, does "not tolerate violations of its core beliefs" and "may cut off a relationship because their value system has been threatened, without giving any indication that anything has changed. The other person may not even be aware of what has happened."[29] Exhibit 12.3 is an excellent example of a Turkish Fi problem-solver. She decides not to work as a Western manager despite a Canadian MBA because the Western business values conflict with her Islamic values.

The strength of Si problem-solving is that it is strongly based on objective data absorbed in detail from and about the external environment. Si individuals tend to be astute observers and have "photographic" memories that record and precisely remember all external environment information they have received, as well as all internal interpretations of that information. Si constantly compares information obtained in the past with present circumstances, situations, and proposals. Memory tends to be eidetic in the sense that the underlying meaning or truth of series of events and/or occurrences is grasped and remembered. Memory exists as a precise, organized, and lasting recollection of events and interpretations. Data retrieval tends to be through sequential recall. Processing tends to be logical, data-driven, and impersonal. Si problem-solvers appear to others as calm, passive, rational, and in control of their reactions.

Fi problem-solving tends to be focused on achieving ideal (utopian) values while avoiding apparent realities perceived and judged as harsh. Fi judges business associates, potential alternative outcomes, events, and interactions on the basis of their conformity to deeply held personal value commitments. Fi is unwilling to compromise value commitments to conform with others' perceptions. Memory is subjective, resisting data or evidence inconsistent with values, and data may be selectively remembered, or re-interpreted to conform with value-based expectations. Fi problem-solvers appear to lack visible warmth or friendliness, preferring to behave harmoniously and inconspicuously, with benevolent neutrality, and perhaps a faint trace of superiority because of their inner commitment to what they perceive as a better world.

The most evident differences between Si and Fi problem-solving are:

1   Si has a better factual and logical basis for its problem-solving, but Fi will reject facts and evidence inconsistent with its deeply held values.
2   Fi will resist conforming to the Si logical process and data-driven approach. Fi memory of evidence presented in the past will be inconsistent with Si memory.
3   Trust-based relationships are difficult to attain because neither side actively promotes friendship as a basis for problem-solving.

In the inevitability of a stressful negotiation, Si has a tendency to lose the ability to distinguish between actual and surreal reality, focusing only on negative possibilities, and feeling that there may be "no way out." Fi may become more distant, or engage in "bossy" hostile personal criticism about violation of key values. Fi may also employ faulty logic, or obsessively focus on facts without being able to satisfactorily order them.

All Western referent nations (Si) versus Iraq and Israel (Ti)

Ti is the predominant problem-solving style preference for Iraq and Israel. If Si is primarily data-driven, and Fi is values-driven, then Ti is characterized by its insistence on conceptual clarity in its commitment to finding "truth" and certainty in the midst of ambiguity and diplomacy. Si, the problem-solving preference for our referent nations of Australia, Canada, Germany, the UK, and the US, was discussed in the previous section. Ni, the problem-solving preference for France (and no other national character except Jordan and the province of Quebec in Canada) was discussed briefly in Chapter 11.

Ti problem-solving is characterized by having as its main goal the search for truth and its principles. It employs a logically straightforward process for clarifying the ideas that will guide and illuminate problem-solving prior to considering facts and evidence. New perspectives are considered more important than new facts and data. Subjective ideas useful for ordering facts and their relationships are more valued than the data itself. The strength of Ti is not its originality but its ability to clearly and precisely organize and present existing information. Ti individuals may appear inflexible, stubborn, inconsiderate, prickly, and difficult to influence because they value honesty ahead of relationships. They do not generally back away from ideas even if they are dangerous to relationships or hurtful of others' feelings. They present their logical assessments of situations as they see them, without caring how their assessments are received. Confronted with unexpected information or situations, they may prefer to withdraw to privately consider them. Ti memory is strong in ordering, structuring, and evaluating information into complex taxonomies for comparison with future new data. However, data that do not fit existing taxonomies may be rejected.

Problem-solving difficulties between Si and Ti would include:

1   Si tends to start with facts but Ti insists on starting with clarification of the ideas that will be used to interpret facts, and factual information is considered less important than conceptual organization.
2   Si will have a more accurate memory of relevant information, while Ti may have rejected information that did not fit their understanding of a situation. Ti, is, however, indifferent to others' reactions to Ti analysis and presentation.
3   Relationships will be difficult because neither Si nor Ti problem-solving values building close trust-based relationships, and both employ impersonal analysis that may be insensitive to the others' needs and expectations.

In an inevitably stressful negotiation, Ti may become very sensitive to criticism, and feel a victim of a lack of appreciation and friendship. Si begins to focus only on negative possibilities and to feel there is "no way out" and no way to find a positive compromise.

CULTURAL ASPECTS OF DOING BUSINESS IN TURKEY[30]

Turkey is located at the crossroads of Europe and Asia. Western Turkey is located in Europe and borders several Balkan countries. Eastern Turkey, comprising the far larger Anatolian peninsula, borders on Middle Eastern countries. Due to its strategic location at the junction of Europe and Asia, Turkey has historically played a significant role in bridging Western countries into the Middle East. Over the past several decades, Turkey has unsuccessfully sought membership in the European Union several times. More recently, it has begun to assert membership in, and influence over, the Middle Eastern regions that were part of the Turkish Ottoman Empire until after World War I. These include present-day Syria, Jordan, Lebanon, Israel, and Iraq. At the time of writing, Turkish armed forces are engaged in the war against ISIL (or ISIS) in northern Syria.

The Republic of Turkey was established in 1923 after the last sultan of the Ottoman Empire was overthrown. Mustafa Kemal Ataturk became the first president of the Republic, moving the capital to Ankara and introducing fundamental reforms, including the Turkish alphabet derived from the Latin alphabet and the dress laws. The reforms of Ataturk were intended to lead the country out of its "dark" past into a more Western and secular future. Contrary to other Middle Eastern countries, Turkey adapted a secular constitution and turned its face to the West.

Religion

Turkey, known as *Anatolia* in Roman times, is a secular country with no official state religion, though it is a country where a synthesis of Islamic traditions and Western thought is prevalent in society. Secularism is a fundamental pillar of the Turkish Constitution. Ironically, the Turkish government, with the support of the army, has sought to remove religion from the public sphere since the inception of the Republic. The Islamic headscarf was banned in universities by dress regulations put into effect in 1984 by the High Education Council (YOK). This edict was canceled in 2008.

In many Turks' minds, being secular is viewed as being patriotic to the Republic. Thus, it is highly likely that you will find people with very secular beliefs who do not practice Islam. This is especially likely in metropolitan cities such as Istanbul, Izmir, and Ankara. Alcoholic beverages are readily available across the country, despite being banned by Islam, and are commonly consumed in secular and Westernized social circles. Still, Turkey is a dominantly Muslim country and Turkish culture is largely affected by Islamic traditions. Turks, even those not practicing Islam, respect the Islamic roots of the Turkish culture. They fast at least one day in the holy month of Ramadan and do not drink alcohol on particularly holy days of Ramadan.

Social customs

Turkish culture is a blend of traditional and modern values, sharing stronger ties with the East through traditions and religious values, and connecting to the West through the inspiration of modernity. Turks adhering to Islamic values have more similarities with people from the Middle East with respect to particular aspects of their daily lives than do secular Turks. Still, Turkey may be viewed as a model for outward-looking Islam because even many conservative Turks may embrace modern values.

The following gestures should be noted when in the company of the Turkish:

- Formal forms of address should be used unless you become a close friend of a Turk. Avoid addressing an elderly person by his/her first name. It is regarded as disrespectful to her/his age and life experiences. Add "Bey" (Mr.) or "Hanim" (Miss).
- Shoes are not allowed in the majority of houses because they may be dirty. Slippers will be provided to guests at the entrance.
- An appropriate greeting from man to woman is either a nod or a "dead fish" handshake with as little contact as possible. Avoid offering a handshake to conservative Muslim women, who may be identified with a headscarf or a conservative outfit. As a sign of respect to the elderly, younger people kiss their hand and press it to their forehead.
- "Saving face" is very important both in social life and business interactions. Turks are sensitive to criticism and it is rude to criticize someone in public, as criticism may be seen as hostility. Core values such as shame, honor, and loyalty are important to Turks.

Work values and business relationships

Turks are commonly relationship-oriented in their business dealings. It may take some time for you to close a deal with Turks if you have just started building a relationship, or have not been referred by a mutual friend. Turks usually prefer to do business only with those they know and like. Third-party introductions are key to creating new contacts and widening business networks. Turks would like to establish long-term relationships so it is essential for outsiders to build trust and show willingness to maintain a long-term relationship.

Turkish women in the workforce are growing in number. Especially in metropolitan cities, large domestic and/or international firms employ many young Turkish women. These highly educated Westernized Turkish women are career-oriented and willing to postpone marrying until their late twenties and thirties.

Comparing American and Turkish work values[31]

Turkey scored high on Hofstede's *power-distance scale*, suggesting that Turks "expect and accept that the power is distributed unequally."[32] Subordinates are expected to do what they are told by their superiors. Subordinates are afraid of disagreeing with their superiors and there is little consultation between subordinates and superiors. The boss generally has ultimate decision-making authority over his/her subordinates, and the latter are generally comfortable with the superior's authority.

In contrast, Americans generally scored much lower than Turks in power-distance. This creates the possibility that Americans will behave in ways that may make Turks feel uncomfortable. Rank and status will likely be much more important to Turks than to Americans, and Americans will be well advised to pay more attention to formalities than they would at home in the US. Americans, and other foreigners, that did not visibly respect rank, status, and formalities would seem disrespectful to Turks, and possibly not be seen, themselves, as having high status. Exhibit 12.6 details differences related to power-distance.

The *individualism–collectivism* scale measures the extent to which persons see themselves as individuals whose identity is separate from their various works, or primarily as members of a social group. Turkish culture scored high on *collectivism*—as high as China. By contrast, the US was the second most *individualist* nation after Australia. Turks could be expected to exhibit and expect respectful and loyal behavior between people in the same groups. In more conservative parts of Turkey, group orientation is still so strong that it may be regarded as rude to express your individual opinion.

However, this strong difference between Americans, and other similar foreigners, and Turks means that many American assumptions about managing, motivating, and training personnel must be carefully scrutinized before implementation. Collectivist Turks may feel uncomfortable, or be unmotivated, or even resist management practices based on individualist assumptions. Exhibit 12.7 details some key practical differences.

EXHIBIT 12.6 BEHAVIORAL DIFFERENCES BASED ON POWER-DISTANCE

Low power-distance (Americans)	High power-distance (Turks)
People value independence over conformity	People value conformity over independence
Managers accept support of subordinates	Managers reject assistance from subordinates
Consultative decision-making with subordinates is the norm	Superiors consult with peers but not with subordinates
Subordinates are relatively unthreatened by disagreement with superiors	Subordinates fear authority and avoid disagreements
Subordinates cooperate rather than compete	Subordinates compete for the attention and favor of the superior
Education signals accomplishment	Education signals greater social status
Social policies are intended to reduce inequalities	Social policies support and reinforce inequalities

Source: Drake, B. *Cultural Dimensions of Expatriate Life: Turkey.* Cultural Dimensions Press, 2010.

EXHIBIT 12.7 BEHAVIORAL DIFFERENCES BASED ON INDIVIDUALISM VS. COLLECTIVISM

Individualism (Americans)	Collectivism (Turks)
Individual achievement and earned merit are the basis of social standing	Birth circumstances, ethnicity, and gender confer social standing
Strong social and legal support for individual rights	Legal structures protect group and community standards
People are expected to act on their own behalf	Individuals defer to group interests
Individuals can hold and express unpopular opinions	Individuals cannot express unpopular opinions without threat of sanction
Individual decision-making is admired	Consensus decision-making is preferred; individual decision-making is dangerous
Loyalty to the company not expected; pay for performance is expected	Loyalty to company and superiors is more valued than performance
Individuals work better alone	Individuals perform better in groups
Efficiency and productivity is valued above participation and attitude	Participation and attitude are valued more than efficiency and productivity

Source: Drake, B. *Cultural Dimensions of Expatriate Life: Turkey.* Cultural Dimensions Press, 2010.

Masculinity–femininity, or what has been called *task/relationship* orientation, is the extent to which goal attainment is achieved either by nurturing and supporting people (femininity or relationship), or by controlling and dominating people (masculinity or task). In *task* cultures like the US, individuals are valued because of what they can do. They demonstrate their capabilities through having skills or knowledge, and accumulating power and/or wealth. In *relationship* cultures like Turkey, people are valued for who they are. Their personality, character, appearance, behavior, and family are all part of the equation.

Americans with a strong task orientation want to get the job done quickly and right the first time. They may experience resistance in Turkey, where time is usually taken to get everyone involved in agreement. Exhibit 12.8 suggests some key American–Turkish differences on task versus relationship.

Turkish culture scored very high on *uncertainty avoidance*–one of the highest scores of any country. Turks minimize uncertainty and ambiguity by adhering to social norms and rules. "Strictness of the rules" is an important element in the uncertainty avoidance construct.[33] Turkish business people have a need for rules, formalization, and structure. This translates into resistance to change, structured learning and training situations, and less flexibility in meetings. It also suggests that you need to be patient with your Turkish business

E X H I B I T 12.8	**EXHIBIT 12.8 BEHAVIORAL DIFFERENCES BASED ON TASK VS. RELATIONSHIP**	
	High task (Americans)	**High relationship (Turks)**
	Work relationships more important than social relationships	Social relationships take priority over work relationships
	Family commitments less important than work commitments	Family commitments take precedence over work commitments
	Achievement measured by accomplishment, possessions, power	Achievement measured by friendships, peer recognition, respect
	Demonstrated expertise determines professional recognition	Peer recognition determines professional recognition
	Criticism may be constructive or destructive	Criticism is usually interpreted as negative

Source: Drake, B. *Cultural Dimensions of Expatriate Life: Turkey.* Cultural Dimensions Press, 2010.

partner as it will take some time for him/her to trust you for a long-term business relationship, or to make a decision. By contrast, Americans scored low on uncertainty avoidance. Exhibit 12.9 indicates some likely differences between Americans and Turks due to this work value.

EGYPT

Ancient Egypt was one of the five cradles of human civilization, along with ancient Anatolia, Sumer, the Indus Valley in India, and China. Its earliest settlements, found by archeologists, date to 3500 BCE. The great pyramids at Giza were built between 2600 BCE and 2500 BCE. Later, Egypt was a rich and prized possession for many empires, including the Assyrians, Babylonians, Persians, Greeks, Romans, and even the French under Napoleon, and the British in the twentieth century. Egypt gained its independence from the British in 1953.[34]

The people and their homeland

Most of Egypt is high, dry plains, rugged hills, and mountains, stretching along the Red Sea Coast to the valley of the Nile, with desert beyond to the west. The population of the Old Kingdom was less than two million; today's Egypt has more than 85 million, who are 90 percent Sunni Muslim and 9 percent Coptic Christian. The official language is Arabic, but English and French are widely understood because of the colonial past.

EXHIBIT 12.9 BEHAVIORAL DIFFERENCES DUE TO UNCERTAINTY AVOIDANCE

Low uncertainty avoidance (Americans)	High uncertainty avoidance (Turks)
Readiness to accept and take risks	Strong reluctance to take risks
Emotional resistance to change is low	Change is resisted emotionally
Loyalty to boss only concerns personal relations	Loyalty to boss determines personal success or failure
Conflict accepted as normal; losing a round is OK	Conflict is a threat because you could lose
Compromise is an acceptable outcome from conflict	Compromise is a sign of weakness and the same as losing
Formal rules can be broken with sufficient reason	Only the highest in authority can break rules
Career changes are growth opportunities	Career changes are evidence of failure or inability
Managers expect to give direction and offer support	Managers are expected to give and enforce orders
Subordinate initiative is valued and supported	Subordinate initiative is feared and discouraged

Source: Drake, B. *Cultural Dimensions of Expatriate Life: Turkey.* Cultural Dimensions Press, 2010.

Political and social conditions

After the late President Sadat signed a peace treaty with Israel (March 25, 1979), brokered by US President Jimmy Carter, Egypt was for many years both the target of Arab economic reprisals and the recipient of significant foreign aid from the US. To curb attacks of Islamic militants in the area, President Mubarak hosted a summit in Cairo at the beginning of Ramadan in 1995. Prime Minister Yitzhak Rabin of Israel, PLO leader Yasser Arafat, and King Hussein of Jordan joined him in the pursuit of elusive peace and prosperity for the Middle East. In a collective communiqué, "The four parties condemned all outbreaks of bloodshed, terror, and violence in the region and reaffirmed their intentions to stand staunchly against and put an end to all such acts." Ironically, Rabin was assassinated that same year by a Jewish fundamentalist who opposed this reconciliation. But Egypt has continued to cooperate as a peace-broker in a region where nations have more to gain by peaceful collaboration than from continuing conflict.

In 2011, as the "Arab Spring" movement for democracy swept through the Middle East, the Mubarak government was overthrown by a nonviolent peoples' uprising that the army did not attempt to quell. Mohammed Morsi, the candidate of the conservative Muslim Brotherhood, won in a democratic election despite the active protests of the secular minority. The army deposed Morsi within a year due to a general fear that he intended to impose conservative Muslim Sharia law as part of a rewritten Egyptian constitution. Morsi had also allowed persecution of Egypt's Coptic Christian minority. The army continues its rule in 2016.

The economy and business[35]

Egypt is a relatively poor country with a GNP (PPP) of only approximately $538 billion in 2012, and a per capita GDP (PPP) of $6,700; 20 percent of the population live below the poverty line. Its workforce of 27.3 million currently suffers from 12.5 percent un-employment.

In 2012, Egypt exported only $8.4 billion of goods—mainly petroleum products, cotton, textiles, metal products, chemicals, and processed foods. These were primarily received by Italy (8.7 percent), India (7.3 percent), Saudi Arabia (6.1 percent), the US (5.2 percent), and Turkey (4.9 percent). Egypt imported $58.8 billion of goods—mainly machinery and equipment, food products, chemicals, wood products, and fuels. These came primarily from the US (10.7 percent), China (9.1 percent), Germany (6.3 percent), Italy (5.1 percent), Kuwait (4.7 percent), and Turkey (4.4 percent). Egypt's trade balance is a concern, given that in 2012 its reserves of foreign exchange were only $15.3 billion.

Social life

This is oriented toward extended families and public gatherings, with a strong sense of distance. Prepare for a slower way of life, including decision-making, and a lack of punctuality in keeping appointments. People follow the Islamic calendar. Five national holiday dates are fixed, whereas Ramadan and Islamic New Year are variable since they follow the lunar calendar. The work week is from Saturday through Wednesday, with no business conducted on Thursday and Friday (Muslim Holy Day). Business hours vary, but typically in summer are 8 a.m. to 2 p.m.; in winter 9 a.m. to 1 p.m.; and 5 p.m. to 7 p.m. all year.

SAUDI ARABIA

The Arabian Peninsula is the heartland of Islamic culture. After hundreds of years of subsistence living, a nomadic, patriarchal, and impoverished society has been transformed suddenly into a more prosperous, educated, and internationally oriented one. Within this whirlwind clash between tradition and modernization, the affluent kingdom founded on Islamic principles has experienced cataclysmic change. Popular magazines have described the nation as a desert super-state—a rich, vulnerable, feudal monarchy being hurtled into the space age.[36] In 2017, Sunni and Arab Saudi Arabia vies with Shiite and Persian Iran to be the preeminent Islamic power in the Middle East.

The people and their homeland[37]

Approximately 90 percent of the Saudi people are Arabs, with a 10 percent minority of Afro-Asians. The kingdom's population has risen rapidly to almost 27 million, with an average age of 25.7. The population is 100 percent Muslim, and Arabic is the official language, though English is widely used for commercial activities. The country occupies four-fifths of the Arabian Peninsula, a landmass of 850,000 square miles, making it geographically one of the largest countries in the region. Geographically, it is a harsh, rugged, desert plateau. Saudi Arabia is reputed to have the greatest oil reserves of any nation, at 261.8 billion barrels.

Riyadh, the royal capital of some 3.5 million, is a modern desert city with new freeways, hospitals, schools, shopping malls, and one of the largest airports in the world. The Red Sea port city of Jeddah is the nation's leading commercial center and hub of the country's 8,000-mile highway system. Jeddah's huge $10 billion airport handles the two million Muslim guests annually en-route to Saudi holy places such as Mecca.

Political and social conditions

Abdullah bin Abdul Aziz, the sixth king of the Saud dynasty, rules today with assistance from a royal family of some 30,000, of whom 7,000 are "princes." About 500 princes are in government service, but only around 60 are thought to be involved in decision-making. Tribal connections are maintained through the Saudi National Guard. The combined wealth of the Al Saud family is estimated to be in the hundreds of billions of dollars.

In Saudi Arabia, Islam permeates Saudi life—Allah is always present, controls everything, and is frequently referred to in conversation. The kingdom follows a form of strict Islamic conservatism called *Wahhabism*.[38] It is among the most restrictive of Sunni Muslim states. Islamic Sharia law governs national life and behavior. A judiciary interprets and advises the king on this law and in other matters. Seven hundred judges preside over the Sharia courts, the backbone of the legal system, but the bane of reformers. The *Majlis al-Shura* is a consultative council of 100 appointed members, broadly representative of the kingdom's diversity, except it excludes women. Although there are no elections or legislature, the king and his provincial governors of provinces govern by consensus, but with absolute authority. It is a system based on trust. Any citizen may receive an audience to make requests, or lodge complaints. Internationally, the king opposes Western democracy and its institutions, while gently nudging his country forward on social matters without unduly offending conservatives.

The role of women

Islam limits the number of wives a man may have by imposing restrictions on divorce, and ensuring a woman's rights to property and inheritance from her husband or father. Men may divorce their wives with a simple oath, while women must plead before an all-male, extremist

Wahhabist judiciary, and mothers have no right to custody of the children. Husbands may deny wives the right to travel, work, or study at university. Following the impact of the first Gulf War with Iraq, women began a quiet revolution.

With advanced education, Saudi women have begun to enter the business world and the professions, especially teaching, along with social and public services. Though women today make up over half of university enrollment, they number only a fraction of the workforce. The so-called invisible women are said now to control as much as 40 percent of private wealth, much of it inherited under the law. Despite social limitations on women, as well as bans on their driving, travel, and political activity—all enforced by the *mutawa* or religious police—cosmopolitan female Saudis slowly forge ahead.

The economy and international trade[39]

The Saudi economy is oil-based, and the government exercises strong controls over major economic activities. In 2012, the GDP was $740.5 billion, with a growth rate of 6 percent, a GDP per capita of $25,700, and a 10.7 percent unemployment rate. The country exported a value of $381.5 billion, mainly petroleum products, to Japan (13.9 percent), China (13.6 percent), the US (13.4 percent), South Korea (10.2 percent), India (7.8 percent), and Singapore (4.8 percent). It imported $136.8 billion, primarily machinery, foodstuffs, chemicals, vehicles, and textiles, from China (12.8 percent), the US (11.9 percent), Germany (7.1 percent), South Korea (6.0 percent), Japan (5.6 percent), and India (4.9 percent). In 2015–16, the Saudi government planned to diversify its economy from its reliance on oil due to Western concerns regarding climate change.

International political issues

In the political caldron of the Middle East, Saudi Arabia is the main Sunni banker and power-broker that confronts Shiite Iran with the help of its staunch ally, the US. Saudi Arabia supported the Allied consortium that dislodged Iraq from its occupation of Kuwait in the First Gulf War, and again in the Second Gulf War when Saddam Husain was overthrown. The Saudi position on Israel has been relatively moderate, though it supports the movement for a Palestinian homeland. American troops have protected Saudi Arabia from its regional enemies. While many American troops have been removed, the country is criticized by fellow Muslim nations because of its eight decades of close ties to the US. Osama bin Laden, the former leader of Al Qaeda, was originally a Saudi dissident.

IRAQ REVIEW

Iraq is another Islamic Arab state. It is the land of ancient Mesopotamia, between the Tigris and Euphrates rivers. The ancient city of Babylon was located here, with a population reputed to have been as high as 500,000 in its heyday—2,400 years ago under King Nebuchadnezzar.[40] Ancient Sumer was also located in what is now Iraq.

In 1921, the British established Iraq as a monarchy with a figurehead king. The new political entity was created out of three Ottoman, ethnically diverse provinces—Shiite, Sunni, and Kurd. An army coup installed dictator Saddam Hussein, a Sunni, in 1979. He fought a war with the Iranians, practiced genocide on his own citizens, and invaded Kuwait in 1990. This provoked UN sanctions, and two invasions by the US and its coalition partners—the Gulf Wars of 1991 and 2005—in which the regime and its large armed forces were quickly defeated both times.

The occupation of Iraq by American and coalition troops triggered a serious insurgency by locals and foreign terrorists. While the majority of the population was Shiite, much of the subsequent terrorism was Sunni in origin, trying to maintain some semblance of its former influence under Saddam Hussein, a Sunni. Saddam Hussein was eventually captured, put on trial, and executed by the new democratically elected government. Iraq's majority are Shiite Muslims who share power with the minority Kurdish Islamic parties and some Sunnis who together govern along ethnic and sectarian lines. In recent years, Shiite and Kurdish Iraq have been locked in combat with Sunni Daesh for control of north-central Iraq. Daesh, or ISIS, is rumored to be composed in part of former army officers of the army of Saddam Hussein, decommissioned by the US after the Second Gulf War.

Iraq's population of approximately 32 million is 97 percent Muslim (Shia 65 percent, Sunni 32–37 percent). Ethnically, the population is 75–80 percent Arab, with a Kurdish minority of approximately 15–20 percent. Both Arabic and Kurdish are official languages.

The Kurds in Iraq have gained a measure of autonomy and peace for their mountainous northern region, and are currently cooperating with the central government in Baghdad. Their goal is to control some nine billion barrels of crude oil in Iraqi Kurdistan, and eventually gain independence to form a new state for Kurds within the borders of Syria, Turkey, and Iran—something vehemently opposed by those three nations.

In 2012, Iraq exported a value of $88.3 billion, mainly petroleum, to India (22.5 percent), the US (22.3 percent), China (13.4 percent), South Korea (11.7 percent), and Japan (4.8 percent). It imported $ 56.9 billion, mainly food, medicines, and manufactures, from Turkey (25.3 percent), Syria (18.3 percent), China (11.7 percent), and the US (7.4 percent).[41]

IRAN REVIEW[42]

A businessperson or other visitor to Iran is "welcomed graciously," which is part of the Iranian and Persian tradition for thousands of years, as a center of trade and civilization. Iranians have a deserved reputation as skilled negotiators who rely on charm and being informed, and seem to enjoy the "art of bargaining." Traditionally, Iranian and Persian culture respects cultivation of relationships as part of deal-making, to get acquainted while determining the "value" of what is being bought and sold. Iranians know how to insure they are "not put in a position of weakness relative to the other" during a negotiation or the outcome. But after the end of P5+1 (UN Security Council + Germany) sanctions (except the US), Iran's priority is to develop its economy—e.g., oil, energy development, and solar power. Chinese and European companies, and MNCs like Royal Dutch Shell, are now involved in Iran. Iran welcomes companies of all sizes, and individual businesspersons.

However, Iran's intent to quickly revive its economy should not be assumed to be an opportunity to take advantage, just as Iran's low-key graciousness is sometimes misread. It is advisable, as usual, for foreign businesspersons to be alert in negotiations, to aim to encompass the interests of both sides, and to expect the "repartee gamesmanship" Iranians excel at. There are reports from experienced foreign businessmen that before the Iranian Revolution an agreement finalized would sometimes be merely a plateau for the Iranians to then start more bargaining. Iran has rushed to finalize new agreements with incentives.

Iranians routinely "emanate goodwill" and confidence, which may reflect conditioning for centuries that Iranians foster loving ties with family and friends; and are considerate and disciplined workers; and habitually rely on "dialectical problem-solving" to seek consensus when there is dispute. The society also fosters maintenance of citizens' active devotion to Islam.

Each Iranian acts as a part of the cohesive society, at once humble as a good Muslim, and proud of the history of Iran and Persia as a continuous great civilization known for learning, trade, poetry, and fine arts including sculpture and uniquely exquisite rugs and miniature paintings never surpassed. The richly detailed lyrical complexity of Persian arts and the intricate designs of Islamic architecture and Koranic calligraphy are a visual embodiment of the grace, lyricism, and disciplined emotional expressiveness of the culture—also manifest in the manners and sensibility of the people.

Iranians are highly educated and proud of Iran's modern capabilities with advanced technology, and they particularly object to insinuations that Iran is not equal to other nations. Iran's missile and nuclear development is in part aimed to prove that Iran deserves acceptance as a respected regional power. A foreigner seeking to do business would often be brought into a friendly personal relationship that may include going to the Iranians' home for tea and food, to build bonds of trust. He would thus be ushered into the Iranians' world of solid ties that would include expectations of respect and fidelity. Iranians are sensitive to slight, impoliteness, or comments deemed to "belittle" Iran. They object to what they deem "mistreatment" of Iran for many decades.

Iranians can be misjudged due to their embrace of "dichotomies." For example, Iranians see no contradiction between their orientation to being highly rational and pragmatic, and belief in the mystical power of Shiia Islam. Iranians accept the necessity for the public "shared social space" to be strictly guarded to foster Islamic piety, including rules for dress and behavior, yet at home Iranians may dress casually and dance (some Westerners have deemed that hypocrisy but Iranians disagree). Iranians respect and promote equality, and also accept hierarchy. They respect differences in power but reject condescension in communication and expect "person-to-person" problem-solving in mutually respectful dialogue despite differences. They value friendship, and like mixing friendship with business. They often have strong and clear beliefs (sometimes doctrinaire), while being known as patient, restrained, calm, and charming (national traits). Iranian culture is evident in all religious and ethnic groups.

Iranians value honesty and moral virtue, which are tenets of Shiia Islam, but Shiites also have a tenet, "Takiyya," that "permits deceit" if one is threatened (which developed historically when Shiites were targeted to be killed for their beliefs). Many Shiites believe that being a good Muslim is a righteous path that can transcend evil and bring Divine harmony into daily life, with good works and loving relationships and spiritual emphasis.

A foreign businessperson creating a partnership with Iranians should be respectful of Iranian sensibilities, and how Western "spontaneous habits in friendship" would be antithetical to Iranian culture. Thus effort should be made to avoid "being loud, raucous, crude, cursing, drinking alcohol, making sexual references or sexual advances, or joking about Iran or Islam." What Iranians deem sacred is a central concern and includes the primacy of Islam, the privacy of females and children, and protection of Iranian national honor.

The secret of successful business ventures in Iran is to balance the subjective and objective—personal rapport and connection in friendly respectful relationships; and coming to clear agreements without ambiguity, using an international lawyer who knows the law of Iran, and US law, and that of his home nation. Written contracts are still essential (and are also required by Shiia Law) with good translation and no ambiguity. Experts advise a foreign investor to use a neutral bank, ideally Swiss, getting a Letter of Credit guarantee, and Americans should contact OFAC at the US Treasury Department. Iranians are known for perseverance, and strategic wisdom, and they believe they can develop their economy despite ongoing US sanctions with the help of friendly nations.

A Western approach to negotiating terms for agreements often assumes that a more powerful nation can impose what it wants, as if it is the center of a transaction and the other side's role is to capitulate (a "Copernican" orientation that Iranians usually resist, but now their priority is to attract many new business partnerships to help counter residual or new sanctions). Iran ordinarily favors creating business relationships in which transactions reflect both sides' concerns from the start, each side aiming to bridge both sides to achieve consensus, noting "how one side's position contributes to the other side's relative position" (a "Heisenbergian" orientation).

In Iran, religious devotion is part of a strategy of "maintaining good relationships" in the "shared social space" of the community, that supports "being a good Muslim" and worship of Allah that brings the Divine into daily life. Effort "to be morally virtuous" is part of the mindset of all, and insures social decorum, with habits of responsibility and reliability; being considerate and fair; treating fellows excellently and courteously; being gracious and polite with unusually harmonious social interactions; working effectively; and following codes of dress and behavior that protect the communities' affirmation of piety. Such values are the bedrock of Iranian society for centuries and is the strength of Iranian society. Those Iranian character traits can be of benefit to any foreign business based in Iran.

Iranians are free-spirited, which may result from their convictions, solidarity as a nation, routine personal discipline, and acceptance of authorities and rules that proscribe an Iranian Shiia Islamic way of life. Iranian young men can be seen congregating in groups, without arguments, with modulated exuberance, and innocent freshness. Iranians rarely suffer from "Western psychological problems."

A potential difficulty for a foreign businessperson is to adjust to the strict decorum expected in the Shiia Muslim "shared social space" that is a central feature of Iran, for Iranians and visitors. All are part of the shared social space, which is organized to foster Islamic principles of "how things should be done." The majority of Iranians are Shiites and their focus is to seek to "be a good Muslim"–in mind, heart, and action, and to follow the 5 pillars of Islam, including prayer 5 times a day. The act of prayer furthers cultivation of good thoughts and "purity of consciousness," and to counter evil and temptations, and guide "right action"–the goal being *to emulate Mohammed* ["peace be upon him"–a phrase that Muslims expect must follow mention of the Prophet's name in writing or speaking; a rule among the devout anywhere as a sacred obligation]. In prayer, each Muslim offers himself to Allah in complete submission, seeking "oneness"–without an intermediary.

Principles and goals of Islam are inseparable from "the doing," praxis. Iranians believe that: the sum total of everyone's efforts to be a good Muslim is a positive force that unites them and empowers them to make a society that is good for all. The foreign businessman who can affirm this "way of life" will find Iranians make good business partners and employees.

Dress and behavior of Iranians–and foreigners–is thus uniformly "non-provocative" and neutral. Men wear dark, loose clothes, high necked; the top garment or jacket should cover to mid thigh over loose pants. Women dress in ankle-length robes or skirts of any color that shows no body shape, and a headscarf. Only the face and hands are personal adornment. There is almost complete absence of what government and religious leaders reject as "Western decadence" including promotion or allowance of "values of narcissism, entertainment that lauds crime, violence, sexual immodesty and promiscuity, the trivial and frivolous, and commercialism". Such "Western decadence" is deemed to "dilute the spiritual core of the person." Without such distractions, a "concentrated persona results" and the fundamentals of the personality can be freely expressed in the narrowed spectrum of what is permitted. The religious Iranian may thus be regarded as vividly expressive with a glow of "spiritually concentrated consciousness"–a phenomenon also seen in people who live in other religious communities.

Some women have businesses in Iran; a foreign businesswoman will be a pioneer, and should have impeccable credentials and demeanor. The Koran affirms the equality of women.

Some young people wonder if they are "missing something" and they use the Internet and are interested in Western culture. But it is telling that Iranian students who attend school in the West stay in groups and follow Iran's cultural norms, and do not give up their cultural restraints. Education is valued, and is universal and respected in Iran, family ties matter and children respect their parents' views and expectations, and Islamic strictures to "avoid temptation."

Iran seeks good relationships with foreign businesspersons while also protecting its values and culture. A foreign businessperson would be the emissary of foreign culture that could be subversive and disrupt the balance Iran has achieved in protecting Iran from foreign influences that undermine Islam and Iranian traditional culture. Whoever does business in Iran will be instrumental in enabling Iran to develop its economy and knowledge, with foreign investment a factor, but without Iran having to sacrifice its own culture and religious beliefs.

ISRAEL REVIEW

Israel[43] is the only predominantly non-Muslim state in the Middle East. It was founded in 1948, by a UN Resolution, as a Jewish homeland for Jews that had survived the Nazi Holocaust during World War II. This represented the re-establishment of a Jewish state that had existed from the time of King David (1000 BCE?) to the Roman expulsion in the first century CE.

The Arab states surrounding Israel launched wars to eradicate the Jewish state in 1948, 1956, 1967, and 1973. Israel won these wars but peace has never been fully achieved because Israel has continued to occupy territories that the Palestinian refugees–the descendants of Palestinians who fled Israel during the 1948 war–claim for themselves for a Palestinian homeland. Currently, there are two territories–Gaza and the West Bank–with limited Palestinian self-rule under the authority of the Israeli government. The establishment of a full peace has defied solution because, on the one hand, Israel has claimed territories on the West Bank to protect itself from Palestinian terrorists that see themselves as freedom fighters. On the other hand, these Palestinian terrorists and their allies in Iran, Syria, and other nations, have refused to declare Israel's right to exist as an independent Jewish state. A sticking point has been the refusal of Israel to cede the old city of Jerusalem as part of a peace agreement. The old city contains the most revered sacred spot of Judaism–the Wailing Wall–that Jews were forbidden to worship at when it was part of Jordan in 1948–1967. Israel has sworn never to part with the Wailing Wall, come what may.

In 2013, Israel's population of 7.7 million was 76.4 percent ethnic Jewish, the remainder being mostly Arab. Hebrew is the official language, though Arabic is officially recognized for the Arab minority, and English is common. The main religions are Jewish (75.6 percent) and Muslim (16.9 percent).

Economy and international trade[44]

Israel has a First World technologically advanced economy. Recent natural gas finds off its Mediterranean coast have offered it energy security despite Arab hostility. In 2012, its GDP was $247.9 billion, with a per capita GDP of $32,200, and a 2.9 percent growth rate. However, 23.6 percent of the population lived under a poverty line of $7.30 per day. In 2012, exports of $64.7 billion were recorded, primarily machinery and equipment, software, cut diamonds, agricultural products, chemicals, textiles, and apparel. These exports went primarily to the US (28.8 percent), Hong Kong (7.9 percent), Belgium (5.6 percent), the UK (5.0 percent), India (4.5 percent), and China (4.0 percent). Israel imported $77.6 billion, including raw materials, military equipment, investments, rough diamonds, fuels, grain, and consumer goods. These came from the US (11.8 percent), China (7.4 percent), Germany (6.2 percent), Belgium (6.1 percent), Switzerland (5.4 percent), and Italy (4.2 percent).

Doing business in Israel

Israel's economy is primarily secular. While the suggestions about Islamic and Arab culture made in this chapter would apply to the Arab minority, most Israeli business is conducted on a different basis. It's interesting to see what the Israelis say about themselves. The Israeli Economic and Cultural Office in Taipei offers the following observations for Chinese considering doing business in Israel:[45]

> The Israeli, who is often perceived as being arrogant, aggressive, and pushy, is actually being direct and honest. And the American, European, or Asian, who are seen by the Israeli as being artificial, phony and weak are actually displaying politeness and respect. If both sides are to go into a commercial venture, without taking the time to understand each other's cultural traits, they are heading for disaster. . . .
>
> Israeli society is what is referred to as a polyphonic culture (relationship-oriented), in contrast to American, Taiwanese, British, or German culture, which are monochronic (rule-oriented). In the relationship-oriented Israeli culture, feelings and emotions are primary, while intuition and objective facts are secondary! Israeli culture can be viewed as witnessing one large family. In a family, one can dismiss formality and act in a direct, immediate and honest fashion. What can be excused in a "family" as being direct is often interpreted outside of the family or Israel's borders as being rude or impolite.

Recommendations for dealing with Israelis include the following:

- *Greetings.* Israel is a very touchy and feely society. However, they do not usually shake hands. Physical contact is made with a smile and direct eye contact. Israelis may stand closer to you than you feel comfortable with. If you step back, however, communications will not be as smooth.

■ *Gestures*. Israelis signal readiness for immediate action by sitting, leaning forward, ready to stand. If they lean back, hands crossed behind their heads, this is a sign of greater informality and improved relationship. If they place their hand up, palm toward their body, and shake it, they are signing "Please wait a moment."

■ *Time*. Israelis, especially Sabras (but not usually Israeli Arabs), are impatient. Meetings can be spontaneous. Punctuality is relaxed and you should allow 15–20 minutes in case a contact is late. Israelis will not "do" breakfast or lunch. They may prefer to eat in their offices while meeting. During a meeting, an Israeli may take phone calls and speak to others about other matters. This is not intended as rude, impolite, or arrogant. Israeli society is very informal and Israelis normally multitask.

■ *Social occasions*. Find out if your Israeli counterpart is religious or "observant." If so, respect their values and go to a "kosher" restaurant. Do not speak about the Israeli government, politics, or religious issues. If they do, be a good listener.

■ *Negotiations*. Be prepared for tough but friendly negotiations. Israelis love to bargain and their first offer may be ridiculously low. Get agreements in writing. A handshake is not enough.

■ *Gift giving*. If you are invited to an Israeli home, it is appropriate to bring flowers, chocolates, or wine. Framed pictures of yourself with your Israeli counterparts are an excellent gift and wall decoration, reminding the Israeli of the personal ties he/she shares with you.

MIDDLE EASTERN REACTIONS TO WESTERNERS

Peoples from ancient civilizations, like Egypt, Persia, Turkey, and Arabia, are proud of their past—its history, art, poetry, literature, and cultural accomplishments. Unfortunately, many Westerners and Asians carry distorted cultural images or stereotypes about people from the Middle East and their contributions to human development. North American and European media have been particularly inept, slanted, and at times false in their presentations about the Middle East and Arabs.

There is deep underlying suspicion in the Middle East against former European colonial powers, especially the British and French, who once ruled much of the area. But insensitive American behavior toward Middle Eastern peoples and their religion explain, in part, reactive "anti-American" campaigns abroad that undermine both political and business relationships. Currently, resentment centers on America as the only superpower capable of military intervention in the region, especially the US coalitions that went to war against terrorism twice in Iraq, support of Israel against Palestinians, as well as against the Taliban in Afghanistan. Both Arabs and Westerners are given to distorting each other's actions, behavior, and beliefs, thus promoting mutual xenophobia. The global terrorist movement among Islamic militants rose partially out of fear of Western culture and values destroying or undermining traditional Arab culture.

As they see us

Seventy percent of the world's oil reserves are in the Middle East. This results in an influx of Europeans, Americans, and even Asians into the region. Here is a summary of the feedback about foreigners from the Arab perspective:

■ Many foreigners express superiority and arrogance. They know the answers to everything.
■ Many do not want to share the credit for what is accomplished by joint efforts.
■ Many are frequently unable or unwilling to respect and adjust to local customs and culture.
■ Some fail to innovate to meet the needs of local culture, preferring to seek easy solutions based on the situation in their own homeland.
■ Some individuals refuse to work through the normal administrative channels of the country, and do not respect local legal and contractual procedures.
■ Some tend to lose their democratic ways when on foreign assignments, becoming instead more autocratic and managing by instilling fear in subordinates.
■ Westerners are often too imposing, aggressive, pushy, and rude.
■ There is frustration over American and European imbalance in support and aid for Israel, in contrast to the Palestinian cause and human rights.

CONCLUSIONS

Peace is an elusive goal in the Middle East. For more than half a century, the central conflict was between Israel's right to exist and the need for a Palestinian Arab state. In 2016, Israel is at peace with its neighbors Egypt and Jordan, but Palestinians still fire missiles into Israel from Gaza, and Israel retaliates. The Syrian civil war shows little sign of ending, with Russia and Shiite Iran supporting the government, and the US and Saudi Arabia supporting the insurgents. ISIS (or ISIL) fights against all sides and has recruited many Westerners to its armies through internet propaganda. The Middle East is, however, critical for world peace and prosperity, so global organizations will continue to seek commercial opportunities and relationships there.

While each country in the Middle East is unique and different, we have provided an overview mainly of differences between a referent group of Western and Middle Eastern nations in terms of their preferences for problem-solving, communications, attitudes about negotiations, and the importance attached to trust-based relationships. We have reviewed Islamic culture and its expectations about business ethics, as well as Arab culture applying as it does to the majority of nations in the area. The Middle East is a promising area for the growth of international business and trade in the twenty-first century, given the emerging economies of Turkey, Saudi Arabia, and Egypt, as well as the high-tech sector in Israel.

MIND STRETCHING

1 Have you ever read the Qur'an, eaten Middle Eastern foods, or made friends with an Arab, whether a Muslim or Christian?

2 Figure out your Jungian attitude/function type for problem-solving and communications. Do a free personality test.[46] Then use Exhibit 2.8 in Chapter 2 to determine whether you are Si, Fi, Ti, or Ni, and whether you are Se, Fe, Te, or Ne. Do the descriptions make sense in terms of how you problem-solve and communicate? Try working with a friend or friends that have both similar and different types to you. Do you work better with people that have the same preferences? Do you have predictable difficulties working with people that have different problem-solving and/or communication styles than you?

3 What major differences do you perceive between Turkey and Saudi Arabia?

4 How could the implementation of synergistic relationships benefit Iran, Iraq, Lebanon, Syria, Palestine, and Israel?

5 What are your reactions to the following quotation?

> Some Western commentators go to great length to portray Arab societies as backward or feeble. … But the West's inability to deal productively with the allegedly simplistic Arab culture actually highlights the weakness of the West's own condescending logic. In reality, there is no naiveté in the Arab world about its centrality in future success or failure of globalization, both geographically and geologically. It will not be, as some commentators claim, left behind.[47]

NOTES

1 Said, E. W. *Orientalism*. New York: Vintage, 1979.

2 Mahmood, K. *Islam Inc.: Rebuilding Islamic Business*. worldfutureonline, 2012.

3 Mann, C. C. "The Birth of Religion," *National Geographic*, June 2011, http://ngm.nationalgeographic.com/2011/06/gobekli-tepe/mann-text (retrieved April 10, 2017).

4 www.globalintelligence.com/insights-analysis/emerging-markets (retrieved April 10, 2017).

5 Hunziker, M. *Depth Typology: C. G. Jung, Isabel Myers, John Beebe and the Guide Map to Becoming Who We Are*. Clayton, NC: Write Way Publishing, 2016.

6 Inkeles, A. *National Character: A Psycho-Social Perspective*. New Brunswick, NJ: Transaction Publishers, 2015.

7 Esposito, J. L. *The Oxford History of Islam*. Oxford: Oxford University Press, 2000. Armstrong, K. *Islam: A Short History*. New York: Modern Library, 2000. Lunde, P. *Islam: Faith, Culture, and History*. Fremont, CA: DK Publishing/Rumi Bookstore, 2002. Aslan, R. *No God But God: The Origins, Evolution, and*

Future of Islam. New York: Random House, 2005. Brown, B. A. *Noah's Other Son: Bridging the Gap Between the Bible and the Qur'an*. London: Continuum International, 2005.

8   Mahmood, *Islam Inc.*

9   This section was written by Zeynep Arslan, formerly an accounting executive at KPMG, Vancouver, Canada branch, and now an instructor at Columbia College, Vancouver, Canada.

10   Khan, M. Z. *Islam: Its Meaning for Modern Man*. Bungay: Richard Clay, 1962.

11   Ahmad, S. and Gazdar, M. *40 Islamic Principles for Successful Management*. London: HotHive Publications, 2009.

12   Ibid.

13   Beekun, R. I. and Badawi, J. *Leadership: An Islamic Perspective*. Beltsville, MD: Amana Publications, 1999. See also Beekun, R. I. *Islamic Business Ethics*. Herndon, VA: International Institute of Islamic Thought, 2006.

14   Kasule Sr., O. H. "Leadership Module, General Theme: Leadership Workshop 1," in *Muslim Leaders' Forum 98 Handbook*. Kuala Lumpur: Tarbiyyah and Training Center, International Islamic University Malaysia, 1998, p. 3.

15   Greenleaf, R. *The Servant as Leader*. Indianapolis, IN: Greenleaf Center for Servant Leadership, 1970, p. 7.

16   Abu Hurairah, in *Sahih Muslim*, hadith no. 4542.

17   Islam prohibits involvement in conventional Western financial services based on interest, speculation, or gambling. Certain food products (pork) and beverage industries (alcohol) are prohibited, as well as the tobacco, weapons of mass destruction, pornography, and cloning industries. Muslims are enjoined to avoid these activities regardless of their apparent self-interest.

18   Mernissi, F. *Los Angeles Times*, June 8, 1990, p. VII/25.

19   Ali, A. H. *The Caged Virgin: An Emancipation Proclamation for Women and Islam*. New York: Free Press, 2006. AlMunajjed, M. *Saudi Women Speak: 24 Remarkable Women Tell Their Success Stories*. Riyadh: Institute for Research and Publishing, 2007.

20   Jung, C. G. *Personality Types*. Princeton, NJ: Princeton University Press, 1976.

21   Von Franz, M.-L. and Hillman, J. *Lectures on Jung's Typology*. Woodstock, CT: Spring Publications, 2015.

22   Inkeles, *National Character*.

23   Massey, B. *Where in the World Do I Belong?* USA: Jetlag Press, 2006.

24   Jung, *Personality Types*.

25   Von Franz and Hillman, *Lectures on Jung's Typology*.

26   Inkeles, *National Character*.

27   Massey, *Where in the World Do I Belong?*

28   Burger, J. M. *Personality*, 6th edn. Toronto, ON: Thompson Wadsworth Learning Nelson, 2004.

29   Haas, L. and Hunziker, M. *Building Blocks of Personality Type*. Eltanin Publishing, 2014, pp. 104, 106.

30   The Turkey country review was written by Zeynep Arslan, formerly of KPMG, and currently a lecturer at Columbia College in Vancouver, as well as an occasional sessional lecturer in the Beedie School of Business, Simon Fraser University, Vancouver, Canada.

31   See Drake, B. *Cultural Dimensions of Expatriate Life: Turkey*. Cultural Dimensions Press, 2010.

32   Hofstede, G., Hofstede, G. J., and Minkov, M. *Cultures and Organizations: Software of the Mind*. New York: McGraw-Hill, 2010.

33   Altuncu, Y., ÖzAktepe, S., and Islamoglu, G. "Preliminary Study for the Development of Uncertainty Avoidance Instrument in Turkey," *Journal of Business, Economics & Finance*, Vol. 1, No. 4, 2012.

34   Goldsmith, A. *Brief History of Egypt*. New York: Checkmate Books, 2008. Bradley, J. R. *Inside Egypt: The Land of the Pharaohs on the Eve of a Revolution*. New York: Palgrave Macmillan, 2008. Sayyid-Marsot, A. L. *A History of Egypt: From Arab Conquest to the Present*. Cambridge: Cambridge University Press, 2007. Brewer, D. J. *Egypt and the Egyptians*. Cambridge: Cambridge University Press, 2007.

35 CIA, *CIA World Factbook 2013*, www.cia.gov/library/publications/the-world-factbook (retrieved April 10, 2017).

36 Bowen, W. H. *The History of Saudi Arabia*. Westport, CT: Greenwood Press, 2007. Vivano, F. "Saudi Arabia on the Edge," *National Geographic*, October 2003, pp. 22–23. Al-Rasheed, M. *Contesting the Saudi State: Islamic Voices from a New Generation*. Cambridge: Cambridge University Press, 2006. Rodenbeck, M. "A Long Walk: A Survey of Saudi Arabia," January 7, 2006, 12-page insert, www.economist.com/surveys (retrieved April 10, 2017).

37 CIA, *CIA World Factbook.*

38 "Analyses – Wahhabism: Saudi Time Bomb?" www.pbs.org/pages/frontline (retrieved April 10, 2017).

39 Ibid.

40 http://truthmagazine.com/archives/voulume44/V44021708.htm (retrieved November 7, 2016).

41 CIA, *CIA World Factbook.*

42 The Iran review was written by Galeyn Remington, Chairman of GRPI Pre-Negotiation Initiatives. Remington was pioneer of pre-negotiation strategy in 1981–1982; is a specialist in international and intranational negotiation deadlock; and has experience working on deadlock negotiations in the Middle East (and other international and intranational negotiations).

43 Gordis, D. *Israel: A Concise History of a Nation Reborn*. New York: Ecco, 2016.

44 CIA, *World Factbook.*

45 www.moital.gov.il/NR/exeres/3614E1A7–2D84–4F27-A4DC–3585A6F6450E.htm (retrieved April 10, 2017).

46 Go to https://16personalities.com. As a back-up, use the "Keirsey temperament sorter" (www.keirsey.com/sorter); it's free as long as you do not buy all the reports.

47 Khanna, P. *The Second World: Empires and Influence in the Global Order*. New York: Random House, 2008.

13 DOING BUSINESS IN LATIN AMERICA

The debate over the causes of Latin America's economic failures relative to the success of Canada and the US has been a recurrent focus of Latin American intellectuals, and there are enough explanations to suit everyone. At the beginning of the nineteenth century, they blamed their Iberian and Catholic roots. Around the middle of that century, the shortcomings were attributed to the demographic weight of a native population that was supposedly opposed to progress. At the beginning of the twentieth century, and particularly around the time of the Mexican Revolution in 1910, it was said that poverty and underdevelopment were caused by an unfair distribution of wealth, above all by the peasants' lack of access to land. Starting in the 1920s and accelerating thereafter, "exploitative imperialism" was blamed.

During the 1930s and 1940s, the view was espoused that Latin America's weakness was a consequence of the weakness of its governments. Experience demonstrated in the 1980s that all these arguments were false. So who, in fact, is responsible? One possible, although partial, answer is "the elites," the groups that lead and manage the principal sectors of a society—those who act in the name of certain values, attitudes, and ideologies that, in the Latin American case, do not favor collective progress.[1] Now, in the twenty-first century, there has been no serious conflict between any two South American countries, aside from stand-offs like the 2008 Andean diplomatic crisis. At the same time, almost every Latin American country is constantly at war with itself over its raison d'être, leadership, resources, and social stability.[2] Good examples are Brazil and Venezuela.

After reading and studying concepts, examples, and illustrations in Chapter 13, readers should:

1   Be more informed of aspects of the business culture in Latin America.
2   Be aware of some of the strengths of NAFTA for Mexico, the US, and Canada.
3   Be better prepared to work with Mexicans, Brazilians, and other Latin countries.
4   Be committed to learn more about any country in Latin America before doing business in that country.

LATIN AMERICAN OVERVIEW

Latin America extends from Mexico in the north to the southernmost regions of Argentina and Chile that approach Antarctica in the south; it includes both North and South America. It is, furthermore, a region of the world in which Romance languages (principally Portuguese and Spanish) are spoken as official languages. Many countries in this part of the world differ widely in terms of their history, socioeconomic status, education, governance, and society. Regardless, there are commonalties and overlapping cultural themes in Latin American countries, such as the influence of the Catholic Church and shared linguistic heritages: for many, family values and established gender roles are also part of the Latin American experience.

The Americas have been inhabited for thousands of years. However, archeologists do not know the origins of the region's earliest inhabitants.

We will begin our examination of the diverse cultures in the southern parts of the Americas with their Aboriginal descendants, the so-called "Amerindians." Many are descendants of ancient, highly developed people and civilizations, such as Aztecs, Inca, and Maya. Many countries in the region today, including Mexico and Bolivia, have large indigenous populations.

Global and local developers frequently impinge upon the rights and lands of such native people in the name of economic development. Agencies like the World Bank are now demanding the inclusion of programs that protect the rights of Aborigines before they fund economic development projects in the Amazon. Indigenous peoples are struggling to survive civil and guerrilla warfare.

This chapter presents an overview of Latin America, including specifics principally about Mexico, Brazil, as well as some information on Argentina. In addition, information will be presented on the principal cultural themes and conditions that affect doing business in or visiting this part of the global market. Finally, we examine some of the challenges for pan-American cooperation in the decades ahead.

Sometimes the rebels seek haven or recruits among the Indians, while the government troops destroy the native villages. The Amerindians are often caught in the middle of various sociopolitical revolutionary struggles currently taking place regionally, as in Venezuela. As the original European colonies of the last six centuries were gradually replaced by the contemporary nation-states, many of the southern countries of the Americas have failed to keep up in economic development with their rich neighbors to the north, the US and Canada. Despite their natural beauty and resources, the Latin countries have been plagued by poverty, despotic governments, bloody revolutions, and profound social unrest. Part of this has been caused by the financial mismanagement of their enormous natural and human resources, and partly by the unequal distribution of wealth and power that is concentrated among less than 5 percent of the total population—the upper-class, educated "elites." In the twentieth century, some progress was made in the growth of a middle class, the adoption of democracy, and free enterprise, the latter especially because of NAFTA (North Atlantic Free Trade Agreement), the Organization of American States, and MERCOSUR (Mercado Común del Sur).[3] Today, smaller Latin countries can attract the attention of other players in the global marketplace.

In the past, a convenient way to designate economic development in countries throughout the planet was to associate them with the First, Second, or Third Worlds. The First World was composed of the rich nations, such as those that attended the G8 meetings. The Third World was simply the poor, somewhat unstable nations. The Second World was composed of the Eastern Bloc countries formerly under Soviet domination. With the demise of the Soviet Union, many of these post-communist states are transitioning into the "First World" category, especially those that have become members of the European Union. In the geopolitical marketplace, Paraga Khanna suggests a redefinition of the label Second World as the undeveloped swing states that are determining global order.[4] He sees such nations as the tipping point that will determine the twenty-first-century balance of power. There is a shift of influence from the North–South to the East–West. Many of these new Second World states are found in Latin America. They include resource-rich nations like Bolivia, Colombia, and Venezuela, as well as the Andean bloc of countries. The big power investors in these states are now China, Japan, and the European Union, in addition to the US.[5] We end this opening section with a profile of Latin America (Exhibit 13.1) and its diverse people and culture.

In summary, the Latin American people are transitioning in this twenty-first century. They are in the process of modernizing their economies, social institutions, and infrastructures. Because of their cultural heritage, many of these countries are popular as tourist destinations, where visitors may appreciate a wide spectrum of human development—from ancient cities like Machu Picchu in the Peruvian Andes, to the Galapagos Islands off the coast of Ecuador, to nascent space programs in Mexico and Brazil.

EXHIBIT 13.1 LATIN AMERICA: PROFILE

Population landmass

- Approximately 8,134,980 square miles (depending on the definition used)

National cultures

- 19 countries
- One commonwealth (Puerto Rico)
- 13 sovereign states in the Caribbean
- Many indigenous cultures

Major cultural inputs

- Native Indians—descended from ancient, highly developed civilizations that flourished prior to European arrival (e.g., Mayan, Incas, Aztecs)
- European—in most countries, largely Spanish with lesser influences of Germans and Italians; except in Brazil where dominant influence was Portuguese
- African
- Asian—ancient Polynesian influence and some Japanese influence

Sociopolitical developments

- Napoleonic Code of Laws
- Feudalistic societies of Spain/Portugal imposed by conquerors on developed Indian civilizations
- French/Austrian Empire imposed on Mexico, the latter being the center of revolutions in 1821, 1824, and 1838, which impacted South America
- Family-oriented with authority centered in the father and often extended to the "father of the nation"
- Universities and republics from the nineteenth century, with great dependence on military institution controls
- Problems of social class integration—although there was much intermarriage of the races, the powerful elites from an economic/social/political standpoint control and dominate the poor, often peasants of Indian heritage
- Economically and technically developing, and in the process of moving from the agricultural through the industrial stage of development; energy discoveries and development in Mexico can dramatically forge a new relationship with its neighbors
- Despite significant growth in spiritualism and Protestantism, the Roman Catholic tradi-

E
X
H
I
B
I
T

13.1

tion is still dominant, but undergoing a profound role change—instead of traditional support for the oligarchy, many clergy provide some leadership in a movement for social justice

▪ The long embargo between the US and Cuba is over, and both countries have an embassy in the other country

CENTRAL AMERICAN COUNTRIES

On the western side of the Caribbean Sea is a land bridge between the northern and southern continents of the Americas that also borders the Pacific Ocean in the west. The seven nations located between Mexico and Colombia are usually referred to as Central America. The future of these countries depends on whether they can capitalize on their geographical position in order to become a corridor of intercontinental globalization!

If ever there was a need and case for synergy, it is in these Central American states, with some 41.7 million people. The nineteenth-century federation called the Federal Republic of Central America may have been premature, but it provided a cooperative model for the future—if not politically, at least economically. Only by collaboration can this group of countries overcome their chronic poverty, illiteracy, and internal strife. Perhaps local business leaders and global managers may succeed in raising the standards and quality of living for the populace. Sandwiched between North and South America, this strategic area cries out for new solutions and contributions from its neighboring nations, with their Anglo and Latin cultures.[6] Adjoining to the east are the many small island nations scattered across the Caribbean Sea, the largest of which is Cuba.

A hopeful Central American trend is toward greater integration of the nation-states. The region is finally moving toward some form of federal get-together, as the dream of Simon Bolivar. The isthmus' five current free market governments have a Central American Free Trade Agreement (CAFTA); they include Costa Rica, Nicaragua, Honduras, El Salvador, and possibly Panama, with the US and Canada as participants to lower their tariffs on CAFTA exports. Since 1821, the isthmus' seven small countries have been trying to become more unified. What is different at this time is the unstoppable trend toward economic integration from the bottom-up, along with regional business consolidation. The area's growth in financial services and tourism is stimulating modernization of infrastructure, such as joint national projects, like the new container port of La Union in El Salvador. Regional law enforcement is improving in its battle against the *maras*—dangerous, well-organized regional gangs.[7]

Education

Colegios are numerous and offer the equivalent of junior college in the US. Upper classes tend to send their offspring to private schools and universities, often conducted by the orders of the Catholic Church. Although literacy is increasing, many in the overall population do not receive more than a very few years of primary education; notable exceptions are found in the larger countries that provide more education. There is rigorous examination competition for university entrance. Technical education also is on the increase, as well as the use of mass media.

Panama, which has never considered itself a part of Central America, has been spared from regional strife and might become a laboratory, along with Costa Rica, for the creation of models that would influence the other states to join in a regional entity for self-improvement. Application of new techniques to promote social peace and reduce internal political violence, as in El Salvador and Guatemala, should become the concern of pan-American social scientists. Simplistic, anticommunist, and military approaches will not solve the region's problems or tap its vast, undeveloped human and natural resources. China appreciates such resources, so is very active in the region in terms of investment, trade, and building factories.

SOUTH AMERICAN CULTURAL DEVELOPMENT

As the global manager flies over the 12 countries that compose the southern continent of the Americas, he or she is struck by the immensity of this land mass and the potential resources below, especially in Brazil and Argentina. Among the 387 million people living on this continent, nine countries have, in addition to their ancient native heritages, descendants from Africa and Asia, and a European cultural base (e.g., Spanish, French, British, Italian, and Dutch). One nation, Brazil, enjoys both Portuguese and African languages and cultural influences. Centered between the Atlantic and Pacific Oceans, South America is shaped like an elongated triangle of some seven million square miles that extends down to the apex of Cape Horn.

South America is a place where we can simultaneously be amazed at the beauty of the pre-Colombian artifacts and civilization, or the very modern and colorful artworks and highrise architecture. Yet, visitors are also appalled by the poverty of the masses and the great wealth of the few, by the violence and terrorism, and by the dominance of a powerful military or dictators. But outsiders are also encouraged by the progress in democratic institutions, education and literacy, health services and population control, changing the images and aspirations of South Americans.

Despite the great diversity in Latin America, there are common themes and patterns. After the development of fairly sophisticated Amerindian civilizations, there was a period of European colonization and exploitation from the fifteenth through eighteenth centuries, followed by wars of independence and attempts at federation during the nineteenth century. Since the early twentieth century, Latin American nations have been engaged in internal and external conflicts. But the last half of that century saw relative peace and significant economic progress among many nations of Central and South America.

With the exception of Suriname in South America's northeast, these countries also share another factor—a Roman Catholic cultural tradition that pervades not only their history but also their way of life and thinking. At first, the clergy protected and educated the indigenous people. Their network of Franciscan, Dominican, and Jesuit missions became agricultural and trading centers and, eventually, the great cities of South, Central, and North America's southwest. With the passage of time and increase in wealth, the Church became part of the establishment, despite the notable successes of priest revolutionaries, like Father Miguel Hidalgo, who espoused the causes of nationalism and freedom for the peasants. As a major landowner itself, the Church has not only supported the oligarchy but also opposed population control, divorce, and social change. The growth of the militant theology and activities in the Latin American Church caused the late Pope John Paul during his visits to the southwestern hemisphere to protest social inequities, while warning the clergy to concentrate on their spiritual mission. In any event, no modern manager operating in Latin America can afford to ignore the Catholic Church as a cultural force. Cooperation and collaboration for social improvement in Latin America will be significantly advanced when business cooperates with all institutions for human development. The new brand of Christianity on the rise there is "Evangelico," principally Pentecostal, with a fundamentalist view of scriptural teachings. In the twenty-first century, Protestants have now risen to 50 million people on that continent. With a conversion rate of 400 per hour, demographers predict Latin American will be newly evangelical before the end of this century.

The "born again" movement matches the transition toward industrialization and urbanization. The religious cultural shift is toward self-reform, spiritual empowerment, and responsibility for improving one's own life now, not just in the hereafter. A powerful tool for this religious revolution is satellite television, beamed southward from what is left of Protestant America's "Bible Belt." Four hundred years of authoritarian Christianity may be overturned in a single generation, and Latin American people will never be quite the same again.

A positive development within South America has been the creation of a partial common market, called MERCOSUR. It originated in 1985 when Argentina and Brazil signed an economic integration agreement. This trade bloc was expanded in 1991 by the Treaty of Asunción, which added Paraguay and Uruguay. In 2006, Venezuela became a full member, while Chile, Bolivia, Colombia, Ecuador, and Peru are associate members without full access and voting rights. This restriction is because these nations are also members of CAN, the Andean Community of Nations, which is a smaller trade bloc. Presently, some 250 million people benefit from this trading security, which has a collective output of $1.1 trillion. Ultimately, it is hoped that all the nations in South America will become associated with this trade and business network.[8] Whether this common market will ever evolve as the European Union did is an open question.

EXHIBIT 13.2 CHINA'S ROLE IN LATIN AMERICA

While the US is losing its influence in Latin America, former outsiders, such as China, are assuming a greater role in hemispheric affairs. Their economies have been growing at a reasonably healthy rate. In 2005, the US presidential administration, opposed by Venezuela and Bolivia, failed again to get a majority for its candidates in the Organization of American States, a 35-country entity. While Washington did succeed in signing a free trade deal with Central America and the Dominican Republic at the Mar del Plata Summit, the presidents of both Argentina and Venezuela made speeches against the US, blaming it for the region's ills.

Meanwhile, China is emerging as one of the largest trading partners of South American countries. China is developing a commercial and strategic presence in the region. It seeks Latin American resources—raw materials, like iron ore, minerals, oil, soy beans—that have significantly impacted the economic growth of Brazil and Argentina. A Chinese firm now operates port facilities at both ends of the Panama Canal and essentially controls that waterway relinquished by the US. China has also renovated Central American ports and factories to expedite delivery of its goods to the US. It assists Latin states with infrastructure improvements and export revenues, so that the local government can improve social safety nets and empowerment provisions. This Asian superpower is offering Latin countries a new way of doing business without a ticket of codes and regulations. Imperialistic *El Norte* no longer rules the hemisphere.

Source: adapted from Parag Khanna's *The Second World*. New York: Random House, 2008. Andres Oppenheimer, "China Topping in Latin America," *Miami Herald*, reproduced in the *San Diego Union-Tribune*, December 30, 2005, p. B8.

The former president of Mexico, Felipe Calderdón, stated the continental challenge well:

> Latin America faces a critical choice between the past and the future, between returning to authoritarian rule or strengthening democratic systems, between protectionism and more open markets, between the wastefulness of populist measures and a responsible balance in public finances.[9]

There is also a growing global interest in the Latin American market, both for exports and imports. Exhibit 13.2 provides one indicator of this trend.

MEXICO[10] AND NAFTA

An informal survey

In 1993, prior to the passage of NAFTA, common people in Mexico, from factory and construction workers to domestic servants, to university students, to professionals, were asked what results they expected NAFTA to achieve. Far from a formal survey, the results were nonetheless enlightening.

Almost everyone said they expected that the selection of consumer goods would go up and prices would come down. Many also hoped that wages in Mexico would increase to a level close to those in the US and Canada, bringing Mexico up to First-World standards. Most thought that this process would take around 25 years, while some believed it could happen sooner. In short, they thought that NAFTA would provide hope, economic development, and a better life for Mexicans. NAFTA was to make Mexico, in economic and social terms, more like its neighbors to the north—a more prosperous society with a larger middle class.[11]

US nationals, on the other hand, were told by Ross Perot to expect a "giant sucking sound" from jobs leaving the US. Canadians believed they had already seen the loss of jobs to the US after the implementation of the free trade agreement, and expected more of the same. Were these expectations realistic, or merely the reaction of the uninformed or misleading propaganda? The majority of the dialogue surrounding NAFTA has focused on jobs and job creation because trade is something tangible. The real issues beyond job creation and destruction are associated with rapid change in the structure of the economy and with new technologies, but these issues are harder to grasp.

Much has happened since NAFTA went into effect. Globalization has accelerated at a breakneck pace. To be world class demands the same competencies of all managers and all companies, regardless of national origin or workplace location. A common global business language has emerged that helps transcend common cultural misunderstandings. Now more than ever, some things are just plain and quantifiable, not subject to interpretation, right or wrong. In effective global organizations, the days when poor results could be hidden behind the smokescreen of "cultural differences" are gone. Management that has relied on this comfortable and convenient, but intellectually weak, explanation for underperformance will need to effect a radical transformation or be left behind.

At the same time, effective global organizations recognize and exploit the value of employee diversity and seek to attract, develop, and retain the best talent in the world, regardless of gender or nationality. Companies that are successful in the NAFTA region have broken down mental barriers based on age-old stereotypes, cast aside feel-good cultural excuses for underperformance, and adopted an attitude of partnership with business associates in North America. Companies that have not, and examples are numerous, have suffered significant opportunity costs, erosion of competitive position, and quantifiable financial losses. While tariff rates and customs procedures might be going through a period of incremental transition, management in North America is going through nothing less than a *transformation*.

This transformation was quickened after the tragic events of September 11, 2001. NAFTA has achieved much in the past, but much remains to be accomplished in the future, with issues ranging from infrastructure to social problems. The implications of ease or difficulty of travel between NAFTA countries are being explored. There will be implications for the 3,600 maquiladora plants throughout Mexico, with the largest number located in the border states of Baja California, Sonora, Chihuahua, Coahuila, Nuevo Leon, and Tamaulipas.

The focus in this chapter, on Mexico, is not to debate the merits of NAFTA but to provide information on aspects of the culture in Mexico. In Chapter 18 we cover cultural aspects of doing business in the US and Canada.

The culture of Mexico

Culture is a "problem-solving tool" and it is "everything we think, do, and have" as members of our society: our attitudes, values, beliefs, faults, traditions, habits, and customs.

Exhibit 13.3 illustrates some cultural differences over a number of variables, starting with family, between Mexico and Canada and the US. Remember, these are generalizations of aspects of national characters that are accurate for most Mexicans, Canadians, and Americans.

Stereotyping

Stereotyping is a normal human trait, which in essence categorizes information to promote better understanding and to avoid information overload. It is difficult to be aware of. In fact,

EXHIBIT 13.3 KRAS' CULTURAL FACTORS

Variable	Mexico	Canada and the US
Family	Family is first priority. Children sheltered. Executive mobility limited.	Family usually second to work. Children independent. Executive mobility unrestricted.
Religion	Long Roman Catholic tradition. Fatalistic outlook.	Mixed religions. "Master of own life" outlook.
Pedagogical approach	Memorization. Theoretical emphasis. Rigid, broad curriculum.	Analytical approach. Practical emphasis. Narrow, in-depth specialization.
Nationalism	Very nationalistic. Proud of long history and traditions. Reluctant to settle outside Mexico.	Very patriotic. Proud of "American way of life." Assumes everyone shares his/her materialistic values.
Emotional	Sensitive to differences of opinion. Fears loss of face. Shuns confrontation.	Separates work from emotions. Sensitivity seen as weakness. Puts up tough business front.
Etiquette	"Old World" formality. Etiquette considered the measure of breeding.	Formality often sacrificed for efficiency. "Let's get to the point" approach.
Grooming	Dress and grooming are status symbols.	As long as appearance is reasonable, performance is first.

EXHIBIT 13.3

	Variable	Mexico	Canada and the US
E X H I B I T 13.3	Status	Title and position more important than money in eyes of society.	Money is main status indicator and is reward for achievement.
	Aesthetics	Aesthetic side of life is important, even at work.	No time for "useless frills."
	Ethics	Truth tempered by need for diplomacy. Truth is a relative concept.	Direct yes/no answers given and expected. Truth seen as absolute value.

Source: adapted from Kras, E. *Management in the Two Cultures: Bridging the Gap Between the U. S. and Mexico.* Yarmouth, ME: Intercultural Press Inc., 1995. Retrieved from: www.mexconnect.com/mex_/culxcomp.html.

as ethnocentrism and stereotypes promote a feeling of belonging to one's own group, the process of overcoming their debilitating effects when conducting business with people of different cultural groups is dependent on an ongoing effort to understand others as they understand themselves.

Joseph Campbell states: "The only way that you can describe a human being truly is by describing his imperfections."[12] It is natural for members of one culture to form exclusionary attitudes toward those of another, if such attitudes promote the success of the society or justify discriminatory behavior toward nonmembers.

Such attitudes, or stereotypes, are often based not on personal experience or observation, but rather on rumors, hearsay, incomplete and one-sided stories, and other types of non-empirical evidence. National stereotypes are frequently based on racism and prejudices and have attained acceptance as a set of values, beliefs, and attitudes forged through common experience.[13] There is a long and rather vicious history of stereotyping in North America, most notably between Mexicans and Anglo-Americans. Such stereotypes "rather than reflecting original responses to unique situations, have become part of day-in, day-out existence" and "rest on the distinction of what in the eyes of the would-be exploiters of other humans is the civilization of the former and the barbarism of the latter."[14]

Stereotyping not only has emanated from North America, but has been vigorously responded to by Mexico and Latin America. Indeed, by their stereotyping, Latin Americans have demonstrated that the "most prevalent form of racism in the world in recent decades has been anti-Americanism."[15]

Profile of Mexican negotiations

In Chapter 4 we described the 12 variables that we believe are present in all negotiations. What follows are those variables as applied to Mexican businesspeople.

EXHIBIT 13.4 HISTORICAL STEREOTYPES

Value affected	Mexican view of North American	Mexican view of self	North American view of Mexican	North American view of self
Self-control	Cold, insensitive, emotionless	Deal passively with stress, saying "ni modo" when something doesn't go according to plan	Emotional, volatile, feminine, undisciplined	Rational, calm, masculine, deals actively with stress through discipline in life
Type of civilization	Condescending, contradictory, not credible	Traditional; technically inferior, morally superior	Primitive, in need of instruction on "how to do things"	Advanced, responsible for showing others how to have democracy and free trade
Racial attitude	Indiscriminate racism. Can't distinguish high-class Mexican from Indian	Social classes have subtle shades; whiter is better; the masses cannot be elevated anyway. North Americans should be able to distinguish between high and low classes and accept high as equals	Indigenous people are inferior, and mestizos combine the worst features of both races. The treatment of the lower classes is unjust, and therefore high classes deserve no respect	Racially superior. Culturally heterogeneous, but racially homogeneous. In Canada, multicultural intermixing normal; in the US multicultural intermixing accepted
Honesty and trustworthiness (high-/low-context)	Manipulative, tactless, have ulterior motives against Mexico; can't be trusted	More important to be nice than objective; OK to bend truth or retain information if people's feelings are preserved (high-context)	Dishonest, indirect, sneaky, not trustworthy	Honest, direct, principled, literal (low-context)
Character	Aggressive, at times brutal and abusive	Brave, but overpowered like "niños heroes"	Submissive, weak	Dominant, strong
Time orientation	Obsessively future-oriented. Doesn't know how to relax. Unrealistically believes time can be mastered	Lives in and enjoys present, respects past, awaits a future to be determined by God's will: "si Dios quiere"	Lives too much in present, while dwelling on the past; surrenders own will and ambition to chance, procrastinating	The present is the birthplace of the future; planning, action-oriented. "All the flowers of all the tomorrows are in the seeds we plant today"

EXHIBIT 13.4

Value affected	Mexican view of North American	Mexican view of self	North American view of Mexican	North American view of self
Social classes	Although morally corrupted, economically and perhaps racially superior	Exclusive, but more cultured and civilized at top levels; money not only determinant of status for "gente decente" (decent people)	Chaotic, inefficient, unjust; high classes lack character and low classes lack potential	Orderly, efficient, fair; upward mobility is possible to anyone who has money to enter
Religion	Profess a false religion	Repository of higher moral values	Passive Christianity (Catholicism); God's faithful servant	Active Christianity (Protestantism). God's appointed steward
Orientation to nature	Destructive, futilely trying to control what only God can master	Nature merely "is," a creation of God that man can ultimately neither influence nor control	Man cannot control nature; fatalism seen in failing to try. Evidence is economic underdevelopment	Man can and should manage and perfect nature; optimistic due to results of economic progress
National intent	Intervention, imperialism, subversion	Sovereignty, respect, recognition	Lacking vision, discipline; needs help to reform flawed political and economic systems	Good-natured missionary, helpful, showing others "the way"
Work ethic	Obsessive materialism, don't know how or when to relax	Work not inherently redeeming; something that must be done	Lazy, work is bad as seen in Mexican sayings: "Do not do today what you can do tomorrow," and "Work is sacred; don't touch it"	Work is the measure of a man as seen in sayings: "Never put off until tomorrow what can be done today," and "An idle mind is the devil's workshop"

Source: data based on selected observations from: Acuna, R. *Occupied America*. New York: Harper and Row, 1981. Condon, J. *Good Neighbors*. Yarmouth, ME: Intercultural Press, 1997. Diaz-Guerrero, R. *The Psychology of the Mexican*. Austin, TX: University of Texas Press, 1975. Paz, O. *The Labyrinth of Solitude*. New York: Grove Weidenfelds, 1985. Pike, F. B. *The United States and Latin America: Myths and Stereotypes of Civilization and Nature*. Austin, TX: University of Texas Press, 1992. Riding, A. *Distant Neighbors*. New York: Knopf, 1985.

BASIC CONCEPT OF NEGOTIATION PROCESS

Negotiating in Mexico is a complex and long procedure, covering several stages. First, the parties involved must determine if they, as individuals or organizations, can do business together. Establishing a warm working relationship with one's counterparts is essential to the process and facilitates the negotiation.

At the negotiation table, because of past historical context, a Mexican negotiator is wary of being taken advantage of by an American *gringo*. The Mexican pride, *machismo*, will not allow this to happen. It is important for a negotiator to be sensitive to any obvious or implied messages regarding Mexican self-esteem.

Connections in Mexico are very important, and the government has a significant influence in private business matters. Permits are required for just about every business transaction. As a result, a government official might elicit a *mordida* ("a little bite," i.e., a bribe) to complete the transaction.

SELECTION OF NEGOTIATORS

Negotiators are selected primarily on status. Family connections, personal or political influence, and education are critical. Hence, the importance of *ubicación* (where one is plugged into the system) becomes evident. Mexican negotiators tend to be high-level, male, and well-connected.

ROLE OF INDIVIDUAL ASPIRATIONS

Whether Mexicans are individualists or collectivists seems to depend on the social arena. In business, and with other men, Mexicans tend to be competitive, set on pursuing individual goals and needs for their personal recognition. Often, they feel they owe loyalty to their patron, but they seek to project a public image of significance and power.

CONCERN FOR PROTOCOL

Mexican culture is dominated by courtesy, dignity, tact, and diplomacy. Protocol is important and social competence is as critical as technical competence.

SIGNIFICANCE OF TYPE OF ISSUE

For Mexicans, relationship-based and personal/internal issues tend to predominate and affect the negotiations, and Mexicans emphasize the social and personal aspects of their relationships with the people they encounter, including businesspeople.

Many Mexicans resent what they see as a long history of unfair treatment by North Americans, and personal honor or dignity may be a factor within the Mexican negotiating team.

COMPLEXITY OF THE LANGUAGE

Communicative context is formed by body language and emotional cues, not just the words spoken. Mexicans communicate with hand movements, physical contact, and emotional expressions, making Mexicans high-context communicators.

All Latin American cultures embrace closeness. People stand close to each other, sit close to each other, and often touch each other.

NATURE OF PERSUASIVE ARGUMENT

Emotional arguments that are overly dramatic and patriotic are considered persuasive. Along these lines, there is the concept of *proyectismo* (constructing plans without critical analysis and assuming in time all will be accomplished). Perhaps much of this stems from the twin origins of Mexican culture: the Indian, based on magic and superstition, and the Spanish, based on imposition, dogma, and faith.

VALUE OF TIME

There is a relaxed polychronic attitude toward time. Although time is a concern, Mexicans do not allow schedules to interfere with experiences involving their family or friends. The culture is more people-oriented than task-oriented.

BASES OF TRUST

Evaluations of trustworthiness are based initially on intuition and then later on one's past record. Negotiations should take place within a generally trusting atmosphere. Trust must develop through a series of frequent and warm interpersonal transactions, either socially or business-oriented.

RISK-TAKING PROPENSITY

Mexicans tend to be risk-avoidant. They will try to work something out to avoid risk as much as possible. Mexicans tend to be very pessimistic in any situation in which there is some amount of risk.

INTERNAL DECISION-MAKING SYSTEM

Decision-making is highly centralized in government, companies, and within negotiating teams. Mexican leaders tend to make decisions without concern for consensus. Individuals with *palanca* (leverage) tend to be well positioned, expressive, and forceful with their opinions and decisions.

FORM OF SATISFACTORY AGREEMENT

The only way to be certain that a business agreement has been reached in Mexico is with a written document. Agreements in Mexico fall under the Civil Code, the Commercial Code, or the Law of Commercial Companies.

BRAZIL

Since it is impossible to cover all countries in South America, we have first selected Brazil for a detailed cultural analysis because it is the largest in terms of population, land mass, and economy.

Historical, political, and economic overview

Brazil is a federated republic of more than three million square miles. First inhabited by nomads from Asia millennia ago, the indigenous people evolved into tribal groups, which today are called Amerindians. The civilizations they developed included empires, such as the Inca, which stretched from Colombia to Argentina. The first Europeans to discover Brazil may have been Jean Cousins in 1488 or Christopher Columbus in 1498. But Portuguese claimed the land in 1500 when their fleet of some dozen ships under the command of Pedro Alvarez Cabral arrived mistakenly in what is called today the state of Bahia! For almost four centuries, Portugal maintained control of Brazil, exploiting many of its resources. Gold, gems, rubber, cocoa, cattle, and other products were shipped to the homeland or abroad. Portuguese noblemen ruled in 12 areas of the colony, and established a plantation economy. This led to the import of some four million African slaves to work in the land. In 1615, Brazil became the seat of the entire Portuguese empire. When the emperor returned to Portugal, his son Pedro II declared Brazil an independent nation in 1822. In 1865–1870, the country engaged in a ruinous war with Paraguay. His 49-year reign transformed the country into a modern state, including the freeing of the African slaves in 1888.

When the military overthrew the monarchy, they declared Brazil a republic in 1889. By the twentieth century, the nation had experimented with various forms of governance—from military rule to dictatorship to democracy, which prevails today. Between 1955 and 1960, the president, Jucelino Kubitcheck, undertook major construction projects, including building a new capital, Brazilia, in the middle of this vast country. From 1945 to 1964, a military coup took over the government and produced the "Brazilian Miracle," when the economy grew by as much as 11 percent per year. The sinister side was that this regime arrested, imprisoned, and killed its supposed opponents, forcing many into exile, especially artists and academics. Finally, the military dictatorship was replaced by the election of Fernando Collor de Mello as president in 1990. After he was later impeached, Fernando Cardoso, a sociologist and former minister of the economy, was chosen as head of state. During his term from 1995 to 2001, many economic and social reforms were undertaken, some of which still benefit the society and its citizens.[16]

Today's federated republic has a bicameral National Congress with a Federal Senate and Chamber of Deputies. The latter's 513 members are elected by proportional representation and serve four-year terms. Besides this legislative branch, the judiciary consists of the Supreme Federal Tribunal, with 11 members appointed by the president for life and confirmed by a vote of the Senate. There are many political parties, and passing reforms is difficult; governance is by coalitions and concessions. The country has formal relationships with many international organizations—such as the United Nations, World Trade Organization, World Bank—and economic partnership with its neighbors through MERCOSUR, a regional trade group.

The Brazilian presidential election on October 27, 2002, was a milestone. For the first time, a simple man from a poor family was successfully elected to the highest position in Brazilian politics. Luiz Ignácio Lula da Silva, known as "Lula," was one of the founders and foremost leader of the metallurgical union and the Workers' Party (PT). The year 2016 was also a milestone as Lula's handpicked successor, Dilma Rousseff, earlier won the election but was impeached by her colleagues. Historically, Brazilian presidents have come from the elite class. Because of his origins, and because a significant percentage of the population lives below the official poverty level, former president Lula chose to focus his administration upon the "Zero Hunger" program, while seeking solutions to critical social problems: improving education; century-long land reform problems; cleaning up rampant corruption and crime; reducing unemployment and reformulating the pension and benefit system; curbing inflation, and national debt problems; and jump-starting a stagnant economy. His first term enjoyed many accomplishments, but was hampered by corruption scandals within the Workers' Party. As a result, changes are occurring now that have never before been seen in the country's long history. The battle is between progress and inertia, especially in a stifling government bureaucracy and regulatory environment. The country is in the midst of a slow economic metamorphosis from unequal and hierarchical to more universal and equalitarian conditions. Brazil hosted the 2016 Summer Olympic Games in Rio de Janeiro.

In the twenty-first century, Brazil is a large democratic and stable society, rich in resources, with a strong economy. Yet, having won a second term until 2010, former president Lula was trying to expand upon the stability and predictability his administration had established. Two economic programs have been successful. The consolidation of sugar and ethanol production has alleviated energy needs and powers automobiles, while creating a new export business. Biofuels and flex-fuel cars, operating on both ethanol and gasoline, are now big businesses. Biotech laboratories are springing up everywhere, and researchers are studying new possibilities, ranging from drought-resistant soya to new energy sources. Brazil is learning to capitalize on nature's sun, water, and soil, and its corporations are becoming multinationals. The other success story is *Bolsa Familia*—a benefit program that gives federal cash (95 reais per month) to poor parents who ensure that their children stay in school and take them to clinics for health tests. This conditional cash plan now reaches 46 million people. In 2008, Petrobas, the state oil giant, announced the development of a new field containing 5–8 billion barrels of light, sweet crude oil. Known as *tupi*, this offshore rich resource is located under a layer of salt deep beneath the floor of the Atlantic Ocean.

Since it sits up to 7 km below sea level, with some fields 350 km off the coast, pumping this oil will be a complex technological challenge. In the waning days of his administration, President Lula seeks to have income from this new enterprise devoted to education.

Protecting the Amazon

Brazil's 3.3 million square miles of Amazon rainforest, 40 percent of its national territory, is a world resource in need of careful management. Unregulated agriculture, mining, and logging threaten this greenbelt—destruction in the Amazon forests contributes to pollution and three-quarters of the country's carbon emissions. So those who would preserve this rich environment and its indigenous people are contributing to the government's new Amazon Fund. Size and accomplishments make Brazil the continent's natural leader, but it could lead the environmental movement by preserving the earth's largest ecosystem in the Amazon Basin.[17] This could be the capstone in the energy leadership Brazil already demonstrates!

The Amazon forests are shared with several of Brazil's neighbors, including Peru and Colombia. Here, as elsewhere in Latin America, the government owns the subsoil and any oil, gas, and minerals found there. All these Amazon nations are attempting to use the rainforest for oil and gas exploration. In all cases, an improved policy is needed to reconcile national interests with those of the environment and local inhabitants, usually Amerindians. NGOs are urging industries to watch over the jungle as they would the ocean, to use helicopters and aero imaging, instead of building logging roads or pouring waste into the rivers.

The people

SOCIAL STRUCTURE, RACE, VALUES, AND RELIGION

Brazil is a spectacular country in both social contrasts and geographical size. First-World living conditions are seen in upper-class neighborhoods; across the street from the massive electronically operated skyscrapers, people live in *favelas* (shantytowns), sometimes with not even the most basic of services. An estimated four million people live in these shantytowns in the cities of Rio de Janeiro and São Paulo alone. Another contrast is in the people's skin tone—a complete spectrum of skin colors, from black to white, and all hues in between. Although 47 percent of the people consider themselves to be "white" (primarily descendants of Portuguese, German, Italian, Spanish, and Polish, as well as Lebanese and Japanese), only 7 percent consider themselves to be "black"; it is estimated that about 45 percent of the population has some degree of African ancestry. With 50 percent of its total population under 20 years of age, Brazil is a very "young" and diversified country. Here, segregation is more class-based than race-based.

A prevalent cultural generalization concerning the people of Brazil is that they are a warm, friendly, and emotionally sensitive people who are generous and receptive to foreigners. The Brazilian class structure is based on economics. While the highest 10 percent of the population enjoys 47 percent of the country's consumption share, the lowest 10 percent only has 1 percent. The rich in Brazil consists of both the old wealthy class and a new affluent class made up of mainly the descendants of poor immigrants from Europe who built empires of riches. Perhaps more important in Brazil than in any other Latin American country, the family has been the single most significant institution in the formation of Brazilian society. The meaning of family in Brazil is not limited to the immediate family, but instead includes the entire *parentela*, or extended family, from both the mother's and father's sides. This group can consist of hundreds of people, and it provides the foundation of the individual's social structure. It is not unusual to see many generations living together under one roof, or at least in the same town or city. It is customary for children to live with their parents until they marry, although this has been changing, especially in the big cities. Loyalty to one's family is the individual's highest ranking obligation. Although the traditional family is usually male dominated, for economic reasons many women work outside the home, and single-parent families are common. Other traditional dominant values in the Brazilian society include community, collectivism, procreation, and a hierarchical society. And in a hierarchical society, it is always important to know who one is talking with.

A traditional value that has its basis in the Catholic Church is one of fatalism. Evidence of this can be found in expressions that are very common in everyday conversations, such as "*se Deus quiser*" ("the Lord willing"). The Brazilian attitude is the result of a history full of unpredictable changes and circumstances over which the individual has had little control. Some examples of more recent circumstances of this type include electricity and water shortages that have resulted in periods of blackouts and lack of water supplies. Even though the Catholic Church has had a profound effect in the formation of the dominant values found in Brazil, a large percentage of Brazilians are only nominally Catholic. Brazilians are very accepting of different religions, and some even practice more than one type of religion. Additionally, though they profess to have at least some alliance to the Catholic Church, Brazilian Catholics have adopted many traditions of Afro-Brazilian religions as well, with offerings made at intersections, even on the busiest of streets in the largest of cities. Brazilians' religious tolerance is evident in the rapid growth of Protestant evangelism.

Cultural characteristics of business

Brazil is rich in both natural and human resources. However, doing business in Brazil can be a challenging experience due to economic uncertainties involving inflation, currency exchange, and interest rates, among other things. At the same time, working in Brazil can be enjoyable and exciting because of the immense economic opportunities that the country offers. Brazil's diverse economy produces everything from automobiles and airplanes to shoes and orange juice. The service and high-tech industries are rapidly growing. By understanding this culture better, it is easier to avoid committing blunders that could potentially lead to negative results in business situations. One of the biggest mistakes that can be made is to consider Brazil to be just another country in Latin America, and to assume that what works in Chile or Mexico or Panama will also work in Brazil. One of the most blatant differences is that it is the only country in Latin America in which Portuguese is the official language. In addition to this example, there are innumerable subtler cultural differences.

GREETINGS

Handshakes are the appropriate form of greeting between men and women in a business setting. However, because Brazilians are warm and friendly people who feel free to show their affection in public, one or two kisses on the cheeks are common between a man and a woman as well as between two women. Women sometimes will kiss three times if one of the women is not married. This is said to bring good luck in finding a husband. Men do not kiss, but it is normal for acquaintances to pat each other on the back or on the arm while shaking hands. It is usual for men and women who are friends to hug each other when they meet. Brazilians touch each other more and for longer periods of time than is acceptable in some other cultures. Upon arriving and before leaving, it is important to greet and say goodbye to each individual, while refraining from use of impersonal statements like "Hi/Bye, everyone!"

NAMES AND TITLES

Most Brazilians are less formal than people in the other Latin American countries; consequently, titles are not always used. First names are used routinely, but it is a good idea to let the Brazilian ask you to call him by his or her first name before doing so. Often, a title is used with a first name, such as *Dona* (Lady) Maria or *Senhor* (Mister) John. *Doutor* or *Doutora* (Doctor) is commonly used to express respect even if the person is not a doctor or PhD (especially with older folks). First and last names may be made up of two or more names. Take the example *Luis Henrique Meirelles Reis*. In this case, it appears that *Henrique* is the middle name, but friends and family will call him *Luis Henrique*. Furthermore, a first name may be a combination of the mother and father's first names. An example of this is *Carlene*, which is a combination of *Carlos* and *Marlene*. A person's compound last name may be a combination of the mother's maiden name followed by the father's last name. This order is different from the order used in Spanish-speaking countries. It is not uncommon for a person's full name to be made up of five or six individual names! Another interesting point is that in the Portuguese language there are two words for the English word *you*. The use of *o senhor* or *a senhora* denotes more respect than the use of the casual *você*.

HOSPITALITY AND ENTERTAINING

Brazilians are well known for being courteous and hospitable. They endeavor to make visitors feel welcomed and comfortable. Expect to be offered limitless very small, but very strong, cups of coffee, both in the office and while visiting someone's home. It is polite to accept the coffee, but it is not considered rude to politely refuse it. Brazilians will often keep offering even if they think that you don't want any more. Do not feel that it is necessary to keep accepting more food or drinks just because your host continues offering! It is just a way of being polite. It is also usual for a person who is about to begin eating to offer some of his food to others. This is only done to show consideration to those around him, and the person offering the food probably has no intention of sharing, but instead expects a polite "No, thank you" in return. Although Brazilians do entertain in their home, among co-workers it is more common to go out for lunch, drinks, or dinner. It is normal for the person who invites to pay, but it is just as normal for the bill to be split equally among all present, regardless of who ate what. Toasts are common in Brazil, but they are not an elaborate ceremony as they are in some cultures. To make a toast, simply lift your glass and say "*Saúde!*" ("Health!"). Never tap your glass with a piece of silverware to get your group's attention before making a toast. Another form of behavior that is not considered polite is to snap your fingers or hiss to get a waiter's attention. Even though this action might be seen in some restaurants, it is not typical behavior.

APPEARANCE, HYGIENE, AND DRESS

Considered by many to be very beautiful people, Brazilians in general are extremely concerned about their appearance. They go to great pains to keep in good physical condition by working out in health clubs, running in parks or along the beaches, and undergoing plastic surgery. It is usual for both women and men to keep their fingernails and toenails neatly manicured, and a visitor doing business in Brazil should do the same. Due to the typically hot weather, it is not uncommon for Brazilians to take two showers every day, one in the morning and another before going to sleep at night. Brazilians also like to brush their teeth after every meal, so it is not unusual to see people brushing their teeth in the restrooms of restaurants or companies.

Dressing for work in Brazil depends on the employer codes, but the standard dress for men is a dark- or light-colored two-piece suit, shirt, and tie. Many companies have adopted the casual Friday concept, and some have casual day every day. While men in the Brazilian workplace dress in much the same way as their American counterparts in general, the same may not be true for Brazilian women. While many Brazilian businesswomen do wear suits, they also dress in a variety of other ways. For example, it is not unusual to see women dressed in low-cut, tight, transparent tops, even with spaghetti straps (or no straps) in the office. Sundresses are also common. Often, women will wear sandals without pantyhose. One important point is that a woman's purse and shoes should always match. Brazilian women in general prefer a more natural look, and little if any make-up is worn. It is also not uncommon to see a woman come to work without drying her hair. Usually, visiting business-women from abroad dress more conservatively than described before. Outside the work-place, dressing is usually casual. During the weekends, even at some fine restaurants in São Paulo and Rio de Janeiro, men wear khaki shorts, slacks, or jeans, and either a button-down or polo-type shirt. Keep in mind when traveling to Brazil that the seasons are opposite; when it is freezing cold in the northern hemisphere, it is quite hot in Brazil.

GIFTS AND BRIBES

Doing business in Brazil does not require gift giving, but since Brazilians regard business relationships as personal relationships, they value all acts of generosity, including receiving presents from their visitors. It's a good idea to try to personalize the gift as much as possible due to the fact that Brazilians appreciate the attention and thought that goes into selecting the right present. Some appropriate gifts include calendars, chocolate, wine, top-quality scotch whiskey, name-brand perfume, or anything unique from the visitor's country that may not be available in Brazil.

When does a "gift" become a "bribe"? This is a difficult line to determine, so it is best for a visitor to err on the safe side and not participate in this practice. Although it is true that bribes have traditionally sometimes been given in Brazil, things are changing. If you are not familiar with the culture's subtleties, you could get into trouble either by offending someone by offering the bribe or by not offering the right thing. For this reason, it may be beneficial to hire a *despachante* to help you. *Despachantes* are specialists in knowing what is appropriate and cutting through the endless bureaucracy that can be found at any level of government. A tactic that is very useful in Brazil is *jeitinho*, which is a term that means "getting around obstacles in order to obtain what you want." Another Brazilian tradition is the *cafezinho*, literally meaning "little coffee." This is a small tip that you give someone when they help you out. If you offer to pay someone for doing a favor for you and he tells you that a *cafezinho* would be fine, he really is not asking for coffee!

TIME

Brazilians' idea of time is more flexible than it is in some cultures. Although in the workplace punctuality is considered important in theory, in reality it is common for meetings to start 5–20 minutes late (or more). One reason for this (or maybe more of an excuse) is the unpredictable traffic found in the big cities. Once the meeting does start, it is important to spend some time with small talk. Some topics appropriate for small talk include family (only if you have met the family previously), current events, the weather, any positive topic, and sometimes soccer, depending on the person you are talking to. In general, negative and controversial subjects should be avoided because they could lead to feelings of embarrassment and an uncomfortable situation. Expect to spend a long time in meetings before any results are produced. Brazilians are not always very direct; in their opinion, it is important to establish personal relationships and a sense of trust before doing business with someone. Time in social situations is seen in a different way. Parties always start later than the time shown on the invitation. If you receive an invitation for dinner at someone's home, you should arrive no more than 15 minutes late; do not come early or exactly on time because the host may not be ready to receive you.

COMMUNICATION: VERBAL AND NONVERBAL

While Portuguese is the official language, many distinct dialects exist in different parts of the country. Accents and even the meaning given to words vary from region to region. Moreover, there are many subcultures in Brazil who still use the language of their ancestors. It is common to hear German and Polish spoken in the South, Italian and Japanese spoken in São Paulo, and Spanish spoken along the borders of neighboring countries. Among the members of the "international business subculture," English is definitely the official language. Individuals in managerial positions at global companies often have some degree of proficiency in English.

Brazilian communication style is very expressive and animated. The norm is to speak fast, without much time between words. Due to variations in the pitch and volume of the voices, a dialogue may resemble more a song than a conversation. Depending on the topic, it may even appear that a fight is about to break out—but, more often than not, it is just an emotionally friendly discourse. Furthermore, Brazilians like to say one thing, give examples or details, and then rephrase the sentences many times, repeating the same idea over and over again. Foreigners may find this style of communication to be confusing, unorganized, or misleading.

The Brazilian writing style shares many characteristics with their oral communication style. Comma splices and run-on sentences, considered incorrect in English, are common in Portuguese writing. Brazilians also use the indirect style of digression more than other cultures do. This sometimes can make it difficult to understand the writer's line of thought.

The concept of low- and high-context communication styles involves both verbal and nonverbal communication aspects. While Brazilians generally are more low-context than the Eastern and Middle Eastern countries, they are usually more high-context than the US and northern European countries. Although Brazilians use words profusely, at times they can be very indirect in expressing their feelings. Therefore, it is imperative that the visitor be aware of the possible underlying meanings in communicative exchanges in order to avoid serious misunderstandings.

While it has been said that nonverbal communication accounts for about 70 percent of all communication, this percentage can be even higher when members of different cultures try to exchange information, especially if one does not speak the local language. At times, the nonverbal forms of communication carry more weight in a conversation than the actual words. One form of nonverbal communication is eye contact. Brazilians in general, and especially among individuals who hold the same status level, look each other in the eye when speaking. However, it is also common for a person from a lower class to look down when speaking to someone he considers his superior. This is a form of showing respect, and should not be looked on with suspicion.

In public places, it is not unusual for people to stare at others for lengths of time that may make members of different cultures uncomfortable.

Silence during conversations has no room whatsoever in Brazilian communication, and the use of interruptions in discussions is common in Brazil. While this may be considered rude in some cultures, there are situations in which a person might use interruptions to show enthusiasm and interest in the conversations. In this country, close physical contact is the norm. An individual's personal distance is short, and touching during a conversation is considered normal. It is common for pedestrians walking on crowded city streets to brush or even run into each other without apologizing. Brazilians like to talk with their hands; it is almost impossible for them to have a conversation without moving their hands to help express themselves. Consequently, the use of hand gestures is widespread. The following is a description of some of the most commonly seen gestures in Brazil:

- The "OK" sign used in the US is considered extremely vulgar, especially when the three extended fingers are held parallel to the ground, close to the chest, with the palm up.
- Extending the middle finger upward is also vulgar.
- Hitting an open palm into a clenched fist sends the same message as the two examples above.
- Extending the index and little finger upward while making a fist with the other fingers means, "Your wife/girlfriend is cheating on you."
- Opening and closing all fingers together many times with the palm up means that a place is crowded or full.
- Pulling the lower eyelid down with the index finger means "pay attention!"; "watch out!"; or "I am watching and paying attention."
- Brushing the fingertips of one hand under the chin and continuing to move the hand out in an outward direction, palm facing inward, means "I don't know."
- Snapping all fingers on each other while moving the hand up and down quickly adds emphasis to what is being said.
- Snapping the thumb and middle finger, pointing the fingers inward while moving the hand from the chest to the shoulder at ear height means "a long time ago."
- Wiping the fingers of one hand with the fingers of the other hand, in a downward direction in front of the chest with palms facing upward, means "it doesn't matter."

WOMEN'S ROLE IN BUSINESS

Though, traditionally, Brazil shares the *machismo* characteristic that is common throughout Latin America, the reality in Brazil today is very different. In many situations, women need to work outside the home to help support the family. This is especially common in big cities. More and more, women are achieving upper-management positions, and even director-ships. However, it is still rare to see women presidents in large companies, both domestic and international. Women are also gaining greater roles in political areas, such as obtaining the position of city mayor or state governor. Women are also serving at the national level of government as cabinet and Supreme Court members.

NEGOTIATING IN BRAZIL

Although a sense of fatalism exists in Brazil due to a feeling of lack of control over one's own future, and the "get rich quick and get out quick" philosophy can still be found, the general attitude while doing business and negotiating in Brazil is more along the lines of "take your time." Negotiations cannot be rushed in this country. Business is done with friends, and friendships take a long time to build. Because personal relationships form the basis of trust in business deals, nepotism and giving preference to friends is common in both companies and government. The following are some characteristics of negotiating styles in Brazil:

■ *Particular over universal.* When making decisions, Brazilians like to look at the details involved in each particular situation, instead of applying universal rules or patterns of behavior to all situations.

■ *Relationship over task.* Brazilians feel that a good relationship must be in place before anything can be accomplished, and it is never a good idea to damage a relationship that is intact, even if it means not completing a task.

■ *Polychronic over monochronic.* Brazilians tend to view the concept of time in a poly-chronic way, often discussing the details of a proposal in a random order instead of in a sequential manner.

■ *Indirect over direct.* Seemingly a contradiction, Brazilians are a very emotional and affective people, but their style in both personal and business affairs is very indirect. Brazilians are usually nonconfrontational and believe in face-saving.

■ *Group over individual.* Although this depends on the circumstances, Brazilians feel the group and relationships within the group are more important than individual aspira-tions. This has implications concerning methods of motivation. Sometimes an indi-vidual manager would prefer to share a bonus with subordinates or co-workers instead of keeping it all for her/himself.

■ *Flexible over inflexible.* Due to constant changes in Brazilian laws, as well as the uncertainty brought by fluctuations in exchange rates, interest rates, and inflation rates, Brazilians have become very adept at "going with the flow." They consider people who always follow standard procedures to be unimaginative and lacking intelligence.

ARGENTINA

The second-largest nation on the continent of South America is Argentina, in terms of population, landmass, and economy. Geographically, it is bounded by five other Latin countries—Bolivia and Paraguay to the north, Uruguay and Brazil to the east, and Chile to the west. This most southern country extends with its neighbor Chile to the tip of Cape Horn, where the Atlantic and Pacific Oceans converge. It is the eighth largest national state in the world; its people dance to the *tango* and the tune of free market enterprise. It is a founding member of a South American trading group known as MERCOSUR. Buenos Aires in the northeast is its beautiful capital city. Beside this federal city, the country is divided into 26 provinces.

Cultural influences

■ *Inhabitants.* About 3 percent of the population descends from the original "Amerindian" people, who now live largely in remote areas. This percentage includes *mestizo* (mixed) and other nonwhite groups. The remaining 97 percent are of European stock, largely Spanish and Italian ancestry. Argentina's cosmopolitan and progressive citizens express intensive opinions about world affairs, their government, its police, politics, and taxes, but usually avoid personal public criticism, except among trusted friends. Gregarious by nature, Argentineans are noted for their respect of the individual, acceptance of failure, and lack of punctuality.

■ *Geography.* Argentina, over a million square miles, has a large plain that rises above the Atlantic Ocean and extends to the towering Andes Mountains to the west. The northwest is home to *chaco*, or swamp land, and the great rivers of the *Plata* system. The rolling *pampas*, or prairies, are in the central part, featuring ranches and cowboys, and famous for wheat growing and cattle raising. Sheep raising occurs in the southern tableland of Patagonia. Although its climate is generally temperate, the *Chicao* region is subtropical, while in southern Patagonia the winters are quite cold. The country's expansive capital is the largest in Latin America, with the world's largest boulevard, elegant retail shops, and 150 parks!

■ *History and governance.* After the Amerindian civilizations flourished, the Europeans entered this land's Rio de la Plata area by way of the Spanish influx in 1516. By 1580, they had established Buenos Aires as the center of their government on the central east coast, adjoining Uruguay on the Atlantic Ocean. In 1810, a tradition of revolutionary revolts and military *juntas* began as a continuing struggle for governmental control. By 1816, Argentina gained independence from Spanish colonial rule under the leadership of its national hero, General José de San Martin. The economy prospered because of rubber plantations and beef production until the end of World War II, when Argentina's unique position of neutrality ended. After decades of instability, Colonel Juan Peron became president in 1946. Under his dictatorship, and with the help of his wife, Evita, the poor supposedly benefited, while the unions, military, and the economy declined. So much so that Peron was forced into exile in 1955. When a provisional military government fared no better, he managed to return to rule with the assistance of the Peronist party, which still has influence there—Peron was elected president, with his second wife, Maria, as vice-president. Within a year he was dead from natural causes, and his widow became the first woman to head a national government in the Western hemisphere. In 1976, her administration ended with a bloodless coup and the establishment of martial law.

Then the ruling military *juntas* were responsible for a campaign supposedly against terrorism, which itself resulted in thousands of kidnappings, arrests, assassinations, and executions. The military's loss of the war against the British over possession of the Falkland Islands brought a return to civilian rule and democracy in 1983 with the election of President Carlos Menem. Sweeping economic reforms and various international agreements brought a measure of prosperity. But in 2001, defaults on $95 billion in bonds led the subsequent administration of President Nestor Kirchner into conflict with the International Monetary Fund over international loans and repayment of a $14.8 billion debt with the IMF. As industrial production shrunk in 2003, Argentina was forced to restructure debt and promote economic reforms, despite $12.3 billion in foreign reserves. In 2007, Kirchner's wife, Cristina Fernandez de Kirchner, was elected chief of state for four years. Presently, a bicameral National Congress consists of the Senate—72 members elected by direct vote to serve a six-year term—and a Chamber of Deputies elected by popular vote for four-year terms. The Supreme Court includes nine justices appointed by the President and elected by the Senate. The nation is also a member of numerous international and regional associations, including the World Trade Organization. Argentina continues to claim Islas Mavinas off its southeast coast, which the United Kingdom continues to administer under the name of the Falkland Islands.

Religious and social life

The observations made elsewhere in this chapter on Latin America also apply, for the most part, to spiritual and social life most evident in Argentina. For example, 95 percent of the people are nominally Roman Catholic, but only 25 percent are regular practitioners, while the remainder limit their participation to special occasions. Foreigners and minorities are free to practice their preferred religions. Again, Latin social customs are prevalent here, such as those described in the next section. The *Señores* (men), *Señoritas* (unmarried, usually younger women), and the *Señoras* (married, usually older females) typically shake hands while nodding to show respect. Close friends among males may embrace, while females will kiss one another on the cheeks and shake with both hands. First names are only used with close acquaintances. Ordinarily, females do not speak to strange males without an introduction. Normally, Argentineans do not yell at one another from a distance, but simply raise a hand and smile.

Upper-class Argentineans are proper, with reserved manners, yet friendly. Social etiquette in this country requires one not to open a conversation with a question, but to start with a greeting. Wait for an invitation to be seated in an office or home. The locals appreciate compliments about their children, décor, and gardens. They also eat in the European style, with knife in the right hand and fork in the left. It is considered bad manners at the dinner table to place your hands in your lap, to use a toothpick, to clear your throat, or blow your nose—rather, you should excuse yourself and go outside the dining area for such purposes. Beef is a favorite dish. Waiters will respond if you raise your hand and index finger. Dress is elegant but conservative—men's hats are removed when in buildings, elevators, or the presence of women. In families, the elderly are respected, the wife is the household manager, and deference is shown to the father as the head of the family. When meeting an Argentinean, it is advisable not to question the person as to his/her career or how he or she earns a living; their occupation will be revealed when they are ready. Generally, in Argentina, business hours are 8 a.m. until noon; then 3–9 p.m. Retail stores are usually closed on Sundays. Soccer is a favorite sport, followed by racing, boating, basketball, and horseback riding.

Social challenges

Like other countries in both North and South America, Argentina has its social inequities and difficulties. Approximately 23 percent of the population lives below the poverty line, and there is no strategy to reduce that percentage. It is also a transshipment center for illegal drugs to Europe, along with money laundering in the Tri-Border Area. There is also a lack of vigorous confrontation of law enforcement corruption. Argentina is also a source, transit, and destination country for trafficking of people in forced labor and sexual exploitation. However, their Congress enacted new federal anti-traffic legislation aimed at protecting human rights. Despite its advantageous climate and resources, Peter Khanna views Argentina as a new Second World entity.[18]

However, this nation, so rich in natural resources, is a world leader in environmental protection, especially in the setting of voluntary greenhouse targets. It is also an active participant in numerous international conservation programs. Argentina now has much to gain in emulating and cooperating more with Chile, its neighbor, with a Pacific coastline of some 3,000 miles that is a gateway to overseas markets. Today, Chile consistently demonstrates 5 percent annual economic growth. It was governed by a successful center-led coalition and a progressive female president, Michelle Bachelet. In the twenty-first century, Argentina continues to be a land of promise with enormous potential!

LATIN AMERICAN CULTURAL THEMES

Central and South America are made up of many nations and cultures. In addition to the Amerindians' cultures and languages, the Spanish heritage and language dominate, except for Brazil, where the Portuguese language and culture are prevalent. Across the Americas, other European cultural inputs are German, Irish, Italian, as well as African and some Asian influences. Some countries, such as Mexico, Bolivia, Colombia, and Brazil, have strong manifestations of ancient cultures of indigenous tribes. The latter people are growing in influence, with improved education and economic opportunities. For example, in 2005, the newly elected president of Bolivia, Evo Morales, had a powerful mandate because of his indigenous origins. He gained political support from the poor, the Andean Indians, and the *mestizos* (mixed race). Global managers realize that all the countries and people south of the US border are not basically the same. Communication and business practice have to be adapted to local circumstances. Generalizations regarding Latin America are dangerous. Many of the countries differ greatly in socioeconomic status, educational levels, governance, and composition of the population. However, the following observations from the late Alison Lanier's classic *Living in Latin America* and others may prove helpful.[19]

Social customs

- *Shaking hands.* This is the same as in Europe. If there are several people in the room, with a little bow, go around to each person and shake hands. The "Hi, everybody" is considered rude and brash. "So long; see you tomorrow" is equally poor. The *abrazo* (embrace) is a greeting used with individuals one knows well.
- *Pleasantries.* Nobody rushes into business. As a foreign businessperson, take your time and ask about your colleague's family's health, the weather, or perhaps the local sports team.
- *Expressing gratitude.* Send "thank you" notes promptly after any courtesy. Flowers are often presented as an expression of appreciation.
- *Time.* Latin Americans may appear often to be late for appointments, according to North American standards, but they expect North Americans to be on time. Business hours normally begin about 8 or 9 a.m., depending on local custom. A lunch break or *siesta* may extend from 12 to 3 p.m. Their offices and stores usually close about 6–8 p.m. Dinner may begin at 8–9 p.m. As a guest, it is appropriate to arrive a little late rather than on time.
- *Party traditions.* Traditionally, women congregate on one side of the room and men on the other, but that is changing. For large formal affairs, invitations are written by hand. Flowers are often sent before a large affair. At a smaller party, you should take them to your host or hostess.
- *Privacy.* There are often closed doors, fences, and high walls around homes, especially of the more affluent. Knock, and wait to be invited in. Do not drop in on neighbors, for this is not customary. Personal security is very important, so the more affluent may have bodyguards and a security system.
- *Questioning.* Some North Americans get to know people by asking questions. However, in Latin America it is safer to talk about local issues of interest. Personal questions are often interpreted as prying.

- *Space.* Latin speaking distance is closer than North American speaking distance. Instead of handshakes, men often embrace.
- *Class and status.* People may not be served on a first-come, first-served basis. Their place in society may determine the order of preference as to serving and seating.
- *Business practices.* The pace in Latin America is traditionally slow, relaxed, and less frenetic, especially when negotiations are under way. Normally, decisions are made at the top. Brazilians, for example, do not like quick, infrequent visits. They like relationships that continue. This implies a long-term commitment in Brazil. Deals are usually concluded in person, not finalized over the telephone or by letter or electronic mail. Again, do not call anyone by his or her first name unless the person has invited you to do so. When in doubt, be formal. Dress conservatively, and use business cards of good quality and in the local language.

Cultural themes and patterns

Themes are basic orientations that are shared by many or most of the people in the region. They are beginning points for understanding, and they sometimes form a pattern of behavior.

- *Personalismo.* For the most part, a Latin's concerns are family, personal friends, hobbies, political party, and possibly sport, such as the local bullfight. But transcending all these is the concern for oneself. So, to reach a Latin, relate everything to him or her in personalized terms.
- *Machismo.* It means "maleness" and is an attitude that men have toward women. The macho is aggressive and sometimes insensitive; machismo represents power. Machismo is made up of virility, zest for action, daring, competitiveness, and the will to conquer. How is it translated into daily business life? A man must demonstrate forcefulness, self-confidence, visible courage, and leadership with a flourish. The machismo concept is implanted early in childhood and varies from country to country. Saving face and honor are important concepts for Latin males. Never criticize family or friends.
- *Femaleness.* Traditionally, women were "up on a pedestal" to be carefully protected by the male who was in charge. Yet, the female may actually control the home, children, and husband. As women in Latin America become better educated and pursue careers, their historical roles in the family and society as wife and mother are changing. For example, in 2005, Michelle Bachelet was elected President of Chile, only the third woman to be so elected to national office in Latin America—the first who was not the widow of an illustrious husband. Instead, this moderate socialist was a twice-separated mother of three children. In her socially conservative country, she previously served in the national government as Minister of Health and Defense. Realize that in some countries, like Venezuela, there is the "public" wife who runs the home and its finances, as well as raises the children, and the "private" wife, or mistress, who is for male pleasure.

- *Desires to get rich quick–fatalism.* There is instability in many Latin American economies, and, as a result, there is a boom-or-bust attitude. Many desire to make it rich by speculation, manipulation, or gambling. As a result, some Latin businesspeople are less interested in stable growth than are US businesspersons. Related to this is the Latin American tendency to let chance guide their destiny. Most are convinced that outside forces govern their lives. They are willing to "accept the inevitable." Don Quixote, who followed his quest whether or not it appeared hopeless, seems like a foolish man to many foreigners. To most Latin Americans, he is heroic. He was "bowing to fate," "taking what comes," and "resigned to the inevitable." Their attitude is: "what will be, will be, God willing."

- *Good manners, dignity, and hospitality.* Latin Americans are much like Europeans in this respect. They are more formal and more elaborate. They shake hands on meeting and departing. In Latin America, the work one does is directly related to the social class one is in, "high" or "low." Latin Americans are, by and large, stratified societies. Latin Americans are born with a sense of place, but the two classes of very rich and very poor is giving way to a growing and more affluent middle class. Latin people have enriched cultures because of their skills in music, art, and architecture. At the same time, Latin Americans are warm, friendly, and hospitable. They like to talk and want to know about a visitor's family and interests.

- *Human resources.* Aristocratic values, late industrialization, and strong central governments have combined to create an imbalance in human resource supply and demand in South America. Large numbers of South American workers have no industrial skills, but there is an oversupply of professional and white-collar workers; there is, in particular, an acute shortage of trained managers. Part of the problem lies in a centuries-old university curriculum with an overemphasis on lawyers and engineers, which is very much in need of modernization. The global market, foreign investments, and increase in high technologies are facilitating the emergence of a pan-American knowledge culture.

- *Authoritarianism and egalitarianism.* Signs of respect can be determined in both tone of voice and manner that denote grades of inferiority and superiority in a hierarchical society. The *patron* is the man of power or wealth who sustains loyalty from those of lesser status. He can be the employer, the politico, the landowner, and, in other cases, the money lender or merchant. Authoritarianism does not allow for questioning. The *patron* knows everything and is all-powerful. To play these roles, one has to be respectful in a subservient position. However, as the middle class continues to grow in size and strength, authoritarianism is less prevalent. Latin America is going through a social revolution in which agricultural and traditional societies are giving way to modern industrial and technological economies. The impact of Roman Catholicism is strong in the Latin cultures, but lessening as a force in the daily lives of people, especially in the urban areas. The profound social, economic, and political changes underway are altering many of the above customs and influences, especially among the younger generation. Democratization, worldwide communications, international exchanges, and contemporary realities are transforming Latin America. Its global managers are sophisticated in the ways of international business, and may not illustrate, at least on the surface, the typical social or cultural characteristics of the region.

CHALLENGES FOR PAN-AMERICAN COOPERATION[20]

The prospects for pan-American synergy in the twenty-first century are encouraging. Inflation is still a major problem, coordination of economic policies is distant, but barriers to trade are being reduced, and governments are committed to cutting fiscal deficits. There has also been relative peace between the nations of the Western hemisphere, despite internal upheavals within various Latin American states. Yet, political factions often block hemispheric efforts toward shared energy and trade exchanges.

There have also been some noble efforts toward economic cooperation that lay the groundwork for real collaboration in the future. It takes time for such diverse cultures to learn the value and skills of joint endeavors. But the ground for synergy has been broken in such undertakings as the Organization of American States, the former Alliance for Progress, the Central American Common Market, the Andean Pact, NAFTA, and MERCOSUR. All such cooperative arrangements seek to collaborate in common economic and trade policies that are more market friendly, while reducing protectionism. Another hopeful sign is the shift away from unilateral foreign aid to sharing of resources through multilateral institutions, such as the World Bank and the Inter-American Development Bank. Lately, the concerns of the various Latin American nations have shifted more to the social arena, with the establishment of such entities as the Inter-American Commission on Human Rights. Another reason for optimism about the future of relationships is the Pan-American Development Foundation (PADF). Its objective is to help the lowest-income people in Latin America and the Caribbean to participate productively in the socioeconomic and cultural development of their societies. The PADF activates the involvement of the local private sector, especially the business community, through the formation of national development foundations in the various countries.

Underlying all of Latin America's difficulties is the need for integral development in the areas of education, healthcare, and opportunities for self-development. The interdependence of North and Latin America and their need for each other are obvious. Economic development is now more horizontal in the Americas, and not just vertical. Those with vision will set goals to close the pan-American poverty gap by around the middle of the twenty-first century.

Achieving synergy within Latin America requires leaders able to do the following:

■ Better manage the national resources of all states in the hemisphere by more effective collaboration of public and private sectors in each country, and between north/south regional relations.

- Manage the transfer of technology and information for mutual development of North American and Latin American people.
- Contribute to economic and social development of Latin America through the exercise of corporate social responsibility by multinational enterprises on both continents.

Meeting the challenges of globalization has increased support for the proposed South American Community of Nations (SACN), perhaps as a replacement for the less-effective Organization of American States (OAS).

The OAS is a regional organization that has all of the 35 independent states of North and South America as members.[21] The Charter of the OAS was signed in Bogotá, Colombia, on April 30, 1948, which is the founding date of the organization. Operating out of its headquarters in Washington, DC, the OAS promotes the values described in Article 2 of its Charter, which include, but are not limited to, security, representative democracy, conflict resolution, and interregional collaboration.[22] The OAS is in a unique position to affect politics and economics across the Americas.

A number of the OAS's online resources are notably pro-business. In the field of intellectual property, the Directory of National Authorities on Intellectual Property helps to promote the image of the Americas as a safe place in which to invest, in addition to providing essential contact information. The Foreign Trade Information System publishes the texts of trade agreements, in addition to detailed information regarding intellectual property.[23] The OAS's efforts to promote sustainable development and to root out corruption are also worthy of careful analysis by those interested in investing in the region.

CONCLUSIONS

This chapter provided global managers with an overview of doing business in Mexico, Brazil and Argentina. To improve the quality of life for all of the Americas' inhabitants, effective and ecologically controlled utilization of resources on these twin continents is a major management challenge. Trained and experienced managers in transnational enterprises throughout pan-America may be able to accomplish in the decades ahead what politicians, dictators, revolutionaries, and soldiers have failed to accomplish in the past centuries—cooperation and collaboration for the common good. The potential of Latin America can be actualized.

MIND STRETCHING

1 What is most striking to you in the contemporary development of Mexico?
2 Why do the Central American states need to implement their negotiations for regional economic trade and development?

3   What is the significance of Portuguese culture and language in Brazil, in contrast to Spanish culture and language elsewhere in Latin America?

4   How do you envision the future of indigenous people or Amerindians in Latin America?

5   Why are North America, Europe, China, and Japan so interested in Latin America?

6   What are the implications of so many Latin Americans migrating to the US and Canada?

7   Why does Latin America have to act as a trading bloc with Asia, Europe, and North America?

8   How can Latin Americans expand their business relationships with Africa, the Middle East, and Russia?

NOTES

1   Montaner, C. A. "Culture and the Behavior of Elites in Latin America," in L. E. Harrison and S. P. Huntington (eds.), *Culture Matters*. New York: Basic Books, 2000, pp. 57–58. Also refer to Chong, N. and Baez, F. *Latino Culture: A Dynamic Force in the Changing American Workplace*. Boston, MA: Nicholas Brealey/Intercultural Press, 2005.

2   Khanna, P. *The Second World: Empires and Influence in the New World Order*. New York: Random House, 2008.

3   Abbott, J. and Moran, R. T. *Uniting North American Business: NAFTA Best Practice*. Burlington, MA: Elsevier/Butterworth-Heinemann, 2002.

4   Khanna, *The Second World*.

5   Cardoso, F. and Bell, P. *A Break in the Clouds: Latin America and the Caribbean in 2005*. Washington, DC: Inter-American Dialogue, 2006. Fay, M. (ed.). *The Urban Poor in Latin America*. Washington, DC: World Bank. De Ferranti, D. et al. (eds.), *Inequality in Latin American and the Caribbean*. Washington, DC: IBRD and the World Bank, 2005. Paige, J. *Democracy in Central America*. Cambridge, MA: Harvard University Press, 1998.

6   Cardoso and Bell, *A Break in the Clouds*; Fay, *The Urban Poor in Latin America*; de Ferranti et al., *Inequality in Latin American and the Caribbean*; Paige, *Democracy in Central America*.

7   See "Together Again, After All These Years?" *The Economist*, May 14, 2005, p. 41.

8   Klonsky, J. and Hanson, S. *Mercosur: South America's Fractious Trading Bloc*. Washington, DC: Council on Foreign Relations, 2008. www.cfr.org/publications/12752/mercosur.html.

9   Calderon, F. "Mexico's Road," *The World in 2008*. www.economist.com/theworldin/2008.

10 Much of the information on Mexico is updated from Abbott, J. D. and Moran, R. T. *Uniting North American Business: NAFTA Best Practices*. Burlington, MA: Butterworth-Heinemann, 2002. Used with permission.

11 Public Citizen, *School of Real-Life Results Report Card*, December 1998; Student: *North American Free Trade Agreement*; Grading Period: January 1, 1994, to January 1, 1999.

12 Campbell, J. *The Power of Myth*. New York: Doubleday, 1988, p. 4.

13 Moran, R. T. and Stripp, W. G. *Dynamics of Successful International Business Negotiations*. Houston, TX: Gulf Publishing Company, 1991, p. 43.

14 Pike, F. B. *The United States and Latin America: Myths and Stereotypes of Civilization and Nature*. Austin, TX: University of Texas Press, 1992.

15 Ibid., p. 46.

16 The material on Brazil was originally written by Kristine Elaine Menn. She has lived in São Paulo, Brazil, since 1992, where she works as a consultant and teacher of cross-cultural communication and English. Subsequently, the authors have updated and added material to this section.

17 Unger, B. "Dreaming of Glory: A Special Report on Brazil," *The Economist*, April 14, 2007, p. 16. www.economist.com/specialreports.

18 Khanna, *The Second World*.

19 Barshefsky, C. et al. (eds.), *U.S.–Latin American Relations: A New Direction for a New Reality*. Washington, DC: CFR, 2008 (Task Force Report #60), www.dfr.org/publication/. Morrison, T., Conway, W. A., and Douress, J. J. *Dun & Bradstreet Guide to Doing Business Around the World*. Paramus, NJ: Prentice Hall Press, 2008. Axtell, R. E. *Gestures: The Do's and Taboos of Body Language Around the World*. White Plains, NY: Wiley, 2008. Stephenson, S. *Understanding Spanish-Speaking South Americans*. Boston, MA: Nicholas Brealey/Intercultural Press, 2003. Lanier, A. *Living in Latin America*. Boston, MA: Nicholas Brealey/Intercultural Press, 1988. Gordon, R. *Living in Latin America*. Skokie, IL: National Textbook, 1976.

20 Skidmore, T. E. and Smith, P. H. *Modern Latin America*. New York: Oxford University Press, 2005. Burns, E. B. and Charlip, J. A. *A Concise Interpretive History of Latin America*, 8th edn. Upper Saddle River, NJ: Prentice-Hall, 2006. Goodwin, P. B. *Global Studies: Latin America*, 13th edn. New York: Dushkin, 2008.

21 OAS, "OAS: Member States," www.oas.org/en/member_states/default.asp.

22 OAS, "Charter of the Organization of American States," www.oas.org/dil/treaties_A–41_Charter_of_the_Organization_of_American_States.pdf.

23 OAS, "OAS: Intellectual Property," www.oas.org/en/topics/intellectual_property.asp.

14 DOING BUSINESS IN EAST ASIA

Chinese military strategists learned that the highest principle of all was flexibility. . . . Good strategists, like water on rock, yield to the terrain in order to wear away the most unyielding of obstacles. They don't simply confine themselves to stratagems that ostensibly fit their circumstances, rather they mix and match according to actual conditions. . . . In short, the ultimate rule for applying these stratagems is to follow no rule.

Gao Yuan[1]

The cognitive mind conceives constants in the flux of phenomena and flow of events, but in the context of combat, where instantaneous adaptation to the unexpected is essential, this "freeze-frame" function of cognition, otherwise necessary for ordinary life, becomes a fatal handicap. As a Zen saying describes it, "As soon as you call it thus and so, it has already changed." Therefore the moment-to-moment presence of mind produced by Zen training is valued for overcoming. . . entanglement in conceptualization.

Zen Master Takuan[2]

Korean men are very emotional when making business decisions. If you strike the right emotional cord, the Korean decision-maker will often respond favourably simply on impulse. On the other hand, a Korean, unlike Japanese, will not be polite when you get on his wrong side. Korean tempers can get awfully hot.

Chin-ning Chu[3]

L
E
A
R
N
I
N
G

O
B
J
E
C
T
I
V
E
S

After reading and studying the concepts, examples, and illustrations in Chapter 14, readers should be able to understand and appreciate:

1   The requirements for building trust- and respect-based business relationships in all three countries as a necessary condition for business, and the differences in relationship-building processes between China, Japan, and Korea.

2   The requirement to save face for Chinese and Korean business counterparts, and how both giving and saving face is even more important for doing business with the Japanese.

3   Issues related to spoken language, nonverbal communications, meeting protocol expectations, negotiations strategies, and decision-making processes, and how these issues differ for Chinese, Japanese, and Korean businesspeople, presenting different challenges for Western counterparts.

4   Differences in genetically based psychological national character preferences for problem-solving, and communications between Japanese and Koreans on the one hand, and Chinese on the other hand, and how these differences affect the interactional process with Westerners.

5   Gender roles, particularly the position of female expatriates in each country.

Separate sections for China, Japan, Korea, and Hong Kong discuss important cultural differences in greater detail.

INTRODUCTION

This chapter is concerned with three of the most successful economic powers and trading nations in the world—China, Japan, and South Korea (Korea). Hong Kong is also included, despite being a part of China, because its business culture is very different from that of China. Hong Kong is, as a separate administrative unit, the seventh greatest international trading economy in the world (exports + imports) ahead of South Korea. At first glance, there are many similarities between the Chinese, Japanese, and Korean business cultures. Many Westerners do not accurately differentiate between them. This is a mistake. There is no unified "Asian" business culture. The conditions Westerners will encounter trying to successfully build relationships and make deals in the three countries are often quite different.

The purpose of this chapter is to help Western businesspeople, students or professionals, understand these differences through direct comparisons, as well as shorter country-specific discussions. There is additional coverage of Chinese (and Japanese and

Korean) Confucian philosophy and its relationship to business ethics in Chapter 9. All three countries are strongly Confucian. Confucianism is an ethical philosophy that teaches morality and governs all interpersonal relationships. There is detailed discussion of Chinese and Japanese strategic thinking, compared to Western, in Chapter 11.

The twenty-first century has been called "The Century of the Pacific," to be led by China.[4] The People's Republic of China (China) has risen from Third World status in 1979 to become the world's largest economy, measured by purchasing power parity (PPP),[5] and second largest behind the US in GDP.[6] China is a twenty-first-century superpower. It has the largest population of any country, and the largest armed forces. It is a nuclear and space power. It is a global economic power with the most exports, second most international trade, and a huge balance of payments surplus. China is also the world's oldest continuous civilization, with over 4,000 years of recorded history; its oldest dynasty, the Hsia, dates to 2200 BCE. Exhibit 14.1 compares the three nations, and Hong Kong, to the US to show their relative importance as international markets.

The Japanese economy was the world's second largest for decades until it was surpassed by China in 2010,[7] and it remains comfortably the world's fourth largest by GDP.[8] After decades of stagflation following the collapse of the Japanese economic boom in the early 1990s, and recent years of deflation, the Japanese government embarked in 2013 on policies intended to devalue the yen and improve global trade competitiveness. Japan's relationship with China is paradoxical. On the one hand, China expresses deep political antipathy about Japan's treatment of China during what the West calls World War II. China also seeks by political and military pressure to force Japan to cede to China the Sekaku Islands, known in China as the Diaoyudao Islands. On the other hand, the bilateral trade relationship between China and Japan is the second largest in the world after that between Canada and the US.

South Korea's economy would be considered impressive in size if Korea was part of the European Union (EU) rather than positioned between China and Japan. South Korea's

EXHIBIT 14.1 WORLD TRADE COMPARISONS, 2015

	United States	China	Japan	Hong Kong	South Korea
Exports, 2015 (billion)	$1,510	$2,143	$622	$510	$549
Exporter rank	#2	#1	#4	#7	#5
Imports, 2015 (billion)	$2,273	$1,576	$627	$529	$429
Importer rank	#1	#2	#4	#7	#9
Total trade, 2015 (billion)	$3.783	$3,719	$1,249	$1,034	$977

Source: CIA, *The World Factbook*. www.cia.gov/Library/Rankorder (retrieved November 16, 2016).

E X H I B I T 14.1

economy, 14th largest in the world by PPP, is 85 percent as large as Italy's, and 15 percent bigger than Spain's.[9] Korea has ambivalent relationships with both Japan (due to Japanese treatment during World War II) and China (due to Chinese support for the Kim Jong Un regime in North Korea). Gifts given by Westerners to Korean counterparts, for example, should not come from Japan.

CHINA, JAPAN, AND KOREA COMPARISONS[10]

A useful way to understand Chinese, Japanese, and Korean business attitudes and practices is through directly comparing how they differ from each other. There are many surface similarities, but these mask intrinsic differences. For example, all three cultures are strongly Confucian in philosophy, but Confucian philosophy varies in its interpretation between the three. In China, the Confucian follower is expected to maintain his/her complete loyalty to his/her leader, and in return the leader always has the best interests of his/her followers in mind. If the leader betrays his/her duty to the follower, she/he is encouraged to rebel.[11] In Japan, however, the follower is expected to remain loyal even if his/her leader does not have his/her interests at heart, even to the point, until recent times, of hara-kiri (suicide). In Korea, absolute reverence is owed to those most senior in age. In Japan and Korea, Confucianism is derived from the Confucian sage Mencius, who believed human nature was good and recommended treating everyone with benevolence. In China, it is derived from the Confucian sage Xunzi,[12] who believed human nature was evil and recommended testing the virtue of others with invitations to ethically dubious practices.[13]

Similarly, Katz[14] and others[15] observed that trust-based relationships were critical in all three countries before any business could be negotiated, and that communications were always indirect. However, the processes for building these relationships differ from country to country, and the Japanese are far more indirect than the Chinese. Koreans are usually indirect but under certain circumstances may become very direct and even aggressive. Therefore, the purpose of this section is to compare and contrast Chinese, Japanese, and Korean practices to make apparent their practical differences. A second purpose is to highlight how Western, and especially American, practices may hinder communication, relationship-building, and negotiations.

Trust-based business relationships

Katz[16] observed that trust-based business relationships were very important for doing business in Korea, and critically important in China and Japan. In all cases, the expectation is that strong bonds will need to be demonstrated prior to any agreements or deals being closed, and that these bonds will develop into genuine friendship over time. In Korea, businesspeople strongly prefer to do business with foreign counterparts with whom they have already developed trust-based relationships. These relationships may be developed to some degree *during* the negotiation process. If Koreans do not spend extensive time building relationships then it is probable that they are only interested in a short-term benefit and the relationship will be disposable. In China and Japan, deep relationships based on trust, shared goals, mutual benefits and constructive handling of controversy or disagreement must be built *prior* to doing any business, regardless of the time it takes. These relationships become key success factors for their Western counterparts, ensuring long-term success.[17]

A necessary precondition for a relationship is respect. In the West, one receives respect on the basis of one's accomplishments and/or education, but Chinese, Japanese, and Koreans all value humility, disapproving of what they perceive as boastfulness. In China, one is respected on the basis of one's greater age, higher rank, and to a lesser extent, one's achievements. The Chinese admire personal traits of patience and ability to socialize. In Japan, the criteria are age, status, and rank, but not achievements. The Japanese admire loyalty, commitment to one's team or company, and the ability to socialize. In Korea, respect depends mainly on advanced age and status. Koreans admire sincerity, persistence, and ability to get along. Because of the importance of humility, however, these traits must be demonstrated rather than simply claimed. For example, even internationally experienced Chinese tend to regard the American rush for quick closure and results as arrogant and rude, and Westerners' claims to competence based on personal education and/or relevant experience as showing off. Being humble means deflecting praise by insisting that one is not worthy, or that others are more worthy. The same is true for the Japanese. In Korea, one should also make a point of showing great respect to the most elderly business counterparts since age-based status is so important.

A second precondition for relationship-building is face-saving, very important in China and Korea, and even more important in Japan. Causing any embarrassment, or perceived disrespect causes loss of face. Loss of face literally means that when others see your face they see you differently, remembering the negative association. In China (and Japan), interpersonal harmony is a critically important value. Any negative feelings or criticism directed at another is perceived as disharmony and causes the recipient loss of face. As a result, emotional restraint, or a "poker face," is a highly valued attribute. Your reputation depends on your ability to control your emotions and remain friendly, regardless of how others receive you. If you need to discuss a difficult topic with an individual counterpart, you should do it privately and find words to convey it positively and with respect. For example, instead of criticizing a weakness, you can praise a number of positive strengths and conspicuously make no mention of what you perceive as the weakness. Your Chinese counterpart will get your point. Additionally, in China a person's face is also his/her company's face. An injury to your counterpart's face may endanger the entire inter-company relationship. An injury to a company's face may hurt possible relationships with other companies as well. Canadian companies that withdrew from northern China at the time of the Tiananmen Square incident, on Canadian government advice, found later that even in southern China they had lost face.

In Korea, the issue of face is much the same, except that Korean negotiators can become much more emotional and aggressive than negotiators in China or Japan. In the West, it would be common to respond emotionally in return, or at least to signal one's feelings nonverbally. Saving face, however, means keeping your cool and never showing if you feel upset, even in your body language or tone of voice. Additionally, you should also not injure the face of your competitors whom the Koreans are probably considering as alternatives. This demonstrates modesty. Any demonstration of loss of composure will likely harm your prospects. The Chinese say "Three strikes and you're out," applying that baseball analogy to giving ignorant Westerners just three chances.

In Japan, face is even more important to relationships than in China or Korea. In addition to saving your counterpart's face, it is also a good idea to give face. Giving face means treating your counterparts with great respect and genuinely praising them, and their organizations, for positive steps and outcomes along the way. A common pitfall for Westerners, however, is to offer praise to an individual person. The Japanese work in teams and you would normally only meet with an individual counterpart if the two of you had long history and strong trust. Picking out one Japanese from his/her team for praise paradoxically causes him/her loss of face through embarrassment in front of his/her team. So, face is given by praising the team or organization. If you want to praise an individual, it should be done privately and will be appreciated. Giving face also means that you may have to pretend that your counterpart understands what you have said even when you suspect she/he does not—following up with questions and clarifications until the communication has finally succeeded.

Apologies are another strategy for giving face and maintaining harmony. In Japan, it is common to apologize often and in detail even for small missteps like being a bit late. Apologizing demonstrates modesty and humility, while respecting the relative importance of your counterpart's face. This is a difficult practice for Americans and most Western Europeans, who are not used to apologizing for what they regard as trivial concerns. Canadians are often well-received because apology is common in Canadian culture.

You should remember that you can only request a favor, or that a counterpart go out of their way to help you, if you already have a trust-based relationship, or if your position is being vouched for by someone who already has such a relationship—an intermediary. Without the relationship, the request will be seen as inappropriate and ignored. If the relationship exists, then your request will be honored as part of what is called "guanxi" in China, or "amauru" in Japan.[18] Guanxi is a form of reciprocal altruism that drives cooperative social interactions between networks of individuals that support each others' aspirations through providing gifts and favors for each other.[19] Requests from guanxi partners within an individual's network are non-negotiable and will always be fulfilled within the ability of the individual providing the favor or gift. Guanxi can "open doors" through political influence, or "solve problems" by bypassing legal requirements. Westerners may also "close doors" by limiting their commitment to their guanxi partners. It is considered inappropriate in East Asia to negotiate the terms of fulfillment, or plead inability to help, or that circumstances have made it impossible to comply. You should also remember that if you have used an intermediary to vouch for you, and then you prove unreliable, it will cause loss of face for your intermediary, and damage your relation with him/her and all his/her network of guanxi friends.

The time required to build these relationships is potentially difficult for Western businesspeople to accept. Most Western business cultures regard relationships with counterparts as only moderately important and not a precondition for doing business.[20] Westerners generally do not believe that they need to trust a counterpart to do business with him/her because their subsequent cooperation will be monitored by the contract and will be legally enforceable. American salespeople are known for bringing final contracts to a first meeting with a new client.

East Asians, however, have a different view of contracts, understood to be flexible if conditions change and governed by the relationship between the parties rather than by law. A Western company that allows its relationship with a Chinese or Korean supplier to deteriorate while the contract is still in force will probably find that ultimately the contract will not be fulfilled, and that it will be very difficult to sue a local company in China or Korea. A Japanese company in the same circumstances will probably honor the contract terms but the relational damage will preclude further business and give your company a bad name in Japan. With Chinese clients, stopping in from time to time to ask how they are doing with the product you sold them will be appreciated. With Japanese, stay in touch more frequently, adding email or telephone consultations.

Communications issues

There is some truth to the belief that English has become the common language of international business, and that business negotiations are often conducted worldwide in English. Where this "reality" breaks down is for your foreign counterpart; English is generally his/her second (or third or fourth) language and his/her comprehension may be limited. This problem is compounded in China, Japan, and Korea because to admit that you do not understand causes loss of face.

In China, many business counterparts pride themselves on speaking English, but command of the language is limited. Your Chinese counterpart will probably bring an interpreter but you should have your own interpreter as well, and you should understand that many Chinese interpreters are also not proficient. You should inquire in advance whether your translator should be proficient in Mandarin Chinese or another dialect, or both. Over 70 percent of Chinese speak Mandarin, but the common dialect in Guangdong province is Cantonese. We have found that northern Mandarin-only translators are not well-received and are ineffective in Guangzhou due to regional resentments. Your interpreter will help you understand the subtleties being communicated, and also what your counterparts are discussing across the table from you. Occasionally your interpreter will tell you that your counterpart's interpreter incorrectly translated your message. Incorrect translation may occur because a Chinese translator does not know the Chinese words for technical English business jargon. Correcting mistakes is, however, a problem because of face issues. You may have to offer elaborations and suggest that your translator translate for you because of greater technical familiarity. In Korea it is much the same as in China. Go slow, and let your interpreter translate your message piece by piece. Ask questions to ensure you are understood.

In Japan, English is taught in the school system from age 12, but Japanese students become more proficient in written English than spoken. You should approach negotiations by preparing written English-language proposals and sample clauses as you would negotiating with Canadians (see Chapter 18). Speak slowly and confirm key points in writing—for example, on a flipchart or whiteboard. Interpreters may be a problematic issue in Japan because they will be seen as a new member of your team, and an outsider. If they have not participated in the initial relationship-building, this will have to be done again. Your translator should be someone from your company who participates from the beginning.

Chinese, Japanese, and Korean counterparts all expect to engage in low-key, quiet, and respectful conversations. They all regard loud voices and emotional over- or undertones as lack of emotional control, a bad sign for a potential business associate or partner. This is an especially difficult lesson for American counterparts who associate loud voices with seniority and strong leadership. Chinese counterparts may become silent for periods of time, especially after a proposal has been made, and this may be a technique to encourage nervous concessions from Westerners who feel uncomfortable when there is not an immediate reaction. The Japanese may also become silent—for 10 seconds or even a minute—and this should not be taken either as agreement or disagreement. This is also a difficult point for Western and especially American negotiators who may interpret silence as agreement or the end of discussion rather than thoughtful consideration that should be respected. If Koreans are silent or appear distracted, it is possible they do not understand and await clarification.

Koreans communicate relatively indirectly though they can become quite direct and emotional in the heat of negotiations. The Chinese are more indirect and generally emotionally restrained. The Japanese are the most indirect and restrained. Indirect communication does not mean "vague," though Westerners often interpret it that way.[21] An observed cultural difference between Asian and Western cultures is the use of "spiral" or holistic versus "linear" logic.[22] Spiral logic is an element of high-context cultures (see Chapter 2) "with individuals circling indirectly around a topic, considering it from all angles and viewpoints"[23] without naming it—but it becomes obvious to everyone (on the Asian team). One interprets what is not being said by "reading between the lines,"[24] and interpreting body language and facial expressions. By contrast, Westerners, and particularly Americans, employ very literal linear logic and do not assume a connection between concepts until it has been clearly stated.

To a certain degree, indirect communication is used to maintain the important values of face and intergroup harmony. Neither Chinese, nor Japanese, nor Koreans will say "no" directly when they oppose a proposal because open disagreement and direct confrontation are discouraged. If the Japanese say "It will be very difficult" or "I am not sure. . ." it likely means "no" and indicates serious problems needing further discussion. In addition, Chinese, Japanese, and Koreans are not committed to dualistic thinking, unlike Westerners. They do not believe that there is one answer that must be right and that this necessitates that other answers must be wrong. They are more likely to proceed dialectically (thesis + antithesis = synthesis), combining elements from different alternatives to produce a wholly new possibility. This is an especially difficult lesson for Americans and Western Europeans, who are dualistic thinkers and not, as a result, as open to compromise.

Nonverbally, the Chinese are the most restrained, even interpreting crossing your legs under the table as a lack of self-control. You should not move your hands when you speak to Chinese counterparts as they do not, and it may confuse. For the Japanese, even scratching your head or frowning may be interpreted as either apprehension or rejection, and they will watch you closely (and you should watch them). In China, you should minimize eye contact as a sign of respect. In Japan, you should minimize eye contact with more senior Japanese counterparts, but make eye contact occasionally with equals. In Korea, you should make frequent eye contact to communicate sincerity and willingness to trust. However, American-style constant eye contact should be avoided even in Korea, where it is interpreted as hostile and aggressive. In all three Asian cultures, the only physical contact should be shaking hands. Americans should avoid their common physical gestures (e.g., touching a counterpart's back) intended to communicate friendship.

Meeting planning and process

In all cases, you should employ an intermediary to arrange the initial contacts and meetings. In China, this intermediary should be a respected local person with whom you already have a good trust-based relationship, or with whom you are able to build such a relationship. Canadians, for example, may use the Canada–China Business Council (CCBC), with its offices in Vancouver and a relationship network in China. We have used the CCBC to meet with senior government and business officials in north and central China, but we needed at the last moment to find alternative arrangements through local government for southern China. Make sure your intermediary is able to establish connections senior enough to be useful. In Korea, the process is similar but the intermediary should have a strong relationship with the specific Korean organization you are interested in, or suspicions may be raised. In Japan, your intermediary should not be perceived to have a lower rank than those you want to connect with in a Japanese company, and should not work for that company, or yours. If you cannot find such a person in Japan, it is permissible to call directly, but not to make contact by letter or email. This is a lesson especially for American businesspeople valuing speedy closure and relying most on electronic connections.

For both China and Korea, a senior executive should lead your team. She/he should be as senior as the Chinese or Korean team leader. You should inquire who will be on the counterpart team, and match your team to theirs on status and rank. When the teams enter the room, members enter in hierarchical order, led by the team leader; your team should enter the same way. For Japan, a senior executive should attend the first meeting to signal senior management support, but is not required for subsequent meetings. Japanese teams do not enter hierarchically and it may be difficult to pick out the team leader. She/he may be the one who says the least, whereas the Chinese and Korean team leaders will lead their discussions.

Meetings will begin with some small talk. Chinese and Japanese delegates will appreciate some bit of humor to break the ice, but this is inadvisable in Korean meetings. Western style set-piece jokes should be avoided in all cases because humor is based on cultural disjunctions that may not apply in other cultures, producing incomprehension and requiring lengthy explanations. With Chinese and Korean meetings, you should let your counterparts set the pace and follow along—a difficult lesson for American cultural expectations of speed and quick resolution. In Japanese meetings, the Western side will be expected to begin with a general "state of the union" presentation that emphasizes the status, size, and accomplishments of your company, and the general nature of the business you have in mind. These presentations should be prepared in detail in advance. The Japanese expect a great deal of detail and will not be under time pressure for an early result. Bring all potentially useful background information and have written copies for all participants. In Chinese meetings, we have found that the Chinese team leader begins discussions with this initial "state of the union" summary at the conclusion of the initial small talk.

Westerners should understand and accept that the purpose of initial meetings is to build relationship by beginning to establish trust, shared goals, potential mutual benefits, and to see how controversy or disagreement will be handled. Subsequent meetings will test these observations and feelings as substantive issues are introduced. No decisions will be made—likely at any meeting—but decisions made by teams after meetings will be communicated at subsequent meetings. This is a difficult lesson for Western negotiators who often believe that they can "close" their counterparts by answering all objections through logical argument and appeals. It is especially difficult for American and Western European negotiators who believe they have the "right" product, service, or technology answers, and are under time pressure from home for quick results.

Westerners may also find difficult the Chinese and Korean penchant for "holistic" negotiations that jump back and forth between topics without resolution, rather than dealing with issues in a "logical" sequential order. The Chinese, in particular, are comfortable with a high level of initial vagueness—far more so than Westerners with their sequential approach—and only expect details to be fully clarified after general agreement is reached in the late stages of negotiations. In addition, Chinese, Korean, and Japanese negotiators may appear to acquiesce to arguments made in one meeting, only to raise the same issues in subsequent meetings long after Western negotiators thought they had agreement. This is usually the case when Westerners take strong, uncompromising positions and the acquiescence signaled the need to maintain intergroup harmony rather than agreement. This will occur again and again until the Western side finally understands there will be no deal until compromises are made.

Negotiations

There will be no serious negotiation for a deal in either China or Japan unless the Asian side is confident that a long-term trust-based relationship has already been established with their Western counterparts. In Korea, there will only be serious negotiations if the Korean side is confident that by the end of the bargaining the relationship will have proven itself to be long term and trust-based.

Negotiation styles vary considerably between China, Japan, and Korea. While long-term relationships, commitments, and benefits are especially valued in all three, only in Japan are the negotiation practices usually cooperative, as if the two sides were engaged together in joint problem-solving as would be the case in many Western countries. In China, negotiators often become quite competitive and even adversarial, battling over seemingly small potential gains. Korean negotiators can become very emotional, aggressive, and adversarial but, oddly, do not see this as contrary to the maintenance of a trust-based relationship. Perhaps Korean negotiators see their aggressive behavior as the true test of whether a trust-based relationship actually exists by testing it under fire. Counterparts who trust will remain calm, friendly, and patient even when the going gets tough. Westerners must remain emotionally restrained and under control when faced with Korean emotion and aggression, or Chinese unemotional competitiveness. If Westerners lose their self-control and meet fire with fire, as would be common in the West, the deal will likely fail because the relationship proved itself wanting. Abramson[25] argued that the principle goal of Chinese negotiators was a trust-based relationship, but that if this goal was not reciprocated, then Sun Tzu military-style strategies (see Chapter 11) would be deployed to target the perceived enemy. Haggling, or extreme competitive bargaining, consisting of repetitive and insistent small, incremental requests for concessions,[26] is a common behavior for Chinese and Korean negotiators, but uncommon in Japan. Apparently corrupt practices—requests for bribes, favors, and gifts—are fairly common in China, somewhat common in Korea, but rare in Japan.

Despite their fierce bargaining, Chinese negotiators will want to preserve the trust-based relationship that they believed existed before bargaining commenced. They will be ultimately willing to compromise to maintain the relationship as long as their Western counterparts remain calm, friendly, and persistent, and do not take the competitive process personally. Westerners should not make too-big concessions early because negotiations will proceed in several stages with each new group of Chinese negotiators eager to extract further concessions to increase their face. Westerners should negotiate team-on-team and not as an individual pitted against a Chinese team. Chinese teams include skilled bargainers capable of outmaneuvering even well-prepared Westerners. Chinese preparation can be extraordinary, perhaps because of their guanxi relationship networks that may have members from many companies. They will likely know how much a product/service has been sold for in other markets, and have a good idea how much you might be willing to concede on price to get a deal. Chinese negotiators are skilled in exploiting disagreements between counterpart team members so the latter should guard not only their words, but also their body language, and what they say on social occasions, because the Chinese keep track. Prices commonly move 40 percent or more from your initial offer to a final agreement so you should make allowance for that. Westerners should expect to win concessions from the Chinese side in return for agreeing to requested concessions. An effective strategy for doing so is to ask for new concessions in areas already agreed. This is a Chinese approach that will seem agreeable to them. In addition, Chinese negotiators may concede additional benefits like greater profitability in a second negotiated deal after a relationship has proven itself in a first contracted period.

Korean negotiators may become emotional as well as competitive and aggressive. They may focus more on short-term benefits than either the Chinese or Japanese. However, the Korean negotiators will be willing to compromise to build an effective long-term relationship. Korean business culture considers buyers and sellers as in a mutual dependency relationship and searches for win–win solutions that benefit both sides. Korean culture supports win–win negotiation practices to maintain mutual face. Again because of Korean haggling, Westerners should not make too-big early concessions because prices will move more than 40 percent from initial offer to final agreement. Worse, Westerners that go too quickly to their "drop-dead" final price will find that their Korean counterparts may be offended, and even suspicious that the Westerners are uninterested in the relationship. As with the Chinese, Westerners who make concessions should ask for Korean concessions in return even in areas already agreed. A common Western approach is to prepare several alternative options where different prices are achievable given sets of specific Korean concessions in return, but you must resist "cherry-picking" by the Korean side.

Even though the Japanese appear cooperative and willing to engage in joint problem-solving, there is one caveat. The Japanese believe that buyers are in the driver's seat and there is a strong expectation that sellers will do everything they can to fulfill buyer needs. Some Japanese buyers may demand to see the seller's cost structure and offer a defined margin above that as a profit. At the same time, if the relationship has borne itself out as trusting and cooperative, and the seller has done its best, Japanese business culture expects that both sides will take care of each other—the same as the Korean buyer/seller mutual dependency—and the buyer will ensure that the seller makes a reasonable profit. In these circumstances, Japanese buyers may be expected to be willing to cooperate and compromise as to the nature of the profit.

Westerners should negotiate team-on-team with the Japanese. Unlike with the Chinese, this is because different aspects of a contract may be led by different Japanese team members; for balanced status, the foreign counterpart who leads from the other side should be the same status as the opposite team leader.

Despite the Japanese ostensible commitment to cooperation, negotiators will try to wear each other down to obtain concessions. Westerners should not make big concessions early because it may be taken as either poor preparation, or disinterest in the process, neither of which reflects well on the overall relationship. Unlike the Chinese and Korean competitive negotiation practice, the Japanese are very formal. They frown on haggling, but every proposal must be priced in detail and foreigners must explain the rationale behind every price. As a result, prices may move between 25 and as much as 40 percent from initial offer to final agreement, with the Japanese expecting to obtain most concessions fairly late in the process. Again, Westerners should ask for Japanese concessions to match their own, and be willing to revisit agreed-upon areas of the contract to get them. Some Japanese believe, however, that there should be no concessions required because both sides should have made their best offer sincerely at the very beginning. These folk should be treated carefully because the apparent lack of sincerity in a high initial offer is a bad sign for the trust-based relationship.

The Chinese, Japanese, and Koreans all believe that privileged information will produce bargaining advantages. Full information is rarely freely shared. This is a very different attitude from that commonly held by Euro-Americans, many Western Europeans and Latin Americans, and Thais, where information is more freely shared as part of a joint problem-solving process.[27] As a result, Westerners may share too much. In China, Westerners should protect their intellectual property (IP), giving no access until the deal is completed. The Chinese legal framework for protecting IP is comprehensive but poorly enforced. In Japan, Westerners should make sure they do not surprise the Japanese team with new and important information. Japanese teams do not react well to such surprises. You should informally share the surprise prior to the meeting where it will be discussed. Koreans will share more information as they come to believe in the strength of the relationship.

Westerners should not exaggerate claims about their organizations, products, services, or prices. All claims will be investigated. Chinese negotiating teams often want to do site inspections of Western facilities. One Canadian company discovered that the Chinese side of their negotiation was simultaneously negotiating in other locations with their direct Western competitors and using that information and those offers to beat each Western company down in price. On the other hand, do not be surprised if Chinese negotiators are not fully accurate in their own claims and attempt to mislead. Verify everything. One Canadian company reported that in China even bank records could be falsified if you were friends with the right people. In Korea as well, misleading claims and information are not uncommon. In Japan, untruths are rare, and attempts to mislead less frequent. It should be needless to say that if you catch a counterpart Asian negotiator in what seems to you clearly a lie, you should not say so at the negotiation. This would be a colossal loss of face and likely the end of discussions. It's also important for Westerners not to try to bluff, because if caught you will lose face, and it could "kill" all trust.

One serious error Westerners make is to think that a deal may be successfully concluded in a single visit, and then to negotiate as if faced with serious and immediate deadlines. This hurried deadline will be obvious to Chinese, Japanese, and Korean negotiators who will stall so as to magnify the time pressure. Near the end of the visit, there will likely be demands for major discounts that will be called "compromises." On the Westerners' last day, there may be demands to renegotiate the whole deal. Chinese negotiators have been known to drive to the airport with their Western counterparts haggling for further concessions the whole way. Westerners must accept that they will likely make multiple trips, and accept all these ploys in good humor while maintaining their emotional control. Continue to emphasize the mutual benefits of what has been discussed. Remain willing to be flexible—willing to compromise in return for concessions from the other side.

In the event of a serious dispute, Chinese companies have long been willing to agree to third-party arbitration in a neutral mutually agreeable country. In Japan, the best neutral third-party arbitrator would be whoever introduced the two sides at the beginning of the process. She/he will be motivated to find a fair solution because she/he loses face if the relationship fails. In Korea, third-party arbitration is not a good idea because it communicates that the relationship is not strong, and without that there will be no deal. You should work to emphasize the value of the personal relationship and try to build greater trust. Try to refrain from logical reasoning or arguing. The Koreans will not decide on the basis of Western "logic" and arguing hurts the relationship.

Decisions

There are some Chinese entrepreneurs that are sole decision-makers for their companies. However, the majority of Chinese, Japanese, and Korean decisions are made away from the negotiating table in a consensus group process. Groups involve many stakeholders, including, in China, political or other individuals in guanxi relationship networks with the decision-makers. When the global fast-food giant McDonald's was blocked from entry into Shanghai, it eventually discovered that the resistance was not from the mayor and council, ostensibly the decision-makers, but from a nonpolitical person the mayor held in deep regard. In China as well, there is still a central economic planning process, and the central (and provincial, and city) bureaucracies have great influence over company decisions. Westerners should remember that any local Communist Party or government official that seems to be involved around a negotiation should be invited and treated as an important negotiation stakeholder. This would not be the case in Japan, but government ministries do organize think-tanks intended to support the corporate sector.

Westerners tend to have two misunderstandings about East Asian decision-making. First, they believe that somewhere, hidden from view, there is a central leader or boss that will make the final decision. Westerners believe this because in the West it is often the case. In China, Japan, and Korea to a large degree, there is no such person. The senior Japanese leaders will orchestrate the process of consensus-building. It is a slow process, identifying all the required stakeholders, building trusting relationships between them, exchanging all relevant information, negotiating, and eventually deciding. In Korea, the process is the same except that the most senior leaders, while not deciding, do have a lot of influence, and usually that final say.

Second, Westerners believe that the final decision will be based on universal principles (free trade, free market economy, democracy, etc.), logic, and empirical evidence because those are universal Western decision-criteria. The Chinese and Koreans, however, will decide on the basis of the situation they are dealing with, regardless of any universal principles. They will likely weigh their feelings and their experiences at the bargaining table—the relationship for example—ahead of any objective and empirical evidence. Government influence, or "communist" political ideology (in China) may force a dogmatic decision regardless of practical preferences. While the Japanese do analyze objective evidence and factor it into their decisions, they also highly value their personal feelings and their experiences at the negotiation table. The Japanese are also reluctant to embrace change that is perceived as risky. Westerners' number-one task, besides maintaining relationship, in influencing a positive Japanese decision is to find them ways to reduce perceived risks.

Gender roles

Gender roles have traditionally represented the male/female dichotomy. Gender has more recently become an aspect of personal identity regardless of whether a person was originally born as, or in, a male or female body. These days "queer theory" recognizes multiple genders beyond male and female.[28]

Foreign women are likely to have few problems in China if they behave professionally in business and social situations. They should avoid appearing overly aggressive and understand that while Mao Zedong granted women equal rights, things have moved somewhat in the other direction since his death in 1976. China has traditionally frowned on intimate relationships between Chinese and Caucasians. Asian women, and particularly overseas Chinese, are likely to be perceived as Chinese, as opposed to foreign, women. Homosexual activity was decriminalized in China in 1997, and declassified as a mental disorder in 2001.[29] LGBT individuals in China have no legal protections against discrimination, employment discrimination, cannot serve in the military, or donate blood, and transgendered individuals will not be recognized as their preferred sex without surgery.

Foreign women may be treated better in Japan than foreign men in the sense of being better able to obtain information. This is the polite Japanese way to treat women. Business socializing may be difficult because Japanese men socialize routinely only with other men. Being perceived to behave aggressively will be a major issue of impropriety for a foreign woman. There are no Japanese laws against homosexuality. In 2003, Aya Kamikawa became the first openly transgendered individual to be elected an official in Tokyo.[30] There are, however, no legal protections for LGBT persons against discrimination, employment discrimination, housing discrimination; they cannot donate blood, and transgender status is only recognized after surgery.

Foreign women may find themselves in some awkward or difficult situations in Korea, though foreign women are treated differently from Korean women. You should tell your Korean counterparts well in advance of a negotiation if there will be a woman on your team so they can prepare and adjust. Same-sex relationships are legal in Korea but a Pew survey in 2015 found that 57 percent of Koreans disapproved of homosexuality, while only 18 percent approved.[31] Pew concluded that you could not admit openly in Korea that you are gay. LGBT individuals have no legal protections against employment, housing, or general discrimination, and cannot serve in the military, but can donate blood.[32]

National character and problem-solving styles[33]

In previous chapters, we discussed psychosocial national character[34] in terms of four extra-verted communication styles (Chapter 2), and four introverted problem-solving styles (Chapter 11) based on Jungian personality research.[35] In Chapters 12, 15, and 18 we combine the problem-solving and communication styles to produce comparative national characters for the national cultures being discussed in those chapters. When we do the same here for China, Japan, and Korea, we find some significant differences. We also use a group of English-speaking (US, UK, Canada, Australia) and EU (Germany, UK) referent nations for comparison, representing those countries where *Managing Cultural Differences* is most likely to be used as a resource. In this section, we limit our considerations to the four introverted problem-solving styles.

According to Massey,[36] the predominant problem-solving style in both Japan and Korea, as well as all six of our Western referent nations, is Introverted Sensing (Si), whereas in China (including Hong Kong) it is Introverted Feeling (Fi). In Chapter 11, Si was defined as follows.

> *Introverted Sensing (Si)*: Si individuals work quietly, systematically, and in-depth to achieve useful results. They deal in facts and details in a careful and orderly fashion, even reporting a photographic memory for details. Si individuals are thorough and conscientious but discount any data that are not sensory. They distrust imaginative people that are less accurate with facts... They value efficiency and cost effectiveness.

Fi was a very different problem-solving process based on quite different criteria. It was defined in Chapter 11 in the following way.

> *Introverted Feeling (Fi)*: Fi individuals base their decision-making on their feelings and their belief that their actions will support strongly held personal values. These values may or may not conform to their society's values, but if not, Fi individuals will resist peer pressure and maintain their own value commitments. They seek harmony and order, influencing others through their actions more than their words. Because their feelings are introverted and not externalized, they may appear unemotional, or indif-ferent... However, they are flexible, modest, nonjudgmental, and forgiving, tending to mediate conflict by affirming the value of all sides.

Si problem-solving emphasizes objective factual analysis, distrusting creative problem-solvers with imaginative solutions that may not be supported by the existing evidence, and valuing efficiency, cost-effectiveness, and tried-and-true traditional alternatives. Fi problem-solving places value-commitments ahead of objective analysis. Haas and Hunziker[37] observe that Fi people are emotionally committed to their core beliefs, will not easily tolerate violations of them, decide on "gut-feel" rather than logical analysis, and may emotionally cut-off a relationship due to value issues without any visible indication that they have done so. They will resist data that appear to conflict with their values, while not having strong opinions about subjects that appear unrelated to their values.[38]

The Japanese and Korean Si problem-solving will seem very familiar to American, British, Canadian, Australian, and German businesspeople once they acclimatize to the cultural differences described above. The strength of Si is that it is data-driven, recording and remembering all objective data about situational aspects of the external environment, and also recording all evaluative interpretive analysis applied to that evidence. It is also very strong at comparing past and present situations to gauge objective levels of performance, effectiveness, and effect over time. In addition to accurate observation and precise memory, it tends to search for root causes of objective effects. If the Japanese and Koreans decide on the basis of their feelings about relationship, and their experiences at the bargaining table as described above, the Si problem-solving style guarantees that the objective evidence presented by their negotiation counterparts will play an important role in determining their feelings about how to proceed.

The Chinese Fi problem-solving will seem very alien, as if the Chinese do not seem to know what they are doing, not following Western problem-solving processes that Westerners often regard as universal. In Chapter 11, however, Exhibit 11.14 indicated that of the world's greatest trading nations, 14 predominantly preferred Fi problem-solving, and 14 preferred Si. The problems Westerners will encounter dealing with Chinese Fi will be repeated in India, Russia, Italy, Spain, Brazil, and Mexico, to name just a few. It is not surprising to find the Chinese at odds with the Japanese and Koreans since the latter have the same difficulties with Fi as Westerners. Fi devalues objective or impartial evidence in favor of supporting values about how the world should be. Fi individuals tend to be idealistic and to hope for external conditions that fulfill their idealism while avoiding realities that they regard as harsh and undesirable. Evidence about people, products/services/technology, and events are judged in terms of their conformity with internally held values, and there is strong unwillingness to change value-commitments to conform better with others' expectations. In fact, Fi individuals tend to select information that supports their value-based analysis.

The Chinese Fi problem-solving style is an immense challenge for Western negotiation counterparts committed to a Si style. A Western Si problem-solver will marshal all relevant data and its interpretation so as to ensure that his/her Chinese counterpart will have the most accurate view possible. She/he will not present this evidence in the context of values because she/he regards values as subjective, and therefore irrelevant to objective evaluation. On the other hand, a Chinese Fi problem-solver will, as described above, be comfortable in the earlier stages of negotiations with a relatively high level of vagueness related to details, and with switching back and forth between topics. She/he is trying to establish the values and principles that should govern the evaluation of the facts as they emerge later. Fi and Si have an enormous probability of immensely frustrating each other because they are based on entirely opposite standards of evaluation—governing values versus governing evidence.

Please note that the specific problems encountered in negotiations between Si and Fi problem-solving are described in detail in Chapter 12 on the Middle East. It is a major issue for Westerners dealing with Saudi Arabian and Turkish counterparts, and well as Chinese.

National character and communication styles[39]

In Chapter 2 we discussed four Jungian[40] extraverted attitude-functions that produced four universal communication styles that affect human communication preferences, with one style predominantly characteristic of every national character. Again, thanks to Massey,[41] the predominant communication style preferences for more than 100 national cultures have been identified, including China, Japan, and Korea. Again, please note that "predominant" simply means the style that most often occurs on average in a national culture.

According to Massey, the predominant communication style in both Japan and Korea is Extraverted Feeling (Fe), described in Chapter 2 in the following way.

> *Extraverted Feeling (Fe)*: Fe individuals are concerned to conform to established cultural patterns and societal norms of interaction and relationship. Their behavior is generally polite, considerate, and sensitive to the needs and expectations of those around them. Fe individuals understand situationally appropriate behavior, and build friendly relationships based on cooperation, shared interests, mutual benefits, and developing trust. They have a value commitment to altruism and will sacrifice their own interests for others. Fe individuals have a knack for maintaining harmony in relationships. They are skilled in establishing empathy and rapport, cooperating, saying the right thing at the right time, and serving others.

In contrast, the predominant communication style in China (and Hong Kong) is Extraverted Sensing (Se). This is described in Chapter 2 as follows.

> *Extraverted Sensing (Se)*: Se individuals have an extremely accurate sense and memory of factual information about the external environment. They seek specifics and details related to their involvements and remember even the smallest elements. Therefore, they have a very accurate memory of what was previously communicated. Se individuals focus on the facts and have little interest in theory or precedents, and do not want to be limited by others' rules or expectations.

Both Fe and Se are quite different communication processes from the Extraverted Thinking (Te) that is the predominant communication style for all our group of English-speaking (US, UK, Australia) and EU (Germany, UK) referent nations. Canada was excluded this time because its predominant style is Fe, the same as Japan and Korea. These referents were chosen as representing those countries where *Managing Cultural Differences* is most likely to be used as a resource. Te is described in Chapter 2 in the following way.

> *Extraverted Thinking (Te)*: Te individuals understand the external environment to be governed by logical and structured processes of cause and effect. Their goal is to organize the external environment and its inhabitants. They tend to see things very dualistically, definitely in terms of "black and white" and "true and false," and have logical and impersonal reasons for their assertions and actions. Anyone and anything that agrees with their reasoning is "right." Anyone and anything disagreeing is "wrong." Te individuals are strong in planning, organizing, directing, and controlling capabilities with a strong need for closure. They do not regard their feelings for others as important, and are not good at giving positive feedback.

These Fe and Se communications styles represent a great challenge for Westerners predominantly committed to Te-style communications. As an aside, Japanese and Korean (and Canadian) Fe communicators would be as challenged by the Chinese Se preference as are Western Te communicators, and vice versa, though for different reasons.

In a nutshell, Fe communicators are primarily interested in building trust- and cooperation-based relationships and are willing to compromise to serve others' needs to some extent to do so. Te communicators do not particularly value relationships, being more concerned with objective facts and analysis. They seek to organize physical sensory data by applying theoretical interpretations they believe, proven analytical tools, scientific method, policies and standard procedures, to achieve a fast decision, and speedy implementation in directions they have already envisioned. Se communicators also value sensory information over relationships, but reject filtering their observations through theoretical or methodological interpretations. They are extraordinarily perceptive of detail, practical, and realistic. They resist quick closure and others' attempts to organize or control outcomes.

Western Te communicators logically organize their perceptions of external environments in terms of cause and effect, expressing these relationships in logical and structural terms. Their communications are about objective data and generally accepted ideas, and not particularly sensitive to their effect on other people. We could say that Te individuals are more oriented toward accurately reporting information as they perceive it, than to the effect of their communications on those they are interacting with. It is an important lesson for Westerners that this communication style that they regard as logical, factual, and honest, is perceived by Japanese and Koreans as abrasive, insensitive, and unconcerned with the relational dynamics the Japanese and Koreans hope to establish as a precondition for business. It does not help Westerners that they may become easily frustrated when their appeals to objectivity appear to fall on deaf ears. Expressions of frustration may cause loss of face, and indicate an emotionally unstable person unsuitable as a business associate.

In addition, Te communicators tend to be motivated by the dualistic thinking common to Western European cultures,[42] and are usually guided by a ruling principle (for example, free trade, democracy, equality) that they believe to be correct or right. Dualism is a black-and-white logical process for determining "right" from "wrong" that allows for no shades of gray. Te communicators assume, and will insist, that anything in disagreement with their ruling principle is "wrong." This means that they are naturally resistant to the consensus-building or compromising that Fe communicators prefer, and that their communications will generally be perceived by Fe communicators as self-interested because of the insistence of Te that their way is the only way. The Fe style, by contrast, is open to many shades of gray, and does not see the world as "black" or "white."

All this makes it challenging for Te communicators to build trust-based relationships with Fe counterparts because the latter will dig their heels in if their Te counterparts refuse compromise while behaving insensitively. A typical Japanese response—similar to Canadians (see Chapter 18)—would be to avoid direct confrontation, while delaying and obliquely undermining Western Te propositions. A typical Korean response would likely be more direct and assertive. Worse, Te communicators feel the need for early closure and forward movement in the directions they desire, so it is not unusual for them to be beset by early deadlines, and unwilling to spend the time to understand others' viewpoints. They are in a hurry to implement their plan, get things organized, and produce results through their own leadership.

Please note that the specific problems encountered in negotiations between Te and Fe communicators are described in detail in Chapter 18 on Canada and the US. It is a major problem for Canadians and Americans despite their many cultural similarities.

The Chinese Se communications style is also challenging for Western counterparts. Both Se and Te communicate relatively impersonally in terms of objective data. If anything, Se evidences a better memory for objective facts and minute details than Te. Where the two differ significantly is that Te is theory-driven, and deductive in logical process, whereas Se is data-driven and inductive.

Te communicators are theory-driven because they are guided by their ruling principle, which is essentially a theory for dividing possibilities or situations into "good" or "bad" based on dualistic principles. They are deductive because they start with this theory and then classify on its basis. By contrast, Se communicators are completely data-driven, and only concerned with achieving specific effects in the situation being considered based on the evidence. They have no patience for abstract theory divorced from situational realities, and will not accept others' rules, like cause and effect, for how their perceptions should be organized.

There is, however, a "twist" that further complicates the negotiation task for Western negotiators dealing with their Chinese counterparts. There is an interaction effect between the introverted problem-solving style, and the extraverted communication style. You see your counterpart's communication style because that is how they communicate with you. You can only infer the other person's problem-solving style because that's how they are thinking while communicating with you using the style you can see.

Westerners' Si problem-solving style is predominantly data-driven, and their Te communication style is very impersonal and concerned with communicating data and evidence, albeit organized around theories of how the world works. The Chinese predominant Se communications style is extremely data-driven with no apparent theoretical interest at all. The Se seems to fit the Western styles of problem-solving and communicating once the Westerners slow down from their need for early closure and quick results, and put aside their insistence on a ruling principle the Chinese will not accept. The Se communicates only an interest in a detailed examination of the proposals being made. Westerners would assume that the Chinese decision-criteria and their own would largely be data-driven.

However, the unseen Chinese Fi problem-solving process discounts the value and importance of the data in favor of the values held by the Chinese decision-makers. Having discussed the objective data in minute detail, the Chinese will retire to their consensus decision-making process where the most important decision-criteria will be their feelings about whether their principal value-commitments will be upheld by the proposed deal, based on their experience at the bargaining table. Westerners will erroneously believe, based on Chinese Se communications, that the Chinese decision will be made based primarily on the data and analysis. From the Chinese perspective, however, the data-driven discussions at the bargaining table are a testing ground for evaluating the quality of the relationship, and whether they may trust these Westerners based on their behavior in trying circumstances.

CHINA

> The Chinese miracle is the most amazing story of economic growth in world history, but it is also a uniquely Chinese story that perhaps no other nation could have written. . . . Nothing about a visit to China is quite as striking as their incredible infrastructure, beginning with the airport. . . . Its [Terminal 3 at the Beijing International Airport] the second largest airport terminal in the world after Dubai, and the third largest building in the world by area. The Chinese completed it all in about 4 years, about 3 times as fast as it would have been completed anywhere else I can think of. How did they do it? Well, they worked 24 hours a day, 7 days a week, 365 days a year. It is a massive, glistening, clean, elegant, and super-friendly place.
>
> Peter Rodriguez, Darden School of Business[43]

The emergence of China as a world superpower over the last 40 years is an amazing story. In 1979, Deng Xiao Ping, China's president and leader, initiated the "Open Door" policy for a Third World nation. Today, China is a political, military, and space superpower rivaling the US in political prestige and influence. Additional coverage of China is found in Chapters 9 (Confucian ethics), and 11 (Chinese strategic thinking).

Cultural guidelines for business in China

China is a culture that values harmony in interpersonal interactions. Perceived conflict is easily interpreted as loss of "face" or disrespectful. Chinese are not comfortable making recommendations or suggestions publicly. By using one-on-one communication and understanding nonverbal signals, one can usually determine the true meaning in conversation over time. In the Beijing office of Nortel back in the 1990s, a Chinese vice-president observed that his American counterparts had insisted that a particular American marketing plan would work. The Chinese executives observed that it would not work in China, and were confronted with demands to explain why not. Confronting areas of disagreement is a normal American problem-solving approach, but direct confrontation is seen as disrespectful in China. The vice-president said that the Chinese executives said, "Well, give it a try if you are so sure," to avoid an uncomfortable situation. It didn't work, and later the Americans confronted the Chinese again. "Why didn't you tell us?" they asked. The Americans were poorly prepared for dealing with Chinese culture. The episode reduced the willingness of the Chinese executives to help Nortel become successful in China, and eventually it folded.

Yet, personal development and growth, as well as monetary reward, are important motivators for Chinese employees. Good training programs are very attractive to them, and often they are willing to take less pay for educational and career opportunities. A detailed and clear reward system is important to such workers. Exhibit 14.2 is about a man who succeeded as an entrepreneur despite Communism's economic reformation.

Experienced China traders advise that when it comes to doing business, *throw away the rulebook, and expect the Chinese to be one step ahead of you!* The local business environment is eccentric and often apparently nonrational, causing managers and negotiators from abroad to make false assessments of the situation. Exhibit 14.3 is about the latest generation of entrepreneurs that have thrown away the old rulebook and succeeded.

Corruption

China was ranked 72nd of 150 nations on a worldwide corruption index conducted by World Audit.org in 2015.[44] In 2013 it had been ranked 61st. New Zealand, Denmark, and Finland were tied for being the least corrupt. North Korea and Somalia were tied in 149th and last place. Japan was 16th and South Korea 32nd. Canada was 9th, Germany and the UK tied at 10th, Australia 12th, the US 14th, and France 19th.

In 1993, China officially began an anticorruption campaign. Progress has been made. In 1998, the former mayor of Beijing was jailed on graft charges. In 2011 two former vice-mayors from eastern China were executed on bribery convictions. President Xi Jinping has made anticorruption a hallmark of his presidency.[45] However, despite these show trials, fraud is endemic. Jamie Flor Cruz of CNN wrote: "corruption is so entrenched that honest officials are now part of a minority that risks being left behind. It is a system where corruption

EXHIBIT 14.2 PIONEERING ENTREPRENEUR AND CAPITALIST

The 2005 obituary of Rong Yiren was a unique account of a Chinese anomaly about the scion of a family commercial empire founded in 1902. His death at 69 raised the question of how this Chinese billionaire, who was not a known member of the Communist Party, ever became vice-president of the People's Republic and twice chairman of the National People's Congress. More intriguing is how he managed to regain his wealth after ceding his family's business holdings after the 1949 revolution, and losing the rest during the Cultural Revolution of 1966–1976. Yet, within a decade or so, he arose as one of the 50 most charismatic businessmen in the world, and one of its richest by a 1999 reckoning of *Fortune* magazine. All this despite his family fleeing to Taiwan and the US, leaving him alone in the middle of the century to run 24 flour mills, textile, and printing plants employing 80,000 people.

Mr. Rong presented himself as a "patriotic" capitalist who remained to help China end its poverty by shifting to a market economy. When he gave the Party what it wanted, he subtly asked for a favor in return. The astute and handsome executive not only survived, but along the way became vice-mayor of Shanghai, and in 1959, vice-minister for the textile industry. Through guanxi, or personal connections, he positioned himself to creatively help Deng Xiaoping open windows to the capitalist world. Educated under the British system at Shanghai's St. John's University, this graduate became Deng's symbol of the new Chinese entrepreneur.

In 1979, at the Party's behest, he founded CITIC as an investment arm of the state to acquire telecoms, utilities, and highways. When a Special Economic Zone (SEZ) was established in southern China for foreign investments, CITIC was there to exploit the property boom. Rong, roving extensively, found the foreign concerns willing to invest in China, and lured them to the SEZ. This sophisticated executive did well for his country and himself. In 2000, *Forbes* estimated the wealth of Rong and his son, Larry Yung, now head of CITIC-Pacific, to be $1.9 billion. Their conglomerate boasts global assets of $6.3 billion, and includes 200 affiliated enterprises. And, in the process, China has been moving steadily toward a free enterprise system!

Source: adapted from "Obituary: Rong Yiren," *The Economist*, November 5, 2005, p. 94.

is the rule rather than the exception."[46] When China's new president, Xi Jinping, took office in 2013, he guaranteed a major battle to reduce corrupt practices, and punish any official that was apprehended. The dining and entertainment industries in Beijing have recently suffered major reversals as officials wait to see if Mr. Xi is serious.

E
X
H
I
B
I
T

14.3

EXHIBIT 14.3 YOUNGER GENERATION OF CHINESE ENTREPRENEURS

Shantou, a once-poor district in southern China, is the birthplace of one of the mainland's richest men. As a deprived boy, Wong Kwong Wu recycled bottles after school to supplement his family's income. At 16, he and his elder brother left to seek their fortunes, ending up in Beijing where they opened a clothing store called Gome. At 17, Mr. Wong switched its emphasis to home appliances and consumer electronics. In 1992, the brothers split the business—the elder went into commercial real estate and the younger kept the retail store. By 2005, they were both rich and jointly owned the skyscraper Eagle Plaza and the block that houses it in North Beijing. Today, Gome is a prosperous electrical appliance retailer with 437 stores in 132 cities and $3 billion in revenue. A clear leader in the 500 billion yuan electrical appliance market, the company now seeks foreign partners for further expansion. At 36, Wong himself was worth some $1.7 billion. Having acquired this wealth within socialist China, the young billionaire has become one of Beijing's biggest residential developers. "The beauty of property over retailing," he smiles, "is that you don't have to deal with so many people!"

Yet Wong lives frugally—he, his wife, and children live in a commonplace apartment. Although he is driven around in a stretch Mercedes for meetings on the move, personally he is a workaholic given to self-denial. Like many young Chinese entrepreneurs, Wong is sensitive to a regime still ambivalent about private property and the rapid rise in private wealth. Conspicuous consumption is still to be indulged in cautiously, especially given President Xi Jintao's promise to root out corruption by identifying those living beyond their means.

Source: adapted from "Face Value: China's Uneasy Billionaire," *The Economist*, February 4, 2006, p. 60.

The cultural practice of guanxi

Guanxi, or social networking, is perhaps the most important Chinese cultural practice affecting the performance and success of foreign businesses in China. Guanxi relationships are characterized by trust and personal relationship between two parties. They are intended to result in a reciprocal flow of transactions and benefits between the parties.[47] Guanxi is variously understood as social networking, a web of interpersonal connections, a pervasive lubricant intended to increase the efficiency and effectiveness of business relations, and an essential informal governance method for ensuring fairness of treatment.[48]

Abramson and Ai[49] reported that successful guanxi relationships with local Chinese counterparts were more important to the success of Canadian firms than willingness to invest in local Chinese operations, or lower levels of perceived environmental uncertainty. A recent meta-analytical study of 53 quantitative studies of guanxi by Luo, Huang, and Wang[50] confirmed that guanxi does enhance MNE organizational performance in China. Guanxi with business associates enhanced operational performance. Guanxi with government officials enhanced economic performance.

Chen, Chen, and Huang[51] reviewed 200 previous studies of guanxi and concluded that the basis for the success of guanxi is personal relationships. They observed that scholars have been debating whether guanxi will remain a key aspect of doing business in China, or whether the development of more impartial legal and regulatory institutions will make reliance on guanxi unnecessary. While this discussion has not been resolved, it seemed evident that guanxi was deeply rooted in Chinese culture.[52] It continued to have a significant role in economic activities despite reforms,[53] and the number of Chinese businesspersons building guanxi connections within China was increasing.[54]

Guanxi[55] takes a somewhat different form in northern China than in the south. The tendency is for guanxi in the north (Beijing, Tianjin) to focus on developing heartfelt ganqing, whereas there is more focus in the south on the exchange of reciprocal gifts and favors. However, the development of ganqing is the dominant form throughout China.

In its dominant form, successful guanxi demands the development of trust between partners based on the demonstration of long-term reliability and competence. Both parties must feel that they share common goals, and will receive mutual benefits, and that any disagreements will be resolved through constructive means that will benefit both sides. Gifts and favors are exchanged, but they are symbolic of the feelings of personal consideration developing between the parties. Gifts and favors may entail taking someone out for lunch, remembering someone's birthday, and/or attending dinners and/or social events that honor one or the other. Government officials in Beijing are allowed to receive simple and inexpensive gifts, usually in the range of $10–20, but are required by their regulations to refuse gifts of greater value.

As trust develops, so do feelings of ganqing. Individuals joined by heartfelt ganqing tend to put their friend's needs ahead of their own. In such an intersubjective[56] or I/thou[57] relationship, the buyer would buy generously because she/he knows it would benefit the seller, but the seller will generously not sell unless she/he knows it would truly benefit the buyer.

JAPAN

Contemporary Japanese culture is considerably different from previous, traditional notions of it and from most people's current stereotypes, including those of the Japanese themselves. Japan is commonly and stereotypically known as a land of nobility and chivalry, with values such as honor, pride, and perseverance. These form a moral code of everyday living that has permeated Japanese society for generations, even centuries. Yet contemporary Japanese culture (especially for younger Japanese) seems to operate from different values, attitudes, beliefs, norms, and behaviors. In short, Japan is evolving into a society with a different culture.

D. Matsumoto[58]

All these Japanese can get along fine without God. They are able to live in ambiguity, in perfect indifference to the church, to the pain of sin, and to the desire for salvation—to everything we whites believe to be essential to human beings. Why is it? Why?

S. Endo[59]

Japan is the epitome of the Far East and its enigmas. Because Japan is going through profound economic and social transformation within a generation or so, its cultural specifics must be viewed in that context. Realities of their participation in the global market and media are only two of the driving forces altering cultural preferences in that traditional society, especially among the new generation. Additional coverage on Japanese strategic thinking is found in Chapter 11.

Relationships

A nation the size of Montana, Japan is cohesive and crowded, which accounts for its rituals of bowing and politeness in crowded urban areas. Japanese relationships are familial and group-oriented instead of individualistic. Japanese value group relations and harmony. Group leadership is more highly regarded than individual initiative. There is a tendency toward clannishness based on family or group connections. One needs to know one's place and be comfortable with it.

Personal relationships score highly with Japanese, and future relationships depend on how you respond in the first encounter. Cut-and-dried relationships with business contacts are inadequate and must be supplemented by a social relationship for maximum effect. This usually means gift giving,[60] entertaining the client with a "night on the town" but not at one's home. Part of the Japanese manager's reward is a generous budget for entertaining. When away from home on business, the Japanese businessperson expects to be entertained lavishly (meals, theater tickets, etc.), but repays this kindness without reservation.

With regard to international relationships, Japan has close emotional and economic ties to the US, but is suspicious of aggressive Americans. The Japanese fear China, yet they are emotionally allied and identify with the Chinese. China has been an important location for offshoring expensive Japanese manufacturing jobs. China was Japan's leading export market and leading source of imports in 2015. This has started to change with the recent upsurge of anti-Japanese feeling in China.

In business relationships, there are two Japans—officialdom and intellectuals (e.g., politicians and businesspersons). In both, decision-making tends to be consensus-oriented, and slow. Senior people have more influence. There is a symbiotic relationship between government and business—cozy but not constricting.

In the context of social relations, Japanese tend to be clean, polite, and disciplined. Sociality and self-control disguise a highly emotional quality of the Japanese character and relationships. While the Japanese are sensitive to what others think or expect of them, and have a keen sense of right and wrong, they find it difficult to deal with the unexpected and strange, and so may smile or laugh when feeling unsure or uncomfortable.

Again, youth epitomizes the culture in transition. They are energetic and productive, yet anxious for change, gaining a new sense of "I/my/me-ness," while the pattern for their elders is "we-ness." The general gap between the generations is very wide. For example, younger university graduates are more open to entrepreneurship, especially in information technologies.

Attitudes and beliefs

The typical Japanese character[61] is diverse, with a sense of poetry and of the ephemeral. There is a concern for the transitory, inconclusive qualities of life, for nature, and its observation. It is actively curious, energetic, and quick, with a sense of delicacy and wistfulness. One manifestation is in the art of flower arrangements.

Although many Japanese will not admit to being religious, and the usual attitude is syncretic, there are three religious philosophies of life that are pervasive and that influence their behavior. Confucianism[62] and Buddhism were both introduced from China around the end of the eighth century CE. Confucianism and Buddhism are both discussed in Chapter 9.

Shintoism[63] is native to Japan. It teaches respect for nature and counsels harmony between mankind and nature. Shinto minor deities are found in shrines (*jinja*, distinguished by red wooden archways), and in nature itself (e.g., mountains and rivers). The dominant religious thrust is the syncretic convergence of Shintoism and Buddhism. Individuals are baptized, honored as children, and married in Shinto ceremonies. They are buried in Buddhist ceremonies.

Buddhism is the largest conventional religion in Japan, while Christianity has had a limited impact (except with Christmas celebrations and decorations in retail stores). The crusading Buddhist Soka Gakkai sect is also a political party that fights inequalities in the social structure, while enshrining the idealistic, self-denial, and the espousal of the underdog.

Values and standards

The dominant Japanese ethos includes familial relationships, loyalty, conformity, and the collective good. Japanese personality is generally self-confident and flexible, demonstrating a sense of order, propriety, and appropriate behavior. There is a tendency toward diligence and thrift, balanced by a fun-loving approach which, at times, seems almost frivolous and extravagant.

In outlook, the Japanese are cautious and given to stalling tactics. They are also insular, which is manifested by the in-group tendency. The rigid, ossified Japanese class system is disappearing. Most Japanese regard themselves as middle class.

Japanese value peace, harmony, and economic progress, ensured somewhat by the fact that only 1 percent of the nation's gross national product is devoted to defense spending. Japan is precluded by its constitution to have offensive military capability. This culture highly regards new ideas and technologies, swallowing them up until they are Japanized (internalized) after careful, detailed examination. The success of Japanese communications and automotive industries confirm this value.

Japanese prefer congenial, known surroundings, and seek to create an atmosphere of well-focused energy and disciplined good cheer. A basic standard of Japanese life is to work and play hard—work particularly for the good of the family or company family, and maintain controlled competition and cooperation in the process. Then play hard—one-night, or one-weekend holidays are common, often at traditional hot-spring hotels.

Postwar Japanese have feared foreign military involvement, but have been willing to engage in humanitarian endeavors sponsored by the United Nations. However, because of the pressure from China and the North Korean nuclear threat, Prime Minister Shinzo Abe hopes to revise the Japanese Constitution to allow for better military capability and the freedom to use it. A current debate in Japan concerns nuclear weapons. The US has guaranteed Japan's nuclear security for many years but the question in Japan is whether the US would go to war with China to defend Japan.

SOUTH KOREA

At the end of hardship comes happiness (Go-saeng Ggeuteh naki eun-da).

Korean proverb[64]

The Korean Peninsula lies south of China, with the Yellow Sea to the west and the Sea of Japan to the east. Manchuria and Russia lie to the north. Korea is very mountainous, and Koreans proclaim that if the land could be rolled out flat it would be as big as China.

Today, the Peninsula is divided between North and South Korea, separated by the demilitarized zone, as an outcome of the Korean War in 1953. There has never been a peace treaty signed between the North and the South and both sides remain militarily ready to resume the conflict at any time. The American armed forces have a real physical presence in the South, intended to ensure that this does not happen. Exhibit 14.4 describes the North Korea situation.

Cultural characteristics

If one were seeking a national characteristic for the Korean people, one would choose *resiliency* to describe their ability to survive hardship and to sacrifice. A vital concept to understand in Korea is *kibun*, one of the most important factors influencing the conduct and the relationship with others. The word literally means *inner feelings*. If one's *kibun* is good, then

EXHIBIT 14.4 NORTH KOREAN NIGHTMARE

In the twenty-first century, the international community has been concerned about North Korea's ability to create nuclear power and weapons. Numerous six-party negotiations by America, South Korea, Japan, China, and Russia with this rogue regime have ended in discord. Despite promises of food and other aid, Kim Jong Il and his militarists resisted, until recently, attempts to coax better behavior. But that is not the only problem neighbors have with this wily and cruel administration, which permits its own population to starve. There are a range of other complaints about its criminal activities, ranging from kidnappings of Japanese nationals from Japan, and production of fake drugs, to money counterfeiting and laundering, to illegal trade in endangered species, missiles, and other weapons. This racketeering state, responsible for tons of illicit goods and fake currency throughout Asia, has seen its diplomats expelled from a variety of countries. The US slapped sanctions on North Korea for illicit weapons proliferation. Up to 40 percent of the state's exports result from its criminal sector, earning up to $1 billion in ill-gotten gains. Meanwhile, South Korea has quietly negotiated with northern officials to provide material assistance, while lessening restrictions on the exchange of citizens throughout the peninsula. Aside from North Korean elites, many face malnutrition and even starvation. These harsh realities force northerners toward improvisation in order to survive, while the elites have access to well-stocked larders and foreign consumer goods in Pyongyang.

North Korea survives because it is a buffer state. China fears a unified Korea, and potentially having US armed forces at the Chinese border. Also, South Korea is ill-prepared for the collapse of its northern neighbor, and any eventual integration of the two Koreas will challenge the South to provide huge resources to the North. Further, their compatriots from the North will face severe culture shock when they try to acculturate to the modern world. A positive development is that the demilitarized zone (DMZ) has become a wilderness zone with flower and fauna that the Peace Forum wants to keep undeveloped as a "Peace Park."

In 2013, however, the DMZ was fully re-militarized as the new northern dictator, Kim Jong Un, solidified his position by canceling the 60-year-old ceasefire, and threatening the South, Japan, and the US with nuclear war. Neither South Korean residents of Seoul, nor Chinese netizens were impressed by the latest North Korean bluster. A series of Mr. Kims, all North Korean dictators, have been crying wolf ever since the early 1950s.

Source: adapted from "Asia: North Korea and Those Six-Party Talks: A Frustrating Game of Carrots and Sticks," *The Economist*, February 11, 2006, pp. 39–40. Dominic Ziegler, "The Odd Couple: A Special Report on the Koreas," September 28, 2008, 19-page insert. Also see "A Look at What North Korea Vow to Scrap Armistice Means," *The Asahi Shinbun*, http://ajw.asahi.com/article_korean_peninsula?AJ201303060098 (retrieved April 11, 2017).

one functions smoothly and with ease. If one's *kibun* is upset or bad, then things may come to a complete halt, and one feels depressed. The word has no true English equivalent, but "mood" is close. In interpersonal relationships, keeping the *kibun* in good order often takes precedence over all other considerations.

In business situations, individuals try to operate in a manner that will enhance the *kibun* of both persons. To damage the *kibun* may effectively cut-off relationships and create an enemy. One prefers not to do business with a person who has damaged one's *kibun*. Much of the disturbance of *kibun* in interpersonal relationships has to do with lower-class persons disturbing higher-class persons, or younger persons not showing sufficient respect for older persons. Thus, for example, a teacher can scold a student in the class and no individual feels hurt, so no one's *kibun* is especially disturbed. A student that resists his/her scolding will damage the teacher's *kibun*.

Proper interpersonal relationships are all important among Koreans, but there is little concept of equality in relationships. Relationships tend to be vertical rather than horizontal, and each person is in a relatively higher or lower position. It is essential for one to know the levels of society and to know one's place. In relationships, it is often necessary to appear to lower oneself in selfless humility and give honor to other people. To put oneself forward is considered arrogant and worthy of scorn. Koreans will seek to determine the age of a foreigner to determine their proper relationship.

Confucianism's emphasis on hierarchy has also influenced relationships. Confucian thought is that one should rank the public higher than the private; one's business or government duties come before one's personal considerations. Protocol is also important to Koreans. When meeting others, if you do not appreciate a person's actual position and give it due recognition, then one might as well withdraw on some pretext and try to avoid future contacts. A representative of another person or group at a meeting is treated with great care because that representative may be sensitive to slights, either real or imagined, and report it back to his or her colleagues.

This is very difficult for Westerners to understand, but a Korean who fails to observe the basic rules of social exchange is considered by other Koreans to not even be a person. She/he is an "unperson" or "unable." Koreans show very little concern for an unperson's feelings or comfort. Thus, such an unperson is not worthy of much consideration. However, even with unpersons, every effort must be made to remain within the framework of polite relations. This need to remain within the "rules" of social exchange and interaction was forcefully demonstrated in the crash of Asiana Airlines Flight 214 at San Francisco Airport in July 2013 (see Exhibit 14.5).

EXHIBIT 14.5 KOREAN CULTURE MAY OFFER CLUES TO ASIANA CRASH-LANDING

When Asiana's Boeing 777 flight crash-landed in San Francisco in July 2013, initial reports suggested that Korean culture might be partly to blame. The plane was traveling too slowly and at too low an altitude on its final approach and its tail struck the seawall just before the runway. Two died and 180 were injured.

According to Thomas Kochan, a professor at Sloan School of Management, "The Korean culture has two features: (1) respect for seniority and age; and (2) quite an authoritarian style. You put those two together and you may get more one-way communication—and not a lot of it upward." Subordinates are expected to speak to superiors using honorific forms that require more words and an oblique approach. In the seconds before the crash, the cockpit voice recorders did not register any discussion about the fast-developing crisis between the pilot and co-pilot of Flight 214. It will, however, be months before a full investigation reveals exactly what happened.

Both the pilot and the co-pilot were well-qualified. However, the pilot was just learning how to fly a Boeing 777. It was his first landing of a Boeing 777 at San Francisco Airport, known to be a challenging place to land. By contrast, the co-pilot had considerable experience flying Boeing 777s and landing them at San Francisco.

The early speculation was that the co-pilot did not have the time to find the appropriate words and oblique approach required of him to correct his superior's unskilled landing approach.

Source: Wee, H. "Korean Culture May Offer Clues in Asiana Crash," *CNBC*, July 9, 2013, www.cnbc.com/id/100869966 (retrieved April 11, 2017).

HONG KONG[65]

The Hong Kong story began when imperial Britain's "gunboat diplomacy" approach to trade met with imperial China's protectionist policies in 1839. The resultant First Opium War ended with the Treaty of Nanking in 1842, which granted, among other trade concessions, the cession of Hong Kong Island to Great Britain. Britain's strategy was simple: Hong Kong was to be a free port that facilitated liberalized trade with China and served as a bastion of British imperial power and influence in Asia. In subsequent conflicts the British gained additional territory (Kowloon Peninsula in 1860, and a 99-year lease of Lantau Island and New Territories in 1898) in what the Chinese later called "unequal treaties."[66]

In the ensuing "Century of Humiliation," China endured continuous military, political, and economic upheaval[67] while Hong Kong remained largely unaffected under British rule. Hong Kong's economic rise started after World War II. During the 1950s, waves of refugees fled Communist China and brought with them skills and capital. Many foreign firms also moved offices from Shanghai, which paved the way for Hong Kong to diversify into light manufacturing from entrepôt trade.[68] In response to the aftermath of the political violence triggered by China's Cultural Revolution in the late 1960s, the colonial government, led by Governor MacLehose, implemented a wide range of social policies during the 1970s that became the foundation of modern-day Hong Kong society.[69] The dramatic end of the Cultural Revolution and the re-emergence of Deng Xiaoping ushered in a new era of economic reform in China. Against this backdrop the question of Hong Kong's political future emerged in the early 1980s as the 99-year lease of Lantau Island and New Territories was set to expire in 1997. In 1984, China and Great Britain signed the Sino-British Joint Declaration that would see the sovereignty of Hong Kong returned to China under a "one country, two systems" policy framework championed by Deng.[70] Economic prosperity continued throughout the 1980s and mid-1990s. During this time the colonial Hong Kong government gradually introduced elected representatives in various administrative and legislative bodies in the city.[71] The aftermath of the Tiananmen Square protests of 1989 marked the start of the pro-democracy movement in Hong Kong.[72]

The manufacturing industry moved north subsequent to the 1980s and the economy became service-based. Tourism, financial services, and trade are now the key industries.[73] China's re-emergence, both economically and politically, has had significant impacts on Hong Kong since 1997. The ever-tighter embrace of the mainland is threatening its autonomy and openness.[74]

Present-day Hong Kong is one of the most competitive and most *laissez-faire* economic entities in the world. Many credit this success to the "positive non-interventionism" that was the hallmark of British economic policy for Hong Kong.[75]

Core values

Hong Kong people pride themselves on being different from their mainland compatriots. A survey in 2014 showed that "rule of law," "freedom," "just and corruption-free," "democracy," and "social stability" are the top five Hong Kong core values.[76] History, economics, religion, and the free movement of people, ideas, and goods have significant influences on Hong Kong people's core values. Hong Kong is a metropolitan megacity that is rich in cultural diversity. Many Hong Kong people were either educated abroad or have dual citizenship with countries like Canada and Australia.[77] Hong Kong people understand and speak English, and cultural influences from Western countries, particularly the US and Britain, are highly visible. Japan and Korea are two close neighbors with significant influences in entertainment and popular culture.

Trust, tradition, reverence for elders, loyalty, morality, shame, and integrity are fundamental cultural values of Hong Kong people. The concept of "one of us" or "our people" is key to any business relationship. To be accepted as "one of us," one has to be trusted and demonstrate all the desired cultural values. Once accepted you are part of your contact's circle of contacts, and such networks are crucial in developing business relationships in Hong Kong.

Cultural interactions

Hong Kong people are highly adaptable and understanding of cultural differences. If there is ever any doubt about anything, ask and you will be enlightened. Some published checklists of dos and don'ts are based on time-honored myths, half-truths or are simply out of date. The one constant in Hong Kong is change. Some cultural norms have evolved and some older cross-cultural taboos (particularly those with historical references) may not even be recognized by the younger generation. Hong Kong's diversity makes any cultural assumptions dangerous. Hong Kong people are also inquisitive. As much as you want to learn about them, they want to learn about you. While cultural differences are important, the context and the social situation in question may also be highly relevant.

Business meetings

■ Punctuality is expected and respected. While most Hong Kong people value time as money, be understanding if your contact is slightly late. Traffic is the most commonly accepted excuse.

■ Dress appropriately in business attire. First impression is critical and may have a lasting impact. How you dress is also seen as the respect you have for your contact and how much you value the relationship. This is such an important aspect of Hong Kong culture there was a popular local song in the 1970s that says "people salute your clothes before they salute you."

■ A firm handshake while establishing eye contact signals trustworthiness and sincerity. A smile can be disarming and set the right tone for the meeting. Hugs and other types of body contact (e.g., high-fives, kisses, and pats on the back) are not common except among very close friends or family.

■ It is considered to be polite to inquire about a person's health or family. While you are not expected to relate intimate details, a curt answer or not reciprocating the sentiment is considered rude.

■ Bring business cards with both Chinese and English translations. It is considered a signal of reverence and respect to both present and accept business cards with both hands. Make sure your cards are properly printed and do not use cards with corrections, which is considered unprofessional. Handle a received business card with respect and care in the presence of the person who gave it to you.

■ Typical Western meeting etiquette applies and people with a senior ranking (professionally or socially) speak first and set the tone and direction of the meeting. Personal interaction and follow-up are important in building a business relationship.

■ Hong Kong people may appear to speak loudly and a soft voice may signal disinterest or weakness. Hong Kong people develop their own "lingo," which can be a mix of English and Cantonese words with deep cultural references (similar to slang in Western cultures.)

■ Modesty is a virtue to Hong Kong people and compliments are usually politely denied (but appreciated). Showing modesty when you receive a compliment will show your sincere desire to be accepted as "one of us."

Negotiations

■ Hong Kong people are more direct in expressing their ideas and positions than their mainland China compatriots, but are still not as blunt and direct as people from Western cultures. Avoid appearing to be brash and overbearing. Being able to "read between the lines" is crucial in business meetings. For example, if your contact were telling you about a bad experience with a former business partner, you may develop a sense of what your contact expects from a business partner. It could be your host's indirect way of expressing their expectations of you.

■ Expect negotiations to be detailed. They may progress slowly. It is not usual for your counterparty to seek consensus among themselves during negotiations. The word "no" is a strong signal of disagreement and may discourage further discussion, so avoid using the word if at all possible. Please also realize "yes" or any affirmative response may simply be your host's way to acknowledging your position.

■ Business negotiations involve give and take and the value of your relationship can be a reason for concessions. Be prepared to compromise.

Dining

■ Hong Kong has a unique food culture and dining is an important business function. Do not refuse an invitation to go for lunch or dinner. If taken to your host's "favorite restaurant" (or a restaurant your host has a relationship with), avoid criticizing the food or service (to show appreciation and respect). You do not wish your host to "lose face."

■ Fighting for the check is a common scene in Chinese restaurants. The key is to be gracious of your host's hospitality and reciprocate appropriately. Sharing business meals is a common way to establish relationships.

■ Be upfront about your dietary requirements and most hosts will understand and try to accommodate.

Comparing Hong Kong, Japanese, and Korean cultural behavior

■ Japanese and Korean people differ significantly in mannerism, gestures, and body language. They are considerate of others and, in general, quiet and reserved in public. Hong Kong people tend to be more rowdy and less conscious of others around them in public places. It is common to see Japanese and Korean people take a slight bow when greeting each other, while you rarely see a Hong Kong person doing the same.

■ Chinese, Korean, and Japanese share some Chinese characters but they are very different languages. Hong Kong people can read some Japanese signs without knowing Japanese as some of these characters have the same meaning in both languages.

■ Japanese people obey traffic signs and crossing signals even if there is no traffic. It is common to see Hong Kong people jaywalking. Eating while walking is a common sight in Hong Kong, but is considered to be impolite in Japan.

■ Japanese people almost never litter and the streets are always clean. Hong Kong streets are almost always clean too, thanks to the local sanitation department.

CONCLUSIONS

China, Japan, and Korea are fraught with cultural and personality differences that make relationship-building and negotiating deals very challenging. Yet these three economies are some of the largest and/or fastest growing and there are great incentives encouraging Westerners to learn to overcome the difficulties.

Not all Westerners will feel comfortable in China, Japan, or Korea because the predominant styles of individual problem-solving and communications are so different from Euro-North American norms. Seagal and Horne[78] observed that only a small percentage of Westerners had the same personality preferences as the majority in China, or Japan, but this minority felt more comfortable in East Asia than at home. The majority of Westerners who come to this region must be very careful to behave in more personal, and less impersonal, ways than is common in their own cultures. They will not achieve effective business outcomes if they do not take the time to build trust-based relationships and give others face through treating everyone with respect and consideration. In China, they will have to respect the values that are the Chinese decision-criteria. In Japan, they will have to be open to compromise. In Korea, they will have to be careful to respect age and seniority as key values.

The social situation in Asia is normally peaceful, but also very dynamic, often volatile. Traditional societies are in transition to a technological and knowledge culture. Unfortunately, historical grievances have come to muddy the relationships between China and Korea, on the one hand, and between China/Korea and Japan on the other. Chinese support for North Korea causes additional tensions between China and South Korea/Japan. China is becoming the predominant power in the region, and American influence may be waning to some degree.

MIND STRETCHING

1   Imagine you are on a team negotiating with Chinese, Japanese, or Korean counterparts. What kinds of specific difficulties would you face based on your own preferences? Which nationality would you find most difficult to successfully deal with? Why?

2   Think about your own approach to problem-solving. Do you rate values or objective data more highly? How do you persuade someone who thinks differently from you?

3   Think about your own style of communications. Do you prefer to just say what you think based on the evidence? Do you try to get along with other people by "softening" your message and being willing to compromise? Is one approach better than the other?

4   Why is it important for you to increase your knowledge and skill in Asian cultures, languages, negotiation styles, and business practices?

5   How would you build guanxi relationships in China? How is relationship-building similar and also different in China versus Japan or Korea?

NOTES

1   Yuan. , G. *Lure the Tiger Out of the Mountains: The 36 Stratagems of Ancient China*. Singapore: Simon & Schuster, 1991, p. 20.

2   Zen Master Takuan, "The Inscrutable Subtlety of Immovable Wisdom," in T. Cleary (ed.), *Soul of the Samurai: Modern Translations of Three Classic Works of Zen & Bushido*. Tokyo: Tuttle Publishing, 2005, p. 101.

3   Chu, C. N. *The Asian Mind Game: Westerner's Survival Manual. Unlocking the Hidden Agenda of the Asian Business Culture*. London: Stealth Productions, 1995.

4   Smambaugh, D. (ed.). *Power Shifts: China and Asia's New Dynamics*. Berkeley, CA: University of California Press, 2005. Kleveman, L. *The New Great Game: Blood and Oil in Central Asia*. New York: Atlantic Monthly Press, 2003. Ringmar, E. *The Mechanics of Modernity in Europe and East Asia: The Institutional Origins of Social Change and Stagnation*. London: Routledge, 2004. Covington, R. "Hearts of the New Silk Road," *Saudi Aramco World*, January/February, 2008, pp. 18–33.

5   "China Economy: Already Larger than U.S.," *The Globalist*, September 26, 2015, www.theglobalist.com (retrieved November 18, 2016).

6   "China Stumbles in Race to Pass U.S. as World's Biggest Economy," *Bloomberg News*, January 29, 2016, www.bloomberg.com (retrieved November 18, 2016).

7   Barboza, D. "China Passes Japan as Second-Largest Economy," *New York Times*, August 15, 2010, www.nytimes.com/2010/08/16/business/global/16yuan.html?pagewanted=all&_r=0 (retrieved June 24, 2013).

8   World GDP Ranking 2016, www.statisticstimes.com (retrieved November 18, 2016).

9   CIA, *The World Factbook*, www.cia.gov/Library (retrieved November 16, 2016).

10 The comparisons between Chinese, Japanese, and Korean practices are an amalgam of information found in the following sources unless otherwise footnoted: Chu, C. N. *Thick Face Black Heart: The Asian Path to Thriving, Winning & Succeeding*. London: Nicholas Brealey Publishing, 1996. Davies,

R. J. and Ikenu, O. *The Japanese Mind: Understanding Contemporary Japanese Culture*. Tokyo: Tuttle Publishing, 2011. DeMente, B. L. *The Korean Mind: Understanding Contemporary Korean Culture*. Tokyo: Tuttle Publishing, 2012. DeMente, B. L. *Etiquette Guide to Japan: Know the Rules that Make the Difference*. Tokyo: Tuttle Publishing, 2011. DeMente, B. L. *Japan's Cultural Code Words: Key Terms that Explain the Attitudes and Behavior of the* Japanese. Tokyo: Tuttle Publishing, 2011. DeMenete, B. L. *Chinese Etiquette & Ethics in Business*. Lincolnwood, IL: NTC Business Books, 1990. Fang, T. *Chinese Business Negotiating Style*. London: Sage Publications, 1999. Katz, L. *The Global Business Culture Guide*. Charleston, SC: CreateSpace, 2014. Kipnis, A. B. *Producing Guanxi: Sentiment, Self, and Subculture in a North Chinese Village*. Durham, NC: Duke University Press, 1997. McNeilly, M. R. *Sun Tzu and the Art of Business: Six Strategic Principles for Managers*, revised edition. Oxford: Oxford University Press, 2012. Morrison, T. and Conaway, W. A. *Kiss, Bow, or Shake Hands*, 2nd edn. n.p.: Getting Though Customs (www.getcustoms.com), 2015. Pye, L. *Chinese Negotiating Style: Commercial Approaches and Cultural Principles*. Westport, CN: Quorum Books, 1992. Wang, J. G. *Westerners Through Chinese Eyes*. Beijing: Foreign Languages Press, 1995.

11 Mencius, *Mencius*, 2010.

12 Twohey, M. *Authority and Welfare in China: Modern Debates in Historical Perspective*. London: Macmillan, 1999.

13 Watson, B. *Xunzi: Basic Writings*. New York: Cambridge University Press, 2003. See also Kline, T. C. and Ivanhoe, P. J. (eds.), *Virtue, Nature and Moral Agency in the Xunzi*. Indianapolis, IN: Hackett Publishing Company, 2000.

14 Katz, *The Global Business Culture Guide*.

15 Many have observed this based on empirical research, though some have argued that Chinese negotiators rely more on Sun Tzu strategy than trust-based relationships. This discussion is surveyed in Abramson, N. R. "Do the Chinese Seek Relationship? A Psychological Analysis of Chinese–American Business Negotiations Using the Jungian Typology," *Journal of Global Business*, Vol. 16, No. 31, 2005, pp. 7–22.

16 Ibid.

17 Abramson, N. R. and Ai, J. X. "Canadian Companies Doing Business in China: Key Success Factors," *Management International Review*, Vol. 39, No. 1, 1999, pp. 7–35.

18 "Guanxi and Amauru, the Driving Force of Social Interactions in China and Japan?" www.thinkingchinese. com/guanxi (retrieved November 20, 2016).

19 See Abramson, N. R. and Ai, J. X. "Using Guanxi-Style Buyer–Seller Relationships in China: Reducing Uncertainty and Improving Performance Outcomes," *The International Executive*, Vol. 39, No. 6, 1997, pp. 765–804. See also Abramson, N. R. "Building Effective Business Relationships in China: The Case of Richmond Engineering," in P. W. Beamish and A. E. Safarian (eds.), *North American Firms in East Asia*. Toronto, ON: University of Toronto Press, 1999.

20 Katz, *The Global Business Culture Guide*.

21 Ibid.

22 Jung, J. "Doing Business the Chinese Way: Eastern and Western World Views and Business Practices in China," University of Delaware Research Briefs, Issue 3, January, 2009, www.udel.edu (retrieved November 21, 2016).

23 Fritz, R. "Multicultural Effects on the Workplace," *Chron Small Business*, www.smallbusiness.chron. com (retrieved November 21, 2016).

24 Katz, *The Global Business Culture Guide*.

25 Abramson, "Do the Chinese Seek Relationship?"

26 Katz, *The Global Business Culture Guide*.

27 Ibid.

28 Wilchins, R. *Queer Theory, Gender Theory*. New York: Riverdale, 2014. Borden, J. *Transgender Complete: A Virtual Handbook*. n.p.: Joanne Borden, 2015.

29 "LGBT Rights in China," www.equaldex.com (retrieved November 21, 2016).

30 "Homosexuality in Japan," https://en.m.wikipedia.org (retrieved November 21, 2016).

31 "The Problem with Being Gay in South Korea," CNN, October 18, 2015, www.cnn.com (retrieved November 21, 2016).

32 "LGBT Rights in South Korea," July 10, 2015, www.equaldex.com (retrieved November 21, 2016).

33 Descriptions of problem-solving types presented in this section are derived primarily from: Sharp, D. *Personality Types: Jung's Model of Typology*. Toronto, ON: Inner City Books, 1987; and Thompson, H. L. *Jung's Function-Attitudes Explained*. Watkinsville, GA: Wormhole Publishing, 1996.

34 Inkeles, A. *National Character: A Psycho-Social Perspective*. New Brunswick, NJ: Transaction Publishers, 2015.

35 For some of the most recent leading-edge Jungian personality research, see: Hunziker, M. *Depth Typology: C. G. Jung, Isabel Myers, John Beebe and the Guide Map to Becoming Who We Are*. New York: Write Way Publishing Company, 2016; Beebe, J. *Energies and Patterns in Psychological Type: The Reservoir of Consciousness*. London: Routledge, 2016; Haas, L. and Hunziker, M. *The Building Blocks of Personality Type*. USA: http://eltaninpublishing.com, 2014.

36 Massey, B. *Where in the World Do I Belong?* USA: Jetlag Press, 2006.

37 Haas and Hunziker, *Building Blocks of Personality Type*.

38 Ibid.

39 Descriptions of problem-solving types presented in this section are derived primarily from: Sharp, *Personality Types* and Thompson, *Jung's Function-Attitudes Explained*.

40 Jung, *Personality Types*.

41 Massey, *Where in the World Do I Belong?*

42 In Massey's analysis, there are no predominantly Te cultures except in Western Europe and the US.

43 Rodriguez, P. *China, India, and the United States: The Future of Economic Supremacy*. Chantilly, VA: The Great Courses, 2011, p. 21.

44 World Audit, "World Democracy Audit, 2015," www.worldaudit.org (retrieved November 22, 2016).

45 Wiki, "Xi Jinping," https://en.wikipedia.org (retrieved November 22, 2016).

46 http://factsanddetails.com/china.php?itemid=303 (retrieved June 27, 2013).

47 Yeung, I. and Tung, R. "Achieving Business Success in Confucian Societies: The Importance of Guanxi (Connections)," *Organizational Dynamics*, fall, 1996, pp. 54–65.

48 Luo, Y., Huang, Y., and Wang, S.L. "Guanxi and Organizational Performance: A Meta-Analysis," *Management and Organization Review*, Vol. 8, No. 1, 2012, pp. 139–172.

49 Abramson and Ai, "Canadian Companies Doing Business in China."

50 Luo et al., "Guanxi and Organizational Performance."

51 Chen, C. C., Chen, X. P., and Huang, S. "Chinese Guanxi: An Integrative Review and New Directions for Future Research," *Management and Organization Review*, Vol. 9, No. 1, 2013, pp. 167–207.

52 Fei, H. *From the Soil, the Foundations of Chinese Society*. Berkeley, CA: University of California Press, 1992.

53 Wank, D. L. "Business–State Clienteleism in China: Decline or Evolution?," in T. Gold, D. Guthrie, and D. Wank (eds.), *Social Connections in China: Institutions, Culture, and the Changing Nature of Guanxi*. Cambridge, MA: Cambridge University Press, 2002, pp. 97–115.

54 Chen, X.-P., Li, X., and Liang, X. "Why Do Business Leaders Pursue Political Connections in China? Economic Benefits or Psychological Placebo?" Academy of Management Conference Paper, San Antonio, August 2011.

55 Abramson and Ai, "Using Guanxi-Style Buyer–Seller Relationships in China."

56 Marcel, G. *The Mystery of Being, Volume I: Reflection and Mystery*. South Bend, IN: St. Augustine's Press, 2001.

57 Buber, M. *I and Thou*. New York: Charles Scribner's Sons, 1986.

58 Emmott, W. "The Sun Also Rises: A Survey of Japan," *The Economist*, October 8, 2005, 18-page insert, www.economist.com/surveys (retrieved April 11, 2017). See also Gordon, A. *A Modern History of Japan*. Oxford: Oxford University Press, 2008. Reiber, B. and Spencer, J. *Frommer's Japan*. Hoboken, NJ: John Wiley, 2008. Matsumoto, D. *The New Japan*. Boston, MA: Nicholas Brealey/Intercultural

Press, 2002. Hall, E. T. and Hall, M. R. *Hidden Differences: Doing Business with the Japanese.* Garden City, NJ: Anchor/Doubleday, 1987.

59 Endo, S. *White Man, Yellow Man: Two Novellas.* New York: Paulist Press, 2014. The words are from the diary of the apostate Durand, defrocked and excommunicated by the Roman Catholic Church for a relationship with a Japanese woman in the novella *Yellow Man.* Endo has been called the Japanese Graham Greene. He was a preeminent twentieth-century Japanese novelist.

60 March, R. M. *Reading the Japanese Mind: The Realities Behind Their Thoughts and Actions.* Tokyo: Kodansha International, 2001.

61 Lie, J. *Multiethnic Japan.* Cambridge, MA: Harvard University Press, 2013.

62 The status of Confucianism as either a philosophy or a religion is debatable. While there are many temples built to Confucius in China, most have regarded it as a philosophy, or way of life intended to teach individuals to engage in ethical thinking and actions. There are those who regard Confucianism as a religion and this view seems to be becoming more common in recent times. See Sun, A. *Confucianism as a World Religion: Contested Histories and Contemporary Realities.* Princeton, NJ: Princeton University Press, 2013.

63 Kasulis, T. P. *Shinto, The Way Home: Dimensions of Asian Spirituality.* Honolulu, HA: University of Hawai'i Press, 2004.

64 Korean proverb #4: "Stressed about a business project? Use these wise words to encourage and not give up. With hard work there is always success. Fighting!" www.seoulistic.com (retrieved December 15, 2016).

65 This section on Hong Kong was written by Anthony Chan, PhD, lecturer at Simon Fraser University, Beedie School of Business, Strategy Area Group, Burnaby, British Columbia, Canada.

66 "How Did the Chinese Government Settle the Question of Hong Kong through Negotiations?" The Commissioner's Office of China's Foreign Ministry, November 15, 2000.

67 Schiavenza, M. "How Humiliation Drove Modern Chinese History." *The Atlantic*, October 25, 2013.

68 "Hong Kong: A Success Story," Foundation for Economic Education, First National City Bank, March 1, 1960.

69 Yep, R. and Lui, T. L. "Revisiting the Golden Era of MacLehose and the Dynamics of Social Reforms." *China Information*, Vol. 24, No. 3, 2010, pp. 249–272.

70 "1898 and All That: A Brief History of Hong Kong," *The Economist*, June 26, 1997.

71 Jacobs, A. "Hong Kong Democracy Standoff, Circa 1960," *New York Times*, October 27, 2014.

72 Cheung, G. "June 4, 1989 Events in China Still Have a Profound Effect on Hong Kong's Political Scene," *South China Morning Post*, May 26, 2014.

73 Dodsworth, J. and Mihaljek, D. "Hong Kong, China: Growth, Structural Change, and Economic Stability During the Transition." International Monetary Fund, August 1997.

74 Levin, N. and Yung, C. "An Era in Hong Kong Is Ending, Thanks to China's Tight Embrace," *Wall Street Journal*, September 23, 2016.

75 Ibid.

76 Chinese University of Hong Kong (CHUK), Communications and Public Relations Office. (2014). "CUHK Releases Survey Findings on Views on Hong Kong's Core Values," press release, www.cpr. cuhk.edu.hk/en/press_detail.php?id=1915 (retrieved November 25, 2016).

77 Marlow, I. "Young Chinese-Canadians Move to Hong Kong for Job Opportunities: Survey," *The Globe and Mail*, June 17, 2014.

78 Seagal, S. and Horne, D. *Human Dynamics: A New Framework for Understanding People and Realizing the Potential in Our Organizations.* Waltham, MA: Pegasus Communications Inc., 1997.

15 DOING BUSINESS IN SOUTH AND SOUTHEAST ASIA, AND AUSTRALIA

Westerners generally cannot rid themselves of (their) sense of superiority. They still consider their values and political and economic systems better than any others. It would not be so bad if it stopped at that; it seems, however, that they will not be satisfied until they have forced other countries to adopt their ways as well. Everyone must be democratic, but only according to the Western concept of democracy; no one can violate human rights, again, according to their self-righteous interpretation of human rights. Westerners cannot seem to understand diversity.

Mahathir Mohamad[1]

Business seems to have lost its genuine sense of connection to humanity, nature, and its institutional credibility, which is the larger context within which it operates. It has lost its sense of Being. Many business leaders seem to have distanced themselves from the rest of the world, and the impact of business decisions on the world outside the company rarely appears to be a central factor. Such a sense of separation is one major reason for the great ecological, humanitarian, and institutional crises that threaten our very existence and well-being.

Ram Nidumolu[2]

After reading and studying the concepts, examples, and illustrations in Chapter 15, readers should be able to understand and appreciate:

1 Differences in national character between the six nations and how these differences affect the predominant problem-solving and communication styles foreign businesspeople will experience. National character is defined as personality or cultural characteristics particularly characteristic of a nation.[3]

2 Predictable difficulties English-speaking businesspeople will face because of differences in national character between their nations and those in this region.

3 Cultural conditions, and resultant effective negotiation strategies and behaviors, for each of the six countries.

LEARNING OBJECTIVES

INTRODUCTION

The twenty-first century has been predicted to be "the Century of Asia"[4] or the "Pacific Century"[5] in the same way that the twentieth was the American Century, and the nineteenth was the British Century. The Asian Development Bank has predicted that by mid-century three billion Asians will have the same standard of living as now enjoyed in the European Union (EU), and that Asia will account for over half of all human economic output.[6] Until the last edition of *Managing Cultural Differences*, all of Asia was covered in a single chapter. Now there are simply too many Asian national economies of importance for international business to deal with them all in one chapter. In Chapter 14 we discussed East Asia, with China, Japan, South Korea, and Hong Kong. In this chapter, we continue our Asian survey with South and Southeast Asia, including India, Australia, Singapore, Malaysia, Thailand, and Vietnam.

While the East Asian economies' impact on international trade is larger, these six national economies are all in the top 25 nations that account for well over 95 percent of all international trade (see Exhibit 15.1). While China ranks second behind the US in total trade, and either just ahead (measured by PPP) or just behind (measured in GDP) the US in total economic activity, Rodriguez[7] predicts that by the middle of the twenty-first century, India will have the world's largest economy, followed by China. Singapore is important because since the time of Deng Xiaoping, China's long time president after Mao Zedong, Chinese leaders have considered Singapore their model for economic, political, and social development.[8] According to Bloomberg,[9] investors poured $50 billion into developing emerging markets in 2016, and Thailand was the 3rd most promising worldwide, with GDP growth of 25.9 percent since 2013. Malaysia is the 6th most promising emerging market, with GDP growth of 21.8 percent in the same period, as well as being the economic model

EXHIBIT 15.1 EXPORTS, IMPORTS, AND TOTAL TRADE AND NATIONAL RANKING, 2015 ($ BILLIONS)

Country	Exports	Imports	Total Trade	Rank
India	272.4	409.2	681.6	13
Singapore	377.1	294.5	671.6	14
Australia	188.3	207.7	396.0	21
Thailand	212.1	177.5	389.6	22
Malaysia	175.7	147.7	323.4	24
Vietnam	162.1	154.7	316.8	25

Source: Central Intelligence Agency, *The World Factbook*, www.cia.gov/Library/rankorder (retrieved November 29, 2016).

espoused by developing Islamic countries.[10] By contrast, Turkey is 7th, Russia 9th, Mexico 16th, and Brazil 17th. Vietnam is also growing rapidly in international importance. In 2013, it was ranked 37th in exports, as opposed to 24th in 2015.[11] Australia is an important trading partner for English-speaking businesspeople, who will experience it as a less risky business environment (see Chapter 3) because of its cultural similarities to the US, UK, and Canada.

The purpose of this chapter is to acquaint you with economic, social, and cultural conditions in these South and Southeast Asian countries. Several, including India and Thailand, are throwing off traditional forms of social organization to achieve free market economies. Others, like Vietnam, have abandoned their centrally controlled economy for the quickly expanding benefits of free enterprise.

Our central purpose, however, is to offer criteria for negotiating successful and profitable business opportunities in these nations. We have tried to identify the most important factors for doing business, and the ways that these may be achieved. For most of these nations, the most important factor is building trusting and cooperative business relationships with local business counterparts.

GENERAL CONSIDERATIONS

South and Southeast Asia require careful consideration for those intending to do business there. The regions contain countries where it is relatively easy to do business, but also countries where business conditions are very challenging. Exhibit 15.2 provides country rankings for ease of doing business for each year from 2009 through 2013. There were a total of 185 countries, worldwide, included in this analysis, so the rankings are out of 185.

EXHIBIT 15.2 EASE OF DOING BUSINESS (WORLD RANKINGS)

Country	2009	2010	2011	2012	2013 (estimate)	Five-year average
Singapore	1	1	1	1	1	1.0
Australia	9	9	10	15	10	10.6
Thailand	12	12	19	17	18	15.6
Malaysia	21	23	21	18	12	19.0
Vietnam	91	93	78	98	99	91.8
India	132	133	134	132	132	132.6

Source: The World Bank, "Economy Rankings," www.doingbusiness.org (retrieved October 23, 2012).

Singapore was consistently judged to be the easiest country in the entire world in which to do business. Australia also seemed to be a promising location to do business. India, despite its economic promise over the next decades, was judged to be a very difficult business environment, as was the rapidly expanding Vietnam. Conditions were becoming easier in Malaysia and more difficult in Thailand, but both were consistently on the more promising side of the scale..

Ease of doing business is generally understood to be a function of how much uncertainty MNEs face when they enter a new business environment. There is usually uncertainty related to differing political, economic, social, technological, and cultural factors. Uncertainty is reduced over time as MNEs and their staff become familiar with local conditions (see Chapter 4). Exhibit 15.3 is helpful in highlighting the effects of local business regulations on ease of doing business. Again, the rankings are out of the 185 worldwide countries included in the survey.

It is relatively easy to do business in Singapore because it is relatively easy to start a business, investors are well protected by law, and products or services are easily exported without bureaucratic "red tape." Contracts are more enforceable in Singapore than in any of the other countries we are considering in these regions. Malaysia surpasses Australia in terms of the indicators we are considering because investors are far better protected, and products/services far easier to export. Even Thailand is better than Australia on these two indicators. India is challenging because it is very difficult to start up a business, difficult to export, and almost impossible to legally enforce a contract (184th of 185 countries).

We might, however, want to ask the World Bank the question: For whom is it easier to do business? By real GDP growth rate in 2014,[12] there seemed to be an inverse relationship between ease of doing business and economic growth. India (7.6 percent) and Vietnam (6.5 percent) had the highest GDP growth even though according to the World Bank they were the toughest places to do business. Malaysia (4.7 percent) grew faster than Thailand

EXHIBIT 15.3 MEASURING BUSINESS REGULATIONS (WORLD RANKINGS, 1 to 185)

Country	Ease of doing business (2013 est.)	Starting a business	Protecting investors	Exporting products	Enforcing contracts	Average of the five indicators
Singapore	#1	#4	#2	#1	#12	4.0
Malaysia	#12	#54	#4	#11	#33	22.8
Australia	#10	#2	#70	#44	#15	28.2
Thailand	#18	#85	#13	#20	#23	31.8
Vietnam	#99	#108	#169	#74	#44	98.8
India	#132	#173	#49	#127	#184	133.0

Source: International Finance Corporation and the World Bank. "Doing Business: Measuring Business Regulations, Economy Rankings," www.doingbusiness.org/rankings; benchmarked to June 2012 (retrieved February 6, 2013).

(2.5 percent) and Australia (2.4 percent) even though it was rated a tougher environment. Singapore—the easiest country in the world to do business—had the lowest growth rate (2.2 percent); even lower than the US (2.6 percent). We might reasonably expect that the World Bank's ratings concern how easy it is for foreign nationals to do business in these countries. Certainly, some businesspeople must not be finding India such a tough business environment. In 2016, its nominal GDP was seventh highest in the world at $2.25 trillion, but it was projected to be fifth at $3.30 trillion in 2020—47 percent growth over the next four years.[13]

Our view is that for each national culture there is a "national character" consisting of enduring personality characteristics and expectations about how business should be conducted. Inkeles[14] describes national character as a consistent set of dispositions built into the personalities of individuals making up a society or cultural group in a specific area. It is not a function of race or ethnicity but of social proximity. Members of an ethnicity that immigrate to a new national culture take on the national character of the new area over time.[15] This national character represents a predominant set of expectations that will be encountered in a national culture among a majority, or certainly a plurality of local nationals.

If you understand the local expectations about how business is conducted, then your path will be considerably eased. For example, looking at Exhibit 15.3, getting contracts enforced in India is tougher than anywhere else. This would be because the concept of legally "enforcing" contracts is foreign to Indian business culture. It is the strength of the relationship between contract partners, maintained by staying in contact and maintaining trust that ensures that a contract will be honored.[16] Indians also expect that, should market conditions change on either side, both parties to the contract will be willing to be flexible about what it means to honor the contract. Certainly, an American or Western European that did not value building trust-based relationships as a precondition for doing business, or who put no further effort into a relationship once the contract was signed, would have trouble with enforcement. His/her lawyers would find out how difficult it is to achieve an unambiguous result in an Indian court.[17] However, those that understood the Indian business national character and the importance it placed on trust-based relationships would not experience these difficulties.

NATIONAL CHARACTER

National character is a term describing enduring personality differences found when comparing populations in different national states. Since the 1940s, "personality and culture" social anthropologists have made systematic efforts to determine the validity and nature of perceived differences in national populations. In recent years, Inkeles[18] has successfully demonstrated through empirical survey that "modal personalities," or enduring sets of differing personality characteristics, exist in various countries, where they characterize sociocultural systems as well as individuals. Massey's[19] study of cross-national Jungian attitude-function preferences, described in detail in Chapter 2, represents a psychological profile of national character. Bridges[20] showed how even intranational organizations could have characters based on the predominant Jungian psychological preferences of its senior management teams.

Data provided by Massey allow us to identify the predominant national character for the six South and Southeast Asian nations in regard to introverted problem-solving style (see Chapter 11), and preferred patterns of extraverted communication (see Chapter 2). These results are found in Exhibit 15.4.

Exhibit 15.4 illustrates some of the significant challenges for foreign businesspersons in South and Southeast Asia based on national character. The Singaporean and Vietnamese national characters are much the same in terms of their approach to problem-solving, preferences for communications, and how they behave under extreme stress or pressure (see Chapter 2 for discussion of stress outcomes).[21] The Malaysians behave very similarly to the Singaporeans and Vietnamese until they are under high stress or pressure. Then, suddenly, they behave very unexpectedly, causing an unsuspecting Westerner much stress in return. The Australians problem-solve using much the same processes as the Singaporeans, Vietnamese, and Malaysians, but you would never know that from their very different communications processes, and their response to stress is unique in the region. The Thais and Indians problem-solve in similar ways but communicate quite differently, and both are different in their communications from all the other predominant national preferences. They also react differently to stress and both in ways not to be expected from the other four countries.

The sheer diversity of national characters, especially in regard to predominant preferences for communications styles, and reactions under stress is like a microcosm of the

EXHIBIT 15.4 PROBLEM-SOLVING AND COMMUNICATIONS STYLE IN NATIONAL CULTURES

Nation	Predominant problem-solving preference	Predominant communication style	"Inferior" function stressed Character[22]
Singapore	Si (Introverted Sensing)	Fe (Extraverted Feeling)	Primitive Ne (Extraverted iNtuiting)
Vietnam	Si (Introverted Sensing)	Fe (Extraverted Feeling)	Primitive Ne (Extraverted iNtuiting)
Malaysia	Si (Introverted Sensing)	Fe (Extraverted Feeling)	Primitive Ti (Introverted Thinking)
Australia	Si (Introverted Sensing)	Te (Extraverted Thinking)	Primitive Fi (Introverted Feeling)
Thailand	Fi (Introverted Feeling)	Se (Extraverted Sensing)	Primitive Ni (Introverted iNtuiting)
India	Fi (Introverted Feeling)	Ne (Extraverted iNtuiting)	Primitive Si (Introverted Sensing)

Source: data derived from Massey, B. *Where in the World Do I Belong?* USA: Jetlag Press, 2006.

world. There are only four styles in each category in the Jungian attitude-function model[23] and all four are found for communications style and reaction to stress. It is enormously stressful, for example, for a Western businessperson that she/he cannot expect to find the same predictable patterns of problem-solving and communications in countries so close together and in the same regions. Singapore is, after all, an island off the coast of Malaysia connected by a short tunnel. An American or British expat's usual stressed-out reaction, following his/her national character, would likely be primitive Fi, the same as with Australians, but quite different from the other five nations being surveyed.

In the following subsections, we will consider the impact of these preferences on actual behavior. We will do the Singaporeans, Vietnamese, and Malaysians in a group because of their similar problem-solving and communications preferences, highlighting the different responses—Singaporeans and Vietnamese versus Malaysians—under stress. We will do the Indians and Thais in a group because they share the same approach to problem-solving, while highlighting their very different communications styles and reactions to stress. We will do the Australians separately because in other chapters (see Chapters 12 and 14) we have used Australia as one of our referent English-speaking nations to highlight the kinds of negotiations-related problems businesspersons from English-speaking and EU nations would encounter. The national characters of the US, UK, and Germany are much the same in these regards (Si/Te) as Australia. By contrast, Canada is very similar (Si/Fe) to Singapore.

National character: Singapore, Vietnam, and Malaysia[24]

As noted in Exhibit 15.4, Singapore and Vietnam have similar psychological national characters. They are both Si problem-solvers and Fe communicators. They both react to excessive stress by acting out in an "inferior" mode that is usually repressed as repugnant so that they are not fully aware that they will behave this way when they "lose control." In their case, this inferior mode is primitive or poorly developed Ne.[25] It is poorly developed because it is contrary to what is regarded as normal comfortable behavior, and so it receives no developmental practice. Malaysians exhibiting their country's predominant psychological national character are also Si problem-solvers and Fe communicators, but under stress they act out in a Ti inferior mode.[26]

Si problem-solvers have excellent recall of subjective and objective data and factual material. They recall all evidence they have derived about their external competitive environments, and all subjective analysis they have considered in relation to those data. They constantly compare past with present and are easily able to see changes and inconsistencies in their counterparts' presentations. They have to a great degree a "photographic memory" for such information. Si problem-solvers value honesty in their negotiation counterparts and will experience stress when faced with assertions that contradict known evidence. They are also stressed by artificially short deadlines that limit their comprehensive data analysis.

Western businesspeople from the US, UK, Canada, Australia, and Germany are also predominantly Si problem-solvers according to their national characters. The Singaporean, Vietnamese, and Malaysian problem-solving process should seem natural to them. Stress will be caused by Westerners placing too little emphasis on trust-based relationship-building, or trying to rush to a quick decision.

The Singaporean, Vietnamese, and Malaysian Si problem-solving evidential acuity is generally hidden in the background behind their Fe communication preference. Fe is a strong relationship-building style. It requires communications to be governed by polite, courteous, and considerate behavior on both sides. Fe acts as a gatekeeper for what are regarded within a national culture as interpersonal social norms, and violations are considered "wrong" and tend with repetition to damage trust and relationships. Fe communicators are willing, under normal circumstances, to compromise to help meet others' needs, and behave altruistically by sacrificing their own self-interest to some extent. Foreign counterparts who communicate in ways regarded as impolite or inconsiderate cause stress, and Fe communicators have a long affective memory for the emotional quality of relationships.

Therefore, Western businesspeople coming to Singapore, Vietnam, and Malaysia are most likely to encounter local nationals that place a high value on building trust-based relationships based on local social conventions. However, despite the willingness to build friendships, and to sacrifice on behalf of friendship, the local nationals have a strong command over the factual details of negotiations. They will be caused stress either by gratuitous diplomacy that glosses over accurate analysis, and short deadlines, or by interpersonal communications that violate social norms of trust- and relationship-building.

Unfortunately, the American, British, Australian, and German national characters are predominantly Extraverted Thinking (Te) in communication style. In Chapter 2 we described Te in the following way.

Extraverted Thinking (Te): Te individuals understand the external environment to be governed by logical and structured processes of cause and effect. Their goal is to organize the external environment and its inhabitants. They tend to see things very dualistically, definitely in terms of "black and white" and "true and false," and have logical and impersonal reasons for their assertions and actions. Anyone and anything that agrees with their reasoning is "right." Anyone and anything disagreeing is "wrong." Te individuals are strong in planning, organizing, directing, and controlling capabilities with a strong need for closure. They do not regard their feelings for others as important, and are not good at giving positive feedback.

Western Te communications are centered around acceptance of an abstract, theoretical, ruling principle believed to apply universally to all nations, people, organizations, and individuals in "black" and "white" terms. Examples include "free trade," "rule of law," "capitalism," "democracy," and "human rights." The ruling principle is "right" or "good." Its antitheses are "wrong" or "bad" (or even "evil"). For example, the antithesis of "capitalism" is generally accepted to be "communism." Castro's Cuba has been a communist state for over 60 years, boycotted by the US for the whole time. The Soviet Union, another communist state, was the "evil empire"[27] for President Ronald Reagan back in the 1980s.

This idea that there are universally opposing principles, one of which is right and the other wrong, is based on the dualism that is often a part of Western logical reasoning. Te communications use logic, cause-and-effect reasoning, and objective data to order and interpret the external competitive environment as sets of intertwined structured processes. Objective evidence that supports the ruling principle is right. Contrary evidence is wrong. Te communications are intended to provide rationales to persuade recipients of the correctness of this view, understood to be logical and above question.

Western Te communications are also always in a hurry to get to implementation. The ruling principle is a "given," as opposed to open for debate. Westerners from North American and Northern European countries have a strong Te-based need for early closure and forward movement in the direction of its goals. They do not appreciate having to revisit decisions they understood to be decided earlier. The central process goal is to achieve a quick decision that satisfies the ruling principle, so that efforts may focus on planning, organizing, directing, and controlling the implementation. Non-Te friends of Western Te-oriented decision-makers report that they experience Te process as "tyranny" in the sense that conflict results from any failure to cooperate with Te expectations.

Te communicators do not particularly value relationships, being more concerned with objective facts and analysis, proving the urgent need for speedy action in ways proposed. This approach will present Western Te negotiators with two problems of their own making.

First, Singaporeans, Vietnamese, and Malaysians strongly prefer to do business with those with whom they have already built trust-based relationships. Their whole Fe communication style places its complete emphasis on achieving these relationships. Their response to Te disregard of relationship-building will likely be to avoid direct confrontation while slowing negotiations down and obliquely criticizing Te proposals. Second, the Te preference for quick decisions and rapid implementation will be frustrated because there will be no deal without relationship, and because Southeast Asians will not make their decisions at the bargaining table, but later through consensus decision-making.

If the stress of a relationship with foreign counterparts becomes too great, Singaporeans and Vietnamese become likely to act out impulsively in ways that they will later personally judge as irresponsible and even reckless. They may lose focus, feel panic, and make uncharacteristically hurtful comments. They may tend to focus on the negative possibilities inherent in the deals they have been negotiating and pull back sharply from the perceived danger, feeling there is "no way out" that they can see.

Malaysians become likely to act out somewhat differently under stress. They may communicate uncharacteristically excessive criticism in the form of sweeping condemnations of their counterparts and their proposed deals. They may become suspicious of their counterparts' motives and closed to any idea of compromise—normally a strength—making all-or-none judgments based on apparently convoluted logic. They may engage in hair-splitting moralizing while adopting an officious attitude. In all these cases, if your Singaporean, Vietnamese, or Malaysian counterparts begin to act in these ways, you should understand that this is a momentary situation caused by excessive stress (or illness). The best approach is to call a temporary halt, or time-out, to the negotiations, so that your counterparts (and/or yourself) may recover their usual equanimity. Western Te communicators have a tendency under stress to lash out with emotional outbursts that cause loss of face for their Southeast Asian counterparts and damage to relationships. An important lesson for Westerners is that if they manage to control their emotional outburst, they must also control negative body language and voice tone. Body language and voice tone tend to be largely ignored by Western negotiators but would be interpreted as equivalent to lashing out in this region.

National character: India and Thailand[28]

As noted in Exhibit 15.4, the psychological national characters of India and Thailand have similar Fi problem-solving. They differ in both preferred communications style and reactions to stress. This Fi problem-solving style is shared with the Chinese national character, and is discussed in Chapter 14 in some detail.

The principal difference between Fi problem-solving, and Western Si problem-solving is that Fi evaluates and decides on the basis of personally held values rather than objective facts and their interpretation. Indians and Thais are more likely to base their decisions on idealistic values, judging their foreign counterparts—behavior, proposals, and relationships— on the basis of how they believe the world should be ordered and organized. They view external situations occurring in their competitive external environments as manifestations, or appearances, of underlying eidetic values. They tend to resist data inconsistent with their values, and also are unwilling to conform to others' potentially more "objective" interpretations, regarding objectivity as just another form of subjectivity. Fi problem-solvers also have unreliable memories for objective data, which may be selectively remembered insofar as it is consistent with held values. This poses a serious problem for Western Si problem-solvers because they tend to discount values as extrasensory data that are not "real."

For most Indians, the Hindu religion plays a major role in their daily lives, and information will be rejected if it challenges religious beliefs and organizational expectations.[29] Indians evaluate the validity of evidence based on their personal feelings, often based more strongly on religious ideology than on objective facts.[30] Any criticism of Indian poverty, belief systems, politics, the caste system, or unfamiliar business practices will generate negative personal feelings in many Indian counterparts, causing them stress.[31]

Similarly, Thai problem-solving is strongly affected by religious values derived from their faith in the ideologies of Theravada Buddhism.[32] The 95 percent of Thais who are Theravada Buddhists generally evaluate the "truth" of any subject based on their subjective and fatalistic feelings, and their religious faith.[33] Thais tend to be nonassertive and very conscious of others' feelings so that any perceived interpersonal dissatisfaction or conflict causes them stress. A minority, having higher education from foreign universities, will decide on the basis of objective facts.

The predominant Indian Ne communication style hides their largely conservative, religiously based problem-solving. Ne communicators are intuitively creative in seeing possibilities inherent in objective situations. They jump back and forth between ideas in a way that can frustrate more linear Te Western thinkers. They have an ability to easily understand complex ideas and to read between the lines, or see through appearances to possibilities that others have missed. They appear very entrepreneurial in attitude, constantly searching for the widest range of possibilities. However, their initial enthusiasm for new ideas quickly diminishes into boredom, requiring a constant stream of innovative new ideas and implementations. Indian Ne communicators feel stress when Western negotiators insist on logical processes for processing visible reality using factual data, and offering proposals based on conventional and proven ideas, while rejecting Indian creativity based on intuitive interpretations. Western Te processes also tend to rely on conventional, established, tried-and-true approaches that devalue the creative possibilities proposed by Ne-driven negotiators.

In contrast, the predominant Thai Se communication style is very realistic and data-driven. In many ways, it is similar to the Chinese Se communications style described in Chapter 14, except that the underlying Chinese problem-solving is more likely Confucian than Buddhist, and definitely not fatalistic in expectation as is Thai Buddhism. The Thai Se style demands the specifics and details of every proposal. However, it rejects any reliance on abstract or theoretical explanations, a hallmark of Western Te logic. Thai Se negotiators would be caused much stress by Indian counterparts whose communications were based on intuitions about the "true" meaning of objective facts. They would also be stressed by

Western reliance on universal principles, such as "free trade," that the Thais would see as a theoretical construct that imposed a set of behavioral rules or expectations. Se communications tends to reject the imposition of behavioral expectations based on theoretical rationales.

Indians under stress tend to act out by becoming physically exhausted, or sick and being unable to continue. When they feel this way, they tend to withdraw, or feel depressed, having the conviction that there is no trust or relationship, and that their negotiation counterparts do not understand or care about them. Thais under stress behave quite differently. They may become suspicious of others' motives while projecting (or mirroring) these feelings onto their negotiation counterparts so that they attribute malevolent motives to those they are negotiating with. Again, you should ask for a postponement of discussions if these behaviors manifest, and not hold your Thai (or Indian) counterparts to how they behaved when they temporarily "lost it."

National character: Australia[34]

As noted in Exhibit 15.4, the psychological national character of Australia is Si problem-solving, and Te communications. This is similar to the Si/Te national character of the US (see Chapter 18), as well as the other Western referent nations (see Chapters 12 and 14) of the UK and Germany, used for comparative purposes. The Australian Si problem-solving style is similar to that described above for Singapore, Vietnam, and Malaysia, as well as for the US and Canada (see Chapter 18). It is in its predominant preference for the Te communications style that the Australian national character differs from all other Asian nations, and is similar to all our Western referent nations except Canada. Westerners seeking to do business in Australia should be very familiar with Australian problem-solving and communications styles. On the other hand, Australians will face many of the same problems as Americans, British, and Germans when they seek to do business in South and Southeast Asia.

Because Te is in a hurry, and believes it knows the "truth," it is loath to spend the time to build trust-based relationships. Katz[35] observes that Australians (and Americans and Germans) put a much lower priority on building these relationships than members of many other cultures. They are motivated by short-term financial or strategic goals, do not see trust as required, and hope to monitor contracts by legal means as necessary. This causes significant stress for Fe national cultures (Singapore, Malaysia, Vietnam) where a trust-based relationship is usually a precondition for doing any business. Se communications (Thailand) rejects abstract theoretical formulations in favor of situational realities and is stressed by insistence on universal ruling principles. Ne communicators (India) are adept at seeing behind supposed ruling principles to detect the real motives of those trying to control discussions, hurrying them on to predetermined conclusions and outcomes. Ne finds it stressful to be told there is only one right way to proceed when its strength is in finding valid alternatives.

Te has a profound ability to create stressful negotiations with Fe, Se, and Ne by its lack of concern for relationships, its insistence on its universal ruling principles, and its exclusion of alternate courses of action. Perceiving others as uncooperative, controlling, or difficult triggers excessive stress for Te individuals. When Te acts out under stress, its tendency is to take criticism very personally, lose its temper in emotional outbursts including exploding in public, and act as if it "hates" its counterparts. The best course of action when your Te counterpart loses it is to break off discussions for the day to give him/her time to recover. Unfortunately, in India and Southeast Asia, emotional outbursts cause loss of face that may terminate even a well-developed trust-based relationship. In Thailand, direct confrontation is seen as extremely impolite, and losing control of your emotions is considered poor manners.[36] In Malaysia the single most important criterion for establishing a successful trust-based relationship is courtesy.[37] People who lose their tempers are regarded as unable to control themselves, and therefore not to be trusted or even respected. The latter is true in Singapore as well.[38]

INDIA

> You'll likely be dealing with people who speak the Queen's English, and who graduated from top Western universities. You can get lulled into a false sense of security—but for people dressing a little different and talking a little different, they are just like me. That's a completely false premise. There are all kinds of nuances in the culture; implicit cultural norms that we don't know about until we run afoul of them.
>
> Jitendra Singh[39]

India is in the process of becoming an open-market economy. The recent growth has stemmed from economic liberalization including industrial deregulation, privatization of state-owned enterprises, and reduced controls on foreign investment and international trade. This process began in the early 1990s and since 1997 India's GDP has grown at an average 7 percent per year. Slightly more than half of India's workforce is still engaged in agricultural production, but services, especially related to information technology, are the major growth engine accounting for nearly two-thirds of India's economic output. India has capitalized on its large educated English-speaking workforce to become a major exporter of information technology services, and software development workers. Although affected by the global recession of 2008–2009, India's economy rebounded with 10.1 percent growth in 2010 due to strong domestic demand. In 2015, India's GDP of $2.25 trillion was seventh highest in the world, and by 2020 is projected to be third highest by PPP.[40]

Historical perspective

As in East Asia, the sixteenth century saw the Western European nations establishing trading posts in India. The Portuguese efforts were focused upon Goa/Cochin on the west coast, and the French in Pondicherry on the east coast. However, the British were the most successful and expanded their influence and power throughout the subcontinent. They built a colonial infrastructure that remains today in large part, including the heritage of English in a *land of many tongues.* After World War I, nationalism grew in India. Mahatma Gandhi organized a series of passive-resistance campaigns and civil disobedience to British rule. The British reign ended on August 15, 1947. On January 26, 1950, the Indian constitution was promulgated, and the country became a sovereign republic and the world's largest democracy.

Hinduism, the religion of the majority of Indians, believes that birth is destiny. It perpetuates the caste system, separating the social classes by occupations, so that privileges or disadvantages are transmitted by inheritance. For over 5,000 years, the caste system, with its thousands of subsystems, has divided people into four divisions—priests, warriors, traders, and workers. Then there are the untouchables, or *dalits*, excluded because of the nature of their crafts, such as working with leather, and waste disposal.

When industrialization began in twentieth-century India, many untouchables were recruited by foreign investors to learn new skills for factory work. An example of how this injustice is breaking down for some 200 million so classified is the late K. R. Narayanan. Born of a poor southern Indian family and educated by Christian missionaries, he won scholarships to the London School of Economics and proved to be a very talented student. Upon his return, India's first prime minister, Jawaharlal Nehru, found Narayanan a job in the diplomatic service, where he ended up an ambassador to Thailand, Turkey, China, and the US. In 1984, he was elected to parliament from his native Kerala. To the surprise of the elite, he subsequently was elected vice-president and then president, saying: "My life encapsulates the ability of the democratic system to accommodate and empower marginalized sections of society." Today, discrimination on the grounds of caste is illegal, and affirmative action programs are under way.

Business philosophy

Indian business philosophy is also based on Hinduism. Nidumolu[41] recounts a story about two birds, originally found in the sacred Hindu Upanishads, or Holy Books, dating back as early as 1500–1200 BCE. The two birds represent the philosophical dilemma for Hindus, and, according to Nidumolu, the best direction for Indian business, and business everywhere. The first bird represents individual ego and its self-interest. It lives in the lower branches of a tree where it experiences constant anxiety because it has no view or perspective on its world. It is entirely focused on satisfying its immediate physical desires, jumping from branch to branch, and eating whatever fruit it can reach, both sweet and sour. The second bird sits at the top of the tree. It sees clearly how it is related to its entire environment. As a result, it is "free of fear and confident of the future."[42] It represents the universal self, or "Being," shared with all living creatures, and, Nidumolu argues, with businesses since under Indian law businesses are treated as persons with rights and responsibilities. Being is difficult to define, but generally "refers to our essential nature, or quality of existence, which we share with all other living creatures, human or not."[43]

The two birds—self-interested ego and universal self—represent two states of mind, describing the intentions and activities of individual businesses. Nidumolu argued that most business is like the bird in the lower branches. It has lost its understanding of how it is connected to all its stakeholders, including humanity and nature. It has lost its sense of Being. It has become focused solely on its short-term interests, and lost sight of its long-term impacts on human quality of life, and the physical environment. Hindu philosophy, as recorded in the Upanishads, points the way for business to regain its proper connectedness to the world. This regaining of Being is a goal for Indian business, and a way for Hindu philosophy to contribute to universal well-being.

The story exhibits two essential Hindu beliefs relevant to the practice of business. First, many Hindus believe that every creature contains a spark of Being that some would call God. Through reincarnation, a being evolves to a more rarified state and eventually merges its spark into the greater collective Being. If the individual self was a part of the collective self and evolved through multiple individual selves to be united with the collective, then there was a correspondence between individual selves. Each individual self could become any other individual self through reincarnative evolution, and vice versa. This Hindu belief promotes a "profound empathy with all beings in the world and with the world itself."[44]

Second, if businesses are also beings, having been granted legal rights commensurate with individuals, then the role of business leadership is to help them evolve from self-interested short-term perspectives to understanding themselves as "an integral part of an interconnected network of beings (whether individual or collective) that share the same foundational reality."[45] This understanding becomes the basis for the ethical commitment of businesses and their leaders to address the quality of life issues of all their stakeholders, including the natural physical environment. Leaders that understand this correspondence between themselves, their organizations, and all other beings can no longer justify their activities in terms of the short-term self-interested perspectives of the lower bird. They have been freed by the greater perspective of the higher bird "to pursue opportunities such as the perfecting of business, and to know and become who you truly are."[46]

Doing business in India

India has been changed materially by its economic development over the past 20 years, especially in the north, and less so in the southeast. The traditional elements of business culture have, however, remained much the same, with the building of trust-based relationships through networking and face-to-face meetings being critical to business success.[47] Jitendra Singh, a management professor at the Wharton School of Business, commented:

> The United States is a much more transaction-oriented society. When you're doing business, you're there to talk about a particular transaction, and you either do it or you don't. But Indian business is still very much relationship-based. Sometimes being too transactional can be not a smart way to go. Do a lot of homework and figure out who

might be the right people to deal with. There's a very tight network at the top of Indian business, and you need to get access to that network in order to succeed. Finding the right partners can be key, but you need to be diligent.[48]

Pawean Budhwar, Associate Dean of Research at Aston Business School, agreed, saying that the key to success doing business in India was tapping into networks and resources that could provide useful information related to your business interests. "Have persistence," he said, "And don't give up. The mileage to get into India is great. Don't expect it to be a smooth ride. Expect it to be irritating. But once you're there, you'll enjoy it—and you'll make a great deal of money."[49]

Indians regard business as "personal," and trust-based relationships as so important that they are willing to spend significant amounts of time building and testing them.[50] Those hoping to build such relationships with Indians must demonstrate their long-term competence, reliability, and sensitivity for Indian cultural issues. Indian businesspeople tend to be interested in long-term relationships and repeat business rather than short-term opportunities. Individuals in trust-based relationships regard themselves less as individuals with potentially differing interests, and more as members of a friendship group, and they try to conform to group expectations and norms so as to maintain group harmony.

Mutual respect is an important element for these relationships. Respect is derived from age, status, and education. Friendliness, flexibility, humility, and a willingness to compromise are valued personal attributes. Face-saving is important. If you cause another person embarrassment, both you and she/he will lose face, and the relationship may be irrevocably lost. The expression of anger and negative emotions, either in words, voice, tone, or body language, disrupts relational harmony, causing this embarrassment. Westerners find this a difficult lesson to learn since for the most part they do not read others' body language or try to control their own, and may believe that honest expression of emotions is both healthy (reducing stress) and honest. It is best to remain friendly at all times, regardless of what is being said.

Most Indians speak softly and moderately so as not to disturb interpersonal harmony. This is intended to communicate humility and respect for others. Individuals that speak loudly and boastfully are seen as lacking self-control, and therefore as unreliable in long-term relationships. This is a difficult lesson especially for Americans, whose cultural expectation is that leadership is demonstrated with loud voices and that believable self-promotion generates respect. Indians may also interpret loudness as dishonesty.[51] Regardless of your personal ethics, you should avoid criticizing Indian poverty, the caste system, local politics, or any Indian business practices. Having endured hundreds of years of British colonialism and imperialism, many Indians might be sensitive about foreigners' criticisms.

Religion plays an important role in shaping Indian life, and should be respected. Hinduism is the majority religion and very diverse in its beliefs. Many Indians believe devoutly in multiple gods, karma (your current actions will affect your future reincarnations; your actions in previous lives affect your current good or bad luck), and reincarnation. Others believe that the many gods are appearances of an underlying single monotheistic god. Most believe, however, that they are "trapped" in a cycle of reincarnation, and in order to escape from it must become detached from ego involvement. This has potentially an interesting effect on personal ethics because to achieve "Nirvana" (the re-uniting of the individual spark with the collectivist flame, or the individual drop of water with the ocean) one must lose the egoistic desire to commit both bad and good deeds. The caste system is also supported by most variants of Hinduism. The justification for caste is based on belief in karma. A person is reincarnated into a higher or lower caste based on the good or bad actions in their previous lifetime. A person's place in a caste may only be changed in their subsequent reincarnation, depending on the karma produced by their lifetime of actions. An interesting aspect of this belief is that an exceptionally bad person could be reincarnated as a god who is punished by being denied the opportunity to develop through subsequent reincarnations toward Nirvana because gods live much longer than other beings. A minority of Indians are Muslims, mainly Shiite rather than Sunni (see Chapter 12 for Islamic beliefs). About 2 percent are Sikh, believing in reincarnation, but rejecting caste and non-intervention through good deeds.[52]

Negotiating a deal

It is helpful to start with a local intermediary that will introduce you to whomever you have identified as a prospective business partner. This intermediary will help you overcome cultural barriers, and navigate India's complex and mammoth federal and state bureaucracies to get the many necessary approvals. The first meeting with a prospective business associate will be devoted entirely to relationship-building. Business might get mentioned but you should not expect any decisions. Pushing for quick resolutions will be perceived as disrespectful. This is a lesson for those immersed in American business culture (see Chapter 18) who might bring final contracts to an initial meeting.

In subsequent meetings Indians tend to take an holistic approach to negotiations, seeing different elements of a possible deal as interconnected, and jumping back and forth between elements without resolution. This is a difficult approach for Western business-people, who tend to rely on a more linear approach to discussions. Indians tend to look to long-term business relationships, long-term commitments, and win–win solutions for solving potential controversies or disagreements. Indians will share information relatively openly, as do Western businesspeople. However, they love to haggle and final prices will often move more than 40 percent lower from initial offer to final agreement.[53] Arguing is usually a counterproductive approach to disagreements over details. It is generally better to remain friendly and willing to compromise, while emphasizing the value of a trust-based relationship to both sides. When you offer a compromise, you may ask for one in return, including in areas that have already been discussed and agreed.

Indian decision-making

Indians will be open to objective information as long as it does not challenge religious belief or Indian social structures like caste. Indian thinking is associative[54] in the sense that it processes information through seeing patterns and contextual relationships between elements that may seem unrelated to Western logic,[55] relying on free association and not on past experience.[56] Decisions are intended to address existing situations and the people involved rather than universal values or principles, and usually within the expectations of the caste system. Individuals evaluate alternatives on the basis of their personal feelings rather than with objective facts, and there is often a strong commitment to religious ideologies and belief systems. Ultimately, decisions must be confirmed in the decision-making group to preserve intragroup harmony. Within the decision-making group, friendship and kinship count for more than expertise, though higher education is highly respected. Most Indians will be too polite to say "no" and will communicate any rejections or equivocations indirectly. Of course, Western-educated Indians will rely more on logic and objective data in their decision-making.

Quick decisions should not be expected. Any proposed alternatives that oppose religious expectations will not be easy to sell. There is a strong sense of what Westerners would consider "fatalism"[57] or determinism because so much of individual and collective circumstances is understood to be outside of individual control and based on cycles of reincarnation. Since escape from these cycles is based on putting aside egoistic involvement and committing no good or bad deeds, passivity is an appropriate ethical stance.

Unlike in the West, contracts may not be honored if the relationship breaks down after the deal has been signed. You should continue to stay in touch, asking, for example, if your Indian buyers are satisfied, or need help using technology, or have any difficulties that you may help address.

Corruption and ethics

While honesty is esteemed in this vast and poor country, corrupt practices are common. In 2014, India was rated one of the 20 most corrupt countries in the world, slightly better than Iraq.[58] "Baksheesh," or tipping, is the usual way to ensure that things will get done, and is often the way to open doors that might otherwise always remain closed.[59] Corruption and fraud are endemic in all levels of society. Corruption, bribes, or payments for "fixing" exist in everyday life and are something that must be dealt with, even accepted, to get things accomplished. While bribery is a crime punishable by suspension and jail time if convicted, corrupt officials rarely encounter resistance.

Lately, the "Zero Rupee" note has been used by those resisting corrupt practices to condemn bribery. A person who has been asked by an official to present a bribe may offer a zero rupee note, indicating a willingness to ask for a disciplinary hearing that could cause the official to lose his/her job.

Eileen S. Wibbeke examined the issue of ethics from a cross-cultural perspective, urging managers abroad to look beyond Western traditions.[60] For example, her analysis of Hindu ethics pointed out its complexity due to historical and cultural tradition. There are a number of ways a believer may seek spiritual liberation, and there are many Hindu scriptures from which to choose. This religion is flexible, tolerant, and socially important. Some Hindu philosophers teach that an act is *amoral* only if it is not based on informed choices that are freely made.

India's economic success story

India's projected annual economic growth for 2017–2018 is 7.5 percent, higher than that for China.[61] India is the fastest growing G20 economy. Much of India's economic success has been in high-technology industries. Exhibit 15.5 describes the success of high-technology industrial growth in Bangalore.

E X H I B I T 15.5

EXHIBIT 15.5 THE HIGH-TECH REVOLUTION

Bangalore is the center of India's booming information technology (IT) industry. Yet, it is something of a paradox—inside its modern industrial parks, business and living conditions operate at a higher level. Outside, its surrounding urban area suffers from deteriorating infrastructure and attempts at renewal. This city is a global and national hub of sophisticated software and remote services, such as business processing outsourcing (BPOs or call-centers). The old city and local government, however, strains to keep up with the demands of its economic drivers, companies like Wipro and Infosys. These high-tech endeavors employ some 260,000 employees, and leading firms are hiring 1,000 new staff per month. Foreign firms are arriving to set-up businesses at a rate of three per week. No wonder the economic forecasts for this dynamic ecosystem are 25 percent or more annually. However, this city, known for its beauty, lush parks, greenery, and mild climate, struggles to cope with a population that has grown from 800,000 in 1951 to more than 8.6 million in 2012.

This municipality has also become a knowledge center that attracts technical and scientific institutes. Their leaders are the Indian Institution of Science, a world-class university known for its excellence, plus Karnataka, whose 77 engineering colleges alone produce 29,000 graduates per year and spearhead India's space program. A few miles out of town is "Electronics City," a cosmopolitan oasis with amenities to suit the needs of these knowledge workers. These range from "state-of-the-art" remote network management systems and cappuccino bars to lively nightlife.

E X H I B I T 15.5

Urban chaos and commuter nightmares in major cities like Bangalore, Delhi, and Mumbai make second-tier cities very attractive. They are growing fast as postindustrial corporations are attracted to Gurgaib and Noida on the edges of New Delhi; Mumbai's new town; Chennai, formerly Madras; Hyderabad in the south; Pune in the west; Molhali in the north. Even old Calcutta, now called Kolkata, is trying to woo investments for its IT and BPO firms. As successful companies expand aggressively, many move out to less congested areas.

Within attractive IT and BPO campuses, the R&D is either outsourced or extended to new global market niches—for example, processing insurance claims, desktop publishing, remote management and maintenance, backup navigation systems, compiling audits and completing tax forms, transcribing medical records, and financial records and analysis. Predictions are that in a few years many MNEs will have up to 25 percent of their staff in India. Also, security and data protection at these advanced facilities are tight! In 2008, IT and its enabling services employed over four million people who earned up to $65 billion from exports, accounting for 7 percent of India's GDP.

Part of this success is attributed to keeping government out of this new business. Also, India has a big competitive edge in its annual production of two million English-speaking graduates, many of whom benefit from a quality education.

Source: adapted from "Special Report on Outsourcing and IT in India: The Bangalore Paradox," *The Economist*, April 23, 2005, pp. 67–69 (report updated).

To appreciate the new business environment in India, consider the implications of Exhibit 15.6.

EXHIBIT 15.6 INDIA'S TATA ENTERPRISES

E X H I B I T 15.6

One of India's most successful global corporations originated in 1958 with a Parsi family named "Tata." Now, this diversified enterprise operates in 85 countries, and is continually acquiring high-profile businesses. In 2000, it acquired the London-based iconic tea company Tetley. In 2007, it acquired Corus, a European steel-maker. The same year, it acquired for $2.3 billion the legendary automobile marques Jaguar and Land Rover, and their British manufacturing plants, from Ford. Tata Industries reflects great financial strength from both domestic and foreign markets and looks upon these acquisitions as long-term investments. Alan Rosling, the company's chief British strategist, believes that Tata will reap the benefits of Ford's previous efforts with these prestigious automobiles. Due to its Indian origins, he is optimistic about Tata's increasing global research because of its sensitivity to cultural differences, and because it seeks to imitate the world's best corporations.

The Tata Group is an Indian conglomerate that spans countries and products, such as automobile and steel manufacturing, software, and tea production. An example of its innovation in emerging markets is Tata's Consulting Services, specializing in the outsourcing of

E
X
H
I
B
I
T

15.6

business processes of higher value. Perhaps one of Tata's most exciting ventures is the building of a small, inexpensive automobile called the Nano. This car, selling for about $2,500, is intended not only for the massive Indian market but also for emerging markets everywhere. The Nano is to be the "people's car" yet its manufacture uses state-of-the-art virtual design technology. Mr. Tata sees these endeavors as safe and less-expensive alternatives for consumers in both developing and mature economies.

Source: adapted from "A Bigger World: A Special Report on Globalization," *The Economist*, September 20, 2008, 26 page insert.

The manufacturing and industrial sector, however, has not grown in India to the same extent as in China, and this continues to be a problem. Most of the growth in Indian GDP has been in the services sector, contributing approximately 59 percent in 2012 and still growing rapidly, especially in IT and outsourcing. By contrast, the industry and manufacturing sector has remained a relatively constant 20 percent of GDP since the early 1990s. This means that India has not been able to match China's growth, driven by export of manufactures.

More than services or agriculture, India's entrenched bureaucracy and poor infrastructure negatively impact industry. Indian labor costs are high by emerging market standards and legal regulations are restrictive. As Chinese wages have risen, "busy-fingers" labor-intensive industry has fled to places like Bangladesh, but not to India. Indian car manufacturers have been an exception. After the riots in China against Japan in 2012, Nissan was the only Japanese car company whose profits rose significantly and this was because it immediately chose to expand in India and to put a temporary halt to expansion plans in China. Tata's Nano (see Exhibit 15.6), however, has not yet achieved the wide-ranging success it was billed for in 2008, and cannot be exported to either the EU or North America without considerable and expensive improvements in emissions and safety technology.[62] There seems no expectation that there will be any large increase in the Indian manufacturing sector in the near future.[63] Exhibit 15.7 describes conditions in the newly developing India.

Gender equality

India is a male-dominated society and there have been many media reports on sexual assault, including of Western women.[64] There are many Indian women in professional positions with significant authority. Indira Gandhi was Prime Minister of India between 1966 and 1984, when she was assassinated. Foreign female expatriates should have few problems if they act professionally in business and social situations. This would include:

EXHIBIT 15.7 INDIAN GROWTH RATES SLOWING?

On a 4,200 km train ride through 615 stations, one traveler reported that she/he never lost a usable cell-phone signal. Ten years ago, no one would have cared because only 5 percent of Indians had a cell phone. Now, according to Ericsson, 75 percent of Indians have access to one. In addition, of India's 247 million households, two-thirds have electricity, half have television and bicycles, though as yet only 5 percent have cars.

PriceWaterhouseCoopers reports that in 2010, 470 million Indians had incomes between $1,000 and $4,000 per year. This is expected to rise to 570 million within ten years, creating a $1 trillion market for goods and services. Yet, this forecast was made when the economy was booming, when it seemed that in a decade or two India would become a very prosperous country. Now, much slower expansion seems likely.

Growth should be maintained at a higher level than the 3 percent that was normal before the market reforms of the 1990s. Recent years, however, have brought high inflation (8.6 percent in 2011), especially for food. Roads, ports, and railways are overwhelmed. Electricity blackouts are common. Labor has become as expensive as in China, even though the Chinese have, on average, three times the wealth.

The Transport Corporation of India reported in 2012 that every one of India's major road networks was clogged with traffic. Roads are being expanded at 4 percent per year, but vehicle traffic is expanding at 11 percent. Driving from Delhi to Mumbai, 1,380 km, takes three days at an average speed of 21 km per hour. The railways are no better. It is a political necessity to keep passenger fares level but these subsidies are paid for with rising freight rates. The result is that goods are sent by truck on the very overcrowded highways.

Given that the infrastructure seems to have reached its limits, a slowdown in economic growth to 5 percent would be very welcome. It was 7.2 percent in 2011. Cyrus Guzder, a Mumbai businessman, commented, "We should not try to get back to the highest growth path. India hurts when it is growing at 8.5 per cent."

Source: adapted from *The Economist* special report on India; "The Economy: Express or Stopping," *The Economist*, September 25–October 5, 2012, pp. 8–10.

■   not initiating hand shaking as a greeting with Indian men, Hindu or Muslim;
■   engaging in no public displays of affection with men except handshaking (no hugging or kissing);
■   wearing conservative dresses or pantsuits—when jogging wearing long pants; and
■   avoiding wearing leather (belts, handbags, purses), as Hindus revere cows.

Social freedom between the sexes is not appreciated, except within more progressive communities. Normally among traditionalists, a stranger should not speak to a woman if he is not acquainted with her or her family. For a young woman to take the hand of a man who is not her husband is usually objectionable. Bold, emancipated women may dare to indulge in dancing with their husbands, but for her to dance with anyone not her husband would be improper.

AUSTRALIA

Australia has negotiated free trade agreements with South Korea (2014), China (2015), and Japan (2016). It was an active participant in the negotiation of the Trans Pacific Partnership (TPP) that would have included Brunei, Canada, Chile, Japan, Malaysia, Mexico, Peru, New Zealand, Singapore, the US, and Vietnam. At the time of this writing, the TPP seems on life-support because of the possible refusal of the US to ratify the treaty. Australia, is, however, a committed Southeast Asian international trading country (see Exhibit 15.1) and has indicated that if the TPP fails, it will seek bilateral trade treaties in replacement.

There is a close Australian–American relationship, perhaps derived from the two countries being close geopolitical allies since the Vietnam War. This relationship covers the spectrum from commercial and cultural contacts, to political and defense cooperation. Euro-American companies wishing to do business in Australia will find relatively few obstacles, though legal regulations are less helpful in protecting investors' interests, and there is "red tape" to overcome before products may be exported (see Exhibit 15.2).

It is important, however, to remember that while Australians speak English as their first language, and seem to behave much as do Americans, there are differences in language and culture. These should be respected and even appreciated. This respect will cement relationships already predisposed toward friendship, and lead to success in business.

Cultural guidelines for doing business

Although originally founded as a British colony in 1778, and with 92 percent of its population of about 22 million being of European descent, Australia has become a multicultural nation. Asians comprise 7 percent of the population, and Aboriginals 1 percent. As of 2005, Australia was admitting 120,000 immigrants per year, one-third from Asian countries, to relieve labor shortages. Melbourne has become a showcase for multiculturalism, with John So, a Hong Kong immigrant, elected lord mayor between 2001 and 2008.

Australians[65] value modesty and brevity in speech. Foreign businesspeople should keep their presentations short without too much detail. Hard-sell tactics are not appreciated as Australians prefer honesty and resist pressure to buy quickly. State the positives and negatives supporting the purchase of your products or services. Claims perceived as boastful may make you the butt of Australian humor. Offer a reasonable price, recognizing that Australians are not hagglers and prices will move less (20–30 percent) than in other South and Southeast Asian countries from initial offer to final agreement. Australians tend to communicate what they think fairly directly and enjoy an argument or debate. Relationships are valued significantly less than in other countries in the region and can be developed adequately during the course of negotiating a deal, which will be policed in the usual Western way of contracts and lawyers as necessary.

In social situations, Australians respect people who have opinions even if these conflict with their own. Arguments are considered entertaining, and become a way to demonstrate openness and honesty, thereby building trust. There are topics best not to broach, like Australia's treatment of its Aboriginal First Nations, or the Papua New Guinea refugee detention centers[66] that could injure your relationship.

Negotiating

Australian negotiating is intended as a friendly debate that will reach a mutually acceptable outcome that covers both short- and long-term mutual benefits. Most Australians will be willing and intend to compromise and cooperate in a search for win–win outcomes. Negotiations may be conducted one-on-one or between teams. Australian teams are often poorly aligned in terms of internal agreement and this may offer advantages to their foreign counterparts. Information is easily shared, as it would be in the US, Canada, and EU countries, as a way to build trust. Disputes are best handled by offering genuine compromises. Offering to split a difference is one such tactic.

Decision-making

Australians[67] are open-minded about diversity of both cultures and opinions, tending to trust or at least give the benefit of the doubt, unless they are given reason to not. They are analytical and place universal values, legal precedence, and their companies' policies ahead of personal feelings about foreign counterparts and their proposed deals. They are objective and decide on the basis of facts and logical analysis. Feelings or intuitions are generally regarded as unreliable. Nor do Australians have any trouble with directly saying "no" should they decide to refuse a deal. The Australian decision-making process is, however, significantly slower than the American one. The decision will be made with the consultation of top management, who may not have attended the actual negotiations.

Corruption is rare. You should avoid giving gifts or offering favors of more than symbolic value. This may be interpreted as a corrupt practice. A signed contract is usually a dependable guarantee that an agreement will be kept to the letter. Any request to change any element of a contract after it is signed will be resisted, and could be interpreted as bad faith on your part.

Gender equality

Many Australian women hold senior and influential positions in companies. You should always treat women with the same respect as men since, if nothing else, they may be the boss. Foreign women should have no difficulties. LGBT people are protected by employment and service antidiscrimination laws. Same-sex couples enjoy most of the same rights as alternate-sex couples, with the exception of marriage.[68]

SINGAPORE AND MALAYSIA

We have chosen to consider Singapore and Malaysia together because the two countries are tightly interlinked geographically, socially, and in terms of business practices. Singapore is a small city-state only 697 square kilometers in area—approximately 3.5 times the size of Washington, DC. It occupies several islands at the south end of the Malay Peninsula, the main part of Malaysia. Malaysia is approximately the same size as New Mexico in the US.

During the British colonial period, ending after World War II, Singapore and Malaysia were part of the same administrative unit, and they were united as a single nation between 1957 and 1965. They also mirror each other in ethnic composition. Singapore is 76.8 percent Chinese, 13.9 percent Malay, and 7.9 percent Indian. Malaysia is 50.4 percent Malay, 23.7 percent Chinese, and 7.1 percent Indian. In terms of similarity of business practices, Abramson and Ai[69] reported that Canadian companies doing business in Singapore and Malaysia encountered no country-specific factors—differences between the two—that significantly affected their performance.

Singapore[70] is a highly developed First-World free market economy. It has intentionally created a relatively bureaucracy-free and corruption-free business environment, achieving a per capita GDP higher than most developed countries. Singapore's economy depends on export and re-export (transshipping), especially consumer electronics, IT products, pharmaceuticals, and financial services. Singapore has in recent years attracted major investments in the pharmaceutical and medical technology sectors, and is regarded by many as Southeast Asia's financial and high-tech hub. While GDP growth fell 1 percent in 2009 with the impact of the global financial recessions, it rebounded to 14.8 percent growth in 2010 due to renewed growth of exports. In 2011 and 2012, growth slowed to 4.9 and 2.1 percent due to the second European recession in that period.

Malaysia is widely regarded as the ideal Islamic economic state—the one other Islamic countries hope to emulate. Malaysia[71] has transformed its economy since the 1970s from a producer of raw materials to a middle-income country with a multi-sector economy. Malaysia is attempting to achieve high-income status by 2020 by attracting investments in Islamic finance, high-technology industries, biotechnology, and services. Nevertheless, the export of electronics, oil and gas, palm oil, and rubber remain major economic drivers of current prosperity levels. The oil and gas sector currently produces 40 percent of Malaysian government revenues so that Malaysian prosperity has hinged heavily on rising and falling energy prices.

Negotiating[72]

In both Malaysia and Singapore it is critical to build trust-based relationships before attempting to negotiate business. Relationship is such a critical criterion that both Malaysians and Singaporeans will not consider doing business with someone with whom they have not already established a deep and lasting relationship. They expect that such relationships will evolve into true friendships, and if they do not, it is a bad sign for a continued relationship.

In addition, Malaysians and Singaporeans will be unlikely to enter into a new business relationship that would have adverse consequences for an existing relationship. New opportunities must be offered to existing friends before new friends may receive serious consideration. Relationships are based on familiarity, respect, and ultimately trust. Face-saving is critical. Causing embarrassment to one person constitutes loss of face for anyone involved and may terminate a negotiation or even a relationship. Politeness and humility are required at all times and in all circumstances.

While Malaysian culture supports long-term relationships, commitments, and mutual benefits, and ultimately favors win–win solutions, negotiations are often competitive, with much hard bargaining. Malaysians haggle less than some Asians but prices will likely be reduced by between 25 and 40 percent from initial offer to final deal.[73] In the event of dispute or disagreement on terms, resolution is best sought by leveraging existing personal relationships, and emphasizing shared goals and long-term mutual benefits. Another strategy is to use a mediator—it is probably best to use whatever intermediary made the initial introductions. Singaporeans are harder bargainers than Malaysians and love to haggle. In Singapore, prices will be fought down more than 40 percent[74] from initial offer to final deal.

Singaporeans tend to negotiate in a direct and honest fashion. They may employ Chinese-style tactics like using time-pressure against a counterpart who has stated a deadline. They may also insist they are making "final offers" that will almost always prove not to be final if rejected. Extreme "low-ball" offers may be used initially in an attempt to shock a Western counterpart into revealing what she/he really thinks his/her product is worth.

Decision-making[75]

Malay decision-making is strongly influenced by Islam, and relatively closed to outside information contrary to that religion. Information is evaluated subjectively and associatively, relying more commonly on personal perspectives than objective analysis. Subjective feelings are considered to reveal truth especially as influenced by, and therefore revealing, Islamic sureties. Decisions are based on situational dynamics and the value of relationships rather than on universal values or principles. Some more religious Malays use Islamic "guidebooks" that indicate appropriate Islamic solutions to varieties of issues. Malays tend to try to avoid or attenuate perceived conflict and communicate rejections indirectly.

Singaporean decision-makers are also relatively closed to outside information, and are inclined to evaluate information associatively as well. There is, however, a higher preponderance of higher education than in Malaysia and this increases the probability of conceptual and analytical thinking. Singapore has no official religion and Islam is largely confined to the minority of Malays. All Singaporeans, however, are strongly loyal to their nation, companies, and especially to important relationships. Relationships have priority over personal value-commitments. Decisions are made by consensus within decision-making groups. A single individual will not stand against the group's will, risking personal loss of face, or causing others embarrassment. Older decision-makers tend to have more influence.

Gender equality

Singapore is still a male-dominated business culture. Foreign women, however, should have no problems if they act professionally at all times. A Singaporean businessman who invites a foreign businesswoman to dinner is far more likely to want to discuss business, or build a professional relationship, than have any personal agenda. In Malaysia, foreign business-women should dress conservatively and modestly as in an Islamic country.

LGBT rights are unrecognized in Malaysia and some forms of homosexual activity are criminalized. A former prominent Malaysian politician's career was ended when he was imprisoned on sodomy charges. LGBT rights also go largely unrecognized in Singapore.

General cultural guidelines

Hamzah-Sendut, Madsen, and Thong, local Malaysian business researchers,[76] offered more general guidelines for building effective business relationships in addition to the ones above.

1. Circle the outside before penetrating to the center. Direct approaches are not normally appreciated, especially when outsiders are seeking business opportunities for the first time. Westerners tend to be linear thinkers and go straight to the point once initial small talk is done. Asians employ spiral logic, making a series of discussions that triangulate their goals without necessarily stating them. Your Asian counterpart will get the drift. He/she is used to connecting the dots and will anticipate where the discussions are leading.

2. The initial contact is very important. First impressions are seldom forgotten. A letter written in English asking for a meeting is considered cold. It is better to receive a tele-phone call from someone seeking to introduce you. Never send a junior person to make the first contact. It may be seen as disrespectful—a loss of face.

3. Forbearance will achieve more than directness. Be prepared to suggest "trial balloons." Be prepared to achieve nothing unless friendly alliances have been cemented. Accept failure without bitterness. Asians are more adept than Westerners at reading negative body language, interpreted as loss of face for the recipient.

4. Building friendship takes a long time by Western standards. Friendship is built through repeated social engagements, as well as demonstrating competence and long-term reliability. Civil servants should be handled with care to help preserve their profes-sional neutrality.

5. Time is handled differently and you should not be surprised to be kept waiting. You should respond with politeness, flexibility, and generosity.

6. Surprises should be avoided in your dealings with others. Sudden shifts in thinking or action may be perceived as wily or tricky. Tactical maneuvers and bluffing are not considered appropriate. The mood should be conciliatory and not confrontational. From the Asian side, the question is whether a marriage of interests will be appropriate.

7   Meeting agendas should not be rigidly fixed. There should be no artificial boundaries to the development of trust.

8   When doing business with Muslims (Singapore = 14.9 percent; Malaysia = 60.4 percent), remember that Islam is more conservative about the separation of genders and appropriate interactions with females.

9   Negotiations should not be considered as competitive zero-sum engagements. You should not strive to win at the expense of your friend. The objective is agreement. Both sides must sincerely believe they will benefit.

THAILAND

Thailand[77] is characterized by a free market economy, pro-investment policies, strong export industries, and a well-developed economic infrastructure. It has achieved steady economic growth largely due to a mix of industrial and agricultural exports, including electronics, agricultural commodities, and processed foods. Thailand has an extraordinarily low unemployment rate—less than 1 percent—resulting in upward pressure on wages, and the importation of approximately 2.5 million migrant workers. Thai economic policy has been to attempt to stimulate domestic consumption, resulting in a nationwide minimum wage, and attempts to reform the tax code to reduce taxes for the middle class.

Thailand's population of approximately 67 million is 75 percent Thai, and 14 percent Chinese by ethnicity. It is 94.6 percent Buddhist, and 4.6 percent Muslim. Thai is the principal language, though English is the second language of the economic and social elite.

Thai cultural values

There have been relatively few studies of business practices in Thailand and their underlying values. There is one major oddity, as viewed through Western eyes. Thais are reported to place a high value on social harmony, and to behave in friendly, cooperative, and even passive ways, and yet to have a strong undercurrent of individualism that may result in win–lose revenge-seeking behavior under certain circumstances.[78]

Pornpitakpan[79] observed the same. Thais placed a high value on maintaining harmonious interpersonal relationships, emphasized saving face, and preferred working interdependently. There was, however, a "dark side." Thais could behave in rough, rude, competitive, and uncooperative ways especially with those who were not members of their relationship networks or in-groups. These negative behaviors could be directed at foreigners, but also on the streets of Bangkok among Thais themselves. Driving practices are aggressive, with insults and curses shouted from car to car. People push ahead of others who are waiting in queues, or people refuse to queue at all, mobbing forward seeking to get ahead of the others.

Hofstede's[80] cross-national work values research supported the view that Thais were more orderly, cooperative, and relationship-oriented than Americans. The Thais were higher in *power-distance*, suggesting a greater willingness to accept unequal power distribution in organizations. They were higher in *uncertainty avoidance*, suggesting they felt less comfortable in ambiguous situations and would behave in ways to increase feelings of certainty. Thais were considerably higher on *collectivism* (versus individualism), meaning they preferred to belong in their reference groups where they exchanged loyalty for care. Thais were also much higher on *femininity* (versus masculinity) suggesting greater caring for others—putting quality of life ahead of success, income, and status. Thais were also much higher on *long-term orientation*,[81] indicating a higher value placed on the Confucian virtues of persistence and perseverance.

Taken together, these findings suggested that Thais would be more relationship-oriented, and more accepting of structured and orderly relationships, than Americans. Pornpitakpan[82] supported the view that Thais were more relationship-oriented than Americans. Americans who adapted to Thai ways, building personal relationships ahead of business ones, and accepting social invitations, were more attractive to Thais.

VIETNAM

Vietnam[83] has been transitioning from a centrally planned economy to a free market one since 1986. The Vietnamese government has affirmed its commitment to economic modernization, joining the World Trade Organization (WTO) in 2007. This has facilitated the development of more competitive and export-driven industries. Vietnam became a negotiating partner in the now apparently defunct TPP trade agreement in 2010. Between 2000 and 2010, agriculture as a share of national GDP has shrunk from 25 percent to 22 percent. Industry's share has increased from 36 percent to 41 percent. State-owned enterprises still account for 40 percent of GDP.

The global recession of 2008–2009 hurt Vietnam's export economy. However, between 2009 and 2011, GDP grew by an average 7 percent per annum. In 2012, GDP grew by an impressive 12 percent and government policies brought imports roughly equal to exports (see Exhibit 15.1). Foreign direct investment inflows, however, declined in 2012 by 4.5 percent to $10.5 billion. Vietnam currently has issues with high inflation (9.2 percent in 2012) and public debt load (48.2 percent of GDP in 2012).

Vietnam is 85.7 percent Kinh, or Viet, in ethnic origin. Its official language is Vietnamese, but English is becoming increasingly popular as a second language. Only 9.3 percent of the population is Buddhist, and another 6.7 percent Catholic. No religion is the preference of 80.8 percent.

Sociopolitical context

Vietnam has an interesting history often connected with that of Western Europe and the US during the twentieth century. Since the reunification of North and South Vietnam in 1975, and Vietnam's withdrawal from Cambodia in 1989, it has focused on introducing the concept of *doi moi*, or renovation. This term includes private enterprise and the approval of 100 percent foreign ownership of firms and joint ventures, openness to overseas Vietnamese, an interest in tourism, and greater individual freedoms.

Since then, the government has been fully committed to the idea of *doi moi*, and has attracted new investors from Japan, Taiwan, Hong Kong, and Australia. Australia, for example, targeted Vietnam in its "Asian Business Success Program," while billboards with ads for Minolta and Hitachi dominated intersections in Hanoi and Ho Chi Minh City (formerly Saigon).

It was also the 1989 peace treaty with Cambodia that opened up diplomatic talks with the US and the countries of Western Europe. This treaty was the economic turning point for Vietnam. Within months, diplomatic ties had been fully reestablished with China and the above-mentioned countries. Washington opened a diplomatic office in Hanoi in 1991 to coordinate the search for American MIAs (soldiers missing in action). The US lifted most economic sanctions in 1992 and 1993. President Clinton then lifted the trade and investment embargo in February 1994, and since then the US has established itself as a significant investor in Vietnam.

Under the administration of a technocratic government, a top priority has been to fix the corruption that was widespread in government. As the world's 13th largest country by population, the government has shown a strong interest in becoming a market economy and opening itself to outsiders. Furthermore, with the reestablishment of diplomatic relations with the US and other major economic players, business opportunities have increased dramatically over the past years. Those companies who take advantage of conducting business in Vietnam now will be rewarded with a high-growth market of consumers. This economic transformation is described in Exhibit 15.8.

EXHIBIT 15.8 TRANSFORMING VIETNAM

Today, Vietnamese welcome the tourist dollar, even for excursions to their wartime Cu Chi tunnels. Such excursions demonstrate their ingenuity, adaptability, perseverance, and determination to resist foreign invaders down through the centuries.

The period since the 1990s has transformed Vietnam by rapid and relatively equitable development in a free-enterprise environment. You can see this in vibrant Ho Chi Minh City (formerly Saigon), especially downtown at the smart Dong Khoi Street where young, prosperous Vietnamese shop. In what was a poor country, the quality of life has dramatically improved despite choking traffic and constant construction. With the switch from a command economy, gradual financial liberalization and market reforms have been fostering rapid poverty-reducing growth.

E
X
H
I
B
I
T

15.8

E
X
H
I
B
I
T

15.8

The country is still handicapped by legislative and bureaucratic processes, especially with regard to the justice system, and countering Communist Party corruption. Other problems to be confronted are rising inflation, a slumping stock market, need for greater trade, and political liberalization, as well as improvement of corporate governance.

A positive aspect of Vietnamese culture is its flexibility to seek better role models which are then melded into something uniquely Vietnamese. Vietnam is active in the Asia-Pacific Summit, WTO, and ASEAN, all of which provide insights for social and economic change. This is a syncretistic society with increasing entrepreneurship and booming business. Further, foreign MNEs have been permitted to undertake a huge range of projects throughout the land. Refugees, who left in the 1970s as "boat people," are either returning or sending back funds for their families and/or investments.

Nothing reveals Vietnam's remarkable turnaround more than the agricultural sector. The countryside, with 70 percent of the population, now provides 21 percent of exports. But climate change could imperil this progress in agriculture.

The Communist Party, with 3.7 million members, has a congress policy "to be friends with all the people." And this has contributed to a rise in tourism, along with a lessening of restrictions against religious groups and ethnic minorities. With the selling of public assets to private enterprise, the state has become less important as employer and provider, and membership in the Party matters less. As Vietnam continues to open its economy to business and strives to meet the United Nations Millennium Development Goals in poverty reduction, its youthful population is filled with optimism about its future.

Source: adapted from Collins, P. "Half-Way from Rags to Riches: A Special Report on Vietnam," *The Economist*, April 25, 2008.

Doing business in Vietnam[84]

Vietnam is a Confucian country (see Chapter 9). Confucian philosophy emphasizes the importance of hierarchy, relationships, responsibility, and obligation. This philosophy is a vital element in Vietnamese society. It is applied in business culture to maintain interpersonal harmony and the collective good.

The idea of saving face—preserving the dignity of the other—is important. The Vietnamese will do anything to prevent loss of face, including avoiding confrontation or telling others what they seem to want to hear. A foreigner will lose face by criticizing someone in public or by not fulfilling promises.

Vietnam is a collectivist society in which one is expected to place the needs of the group ahead of those of the individual. Family and community concerns take precedence over those of business or individuals. Ties between families and communities will have a significant effect on individual behavior.

Business organizations tend to be hierarchical, following the Confucian model. Ideas and decisions are generated at senior levels and often, the oldest manager has the most influence. Employees are expected to be loyal to the hierarchy, but in return the boss is expected to guard the welfare of the employees and is responsible for their behavior.

Status is important. Supervisors and co-workers should be treated with respect. Titles are important. Status is earned through education and age. It is very important to your acceptance and success to show respect to senior individuals, based on their education, position, and age. At a meeting, the eldest participant arrives first. Status is also based on gender, though this is becoming less pronounced. Most Vietnamese women work in assistant or clerical roles. However, Vietnamese men will treat foreign women in senior roles as equals.

Business relationships are formal and take time to develop. Vietnamese businesspeople prefer to get to know foreign counterparts before serious business talk can begin. You may be treated with suspicion if you try to get right down to business, so several meetings may be required just to become acquainted. It is important to demonstrate competence and reliability at all times.

International business is usually conducted in English, though the Vietnamese appreciate efforts to speak some Vietnamese. It is advisable to have all documents translated into Vietnamese. Face issues may inhibit your Vietnamese counterparts from admitting not understanding. Therefore, it is also useful to have your own translator. French language is an asset since English will not be understood often in rural areas.

Negotiations may be lengthy and time-consuming. The Vietnamese will want to examine all details. They will have to consult within their group, and the entire process will be reviewed at senior levels. The Vietnamese are known for bureaucratic procedures, also slowing down the process. Don't be surprised in actual negotiations if there are long periods of silence. The Vietnamese may think and consider before responding. They may also remain silent in the face of a potential disagreement in order to save their face, and yours. Maintain a soft voice when speaking. Loud voices and extensive hand gestures are considered rude and make Vietnamese uncomfortable. Always accept any tea or food offered by your negotiation partners since not doing so is considered rude.

Introductions are formal. It is helpful to be introduced by a mutual acquaintance, suggesting the value of building relationship networks. Gift-giving is a common practice. Gifts need not be expensive—they simply show appreciation. Fruit and flowers are common gifts, to be wrapped in colorful paper.

CONCLUSIONS

South and Southeast Asia are demonstration models of the complexity and multidimensional aspects of culture. Although we have provided cultural specifics on only a few countries, it is enough, perhaps, to convince global managers of the important distinctions that exist. South and Southeast Asians are very different culturally from Westerners. These differences include language, religion, family, and social attitudes that influence business practice and building effective relationships.

The new market opportunities and diversity in the Pacific Basin alone should motivate us to seek further cultural information, whether we are dealing with Australians who are seemingly Western in outlook, or with Vietnamese who are so obviously different. South and Southeast Asian economies will become more and more important players in the global economy as the twenty-first century progresses.

MIND STRETCHING

1   What seemingly is involved as traditional Asian societies transition into modern ones (e.g., India, Malaysia, Thailand, Vietnam)?

2   What are the commonalities in building effective business relationships in India, Singapore/Malaysia, Thailand, and Vietnam? What are the differences?

3   What cross-border commonalities have you observed in this study of Asian cultures?

4   Why is it important for you to increase your knowledge and skill in Asian cultures, languages, negotiation styles, and business practices?

5   With the expansion of global terrorism and insurgencies in Asia, what cautions should you observe in travel to the region?

NOTES

1   Mahathir, M. and Shintaro, I. *The Voice of Asia: Two Leaders Discuss the Coming Century.* Tokyo: Kodansha Amer Inc., 1996. Dr. Mahathir bin Mohamad was Prime Minister of Malaysia, 1981–2003. Shintaro Ishihara was Governor of Tokyo, 1999–2012.

2   Nidumolu, R. *Two Birds in a Tree: Timeless Indian Wisdom for Business Leaders.* San Francisco, CA: Berrett-Koehler Publishers, 2013.

3   www.oxforddictionaries.com (retrieved November 29, 2016).

4   "Asian Century," https://en.m.wikipedia.org (retrieved November 29, 2016).

5   Borthwick, M. *Pacific Century: The Emergence of Modern Pacific Asia.* Boulder, CO: Westview Press, 2013.

6   "Asia 2050: Realizing the Asian Century," Asian Development Bank, www.iri.edu.ar/cd_anuario_2012 (retrieved November 29, 2016).

7   Rodriguez, P. *China, India, and the United States: The Future of Economic Supremacy Course Guidebook & Transcript.* Chantilly, VA: The Teaching Company, 2011.

8   "China's Love of Lee's 'Singapore Model' Ran Deep for Decades," Bloomberg, March 23, 2015, www.bloomberg.com (retrieved November 29, 2016).

9   "The Top 20 Emerging Markets," Bloomberg, www.bloomberg.com (retrieved November 29, 2016).

10 Mahmood, K. *Islam Inc.: Rebuilding Islamic Business.* n.p.: Wfol.tv, 2012.

11 Central Intelligence Agency, *The World Factbook*, www.cia.gov/Library/rankorder (retrieved November 29, 2016).

12 "List of Countries by Real GDP Growth Rate," https://en.m.wikipedia.org (retrieved November 29, 2016).

13 Statistics Times, "List of Countries by Projected GDP," www.statisticstimes.com/economy/countries (retrieved November 29, 2016).

14 Inkeles, A. *National Character: A Psycho-Social Perspective*. New Brunswick, NJ: Transaction Publishers, 2015.

15 Ibid.

16 Katz, L. *The Global Business Guide*. Charleston, SC: CreateSpace, 2014.

17 See the Indian film *Court*. www.m.imdb.com/title (retrieved November 29, 2016).

18 Inkeles, *National Culture*.

19 Massey, B. *Where in the World Do I Belong?* USA: Jetlag Press, 2006.

20 Bridges, W. *The Character of Organizations: Using Personality Type in Organization Development*. New York: Nicholas Brealey, 2000.

21 Quenk, N. L. *Was That Really Me?: How Everyday Stress Brings Out Our Hidden Personality*. Palo Alto, CA: Davies-Black Publishing, 2002.

22 The "inferior" personality type is the opposite of the dominant (see Chapter 2). It represents behaviors that the dominant personality rejects as unacceptable and repugnant because they run counter to those of the dominant. The inclinations of the inferior are repressed and denied so the inferior is primitive in its behavior because the behaviors have never been practiced. The inferior may overwhelm the dominant under conditions of high personal stress, taking over conscious behavior for short periods. See Quenk, N. L. *Was That Really Me?*

23 Jung, C. G. *Personality Types*. Princeton, NJ: Princeton University Press, 1976.

24 Descriptions of the Jungian attitude-functions are derived from: Sharp, D. *Personality Types: Jung's Model of Typology*. Toronto, ON: Inner City Books, 1987; Thompson, H. L. *Jung's Function-Attitudes Explained*. Watkinsville, GA: Wormhole Publishing, 1996. Descriptions of inferior or shadow functions appearing under stress are derived from Quenk, *Was That Really Me?*; Thompson, *Jung's Function-Attitudes Explained*.

25 The theoretical niceties of Jungian theory regarding the repressed "shadow" personality are beyond the scope of this book. Easy references include Johnson, R. A. *Owning Your Own Shadow*. San Francisco, CA: Harper, 1993; Bly, R. *A Little Book on the Human Shadow*. San Francisco, CA: Harper, 1988. A very clear discussion of stress reactions is found in Quenk, *Was That Really Me?*

26 The reason the Malaysian national character differs in stress reaction is based on intricacies in the Jungian theory, beyond the scope here, having to do with dominant and auxiliary attitude/functions (see Chapter 2 for a brief discussion). In the Singaporean and Vietnamese national characters, Si is the dominant and Fe is the auxiliary. In the Malaysian, Si is the auxiliary and Fe the dominant. This difference in order of priority results in different stress reactions.

27 Birzer, B. J. "The Evil Empire and Ronald Reagan," The Imaginative Conservative, www.theimaginative-conservative.org (retrieved November 30, 2016).

28 Descriptions of the Jungian attitude functions are derived from: Sharp, *Personality Types*; Thompson, *Jung's Function-Attitudes Explained*. Descriptions of inferior or shadow functions appearing under stress are derived from Quenk, *Was That Really Me?*; Thompson, *Jung's Function-Attitudes Explained*.

29 Morrison, T. and Conaway, W. A., *Kiss, Bow, Or Shake Hands: The Bestselling Guide to Doing Business in More than 60 Countries*. n.p.: Getting Through Customs, 2015.

30 Ibid.

31 Ibid.

32 Ibid.

33 Ibid.

34 Descriptions of the Jungian attitude functions are derived from: Sharp, *Personality Types: Jung's Model of Typology*; Thompson, *Jung's Function-Attitudes Explained*. Descriptions of inferior or shadow functions appearing under stress are derived from Quenk, *Was That Really Me?*; Thompson, *Jung's Function-Attitudes Explained*.

35 Katz, *The Global Business Guide*.

36 Morrison and Conaway, *Kiss, Bow, Or Shake Hands*.

37 Ibid.

38 Ibid.
39 Hume, T. "The Secrets of Doing Business in India," CNN: International Edition, February 3, 2012, http://edition.cnn.com/2012/02/03/business (retrieved February 9, 2013).
40 Statistics Times, "List of Countries by Projected GDP."
41 Nidumolu, *Two Birds in a Tree*.
42 Ibid., p. 16.
43 Ibid.
44 Ibid., p. 20.
45 Ibid., p. 21.
46 Ibid., p. 181. See Organ, T. W. *The Hindu Quest for the Perfection of Man*. Columbus, MO: South Asia Books, 1994. Organ discusses the meaning of freedom in ancient Indian philosophy.
47 Morrison and Conaway, *Kiss, Bow, Or Shake Hands*.
48 Hume, "The Secrets of Doing Business in India."
49 Ibid.
50 Katz, *The Global Business Guide*.
51 Ibid.
52 Morrison and Conaway, *Kiss, Bow, Or Shake Hands*.
53 Katz, *The Global Business Guide*.
54 Ibid.
55 "Associational Thinking," www.cerecore.com (retrieved December 2, 2016).
56 "Associative Thinking," www.encyclopedia2.thefreedictionary.com (retrieved December 2, 2016).
57 Morrison and Conaway, *Kiss, Bow, Or Shake Hands*.
58 Transparency International, "Corruption Perceptions Index 2014," www.transparency.org (retrieved December 3, 2014).
59 Morrison and Conaway, *Kiss, Bow, Or Shake Hands*.
60 Wibbeke, E. S. *Global Business Leadership*. Burlington, MA: Elsevier/Butterworth-Heinemann, 2009, pp. 55–71. See also Moran, R. T. and Youngdahl, W. E. *Leading Global Projects: For Professional and Accidental Project Leaders*. Burlington, MA: Elsevier/Butterworth-Heinemann, 2008.
61 OECD, "India: Economic Forecast Summary (November, 2016)," www.oecd.org (retrieved December 2, 2016).
62 Cato, J. and Vaughan, M. "Why Can't I Buy a $2500 Nano in Canada?" *The Globe and Mail*, January 12, 2011, www.theglobeandmail.com (retrieved December 2, 2016).
63 This paragraph is derived in part from *The Economist*, "Special Report India," 12 page insert, September 29, 2012, p. 10.
64 The Associated Press, "5 Men in India Given Life Sentences for Sexual Assault of Danish Tourist," *Toronto Star*, June 10, 2016, www.thestar.com (retrieved December 2, 2016).
65 Morrison and Conaway, *Kiss, Bow, Or Shake Hands*.
66 Reuters, "Australia Agrees to Close Controversial Papua New Guinea Refugee Detention Centre," *The Telegraph*, August 17, 2016, www.telegraph.co.uk (retrieved December 2, 2016).
67 Katz, *The Global Business Guide*.
68 "LGBT Rights in Australia," www.en.m.wikipedia.org (retrieved December 2, 2016).
69 Abramson, N. R. and Ai, J. X. "Practicing Relationship Marketing in Southeast Asia: Reducing Uncertainty and Improving Performance," *Management International Review*, Vol. 38, Special Issue 1, 1999, pp. 113–143.
70 CIA. *The World Factbook*, 2013, www.cia.gov/library/publications/the-world-factbook/geos/as.html (retrieved December 2, 2016).
71 Ibid.
72 Katz, *The Global Business Guide*.
73 Ibid.
74 Ibid.

75 Morrison and Conaway, *Kiss, Bow, Or Shake Hands*.

76 Hamzah-Sendut, T. S. D., Madsen, J., and Thong, G. *Managing in a Plural Society*. Singapore: Longman, 1990.

77 CIA. *The World Factbook*, 2013, www.cia.gov/library/publications/the-world-factbook/geos/as.html (retrieved December 2, 2016).

78 Roongrengsuke, S. and Chansuthus, D. "Conflict Management in Thailand," in S. M. Leong, S. H. Ang, and C. T. Tan (eds.), *Marketing Insights for the Asia Pacific*. Singapore: Asia Pacific Marketing Association and Heinemann, 1998, pp. 167–221.

79 Pornpitakpan, C. "Trade in Thailand: A Three-Way Cultural Comparison," *Business Horizons*, March–April, 2000, pp. 61–70.

80 Hofstede, G. *Culture's Consequences: International Differences in Work-Related Values*. Beverley Hills, CA: Sage, 1984. See Hofstede, G. *Uncommon Sense about Organizations: Cases, Studies, and Field Observations*. Thousand Oaks, CA: Sage, 1994.

81 Hofstede, G. *Cultures and Organizations: Software for the Mind*. New York: McGraw-Hill, 2010.

82 Pornpitakpan, C. "The Effects of Cultural Adaptation on Business Relationships: Americans Selling to Japanese and Thais," *Journal of International Business Studies*, Vol. 30, No. 2, 1999, pp. 317–338.

83 CIA. *The World Factbook*, 2013, www.cia.gov/library/publications/the-world-factbook/geos/as.html (retrieved December 2, 2016).

84 Adapted from Communicaid, "Doing Business in Vietnam: Vietnamese Social and Business Culture," www.communicaid/access/pdf/library/doing-business-in-vietnam (retrieved July 12, 2017).

16 DOING BUSINESS IN EUROPE AND RUSSIA
Great Britain, Ireland, France, Germany, Italy, and Russia[1]

Those fusty old Europeans are engaged in a radical experiment to reinvent themselves—this bid to create a "New Europe" is more than a collection of countries, but less than a unified state. The Maastricht treaty is not yet a teenager, the common currency is barely out of its nappies, a new constitution is being debated, new members have been admitted, and new candidates are under consideration. There is agreement on a united financial recovery strategy, and still talk of a common foreign policy. The euro is doing better than expected as a means of financial exchange.

The Economist, January 22, 2003

Abroad, not only will an inward-looking America unnerve allies from Europe to Asia who have depended on the superpower's stabilizing support: Mr. Trump's stunning victory will send shock waves around the world. Europe will feel the tremors.

Daniel Franklin, *The World in 2017*

After reading and studying concepts/examples and illustrations in Chapter 16, readers should:

1   Appreciate some of the cultural similarities as well as differences within Europe.
2   Learn some of the cultural differences, for example, between France and Italy when they have been neighbors for hundreds of years.
3   Be a little more curious when visiting any European country to explore and learn much more and in greater depth about various aspects of their cultures.
4   Begin reading respected journals or newspapers to follow Great Britain as they exit the EU, and France and other countries as the far-right continues to gain or lose voters.

The principal objective of this chapter is to understand some of the cultural complexities and diversities in the European Union (EU) members. Specifically, two European countries, France and Italy, will be examined in some depth, providing historical perspective and cultural guidelines. We will also cover some general cultural guidelines and generalizations for Europe, with sections on Great Britain, Ireland, France, Germany, Italy, and Russia.

Europe is the world's second smallest continent, bounded to the west by the Atlantic Ocean, to its east by Russia, and to the southeast by Turkey. It ambles from Iceland to Gibraltar—in the north, this landmass is set apart by the Arctic Ocean and in the south by the Mediterranean, Black, and Caspian Seas. Amid its landmass, peninsulas, and islands, it is home to more than 40 countries. Between two major mountain systems, a rolling, fertile plane stretches from the Pyrenees to the Urals. Herein are located some of the world's greatest urban centers, such as London, Paris, Berlin, and Moscow.

The continent has over 800 million people, roughly three-quarters of whom live in urban areas. Home to multiple ethnic groups, some 284 languages are spoken on the continent. (The major branches today include the Italic, Germanic, and Uralic language groups.) For millennia, Europeans have been providing humanity with ideas, ideals, and information that have nurtured the world's cultures and societies.

HISTORICAL PERSPECTIVE[2]

According to the most recent archeological evidence, the earliest fossil remains of the family of animals that includes human beings date back to approximately 1.8 million years ago. For hundreds of thousands of years, Neanderthals had preceded modern humans and shared the continent for roughly 100,000 years with them before becoming extinct. Recently, important fossils were uncovered in the Atapuerca Mountains of northern Spain; hominins were living there some 600,000 years ago—these Europeans may be the last connection to both the Neanderthal and *Homo sapiens.* The wall art and artifacts in caves of northern Spain and southern France confirm the aesthetic sense and tool technology of Stone Age cultures. Migration of peoples from Central Asia some 5,000 years ago brought the Indo-European language groups into the region. Minoan civilization, an important source of Western civilization that emerged on the island of Crete, dates back to roughly 7000 BC; the Minoans produced an impressive culture that was stimulated by trade with Egypt and Asia Minor. Ancient Greece is said to have begun in the eighth century BC (during its archaic period). Classical Greeks enriched the world, especially future European civilization, through philosophy, mathematics, natural sciences, political thought, arts, and architecture. The Greek legacy was bequeathed to the Romans, who became masters of architecture, engineering, law, and military strategy. The Roman Empire was the first attempt at uniting the continent's peoples, and it even extended into what is now the Middle East. Although the Roman Republic survived for only 500 years, their language (Latin), infrastructure, and heritage continue to influence humankind.

EUROPEAN DIVERSITY

Late in the twentieth century, the multinational entities of Europe sought ways to unify their economic efforts through the formation of a European Common Market. As the scope of cooperation increased among the participants (e.g., European Space Agency), the term *European Community* came into use. In 1992, member countries signed the Maastricht Treaty, a road map for establishing an economic and monetary union. Under the umbrella of the EU, three key institutions were created: a European Council, Commission, and Parliament. By 2002, a common currency called the *euro* was put into circulation and adopted by 11 member states.[3]

These endeavors toward union resulted in formal agreements that allow goods, people, services, information, and capital to move freely among member countries. In 2010, EU membership was expanded to 27 nations. There are also three candidate countries who have applied for admission. The original members are Austria, Belgium, Denmark, Finland, France, Germany, Greece, Ireland, Italy, Luxembourg, the Netherlands, Portugal, Spain, Sweden, and the United Kingdom. Jacques Chirac of France observed: "For nearly 50 years, the heart of our continent was split between democracy and dictatorship in a balance of terror. The fracture that started in Europe spread across the planet."[4] Now, the forces for unity and inclusion on this continent are spreading. Despite Turkey being a member of NATO and an EU applicant, it has yet to be admitted.

The central EU themes are to: (1) attain a single market economy of consumers that offers peaceful stability and wealth, as well as political and economic clout; (2) establish Europe-wide institutions and policies; and (3) respect and not fight about differences within this voluntary union. Although Europeans still cherish their diversity, not all is "smooth sailing," as different and competing visions emerge.

As we entered 2017, the euro was down, and voters in Great Britain had voted to leave the EU, the process for which has begun.

To manage the EU and achieve such goals, the European Commission has 27 commissioners appointed by national governments for a five-year term. With headquarters in Brussels, the Commission's administrative body consists of 20,000 officials. Political matters are left to the European Council, made up of 27 heads of government; law and budgetary matters are the concern of the Council of Ministers under a six-month rotating chair under a head of a member state. These are supplemented by the European Parliament in Strasbourg, comprising 754 members, and a Council of Justice based in Luxembourg, which acts as a supreme court. The EU has a plethora of other agencies to advance its social partnership by the four freedoms of movement for goods, services, labor, and capital.

The "internationalization" of the European workforce has been progressing for at least five decades, accelerated by the multinational corporation. Since World War II, more than 30 million workers—mostly from countries in Southern Europe and North Africa—have flowed into Western and Northern Europe (the foreign-born population is large). European businesspeople have always exceled at multilingual skills.

So who is European? It is no longer the typical inhabitants of the last two centuries on that continent. The enlargement of the EU changes demographic factors, such as affluence, poverty, and fertility. Also, the ongoing mass immigration into Europe is altering the composition and culture of its peoples. Many of the new arrivals face not only discrimination, but also civil disorder caused by anti-immigrationists. The EU estimated that 500,000 illegal immigrants are being absorbed yearly. Add to that the many thousands of refugees that request political asylum, and one can see how harmony in Europe could be threatened. Regardless, the Common European Asylum System (CEAS), through legislation, has established fruitful guidelines for the rights of those seeking asylum in the EU and has standardized an applicable definition of the word "refugee."

European perceptions

When we analyze Europe, it is not easy to define a cultural set of beliefs, customs, values, practices, and feelings. While each country therein has its own distinctive culture, there are still commonalities that distinguish the "old world" from other regions. Below is an overview of principal themes on that continent that may alter outsiders' perceptions of them:

■   Europeans have an inherent interest in the quality of life, at all levels of society. There is a predominant humanist belief that people are to be served by progress, and not the reverse. They enjoy socialization with family and friends.

■   Europeans generally have an inordinate sense of reality. When one reflects on the wars and disruptions in Europe in the twentieth century alone, one can understand how Europeans know that tragedy can be just a breath away, and that perhaps only this moment is real.

■ Europeans historically have had to fight their neighbor, whereas Americans have had to conquer the elements to develop their country. European heritage is such that they think long term, in the context of centuries.

■ Europeans have endured. They have survived plagues, atrocities, great wars, and border and government changes. They have lived through many ambiguities, and have the threads of ancient customs and traditions in the fabric of their cultures. They know the fragility of their civilization.

Education/schooling

Educational systems in Europe tend to be very traditional, somewhat rigid in offerings and organization, and resistant to change. While strong in science, engineering, literature, and languages, courses in business, management, and entrepreneurship were only recently and slowly introduced. Here is a sampling of some trends in schooling the next generation:

■ Teachers in the Netherlands and Scandinavia have far less "distance" between themselves and their pupils than do their counterparts in Mediterranean countries.

■ In one of the world's most egalitarian societies, Dutch children are taught to keep low profiles, and that being "first" at something is not necessarily a virtue; whereas in Mediterranean countries, such as Greece and Italy, children tend to be nurtured as special, unique, and implicitly superior individuals. In Britain, it is acceptable to finish first, but only if one can do it without seeming to work harder.

■ In many European countries, such as the UK, educational systems suffer from culture lag and need updating of their instructional systems for an "information society" and a "knowledge culture."

■ Germany's first woman chancellor, Angela Merkel, announced a plan in 2008 to modernize and renew that country's educational system at all levels.

Politics/economics

While there is diversity within Europe's political and economic systems, the EU is a force for standardization. Very gradually, the EU is fostering political integration, as demonstrated by the euro currency. Here are trends to observe there:

■ Countries like Britain and Denmark, with long traditions of relatively nonintrusive government but with respect for the law, have tended to resist proposals for new regulations from EU administrators in Brussels. Yet, once agreement is reached, they have the best record of implementation. But the newest EU members are less resistant and more cooperative, so as to retain EU benefits.

- On the other hand, Belgium, where bureaucracy is oppressive and evading laws/regulations is widespread, ranks among the quickest to propose new EU rules, but has the worst record for implementing adopted regulations.
- In France, many Arab citizens are now eligible to vote in presidential elections, thus influencing the outcome of future governmental policies.
- While some complain that there are too many national entities in Europe, it is also home to many supranational organizations, such as NATO, UNESCO, the OECD, and the European Court of Human Rights.

Europeans seem to be divided in their viewpoint of their world role with regard to transatlantic relations. Some argue that the EU's main weakness lies in inflexible political and economic structures that make it less capable of responding adequately to both globalization and its own enlargement challenges.[5] Yet the EU leaders announced at the turn of the twenty-first century their goals to create *the most competitive and dynamic knowledge-driven economy in the world.* With its expansion in membership, the EU's GDP is some $16 trillion, larger than that of the US. Exhibit 16.1 offers one insight into the growing pan-Europe commercial activities and their impact on the environment.

EXHIBIT 16.1 CROSS-BORDER ALPINE BUSINESS

A recent magazine feature bewailed how the Alps mountain chain is under pressure from the heavy toll of tourism, commerce, pollution, and global warming on Europe's winter playground. Along with artificial snow-making machines, synthetic blankets that reflect solar radiation are being used to slow summer melting. If current temperature trends hold, 50–80 percent of the remaining Alpine glacier ice could vanish by 2100! The whole Tyrolean culture and way of life is under threat. Arrayed across the heart of Europe, the Alps have been intensely used for centuries, but only 17 percent of its 74,000 square miles are protected. Fourteen million people live there, but usable space in Alpine valleys is limited; yet there is an orgy of tasks under way there by humans—factories, train tracks, hotels, houses, churches, ski lifts, farms, parking lots, stores, boutiques, and restaurants, all bound together by concrete roads. Every day, 4,000 tractor trailers thunder through the Mont Blanc tunnel connecting France and Italy. With the cars and buses for thousands of tourists, the small village roads are clogged, and pollution results from all that traffic. The Alps are big business, a sort of factory producing 1.6 million gallons of liquid water; millions of cubic meters of lumber; tons of iron and salt; spectacular cheeses, wines, and apples; amusements, athletic challenges, and artistic inspiration; plus mining and fishing. Seventy-seven million tons of cargo move through these mountains in an average year, and trans-Alpine commercial transport is likely to double by 2020!

E X H I B I T 16.1

E
X
H
I
B
I
T

16.1

The Alps stretch 650 miles across eight European nations, housing some 650 ski resorts. Scientists predict that as the permanent snow line rises along with temperatures, half of these resorts will go out of business. Furthermore, less snow and ice cover means less runoff to feed Europe's major rivers; melting permafrost destabilizes steep slopes and the structures built upon them. The mountains also concentrate fumes and noise from all the vehicle traffic, and their carbon dioxide contributes to the global warming, while the valley walls carry the maddening noise upward. Modern people are negatively impacting this unique environment and culture. Alpine people—known for their stoicism and individualism, crafted for a world of isolation and avalanches—are now coping with a host of modern problems. As the awesome mountains with their beauty and tranquility are the central reality of Alpine life, humanity should cherish and protect them.

Source: Zwingle, E. "Meltdown: The Alps Under Pressure," *National Geographic*, Vol. 209, No. 2, 2006, pp. 96–115.

Immigration and labor exchange

The new EU immigration regulations and job opportunities have attracted to this continent a host of external migrants, legal and illegal. The émigrés come largely from Africa, the Middle East, and Turkey. "Destination Europe" now accounts for over 47 million immigrants from abroad (a 2010 statistic). Though the new arrivals ease labor shortages, they increase the anxieties of Europeans about cultural identities and values. EU countries have dealt with the challenge in various ways—from integrating them into society to legal containment or expulsion. For example, Austria will fine and expel immigrants who fail to attend mandated classes in the German language, while Britain requires those seeking citizenship to pass a test. As émigrés swarm into Western Europe, the nations there are tightening their immigration laws. Many of these "visitors" live together in ghettos, forming new ethnic minorities. So far, European policy has been inadequate, not facilitating integration into their societies and not encouraging assimilation. On the other hand, some of the new arrivals have resisted acculturation, refusing to learn the language and culture of the host country, and not letting their children marry the locals or outside their religious faith. When second- and third-generation children of immigrants are unable to enter the mainstream society, they often resort to protests and riots, such as those happening in France. Unemployment among such youths is usually higher than average, and obstacles are often in place against home owner-ship and adequate education.

Under EU policies, internal migrants seeking work outside their own country in other member nations are free to do so. But such labor exchange, especially from the east, finds an open market that is curtailed, except in Britain, Ireland, and Sweden, who only limit benefit-seekers. Most of the other original 12 members impose transitional arrangements to curb "freedom of movement," which is supposedly a right of all EU citizens. Their governments fear that Eastern Europeans will steal jobs from the locals, but in actuality more often they take work that the locals shun. Germany and Austria are most cautious of opening their labor market, because their countries are on the border of former communist countries whose workers go west for higher wages (e.g., Austria's wages are five times higher than those of Slovakia). Globalization and an aging workforce in Europe could eventually cause greater labor mobility that will prove beneficial, forcing more workforce flexibility among the EU member states.

Multiculturalism[6]

Another EU challenge is to promote multiculturalism among its 27 members, developing a continent-wide application and understanding of Article 9 of the European Convention on Human Rights. While secularism is on the rise in Europe, and church attendance falls, new mosques are opening everywhere on the continent—the UK alone has over 1,000! The Islamic community now represents about 6 percent of the European population, and so the term *Eurabia* arose! In several member countries, violence has erupted between a swelling Muslim minority and the majority populations. Mosques and Muslim gravesites have been vandalized, and complaints rise about discrimination against them. The Muslim global backlash, as seen in the 2006 riots and burnings because of what they perceived as blasphemous, hurtful cartoons against their founder and beliefs originating in a Danish newspaper and reprinted elsewhere, is a case in point. The growing Muslim presence is changing the "face" of Europe, more than the military invasions of the Ottoman Empire in previous centuries.

European Muslims more and more seem to be secular in outlook and supportive of liberal values—countering stereotypes of their coreligionists. They could become leaders in promoting integration of their communities with the mainstream culture, thwarting rising contention between Muslims and other Europeans. Europe's leaders, in general, are also challenged to contain resurgent xenophobic behavior across the continent, from whatever source. With the increasing activities of global terrorism networks, EU states have new concerns about foreign visitors and migrants. Further, Europe's Muslim minorities feel stigmatized for the actions of Osama bin Laden or other criminal Islamic fundamentalists. Although many Muslims assimilate into European cultures, others choose self-segregation, and many are forced, for economic reasons, to live in impoverished "ghettos." Often, they experience cultural chauvinism and discrimination, ranging from unemployment to outright racism and violence against their person and property. Most Muslims have come to Europe seeking the opportunity to improve their lives.

E
X
H
I
B
I
T

16.2

EXHIBIT 16.2 GENERAL TIPS FOR DOING BUSINESS IN EUROPE

- Customer service is the key to success. The standards of Europe in this regard are not up to those in other countries.
- Publish price lists in terms of the local currency.
- Deploy Americans to Europe on the basis of a two-year minimum commitment to establish meaningful customer relations; the staying power of expatriate personnel is a subtle indicator—whenever possible, hire locals and then train them.
- Lease office equipment and computers in Europe because of the electrical differences in power outlets.
- Ensure that sales personnel know their products. Europeans are sophisticated buyers of foreign merchandise.
- Europeans gauge the forethought and commitment of a foreign firm by the way it treats its sales representatives. They perceive the salesperson as a key role, which should be judged on long-term performance; select such representatives very carefully.
- Europeans do not like change, so it is important for the foreign company to project stability and long-range commitment, yet they are attracted to "new" products, processes, and services.
- When able to properly serve the primary market in Europe, remember geographic distances are not great. Assess the secondary markets (Spain and Portugal, Greece, and the Eastern European countries), and respond carefully to all inquiries from such areas.
- Beside cultural, language, and political differences in Europe, be prepared to cope with technical differences (e.g., length of stationery and forms that do not fit standard copying machines, ink that does not reproduce well, different abbreviations).
- European nomenclature and honorific titles are to be observed in oral and written communication (especially spellings in English that differ between British and North American versions).
- Europeans value personal contacts and mementos, so the token gift may create a favorable impression, as may participation in a trade fair that is part of a centuries-old tradition.

WESTERN EUROPE

In Western Europe, we will discuss, in some detail, France, Germany, Italy, and Russia. Most are members of the EU. Further cultural information on all these countries is available from their embassies or on the internet. Many books and magazines also contain cultural and country-specific information (e.g., www.economist.com/countries/cities).

2016/2017: some internal European issues

There are considerable tremors in many countries in Europe and, depending on your perspective, the movement is either good or bad.

- The presidential elections in France in May could see Marine Le Pen of the National Front in a strong position. She waits to leave the EU and euro.
- Great Britain has officially begun the proceedings to leave the EU.
- Putin is a dictator à la czar, who took back Crimea and interfered in Ukraine while the West watched.
- In Austria, the alt-right is challenging but losing, as they also are in other countries.
- In the Netherlands, Wilders of the Party for Freedom (PVV) wants to close the borders, shut mosques, leave the EU, and the euro.
- Angela Merkal may run in 2017 for a fourth term and may find she is the sole opponent of populist issues in Europe.

We continue into some cultural specifics and hints on how to work effectively in Great Britain, Ireland, France, Germany, Italy, and Russia.

GREAT BRITAIN

The United Kingdom of Great Britain (UK) constitutes the main island consisting of England, Wales, and Scotland. It also includes six counties of Northern Ireland known as Ulster. Other outer islands within the UK include the Hebrides, Orkney, and Shetlands. Although English is the principal language, secondary languages or dialects such as Welsh, Scottish, and Irish are spoken in various regions. Apart from many immigrants from British Commonwealth nations, the principal inhabitants are known as English, Welsh, Scots, and Irish.

Historical perspective overview

English has almost become a universal means of communication, especially in business and international travel, as well as within the EU. Even though the sun has set on the British Empire, their global impact has been significant. Not only their language, but their customs, laws, and lifestyles penetrated remote corners of the world and held sway over continents from North America and Asia to the Middle East and Africa. It is still evident in the many member states of the British Commonwealth of Nations.

    The British have been forced to retreat, in many ways, to the confines of their island kingdom and a few small remaining territories, such as the Falkland Islands. And they have been followed home by the multicultural inhabitants of their Commonwealth, who used their privilege of British connections to resettle in the "mother country." Added to this influx from the "colonies" are the transfers of many affluent Middle Easterners to England seeking property, education, health services, and recreation. This reverse migration from the British West Indies, Africa, Asia, and the Indian subcontinent is transforming what was once a largely white, homogeneous, class-conscious society into one that is more heterogeneous, egalitarian, and cosmopolitan.

The exception is Ulster, which has been racked by armed struggles (economic, political, social) between its Catholic and Protestant (Orangemen) communities. Paramilitary operations by extremists from both sides have been the source of conflict, violence, and transgressions of human rights.

Cultural guidelines for doing business in Britain

Commercial policies and practices vary slightly in the UK's four major regions: England, Wales, Scotland, and Northern Ireland. Generally, punctuality is highly regarded and people expect you to be on time for appointments. Typically, the British observe a five-day workweek, Monday through Friday at 9 a.m. to 5 p.m., except for government offices, which are closed between 1 and 2 p.m., but open until 5:30 p.m. Introductions, especially by third parties, are important; once the contact is made, the third-party responsibilities are over. During business presentations and negotiations, one should present objective facts, emphasize product safety, and prepare for market flexibility.

In behavior, the British are normally private and traditional, expecting visitors to observe conventions and maintain decorum. So, initially be businesslike; it is not wise to get too personal. Their reserve causes them to avoid direct conflict and to hesitate to complain or report inadequate service. British people tend to be unemotional and to downplay situations that might cause problems. Their sophistication and politeness may be punctuated with apologies and self-deprecating humor. There are also some differences in English terminology (e.g., the ground floor in the UK is the first floor in the US, and the UK's first floor would be designated the second floor in America), as well as in driving habits (the British drive on the left side of the road but have right-handed motor vehicles).

Depending on where you are in the island kingdom, there are regional behavioral differences, especially among the Scots, Welsh, and ethnic groups. Although largely a Christian nation, Muslims make up 11 percent of the population, while Sikhs, Hindus, and Jews are smaller minorities. There is less class consciousness among the elite, while the average person in the UK is more egalitarian. The "pub" and tabloid newspapers, along with soccer and cricket, are most popular among the masses. Although the queen is held in respect, royalty garners less affection and has diminishing influence.

Britain shares a unique cultural heritage with and affinity for America, its former colony and frequent ally in many wars. It leads in EU market penetration of the US. Its economic approach is based on free enterprise, commitment, and encouragement of international trade. The nation has a low-risk reputation because it normally meets its obligations and liabilities, while protecting intellectual property rights. Although an EU member state, at least for the present time, the country successfully seeks exceptions, like postponing adoption of the euro currency (no longer necessary), retaining the pound sterling as its monetary unit. The UK maintains itself as both a global and EU financial and investment center. Although a strong Anglo-American economic and military partnership exists, the nation is being drawn ever more into the EU. There, the British exercise considerable influence and leadership in economic, trade, and political matters.

With a largely unwritten constitution going back to the Magna Carta, English common law and traditions are observed. Though a democratic, constitutional monarchy, the monarch is nominal head of state, but the influence of the subsidized royal family is largely confined to ritual, ceremony, charity, and tourism. Political power resides in one chamber of a bicameral Parliament, the House of Commons (651 elected members); the scope of the House of Lords is currently under revision. The prime minister heads up the national government, acting through her cabinet and ministers in charge of various governmental departments; the latter appointments depend on which political party or coalitions can command a majority in the Commons. Although a centralized state, a process of devolution is under way, giving more autonomy to regional and government entities. Among a number of political parties, the Labour Party and the Conservative (Tory) Party are dominant.

For the past decade, Britain has had a strong economy and relatively crisis-free prosperity. Its work environment is productive and competitive, slightly ahead of its free-trading partners. The country struggles with its increasing diversity of population and devolution of central governmental powers, along with its role in an expanding EU. London is a world-class city, while the nation and its regions are emerging as major artistic and cultural centers.

Businesspeople who form partnerships with the British should be aware of these tips:

- While often sophisticated and civilized, British leaders are more formal, value privacy, and are somewhat touchy. (Do not initiate conversation about family or work; stick to safe subjects like the weather, sports, or English cultural life.)
- Within the UK's controlled business environment, maintain decorum and avoid casualness in dress and conversation, such as loudness and shouting.
- Family names and titles, along with "sir," are used, and deference is given to the superior or the affluent, including maintaining an appropriate distance.
- Negotiators seek to understand the other's position and are marked by tolerance, compromise, and problem resolution by committees.
- During business days, two breaks are observed, usually for morning coffee or afternoon tea ("high tea" consists of pastries and small sandwiches); lunch or dinner may involve gin and tonic or sherry, with coffee after the meal.
- Fine manners and good etiquette are expected at all social occasions (e.g., holding doors for women, standing when ladies enter a room, not talking business if invited to a club).

To put this in perspective, remember that the younger generation is quite different, breaking with traditions and conventions. Recall that Britain, always known for its literature and performing arts, today is also the home of rock music, pop stars, and mod fashions, superb actors, fine theater, and classic films! Just pick up a British tabloid to get the other side of British lives.

Finally, realize that as a result of globalization, many foreign executives live and work in Britain, heading up some of the top companies there. Of the 50 largest British firms, many are run by foreigners, plus more in middle management. Foreign management also find the UK an attractive place to work, with the pay relatively high and lower taxes. The British business culture is also easier to fit into, whether in its capital London or other major cities.

IRELAND: THE EMERALD ISLE

After 800 years of English occupation, the Republic gained its freedom in 1921, joined the European Community in 1973, and is one of the wealthiest nations in that union. EU trade took the country out from under British control, and it prospered, starting with EU loans and assistance. South Ireland has become the European headquarters of numerous multinational corporations because of the educated labor pool and location. EU labor exchange policy has turned a homogeneous society into a more heterogeneous one, including workers from Eastern Europe and Africa. The EU influence has transformed a male-dominated society into one that offers equal opportunities for women, including politics (two women have become the nation's president). Irish youth now perceive themselves as the *new Europeans*, so the diaspora is over—many overseas Irish businesspersons and professionals are returning to their homeland. Institutions of higher education include the University of Dublin (Trinity College founded in 1590), National University (headquartered in Dublin, with branches in Cork and Galway), and Maynooth Seminary.

Historical perspective overview

Centuries ago, the ancient Celts swarmed out of Central Europe, settling finally in Gaul, Scotland, Wales, and Ireland. Irish tribes were eventually formed into kingdoms, suffering occasional sea invasions from the Vikings, who founded Dublin. With the coming of a Breton missionary, known today as St. Patrick, the inhabitants were converted to Christianity, replacing the druids, priests, prophets, and sorcerers who practiced the Celtic religion of Gaul and Britain. The Irish churches and monasteries were famous for learning, producing wondrous illustrated volumes, such as the *Book of Kells*, now housed in Trinity College, Dublin. The glory days for the Irish were after the fall of the Roman Empire and the rise of Charlemagne, when Western scholarship and literacy were isolated from Ireland. Thus, in these "Dark Ages," Ireland became known as the *land of saints and scholars*, which preserved the knowledge from the Greek and Roman traditions. When the new emperor established stability in Europe, Irish scholars spread throughout that continent, reviving educational and artistic traditions. In fact, this early Irish church was quite liberal and advanced, permitting women into "holy orders" to become lawyers, priests, abbesses, and even bishops. Gradually, as this unique form of Christianity was brought under the rule of the pope in Rome, all that changed as the Catholic Church in Ireland became more bureaucratic and rigid in its administration. Over the centuries, monks, friars, and nuns were the humanitarians who cared for the peasants during famine and disasters. Often, the only educated persons in a village were the clergy and the physicians who became figures of authority. The Roman Catholic Church was a major cultural and educational force, as guardians of the national identity. In contemporary times, this influence is lessening, and its dogmatism is questioned by the people, including religious prohibitions on contraception, divorce, and abortion.

For the last 1,000 years, the Gaels have been fighting for freedom and independence. Thus, the second seminal force in Irish history is the British Empire. After Henry VIII changed England's religion from Catholicism to Protestantism, Ireland was invaded many times by English kings who subjugated the people to their rule. Henry VIII became head of the Church in England, eventually introducing the Anglican religion into this country as the "Church of Ireland." Wealthy monasteries became military targets, the Irish were dispossessed of their property, and Protestant aristocrats took over plantations and estates. In the 1650s, Oliver Cromwell's confiscation of property led to a situation whereby in the eighteenth century the native populations owned less than 15 percent of their own land. The locals' hatred of their oppressors increased when the English failed to help the starving Irish during the potato famines of 1842/1846; one million died, and another one million emigrated, principally to North America and Australia. Matters worsened when the natives were generally denied educational opportunity, and illegal schools were secretly established. Essentially what happened was that a more advanced industrial society took over a rural country suffering from culture lag. Since the sixteenth century, the English gentry have invested heavily in Ireland, transforming the north from an agricultural to an industrial society by bringing in new technologies and Presbyterian factory workers from Scotland, known even today as the "Orangemen."

The Irish never accepted British rule, fighting over and over for their independence under the leadership of numerous patriots. Their pressure for reform, often aided by both English and Irish Protestants, first resulted in Home Rule granted by the English Parliament early in the twentieth century. This became an impetus to Irish investments and protectionism, while World War I brought agricultural and industrial prosperity, even between the years 1915 and 1921 known as "The Troubles." Armed rebellion in 1916 under nationalists like Eamon De Valera and Michael Collins resulted in a treaty that established the Irish Free State in 1921. In contrast to the new republic in the Catholic south, the six counties in the industrialized north were dominated by the majority Protestant Orangemen, who sought to remain a part of Britain. After 1968, their prejudice and exclusionary tactics against minority

Catholics led to serious violence between both sides under the cloak of religious differences.

Today, the Republic of Ireland is a parliamentary democracy, with a president serving seven years largely in a ceremonial role. The bicameral legislature is composed of the *Seanad* (Senate) with 60 members (49 elected, 11 nominated by the prime minister and elected by local universities) who serve five-year terms; and the *Dail* (House of Representatives) with 166 elected by universal suffrage (proportional representation) for a maximum of five years. The *Taoiseach* (prime minister) is the government leader, and there is an independent Supreme Court. Irish representatives are also playing significant roles in the EU, in both its administration and Parliament.

Cultural guidelines for business in Ireland

Ireland's inhabitants have been impacted by Gaelic culture, language, literature, and music. Worldwide, the Irish are known to be loquacious and sentimental, family-oriented and combative, politically astute and skilled in arts and crafts, horse breeding, and farming. Their land offers many natural resources, such as zinc, lead, natural gas, crude oil, barite, copper, gypsum, limestone, dolomite, peat, and silver. Vocationally, the Irish have moved from being primarily farmers, fishermen, soldiers, scholars, and missionaries to bankers and high-technology education providers, as well as leaders in fashion, cuisine and the culinary arts, glass-making, and the performing arts.

The Irish personality may appear complex and at times contradictory. While generally conservative and sociable, they can at times be caustic and sarcastic about authority, as well as rebellious. The people are also known for their fighting spirit, hospitality, friendliness, and generosity. Their humanitarian zeal is reflected in their foreign missionaries and rock stars, who raise funds for global needs. Ostentation is frowned upon, except in giving to charity. When meeting strangers, a favorite pastime is to reveal as little about oneself as possible, while finding out as much as possible about the other person. Given the change-able climate, weather is a favorite topic of conversation, as is the environment. Leisure time is highly valued and structured only in sports.

Socially, the first name is commonly used, while in business the preference is to use the surname. While promptness is expected at work, socially the Irish are more flexible about time. Attitudes toward deadlines are relaxed, unless one emphasizes why a delivery date is important. The 39-hour, five-day workweek is normally 9 a.m. to 5:30 p.m., with lunch usually from 1–2 or 2:30 p.m. There are nine national holidays, with special attention given to Christmas, Easter, St. Patrick's Day, and St. Stephen's Day. Vacations tend to be in July and August, not a good time to schedule key appointments and meetings.

Ireland is a society going through profound transition. The mindset of the younger generation today is quite different from that of the older population, who experienced want and deprivation. The culture is being transformed into a knowledge center, with increasingly diverse participants who come not only from the EU but around the world.

FRANCE

France is geographically the largest country in Western Europe. In medieval times, French royalty and troops moved back and forth from Normandy to the British Isles, exchanging feudal domains. In the late eighteenth and early nineteenth centuries under Napoleon Bonaparte, the *grande armee* extended its control across Europe to Russia. The empire's remnants reveal the scope of France's colonial power and help us appreciate the glory that was France. Begin by looking today at what was once French East Africa, and where the French language is still spoken (Burundi, Central African Republic, the Congo, Djibouti, and, to a lesser extent, Rwanda). The same cultural impact is still evident in Northern Africa (Algeria, Chad, Egypt, Mali, Mauritania, Morocco, Niger, Tunisia, and Senegal); West Central Africa (Benin, Burkina Faso, Cameroon, Congo, Cote d'Ivoire, Gabon, Guinea, and Togo); and even in Madagascar. Recall, too, the influence of French culture and cuisine in such widely separated locations as India (Pondicherry) and Indochina (Vietnam). Today, France still administers certain Caribbean islands, such as Guadeloupe and Martinique; in addition, many islands in Oceania have special administrative arrangements with the French government.

Historical perspectives[7]

Many books have been written on the glorious history of France—from when it was known as Gaul under the Roman Empire, through the Middle Ages when France was gradually united under its own king, and then to its expansion across Europe under Emperor Napoleon. A great contribution toward the establishment of democracy came from its support of the American Revolution, and then through its own French Revolution. France helped to found both the European Common Market and EU, but have a diminished role in the world today.

    The current Fifth Republic of France came into being in 1958, and has been governing by "cohabitation"—a sharing of power between the president with a seven-year term and the bicameral Parliament of the National Assembly and Senate. The president appoints the prime minister, who runs the country on a daily basis, presides over the cabinet, commands the armed forces, and concludes treaties. He has the power to dissolve the National Assembly and assume full power. Two-fifths of members in that National Assembly are on leave from the civil service. Fifty-seven percent of the adult population is either civil servants or their dependents. The various ministries of government employ some two million plus in public service. Confidence is eroding in the nation's lackluster economic formula of higher taxes and higher social charges, especially during the current slowdown in economic growth. Excessive spending on healthcare, continuing widespread strikes, and the country's limited role in world affairs have disillusioned the public. Although France's colonies have diminished, it still administers Tahiti in the Pacific, and has influence in its former possessions in East Africa.

EXHIBIT 16.3 PERCEPTIONS OF FRANCE

The French constitute the most brilliant and the most dangerous nation in Europe, and the best qualified to become an object of admiration, hatred, pity, or terror, but never of indifference!

Alexis de Tocqueville

The average Frenchman is concerned about an elite of bureaucrats, businessmen, and politicians who seemingly run the country to benefit themselves amidst corruption and public scandals.

New York Times, August 1, 1999

The French themselves are horribly muddled over France's place in Europe, over the impact of globalization, and at root, over what it means to be French.... France has an identity problem. It needs the courage to redefine itself.

J. Andres, "A Divided Self: A Survey of France"[8]

The French have a passion for engineering and technology, for research and solutions that push back the boundaries. The Ecole Polytechnique is one of the best engineering schools in the world, and French technology tends to be very sophisticated.

Nani Becalli, CEO, GE Europe

As an American living in France, I personally find the quality of day-to-day life far superior to anything I could afford back home in the USA.

Richard Chessnoff, *The Arrogance of the French*[9]

The biggest lesson of the French riots is that more jobs are needed. In the deprived suburbs, a kind of soft terror rules. When too many young people see nothing ahead but unemployment after they leave school, they end up rebelling. Thus, one rational analysis of the forces that lie behind the riots, car-burning, and street battles that have broken out, first in the banlieues of Paris and then right across France for two weeks. It points to a pressing case for action to build a greater sense of identity with French society among the rioters, most of whom are second-generation Muslims of North or West African origin. There are arguments over why five to six million Muslims there feel alienated—one-third the total in the EU and one-tenth of the country's population. But the answer surely lies in the toxic mix of poor housing, bad schools, inadequate transport, social exclusion, disaffection over discrimination, and, above all, high unemployment. French unemployment has hovered around 10 percent; the average rate among youth is over 20 percent, one of the highest in Europe; among young Muslims in the banlieues, it has been twice as high again. Most of the French elite, on the left as well as the right, have simply ignored the festering problem. There are no black or brown mainland members of the National Assembly; hardly any on television. The yawning gap between the French elite and the ordinary people was a big cause of government's loss of the referendum on the European constitution. The unrest in French cities shows that social and policing policy has failed. France needs to acknowledge its multiracial complexion by adapting its vocabulary, rather than hiding behind "the myth of republican equality."

"French Failure," *The Economist*[10]

E
X
H
I
B
I
T

16.3

France spends 30 percent of its budget on "social protection," and makes it possible for even an illiterate immigrant to live fairly well without having worked a day in his life. Yet shying away from reality by France's ruling class does not change the reality that one of the most civilized nations in Europe is sliding into barbarism. None of the violence was either surprising or unexpected. Indeed, it was an easily predictable denouement of the gradual transformation of hundreds of Muslim enclaves into crime-ridden, self-isolated, anti-societies that have de-facto seceded from French society in virtually every aspect, except for continuing to depend upon the welfare state. This is not merely a local situation, but has implications for much of Europe, in terms of socio-political and economic context. There seem to be three seemingly unstoppable trends: the implosion of the European social-market economy; an unprecedented demographic collapse of the native European populations; and the takeover of the burgeoning Muslim communities in Western Europe by radical Islam. The French and European socio-economic model had much to do with the rise of the Muslim ghetto, and its ongoing implosion will dramatically exacerbate its conflicts with society at large. The new tougher economic climate, combined with ever-present French xenophobia and racism, led to the high unemployment and progressive ghettoization of the second-generation Muslims. With a fertility rate twice that of the natives, the Muslim community in France and Western Europe is growing at 50 percent every decade. The European Union will lose nearly half its native population by 2050, while its Muslim community increases five-fold to 100 million. What is needed is a cultural revolution.

Alex Alexiev, "France at the Brink"[11]

France is a stratified society in need of change, flexibility, and mobility.

CBS Sunday Morning Report on the student protests in Paris, April 2, 2006

A priority of my foreign policy is to further the Mediterranean Union. The goal is to create an area of solidarity involving the environment, cultural dialogue, economic growth, and security. This union should be built upon projects that are ambitious but realistic, showing all the peoples of the Mediterranean that together we can build a shared future of peace.

Nicolas Sarkozy[12]

In July 2008, a Paris summit of 40 heads of state and the EU inaugurated an unprecedented Union of the Mediterranean to achieve the goals stated by Nicolas Sarkozy in Exhibit 16.3, for the benefit of southern and eastern nations bordering the Mediterranean Sea. The hope is to improve their trade with the EU members by joint programs to improve poor infrastructure, an ill-educated workforce, and unemployment. The aim also is to upgrade the environment, climate, transport, immigration procedures, and policing in the region. The summit declaration committed the participants to preventing nuclear proliferation, countering terrorism in all its forms, and promoting democratic principles, human rights, and fundamental freedoms. The French led with Egypt in the effort to establish a UM Secretariat.

Cultural guidelines for doing business in France

IDEALISM

The French tend to believe that the basic truths on which life is based derive from principles and immutable or universal laws. They are concerned with the essence of values. The motto of the French Republic is "Liberty, Equality, and Fraternity." To the French, values such as these should transcend everything else in life. They behave in an individualistic manner. "*Chacun defend son beef-steak*" (everyone protects his own steak). Sometimes they are frustrated and find it difficult to live by these ideals in everyday life, yet the hunger for these altruistic ideals is still present and deeply ingrained in most French people. For example, contrast the French and the American views on sex and money. The French are not easily embarrassed by sex or nudity. But they are embarrassed talking about money, how you get it, or vocational positions and salaries. To them, your job, your income, and such are personal and not the business of others.

PRACTICALITIES

Generally, except for lunch, the French time sense is casual, so people are often late and no offense is normally taken. Although the person in a subservient position is usually prompt, the executive is free to be late. Anticipate a reluctance to make commitments, leading to scheduling at the last minute. Also expect frequent rescheduling of meetings and appointments.

The French enjoy leisure and socialization, as can be seen in their long luncheons, seven official holidays (see www.getcustoms.com), and four or five weeks of vacations (usually in August, when the nation virtually shuts down). Although a land of great medieval cathedrals, over 75 percent of citizens who call themselves Roman Catholic do not see religion as playing a large part in their lives, and may even be slightly anticlerical. While giving lip service to religious toleration, the over five million Muslims in France are treated with mistrust and often only tolerated. Realistically, the country's far-right white extremists, influenced by a colonial past, are xenophobic and hostile toward Arabs. The intensely competitive French educational system puts immigrant children of non-French-speaking backgrounds at a real disadvantage, marooning them between two cultures, even when born in France. French education does impact business—schools are rigorous and value linguistic capability.

French society is stratified, with sharply defined and competing classes, and diversity is just beginning to be appreciated. Despite some female prominence in public offices and the professions, women's rights have come late, and sexual harassment only became illegal in the early 2000s. Foreigners complain of inadequate customer service. Managers and employees are "family" who often unite against outsiders.[13]

SOCIAL STRUCTURE AND STATUS

The French are very status-conscious. Social status in France depends on one's social origins. Outward signs of social status are the level of education, a beautiful house with a well-designed, tasteful façade (not a gaudy one), knowledge of literature and fine arts, and the social origins of one's ancestors.

Social standing and class are very important in France as well. The French social classes are the aristocracy, the upper bourgeoisie, the upper-middle bourgeoisie, the middle, the lower-middle, and lower classes (blue-collar workers, peasants). Social classes categorize people according to their professional activities (teachers, doctors, lawyers, craftsmen, foremen, and peasants), as well as their political opinions (conservative, left-oriented). The mass influx of immigrants, an underclass, into a relatively homogeneous society is altering the situation.

Social interactions are thus affected by these social stereotypes. It is extremely difficult for a French individual to be rid of social stereotypes. They affect personal identity. Unlike an American who can theoretically attain the highest levels of social consideration by working hard and being professionally successful, the French find it difficult to do so. If professionally successful, the French can expect to climb one or two stages of the social ladder in a lifetime, but often nothing more.[14]

COOPERATION AND COMPETITION

The French are not basically oriented toward competition. To them, the word *competition* has a very narrow meaning—practicing a sport at the highest level of international excellence. For example, the French consider superstar professional athletes as involved in competition. The average French person does not feel affected by competition, which can be dangerous to the country's economic welfare. Some years ago during a New Year's Eve television speech, then-President Giscard d'Estaing tried to educate the French and make them face the fact that competition really should affect their lives. He said competition is not just what the French soccer team experiences during the World Cup. The economic welfare of the French people actually depends on how competitive French goods are on international markets. He tried to awaken the French to the notion of competition, so that they would motivate themselves to work harder and be more productive.

When confronted with individuals with a competitive drive, the French may interpret them as being antagonistic, ruthless, and power-hungry. They may feel threatened, and overreact or withdraw from the discussion. Yet, the pyramidal structure of the French educational system exposes French children and adolescents to competition very early.

PERSONAL CHARACTERISTICS

French people are friendly, humorous, and sardonic. The French wish to be admired. French people are more likely to be interested in a person who disagrees with them. Because they want to be liked, the French are very hard to impress and impatient with those who try. A French person, when trying to get a sense of another, looks for qualities within the person and for personality. French people tend to gain recognition and to develop their identity by thinking and acting against others.

TRUST AND RESPECT

Personal honor and integrity are valued in France. A French person trusts an individual according to an inner evaluation of the subject's personality and character. Because social stereotypes are so vivid, an average French person cannot earn respect from members of other social classes merely through work accomplishments and performance.

Regarding privacy, a foreign student living with a French family closed the door to his bedroom after dinner, not realizing that closed doors are considered rude and that the visitor was expected to socialize with the family. Furthermore, when shutters to the outside are closed, this is not a sign of distrustfulness by the French, but a desire for privacy from the passerby.

STYLE OF CONVERSATION

French speakers seldom put themselves forward or try to make themselves look good in conversations. If they accidentally do, they will usually add, "Je ne cherche pas a me vanter mais . . ." ("I do not want to boast but . . ."). Boasting is often considered a weakness, a sign of self-satisfaction and immaturity. In conversations with the French, some may ask their French counterparts questions about themselves. The French will probably shun such questions and orient the conversation toward more general subjects. To them, it is not proper to show characteristics of self-centeredness.

Further, the French are so proud of their language that they expect everyone to be able to speak it—visitors not fluent in that language are advised to apologize for lack of that knowledge and to learn a few key phrases and pronounce the words correctly. Be sure to smile when you use them. Remember that, for centuries, all Western diplomats spoke

French, and it was the language of the Russian czar's royal court. The French are very sensitive about the diminishment of their language in the global market, and the introduction of English words into it.

The French, who may seem contentious, often criticize institutions, conditions, and people they live with. A disagreement can be considered stimulating to a French person. It is not uncommon to see two French people arguing with each other, their faces reddened with what seems to be anger, exchanging lively, heated, and irreconcilable arguments. Then later, they shake hands and comment: "That was a good discussion. We should do it again sometime!" The French tend to think that such arguments are interesting and stimulating. It is also a meaningful outlet for tension and appreciation of humor. They also often add a touch of cynicism to their humor and may not hesitate to make fun of institutions and people.

CONSISTENCY AND CONTRADICTIONS

The French abound in contradictions and are not overly disturbed by them; instead, they relish their complexity. They profess lofty ideals of fraternity and equality, but at times show characteristics of utmost individualism and selfish materialism. On the political scene, they seem continuously restless, verbally criticizing the government and capitalism, yet they are basically conservative.

ATTITUDES TOWARD WORK

Typically, French attitudes toward work depend on whether they are employed in the public sector or in the private sector. In the French bureaucracy and in state-owned concerns, there is little incentive to be productive. Quotas are rarely assigned, and it is virtually impossible to lay off or dismiss employees on the basis of job performance. Massive strikes have caused difficulties when companies have attempted to reform or modernize, or when government tries to pass policies and legislation that many people object to; strikes by university students have actually brought down the government in power. In the private sector, the situation is different. It is true that French workers do not respect the work ethic. They are usually not motivated by competition or by the desire to emulate fellow workers. They frown on working overtime and have four to five weeks of vacation each year. However, they usually work hard in their allotted working time. French workers have the reputation of being productive. Part of the explanation for such productiveness may lie in the French tradition of craftsmanship. A large proportion of the French workforce has traditionally been employed in small, independent businesses where there is widespread respect for a job well done, and many French people take pride in such work. This may also be explained as many have not been employed in huge, impersonal industrial concerns, where craftsmanship may not be so valued. Rather, they often have a direct stake in the work they are doing and are usually concerned with quality.

ATTITUDE TOWARD AUTHORITY

French companies contain many social reference groups that are mutually exclusive. Tight reins of authority are needed to ensure adequate job performance. The lesser emphasis on delegation of responsibility limits accountability and contributes to a more rigid organizational structure. As a consequence, decision-making is more centralized in French companies, and it may take longer before decisions are reached and applied. This may be a source of frustration for foreign executives (especially lower- and middle-management executives) who are working with French executives from a comparable management level. The flow of communication is improved if American executives have direct access to two or three top executives of a French company. This is where the actual decision-making power is. French subordinates tend to view an attempt to track personal progress as an infringement on their territory. The following example illustrates this point. A consultant on a project in the south of France reported the following:

> The main objective of our project was to increase sales of a high-tech product. One of the ideas to accelerate sales was to introduce the use of a daily chart to track each individual's sales progress. The goal was to focus management's and subordinates' attention on specific areas for improvement, as well as ask those who were doing well to share tips to help their colleagues' progress. Although management thought this idea was great, and many of the salespersons agreed that in theory it was a good idea, nine out of ten salespersons loudly objected. The reason? They did not want management—or their colleagues—to be able to track their sales. This idea was never put into practice.

The highest executives of large French companies also have "different" management styles, as the French are judged on personal attributes as well as on performance. It takes poor performance for them to be challenged in their functions by a board of directors or by subordinates. Patterns of authority are stable in French industry. Therefore, because they do not need to justify their actions to the same extent, the very top French executives tend to be more autocratic in their managerial style. Executive functions also have more overtones of social leadership.

It is interesting to compare French and American business magazine interviews of executives. Along with professional experiences and activities, top French executives usually mention details concerning their personal lives, such as former professors who had an impact on them, enriching social and personal experiences, books that influenced their outlook on life, and what their convictions are on political and social issues. On the other hand, top American executives will more likely emphasize the progression of their career in terms of professional achievements. But in this arena of exercising power and authority, French management is also changing because of their involvement in the global marketplace and the foreign acquisitions, mergers, and alliances of French corporations. Obviously, there are considerable differences in the French management style as compared to the style of managers from other countries. Chapter 3 explains some factors present in cross-cultural management.

ORGANIZATIONAL STRUCTURE AND STYLE

The organizational structure of French companies tends to be rigid; the French put less emphasis on control of individual performance. The decision-making process is more centralized in French companies. Important decisions are made only by the top executives, but slowly there is a trend toward team management because of consortia formed with businesses outside the country, such as Airbus.

CONFLICT

The mentally vigorous French have been aptly described as *combative libertarians*; that is, they appreciate strong argument and contradiction. The French, partly because they live in a more closed society with relatively little social mobility, are used to conflict. They are aware that some positions are irreconcilable, and that people must live with these irreconcilable opinions. They, therefore, tend not to mind conflict, and sometimes enjoy it. They even respect others who carry it off with style and get results. The French are also less concerned about negative reactions from those with whom they are in conflict.

French managers also report difficulties in adjusting to life in other countries. The French managers seem to experience problems caused by emphasis in the French culture on pride in their past cultural heritage, causing them to be too critical of people who do not benefit from that same cultural tradition. In their self-descriptions, the French managers feel handicapped by their conditioning to a formal way of thinking and a lack of actual knowledge of other cultures.

The atmosphere today in France is very diverse. There are some pessimists among the elite and intellectuals who are publishing articles and books forecasting the decline of France and its culture. For example, in 2003, Nicolas Bavez published a volume, *New World, Old France*, decrying French nihilism, which he predicts will lead to a *national crisis, unequaled since the agony of the fourth republic.* The increasing number of books and articles on such themes indicates a growing mood of melancholy, gloom, and discontent, evident in the May 2006 rejection of the EU constitution in a national referendum. The people's contrariness is reflected in a recent CSA poll in which 70 percent reported that future generations would live less well than they do today, while 84 percent indicated that they were happy. More intriguing is the rise in the French female fertility rate to 0.09 in 2004, the highest rate in Europe after Ireland—1.94 children per woman.

During this decade, the French have been gripped by antiliberalism, antiglobalization, and anti-Americanism. Though these attitudes are lessening, it would seem that the present disgruntlement of French citizens is caused by the country's political ecosystem where past elite leaders were unwilling to promote necessary change in their society. Yet the French approach to citizenship has its strengths, with its unapologetic approach to national identity, and emphasis on secularism and equality. Exhibit 16.4 lists a few business tips.

EXHIBIT 16.4 BUSINESS TIPS WITH THE FRENCH

1   French handshake is a *firm*, brief handclasp accompanied by a short span of eye contact. When French employees arrive at work, they usually greet their colleagues with a quick handshake, and repeat the process when they leave. Some may kiss their friends of both genders on the cheeks, but this is the exception in a business setting. A French woman offers her hand first. It is considered vulgar to snap one's fingers.

2   French conversation is not linear, and frequent interruption of each other may occur. Conversation is meant to entertain, not just inform, so expect many references to art and argument, as every possibility is explored and articulated, opinions are expressed, and need not be refuted. The French complain that Americans lecture, not converse.

3   Food is important in France, so expect to share meals enthusiastically while doing business with the locals. Whoever initiates the meal is expected to pay, and to make restaurant reservations, except in hotels and brasseries. With an invitation to a person's home for a social occasion, it is polite to bring a gift of wine or flowers (not roses or chrysanthemums, which are more appropriate for funerals).

4   Respect privacy—close doors after you, and knock on them before entering.

5   Be attentive to voices—the French expect you to recognize the person over a telephone by voice alone. As a sign of closeness, avoid saying, "Who is this?" Regulate voice volume, lest you offend with loud or boisterous talk and braying laughter.

6   Neatness and good taste are important in this culture.

Source: Morrison, T., Conaway, W. A., and Douress, J. J. *Dun & Bradstreet Guide to Doing Business Around the World*. Upper Saddle River, NJ: Prentice-Hall, 1997.

GERMANY

Historical overview

The forerunner of today's Germans were the Saxons, whose trade and military excursions took them west into England (Anglo-Saxons) and south into what is now Romania. The foundation of Germany was laid by Teutonic feudal lords. From its Indo-European origins, the Germanic language was not only spoken in Germany, Austria, and Switzerland, but impacted English, Dutch, Flemish, Scandinavian, and other languages. The culture became renowned for exceling in mathematics, natural science, and military science, as well as in the arts and music. Like most European powers in the sixteenth through nineteenth centuries, the Germans were late in becoming empire builders, eventually acquiring overseas colonies that spanned from the South Pacific to West Africa. Its former kaiser was related to the British royal family. Prussian militarism led the emerging nation into a series of conflicts beginning with the Franco-Prussian War, followed by World Wars I and II. After temporary glories, the attempts at cross-border expansionism in the twentieth century resulted in much misery and deprivation for its people. The rise and fall of Adolf Hitler and his fascist Nazi Party (1933–1945) negatively affected not only Germany, but millions of humans, both Jews and Christians, caught up in the fighting and purges, concentration camps, and the Holocaust. These horrible calamities laid waste to the continent and led to the Soviet invasion of East Germany and the establishment of a puppet state (German Democratic Republic [GDR]) under the influence of the USSR. The former capital, Berlin, was divided temporarily among the occupying armies of the American, British, and Russian Allies. In 1949, the west became the multiparty Federal Republic of Germany, adopting the *Grundgesetz* as its basic law, with Bonn as its capital.

In time, the communist GDR government in the east built barriers to protect its German inhabitants from contamination by Western democracies and free enterprise. On November 9, 1989, irate Germans tore down the Berlin Wall, and its elimination marked the end of an era. On October 3, 1990, after 41 years of political division, most of Germany was reunified, and the process of reintegration between its western and eastern populations began. The unified Federal Republic of Germany (FRG) has evolved into a democratic, market-oriented system. Over their 40-year separation, the two Germanys had developed differing cultural values, mindsets, and customs, in addition to opposing economic and political systems. Many in the former West Germany (*weiss*) complained that those in East Germany (*ossis*) lived too long in their socialist world, thus were naive and unsophisticated. Because of totalitarian central planning, those in the west thought that their counterparts in the east were not good as managers or entrepreneurs because they had no experience in a market economy, nor were the easterners grateful for the benefits unity brought. On the other hand, the *ossis* observed that the *weiss* were arrogant and materialistic, for relentless competition made them "hard as nails." Furthermore, they resented westerners securing the best jobs in the east, while unemployment hit women workers disproportionately.

Although these attitudes linger among some, the healing and integration process of the past decades built bridges over this cultural divide.

At the beginning of the twenty-first century, the united Germany, with Berlin again as its capital, has become the largest economy in Europe and the sixth largest export market for US products worldwide. After spending three million euros on the unification process, a physics professor, born in East Germany, was elected the first woman chancellor in 2006. Dr. Angela Merkel now leads a left–right political alliance, and remains the chancellor today.

As a parliamentary democracy with a bicameral legislature, there are two main governing bodies in Germany. The larger *Bundestag* (Parliament) consists of 672 deputies elected for four-year terms from the states, and possesses legislative power. The upper house, the *Bundesrat*, is composed of delegations from the 16 states that function under the *Länder* (state constitutions). Its 68 votes are based on the proportion of populations, and power is limited, except in exercising vetoes over proposed legislation. Germany has a president, but the position is one of honor and a formality, not one of real power, which lies in the office of the chancellor (*Bundeskanzler*). The chancellor is either the leading representative of the party with a majority of seats in the *Bundestag* or the leader of the largest party in a coalition government.

Cultural insights for doing business in Germany

Germans today are a more diverse people as a result of heavy immigration. Traditionally, they have a reputation for being industrious, hard-working, reserved, and perhaps even cold in behavior. Generally, they are perceived as meticulous and methodical, and sometimes militaristic in the preciseness of their actions (linear thinking). At the same time, they have a reputation for quality and exactness—their buses, trains, and planes usually run on time. Detail in planning and project implementation is valued. Some of the world's greatest composers, writers, and philosophers are products of the German heritage.

Germans are very organized. Their attitude is to organize the time allotted to its greatest efficiency, rather than wait and see what happens. Nor are the Germans normally an outward people; they tend to be very private. They maintain a slightly larger personal space around themselves, usually standing six inches further back than do North Americans. The German language is a key to understanding their national personality. The Germans make a strong distinction between an acquaintance (*bekannte*) and a friend (*freund*). Germans will only use *freund* when they really mean it; otherwise it is a *bekannte*. Close family ties are also cherished.

Business context

Germany is one of the original members of what was once known as the European Community. Much of German business practices and laws are directly tied to the regulations and directives from that community or union in Brussels. The principle of collective good is important in the idea of codetermination (*mitbestimmung*). Codetermination allows for worker input into the management of the firm. Any firm with more than five employees should have a worker's council (*Betriebsrat*) that represents the employees and helps them solve various grievances with the firm's management. Any coal or steel firm of more than 2,000 workers is required to have 50 percent of the company's supervisory board composed of workers. There is also a specially chosen labor representative on the management board of the company. This all illustrates an attempt to include a most important part of the economic structure: the worker.

German unions are very strong and provide workers with many more rights than some foreign counterparts. For example, they can become involved in decisions for dismissal. The process of codetermination gives management and workers the opportunity to work together to shape or define the firm's goals, objectives, and responsibilities.

The Germans are among the highest paid workers in the world, and enjoy a high standard of living. They are able to afford the luxuries and extras of life. An important part of this concept is the vast welfare state that supports the German worker. This includes liberal pensions, bonuses, medical and dental care, and five to six weeks of annual paid vacation. Though taxes are heavy, this system has relieved the typical German of many financial worries. But the above factors also contribute to driving up the costs of business and making Germany's products and services less competitive. Currently, Germany is known for its high quality of life and protective benefits for its citizens. But its current weak financial growth has been attributed not just to a downturn in the world's economy, but also to the need for restructuring what has become an overburdened welfare state.

Germany is committed to a free enterprise economy. Government and business work very closely together, as can be seen in the extent of government control/participation in industry. The state holds control or equity participation in hundreds of firms. In the public service arena, the railroads and postal system are now privatized, with the state owning most of the shares. The state also owns a trade monopoly in alcohol. An area that is perhaps the fastest growing in Germany, as well as throughout Europe, is joint government and private business ventures. This means a partnership between private businesses and firms controlled by the government. With denationalization ongoing, this increase in joint partnership ventures is another indication of "collective interest" being an important part of the German business and economic community.

Work practices

The German sense of time requires punctuality for both business and social engagements but does not seem to extend to delivery dates. Goods and services may be delivered late without explanation or apologies. There are 13 national, plus regional, holidays (see www. getcustoms.com). People take long vacations during July, August, and December. Little work is accomplished during regional festivals, such as Oktoberfest or Carnival prior to Lent. The workweek is Monday to Friday, 8 or 9 a.m. to 4 or 5 p.m., but check on banking hours, which normally are 8:30 a.m. to 1 p.m. and 2 to 4 p.m., sometimes extended to 5:30 p.m. On Saturday, shops may close by 2 p.m. except for once per month when they may be open in the evening. The preferred time for business appointments is late morning or late afternoon, and these should be scheduled several weeks in advance.

Social customs

Germans are very knowledgeable and capable businesspeople. They pride themselves on having quality products to offer on the world markets. They are formal in their business dealings, not only with foreigners, but among themselves as well. For the foreigner, it is best to be conservative and subdued, unless you are given the indication to be more informal. The Germans do not like loud people, especially in business, and have little respect for the pushy or brassy businessperson. To them, such behavior reflects a weakness in the person or company. In this culture, business is taken seriously. Germans tend to be exact in their dealings and somewhat more distant in their business relationships.

The handshake is an important part of the German greeting. They shake hands often. The woman extends her hand first. Firm handshakes are preferred. If one is entering a room filled with many people, the person should proceed around the room shaking everyone's hands. Again, a friendly "good morning" or "good day" is appropriate.

In the German language, there are two forms of address, the polite and the familiar. The familiar form *du* is used only for relatives, very close friends, children, and animals. The polite form *sie* is used on all other occasions, including in the business environment. Any foreigner addressing a German should use the polite form. Some Germans who have known each other for years still use the polite form. A German may initiate the usage of the *du* form, although this is not routine. Not only should you use the polite form of speech, but you should also refrain from using first names; *Herr* and *Frau* are more appropriate. Women should always be called *Frau* regardless of their marital status.

The Germans are title conscious, and proper etiquette requires addressing them by their title. Also, those who have attained their PhD are addressed by the term *doktor* (i.e., "Herr Doktor Schmidt" or "Frau Doktor Braun"). Women are called by their first names. The wife of Georg Meyer will not be Frau Georg Meyer, but rather Frau Ursula Meyer. A friend or associate should introduce the newcomer to the group, as Germans prefer third-party introductions.

In some countries, it is quite common to entertain a client for dinner at a fashionable restaurant. A good rule to follow is to conduct business during business hours. The Germans like to discuss things and enjoy a good discussion on the topics of the day. Religion, politics, and nuclear power are freely discussed, but conversations relating to one's private life are only among friends. Bragging about personal achievements and finances should be avoided.

Communications

GESTURES

The Germans are generally restrained in their body movements. They do not wave their arms and hands a lot as in other cultures. It is impolite to talk to someone with your hands in your pockets. It is also considered rude to sit with the bottom of your shoes facing another person. For this reason, German men cross their legs at the knees, rather than with an ankle on the other knee. Most body movements could best be characterized as conservative.

LANGUAGE

German is the official language in Germany, although in border areas other languages are spoken more often. There are many dialects and local variations spoken throughout the countryside, although dialects are generally only spoken in less formal situations with

EXHIBIT 16.5 BUSINESS TIPS WITH GERMANS

1   Guests usually stand until a host enters the room, then remain standing until offered a seat.

2   Avoid chewing gum in public, conversing with hands in pockets, or propping legs on desks or tables.

3   Germans are free thinkers and have a wide variety of interests to discuss on social occasions, such as current events, politics, religion, and sex, but avoid talking about work, private life, personal achievements, or American sports.

4   Be formal in business deals, and avoid haggling or price discounting.

5   Be aware that business responsibility is first to society and the environment, and then to maximize profitability.

friends. *Hochdeutsch*, or the "high" German, is found in all magazines, newspapers, television, and the like. In a business context, your counterpart will avoid the use of dialects. English is the major foreign language taught in Germany, and most businesspeople are conversant in it. With the influx of Turkish workers during the past decade, Turkish is also spoken in some circles.

Exhibit 16.5 provides five concluding suggestions for business success in Germany.

ITALY[15]

This portion of Europe has always been geographically distinctive because it is seemingly shaped like a boot. It has many small islands on its eastern coastline, but the two largest are Sardinia and Sicily to the south.

Cultural guidelines for doing business in Italy

Over millennia, this land was divided into so many independent political entities—each with autonomous governance, ruling families, language dialects, local customs and traditions, as well as cuisines—that the various parts of Italy today are unique in various ways while also sharing some common cultural values. By means of the mass media and the education system, Italy today has grown closer together into a more united country, but it is still rare to find an Italian who will say he is Italian, and not Roman, or Florentine, or Genovese. This tendency demonstrates the strong cultural value of *campanilismo*. It centers on the campanile, or bell tower, that can be found in every village in Italy. Ordinary citizens feel comfortable when they can see the campanile of their own town. The implication is that Italians prefer to stay in their city of origin and will always consider the interests of their campanile in business situations. Yet as an EU member, many cosmopolitan Italian political and business leaders find themselves more involved today in European institutions, as well as the global market. Italians have served as president of the EU and CEOs of global corporations.

What can one say about Italy? Thousands of books have been written about its cultural treasures. Anyone who visits the country falls in love with its picturesque villages and stunning countryside, its historic and beautiful cities, its poetic and dynamic language, and its incredible food and wine. It is the land of art, science, and passion, the land of "saints, scholars, and navigators" (Italian proverb). Apart from Italian contributions to art and architecture, music and literature, this creative people invented many current business practices (e.g., innovations in banking, insurance, and double-entry bookkeeping). Most people would agree that Italian fashion, food, and sports cars are the best in the world. There, we find *La Dolce Vita*, the ability to enjoy everything with art and style. But loving Italy and doing business there are two very different things.

One important thing to realize about Italy is that it has two faces, like the two-faced Roman god Janus—one looking forward and one looking backward. Italy is the vestige of the eternal Roman Empire, yet on the cutting-edge of modern scientific research and many types of technology. It looks backward to its age-old traditions, and looks forward (painfully sometimes) to its position as a strong member of the EU. Italy is frequently in a state of social, economic, and political change. Such transitions attempt to cope with major challenges of immigration, European integration, globalization, and family breakdown. In addition to having two faces, Italy also has two halves. This is due in part to the historical occupations of the areas. The north is well developed into an industrial powerhouse and one of the richest areas of Europe. In contrast, the southern half of Italy, starting just below Rome (known as the *Mezzogiorno*), is one of the poorest areas of Europe. The south is economically depressed and primarily agricultural. It is perhaps Italy's greatest economic problem, with social issues as well. The south embodies the stereotypes that foreigners have of Italy—chaotic streets and violently honking horns with drivers shouting at each other. Mafia criminality also undermines Naples' and Sicily's progress, whereas the north exemplifies the best rendition of Italy as a modern industrial power.

Volumes have been written on the Italian contributions to Western civilization. The West owes its essence and structure to Italy in the many areas of science, economics, navigation, art, architecture, politics, and literature. In every area of study stand many Italian geniuses, including Dante, Galileo, Michelangelo, Leonardo da Vinci, Francis of Assisi, Verdi, and Marconi. Remember that Christopher Columbus (a Genovese navigator) "discovered" America, and don't forget that the name *America* comes from the Florentine cartographer, Amerigo Vespucci! Italians are very proud of their heritage, and it is advisable for businesspeople to know, appreciate, and respect it. Italians also have immigrated in large numbers abroad, especially to North America and Brazil.

The following are some insights about Italian sense of identity and cultural values that affect business. In a recent survey, Italians evaluated themselves in terms of their national character—the top three qualities reported were the art of *arrangiarsi*, creativity in art and the economy, and connection to the family. Interestingly enough, the feature that they reported as the least present was that of civic duty. Now to explain key concepts in the Italian mindset and lifestyle:

■ *Art of arrangiarsi* means to be able to make do, to get by, to work oneself out of any situation. This activity has been elevated to an art in Italy because of the fact that most systems do not function as expected. The cause of this has historical roots, owing to the numerous invaders, conquerors, and imposed systems of foreign governments. In business terms, this could be called "creative problem-solving." The Italians have learned to *arrangiarsi* as a reaction to the formidable system of government, laws, and taxes. It is hard for Americans to understand this idea because they are used to having systems that actually work as expected. Instead, Italians have developed ways to get around the system and accomplish what needs to be done in a creative way, via connections and family ties.

■ *Relationships with family and friends* emphasize family ties, connections, and relationships as bastions against the insecurities of life. Over the centuries, this value and system was a solution to problems imposed by foreign occupation. Today, everything flows from such relationships—from getting a job to opening a bank account; everything depends on connections. The successful foreign businessperson makes it a point to understand the connections and use them.

■ *La cordata* literally means rope or cord, referring to the practice of pulling along friends and family in the climb up the corporate ladder. It is an outgrowth of the relationship/ family value explained above. People who find work in a company or government office immediately seek to be part of a *cordata*, or network. And if they also start their own enterprise, gradually their friends or relatives are involved in some way in the undertaking. The practice is also used to form alliances between companies for buying materials or products. So Italians are very open to synergistic relationships. See Exhibit 16.6 for a few comments on Italy.

■ *Bella figura* literally means *beautiful figure*, but it can make or break a business negotiation. *Bella figura* is the desire to make a good impression, to give a good appearance, and to convey a certain image. It is somewhat like the Asian value of saving face, but encompasses appearance as well as behavior. It is responsible for the fact that Italian fashion, art, and architecture are world renowned and sought after. Italians seek to make a *bella figura* through their appearance, both physical and economic, and their behavior. It is important for managers to remember this in all areas of interaction. Proposals and presentations must look good. Image is key in all areas, including dress and behavior. Status and prestige also matter. The foreign businessperson is advised to imitate the Italians on this one. And be careful not to present a *brutta figura* (ugly figure)—that can mean being obviously drunk, looking slovenly, arriving late, being unprepared, giving an unattractive presentation.

■ *Furbo* is an Italian word that is very hard to translate. It can have negative or positive connotations. It has evolved as a concept that describes how to outsmart one's adversary or beat the system. A funny example is that of the seat belt law. Seat belts are now required everywhere in Italy, and the police will fine motorists if they aren't wearing them. Someone in Naples started producing a sweater that was made with a black diagonal stripe from the neck to the stomach, so that when you wear it, it appears that you are wearing a seat belt. So you outsmart the police. This is being a *furbo*. In business, it is very important to be on your guard, because often someone will try to outsmart you in some way. Beware of the well-developed *furbo*, because he is waiting to rip you off.

Foreigners also need to be aware of the following value orientations among the Italian people.

EXHIBIT 16.6 OBSERVATIONS ON ITALY

E X H I B I T 16.6

The first thing to say about Italy is that, however grubby its politics or flaky its economics, it is still, for most of its inhabitants and visitors, one of the most delightful countries of the world. Its confection of man-made and natural beauty, cultural heritage, and clement climate is second to none. Its people are blessed with charm, humor, and the ability to enjoy, let alone let others enjoy, life. Few have so brilliant a sense of style and fashion, so sumptuous a cuisine and cellar, so strong a tradition of melding hard work with pleasure.

This survey is filled with praise for the globe's sixth largest economy; its relatively strong family life and social cohesion; its top-flight universities and scientists; its manufacturing and high-tech pursuits. Then it points out Italy's continuing problems—government instability and turnovers; Western Europe's worst-performing economy; business failure to be competitive and to effectively use new communications technologies; slow pace of reform in labor markets and in overcoming the North–South income gap; inadequate probity in battling corruption and criminal behavior (e.g., the mafia); lack of foreign investor trust because of the country's rickety and opaque legal system; need for faster decentralization and privatization, as well as for constitutional, electoral, and welfare reforms by the state.

But the report concludes that Italy is still one of the world's most dynamic, enjoyable, and, in many ways, admirable countries.

Source: Smiley, J. "A Survey of Italy—What a Lovely Odd Place," *The Economist*, July 7, 2001, p. 18. Also see the update by Peet, J. "Addio, Dolce Vita: A Survey of Italy," *The Economist*, November 26, 2005, www.economist.com/surveys (retrieved April 13, 2017).

Determinism

Italians are basically fatalistic, *che sarà, sarà*. Because of their long history of natural and political disasters, as well as their experiences with Catholicism, they tend to believe that nothing can be done to prevent things from happening the way they are destined to happen. Insecurity is viewed as a fact of life. This conviction may explain why they tend to live in the moment. Remember that the famous Latin quote *carpe diem* (seize the day) came from Italy; thus, they will take opportunities in the moment without thinking that they have control over their actual success. One source of frustration in business stems from this fatalism. Foreign managers will find it difficult to extract detailed objectives and plans from their Italian counterparts, as the practice of setting precise objectives goes against this deterministic philosophy. Besides believing that they do not control their destiny, they also hate to make mistakes (it causes *brutta figura*), so they do not like to commit themselves too tightly to objectives they are not sure they can complete.

Time sense

Italians are often multitasking. Conducting a meeting, taking a phone call, and signing papers all at the same time are quite common. It can be very stressful for foreigners to be in a meeting that is constantly being interrupted with knocks on the door and phone calls. As far as punctuality is concerned, the north is much closer to Northern Europe in its adherence to meeting times and time allocation; but in the south, time flows at a slower pace, and people tend to be much more relaxed with appointments and schedules. It is common to have many changes of schedule, shifting, canceling, reinstating, and so forth. The best way to handle this is to be flexible and patient. Anticipate schedule changes as a matter of course. However, foreigners are expected to be on time for business and social engagements, while Italians have more latitude in this regard. Again, North Americans and northern Europeans will discover the business environment in the south to be less time-conscious, even more relationship-oriented, and more relaxed.

Normal business hours range from 8–9 a.m. to 1 p.m., and then from 3–6 or 7 p.m. There are 12 national, plus regional, holidays; a city can shut down to celebrate the feast of the local patron saint. July and August are vacation months for firms, and many close during this period.

Action orientation

Italians tend more toward *being* than doing, because of their long past, their traditions, and their propensity to form relationships. They identify themselves with their region, their family, or their soccer team more than with their job. Italians define themselves also by their network of relationships and the connections they enjoy.

Again, there is a pronounced difference between north and south. The north has a greater focus on activity and is more dynamic; the south has an even greater focus on relationships and operates at a slower pace. The key difference between outsiders and the Italian is that individuals do not value themselves here by what they do, but by how well they, their families, and their friends can live on their financial and professional successes.

Communication

Italian culture is high-context, although the north is somewhat less than the south. The Italian language is very colorful and musical. One of the favorite pastimes of Italians is that of talking and engaging in polemical discussions. For visitors, the natives seem to waste a lot of time talking. They usually speak rapidly, at high volume, all at the same time, and in very heated discussions. They are known for their buoyant style, combining emotion, gestures, and volume that create an overall impression of a theatrical presentation. One of their most admired abilities is that of being able to put on a spectacle or show. They tend to keep one eye on the other members of the group so that they can gauge their performance. They are very expressive, or *esternazione*, meaning *expressing* or *venting*, or *letting it all out*. *Esternazione* is reflected in every communication situation. In politics and the media, it means press releases. In private life, it means telling it all. There is no word for *privacy* in the Italian language. For some companies, this can pose a problem, because secret policies, etc., are never secret and are often discussed at the local cappuccino bar with the family, and even with the press. However, it must never be assumed that the Italian businessperson will tell you everything. There is also another Italian quality, *omertà*, which means silence. Here are some communication behaviors to look for in Italians:

- *Indirect versus direct.* In spite of *esternazione*, personal and business relationships can be quite indirect, on the basis of unspoken (high-context) values that everyone (Italian) is supposed to know. Third parties are often used to communicate important messages, especially unpleasant ones. A foreign businessperson must be aware of the hidden cultural assumptions. The best solution for this is to have a bilingual, bicultural person to advise you.
- *Expressive.* Italians have an incredibly well-developed system of gestures. They also have an uncanny ability to yell at each other simultaneously, while somehow communicating a message.
- *Formal.* In spite of whatever stereotypes foreigners may have about the informality of Italians (e.g., drivers screaming and gesturing at each other in traffic jams), the Italians are initially quite formal, both in personal and business relationships. They adore the spectacle of form and ritual, even in business situations. Appropriate titles are always used, such as *Dottore/Dottoressa* (person with a university degree). The businessperson must be sure to know in advance the appropriate titles. When speaking in Italian, the formal style is always used unless otherwise specified. The above tendencies are evident in business cards, which may be of three kinds: formal with all the necessary business information, including titles and degrees; informal without extensive titles, but

which indicates that one has formed a less formal professional relationship; social or visiting card with just the person's name.

Physical contact

Italians are very warm, and it is quite normal to see men hugging each other or sitting or leaning close. Women greet each other with a kiss on both cheeks, usually after the first time they meet. Men shake hands with men and will kiss women who they know on both cheeks. However, Italians have a smaller spatial radius than many foreigners. Part of this is due to the nature of the culture, very relationship-oriented, but also because in many areas space is actually very limited.

Power-distance

Italians tend to follow more traditional roles of hierarchy. They seem to be very egalitarian in their communication style, but they respect hierarchical structure. Status and titles are important. Foreign managers who are more informal must remember to project themselves in terms of their perceived status.

Individualism

Italians pride themselves on being highly individualistic. This comes out repeatedly as being a very important cultural value. But individualism does not mean independent. They are very social and prefer to be in groups, as long as they are still viewed as unique individuals. In negotiating, it often happens that each individual wants to speak, and basically repeats everything that has already been said. If the individuals are denied the opportunity to speak, they go away feeling resentful and undervalued. The result of this individualism is the fact that Italians find it difficult to truly work as part of a team.

Competitiveness

Italians are competitive, even though they put a high stress on relationships. Probably the biggest areas of competition are physical appearance and lifestyle. But Italian business does not have the same drive toward competition that many foreign businesses do, probably because business is based on relationships, which means that client relationships take precedence. It is not common practice in Italian business to give individual awards or single out one individual for commendation. This trait is very much evident in the field of sports.

Structure

Italian life is seemingly highly chaotic, perhaps as a result of the bureaucracy and the lack of overall communication between government offices. Thousands of laws are made in the hope of imposing some sort of control. But, as one writer said succinctly, the Italians are unpredictable, but they love routine. They are highly risk-averse, but they go out of their way to circumvent regulations. Italian companies do not like to take risks. However, experience has shown that if a company is willing to take a risk, it will do very well in Italy.

Thinking

Italians are *deductive* in academic situations, but pragmatic in business negotiations. They tend to decide on the basis of separate situations, and often refer back to other similar situations and results.

Italian systems orientation

ECONOMY

Italy has the eighth largest economy in the world (a 2011 statistic), despite its problems. The government seems to favor privatization and less state control of the economy, though it is required to meet EU standards and regulations. For all its attractions and successful firms, Italy is caught in a slow economic decline, requiring bold political leadership to push needed reforms. The single *euro* currency has broken the country's habit of frequent devaluation, but it is also forcing Italy to change its whole economic model while promoting structural reforms. Some of the biggest economic challenges facing Italy are the following:

- Living standards are falling in spite of increasing costs.
- Too many small, privately and family-owned companies, which contribute to low female participation in the workforce and are often in the wrong industries.
- A backward southern regional economy that is poorly performing and too dependent on the public sector.
- Corruption and violent crime (e.g., Naples), aided by mafia activities, somewhat limited by prosecutions by dedicated magistrates.
- Underdeveloped tourism industry despite the gains the country can make from tourism.
- High unemployment rate, heavy business tax burden, and unwieldy government bureaucracy—the high rate of unemployment is caused by the heavy employment taxes that businesses must pay to employ people legally; high business taxes and red tape discourage foreign investment.
- A very strong black market, whose dimension is really not known. This means that the Italian economy is probably a lot stronger than it appears on paper because of the size of the *mercato nero*.

Further, the amount of foreign investment is significantly less than in other European countries, for several reasons. First, communism exerted a strong influence on the government after World War II, discouraging foreign business. Second, the distribution system of

Italy has a long way to go before it can compete effectively with other European countries. Third, the practice of delayed payment discourages business in all areas. Italian companies usually pay on a 60- to 120-day basis, which ends up frequently translating into 120–160 days. This can cause a significant cash flow problem for foreign companies who are waiting for payment and must finance the delay. As can well be imagined, there is an ensuing snow-ball effect. Delayed payment is rampant in Italy. Currently, the government is trying to solve such problems, but it is unlikely that solutions will be found very soon.

Sociopolitical forces

The Catholic Church continues to be a significant political and cultural force in Italy, even though it has declined in power in the past few years. Italy is primarily Catholic, but a great percentage of the population does not actually regularly practice that religion. However, the Vatican has a strong presence in the formation of government policy, especially in the moral and ethical areas.

Government and political forces

Mussolini once said: "It is not impossible to govern Italians. It is merely useless." Italy is a multiparty parliamentary republic. Because of the large number of political parties (approximately 50 or more), Italy is basically governed by coalitions formed by various parties. One can only imagine the challenge of developing policies with so many parties. There is both a president and a prime minister. Government plays a heavy role in business, as do the labor unions. Foreign managers must be very aware of this added dimension to doing business in Italy, especially its complex justice system.

Legal system

The Italian legal system and bureaucracy is infamously tortuous and slow, as well as contra-dictory. It has been estimated that there are over 500,000 laws in Italy, many of which have never been canceled since Roman and medieval times, as well as the hundreds of new ones that are made every year. This makes the law profession quite attractive, as it is necessary for every business to have a competent lawyer on call. Similarly, tax codes are perilous. The situation is further complicated by the overlay of EU rules and regulations. Such a high number of laws, laughed one Italian businessman, and nobody follows any of them! Thus, the cultural value of *arrangiarsi* flourishes in response to an overloaded system.

Women in business

Traditionally, Italy and its business world have been male-dominated, despite great respect for women and matriarchal figures. Since the 1990s, women have been challenging such attitudes. Although women in commerce and the professions are more prevalent and accepted, their salaries and perks usually are not yet comparable to their male colleagues, even when the women have superior education. However, they are making rapid progress, especially when such career women develop their own personalized management style.

Business–family capitalism

As a great number of businesses in Italy are family-owned, many businesses lack management professionals. The head of the family wants to maintain control over the business. This widespread phenomenon weakens Italy because these businesses do not want to be publicly traded. Because they finance through debt, and because they want to maintain control at all costs, they limit their growth, and subsequently cannot compete in the global market. Yet the genial, amiable, and volatile Italian people will endure and move ahead in the twenty-first century—by most standards, they are wealthy, live long, and their families work together! The tips in Exhibit 16.7 will be helpful for all travelers to consider.

EXHIBIT 16.7 CONCLUDING TIPS FOR DOING BUSINESS IN ITALY

E X H I B I T 16.7

- Start-up: Be aware of possible problems involving laws and taxes.
- Learn Italian.
- Try to find an Italian counterpart to help you through the bureaucracy.
- For the initial contact, a third-party introduction is very helpful; if you can't get that, write directly in Italian.
- Print materials in Italian.
- Meeting: Try to build a relationship. This is a relationship-oriented country, and if you form a relationship, you have a better chance. You do that by taking time, finding out about the other person, and building trust. It is perfectly acceptable to ask questions about family, and expect to answer questions about yours.
- Dress code: Look your best.
- Forms of address: Be formal until the other person indicates that you may speak in the familiar (that is, if you are speaking in Italian).
- Access the *cordata*.
- Get a good lawyer and a good *commercialista*.
- Be flexible.
- Make connections.
- Be patient (things go along at what seems to be a standstill, and suddenly the ball starts rolling).

RUSSIA

Europe borders on Russia and Turkey, both of which provide entry into Asia. In ancient times they connected to a series of trade routes with multiple branches through the heart of Europe and Asia, such as the Asian Silk Road.

The eastern region of the European continent tends to be landlocked. However, this region is also punctuated by mountain systems like the Urals, and rivers such as the Deniester, Dnieper, and Don and Volga, which also empty into the Black Sea. The area also marks where Finland meets Russia, and where in past centuries there were great westward migrations of peoples and their flocks.

From the geopolitical entity known as the USSR, the Russian Federation has emerged since the turn of the millennium, along with its neighbors in the Commonwealth of Independent States (CIS). Together, the CIS has sought to (1) repeal all Soviet laws and assume the powers of that former regime; (2) launch radical economic reforms, including the freeing of most prices; (3) retain the ruble, while allowing new currencies to be adopted in some countries; (4) establish a European-style free trade zone; (5) create joint control of all nuclear weapons; and (6) fulfill all foreign treaties and other obligations of the former communist regime.

Since the Soviet breakup, the countries immediately surrounding the Russian Federation have been in turmoil. Once part of the czar's empire in the Caucasus, these entities struggle to be nations, like Belarus, Georgia, and the Ukraine. They seek a new identity and more independence, while coping with dictators, internal conflict, and serious economic problems. Besides the Russian Federation, the other key Commonwealth player is ancient Ukraine, populated with Slavic peoples since at least 2000 BC. Its name means *borderland*, and its beautiful capital is Kiev, the mother city of the Old Russian Empire, famous for Slavic Orthodox churches, and Cossacks.

Historical perspective

To understand what is happening in contemporary Russia, its regions, and satellite countries, one has to comprehend that vast country's recent history, especially its 1918 revolution. For much of the twentieth century, the totalitarian mindset and policies dominated political, social, and economic life throughout Central Europe. When the Union of Soviet Socialist Republics was founded in 1922, Russia, and eventually its Eastern Bloc allies, ensured that all major government and economic decision-making posts were filled by Communist Party members. These enforced its doctrine of centralism, requiring that decisions made at the top not be questioned by the lower echelons. This led to a situation in which a few people at the peak of the pyramid made almost every significant decision, and local initiative was practically nonexistent. The system restricted enterprise and meaningful contact with world market demand and supply. Its state monopoly sought to prevent capitalist countries from influencing the course of economic activities in the whole geographic area, except for what Western science and technologies its spies could steal.

Some suggestions for doing business in Russia

Whether the remodeled Russia under Vladimir Putin, who has turned his country into a centralized state under his or his cronies' command, will be able to modernize further and peacefully meet the immense needs of its varied peoples is an open question. Obviously, Russia is in the midst of a painful political, social, and economic transition. For centuries, the national cultures were autocratic and totalitarian, and again the economy is stagnating.

Instability and transformation

Some immediate problems facing Russia are as follows:

- Accelerating disintegration of the economy and need for new financial systems and enterprises.
- Deepening crises in food/consumer goods production and distribution, as well as in housing and health services.
- Breakdowns in traditional systems (e.g., legal, banking, business, fuel, and transportation) that hinder foreign investment and entrepreneurialism.
- Extensive job dislocation and rising unemployment.
- Political fragmentation and power-seeking by the republics, such as the independence movement in Chechnya.
- Rising crime and political assassinations by a criminal underground mafia that extends its power even to émigrés in New York and Los Angeles.
- Development of very powerful "oligarchs" who amassed their wealth by seizure or rigged purchasing of state assets.

But Russia has positives, such as:

- Incredible human resources of a literate people with a combination of unique traditions and contributions to the arts and sciences, from music and ballet to space technology and physics.
- Vast natural and material resources, much of which are yet to be developed.
- Sound educational system that provides high-level instruction in mathematics and sciences.
- Codependent economies that foster cooperative alliances.
- Growing interest in preserving and protecting the environment and preventing disasters like nuclear accidents.
- Majority of the population demonstrating for conservative public decisions made in a democratic way, desiring order and discipline, but not totalitarianism.
- Resurgence of religion and some religious tolerance.

Trade and business opportunities

Breaking into Russia takes perseverance and hard work by foreign firms that have succeeded by developing long-range strategies. Although Russia can offer foreign companies and universities much in terms of scientific, technical, and engineering talent, as well as processes, its greatest need from the West is for capital investment, plus management systems and development.

In the past few years, many joint-venture agreements have been entered into by Western and Russian companies and institutions. Corporate giants have proven that successful projects can be accomplished within Russia, as Pepsico, Coca-Cola, Dow Chemical, Marriott, McDonald's, and American Express have demonstrated. Most suffered from the Soviet bureaucracy and their regulations.

Negotiating style and protocol

During the ongoing transition from centralized planning to market economies within Russia, foreigners can expect much confusion, frustration, and uncertainty. In negotiations, the Russians are noted for patience and stalling, considering compromise a sign of weakness. They expect to "play hardball," continually seeking concessions, and revising "final offers"– the longer the foreigner holds out acceptance, the more attractive the offer. Emotional "walkouts" and dire proclamations are part of their process. So, too, are the use of *blat*, or connections who use influence on your behalf, in exchange for favors, monetary or otherwise. Bribery and corruption are major problems.

There are two stages in business negotiations with the Russians. During the first stage, they try to get as many competitive offers as possible and play one supplier against another, before making a final decision. Nothing may happen for a while after the Western firm has submitted its bid. Then the Russians may notify the firm that it is still interested and resume negotiations. Potential suppliers are expected to provide detailed technical explanations of their products, so that the Russians can evaluate precisely what is being offered. Having collected several competitive offers, the Russians are adept at creating competition among the suppliers. Quotations from competitors are revealed to force bidding suppliers to cut their prices.

The second phase of negotiations begins when a supplier has been chosen. This phase is usually shorter than the first one, but it still takes time to settle all the various points in the final contract. Russian negotiators often negotiate with the weakest competitor first. After concessions are obtained from the weakest, the other companies are notified they must also accept them.

Another maneuver used by Russian negotiators is to first fix the final price the supplier is willing to take for its product. Once this price is firmly quoted, the Russians may make additional demands for such extra services as free training of technicians or equipment maintenance, which were not originally included in the producer's description and price.

Experienced foreign companies make it a standing rule to begin contract talks by discussing the articles of the purchasing agreement before any discussion begins on final price. It should also be made clear at the beginning on which points the supplier is willing to make concessions and on which it is not. The longer an executive postpones talking about demands that are of major importance to his or her company, the more forcefully the Russians may oppose them later.

Each agreement made with the Russians should stand on its own accord. Granting a price discount or making concessions to the Russians to win future business simply does not work. A common Russian tactic is to ask for a bulk price for a product and then to apply the lower price per unit from the bulk price to a smaller lot. It is implied, and sometimes even promised verbally, that more purchases will follow. However, Russians will honor only written agreements.

It is important to let Russians know exactly where your firm stands on all issues. The Russians do not respect negotiators who make large concessions because they then believe that initial proposals were inflated or deceptive. The firm should be prepared to stand by its position, and to drop negotiations and cut its losses if necessary. This will impress the Russians far more than slowly acquiescing to their demands. Although the "old" Soviet system may no longer exist, attitudes and cultural perceptions are much more resilient. Russians are very protocol-conscious.

Work environment

The workweek is generally Monday through Friday, 9 a.m. to 5 p.m. Recently, some banks have begun opening on Saturdays and evenings. Retail stores may be open Monday through Saturday from 8–9 a.m. to 8–9 p.m.; food stores are also open on Sunday. Although foreigners are expected to show up on time for business appointments, allowance is made to be 15–30 minutes late for social events. Your Russian counterpart may be tardy or not show up at all—the previous communist system conditioned people to lateness, not promptness, and endless waiting in lines. Now, foreign businesses are training their personnel in attitudes of punctuality and prompt customer service. Also allow for delays because of inadequate transportation and distances.

Typically, Russian officials expect to conduct business with only the highest-ranking executives. On the initial visit, the Western firm's representative is advised to send executives to ensure a favorable first impression. Final negotiations on larger deals should be handled by a key executive to demonstrate the importance the Western firm is placing on this business. Then the locals may be willing for their chairperson or deputy chairperson to enter the negotiations at some decisive stage.

Business tips for Russia

The following are some additional cultural clues that may advance synergistic relations:

- *Consumers* are only beginning to get accustomed to higher quality for higher prices. In addition to a plentiful and consistent supply of quality food, they seek modern conveniences and entertainment. Having been subjected to substandard clothing and outdated styles, they hunger for Western adornments that are colorful, stylish, and practical in their climate. However, business dress is conservative (e.g., suit and tie).

- *Business contacts*—relative to foreign trade, the Russian Market Institute can provide useful data and quotations. Outsiders will have to network and seek direct contacts with new factory owners and entrepreneurs. Emerging there and in the US are consulting firms/publications to facilitate business in Eastern Europe. The internet can be a prime source of this information.

- *Currency challenges*—innovative ways must be developed to convert the volatile ruble and other new monetary units into international hard currency, such as by barter, exchange of services, or third-country transfer.

- *Attention to detail*—because of the Soviet cultural conditioning of the past decades, visitors can expect local officials to give much attention to such matters as seating arrangements and invitations; business cards printed in both Cyrillic and one's own language or English; and the caliber of a technical presentation both in writing and orally. Continuity is an important factor, so the visiting team should designate one person as project manager or spokesman in business dealings.

- *Communication* is facilitated when the foreigner can speak the local language, but many Russians, Ukrainians, and other republic representatives are comfortable speaking English, German, or French. The use of interpreters has both positives (clarifying meaning or building interpersonal relations) and negatives (perceptual slanting by the translator or lack of technical understanding). Orally, Russians may greet foreigners with *gospodin* (Mr.) or *gospozha* (Miss or Mrs.) and ask acquaintances for their *imya* (first name) or *ochestvo* (patronymic). Name listings are similar to those in the West, except for the use of the Russian middle name—a *patronymic* derived from the first name of one's father (e.g., the use of *Ivanovich*, meaning the son of Ivan). Women also add an "a" to their surname, as well as to their patronymic middle name (e.g., *Ivanova* for daughter of Ivan). Customarily, the use of the latter, or first name, is indicative of familiarity and friendship.

- Get to know Russian body language. For example, to the Westerner, the traditional Russian official or executive may appear stiff. Gestures are usually kept to a minimum, and expressions may seem blank and uninterested. Smiles are rare, except between people who are close. This is the public image Russians seem to convey. In private, they are much more expressive. The modest reserve that they publicly project breaks down under more personal surroundings and socialization.

- *Time sense* is quite different in Russia, and the locals dislike the quick tempo of Western business or the attitude that time is money. They use the slower tempo to good advantage, especially in negotiations, business, or socializing. The inhabitants quote old Russian proverbs like, "If you travel for a day, take bread for a week," or

"Patience and work, and everything will work out." Part of this stoicism and slowness is due to inadequate telecommunications and transportation. Within this colossus of a country, even simple technological advances like fax machines can save much time and facilitate communication, while the computer may expedite matters, if the local has one that functions.

■ *National psyche*–Russians have long suffered from a sense of inferiority (for which they overcompensate); in the days of the aristocracy, the Czar's court turned to things French and German to show how civilized and sophisticated they were. Having been often cut off from outside contacts, the Russians also have manifested xenophobia. Totalitarianism also made many citizens feel like prisoners in their own society. The younger generation is more educated, more open, and more cosmopolitan, as well as more disillusioned and cynical.

Russian leaders are generous hosts with food and beverages. Dinners are long and elaborate, and toasts are frequently and generously made to good business relationships and mutual friendships. The visiting foreign businessperson should be prepared to encounter some amiable "imbibing competition" stemming from the Russian prowess for drinking. To better comprehend this complex Slavic people, it helps to read their writers before traveling to Mother Russia.

CONCLUSIONS

In the opening section of this chapter we presented a historical overview of several countries in Europe. The overview includes the ongoing developments within the EU expansion to 27 members, as well as its accomplishments and ambitions.

Well into the twenty-first century, Europeans are likely to be engaged in struggles to (1) gain continental identity; (2) cope with fertility issues of lower birth rates among the traditional inhabitants, and higher ones among the immigrants; (3) control the flow and acculturate these new arrivals from abroad, especially among the Muslim populations; (4) transform their agricultural and industrial cultures to a continental knowledge culture; and (5) operate more effectively within the realities of the global market.

MIND STRETCHING

1   Why is some understanding of European history so important to comprehending EU and related continental developments today?

2   What are the implications of changes in the balance of religious adherents within Europe (e.g., Christianity, Muslims, and Jews)?

3 How is the development of a single continental market strategy in Europe going to affect the global market?

4 Why are the nations in Northern Europe concerned about the less economically developed countries in Southern Europe?

5 What are some of the specific European countries whose cultures facilitate synergistic relations with their neighbors, and which ones are seemingly unsynergistic (e.g., more combative, less cooperative)?

6 What impact do geography and climate in various parts of Europe have on a people's culture and economy?

NOTES

1 Cultural profiles of France, Germany, Italy, and Russia are included in the book. Additional country profiles are on the *Managing Cultural Differences* website.

2 *Europe in Transition: Reshaping a Continent* (a map insert). Washington, DC: National Geographic, 2008. "Europe," *Family Reference Atlas of the World*. Washington, DC: National Geographic Society, 2002. pp. 126–141. Davis, W., Harrison, K., and Howell, C. H. "Europe," in *Book of Peoples of the World: A Guide to Cultures*. Washington, DC: National Geographic, 2008, pp. 192–255. Morrison, T., Conway, W. A., and Douress, J. J. *Dun & Bradstreet Guide to Doing Business Around the World*. Upper Saddle River, NJ: Prentice-Hall, 2009. Also refer to www.nationalgeographic.com

3 *Europe: The State of the Union*. New York: Atlantic Monthly Press, 2008. Pinder, J. and Usherwood, S. *The European Union: A Very Short Guide*. Oxford: Oxford University Press, 2007. Dick, L. *Guide to the European Union*. South Burlington, VT: Bloomberg Press/Economist Books, 2004. Beech, D. *The Dynamics of European Integration: Why and When EU Institutions Matter*. London: Palgrave Macmillan, 2005.

4 This quote can be found in the following articles: Rennie, D. "In the Nick of Time: A Special Report on EU Enlargement," *The Economist*, May 31, 2008, p. 16; Peet, J. "Fit at 50: A Special Report on the European Union," *The Economist*, March 17, 2007, p. 20; Rachman, G. "Outgrowing the Union: Survey of European Union," *The Economist*, September 24, 2004.

5 Storti, C. *Old World/New World: Bridging Cultural Differences—Britain, France, Germany, and the U.S.* Boston, MA: Nicholas Brealey/Intercultural Press, 2003. Brittan, S. "Europe Is Not So Backward After All," *Financial Times*, July 30, 2004. Roger, P. *The American Enemy: The History of French Anti-Americanism*. Chicago, IL: University of Chicago Press, 2005. Chesnoff, R. Z. *The Arrogance of the French: Why They Can't Stand Us and Why the Feeling Is Mutual*. New York: Sentinel Press, 2005. Ver Berkmoes, R. *Western Europe (Multi Country Guide)*. New York: Lonely Planet, 2007.

6 Klausen, J. *The Islamic Challenge: Politics and Religion in Western Europe*. Oxford: Oxford University Press, 2005. Burleigh, M. *Earthly Power: The Clash of Religion and Politics in Europe from the French Revolution to the Great War*. New York: HarperCollins, 2006. Baker, R. W. *Islam Without Fear: Egypt and the New Islamists*. Boston, MA: Harvard University Press, 2003.

7 Guizot, P. G. *A Popular History of France from Earliest Times*, Vol. 1. London: BiblioBazaar, 2008. Porter, D. and Prince, D. *Frommer's France 2008*. Hoboken, NJ: Wiley Publishing Inc., 2007; Asselin, G. and Mastron, R. *Au Contraire! Figuring Out the French*. Boston, MA: Nicholas Brealey/Intercultural Press, 2001. "The Art of the Impossible: A Survey of France," *The Economist*, October 28, 2006, p. 16. "French Decline: Predators and Prophets," *The Economist*, February 4, 2006, p. 6.

8 J. Andres, "A Divided Self: A Survey of France," *The Economist*, November 16, 2002.

9   Chessnoff, *The Arrogance of the French.*

10   "French Failure," *The Economist*, November 12, 2005 pp. 11–12, 24–26.

11   Alexiev, A. "France at the Brink," *The San Diego Union-Tribune*, January 22, 2007, p. G3/5.

12   President of France, President of the European Union, last half of 2008, "France in a Challenging World," *The World in 2008* n.p.: The Economist, 2008, p. 96.

13   For the insights that follow, the authors express appreciation to Gerd-Peter E. Lotao, who first wrote on "Doing Business in France" in the World Trade Notes of *Credit and Financial Management Magazine* (June 1987, p. 10).

14   A previous edition of our book, *Managing Cultural Differences*, was translated into French under the title *Au-Dela Des Cultures* in 1994 by InterEditions, Centre francaise d'exploitation du droit de copie, 3, Hautefeuille, 75006 Paris, France.

15   The authors are grateful to Maryellen Toffle, MIM, a graduate of the Thunderbird School of Global Management, who wrote this section on Italy. Her work resulted, in part, from interviews with Italian professionals, such as management consultant Dr. Luigi Giannitrapani, managing director Marina Zacco, and operations director Dr. Annalisa Bardi. We have updated this material with special acknowledgment to "Audio, Dolce Vita: A Survey of Italy," *The Economist*, November 26, 2005, p. 16.

Resources for the Future: MCD10e readers concerned about the future of the world or a specific region or country will find useful these three sources of information:

1   The annual *State of the Future* report and CD (www.StateOfTheFuture.org). This is an outcome of The Millennium Project sponsored by the World Federation of UN Associations.

2   Foundation for the Future (www.futurefoundation.org). Request information about publications, proceedings, awards, and symposia.

3   The World Future Society (www.worldfuturesociety.org). Request membership for access to their annual forecasts, publications, online exchanges, and conferences.

Resources on Europe: Periodically, *The Economist* magazine publishes special country surveys that are also available as reprints. For latest surveys on any country, see www.economist.com/surveys.

17 DOING BUSINESS IN AFRICA

Africa has been referred to as "the continent of beginnings." Fossils and records of the earliest humans go back more than four million years. What can be considered our early upright ancestor, *Homo erectus*, departed Africa on the long journey that eventually populated the Earth. It now seems likely that every person in today's world comes from a lineage that derives from the ancient Africans. Innumerable cave paintings and petroglyphs, from the Sahara to South Africa, provide clues to the beliefs and ways of life of these age-old hominids.[1]

L
E
A
R
N
I
N
G

O
B
J
E
C
T
I
V
E
S

After reading and studying concepts, examples, and illustrations in Chapter 17, readers should:

1   Be aware of some important cultural aspects of Africans relevant to traveling or doing business in Africa.
2   Understand better the long history of Africa and appreciate that all humans can trace their DNA heritage to Africa.
3   Be aware of any stereotypes they may have of African people.
4   Appreciate the challenges African nations have experienced in the past and may continue to experience in the future.

We need to appreciate Africa as the cradle of human civilization, not just as a continent of economically developing countries. After an overview of African history, this chapter will examine some of the nations and peoples on this diverse continent, and will provide specifics regarding their respective cultures, so as to not only facilitate communications and business with Africans, but also to better understand Africans and some of the challenges they face.

BEGINNINGS

Two hundred million years ago, this landmass split off from the ancient supercontinent of Pangea. Africa is the cradle of all humanity, for we all trace our DNA heritage to this area. *Homo sapiens* first appeared in Africa in an anatomically mature state some 200,000 years ago, probably in what is today known as Omo Kibish in Ethiopia. Genetic data indicate that there were two human migrations out of this continent. The first group went no further than what is now Israel, dying out some 90,000 years ago. Descendants of modern humans left Africa some 70,000–50,000 years ago. By 50,000 years ago, following a coastal route along southern Asia, they reached what is now Australia and became a people known today as Aborigines. Some 40,000–30,000 years ago, human inland migration, apparently via Asia, populated the continent known as Europe. During roughly the same period, these humans migrated into Central Asia, arriving on the grassy steppes north of the Himalayas. They also traveled through Southeast Asia and China, eventually reaching Japan and Siberia. Genetic clues lead us to believe that humans in northern Asia eventually migrated to the Americas. Between 20,000 and 15,000 years ago, sea levels were low, and so were lands that connected Siberia to Alaska; the new arrivals trekked southward down the west coast of what is now America. The DNA marker M168 among today's non-Africans is one indicator used to prove that we all trace our origins to the *mother of the human family–* Africa! Our diverse faces and races ultimately trace their origins through genes back to the first hunter-gatherers.

Africa has largely remained a mystery to the outside world, marked perhaps more by its isolation than by any other feature. This stubborn reality can be traced to the earliest times, and is reflected in the hopelessly misrepresented images of ancient cartographers, whose graphic distortions were as errant as the half-myths and false science that passed for knowledge about the "dark continent." Yet, ancient civilizations flourished in Africa from Carthage in the north to "empires" in the south. Among these was the Kingdom of Zimbabwe, which flourished in the thirteenth to fifteenth centuries; and, in the Niger area, the grand states of the Yoruba, the Ashanti, and the Hausa people prospered. From 900 CE onward, the eastern coastal plains were the homeland of the Swahili culture and language that flourished in the area stretching from Somalia to Zanzibar, including a mix of local peoples, Arabs, and immigrants. From the fifteenth to nineteenth centuries, the search for riches and a route to India brought European explorers and occupiers, beginning with the Portuguese, with the British, French, Belgians, and Germans following. Unfortunately, few Europeans appreciated the civilizations and cultures already functioning there, imposing their own ways on the indigenous inhabitants. Although Africans dispersed by natural migration, they were also forcefully introduced into the Americas, Europe, Latin America, and the Middle East as a result of the inhumane slave trade. The last half of the twentieth century has been Africa's postcolonial period of independence. As the people of the world scramble to utilize African resources, a mature continental civilization may finally come into its own in this twenty-first century!

MODERN AFRICA[2]

There are over 50 countries located on the continent, from Algeria in the Islamic north to South Africa. National identities are diverse for peoples assembled within borders imposed by departed European imperialists. The outsiders' partitioning of Africa in the past two centuries made little attempt to make national borders coincide with on-site ethnic groups and tribes. Boundaries on this continent are continuously being reconfigured as new states emerge. In 1993, Eritrea officially achieved independence from its neighbor, Ethiopia. National names also change frequently; for instance, Rhodesia became Zimbabwe, and Tanganyika became Tanzania. Africa is home to roughly one-third of the world's sovereign states, but only 19 of them here have democratic governments, depending on how the word "democracy" is defined. At least four are routinely classified as failed states–the Congo, Somalia, the Sudan, and Zimbabwe. The World Bank and the IMF currently classifies 39 countries worldwide as heavily indebted poor countries (HIPCs)–33 of these are in sub-Saharan Africa. Most of these countries came into existence in the twentieth century, and currently about half of the governments were formed as the result of coups, principally by the military. In too many African states, the rule of law has been displaced by the rule of the autocrat who seizes power and control. The redrawing of former colonial boundaries need not mean smaller African states; it could simply mean more rational and viable political communities. The long-term scenario emerging from continuing crises may be the gradual change of boundaries between the DRC, Rwanda, and Burundi. Unless the Hutu and Tutsi are partitioned into separate countries or federated into a larger, stable, and democratic political community, they are likely to engage in conflict. One solution for the problems in the region calls for the international community to put together a large package of incentives to persuade Rwanda, Burundi, and Tanzania to create the United States of Central Africa; that way, parts of the DRC could one day seek admission into the new federation. Currently, the African Union acts as a coordinating medium for the continental countries, and strives to encourage regional cooperation, trading, and political stability. Sovereign states with bureaucratic controls are the hallmark of Western European civilization. But such historical experience was largely absent in sub-Saharan kingdoms before the arrival of European colonialism during the past three centuries.

Although Africans had learned to smelt iron by 1500 CE, the industrial stage of development was not experienced by most Africans. They were mainly hunter-gatherers, farmers, and herders; only a small minority lived in urban areas. After a few hundred years of predatory slave-raiding and direct European influence or rule, all African countries have regained their independence from European control since the mid- to late twentieth century. Thus, a dynamic process is under way throughout Africa to develop modern mass societies with the accompanying political, economic, and technological systems. One needs an Afrocentric approach to fully appreciate this heritage and experience. Africans in diaspora may be found on every continent, but there are large populations in both North and Latin America, as well as in Europe. Barack Obama became the President of the United States of America in 2009; his father was a Kenyan from the *luo*-speaking Nyanza Province in Kenya.

Africa is a land of great promise and potential, a continent of immense natural beauty and resources, most of which is still undeveloped. It is a region of contrasts between the primitive and the ultramodern, a place where new industries, technologies, and cities emerge gradually. Yet, in this postcolonial period, it is the misfortune of Africa, which birthed civilization, to remain mired in human suffering and carnage in the twenty-first century. Although this collective of countries is somewhat disconnected from the world by its unmatched sorrows, its rich mixture of people has a distinctly African sense of brotherhood and humor.

The murder of thousands of Namibians by Germans over 100 years ago (between 1904 and 1908) is close to being accepted and recognized by the German government as the twentieth century's first genocide.[3] Over 100 years ago, the area was known as South-West Africa and was one of Germany's former colonies. Namibia and Germany are now negotiating to end a sad chapter of Europe's past in Africa. Germany is expected to apologize and compensate Namibia. Thousands of Herero and Nama people were shot, hung from trees, or died in the desert without water as Germans had sealed watering holes.

For global leaders to be effective in their trade and development efforts within Africa, they must be realistic in their analysis of its peoples and possibilities. First, there is great diversity of tribes, languages, customs, religions, education, and governments. Second,

most of the people here are generous, eager to learn, and hardworking. Their natural buoy-
ancy and flexibility have been dampened by widespread famine, epidemics, exploitation, and
social unrest. The world media often distorts the external image of Africa by its emphasis on
African tragedies—the horror of the mass poverty, the AIDS epidemic, the extensive
droughts, the many civil wars, and the millions of refugees. Often overlooked in these reports
are the success stories—World Bank and UNESCO projects that work at the local levels,
the green revolution that expands agricultural production, the many business enterprises
that flourish, the African foreign students who return to apply their Western education, and
the shift from failed socialism to democratic and market-oriented policies.

   The Economist's "The World in 2017," highlights the following relevant points:[4]

■   Commodities such as oil are busting, and oil exporters of Nigeria and Angola will be
    hurt.

■   Robert Mugabe, at the age of 92 and a despot, is expected to hang on to power until
    he dies.

■   In South Africa, Jacob Zuma continues to be charged with corruption, and the African
    National Congress is expected to face tough challenges to continue its dominance.

■   Gabon, with a population of fewer than two million, has a gross national income per
    person of more than $15,000. Gabon is one of the most prosperous countries in sub-
    Saharan Africa. GDP grew by more than 6 percent per year from 2010 to 2012.
    However, a significant proportion of the population are poor because of inequality in
    income distribution.

■   Egypt receives billions in aid, and tourism and foreign investment are dropping.

■   In Uganda, President Museveni is running for a fifth term after 30 years in power.

■   In Nigeria and other countries such as in Chad and Cameroon, the full-face burqa is
    being forbidden in public.

ASPECTS OF AFRICAN CULTURE

Africa entered this new millennium in a state of intense transition. The changes under way
can also be summed up in three words: *tribalism, chaos,* and *development*.

Tribalism

The tribe is the basic sociological unit of Africa that provides one's sense of identity, belonging,
and responsibility. When tribal members leave rural areas to go to the city for a job or to
study, traditionally their enhanced stature brings with it responsibility for assisting their tribal
brothers and sisters at home. Such social pressure on successful Africans may impose a
burden to augment income by any means, legal or otherwise. Tribal bonds also lead to intergroup conflict, destruction, and corruption. As the force of tribalism deteriorates in modern,

urban environments, Africans search for other substitutes—new institutional loyalties such as membership in a religion, cooperatives, and political parties, often formed along ethnic lines.

For many, tribalism is the bane of independent Africa, with its many tribes and clans involving more than 2,000 living languages. Left over from the colonialists are areas where French, English, Portuguese, and a dialect of Dutch are widely spoken. National leaders seek to transform intertribal hostility into collaborative community endeavors. Tribalism is evident in elections, where voting favors the largest tribes, while the winners are only slowly learning that power should be shared with the minority losers. It is also behind failed attempts at ethnic cleansing, authoritarian regimes, and political corruption. The challenge for many Africans is to build upon tribal heritage, while moving beyond narrow tribal loyalties and constraints for the greater common good of the nation and its economic development.

This issue is closely connected to ethnicity. Perhaps this definition will make our point: An ethnic group is a distinct population whose members identify with each other based on a common ancestry. Such groups are distinguished by common cultural, linguistic, or religious traits. Ethnicity is different from the concept of race, which divides people on the basis of physical or biological traits, such as skin color, which in Africa protects the inhabitants from a strong sun. The point for cosmopolitans to remember is that many African "leaders" exploit tribal and ethnic ties over national interests. Both are used by the "big boys" as a means of staying in power!

Chaos

As Africans seek to move beyond their colonial dependency, while rapidly creating appropriate cultural institutions and opportunities, tumult abounds. The destabilization process is compounded by a combination of factors. Sometimes it is caused by nature, when lack of rain triggers mass famine, or a monkey virus infects entire East African populations through the plague of AIDS, caused by the HIV virus that continues to kill many thousands each day. Because of poor or inadequate water systems, other infectious diseases such as malaria devastate African communities. In June 2003, a group of African presidents appealed for greater help from the rich G8 nations meeting in Evian, France. Foreign governments have spent billions to fight disease in Africa, mainly through the Global Fund, an organization supporting 150 programs to fight AIDS, tuberculosis, and malaria. But other nations have to match that commitment, which the G8 leaders promised to do. But in some African states, such as South Africa, the governments have been unable to use the external resources effectively. Other countries on the continent lack a well-organized and functioning healthcare system. Many immature political entities do not use donor funds effectively because of a lack of medical personnel and inadequate road and communications infrastructure. Sometimes, the disarray and the obstacles to African development come from the following:[5]

■ The rise of extremist Muslim militants and terrorists, as seen in North Africa, the Sudan, Somalia, and more recently elsewhere, such as Kenya.

- Tribal conflicts that escalated into civil wars, as in Rwanda when the Hutu army oversaw the murder of one million Tutsi; in Somalia where tribal warfare led to the collapse of the government and anarchy; and in the Congo and Sudan where geno- cide prevailed and millions died. Distorted ambitions and ideologies of local dictators and guerrillas to crush their opposition in other tribes have led to new tyrannies, such as that which occurred in Uganda, Nigeria, Liberia, Angola, and elsewhere.

- African infighting and the resultant destruction are sometimes attributed to religion, such as when brown-skinned Muslim Arabs from the north of Somalia raid and destroy dark-skinned Christians in the south of a country with hopeless governance.

- Incompetent strongmen who take political power through coups or rigged elections, and use their positions as heads of state to benefit only themselves and their cronies. This lack of authentic leaders has contributed to undermining of national economies and exploitation of the citizenry. Hence, the rule of the "big man" replaces the rule of law, while the average person suffers. The deterioration of Rhodesia when it became Zimbabwe under its dictator, Robert Mugabe; the DRC when ruled by Mobutu Sese Seko; or Uganda under its despot, Idi Amin, are cases in point!

- Failure of the current states in terms of borders, governance, and infrastructure. Before the nineteenth century, Africa had been divided into thousands of kingdoms and chief- doms whose systems of government developed over hundreds of years. For adminis- trative purposes, European colonialists created a few dozen nation-states whose borders often divided tribal lands. On all this was grafted European governance models, such as parliamentary democracy, that were alien to many Africans. The new regimes proved unstable and dysfunctional, with elected governments giving way to authoritarianism, military take-overs, and assignations. The result has undermined the growth of any democratic free-enterprise system, while incumbents became rich and powerful with their private militias and suppressed media, unless they were killed, jailed, or driven into exile.[6]

Often, such internal troubles are exacerbated by outside intervention, as when in past centuries Europeans imposed their controls on the locals; today the influence of European cultures and dependency may still be found in former African colonies of Britain, France, Germany, and Portugal. In the twentieth century, Western powers twice involved Africans in their world wars, as well as in the Cold War between the US and the former USSR. Africans have been involved again, when the United Nations sends relief efforts, but with inadequate peacekeeping troops, to such places as the Sudan, Liberia, Rwanda, and Somalia.

The combination of such problems worsens because of overpopulation, the need for food because of disruption in farming and fishing, systemic corruption, and widespread unemployment. Mass poverty engenders desperation, which may feed political extremity. All of the above factors contribute to the displacement of millions of Africans from their home- lands. Many end up as refugees amid poverty on a gigantic scale. One effect of this chaos is the threat it poses to the ecological environment of the continent. Deserts are widening, broad savannas and their communities struggle to survive. Sometimes the confusion is simply future shock as tribal cultures and rural peoples try to cope with the demands of an urban, postindustrial way of life. Finally, too many postcolonial nation-states and their political leaders in Africa are failing to liberate, protect, and service their own citizens, as well as their country's resources.

But the situation is not all bad—Africans are survivors with remarkable resilience and "make do" capacities. Entrepreneurs abound, humanitarian efforts progress, and some countries are justly and successfully ruled by elected leaders. Peacekeepers and peace enforcers in many cases produce positive results, as in Cote d'Ivoire; the African Union is also training regional brigades.

Development

Africa has been classified as the Third World in economic terms—it contributes only 1 percent of the global economic output. This poor continent is often viewed as a land of tragedy or promise because of its rich natural and human resources that have not been fully developed. The nations here are being crippled by debt to foreign interests. The cause of the current woes goes with past European colonialism and inadequate education of the African people. Because of this historical influence, when the majority of Africa gained independence after the 1960s, many of its "leaders" were ill-prepared to lead their countries. They turned toward state socialism, favoring government intervention in the economy with bureaucratic controls that stifled initiative, killed incentive, and created chronic, artificial shortages. The situation represents a rejection of the continent's heritage of consensual and participatory democracy, which should embrace *free* markets, trade, and enterprise. The full potential of Africa may be realized in this century if Africans are empowered to build an infrastructure on the basis of their own uniqueness and cultures. Development increases opportunity for people. But to actualize these prospects, Africans will have to learn how to (1) practice synergy among themselves; (2) control their populations; (3) advance their literacy, education, and productivity; (4) build infrastructure, especially roads and transportation; (5) promote conservation and ecotourism; and (6) connect with the information age and its technologies. Consider just one reality to be rectified—less than 10 percent of the continent's land is formally owned, and only one in ten Africans lives in a house with formal deeds or titles. But Africa's biggest need is for effective, indigenous leadership at all levels of their society, yet no country is effectively addressing this need.

For foreigners to be more effective in their business and professional relationships with Africans, it is helpful to have some knowledge of the diverse cultures of this continent. In a previous chapter, we described some aspects of Islam, which also dominates North Africa and the Muslim states elsewhere in this area. Within black Africa, there are some common cultural characteristics. The next section will review five dimensions of those African cultures—family, trust/friendship, time, corruption, and respect for elders. This selected analysis may increase awareness and improve interaction not only with Africans, but with the millions of descendants from this heritage who are found throughout North, Central, and South America, as well as in the Caribbean, the UK, and the Middle East. Being cautious with African generalizations is an effective approach as African cultures are not only diverse, but dynamic, changing to ensure survival, as well as to adapt to new times and circumstances.

An example of success

There are many, many examples of business success in Africa. Exhibit 17.1 is a case in point, and illustrates how situations can change when private enterprise is allowed to work.

EXHIBIT 17.1 IMPACT OF TELECOMMUNICATIONS IN AFRICA

First radio, then television, and now mobile telephones are transforming African communications and business. The wireless age is overcoming the obstacles on this huge continent caused by poor roads, unreliable energy, political instability, and corruption that prevented the wiring of landline telephones. The new technologies bypass all this, giving regions and people access to phones they never had before. But Africans use this new communication tool for more than mere talking—shepherds in drought-ridden Sahel are using handheld GPS units and cell phones to alert others to good grazing; in Nairobi, customers avoid long lines at their bank by monitoring their accounts by text messaging; in Ethiopia, teachers are being trained to use solar-powered satellite radios to receive lessons broadcast to their classes; in South Africa, wives at home use cell phones to talk in the evening with their husbands who work hundreds of miles away; healthcare workers use their phones to summon ambulances; fisherwomen who can't read tell their customers to call their cell numbers to order fish; and retailers in the slums can take delivery orders from affluent suburbanites. On a continent where some remote villages communicate by beating drums, cell phones are a technological revolution. Cell operators can't put up phone towers fast enough. This phenomenon is causing a sociological and economic godsend for Africans at large. Today, Africa is the world's fastest growing cell phone market—in 2012, in fact, there were 648.4 million cell phone subscriptions on the continent. Others simply buy cell phone time to make each call—buying wireless phone time is like using the grocery list. Used handsets are sold for $50 or less. All this from a people who typically live on $2 or less per day! Domestic cell companies, like MTB and Conteh, are not only building telecommunications networks, but providing much-needed jobs and national income. International firms, like Vodacom, have 1.1 million subscribers in the Congo, adding a thousand new customers daily, and logging 10,000 calls per day. Bicycle-driven battery chargers are being used in rural areas to provide sufficient electricity to charge the phones. It's all been a boon, not only to business throughout Africa, but also to families who want to connect with one another.

Source: "Making the Connection in Africa: Whatever You Thought, Think Again," *National Geographic*, September 2005. "Africa Calling," *The Economist*, May 26, 2007, p. 74.

CULTURAL CHARACTERISTICS OF AFRICANS[7]

In Africa, there is no single culture. The northern African states of Mauritania, Morocco, Algeria, Libya, and part of the Sudan are closer to the Middle Eastern cultures. The descriptions that follow best apply to sub-Saharan Africa, home of black Africans, like the peoples of Mali, Senegal, Ghana, Congo, Benin, Tanzania, and South Africa. Yet, even their music and musical instruments reflect the diversity of their culture

Family and kinship

The basic unit of African society is the family, which includes the nuclear family and the extended family, or tribe. In traditional African society, the tribe is the ultimate community; no unit has more importance. There may be some loose confederations, but they are temporary and limited in scope. In political terms, the tribe is the equivalent of a nation. It does not have fixed boundaries, but on its sanction rests the law (customary law like English common law). All wars were fought on the tribe's behalf, and the division between "them" and "us" lay in tribal boundaries.

Africans center their communities around villages for food gathering and cultivation. The village elders become judges, mediators, trade masters, and leaders within both religious and tribal life. In some ways, the tribe is more than a nation. In Europe and America, ethical and moral standards are not given by national sanctions, but rest on religious and cultural traditions common to the whole continent. But in traditional Africa, except for areas under Islamic control, the family tribe provides the guidelines for accepted behavior. The tribe bears a moral connotation and provides an emotional security. It is also a source of social and moral sanctions, as well as political and physical security. The tribe provides its members with rules governing responsibilities, explanations of the responsibilities, and guidelines for organizing the society, and, hence, the culture.

The tribe is broken down into different kinship lines. The concept of kinship is important to understanding African societies. It constitutes the primary basis for an individual's rights, duties, rules of residence, marriage, inheritance, and succession. Kinship refers to blood relationships between individuals, and is used to describe relationships in both a narrow and a broad sense. Parents and their children are a special kind of kin group. The social significance of kinship covers a wide social field in most African societies. In Western culture, its significance usually does not extend beyond the nuclear family, but in African culture it embraces a network of people, including those that left the village for urban areas.

The family—father, mother, children—is the ultimate basis of the tribe. But the tribal and family unit organization is being disrupted by changes in the economic organizational structure. The economic organization has tied reward to individual effort, and developed road, rail, water, and air communication networks that have increased the range and speed of contact—thereby increasing the rate of intercultural contact and change. The reorganization has also brought tribes together as territorial units, with greater opportunities for migration from one area to another, but with a corresponding weakening of family bonds and behavior control.

As this newfound mobility moves more people to the large urban areas, they try to maintain some family ties. This involves a responsibility to support family members still in the villages. It also affects Africans' business relationships with managers from abroad in terms of hiring practices and the need for extra income to support those at home. Earnings from business transactions are often used for this purpose.

Trust and friendship

Trust and confidence are essential elements needed for successful enterprise in Africa. It is very important to get to know co-workers as individuals before getting down to actual business activities. With Africans, after family, friendship comes next in importance. Often, a friendship continues after specific business activities end. Socializing outside of the office is common. It is under those relaxed conditions that managers talk politics, sports, and sometimes business.

In Africa, interpersonal relationships are based on sincerity. African societies are normally warm and friendly. People generally assume that everyone is a friend until proven otherwise. When Africans smile, it means they like you. When smiles are not seen, it is a clear sign of distrust. Once a person is accepted as a friend, that person is automatically an "adopted" member of the family. A friend can pop into a friend's place anytime. In African societies, formal invitations and appointment-making are not common.

One of the most important factors to remember when doing business in Africa is the concept of friendship before business. Normally, before a meeting begins, there is general talk about events that have little or nothing to do with the business at hand. This can go on for some time. If the meeting involves people coming together who have never met, but who are trying to strike a deal (an African and a foreigner), the African will try to reach out for friendship first. If, in doing so, the African receives a cold response, he may become suspicious and lose interest in the deal.

In the traditional village culture, Africans share good fortune and food with other members of the community. This is an example of the values that modernization may unfortunately change.

Time and time-consciousness

The way an individual views the concept of time has a major impact on any business relationship. If two businesspeople enter into a situation with complementary goals, abilities, and needs, a successful arrangement can be thwarted if each has different ideas about time. In Africa, time is viewed as flexible, not rigid or segmented. People come first, then time. Anyone in a hurry is viewed with suspicion and distrust. Because trust is very important, individuals who follow inflexible time schedules will have little success. The African wants to sit and talk—to get to know the person before discussing business. Normally, time is not seen as a limited commodity. What cannot be done today can always be accomplished tomorrow. Meetings are not held promptly, and people may arrive several hours late. Often, foreigners misinterpret this as laziness, untrustworthiness, lack of seriousness in doing business, or even lack of interest in the venture. However, lateness in meetings should be perceived as part of African life. It is understood among friends that even though everybody agrees to meet at a given time, they will not actually gather until later.

However, when Africans are dealing with foreigners, they normally try to be on time out of respect for the non-African's concept of time. In the larger cities of Africa, the concept of time is changing. Punctuality is becoming more important. Contact with Western businesspersons has brought an increasing awareness and acceptance of the segmentation of time and its consequent inflexibility. But away from the capital city, time is still viewed in a relaxed and easygoing manner.

Corruption

Corruption in Africa is sometimes related to its poverty, and often results from tribal responsibilities that individuals carry with them when leaving the village for a job or schooling in the city. The enhanced stature of city life brings a responsibility to assist one's tribal family. This obligation often imposes a financial burden on the successful member far in excess of income. The worker is unlikely to resist the pressures of society, and is thus forced to augment income, often by means regarded by foreigners as bribery or corruption. However, to the African, it is not. As long as great disparities in income and standards of living continue, the bribe system is likely to continue, as it has in many developing economies. In Africa, extra income is swiftly distributed through the extended family system to distant relations living in remote places. The tradition of sharing continues even as individuals move away from their tribal origins.

Corruption may arise because of inadequate compensation for work, causing laborers to seek additional income. Many African state governments have been corrupted by greedy political and military rulers who use public monies and offices to enrich themselves and their families at the expense of citizens and foreign businesspersons. Exhibit 17.2, on Jones & Smith Food Company, gives readers an example of the payment of gratuities.

Respect for elders

Age is another important factor to consider in Africa. It is believed that the older one gets, the wiser one becomes—life has seasoned the individual with varied experiences. Hence, in Africa, age is an asset. The older the person, the more respect the person receives within the traditional community, especially from the young. Thus, if a foreigner is considerably younger than the African, the latter will have little confidence in the outsider. However, if sincerity, respect, and empathy are shown, the person will receive a positive response. Respect for elders tends to be the key for harmony in African cultures and village life.

EXHIBIT 17.2 JONES & SMITH FOOD COMPANY

The Jones & Smith Food Company is located in the capital of a large African country. However, they want to expand their headquarters to another state capital. To do this, they need approval from both the federal and the state governments. The company sent a written application a few months ago, but did not get any response.

The manager of the project went several times to the Federal Ministry of Trade and Economic Development, but was always told to come back the next day. Mr. Jones became frustrated and mad at the clerks and officials involved. However, in the process of the argument, one of them said: "This is not America. It's Africa. If you want anything done on time, you've got to give a bribe. Kind of like a gratuity tendered before, rather than after, a service is performed."

Mr. Jones, who is not accustomed to such practices, angrily stormed out of the office. In the car, he narrated the incident to the driver, who advised him to give the "gratuity" or have the proposal denied.

In an emergency meeting, the company's board of directors decided to offer the gratuity. To the company's surprise, the proposal was approved the next day.

But back in Mr. Jones' home culture, a board of directors may frown upon such payments, and home-country laws may consider such bribes illegal.

Young Africans normally do not oppose the opinion of their elders. They may not agree, but they must respect the opinion. In some cases, especially in rural areas, young people are not expected to offer opinions in meetings. The informal and formal interpersonal relationships in Africa are on the basis of cultural norms of various African societies. As Africa modernizes—nearly 40 of its cities have over one million inhabitants—some of the old ways, such as respect and care for seniors, may unfortunately diminish, as is happening with other traditional cultures in transition. African cultural characteristics vary in an urban area, in contrast to classical village life.

CULTURAL SPECIFICS BY GEOGRAPHIC REGIONS[8]

It is impossible here to cover all the cultural aspects of doing business or humanitarian work in all 50 African states. Instead, four major geographic areas of Africa are profiled. We have selected two countries for a more detailed analysis—namely Nigeria as the country with the largest population in Africa, just under 200 million, and South Africa as a country with great natural resources and potential. We will also consider a particular cultural dimension of Africa—business customs, protocols, and prospects.

North Africa[9]

This region contains seven countries: Algeria, Egypt, Libya, Morocco, the Sudan, Tunisia, and Western Sahara. Many classify themselves as republics. Libya, moreover, is a provisional parliamentary republic, and was once a subsumed sphere of Italian influence. Morocco is the only kingdom. Except for the coastal countries, the area can be characterized as one of high temperatures, vast deserts, Muslim religious practice, and French colonial cultural influence. The economies are developing, centered on textiles, food processing, agriculture, and mining; several are better off for producing or processing crude oil and petroleum.

The history of North Africa has been impacted significantly by the Middle East, especially by the culture of the Arabs and Islam. The latter defines the region's ethnicity and languages, particularly among the Semitic-speaking Arabs. From Morocco to East Africa, Arabic is the unifying common cultural influence. Up to 10,000 years ago, we already learned, Egypt gave rise to agriculture and a civilization based upon it. The area has also been known in the past for its nomadic herding, with life centered around the oases, still evident in today's Libya. The sea and the camel became the means for development of North African trading routes. Since ancient times, the making and distribution of bread is a common factor that the Arabs call *aish*, or life. Other regional foods include rice, yogurt, and meat kebabs, along with Mediterranean dishes that feature eggplant, beans, olives, pickles, and pastries. Extended families with arranged marriages are traditional, but are changing with urbanization and modernization, especially with regard to the role of women in society. Oral verse, poetry, and literature are common here as ways of expressing feelings. Pan-Arab movements have occurred in both the past and present, but generally have not succeeded because Arab leaders prefer decentralized power, avoiding domination by others. Abdul Nasser's attempt in 1958 to found a United Arab Republic lasted about four years. The region resists national unity and federalism, as evident in Algeria, Libya, Yemen, and other parts of Africa, such as the Sudan and Somalia.

East Africa[10]

This eastern region encompasses a dozen states, just south of Libya and Egypt, and bordering on the Red Sea, Gulf of Aden, and the Indian Ocean. The states include Burundi, Central African Republic, Congo, Djibouti, Eritrea, Ethiopia, Kenya, Rwanda, Somalia, Sudan, South Sudan, Tanzania, and Uganda. The area starts in the north with the Sahara Desert of Sudan and ends in the south with the Congo and Tanzania. Except for Eritrea and Somalia, the other ten countries style themselves as "republics," despite the presence of dictators or military coup commanders. Although Ethiopia was an ancient empire, most East African states were created as national entities by Britain, France, Germany, and Italy during the nineteenth century. Their borders and names have frequently changed as a result of civil wars and other conflicts. Some geographers place Sudan as part of North Africa, but we prefer to consider it within East Africa, sometimes called the Horn of Africa.

East Africa is a landmass of great natural diversity and beauty, with its deserts and mountains, rivers, and lakes, as well as a long, stunning coastline. It has temperatures and precipitation—from 73 to 89 °F in the north, and from 64 to 69 °F in the south. Except for deserts and barren lands in five northeastern countries, the predominant land use is grassland, woodland, and forest, with some cropland and wetlands. Agriculture is the primary regional industry, along with mining of copper, gold, fluorite, and diamonds. Two manufacturing centers are in Khartoum, Sudan, and Kinshasa, Congo; there is also one processing plant near Lubumbashi, Congo. Resplendent with spectacular landscape, Tanzania has one of the largest populations in the area. The region boasts the natural wonders of Mount Kilimanjaro and Mount Kenya, Africa's highest peaks, as well as Lake Victoria, the second largest lake in the world and the largest on this continent. The latter is the source of the White Nile, the largest branch of the Nile River, which flows northward until it empties into the Mediterranean Sea.

Some of these countries are landlocked—the Central African Republic, Congo, and Democratic Republic of the Congo, but the latter does border on Lake Tanganyika. The remainder have coastlines along the Indian Ocean, Gulf of Aden, and the Red Sea. The land is defined by the Great Rift Valley, a 3,000-mile fault that runs north to south, and was originally formed when massive tectonic plates shifted millions of years ago.

It was from East Africa that humanity spread beyond its origins, moving to all five continents.

West Central Africa

On the Atlantic side of the African continent, the Gulf of Guinea defines the region. Its coastline has a series of exotic names that reveal something of its history—Grain Coast, Ivory Coast, Gold Coast, and Slave Coast. This is an equatorial area of high precipitation (20–40 inches of rain), and high temperatures (75–80 °F). It is a landmass primarily of forest, woodlands, and grasslands, plus mixed-use cropland, and wetland. It is an expanse filled with wildlife and fauna—the major agricultural products are banana, cassava, cattle, citrus fruit, cocoa, coffee, corn, fish, forest products, sheep, sorghum, sugarcane, swine, tea, and tobacco. The area is also rich in industry and mining—aluminum, gold, manganese, titanium, diamonds, manufacturing, petroleum, and processing. West Africa is in the midst of an oil boom today, but, unfortunately, too many corrupt elite benefit instead of improving the lives of the masses. These natural resources are why so many non-Africans have come here, and why it is a target of foreign investment.

Centuries ago, this region experienced the rise and fall of great African empires, like the Mali from the thirteenth century and the Songhay from the fifteenth. Great rivers, such as the Gambia and Niger, flow from the mountains to the shores through forests, savannas, and arid plains to an often swampy coastline.

The region is home to some 14 nation-states, all of which describe themselves as republics. However, their rulers range from democratically elected presidents to dictators and military coup masters. The locale extends from Guinea-Bissau in the northwest corner, south of Senegal, to Congo in the southwest that abuts the Democratic Republic of the Congo. Alphabetically, these countries are: Benin, Burkina Faso, Cameroon, Congo, Cote d'Ivoire, Equatorial Guinea, Gabon, Ghana, Guinea, Guinea-Bissau, Liberia, Nigeria, Sierra Leone, and Togo. The biggest urban center is Lagos, Nigeria. We have chosen Nigeria for a brief cultural analysis. Unfortunately, West Africa continues to be a region of political instability and even civil war, often originating from rebel groups in neighboring countries.

Nigeria

Nigeria's landmass is approximately 356,669 square miles—about twice the size of the state of California. This West African nation is bounded by Benin, Niger, Chad, and Cameroon, as well as the Atlantic Ocean on its southern edge; there have been some border disputes with its neighbors over Lake Chad.

HISTORICAL PERSPECTIVE OVERVIEW

The history of this country and its peoples dates back to the seventh century BCE. In 1861, the British seized the principal city of Lagos, supposedly to end the slave trade then flourishing there. The English social, financial, and political cultural impact has been considerable ever since. Nigeria gained political independence in 1960; it is still a member of the British Commonwealth of Nations, with citizens often traveling to the UK for business, pleasure, or resettlement. English is often the language for business and national affairs, in addition to six different local languages.

Nigeria's rapidly growing population of just under 200 million is composed of 250 tribal groups of which 65 percent are the Hausa-Fulani, Ibo, and Yoruba. These also represent three major language groups (Hausa, Zula, and Swahili). There are five main religious influences present: Muslim (50 percent); Protestant (25 percent); Roman Catholic (12 percent); African Christian (11 percent); and traditional African or indigenous beliefs (10 percent) (all percentages are approximate). As with many African countries, foreign missionaries accompanied European colonists in previous centuries. Today, Christian churches, schools, hospitals, and social institutions have significant influence on the culture, especially in the south, as do comparable Qur anic schooling and enterprises in the north. A quota system guarantees students from the north a share of university places—an undue share, contend the southerners, who view their school system as superior.

CULTURAL GUIDELINES FOR DOING BUSINESS IN NIGERIA

Nigeria's human resources have great potential, and oil is its main income producer today. The literacy rate has risen as a result of the introduction of six years of compulsory education. Over 14 million students are enrolled in elementary and secondary schools and 48 colleges/universities. The Nigerian educational system is based largely on the British system.

SOCIAL STRUCTURE

In Nigeria, the family dominates the social structure. Nigerian tradition places emphasis on one's lineage through the male head of the household. In non-Muslim sections, these familial connections form vast networks that serve as a foundation for one's social identity. Marriage is seen as a way of producing more children to contribute to this lineage or network. Sterility is grounds for divorce. Three forms of marriage exist in Nigeria. Among some Christians and non-Muslims, unlimited polygamy is customary. Wives are acquired through the payment of a "bride price" to the bride's parents. Muslim custom differs in that the number of wives is usually limited to four. Western Christian marriage is relatively uncommon in rural areas, though increasing in the cities.

GROUPS AND RELATIONSHIPS

Among the many tribes, the principal ones are (1) the Hausa, very religious Muslims; (2) the Yoruba, an outgoing, festive people; and (3) the Ibo, excellent merchants, extremely resourceful, hardworking, and conscientious.

The following important attitudes exist in Nigeria, affecting business relationships:

■ *Old family business tradition.* One does not share information because everyone else is a competitor. (This traditional attitude has often been reinforced by subsequent European influences, as opposed to new American management training which encourages the free flow of information, including the sharing of trade knowledge and more open communications. Many young Nigerian businesspeople are US-trained.)
■ *Muslim attitudes.* Predestination rather than free will; reliance on tradition and precedent; mistrust of innovation; unwillingness to take risks; learning by rote rather than by experiments or problem-solving.

COMMUNICATION

A Westerner in Nigeria should not use words such as *native*, *hut*, *jungle*, *witchcraft*, and *costume*. The connotation behind these expressions tends to be that Africa is still a dark continent. Nigeria, as is true with many other parts of Africa, has made great strides in development and is proud of its advancement. Therefore, it is best to remember that a hut is a home and a costume is really clothing. Nigerians want to be friends with foreign visitors, and they are proud to have them in their homes. They will go to great lengths to be a friend, but they do not want to be patronized.

- *Greetings.* Upon meeting a Nigerian business associate, the greeting is Westernized but formal. A simple "Good morning, Mister Opala, how are you?" is accepted as proper. Asking personal questions about one's family is a common practice. Once you have established some degree of familiarity, you can use a first name if the Nigerian initiates it. Always shake hands when greeting someone. It is extremely rude not to acknowledge a person when entering a room or to fail to shake his or her hand.
- *Forms of address.* Nigerians distinguish the levels of familiarity between one another by their forms of address. Friends will call one another by their first names. Older brothers and sisters are very rarely addressed by their first names. An older brother is addressed as N'da and an older sister as N'se, which means "my senior [brother or sister's name]." This is simply a sign of respect toward seniority and age. The expressions *sir* and *ma'am* are always used when speaking to a businessperson, government official, someone older, or someone in a position of authority.

SOCIAL CUSTOMS

Nigerians are a proud and self-confident people. They are extroverted, friendly, and talkative. Nigerians are also known for their hospitality. Consequently, it is possible to make more long-lasting relationships that are less superficial than those in other cultures.

When a friend, acquaintance, or relative becomes ill, it is customary for that person to receive many visitors. Anyone who even remotely knows the sick person will come to visit. It is the Nigerian way of saying, "I want to know for myself how you're feeling."

- *Gender.* As in all of Africa, the role of women in Nigeria is changing with modernization, especially in urban centers. Traditionally, females have always performed the major laboring tasks, from farming to road building. Now, with increased education and opportunity, they are moving up in commerce and industry, as well as in government and the professions.
- *Marriage.* When two people are considering marriage, a proper procedure must be followed. The first step is for the prospective groom to send an intermediary to the woman's home to present the idea of marriage to her parents. Gifts are sent to the woman, and then the man himself comes to the woman's parents to discuss the marriage. If everything is in order with the prospective bride's family, the woman then goes to live with the man's family to make sure this is where she wants to live. If so, the marriage can occur. The dowry involved in the marriage is not a fixed amount. It is an insurance against maltreatment of the woman. It is not until the wife dies and is buried in her natal land that the dowry is paid to her husband, if she has been treated well.

Intermarriage between tribes is rare in Nigeria. There is still rivalry between tribes, and the intent seems to be to try to keep them pure. However, if such an intertribal marriage should occur, oddly enough, the stranger will be treated almost royally by the members of the other tribe. The reason for this is that the nontribe member is viewed as having made a supreme sacrifice by giving up his or her tribe and their traditions and adopting those of the spouse, as they almost always do in this situation.

Most Nigerian cultures are patriarchal. In some areas, particularly the rural ones, polygamy is still prevalent. However, in urban areas, it is much more common to find one-man, one-woman marriages.

TRADITIONS

Nigeria is growing quickly and becoming more modernized and urbanized, but traditions are still very important to the people. Local customs still play a significant role in Nigerian life. One such ritual, though quickly disappearing, is found strictly in the western portion of the country and has to do with tribal marks. When a child reaches the age of two or three years, he or she has the appropriate tribal marks burned into his or her face, very similar to the branding process. These marks reflect tribes or family. When one sees the marks, it is not necessary to ask what the person's last name is or from what tribe he or she comes. It is said that if the child cannot withstand the pain during the ceremony, as there is no anesthesia, he or she is not worthy of that family or tribe. The process is very unhygienic and dangerous and is dying out gradually.

Nigeria is a "right-handed" society. As in many cultures, the left hand is considered unclean, as it is the "toilet hand." It is extremely impolite to extend the left hand to others or to eat with it, even if the person is left-handed.

It is important to reemphasize the matter of age in Nigeria. There is a profound respect for one's elders. Older people are not placed in nursing homes when they become ill. They are taken in by their families, looked after, and revered. The importance of the elderly seems to lie in their capability to pass on family history and tradition.

The custom of eating with one's hands is practiced in Nigeria. If there is a big festival, or even in a private home, where there are foreign visitors not used to this custom, allowances are made and silverware is often provided. However, an honest effort will be greatly appreciated.

BUSINESS TIPS FOR WORKING IN NIGERIA

■ *Meetings.* It will almost always be necessary to deal, in some capacity, with Nigerian government officials. When a meeting is granted, whether with the desired official or someone else, there are important practices to be aware of. First, any significant business transaction is always conducted in person. Any attempt to conduct business either over the telephone or by mail is seen as considering the matter trivial and unimportant. When visiting a colleague's office, tea, coffee, or other refreshments are always available and offered. These refreshments should not be refused, as this may be taken as an offense. Also, refreshments must always be available when the colleague comes to visit the foreign businessperson's office. When commercial visitors are invited to a local colleague's home for dining, if at all possible, the invitation should not be refused.

At state and federal meetings, protocol must be observed. Extreme politeness, respect for authority, and a slower pace are normal. If an authority does not answer your question, it may mean they do not know the answer and do not want to be embarrassed. It is helpful if a foreign businessperson establishes a Nigerian counterpart. One needs expertise in dealing with the Nigerian business community. References should be carefully checked, and choosing someone with influential contacts is important. This local resource will prove invaluable in translating later what was said during a meeting. It takes a long time to become established in the Nigerian business community, and it is who one knows that will make a difference. Connections are important and should be cultivated. When investing in Nigeria, start at the state government level instead of the federal. Each state operates differently, but all want and need business. Consequently, they are very receptive and can greatly facilitate business formalities.

■ *Negotiations.* When conducting negotiations with a Nigerian, the tone of such meetings is generally friendly and respectful. Notice should be taken of titles to be sure the appropriate ones are used correctly. Age is highly respected in Nigeria and often associated with wisdom. Therefore, to maximize chances of success, an older person should be sent to meet with prospective businesspersons. Nigerians assume promises will be kept, so be realistic about delivery dates or price specifications. Furthermore, it is not unusual for a Nigerian worker to try to involve his foreign manager or supervisor in politics. It is much better not to participate in these political discussions as sides will undoubtedly be taken and one's role may be compromised. Subsequently, an air of hostility and tension will be apparent.

■ *Decision-making.* Decision-making is based on a centralized system, and delegation of authority is almost nonexistent. Nigerians cling to authority and are dependent on supervision.

A Nigerian manager in a high-level position may feel obligated to find jobs for his or her family and will not hesitate to "pull strings" to employ them.

■ *Concept of time.* In Nigeria, this can be summed up as unlimited. Lagos, the center of business, is congested, and traffic jams can hold one up for several hours. Consequently, late appointments are common and usually anticipated, and telephone service is sometimes unreliable. Time is, therefore, not of the utmost importance to most Nigerians. As such, punctuality is not prevalent. Although work is important to Nigerians, so is their leisure. Sports are a favorite way to spend time, including the most popular activities of soccer, boxing, and horse racing. Hockey (field), tennis, cricket, polo, golf, rugby, table tennis, and softball are also played.

Southern Africa[11]

The southern tip of the African continent encompasses 11 nations. On the west coast facing the Atlantic Ocean are Angola, Namibia, and South Africa. The latter is the most modern state, bordering on the Indian Ocean, and will be the target for our analysis. Within the region are the small kingdoms of Lesotho and Swaziland. In the region's interior are Zambia, Malawi, Zimbabwe, and Botswana. On the east coast facing the Indian Ocean are Mozambique, plus the island of Madagascar. In this southern area, the largest population centers are along the northwest and southwest coastlines, as well as in the north.

The area's peace and prosperity has been severely constricted by a 30-year civil war in Angola; a lengthy, costly, but successful struggle to overturn the all-white, Afrikaner apartheid government; and the ongoing civil unrest, killings, land grabs, and economic disasters of President Robert Mugabe's administration in Zimbabwe. An exception to this pattern is Botswana, a small, peaceful country of only 1.8 million people, just north of South Africa. It has used its vast diamond wealth wisely to foster education, one of the best on the continent, as well as tourism and a friendly business environment. This country is known to be the least corrupt state, but its sparkling image is marred by a high rate of AIDS and its mistreatment of a most vulnerable ethnic group, the Bushmen, or San, a hunter-gatherer tribal people.

Off the coast of Mozambique is the island of Madagascar, also a part of Southern Africa. Further east in the Indian Ocean are three other small islands. The second of these is Mauritius, an independent republic (Exhibit 17.3).

South Africa[12]

South African society is in the midst of a transformation that could lead to more prosperity, if both the white citizen minority who had been in control and the oppressed black majority now ruling truly share their nation's sociopolitical institutions and power. By their practice of cultural synergy, both may create a multicultural society of equal opportunity.[13] One small indicator of progress is the "Buppies," the growing, upwardly mobile, black professionals. In this multiracial democracy, they can even be found at gatherings of "high society."

HISTORICAL PERSPECTIVE

South Africa has a heritage of pioneering, colonization, wars, and building a modern infrastructure. *Apartheid* is gone—a failed policy of separation of whites and blacks that was internationally condemned and finally abandoned in the 1990s. Three centuries ago, this land became home to Bushmen and Hottentots, Bantu-speaking black tribes. In the mid-seventeenth century, the European whites arrived. First were the Dutch, who built a trading settlement at the Cape of Good Hope. They were joined by Germans and French Huguenot refugees in 1688. Together, these colonists would become known as Boers (farmers). The

E
X
H
I
B
I
T

17.3

EXHIBIT 17.3 MAURITIUS: MULTIDIVERSITY PROGRESS

This isolated island state of only 1,100 square miles gained its independence from Britain in 1968. Then, it was a sugar-based economy with a GDP of $200 per person. But with freedom, the country's GDP has jumped to $7,000 per person and ranks high for good governance. The World Bank has also given the republic a high ranking as the best African country for ease of doing business. With over 100 hotels, it is now a peaceful and popular place with tourists who crave sun, palm trees, and good service. Its capital of Port Louis is an attractive place for offshore banking, hosting 19 global banks. Furthermore, Mauritius is a low-tax gateway for investment into Asia, especially India. The economy also includes food processing, sugar milling, chemical and textile manufacturing, fishing, as well as cattle raising plus the exporting of cut flowers and molasses.

With an economic mindset that welcomes competition, its government has slashed commercial red tape and cut taxes, while reforming labor legislation and promoting itself as a desirable business destination. As a result, unemployment and budget deficits are down, and foreign investments are up. Unfortunately, the republic has to import most of its food and energy, while too much of the economy is concentrated in the hands of a few local conglomerates. These factors are being diminished by a new competition commission and development of new industries. With an independent judiciary and democratic elections, three political parties agree on broad policy directions.

A pluralistic population mix of Africans, Chinese, Europeans, and Indians has religious and cultural differences, but has avoided communal divisions. They speak some seven languages, ranging from English, Creole, and French to Hindi, Urdu, Hakka, and Bojoori. Further, adherents of Christianity, Hinduism, and Islam have learned to tolerate one anothers' beliefs. Surely, a demonstration model for other African nations to emulate!

Source: adapted from "Beyond Beaches and Palm Trees," *The Economist*, October 18, 2008, p. 58.

British invaded and captured the Cape in 1806, gaining formal possession of the colony in 1814 as the result of the Napoleonic wars. To avoid English rule, the Boers migrated to the undeveloped interior of the country from 1835 to 1848, defeating the indigenous Zulu and other tribes in the process. With the discovery of gold and diamonds in that territory, Britain annexed parts of that area that led to the Boer War, which they won in 1902. The British then combined their colonies of Cape and Natal with the Boer Republics of Orange Free State and Transvaal, creating in 1910 the Union of South Africa, today called the Republic of South Africa (RSA).

Thus, this is a nation of four cultural influences or ethnic groups: the native African majority, the minority populations consisting of the Dutch who were to become known as Boers and *Afrikaners*, along with the British and Asian immigrants, the latter mostly from India and designated later as the *Coloureds*. As British power waned, the Afrikaners increasingly took control of the government after the election of their National Party in 1948. During the 1960s, Afrikaners introduced the oppressive apartheid system separating blacks from whites, creating two unequal communities. Another flawed policy was launched that forced settlement for the majority black African population in separate and supposedly independent homelands (e.g., Lesotho and Swaziland). Since the 1960s, domestic turmoil and violence caused by these inhumane political actions brought international protests and boycotts, including trade sanctions by the US and condemnation by the United Nations.

To fight for black human rights, the African National Congress (ANC) was formed in 1955 and eventually coalesced with other black groups' campaigns against the white power government. Finally, the economic and social impact of multinational sanctions led to the resignation in 1989 of the president of the RSA, P. W. Botha. His replacement, F. W. de Klerk, implemented a series of democratic reforms, beginning with the freeing of political prisoners, the desegregating of institutions, and the legal recognition of the ANC as a political party. The outcome was the signing of a peace agreement between the latter and the ruling elite providing for power-sharing, the dismantling of apartheid, and the holding of open elections. In the 1994 election, all RSA citizens voted for the first time, electing ANC leader and former political prisoner Nelson Mandela as president, and de Klerk as vice-president of a multiethnic government. For their peacekeeping success, both men were awarded the Nobel Peace Prize. Since then, a political evolution, not revolution, has been under way.

The RSA is a laboratory of social experimentation that has implications for the whole continent. With the ascendancy of the ANC leadership to the national government in 1994, and a new approach to white/black power-sharing, the inequitable, segregated, apartheid political and social system is very slowly being transformed into a more democratic, multi-party one. Despite an odious and corrosive historical legacy, here the change process and progress are under way. Suffrage policy was at first limited to whites only, and then extended to the *Coloureds*, and now finally includes the blacks, formerly restricted to voting in local "homeland" or township elections. The shift in political parties and power has been from the National Party and Conservative Party to the ANC, the Inkatha Freedom Party (Zulu), and the Democratic Party. Overall, the current government is striving to meet educational and training needs for a global economy and a knowledge society.

Postapartheid presidents have all been from the ANC, and struggle with human resource and economic improvements for all. They have been slow to counter the AIDS epidemic in the country, and to provide human rights leadership relative to nasty regimes elsewhere. With refugees flocking in from nearby Zimbabwe, they have been reluctant to confront its failed president, Robert Mugabe, or to endorse the International Criminal Courts prosecution of Omar al-Bashir, the Sudan's president accused of genocide. They have not implemented the vision of the revered Nelson Mandela when he was elected president: *Human rights will be the light that guides our foreign affairs*. Africa's richest nation has yet to become a "beacon of hope" to the world's oppressed. However, the government has been a leading peace-maker in the New Partnership for Africa's Development, which promotes continental democracy and effective governance through a peer-review system. South Africa has sent troops to mediate conflicts in Darfur, Burundi, the Central African Republic, and Congo. At home, it has adopted a progressive constitution, prohibiting discrimination and promoting civil liberties. Its officials have sought to provide more adequate housing and reproductive healthcare for citizens. Archbishop Desmond Tutu observed that turning a blind eye to oppression outside South Africa is "a betrayal of our noble past. . . . If others had used the arguments we are using today when we asked them for support against apartheid, we might have still have been unfree."[14]

CULTURAL GUIDELINES FOR BUSINESS IN SOUTH AFRICA

Black Africans consist of nine tribal groups—Zulu (the largest), Xhosas, North and South Sothos, Tswanas, Shangaan-Tsongas, Swazis, South Ndebeles, and Vendas. Each has its own special cultural heritage, language, and sense of identity. During the apartheid period, tribal groups were assigned by the racist government to ten ethnic "homelands" that were supposed to have self-rule, but actually were dependent on the white statecraft—these are being dismantled under the new regime. Although English and Afrikaans (a Dutch derivation) are the official languages, the blacks among the four major tribes speak varying forms of Bantu. The whites in South Africa are divided into two groups—the English-speaking descendants of English, Scottish, and Irish settlers, and the Afrikaans-speaking offspring of the Dutch, German, and French colonials; there are also the English-speaking *Coloureds* descendants of early white setters, native Hottentots, imported Dutch East Indian slaves, and indentured laborers from India (Hindi speakers).

SOCIAL CONDITIONS IN SOUTH AFRICA

■ *Family structure* in the black community has been somewhat destabilized by past apartheid policies and its constraints; dislocation caused by job seeking contributes to many people living in poverty. In the black extended family, there is normally great respect manifested toward the elderly and obedience to parents. In contrast, the white community's family is nuclear, close-knit, and privileged, though declining in affluence and influence. The Truth and Reconciliation Commission enabled families from both sides to testify or confess about the brutality of 40 years of the apartheid regime, and to try to move on with reconstruction.

■ *An emerging middle class* is slowly happening among the black community—up to 40 percent of the total population. Affirmative action and black empowerment programs have opened up the job market and management positions. Today, some 70 percent of the workforce is black African.

■ *Lifestyle* is better for many black Africans since the early 2000s—their society is humming with activity and opportunity amid poverty. Among the blacks, one can find more vibrancy, naturalness, and brotherhood, but it is sometimes marred by intertribal conflict and power struggles. The rates of crime, violence, and alcohol abuse are up, again partially because of past Afrikaner practices of uprooting people (e.g., putting migrant laborers into hostels, and paying too many wages in *papsak*, or wine).

■ *Sports* are a positive influence among South Africans. While a prisoner, Nelson Mandela taught himself about rugby because his Afrikaner jailors liked it so much.[15] When he was released from jail, Mandela inspired black Africans in many ways, including sports; he coaxed all his countrymen toward more civilized government and behavior. Having studied the culture of his opponents, he promoted rugby as a bridge across the racial chasm.

■ *Work environment* is gradually improving for all employees. However, in government, the ANC, a former revolutionary party, is still authoritarian and prizes political loyalty. Its officials have not mastered the art of administration and science of management, while being deployed from one job position to another. The shortage of qualified personnel has led to many job vacancies, especially in the financial and banking sectors.

■ *Healthcare and social services* are beginning to deteriorate, though the country has the most organized and functioning healthcare system in Africa. The quality of life for average citizens is being severely undermined by the spread of diseases, especially AIDS. The administration of President Mbeki was absurdly slow in responding to the epidemic of 5.2 million HIV-infected citizens. The UN expects South Africa's GDP by the 2020s to be lowered by 17 percent. With about 1,000 dying daily from this illness, the government is finally waking up to the scourge of AIDS and its implications—a comprehensive regime is under way to combat the pandemic with antiretroviral drugs.

■ *Criminal justice* is weak in South Africa—the system suffers from too many unemployed criminals who either do not get caught, or when they are arrested, are not likely to be convicted. Although the government is spending more on law enforcement, crime statistics show the country to be among the most violent in the world. The old hatred of police lingers, along with a legacy of firearms. Poorly paid police ranks are riddled by corruption, inadequate equipment, insufficient training, and ineptness (about one-quarter are functionally illiterate, and large numbers do not even have a driver's license to drive themselves to crime scenes).

ECONOMIC AND SOCIAL CHALLENGES

■ *Economic development.* South Africa still has the strongest and most diversified economy on the African continent. Although it has only 6 percent of the sub-Saharan people, it accounts for one-third of its GDP. With a diversified economy and First-World financial services, the economy has structurally changed and is more internationally competitive. It is strong not only in minerals and raw materials, but increasingly in high technologies. A strong central bank and an improving legal system, as well as a fair road and transport infrastructure, all contribute to development. Although foreign investments did not grow as anticipated with the lifting of global economic sanctions and diminishing civil protests, the global companies that have come are pleased overall with their experience and are expanding.

The economic situation is well summarized in the township of Soweto, Johannesburg. In what was once a byword for violence and black deprivation, shiny new cars are parked in front of elegant houses protected by security systems. Shopping malls, banks, and tourists are now visible. Black economic empowerment is evident throughout the country.

■ *Twenty-first century needs.* This country produced two of the greatest modern African leaders—Nelson Mandela and Desmond Tutu, both Nobel Peace Prize winners. Mandela, as the first African president, and Archbishop Tutu personified the vision of creating a country with a nonracial future. Together, they established a Truth and Reconciliation Commission, engaging enlightened leadership like theirs, in both the public and private sector. Leadership is South Africa's primary need; leadership that is concerned for the whole citizenry, not just for his/her own community. That type of leadership would address challenges, such as promoting the following:

- *Pluralism and inclusiveness*, which allows for reasonable dissent, compromise, give-and-take, and protection of human rights.
- *Educational and training improvements* at all levels for the development of a more knowledgeable and competent workforce.
- *Rebuilding strong family life and childcare*, especially in those African homes and villages devastated by past apartheid policies and currently by AIDS.
- *Economic development* without graft and corruption that improves the whole society, especially the black African and colored poor.
- *Political diversity and inclusiveness* so that all citizens participate in voting, and parties other than the ANC are given the opportunity for more leadership participation in a government that is less centralized (e.g., Democratic Alliance). As former President Thabo Mbeki stated in 2007, the country needs to pursue a *commonly defined national agenda*, something he was unable to accomplish during his administration. If such a new mission statement for South Africa is ever written, it should emphasize "bridge building" among the many elements needed in a still-divided society (Exhibit 17.4).

BUSINESS TIPS FOR WORKING WITH SOUTH AFRICANS

With a continent as vast and diverse as this, it is difficult to generalize on the preferred business and trade practices. South African business customs, for example, require some flexibility, depending on the circumstances. The white business protocols are comparable to those of Europe and North America, whereas those of Indian heritage may seem more like the commercial environment found in India. However, in what is typically referred to as *black Africa*, whether in the west, east, or south, the following observations may prove useful. These observations supplement those made earlier in this chapter on "Cultural Characteristics of Africa."

EXHIBIT 17.4 THE NEW SOUTH AFRICA

Since the 1990s when the ANC triumphantly took power in South Africa's first multiracial democratic elections, the country has plotted its course to relative stability, democracy, and prosperity. It is even beginning to lead the continent in an entirely new way, urging other nations there to emulate its example. Under Nelson Mandela's leadership, the ANC government campaigned to alleviate poverty and degradation of apartheid victims, without resorting to counterproductive populism. While there have been some improvements, there is growing impatience over the pace of change in South Africa. Mandela's vision of a "rainbow nation" has slowed to a crawl.

Yet, from education to foreign policy to crime-fighting, the inhabitants have found creative solutions to their problems. The government has presided over 87 months of economic growth (currently 5 percent per year), low budget deficits, and low inflation, while trying to encourage free enterprise. Buoyant domestic demand has been accompanied by the sort of foreign investment that some thought would never come. But despite a 5 percent GDP growth, the unemployment rate has risen and has affected 27 percent of the population. Governance policy has provided more money for social program grants, mainly for child support and pensions to some ten million people, as well as for public works, mainly to stimulate job creation, consumer demand, and tourism.

Furthermore, there are hopeful experiments to benefit children from squatters' camps, such as an extraordinary school called Sekolo Sa Bonrokgo in the northern suburbs of Johannesburg. There, 25 dedicated teachers inspire black students to achieve remarkable academic progress. As the lack of quality education is the single most important factor holding back the country's development, such innovations need to be multiplied.

The continent needs a strong South Africa, one prepared to go beyond traditional agendas, and to make a commitment to good governance, human rights, and democracy as enshrined in the goals of the African Union.

Source: excerpted and adapted from Crokett, R. "Chasing the Rainbow: A Survey of South Africa." *The Economist*, April 8, 2006, 12-page insert (www.economist.com/surveys).

■ *Meetings*. Business is normally discussed in an office, bar, or restaurant, but always outside the home. What happens in the home is considered private. When invited to someone's residence for a meal, do not discuss business. When an African is the host of such meetings, he or she will pay for everyone. If a foreigner is the host, he or she should pay. If a foreigner receives an invitation to a *braaivlets*, or barbecue, it is an important part of getting to know business associates better without discussing business *per se*. It is customary for outsiders to bring a token gift, such as a beverage or candy.

■ *Communications*. Most businesspeople have business cards, which are exchanged readily. After some small talk on encountering a foreigner, white South Africans tend to get down to the purpose or agenda for the meeting, whereas those of other races may make long inquiries about your health and family before getting down to business.

■ *Attitudes.* South Africans generally are more low-key in their business discussion, searching for "win–win" opportunities for both parties. They are wary of foreigners who try to take advantage of them, so resist high-pressure and cut-throat tactics, and emotional appeals. Ordinarily, in the world of commerce and government, people do not like to be rushed into decisions about a deal. The local merchants of Indian or Chinese heritage are experienced and shrewd traders, and may be more aggressive in their negotiations.

■ *Seniority.* As indicated previously, traditionally, age commands respect. Age and wisdom are seen as identical, and the norms of the elders must be followed to ensure smooth business dealings. Some of this tribal heritage is retained in some business environments.

■ *Gender.* As women become better educated and involved in business life, the traditional precedent of man before woman is giving way to a more equalitarian approach. This is confirmed by the national policy of affirmative action to ensure equal opportunity.

In Exhibit 17.5, the significant role of China in Africa can be seen. Currently, Chinese presence is even stronger.

EXHIBIT 17.5 CHINA IN AFRICA

During the Cold War, China entered Africa to encourage solidarity with socialistic states there by aiding with infrastructure projects, as well as supporting liberation movements. Now, China rapidly buys up African oil, metals, and farm products to fuel its own economic growth. Chinese officials, businesspeople, and laborers are flocking to this continent in ever-increasing numbers. For example, in 1991 only 300 Chinese foreigners lived in Zambia; by 2008, the number had jumped to 3,000. Similar trends can be seen in other African states such as Algeria, Angola, Congo, Kenya, Morocco, Nigeria, and South Africa. In 2008, the PRC president, Hu Jintao, not only visited some of these countries, but invited 30 African leaders to a Sino-African summit in Beijing!

With China's economy growing on average 9 percent annually, and its foreign trade increasing five-fold, it needs African natural resources more than just ideology and influence. Its trade and investment in Africa is $50 billion or more. China looks for copper and cobalt in the DRC and Zambia; for iron ore and platinum in South Africa; for timber in Cameroon, Congo-Brazzaville, and Gabon; for oil primarily in Nigeria, as well as Congo, Equatorial Guinea, and Gabon. Thus, Chinese trade with African sources continually expands. China also contributes aid and investment to this continent (over $10 million yearly), as well as canceling African debts, thus assisting the development of infrastructure and housing. Further, Chinese aid is straightforward, without the bureaucratic demands of the IMF and World Bank. China builds strategic relationships and agreement with African states. Its assistance includes investments, professional training, and providing Chinese doctors, technicians, and workers to Africa. In sharing its technology, many African states benefit, such as building and launching a satellite for Nigeria. Also, China is becoming a processor of commodities, cheaper goods services, and military hardware to the continent. By buying African, the PRC reduces its own trade deficits and offers competition to Westerners there. Yet, there are concerns for human and economic rights in China's projects—for example, alleged mistreatment of workers in a Chinese-owned mine in Zambia; technical assistance, which necessitates the Chinese remain to maintain railways and pipelines built mainly with Chinese laborers; support for the Sudan government when it commits genocide against its own people in Darfur; resisting democratic reforms in countries ruled by the "big man"; and blocking UN reforms and sanctions against failed administrations, such as that of Robert Mugabe in Zimbabwe. It would appear that this new interloper is no more altruistic than its colonial predecessors on this great continent. In the long term, the ultimate question is: Will China contribute to lifting Africa from a Third-World to a First-World civilization? There can be synergy between China and its African partners that is "win–win" for both partners.

Source: adapted from "China in Africa: Never Too Late to Scramble," *The Economist*, October 28, 2006, pp. 53–56. Khanna, P. "China Moves In," in *The Second World*. New York: Random House, 2008, pp. 188–190.

E X H I B I T 17.5

CONCLUSIONS

When comparing cultures, such as those of America and Africa, and how they affect the business environment or humanitarian service, it is necessary to understand that the US is a low-context culture. It is technologically and futuristically oriented with an emphasis on individual achievement rather than on group participation. In the communication process, a low-context culture places meaning in the exact verbal description of an event. Individuals in such a culture rely on the spoken word. In contrast, Africa's culture is high-context. In the communication process, much of the meaning comes not from the words, but is internalized in the person. Meaning comes from the environment and is sought in the relationships between the ideas expressed in the communication process. High-context cultures, more so than low-context cultures, tend to be more human-oriented and to value the extended family. Perhaps this closing quotation may stimulate readers' thinking about Africa: "No other continent has endured such an unspeakably bizarre combination of foreign thievery and foreign goodwill."[16] The outside world needs to appreciate and give back to Africa for its enormous contributions to humanity and multiple nations.

MIND STRETCHING

1   Why is it important for all members of the human family, now consisting of 6.5 billion people, to appreciate Africa's past, present, and future potential?

2   How has past European colonialism impacted today's Africans, in contrast to present Asian influence on them?

3   What and where is sub-Sahara Africa, and how do its 48 states differ from the rest of the continent?

4   What is the implication of the fact that, in Africa, 900 million inhabitants live in the countryside, while rapid urbanization is under way?

5   How can those who live outside of Africa contribute to development of its human and natural resources, to combating poverty and disease on this continent, and to promoting peace and better governance?

6   What is the connection, if any, between one-third of Africa's countries with soaring oil revenues, and cycles of unrest, violence, and civil wars on the continent?

7   Discuss Acemoglu and Robinson's theory described in chapter 1 of *Why Nations Fail*, as it applies to Africa.

AFRICAN RESOURCES

Beside a search on the internet for Africa or any country therein, consult www.africaguide.com; www.joeant.com/DIR/info/get/7375/18588; and www.sul.stanford.edu/depts/ssrg/africa/guide.html. A very useful learning system is *Africa*, produced by Palm World Voices (www.palmworldvoices.com). This compact packet focuses on African peoples and their business. Each package contains a National Geographic map of African peoples and their music; a booklet with pictures entitled "Africa the Musical Continent"; a visual DVD; and an audio CD on the music of Africa. Inquire about other productions, such as BabbaMaal: Senegal. Specific country reports are available from the Reprints Department, The Economist Newspaper Group, Inc., 111 W. 57th St., 10019. New York, NY 10019, USA (www.economist.com/surveys).

Details on every country in the world, including those in Africa, are available in the CIA *World Factbook* (www.cia.gov/cia/publications/factbook/geos/ct.html). The National Geographic Society periodically publishes updated maps on Africa (www.nationalgeographic/africa). For example, the map supplement to their magazine in September 2001 was entitled "Africa Today," and in September 2005 it was "Africa the Human Footprint." Also see the National Trade Data Bank, International Trade Administration, US Department of Commerce, Washington, DC, 20230 (Tel: 1/800-USA TRADE #4/5; www.export.gov; click on "market research" and then "country commercial guide" and choose a particular African state.) For hard copy or diskette of any African country guide, call National Technical

Information Service (1-800/553-NTIS). There is a country code for information on all nations of Chapters 12–18 (telephone hotline, 1-202-482-1064 or 1860). Major US cities also have local offices of USDC with commercial advisers to provide counseling and resources to businesspersons seeking data or connections abroad in a specific country or area within that target culture. Also consult the local telephone directory under "Government Pages" for the nearest listing of the US Government Offices and the Federal Commerce Department.

NOTES

1   Davis, W., Harrison, D., and Herbert Howell, C. (eds.). *Book of the Peoples of the World: A Guide to Cultures*. Washington, DC: National Geographic, 2002, 2008.

2   Dowden, R. *Africa: Altered States, Ordinary Miracles*. London: Portobello Books, 2008. Meredith, M. *The Future of Africa: A History of Fifty Years of Independence*. New York: Perseus Books/Public Affairs, 2006. Iliffe, J. *Africans: The History of a Continent*. Cambridge: Cambridge University Press, 2007. Pitcher, G. *Lonely Planet's Africa*. New York: Lonely Planet Publisher, 2007. "Africa: Whatever You Thought, Think Again," *National Geographic Magazine*, Special Issue, September 2005. Guest, R. "How to Make Africa Smile: A Survey of Sub-Saharan Africa," *The Economist*, January 17, 2004, p. 16, www.economist.com/surveys. Oldfield, S. (ed.). *The Trade in Wildlife: Regulation for Conservation*. New York: Earthscan, 2003. Peterson, D. *Eating Apes*. Berkeley, CA: University of California Press, 2003.

3   *New York Times*, December 29, 2016, pp. 1, 11.

4   "The World in 2017," *The Economist*.

5   Painter, N. I. *Creating Black America: African-American History and Its Meaning*. Oxford: Oxford University Press, 2006. Hill, K. H. *Religious Education in the African-American Tradition*. Danvers, MA: Chalice Press, 2007.

6   Salgado, S. *Africa*. New York: Tachen, 2007. Obradovic, N. (ed.). *The Anchor Book of Modern African Stories*, 2nd edn. New York: Anchor, 2003. Richmond, Y. and Gestrin, P. *Into Africa: Intercultural Insights*. Boston, MA: Nicholas Brealey/Intercultural Press, 1998. Wiredu, K. *Cultural Universals and Particulars: An African Perspective*. Bloomington, IN: Indiana University Press, 1997; Arnold, M. J., Geary, G. M., and Hardin, K. L. (eds.). *African Material Culture*. Bloomington, IN: Indiana University Press, 1996. Ojisku, U. J. *Surviving the Iron Curtain: A Microscopic View of What It Was Like in a War-Torn Region*. Baltimore, MD: Publish-America, 2007. Lovejoy, P. E. *Transitions in Slavery: A History of Slavery in Africa*. Cambridge: Cambridge University Press, 2000.

7   Ibid.

8   Ham, A. *West Africa*. New York: Lonely Planet, 2006. Vansina, J. *How Societies Are Born: Governance in West Central Africa Before 1600*. Charlottesville, VA: University of Virginia Press, 2005. Falola, T. and Heston, M. *A History of Nigeria*. Cambridge: Cambridge University Press, 2008.

9   Diagram Group, *North Africa: Islam, and the Mediterranean World*. New York: Frank Cass Publications, 2005. Davis, D. *Resurrecting the Granary of Rome: Environmental History and French Colonial Expansion in North Africa*. Athens, OH: Ohio New University Press, 2007.

10 Diagram Group. *History of East Africa*. New York: Frank Cass Publications, 2003. Fitzpatrick, M. and Parkinson, T. *Lonely Planet's East Africa*. New York: Lonely Planet, 2009. Davitt, N. *Kenya: A Country in the Making*. New York: W. W. Norton, 2008. Marcus, H. G. *History of Ethiopia*. Berkeley, CA: University of California Press, 2008. Johnson, D. H. *The Root Causes of Sudan's Civil Wars*. Bloomington, IN: University of Indiana Press, 2002. Flint, J. and de Waal, A. *Darfur: A New History of a Long War*. New York: Zed Books, 2008. Barz, G. *Music in East Africa: Experience Music, Expressing Culture*. Oxford: Oxford University Press, 2004.

11   Meredith, M. *Diamonds, Gold, and War: The British, the Boers, and the Making of South Africa*. New York: Public Affairs/Perseus Group, 2008. Murphy, A., Armstrong, K., Firestone, M., and Fitzpatrick, M. *Southern Africa*. New York: Lonely Planet, 2007. Ehret, C. *An African Classical Age: Eastern and Central Africa in World History, 1000 B.C. to A.D. 400*. Charlottesville, VA: University of Virginia Press, 2001.

12   Cockett, R. "Chasing the Rainbow: A Survey of South Africa," *The Economist*, April 8, 2006, p. 12. Grimond, J. "A Survey of South Africa: Africa's Great Black Hope," *The Economist*, February 24, 2001, p. 16. Sadiman, J. *South Africa's "Black" Market: How to Do Business with Africans*. Boston, MA: Nicholas Brealey/Intercultural Press, 2000. The authors acknowledge that the insights for this profile were partially obtained from: "Culturegram for the Republic of South Africa," *Culturegrams*, David M. Kennedy Center for International Studies, Brigham Young University; Carlin, J. *Playing the Enemy: Nelson Mandela and the Game That Made a Nation*. New York: Penguin Books, 2008. For further information about this nation and its culture, contact the Embassy of South Africa (3051 Massachusetts Ave., NW, Washington, DC 20008, USA) and the South African Tourism Board (747 Third Ave., 20th Floor, New York, NY 10017 or 9841 Airport Blvd., Ste. 1524, Los Angeles, CA 90045, USA).

13   Lewis, R. D. *The Cultural Imperative: Global Trends in the 21st Century*. Boston, MA: Nicholas Brealey/Intercultural Press, 2003. Khanna, P. *The Second World: Empires and Influence in the New Global Order*. New York: Random House, 2008, chapter 21.

14   "South Africa and the World: The See-No-Evil Foreign Policy," *The Economist*, November 15, 2008, pp. 55–56.

15   Carlin, *Playing the Enemy*. Also see "Briefing South Africa: The Long Journey of a Young Democracy," *The Economist*, March 3, 2007, pp. 32–34.

16   Kingsolver, B. *The Poisonwood Bible*. New York: HarperCollins, 1998.

18 DOING BUSINESS IN CANADA AND THE UNITED STATES

There are known knowns. These are things we know that we know. There are known unknowns. That is to say, there are things that we know we don't know. But there are also unknown unknowns. There are things we don't know we don't know.

Donald Rumsfeld[1]

There is nothing more terrible than ignorance in action [Es ist nichts schrecklicher al seine taetige Unwiissenheit].

Johann Wolfgang von Goethe[2]

Americans should never underestimate the constant pressure on Canada the mere presence of the United States has produced. . . . Living next to you is in some ways like sleeping with an elephant. No matter how friendly and even-tempered the beast . . . one is affected by every twitch and grunt. It should not therefore be expected that . . . this Canada, should project itself as a mirror image of the United States.

Pierre Trudeau[3]

After reading and studying the concepts, examples, and illustrations in Chapter 18, readers should be able to understand and appreciate:

1   Differences between Canadian and American business environments in terms of ethics and levels of corruption, quality of life, and ease of starting up and doing business.
2   Differences in Jungian psychology that produce differing national characters between Canada, the US, and the French Canadian province of Quebec (significantly different in itself), and how they affect styles of business communication.
3   Differences in approaches to negotiation that can make Americans look very alien to Canadians, and vice versa.
4   American and Canadian mainstream cultural contexts as well as ethnic subcultures having different issues and concerns from the mainstream.
5   Aboriginal issues that may be leading to a reshaping of the Canadian political environment. Aboriginal nations existing within Canada and the US represent a growing and important emerging market as well as a cultural group that has been discriminated against by mainstream culture since time immemorial. In recent years they have engaged in political action in both countries, asserting their rights to equal treatment with non-Aboriginals.

INTRODUCTION

The US and Canada are considered on both sides of their border to have very similar national and business cultures.[4] To a large extent, this assumption has been supported by a number of older studies showing that American and Canadian values and attitudes tended to cluster together and were different from clusters of other nations and national cultures.[5] More recent studies have highlighted differences. For example, Massey[6] found that the two countries had different psychosocial national characters that particularly affected predominant communication styles. National character was defined as a psychological disposition built into the personalities of individuals making up a society or culture that differentiated their collective thinking and behavior in identifiable ways.[7]

Certainly, the two nations have long shared a very close trade relationship. Since the signing of the Free Trade Agreement (FTA) in 1988, and the inclusion of Mexico in the North American Free Trade Agreement (NAFTA) that superseded the FTA in 1994, Canada and the US have each been the other's top trading partner. In 2015, trade with the US accounted for 71.7 percent of Canadian exports and imports. Trade with Canada accounted for 18.6 percent of American exports and imports. Trade between the two countries was valued at $750 billion in 2015, with Canada the number one trading partner of 35 of 50 American states, and nine million American jobs dependent on trade with Canada.[8] Trade with the US generates about one-quarter of Canadian GDP.

Canadian and American businesspeople have tended to assume that business practices are consistently the same on both sides of the border. When the Canadian ambassador to the US asks his audiences if there is a difference, Americans "politely say no, not really," while Canadians say "the opposite."[9] Yet Canadians have generally assumed, despite mounting evidence, that business strategies that have been successful in Canada will be equally successful in the US—but this has not been the case.[10] Between 20 and 50 percent of successful Canadian businesses that enter American markets are unsuccessful there.[11] Target, the second largest discount retailer in the US, was recently spectacularly unsuccessful at entering Canada. Opening its first store in March 2013, it had 133 Canadian locations by January 2015 when it filed for bankruptcy. It had closed all locations by April of that year.

Certainly, the US is a tempting target for Canadian companies. The largest Canadian regional markets are in the provinces of Ontario and Quebec, but Quebec is a French-speaking province and provincial law requires that business be conducted in French, including product labeling and store signage. It seems easier to English Canadian (Anglophone) businesspeople located in Western Canada to enter nearby English-speaking markets in the Midwest or western US than to manage stores in much more distant Ontario, or to operate in an entirely different language in Quebec.[12] Canada is an equally tempting target for American businesspeople who prefer to do business in a politically stable and English-speaking country where there is less perceived uncertainty (see Chapter 3). Canada's economy is only about the size of California's, but it is 59 percent the size of the UK's (and 124 percent of Australia's),[13] and just across the border rather than across an ocean. However, research has demonstrated that Canadian and American retail purchasers have different cultural expectations, intentionally build different kinds of business relationships, and communicate and negotiate differently. French Canadians communicate differently in business contexts from both English Canadians and Americans, while Chinese Canadians (a rapidly growing cultural minority) conduct their business very much as would be encountered in China (see Chapter 14). Evans, Lane, and O'Grady called these kinds of cultural differences "unobtrusive barriers" to successful commercial relationships.[14]

The purpose of this chapter was to help Canadians and Americans understand how they are culturally different from each other in their approaches to business so that both may be more successful in what is the largest bilateral trading relationship in the world.[15] It is equally important for businesspeople from other countries to understand these differences. Canada and the US are two of the most politically stable markets in the world and represent high investment safety. In addition, because of NAFTA, investments made in products or services that will be produced with more than 50 percent content in

Canada, the US, or Mexico may be sold without duties or tariffs in all three national markets. The first section of this chapter discusses the ways in which Canadians and Americans conduct their business differently. In the second and third sections, the US and Canada are discussed separately in terms of key cultural aspects. Both countries are multicultural, with significantly large cultural minorities that result in regional internal cultures. Within these cultural subgroups, approaches to business and critical issues may substantially differ.

AMERICAN–CANADIAN COMPARISONS

A useful way to understand American and Canadian business attitudes and practices is through directly comparing how they differ from each other. There are a number of studies that compare the two economies, and the ease of doing business in each country. There are studies comparing how Americans and Canadians approach problem-solving, decision-making, and how they are different in the ways they negotiate in the process of building effective business relationships. There are even differences in the ways they define and regulate business ethics. Exhibit 18.1 compares the two nations on a number of economic criteria.

EXHIBIT 18.1 COMPARATIVE ECONOMIC AND SOCIAL INDICES

Index	Canadian economy	American economy
Exports	Ranked 12th	Ranked 2nd (3× more than Canada)
Exports per capita	Ranked 25th	Ranked 50th (3× less than Canada)
Economic importance	Ranked 7th	Ranked 1st
GDP	Ranked 12th	Ranked 2nd (9× Canada)
GDP per capita	Ranked 8th	Ranked 10th (5 percent less than Canada)
GDP value final goods produced	Ranked 88th	Ranked 160th (50 percent less than Canada)
Population in poverty	Ranked 8th	Ranked 34th (61 percent more than Canada)
Public debt	85.4 percent of GDP	70 percent of GDP (22 percent less than Canada)

Source: "Economy Stats: Canada vs. United States," www.nationmaster.com/compare/Canada/United-States/Economy (retrieved November 12, 2016).

Economic comparisons

Economically speaking, the US has a weaker and lower-performing economy than Canada when measured on a per capita basis (see selected indices in Exhibit 18.1). The population of the US is approximately ten times greater than that of Canada. Its GDP, however, is only nine times larger. The US is poorer, with GDP per capita lower than that of Canada, with a higher percentage of its population living below the poverty line despite average American incomes per capita being 25 percent higher.[16] This may not be surprising since real wages for American workers, after inflation, have been flat or even declining for decades, and today's average hourly wage has the same purchasing power as it did in 1979.[17] In contrast, Canadian real wages have grown faster than the average for G20 countries, including at 5 percent per year between 2007 and 2013.[18] Canada is also a stronger international exporter than the US on a per capita basis, suggesting Canadians are oriented more toward grasping business opportunities in the world outside their country than are Americans.

Canadians would argue that their country has sacrificed economically to produce a better and more supportive social environment for all its citizens. Universal Medicare is an obvious example that the US has only incompletely addressed through "Obamacare" which the incoming (in 2017) Republican administration has promised to repeal. Even with Obamacare, approximately 15 percent of Americans still lack health insurance coverage, and those with coverage may pay considerably more than in Canada.[19]

In 2015, Canada had a substantial trade surplus of $15 billion with the US, which received 75 percent of Canadian merchandise exports. Canada was the largest US foreign energy supplier, and the top source for US uranium. Canada's proven oil reserves were the third largest in the world after Saudi Arabia and Venezuela, and Canada was the fifth largest oil-producing country in the world. If and when the Keystone XL pipeline is approved, as promised, virtually all Canadian oil will be shipped to, or through, the US.

Ease of doing business

The World Bank compares a number of statistics on an annual basis, ranking all 190 nations in the world on various criteria related to doing business. The 2017 rankings for the US and Canada are found in Exhibit 18.2.[20] Both countries are in the top quartile of those facilitating business, though for most criteria business has it easier in the US.

This exhibit is, however, more useful for predicting the kinds of problems Americans would face doing business in Canada and vice versa. A problem would be a situation that is unexpected based on one's existing experience. The US seems to generally be an easier place to do business than most other countries, including Canada. Getting electricity seems likely to be a Third World experience in Canada. On the other hand, Canada is an easier business environment for start-up, investor protection, and especially lower taxes. Canada's total tax load, however, is 38.4 percent of GDP compared with 28.2 percent in the US.

E
X
H
I
B
I
T

18.2

EXHIBIT 18.2 WORLD BANK: EASE OF DOING BUSINESS

Topic rankings (of 185)	Canadian rank	American rank
Ease of doing business	22	8
Starting a business	2	51
Dealing with construction permits	57	39
Getting electricity	108	36
Registering property	43	36
Getting credit	7	2
Protecting minority investors	7	41
Paying taxes	17	36
Trading across borders	46	35
Enforcing contracts	112	20
Resolving insolvency	15	5
Average score	39.6	28.1

Source: World Bank Group, "Doing Business: Measuring Business Regulations," www.doingbusiness.org/data/exploreeconomies (retrieved November 12, 2016).

Canadian business taxes are quite low compared to the US—10 percent in Alberta and 11 percent in British Columbia, for example. So, personal taxation is higher.

There are other criteria that favor doing business in Canada over the US. Forbes did its own evaluation of the best countries in the world for business. It evaluated 130 countries on property rights, innovation, taxes, technology, corruption, freedom (personal, trade, and monetary), red tape, investor protection, and stock market performance—all equally weighted. Canada was ranked 7th, behind Denmark, New Zealand, Norway, Ireland, Sweden, and Finland. The US was ranked 22nd, just ahead of Japan and just behind Taiwan. Saudi Arabia was 74th, Russia 81st, China 94th, and India 97th. Iran was the least desirable.[21]

The US News[22] also ranked the overall best countries for business for 2016. It covered a variety of metrics, including adventure, citizenship criteria, cultural influence, support for entrepreneurship, cultural heritage, successful people, openness for business, power, and quality of life. Canada was ranked number 2 after Germany. The US was ranked number 4 after the UK, and ahead of Sweden and Japan. Canada ranked higher than the US despite its $44,800 GDP/capita (PPP[23]) being significantly lower than the American $54,600 GDP/capita (PPP). By contrast, China was ranked 17th, India 22nd, and Russia 24th. Perhaps this result was explained in part by a CNN survey[24] that found that Canada was the 6th happiest country while the US was 13th. Denmark was 1st, and Syria was last at 156th.

Jungian personality types, communication styles, and national culture

In previous chapters we discussed psychosocial national character[25] in terms of four extraverted communications styles (Chapter 2), and four introverted problem-solving styles (Chapter 11) based on Jungian personality research.[26] In Chapters 12, 14, and 15 we combined the problem-solving and communications styles to produce comparative national characters for the national cultures being discussed in those chapters. When we do the same here for Canada and the US, we find that the predominant problem-solving psychological type is Si, or Introverted Sensing, for both countries. In Chapter 11, Si was defined in the following way.

> *Introverted Sensing (Si)*: Si individuals work quietly, systematically, and in-depth to achieve useful results. They deal in facts and details in a careful and orderly fashion, even reporting a photographic memory for details. Si individuals are thorough and conscientious but discount any data that are not sensory. They distrust imaginative people that are less accurate with facts. . . . They value efficiency and cost effectiveness. Others may see them as calm and passive, as if not reacting to events going on around them. They might seem difficult to get to know because they tend to hold their thoughts and feelings within themselves.

Canadian and American businesspeople predominantly approach problem-solving in this same Si way, objectively and with great factual accuracy, discounting extrasensory arguments such as related to beliefs or values, and unproven but creative ideas. Be aware, however, that when we discuss national character, we are discussing the predominant, or most common problem-solving style, and there are three other styles that will be encountered, though less frequently (see Chapter 11).

At the same time, Canadian and American national cultures differ in terms of their predominant extraverted communications style. Americans tend to be Te, or Extraverted Thinking. Canadians tend to be Fe, or Extraverted Feeling. In Chapter 2 Fe and Te were defined in the following ways.

> *Extraverted Feeling (Fe)*: Fe individuals are concerned to conform to established cultural patterns and societal norms of interaction and relationship. Their behavior is generally polite, considerate, and sensitive to the needs and expectations of those around them. Fe individuals understand situationally appropriate behavior, and build friendly relationships based on cooperation, shared interests, mutual benefits, and developing trust. They have a value commitment to altruism and will sacrifice their own interests for others. Fe individuals have a knack for maintaining harmony in relationships. They are skilled in establishing empathy and rapport, cooperating, saying the right thing at the right time, and serving others.
>
> *Extraverted Thinking (Te)*: Te individuals understand the external environment to be governed by logical and structured processes of cause and effect. Their goal is to

organize the external environment and its inhabitants. They tend to see things very dualistically, definitely in terms of "black and white" and "true and false," and have logical and impersonal reasons for their assertions and actions. Anyone and anything that agrees with their reasoning is "right." Anyone and anything disagreeing is "wrong." Te individuals are strong in planning, organizing, directing, and controlling capabilities with a strong need for closure. They do not regard their feelings for others as important, are not good at giving positive feedback.

Canadians tend to behave more politely and considerately, with a willingness to compromise in the interests of building cooperative, harmonious, and eventually trust-based relationships. These values represent their preferred basis for negotiating with others. In contrast, Americans tend to be more aggressive, feeling their beliefs to be "right" and having a strong need for early closure of discussions so as to move quickly to action, which they would prefer to organize and manage themselves. The Canadian style may look like a "push over" for always-determined American negotiators, with its willingness to compromise to achieve harmonious relations. However, Canadians have much experience with Americans and are more likely to avoid head-on confrontations, while undermining American intentions in a holding action, and seeing Americans as hostile when they are just being the way they are.[27] The Fe/Te difference may produce difficult interactions for both sides.

This Fe/Te difference in communication styles is not uncommon in international interactions. Exhibit 18.3 identifies those national cultures with predominant preference for either Te or Fe communication style preferences, including only nations in the top 20 international trading countries accounting for almost 95 percent of world trade.[28] The trade rankings (imports + exports) of the countries are given in parentheses. China, Mexico, Dutch Belgium, Italy, Russia, India, Spain, and Brazil are excluded since they have neither Fe nor Te predominant communications style preferences.

EXHIBIT 18.3 NATIONS PREDISPOSED IN FAVOR OF TE OR FE COMMUNICATIONS STYLES

Extraverted Thinking (Te)	Extraverted Feeling (Fe)
US (#1)	**Canada (#10)**
Germany (#3)	Japan (#4)
France (#5)	South Korea (#8)
UK (#6)	Singapore (#12)
Netherlands (#7)	French Belgium (#16)
Switzerland (#18)	Taiwan (#17)
Australia (#19)	

Source: Massey, B. *Where in the World Do I Belong?* USA: Jetlag Press, 2006.

The preferred Canadian style of communication is more similar to that of Asian rather than European countries. It is a more polite and indirect style, as will be seen, and has contributed to Canada having the reputation as one of the "nicest" cultures in the world.[29] According to Brean,[30] Canadians say "sorry" not so much as an apology as a strategy for achieving smooth, unconflicted, and harmonious interactions. "Once you learn how to properly say 'I'm sorry,' you will no longer be trying to become Canadian, you will have rewired your brain to such a degree that you will actually be Canadian."[31] Nor is it surprising that Canadians would have developed a different, less aggressive and assertive communication style, and possibly a more altruism-preferring gene pool, from Americans. Many immigrants to Canada, starting with the Empire Loyalists in the eighteenth century, left the US for Canada because they could not abide the more aggressive US culture, with its emphasis on competition, survival of the fittest, guns, and self-reliance.

Extraverted Thinking (US) versus Extraverted Feeling (Canada)[32]

The Canadian predominant Fe communication style is governed by the desire and expectation to engage in polite, courteous, and considerate communications. Individuals genetically predisposed in favor of Fe are gatekeepers for social norms and gauge the rightness or wrongness of their intended communications against their expectations as to what constitutes civilized behavior. Their goal is to improve society through positive social discourse and harmonious relationships. Fe individuals generally understand what will be considered "appropriate" behavior in any situation. They tend toward altruism, putting others' needs ahead of their own, and sacrificing their own self-interest. They intuitively "feel" others' emotions and say the "right" thing that those receiving Fe communications need or hope to hear. Fe memory is affective. It remembers relationships and expressed values and emotions. Because of Fe commitment to finding altruistic solutions that allow diverse positions to exist simultaneously in harmony, Fe memory is attuned to others' feelings, and finding shades of meaning that will allow compromises between positions that dualists would argue were either "right" or "wrong." Memory is strong and easily verbalized, so Fe is adept at advocating for workable compromises between potentially intransigent positions.

In contradistinction, Te (see Chapter 12) individuals conform to a "ruling principle" that is believed to represent objective reality, or an objectively oriented intellectual formula that they intend to apply consistently both to themselves and others. Te classifies things and people as "good" or "bad" depending on whether they agree with, or conform to, this ruling principle; for example, "democracy," "free markets," or "self-determination." Te is driven to plan, organize, decide, and direct everything and everyone around them to achieve this conformity. Te needs closure, and forward movement in their approved directions. Te memory is like a relational database of knowledge, principles, and rules, organized by logic, supporting their ruling principle against any opposition. Friends of Te individuals—those closest—report that their friendship is a "tyranny" because Te intends to lead others in the directions they believe to be right.

There will be predictable communications issues between Canadian Fe and American Te.

1   Fe memory is strongest for others' feelings, positive or negative, that guide Fe to find acceptable compromises. Te memory for the objective facts of a situation is more accurate.

2   Fe rarely sees situations as "black and white," and prefers more subtle or flexible communications that allow individuals or groups with different views to compromise. Te rejects this view, believing that its ruling principles are always the correct way forward.

3   Fe seeks harmonious relationships and is willing to altruistically put aside self-interest for agreements. Te is not concerned with harmony and pursues its self-interest as the basis for collective betterment.

In a stressful negotiation, Fe will become cold, theatrical, mechanical, and self-critical. Fe is not an effective strategy for dealing with Te because the latter disavows Fe values and goals, seeking control. When Fe must work with uncooperative or undermining people, the likely eventual reaction is excessive criticism directed in this case at Te. This takes the form of "sweeping condemnation," "sharp, biting, even vicious comments," "mistrust," and a "coolly objective" and distrusting mindset.[33] This attitude of being culturally superior to the US has become part of Canadian culture. Canadians believe theirs is a kinder, gentler, more caring society, with its universal medicare, gun control, less violent crime, and lower poverty levels. In private, Fe will be consumed with self-blame, obsessively searching for the "truth,"[34] assumed to be somewhere between the Fe and Te positions. In contrast, under stress Te takes criticism very personally and expresses its frustration with uncontrolled emotions.

Other psychological differences

One of the first studies to compare the cognitive problem-solving and decision-making preferences of American and Canadian businesspeople was Abramson, Keating, and Lane.[35] This research measured samples of American and Canadian business students using the Jungian-based Myers–Briggs Type Indicator (MBTI) instrument. Significant differences were found on two of the four scales—*sensing versus intuiting*, and *judging versus perceiving*.

1   *Sensing versus intuiting*: A *sensing* person focuses primarily on immediate sensory experience and tends to be more realistic and practical. She/he develops acute powers of observation and a good memory for details. An *intuiting* person is more concerned with possibilities and meanings than sensory information. She/he may not have such an acute memory for details but is likely to be more imaginative, innovative, theoretical, and abstract. Sensing and intuiting are, according to Jung,[36] the two primary modes of gathering information from the external environment.

2   *Judging versus perceiving*: A *judging* person prefers to make relatively quick decisions based on a more limited dataset. She/he is well organized and makes the most
of the information she/he has. She/he tends to seek closure as soon as possible,
aiming for quick action. A judging person would appear decisive and confident. A
perceiving person values the constant possibility of receiving new information relevant
to a decision. Closure and decision-making is delayed to allow time for further information to manifest. A perceiving person would appear curious and adaptable, but relatively slow to commit him/herself.

The study found that American managers were more *sensing* and *judging*. The
Canadians were more *intuiting* and *perceiving*. The Americans would perceive the
Canadians as very slow to make up their minds, and not entirely accurate in their understanding and interpretation of physical evidence. The Canadians would perceive the
Americans as always in a rush, willing to make ill-considered decisions, and relatively
unimaginative and un-innovative. These findings are consistent with Massey's[37] finding that
the Americans were Te and the Canadians Fe. The Canadians would be slower to decide
because they would search for acceptable compromises. Americans would be faster
because their ruling principle was clearly defined and brooked no compromise. Canadians
would be less likely to remember objective facts because they focused on subjective interactional factors.

A second interesting study was that of van Oudenthoven.[38] American and Canadian
managers were surveyed using Hofstede's[39] work values instrument. The Americans and
Canadians were very similar on the *power-distance* and *uncertainty avoidance* scales but
not on *individualism* or *masculinity*. The Americans were closer to the British than the
Canadians on *individualism*, and closer to the Belgians and Greeks on *masculinity* (or task
versus relationship orientation). On the *individualism versus collectivism* scale, Americans
would perceive Canadians as less concerned with personal achievements and individual
rights, and less likely than Americans to stand up for themselves and their beliefs. On the
masculinity versus femininity scale, Americans would perceive Canadians as less competitive, assertive, and materialistic, and less interested in personal ambition and power. This
study supported the view that Americans were more self-interested, and Canadians more
altruistic.

American versus Canadian negotiation tactics and behavior

Both Morrison and Conaway,[40] and Katz,[41] have produced recent analyses of cross-culturally
appropriate business behavior for wide numbers of worldwide national cultures. Both agree
that there are significant differences in how Americans and Canadians negotiate business
deals. Exhibit 18.4 summarizes these differences, combining the two sources, and the
recommendations for how best to approach negotiations with American and Canadian
businesspeople.

EXHIBIT 18.4 AMERICAN VERSUS CANADIAN NEGOTIATION STRATEGIES AND BEHAVIOR

Negotiation criteria	American preferences	Canadian preferences
Negotiation strategies	Points made through accumulation of objective facts.	Facts are accepted as primary evidence.
	Facts may be biased by ideologies or ruling principles like democracy, capitalism, or consumerism. Feelings are not evidence.	Strong faith and confidence in Canadian self-determination and consumerism. Little interest in feelings as evidence.
	Judeo-Christian values heavily influenced by egocentrism and ethnocentrism (own ways and American ways as best ways).	Strong ethnocentrism (Canadian ways best), especially in the French province of Quebec.
Negotiation behaviors	Business is expected to proceed with lightning speed. Salespersons bring final contracts to initial meetings.	Slower pace. Relationship-building, and assessment meetings precede meetings intended to achieve agreement.
	All relevant information is sent electronically prior to meeting.	Americans are believed to practice self-promotion and "hype." They should not inflate product/service benefits.
	Appointments are made by email. Conferences are broadcast live on internet and available for future study.	All materials should be in both French and English if Francophones are involved. In Quebec, French is the legal language.
	Americans keep up-to-date with newest electronic tools for communication.	Canadians are multi-ethnic. English Canadians behave more like British negotiators. French Canadians behave like French. Canada's third largest minority, Chinese, behave often more like Chinese negotiators if their families are more recent immigrants.
	Use of smartphones and cells is common in business meetings, including receiving calls.	
	Normal focus is "bottom line" financial issues, new technology, short-term rewards.	
	Business starts after brief period of small talk. Compliments are used as conversation starters, or "what do you do?" Americans believe you are what you do.	Canadian negotiators will not be rushed by American need for early closure. They will resist.
		"What do you do?" is considered too personal. Sports is a better icebreaker, for men especially.

Negotiation caveats

E X H I B I T

18.4

Americans may sometimes tell mistruths or make misleading claims, calling it "twisting" or "bending the truth." Open lying is considered unacceptable.

Americans may appear aggressive or adversarial. They will not shy away from open confrontation if challenged. Signs of anger or threats indicate things are not going well.

Avoid trying to create time pressure for Americans. Their level of interest will decrease. They will consider other options. Avoid stalling as Americans hate wasting time.

In a conflict, emphasize common objectives, search for mutually acceptable alternatives, and show willingness to compromise.

Always use politically correct vocabulary. Never say "Negro" for African-American, or "Oriental" for Asian-American, or "Latino" for Hispanic. Apologize quickly if someone looks offended.

Avoid aggressive tactics. Canadians regard "bending the truth" as lying.

Canadians will not shy away from open confrontation if challenged. These tactics will deteriorate the American credibility and position, though this may not be stated.

Offering written terms and contract clauses may shorten the bargaining process. Canadians prefer this approach.

Offering compromises helps resolve disputes. Leveraging personal relationships with Canadian counterparts helps as well.

Always use politically correct vocabulary. Apologizing is a good strategy and Canadians will typically apologize in return. Refusing to apologize damages the relationship until apology is made.

Sources: Morrison, T. and Conaway, W. A. *Kiss, Bow, or Shake Hands*, 2nd edn. n.p.: Getting Through Customs, 2015. Katz, L. *The Global Business Culture Guide*. Charleston, SC: CreateSpace, 2014.

Morrison and Conaway[42] offer a number of specific recommendations for American negotiators dealing with Canadian counterparts. These include:

1   Contact Canadian senior executives through a third party, mutual friend, or interme-diary. You will receive a more serious look than if you make direct contact, especially electronically.
2   Focus more on short-term benefits than on long-term benefits.
3   Do not assume that all change will necessarily be perceived as good, or an improvement.
4   Refrain from making extravagant claims. This is the Canadian stereotype of the American businessperson. Your claims will trigger suspicions, and possibly private unstated ridicule.

5   Avoid any sense of being condescending, or talking from a position of assumed superiority. This is also part of the American stereotype in Canada.

6   Avoid the "hard-sell" attempting to save time. Canadian decision-making is slower and
trying to rush it will make it even slower.

7   If your Canadian counterpart is done talking with you today, you are done too and
should simply try to book the next appointment.

8   Avoid appearing either emotional or interrogating. Canadians are emotionally
restrained (Francophones much less so), and find interrogation intrusive.

9   Canadians are often self-critical. Avoid agreeing with their negative self-evaluations.

10   Canadians often apologize even for trivial things. Your best bet is to apologize in turn.

11   Avoid consulting your electronic devises or answering the phone while meeting.
Canadians regard this as rude and boorish.

Cross-national differences in relationship-building activities

Both Morrison and Conaway,[43] and Katz,[44] offer observations on relationship-building
behavior for Americans and Canadians, and how it differs in the two business cultures.
Exhibit 18.5 summarizes these observations.

EXHIBIT 18.5 RELATIONSHIP CRITERIA FOR AMERICAN AND CANADIAN BUSINESS CULTURES

Relationship criteria	American criteria	Canadian criteria
Relationship importance	Only moderately important. Not a precondition for doing business. Even closer relationships may be dropped for a better deal elsewhere.	Only moderately important. Not a precondition for doing business. Francophones prefer to build relationships before doing business. Anglophones hope to maintain long-term relationships. Friends believe it's okay to cooperate and compete at the same time.
Mutual respect	Respect depends on achievements, education, age, and rank—in that order. Admired traits include resourcefulness, perseverance, expertise, and good communication skills. You must treat everyone the same without discrimination. You must wear neat and clean clothing.	Respect depends on achievements and education. Rank and titles are more important than in the US. Admired traits include honesty, ambition paired with humility, tolerance, and reasonableness. An individual must demonstrate his/her responsibility to the community.

Relationship criteria	American criteria	Canadian criteria
Trust	Not discussed.	You must demonstrate long-term personal integrity, dependability to win others' trust.
Conversation preferences	Americans speak loudly. A strong voice is associated with authority and leadership. Hispanics expect you to show your emotions.	English and French are official languages. Polite listeners rarely interrupt others. Periods of silence are for reflection and not negative. Anglophones rarely show emotion. Francophones often show emotion. Talking loud is a sign of emotional perturbation.
Direct vs. indirect communications	The US has several regional subcultures. Northeasterners and West Coasters are direct and dislike vagueness. They openly share opinions on issues. Southerners are more indirect. They highlight positives to soften criticism. They are less direct saying "no."	Anglophones are fairly direct. Francophones are less so. Other minorities may be similar to their national cultures outside Canada. Canada regards itself as a "mosaic" rather than "melting pot" and does not seek uniformity from minorities.
Nonverbal	Americans may signal friendship with some physical contact like back-slapping.	Physical contact is best avoided. Francophones may greet friends with light kisses to both cheeks. Wait for them to initiate.
Processing information	Americans are relatively ethnocentric and closed to most outside information. If a deficiency is identified, then outside capabilities are quickly adopted. Americans are very analytical. Concepts are abstracted quickly. Innovation is usually preferred to traditional methods.	Canadians tend to be well-informed, and open to reasonable discussions. Canadians are fairly analytical, preferring objective information to subjective impressions.
Anxiety and its reduction	Americans have low anxiety about life but high anxiety about deadlines and results. Recognition is the greatest reward. The work ethic is very strong. There are rules for every circumstance. Americans are comfortable with risk, emphasizing self-determination, and survival of the fittest.	Canadians have low uncertainty avoidance. Recognition is the greatest reward. Competitive behavior is expected. There is no felt need to establish strict laws or rules to give structure. Social organizations provide behavioral stability. Canadians have social services equivalent to Western Europe paid for by tax rates similar to the US.

EXHIBIT 18.5

E
X
H
I
B
I
T

18.5

Relationship criteria	American criteria	Canadian criteria
Issues of equality	Personal equality is guaranteed by law but there is considerable ethnic and racial bias against some minorities, especially those perceived as "nonwhite." Some "nonwhite" minorities, like Hispanic, would be considered "white" in Canada.	Personal equality is guaranteed by the Charter of Rights. There continues to be ethnic bias against Aboriginal peoples that has lasted throughout Canada's history. Canada has the highest annual percentage of population immigration in the world. Most minorities are treated with consideration, though they must find their own way, economically, over time.

Abramson[45] conducted a study to determine the activities that Americans and Canadians preferred to use to build and maintain effective marketing and sales buyer–seller relationships. These results are summarized in Exhibit 18.6.

Considerable differences were found, both on marketing mix (product, promotion, price, direct sales, and service) and relationship marketing variables. Americans were much more committed to relational activities. They built and maintained relationships by focusing on developing mutual respect, shared goals, personal trust, and making sure everyone received the expected benefits. Canadians also valued these activities highly but Americans valued them much more highly. By contrast, Canadians were more likely to focus on sharp pricing, and helping out a customer if asked to do so. In Exhibit 18.6, a significant difference is shown as either (>) or (>>), depending on how much more. Similarly, less and much less are (<) and (<<).

E
X
H
I
B
I
T

18.6

EXHIBIT 18.6 BUYER–SELLER RELATIONSHIP-BUILDING ACTIVITIES BY MEAN SCORE

Mean score	American	Canadian
4.6	Build respect–U. S. >	
4.5		
4.4		
4.3		Build respect–Can.
4.2		

Mean score	American	Canadian	
4.1	Advertising and promotion—U. S. >>		E X H I B I T 18.6
	Build shared goals—U. S. >>		
	Build trust—U. S. >		
4.0		Sharp pricing—Can. >>	
3.9	Ensure mutual benefits—U. S. >	Help if asked—Can. >>	
3.8		Build trust—Can. <	
3.7	Sharp pricing—U. S. <<	Advertising and promotion—Can. <<	
		Build shared goals—Can. <<	
		Ensure mutual benefits—Can. <	
		Product R&D—Can. >	
3.6			
3.5	Help if asked—U. S. <<		
	Product R&D—U. S. <		
3.4		Ask for small favors—Can. >>	
3.3			
2.9			
2.8	Ask for small favors—U. S. <<		

Source: Abramson, N. R. "Building and Maintaining Effective Buyer–Seller Relationships: A Comparative Study of American and Canadian Expectations," *Journal of Promotion Management*, Vol. 12, No. 1, 2005, pp. 129–150.

Exhibit 18.6 shows that even though the top activity for both Americans and Canadians was building mutual respect, the Americans worked at it considerably more. They built shared goals to a much greater extent, and did much more to build trust and ensure everyone achieved the mutual benefits expected. Americans also engaged in considerably more advertising and promotion. In contrast, Canadians were very much more likely to rely on sharp pricing, being helpful, and developing their products at the request of their customers. It was interesting that the Canadians were much more likely to ask for small favors, whereas this was an unlikely approach for the Americans.

This study suggested that despite a more assertive national character and a need for quick decisions and early action, Americans were sensitive to the need for trust-based relationships. They would be willing to "go the extra mile" if their Canadian counterparts felt too rushed or pressed.

Business ethics and bribery[46]

Business regulation in Canada requires greater transparency and accountability than in the US. As a result, perceptions of corruption and questionable dealings are lower for Canadian business. Transparency International rated 178 countries on a scale of 0 (highly corrupt) to 10 (very clean), and ranked Canada (8.9/10) the sixth least corrupt business environment after Denmark, New Zealand, Singapore, Finland, and Sweden. The US was ranked (7.1/10) 22nd–still a strong result when 75 percent of countries ranked lower than 5/10. For example, Saudi Arabia (4.7) was 50th, China (3.5) 78th, India (3.3) 87th, and Russia (2.1) 154th.[47]

Bribing government officials is a criminal offense under both Canadian and American law. Under the Canadian *Corruption of Foreign Public Officials Act*, a bribe is defined as a payment of value to a foreign official intended to obtain, either directly or indirectly, a business advantage or opportunity by inducing the official to use his/her position to decide in favor of the bribe-giver. Items of value could include cash, computer equipment, travel, medical supplies, entertainment, or vehicles. A foreign official is a person who holds a legislative, administrative, or judicial position, or performs public duties for a state. This definition includes foreign military officers responsible for procurement decisions. The American equivalent of this Act is the *U. S. Foreign Corrupt Practices Act*.

Not all payments are, however, considered bribes. Public officials in many foreign nations, especially in the Third World, control the granting of licenses. It is a normal practice for them, or their superiors, to increase their income with payments for their favors. Reasonable payments to foreign officials to promote products or to facilitate the performance of contracts are not illegal.

It is similarly legal to offer facilitation payments to induce officials to perform routine acts within the scope of their normal duties. One may pay officials to perform routine functions that they are supposed to be performing as part of their jobs. For example, one may legally bribe an official to receive a visa or work permit. One may pay a harbormaster to unload a cargo from a ship. Such bribery is expensive because it cannot be used as a tax deduction and must use after-tax dollars.

There is, however, no established standard for what constitutes an illegal bribe. Businesses are on their own in making a judgment on the basis of circumstances and local culture. A gift of a bottle of whiskey costing $300 may be appropriate for a senior official, but a collector's bottle worth $100,000 is likely not. The Canadian Revenue Agency does not provide acceptable guidelines as to what constitutes a reasonable payment. Businesses must use their judgment, and that of their lawyers.

By contrast, US authorities provide 120 pages of guidelines defining proper gifts, travel and entertainment expenses, and facilitation payments. These guidelines say, for example, that wining and dining a foreign official is completely acceptable, but spending $10,000 doing so would likely lead to prosecution.

In a similar vein,[48] the US Federal Tax Laws required 72,536 pages to be fully stated in 2014. By contrast, the Canadian Income Tax Act and Regulations filled only 4,047 pages the same year. US culture is very bureaucratic and rule-oriented, with specific rules for virtually every possible circumstance. Canadian culture is more likely to rely on more general principles, relying on citizens to apply them appropriately in the situations they encounter.

THE UNITED STATES OF AMERICA

> America is great, not because it is perfect, but because it can always be made better—and that unfinished work of perfecting our nation falls to each of us. It's a charge we pass on to our children, coming closer with each new generation to do what we know America should be.
>
> Barack Obama[49]

The US is the most technologically advanced and largest economy in the world.[50] It is a free market economy in the sense that private individuals and businesses make most economic decisions, and governments, both federal and state, buy most of their goods and services from the open marketplace. American companies have greater flexibility than companies from Western Europe or Japan in making expansion plans, laying off unneeded employees, and developing new products. American firms are at the technological leading edge, especially in the computer, medical technology, aerospace, and military industries. Other industries of note include petroleum, steel, motor vehicles, telecommunications, chemicals, electronics, food processing, consumer goods, lumber, and mining. The industrial production growth rate in 2011 was 4.1 percent.[51]

While it appears that the US runs a significant annual current exchange deficit due to the much higher level of imports to exports, this is only partially true. Foreign companies that set up wholly owned manufacturing plants in the US are allowed to import parts and assemblies from their foreign suppliers for products to be sold either in the US as American products, or for re-export to foreign markets. In 2012, the US had $2.82 trillion in foreign investment, and had invested $4.77 trillion outside the US. The government held $148 billion in foreign exchange and gold, the 17th largest amount of any country.

In recent years, the US has experienced political turbulence perhaps because of the relative decline of the middle class—that one-third of Americans earning middle income, as opposed to the one-third earning upper incomes and the one-third earning lower incomes.[52] Between 2000 and 2014, the share of adults living in middle-income households decreased in 203 of 229 American metropolitan areas based on government data. The average decrease was 4 percent. As a result, the middle class may no longer be the economic majority in the US. This decline has been incorrectly attributed to globalization and the emergence of free trade agreements that have allowed the importation of goods without tariffs, and the resultant offshoring of high-paying manufacturing jobs to foreign countries with much lower wage rates. These jobs had been held by often less well-educated "white" males of middle income, and their replacement jobs, when available, were often part-time, in service industries, at much lower wages. These trends have left many Americans angry and in despair, attributing their misfortune to the decline of American manufacturing, and the transfer of their jobs to places like Mexico and China. The existence of millions of undocumented "illegal immigrants" unprotected by American labor law and forced to work for less than the minimum wage exacerbated the problem by keeping low- and middle-income wage rates down. Walshe[53] called the plight of undocumented immigrants the emergence of a "slave" class in the US.

Research has shown, however, that American manufacturing has not declined as a result of globalization. The US Department of Commerce has reported that since 1979 American factory production has more than doubled to $1.91 trillion in 2015, even though more than seven million factory jobs were lost in the same period.[54] US manufacturing, measured in 2009 dollars adjusted for inflation, is the world's second greatest after China. Deloitte has predicted that US manufacturing will overtake China by 2020.[55] The loss of manufacturing jobs has been caused by robots replacing human workers, resulting in the reduction of labor costs in the US of 22 percent, and increased international cost competitiveness.[56] The trend is expected to continue as the cost of robot technology declines. A robotic spot welder that cost an average of $182,000 in 2005 cost $133,000 in 2014, and is predicted to cost $103,000 by 2025.[57] On the plus side, American MNEs have less incentive to offshore their manufacturing operations to low-wage countries, and have begun to bring their plants back to the US, preferring to avoid nations with greater political instability and uncertainty. Energy pricing and rising foreign wage rates are also factors. Chinese wage rates have, for example, risen an estimated four- to five-fold since the beginning of the century. When energy costs are more than the equivalent of $100 per barrel of oil, it is cheaper to manufacture in the US when the cost of sea transport from China is included in the costing.

Historical context

The US originally consisted of 13 British colonies located along the eastern seaboard of what is now the US. The US achieved independence from Britain through the American Revolution (1776–1783). A major cultural difference between the US and Canada was that Canada at that time consisted of British colonies that remained loyal to Britain. Americans who opposed the Revolution fled to Canada.

The twentieth century witnessed America becoming a world power, the deciding force in both World Wars I and II. The US swung from isolationism and non-ratification of the League of Nations to internationalism and formation of the United Nations. During this time, citizen movements ensured:

1   the guarantee of women's suffrage by a Constitutional amendment granting women the right to vote;
2   the end of prohibition laws against alcohol consumption; and
3   the protection of African-American citizens in the Civil Rights Act of 1964 and the Voting Rights Act of 1965.

After World War II (1939–1945), the US led in establishing international structures and economic policies, such as the International Monetary Fund, the World Bank, and

NATO. Its chief rival was the Soviet Union, and the two countries engaged in a geopolitical Cold War that resulted in the demise of that Communist government in 1991. During those years, the US, like Russia, conducted "witch-hunts" against supposed Communist infiltrators during the McCarthy period (1947–1954), which questioned the loyalty of anyone with leftist political sympathies.[58] It also engaged in a series of regional wars in Korea (1950–1953); Vietnam (1961–1973); Iraq (1991; 2003–2012); and Afghanistan (2001–?). In America, these major military conflicts not only weakened the nation's economy and vastly increased American federal debt, but also resulted in significant countercultural movements and public protests.

In the twenty-first century, the attack of Middle Eastern terrorists on September 11, 2001, against New York City's Trade Center and Washington, DC's Pentagon building changed the nation and its citizens. That event led to a declaration of war on terrorism worldwide. It contributed to the nation's concern about improving security for its citizens, limitations on immigration and human rights, as well as neglect of domestic concerns. Wars in Afghanistan and Iraq lowered the high esteem many foreigners felt for the US.[59]

American cultural insights[60]

The citizens of the United States of America refer to themselves as "Americans." The US has been referred to as a "melting pot" culture, where people come from many places and meld into the mainstream European cultures of the US. The "salad bowl" metaphor is perhaps more appropriate and accurate. It recognizes the contributions of the Native American, African, Asian, and Latin cultures, each maintaining its unique cultural markers, while striving to work and live in harmony.

It is true that the US is a land of immigrants. German-Americans are the largest grouping at 49.8 million.[61] In 2000,[62] the Irish (30.5 million), English (24.5 million), African-American (24.9 million), Mexican (18.4 million), Italian (15.6 million), and First Nations (7.8 million) were the major ethnicities. The last census confirmed that nearly 40 million people now in the US were foreign-born. This makes the US a multicultural society with a variety of ethnic micro-cultures. Although English is its only official language, Spanish has emerged as a de facto second language, especially in the Southwest and Florida.

By 2050, the US census forecasts that minorities in this country will become the majority. By then, the American population is expected to number 438 million, including some 40 million of Asian heritage. It is estimated that "whites" will make up only 46 percent of the US population, while one in three Americans will be Hispanic. In Canada, Hispanics would be considered by many to be "whites." An element of American culture is a rather morbid fascination with dividing ethnicities by "race" as a basis for ascribing status.

American cultural profile

There are some general cultural characteristics associated with most Americans. The over-view of the dominant mainstream culture reveals that citizens of the US tend to be:

- *Goal- and achievement-oriented*: Americans are optimistic, and think they can accomplish just about anything, given enough time, money, and technology.
- *Highly organized*: Americans prefer a society that is strong institutionally, well organized, and secure.
- *Freedom-loving and self-reliant*: Americans fought a revolution and subsequent wars to preserve their concept of democracy, so they resent too much control or interference, especially by government or external forces. They strive through law to promote equal opportunity and to confront their own racism or prejudice. Americans also idealize the self-made person who rises from poverty and adversity. Control of one's destiny is popularly expressed as "doing your own thing." Americans think, for the most part, that with determination and initiative, one can achieve whatever he or she sets out to do, and can thus fulfill individual human potential.
- *Work-oriented and efficient*: Americans generally possess a strong work ethic. They are very time-conscious and efficient in doing things. They tinker with gadgets and technological systems, always searching for easier, better, more efficient ways of accomplishment.
- *Friendly and informal*: Americans reject the ascribed privileges of royalty and class, but do defer to those with affluence and power. Media celebrities impress many Americans. Although informal in greeting and dress, they are a noncontact culture (e.g., they usually avoid embracing in public).
- *Competitive and assertive*: Americans in play or business generally are so oriented because of their drives to achieve and succeed.
- *Values in transition*: America is a dynamic and open society. Traditional American values of family loyalty, respect and care of the aged, marriage and the nuclear family, patriotism, material acquisition, forthrightness, and the like are undergoing profound re-evaluation.
- *Generous and altruistic*: Although Americans seemingly emphasize material values, they are a sharing people, as has been demonstrated in the Marshall Fund, foreign aid programs, refugee assistance, and their willingness at home and abroad to espouse a good cause and to help neighbors in need. Volunteerism is alive and well in the US.

These cultural characteristics have become less characteristic of all Americans because of its advancing multicultural composition. Exhibit 18.7 indicates some of the contrary cultural values that foreign businesspeople may encounter, depending on with whom they are doing business.

EXHIBIT 18.7 CULTURE CONTRAST

Host country value	US value
Japan: group orientation	Individualism
Guatemala: flexible time sense	Punctuality
Saudi Arabia: relationship focus	Task/goal orientation
Switzerland: formality	Informality
India: stratified class structure	Egalitarianism
China: long-term view	Short-term view
Germany: structured orderliness	Flexible pragmatic
France: deductive thinking	Inductive thinking
Sweden: individual cooperation	Individual competition
Malaysia: modesty	Self-promotion

Source: Wederspahn, G. M. *Intercultural Services: A Worldwide Buyer's Guide and Sourcebook.* Burlington, MA: Butterworth-Heinemann/Gulf, 2000, pp. 41–42.

E
X
H
I
B
I
T
18.7

Social change is also having an effect on American culture. Exhibit 18.8 indicates some of these more recent changes.

EXHIBIT 18.8 AMERICA'S CHANGING CULTURE

5.2 million Americans are estimated to be living overseas.

5.7 million unmarried, heterosexual couples live together.

65 percent of population is urban, 33.6 percent suburban, and the remainder other (e.g., rural).

27 percent of the high-income males report a work week up to 50 hours.

33 percent of the females and 25 percent of the males are college graduates; both in the age group 25–29.

77 percent work in the service sector; 20 percent in industry; 3 percent in agriculture.

46 percent of the workforce are civilian women.

67 percent of children live with two parents; 28 percent with one parent; 5 percent other.

31 percent of college freshmen describe themselves as liberal in their political/social outlook.

20 percent of the population will be age 65 or older in 2050.

45 percent of the population by 2050 will be "white," 31 percent Hispanic, 14 percent African-American, 10 percent Asian.

80 percent today accept interracial marriage among Americans, while 45 percent of voters under 30 accept gay marriage rights.

Source: Newsweek Magazine Special Inaugural Issue, January, 2009, entitled "Obama's America: Where We are Now." The data are based on a Newsweek poll, plus information from Pew Research Center, US Census Bureau, Congressional Research Center, and Environmental Systems Research Institute.

E
X
H
I
B
I
T
18.8

Micro-cultures in the US[63]

Thus far, the emphasis has been on the majority American macro-culture. However, American culture is in transition. The emergence of a polyethnic society is most evident in Los Angeles, where a cacophony of 160 languages is spoken today. Undocumented immigrants now comprise up to 2.4 percent of California's population. The transformation of minorities into majorities is also taking place in Texas, Arizona, New York, Nevada, New Jersey, and Maryland. For now, these micro-cultures–African-Americans, Aboriginal First Nations, Hispanics, Chinese-Americans, Vietnamese-Americans, Muslim-Americans, and so on–are socially, economically, and physically challenged by the mainstream culture. Those who have been part of the majority will have to change their sense of identity as they themselves become minorities and find themselves sharing power and influence with "people of color" if American institutions are to retain their effectiveness.[64] Mainstream cultural norms and standards are being altered as minorities move up into full equality.

There are three substantial minority groups (African-Americans, Aboriginal First Nations, and Hispanic-Americans) distinguished by their physical, as opposed to cultural, characteristics. According to Gudykunst and Kim,[65] there are five characteristics of minority group membership:

1   Members of minority groups are treated differently from members of a majority group by members of the majority group. This inequality usually takes the form of prejudice, discrimination, and even segregation.
2   Members of minority groups have either physical or cultural characteristics that make them stand out from the majority group.
3   Because minority groups stand out from the majority, membership in them is not voluntary.
4   Members of a minority group tend to associate with and marry other members of their group.
5   Members of a minority group are aware of their subordinate status, which leads to strong group solidarity and gaining a sense of ethnic identity.

African-American

Racism is an explosive issue in American life today. To begin a serious dialogue regarding race, one must establish the terms for racial issues. As long as African-Americans are viewed as "them," the burden falls on the persons of color to do all the "cultural" and "moral" compromising, so healthy race relations are hampered. African-Americans represent about 15 percent of Americans. In six southern states–Mississippi, Louisiana, South Carolina, Georgia, Maryland, and Alabama–and the District of Columbia, African-American numbers are far greater. In Washington, DC and Detroit, Michigan, African-Americans are the majority.

African-Americans are made visible by their skin color, represent the main cultural group forced into slavery in the US prior to the American Civil War (1861–1865), and have generally remained as "second class" citizens since despite advances inspired by Dr. Martin Luther King in the 1960s. Currently they are the principle victims of police shootings that have inspired the "Black Lives Matter" movement in recent years. African-American prosperity lags that of "white" Americans:

- In 1969, African-American family income was 60 percent of "white" family income. By 2005, it had risen to 65 percent, though for the university-educated, the difference was smaller.[66]
- In 2014, the median family income for American "whites" was $71,300 versus $43,300 for African-Americans. For university-educated "whites," median family income rose to $106,600, significantly higher than for households headed by African-American college graduates at $82,300.[67]
- The racial wage gap between "blacks" and "whites" is diminishing because of increasing deregulation and competition in financial institutions.
- The number of African-Americans elected or appointed to office at all levels of government has increased dramatically, including to the US Supreme Court and Attorney General, as well as the presidency itself.
- The number of African-Americans completing secondary school, college, and post-graduate studies is rising steadily.

When an African-American, Barack Obama, was elected president (2008–2016), civil rights leaders believed that circumstances would improve for all African-Americans. This has not occurred, as evidenced by the many unjustified shootings of African-Americans by police in recent years.[68] Yet Americans seem to be in far greater danger of gun violence from each other than from police. In the first ten months of 2016, in Chicago, for example, 624 citizens were murdered, 557 by guns. This was 20 more than in all of Canada in 2015. Canada has 3.5 times the population of Chicago (35 million vs. 9.9 million).

Aboriginal First Nations

The Aboriginal First Nations' people lived in North and South America before the Europeans began to arrive with the Vikings in about 1000 CE and Columbus in 1493 CE. They are known as First Nations because they were the original inhabitants, possibly having arrived from Asia over a land bridge from Siberia more than 20,000 years ago. Aboriginals are distinguished from First Nations by descent from ethnic intermarriage over centuries.

There are many fundamental differences between tribal culture and the dominant US culture. The following contrasts five of these differences between the mainstream culture and that of Native Americans:

■ In the mainstream, time is to be saved, and spent. People are paid for their time and generally view time as a commodity and a continuum. For Aboriginals, time is relatively less scheduled. Aboriginals may go faster or slower depending on their priorities or need for mutual agreement prior to action.

■ In the mainstream, decision-making is based on authority. Some have authority to make decisions and others do not. Authority in Native American cultures is also hierarchical, but there is more emphasis on achieving consensual community decision-making.

■ In the mainstream, people are generally future-oriented and believe strongly in progress. Virtually any technological advance is greeted with enthusiasm. No opportunity for development is eschewed. First Nations seek to maintain their traditional culture and values and generally will not support development that will interfere with their values or land.

■ In the mainstream, Americans have come to prefer to live in urban settings, believing there to be greater opportunities for economic advancement, social welfare, and entertainment. Aboriginals tend to prefer to live in rural settings, both as a means of protecting their cultural integrity, and because the American government forced them in previous centuries to live on relatively marginal value reserve lands.

■ In the mainstream, people make decisions by confronting those that disagree. It is not uncommon for interested parties to interrupt each other, and to battle over areas of disagreement. In First Nations' culture, people are careful to share speaking time, speaking calmly; interruptions are considered rude and unacceptable.

Hispanic-American

Broadly defined, a Hispanic-American is an immigrant to the US, or one whose ancestors came from Spain or Latin America. Many still speak Spanish and may reflect the cultural images of both Spain and the indigenous peoples of Mexico, Central, and South America. The Hispanic cultural influence in the US is most evident in California, Florida, Nevada, Arizona, Texas, Puerto Rico, and Guam. In 2011, Latinos represented 16.3 percent of the US population,[69] having grown by 43 percent over the previous decade, and are predicted to be one-third of the American population in 2050.[70] Approximately 65 percent have origins in Mexico, 12 percent in Puerto Rico, 12 percent in Central America and other Latin countries, 8 percent in Cuba, and 5 percent in the Dominican Republic.

From a Canadian point of view, Spanish would be considered "white." People of mixed European and indigenous ancestry would be considered Metis (usually English or French and First Nation in Canada). They could easily "pass" for "white" in Canadian society unless they preferred to pursue their newly granted Aboriginal Metis treaty rights to land and social assistance. These rights were established in a landmark Canadian Supreme Court decision in 2013.

It is difficult to generalize about Latin-Americans, but they are gaining political power and representation as greater numbers begin to vote. Although many are bilingual, they gain some cohesiveness through the Spanish language, Roman Catholicism, and family values. They are moving rapidly into middle-class status and home ownership. In most states, the number of Hispanic-owned businesses has doubled, and their purchasing power is likely to triple by the end of this decade. Hispanic buying power in the US reached $1 trillion in 2012 and is predicted to rise to $1.5 trillion in the next five years. The Hispanic consumer market—large and growing—has a reputation for brand loyalty, particularly when shopping for food and clothing.

THE DOMINION OF CANADA[71]

> An education system isn't worth a great deal if it teaches young people how to make a living but doesn't teach them how to make a life.
>
> David Suzuki[72]

Canada is very similar to the US in being a democratic, affluent, high-technology oriented, industrial society with a $1.45 trillion plus economy (GDP measured as PPP) in 2012. As a rule of thumb, Canada has almost exactly one-tenth the population of the US, and Canadians measure how they are doing economically by multiplying Canadian figures by a factor of ten. Since the US GDP was $15.66 trillion in 2012, Canadian commentators reported that there was a productivity gap between American and Canadian workers.[73] Now that US GDP is only nine times greater, the productivity gap has disappeared for the time being.

However, Canada is a very successful trading nation—possibly more so than the US. While the US was the third most successful world exporter in 2011 ($1,497 billion), and Canada the eleventh ($463 billion),[74] Canada exported about three times more per capita. Canada's principal trading partner was the US (73.7 percent of exports in 2011).

The reason Canada both imported and exported crude oil, despite having the world's third largest oil reserves, is because of its tight economic integration with the US. Most Canadian oil is produced in the western prairie regions of Alberta and Saskatchewan. Existing pipelines flow north–south to Texas, where the bitumen oil is processed. Eastern Canada is supplied by sea from the Middle East because there is no east–west pipeline. Such a pipeline is currently being considered, as is one from Alberta through British Columbia to the west coast for shipment of oil to China and Japan. A recent irritant between Canada and the US was the refusal of the Obama administration to approve a pipeline from Alberta to the Gulf of Mexico for environmental reasons. Now, going forward, it appears that this pipeline will be approved, giving Canada better access to world markets. Canada is the fifth largest oil-producing country in the world.

There are regional differences in trade orientation within Canada. The province of Ontario has always been the industrial and manufacturing heartland of Canada. Most Ontario trade has historically been with the US. By contrast, British Columbia, on Canada's west coast, has become very Pacific Rim-oriented in its trade focus. This has been facilitated by British Columbia's major city, Vancouver, being a popular spot for Asian immigration (approximately 42 percent visible minorities; including 20 percent ethnic Chinese and 10 percent various South Asian).[75] In 2012, only 45.8 percent of British Columbia's exports went to the US, while the rest went to China (19.4 percent), Japan (13.5 percent), Europe (6.5 percent), and South Korea (6.1 percent).

Social context

Canada is also a multicultural society, perhaps more intentionally so than the US. While the US prided itself for many years as a cultural "melting pot" and only recently found itself a "salad bowl," Canada has long regarded itself as a "cultural mosaic."

Canada's most defining feature is its multicultural ethnic diversity. Up to the present day, the British (Anglophones) and French (Francophones) have maintained their separate cultural identities, and when Canada became a national entity in 1867, English and French both became official languages. In recent times, the Anglophones and Francophones have been joined by a vast influx of immigrants (Allophones). Canada currently accepts upwards of 300,000 to 350,000 new immigrants per year—approximately 1 percent of its total population. Statistics Canada reported that according to the 2001 Census, Canada had 34 ethnic groups with at least 100,000 members, and ten of these had memberships of one million plus (see Exhibit 18.9). In 2006, 20 percent of the Canadian population was foreign-born, and this element of the population was increasing four times faster than the native-born population.[76] In 2015–2016, Canada accepted 25,000 Syrian refugees, flying them to Canada in a matter of weeks as a humanitarian gesture, while the US still debated whether it is safe to do so, given fears of "Islamic" terrorism.

Micro-cultures: First Nations and Aboriginal

In the context of business opportunities, Canada contains several micro-communities of interest. The First Nations are a genuine emerging market within Canada. One and a quarter million Canadians are classified as having Aboriginal ancestry. Three-quarters of these people live on reservations. The federal government groups First Nations classified people into four categories—status (registered formally under the Indian Act); non-status (persons who have not registered with the government); Metis (descendants of mixed Aboriginal and European ancestry); and Inuit, a distinct cultural group who generally live in the far north and speak primarily their own language, Inuktitut.

EXHIBIT 18.9 LARGEST ETHNIC IDENTITY GROUPS IN CANADA

Ethnic origin	Percentage	Population (million)	Area of largest proportion (percent)
English	21.03	6.57	Newfoundland (43.2)
French	15.82	4.94	Quebec (28.9)
Scottish	15.11	4.72	Prince Edward Island (40.5)
Irish	13.94	4.35	Prince Edward Island (29.2)
German	10.18	3.18	Saskatchewan (30.0)
Italian	4.63	1.45	Ontario (7.2)
Chinese	4.31	1.35	British Columbia (10.6)
First Nations	4.01	1.25	Northwest Territories (36.5)
Ukrainian	3.87	1.21	Manitoba (14.8)
Dutch	3.32	1.04	Alberta (5.3)

Source: Wikipedia, Demographics of Canada, 2011.

Canadian courts have held that First Nations' people deserve compensation for guarantees made to them by the British Crown in treaties that were subsequently not honored. In addition, the federal government confiscated some tribes' hereditary lands in the past without legal ratification in the form of treaties. Courts have held that treaties must be agreed to, and compensation paid to address these ancient wrongs. There is no unified First Nations plan for negotiating these treaties, and no central authority that speaks for all the 700+ bands in Canada. Ultimately, each pursues its own interests, independently if necessary.

Conditions on First Nations' reserves are generally terrible, with high unemployment, substance abuse, high rates of suicide, poor housing conditions, poor schooling resources, and so on. Many reserves are located in rural and/or wilderness locations where it is difficult for the federal government to provide adequate services. Many First Nations' people want to put their full efforts into negotiating treaties as a means of obtaining the financial compensation needed to develop their resources and improve their living conditions. The *Idle No More* movement that began in 2012 and continues today has been an effort by Aboriginal leadership and young Aboriginals to pressure a government believed to be insincere in its negotiating strategies, and not committed to finding equitable solutions. In addition, the *Truth and Reconciliation Commission of Canada* reported in 2015 that the Canadian government had systematically discriminated against Aboriginal Canadians by seizing

Aboriginal children and sending them to residential schools where they were not allowed to see their parents or speak their native languages, and where many were sexually abused.[77] Many Canadians of all ethnicities were appalled at these findings and now support improved conditions for Aboriginals in Canada.

A smaller number of First Nations people believe that their social and economic conditions need to be addressed with whatever resources are available to them currently. Each band receives annual financial allocations from Indian and Northern Affairs Canada (INAC), the government department responsible for managing the Indian Act. In 2011–2012, INAC's budget was CAN$7.3 billion.[78] If a band chief is elected that supports the goal of immediate development, then that band will initiate plans to attempt to build a piece of infrastructure, or support local business initiatives to develop the band economy.[79] Generally, such bands find that in addition to inadequate financial resources, they lack managerial and organizational capabilities necessary for an effective business.

The serious needs of bands and the desire to address them, plus the lack of First Nations managerial resources, and substantial government funding have spawned an industry in Canada. Many consultants have found opportunities doing needs assessment, planning projects, providing managerial capabilities, and even supporting the treaty negotiations from the Aboriginal side.

Micro-cultures: Asian

Vancouver, British Columbia, is Canada's third largest city. Of a total population in the Greater Vancouver Regional District of 2.3 million, 52 percent do not speak English as their first language due to the effects of immigration. Almost 30 percent of the city's population is of Chinese heritage. Many of these Chinese people emigrated from Hong Kong prior to the return of the British colony to China in 1997. Other significant Asian groupings include South Asian (mostly Punjabi, 5.7 percent), Filipino (5.0 percent), Japanese (1.7 percent), Korean (1.5 percent), as well as sizable numbers of Vietnamese, Indonesians, and Cambodians. In Vancouver, the second language after English is Mandarin or Cantonese. Canada's second official language, French, is almost never heard spoken. Canada's largest city, Toronto, gets three immigrants for every two in Vancouver, and also has a high Asian population.

Some Vancouver neighborhoods are more Asian than others. Richmond's population would make it the fourth-largest city in British Columbia, and its 60 percent immigrant population is the highest in Canada. More than half its population of 190,000 is Asian, including Chinese (43.6 percent, mostly originally from Hong Kong, Taiwan, and China), South Asian (8.0 percent), and Filipino (5.5 percent). Richmond has two Buddhist and two Sikh temples.

This strong Asian representation has made Vancouver (and Toronto) a remarkably multicultural city. Multicultural and multiracial marriage is becoming common, especially among younger people. It has also produced many opportunities for doing business in

China or India, and for attracting Asian businesspeople to Vancouver. This explains why British Columbia exports significantly more to China, Japan, and South Korea, and significantly less to the US and Europe, than the rest of Canada.

CONCLUSIONS

Despite their many similarities, there are also many differences between the US and Canada. Many of those differences may stem from the fact that the US has been a world superpower—political, military, and economic—for most of the past century. For much of that time, Canada stood in America's shadow, largely invisible to people living on continents other than North America. Former Prime Minister Trudeau's comment, at the beginning of this chapter, about Canada being in bed with an elephant is very insightful regarding Canadian identity. Canadians are very sensitive about what is going on in the US. At the same time, they assert themselves by feeling superior whenever the US suffers some setback. Exhibit 18.10 is suggestive of this very Canadian attitude.

EXHIBIT 18.10 A PERSONAL RECOLLECTION, TRAVELING IN CHINA

When I was traveling in China doing research in the 1990s, I met a senior Chinese official who tried to explain to me about Chinese foreign policy. He said: "We love the Americans—they are far away. We hate the Japanese—they are very close. It's easier to get along harmoniously with those far enough away that they can't make trouble for us too easily." I said: "I know how you feel. We Canadians love China. You are far away. But the Americans are very close."

Canada is a staunch ally of the US. It always will be because the two countries' interests are completely intertwined. On the one hand, Canada sometimes feels forgotten as America chases its other friends. On the other hand, it may be a blessing when the elephant isn't thinking of you and goes off on his way.

Americans and Canadians do more business together than any other two nations in the world. Too often difficulties arise in their relationships because both parties mistake the other for themselves. We hope the contents of this chapter will help you recognize how Americans and Canadians are different, as an aid to building even stronger relationships.

E
X
H
I
B
I
T

18.10

MIND STRETCHING

1 Many Americans seem to be anxious about how the world perceives them, and are disturbed by what seems to be America's declining image and position in many countries. Some wonder if the end is near for US dominance or influence. The following are some quotations from recently published materials that are worth considering. What do they say about the position of the US in the world community?

- ▪ "In Muslim and developing countries, the image of America is skewed by north/south, east/west economic inequality; by longstanding, direct grievances over foreign policy."
- ▪ "In developing countries … there is much greater awareness now than there used to be of the nature and pervasiveness of imperialism. As a result, in some countries there is mounting reluctance to conform to ideals 'born in the USA.'"
- ▪ "One of the trickiest files for the prime minister (of Canada) will be relations with the US. The two countries are drifting apart."

2 Consider how a typical American businessperson would be received in Canada? How is she/he likely to be treated? What must the Canadians be thinking of him/her? How should an American businessperson behave to receive the best results in a negotiation with Canadians.

3 Now consider how a Canadian businessperson will be received in the US. How should she/he behave differently than usual in order to be effective?

NOTES

1 Donald Rumsfeld, Secretary of Defense under George W. Bush, gave this answer at a US Department of Defense news briefing on February 12, 2002. He was answering a question concerning lack of evidence linking the Iraqi government of Saddam Hussein with the supply of weapons of mass destruction to terrorist groups. "There are known knowns," https://en.m.wikipedia.org (retrieved November 8, 2016).

2 Morrison, T. and Conaway, W. A. *Kiss, Bow, or Shake Hands*, 2nd edn. n.p.: Getting Through Customs, 2015.

3 www.canada4life.ca/quotes.php (retrieved April 12, 2017). Pierre Trudeau was Prime Minister of Canada, 1968–1979, 1980–1984.

4 Root, F. R. *Entry Strategies for International Markets*. Lexington, MA: Lexington, 1987.

5 See Ronen, S. and Kraut, A. J. "Similarities Among Countries Based on Employee Work Values and Attitudes," *Columbia Journal of World Business*, Vol. 12, 1977, pp. 89–96. Also see Hofstede, G. *Culture's Consequences: International Differences in Work Related Values*. Beverley Hills, CA: Sage, 1980. Both studies observed that national cultures could be grouped into clusters of cultures that were more alike than cultures grouped into other clusters. Canadian and American cultural values were generally closer together, as were English-speaking countries including the UK and Australia.

6 Massey, B. *Where in the World Do I Belong?* USA: Jetlag Press, 2006.

7 Inkeles, A. *National Character: A Psycho-Social Perspective.* New Brunswick, NJ: Transaction Publishers, 2015.

8 Hasselback, D. "Canada Braces for Life with a New America," *Vancouver Sun*, November 11, 2016, p. C3.

9 Bothwell, R. *Your Country, My Country: A Unified History of the United States and Canada.* New York: Oxford University Press, 2015.

10 Evans, W., Lane, H., and O'Grady, S. *Border Crossings: Doing Business in the US.* Scarborough, ON: Prentice Hall Canada, 1992.

11 Pitts, G. "Jean Coutu Goes Where Others Fear to Tread," *The Globe and Mail*, April 7, 2004, pp. B1, 17.

12 Abramson, N. R. "Configuration, Coordination, Learning and Foreign Market Entry: A Study of Canadian Software Companies Entering the United States." London, ON: University of Western Ontario Doctoral Dissertation, 1992.

13 "List of Countries by GDP (nominal)," www.en.m.wikipedia.org (retrieved November 11, 2016).

14 O'Grady, S. and Lane, H. W. "The Psychic Distance Paradox," *Journal of International Business Studies*, Vol. 27, No. 2, 1996, pp. 309–333.

15 "Canada-United States Trade Relations," www.en.m.wikipedia.org (retrieved November 11, 2016).

16 Bothwell, *Your Country, My Country.*

17 Desilver, D. "For Most Workers, Real Wages Have Barely Budged for Decades," Pew Research Center Fact Tank, October 9, 2014, www.pewresearch.org (retrieved November 12, 2016).

18 CBC News, "Canada's Dismal Wage Growth Still Better than Most of G20," www.cbc.ca (retrieved November 20, 2016).

19 Truecost, "List of Countries with Universal Healthcare," https://truecostblog.com (retrieved November 12, 2016).

20 World Bank, "Doing Business 2017 Economy Rankings," www.doingbusiness.org (retrieved November 12, 2016).

21 "Best Countries for Business," *Forbes Magazine*, www.forbes.com (retrieved November 8, 2016).

22 "Overall Best Countries Ranking," *US News*, www.usnews.com/news (retrieved November 12, 2016.

23 PPP is purchasing power parity. GDP is an unreliable measure of comparative prosperity because the same value of currency buys a variable amount in different countries. PPP attempts to equalize for this difference.

24 Hetter, K. "Where Are the World's Happiest Countries?" CNN, March 21, 2016, www.cnn.com (retrieved November 8, 2016).

25 Inkeles, *National Character.*

26 For some of the most recent leading-edge Jungian personality research see: Hunziker, M. *Depth Typology: C. G. Jung, Isabel Myers, John Beebe and the Guide Map to Becoming Who We Are.* New York: Write Way Publishing Company, 2016; Beebe, J. *Energies and Patterns in Psychological Type: The Reservoir of Consciousness.* London: Routledge, 2016; Haas, L. and Hunziker, M. *The Building Blocks of Personality Type.* USA: Eltanin Publishing, 2014.

27 Hunziker, *Depth Typology.*

28 These 20 nations are identified in CIA, *The World Factbook*, 2013, www.cia.gov/library/publications/the-world-factbook (retrieved November 8, 2016).

29 Johanson, M. "Why Canada Has the Best Reputation in the World," July 7, 2013, www.ibtimes.com (retrieved November 12, 2016).

30 Brean, J. "The Use and Abuse of 'Sorry': Americans Do Not Say It, the British Do Not Mean It and Canadians Overdo It," *National Post*, June 27, 2014, www.news.nationalpost.com (retrieved November 12, 2016).

31 Ibid.

32 Descriptions of Fe and Te are derived from Sharp, D. *Personality Types: Jung's Model of Typology*. Toronto, ON: Inner City Books, 1987. See also Thompson, H. L. *Jung's Function-Attitudes Explained*. Watkinsville, GA: Wormhole Publishing, 1996.

33 Quenk, N. L. *Was That Really Me: How Everyday Stress Brings Out Our Hidden Personality*. Palo Alto, CA: Davies-Black Publishing, 2002, p. 153.

34 Ibid., p. 155.

35 Abramson, N.R., Keating, R.K., and Lane, H.W. "Cross-National Cognitive Process Differences: A Comparison of Canadian, American & Japanese Managers," *Management International Review*, Vol. 36, No. 2, 1996, pp.123–147.

36 Jung, *Personality Types*.

37 Massey, *Where in the World Do I Belong?*

38 van Oudenhoven, J. P. "Do Organizations Reflect National Cultures? A 10-Nation Study," *International Journal of Intercultural Relations*, Vol. 25, 2001, pp. 89–107.

39 Hofstede, G. *Culture's Consequences: Comparing Values, Behaviors, Institutions and Organizations Across Nations*. Beverley Hills, CA: Sage, 2003.

40 Morrison and Conaway, *Kiss, Bow, or Shake Hands*.

41 Katz, L. *The Global Business Culture Guide*. Charleston, SC: CreateSpace, 2014.

42 Morrison and Conaway, *Kiss, Bow, or Shake Hands*.

43 Ibid.

44 Katz, *The Global Business Culture Guide*.

45 Abramson, N. R. "Building and Maintaining Effective Buyer–Seller Relationships: A Comparative Study of American and Canadian Expectations," *Journal of Promotion Management*, Vol. 12, No. 1, 2005, pp. 129–150.

46 Krishna, V. "The Dangers of Bribery," *Financial Post*, February 14, 2013, p. D4.

47 Transparency International (TI), "Corruption Perceptions Index 2010," www.transparency.org (retrieved November 11, 2016).

48 Moody, K. G. C., Berg, R. A., Barba, P., and Marino, A. *Renouncing Your U.S. Citizenship*. Vancouver, BC: Moodys Gartner Tax Law presentation, November 29, 2014, p. 8.

49 Obama, B. "What I Want for You and Every Child in America: A Letter to My Daughters," *Parade–The San Diego Union Tribune*, January 18, 2009, pp. 4–5. Barack Obama was the 44th President of the United States.

50 CIA, *World Factbook*.

51 Ibid.

52 "America's Shrinking Middle Class: A Close Look at Changes Within Metropolitan Areas: The Middle Class Lost Ground in Nearly Nine-in-Ten Metropolitan Areas Examined," Pew Research Center, May 11, 2016, www.pewsocialtrends.org (retrieved November 14, 2016).

53 Walshe, S. "Stop Allowing the Wealthy to Treat Undocumented Immigrants Like Slaves," *Guardian*, March 13, 2013, www.theguardian.com (retrieved November 14, 2016).

54 Wiseman, P. "Rise of the Machines to Blame for Job Losses: It Isn't China or Mexico Sapping Positions from U.S., It's Robots," *Vancouver Sun*, November 5, 2016, G3.

55 Ibid.

56 Ibid.

57 Ibid.

58 Fariello, G. *Red Scare: Memories of the American Inquisition: An Oral History*. New York: Avon, 1995. May, G. *Un-American Activities: The Trials of William Remington*. New York: Oxford University Press, 1994. Schrecker, E. *Many Are the Crimes: McCarthyism in America*. Princeton, NJ: Princeton University Press, 1998. Some Americans still defend the memory of McCarthy and there is evidence there were some Soviet infiltrators. See Weinstein, A. and Vassiliev, A. *The Haunted Wood: Soviet Espionage in America–The Stalin Era*. New York: Modern Library, 2000.

59 Maddox, B. *In Defense of America*. New York: Little, Brown, 2008. Tyler, P. *A World of Trouble: The White House and the Middle East—From Cold War to the War on Terror*. New York: Farrar, Strauss and Giroux, 2009.

60 Campbell, J. *U.S.A.* New York: Lonely Planet, 2009. For US Census Information, visit www.census.gov/main. Also see Sayre, A. P. *Welcome to North America*. Brookfield, CT: Millbrook, 2003.

61 Bass, F. "U.S. Ethnic Mix Boasts German Accent Amid Surge of Hispanics," *Bloomberg*, March 5, 2012, www.bloomberg.com/news/2012-03-06 (retrieved November 12, 2016).

62 http://names.mongabay.com/ancestry/ancestry-population.html (retrieved November 12, 2016).

63 Gudykunst, W. B. and Kim, K. Y. *Communicating with Strangers: An Approach to Intercultural Communication*, 3rd edn. New York: McGraw-Hill, 1994.

64 Hewlett, S. A. "Too Many People of Color Feel Uncomfortable at Work," *Harvard Business Review—HBR Blog Network*, October 18, 2012.

65 Gudykunst and Kim, *Communicating with Strangers*.

66 https://en.m.wikipedia.org/wiki/African-Americans (retrieved April 12, 2017).

67 Vega, T. "Blacks Still Far Behind Whites in Wealth and Income," June 27, 2016, www.money.cnn.com (retrieved April 12, 2017).

68 "Murder No. 605: Chicago Has Seen a Spike in the Number of Murders this Year, and It Just Crossed a Terrible Threshold," *Maclean's*, November 14, 2016, p. 34.

69 "Hispanic Population in the U.S.," Pew Research Center, March 30, 2011.

70 CIA, *World Factbook*.

71 The founding fathers of Canada intended to create the Kingdom of Canada. The name Canada was derived from an Iroquois word, "Kanata," meaning settlement, village, or land. The word "kingdom" was changed by the British colonial office in London for fear of antagonizing the US. "Dominion" was substituted, taken from the Christian Bible (Psalm 72:8).

72 Tucker, E. "Top 10 Memorable David Suzuki Quotes," *Global News*, April 13, 2012, www.globalnews.ca (retrieved December 14, 2016). David Suzuki is a Canadian icon—an environmentalist and professor who has taken a leading role on battling climate change.

73 Simpson, S. "Innovation Key to Close Canada's Productivity Gap," *Calgary Herald*, February 19, 2013, www.calgaryherald.com/business (retrieved November 15, 2016).

74 http://en.wikipedia.org/wiki/List_of_countries_by_exports (retrieved November 15, 2016). These figures are based on the CIA's *World Factbook*.

75 Roy, R. "Vancouver's Multi-Ethnic Population," *Vancouver.com*, http://2vancouver.com/en/articles/vancouvers-multi-ethnic-population (retrieved November 15, 2016).

76 Statistics Canada. "Study: Projections of the Diversity of the Canadian Population," March 9, 2010, www.statcan.gc.ca (retrieved November 15, 2016).

77 "Truth and Reconciliation Commission (Canada)," https://en.wikipedia.org/wiki/Truth_and_Reconciliation_Commission_(Canada) (retrieved November 14, 2016). See also Truth and Reconciliation Commission of Canada, *Final Report of the Truth and Reconciliation Commission of Canada, Volume One: Summary: Honouring the Truth, Reconciling for the Future*. Toronto, ON: Lorimer, 2015.

78 Assembly of First Nations; British Columbia Assembly of First Nations, "First Nations' Revenues," www.bcafn.ca/toolkit (retrieved November 15, 2016).

79 See Abramson, N. R. and Ai, J. X. *Royal Bank: Hagwilget Band Case Series* in the instructor online teaching materials. These cases detail negotiations initiated by the Hagwilget Band in Hazelton, BC, to obtain a Royal Bank branch on the Hagwilget Reserve.

INDEX

Page numbers in **bold** refer to exhibits and images.

Taylor & Francis eBooks

Helping you to choose the right eBooks for your Library

Add Routledge titles to your library's digital collection today. Taylor and Francis ebooks contains over 50,000 titles in the Humanities, Social Sciences, Behavioural Sciences, Built Environment and Law.

Choose from a range of subject packages or create your own!

Benefits for you

» Free MARC records
» COUNTER-compliant usage statistics
» Flexible purchase and pricing options
» All titles DRM-free.

Benefits for your user

» Off-site, anytime access via Athens or referring URL
» Print or copy pages or chapters
» Full content search
» Bookmark, highlight and annotate text
» Access to thousands of pages of quality research at the click of a button.

REQUEST YOUR **FREE** INSTITUTIONAL TRIAL TODAY

Free Trials Available
We offer free trials to qualifying academic, corporate and government customers.

eCollections – Choose from over 30 subject eCollections, including:

Archaeology	Language Learning
Architecture	Law
Asian Studies	Literature
Business & Management	Media & Communication
Classical Studies	Middle East Studies
Construction	Music
Creative & Media Arts	Philosophy
Criminology & Criminal Justice	Planning
Economics	Politics
Education	Psychology & Mental Health
Energy	Religion
Engineering	Security
English Language & Linguistics	Social Work
Environment & Sustainability	Sociology
Geography	Sport
Health Studies	Theatre & Performance
History	Tourism, Hospitality & Events

For more information, pricing enquiries or to order a free trial, please contact your local sales team: www.tandfebooks.com/page/sales

Routledge
Taylor & Francis Group

The home of
Routledge books

www.tandfebooks.com

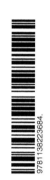